An Introduction to Programming

A Structured Approach Using PL/I and PL/C

Third Edition

Richard Conway
David Gries
Cornell University

contributions by
John E. Dennis and Jorge Moré

Little, Brown and Company
Boston *Toronto*

Library of Congress Cataloging in Publication Data

Conway, Richard Walter
An introduction to programming a structured approach using PL/I and PL/C

Bibliography: p. 707
Includes index.
1. PL/I (Computer program language) 2. PL/C (Computer program language) 3. Structured programming. I. Gries, David joint author. II. Title.
QA76.73.P25C65 1978 001.6'424 78-21901
ISBN 0-316-154148

Library of Congress Catalog Card No. 78-21901

ISBN 0-316-15414-8

9 8 7 6

BP
Published simultaneously in Canada
by Little, Brown & Company (Canada) Limited

Printed in the United States of America

An Introduction to Programming

Little, Brown Computer Systems Series

Gerald M. Weinberg, *Editor*

Basso, David T., and Ronald D. Schwartz
Programming with FORTRAN/WATFOR/WATFIV

Chattergy, Rahul, and Udo W. Pooch
Top-down, Modular Programming in FORTRAN with WATFIV

Coats, R.B., and A. Parkin
Computer Models in the Social Sciences

Conway, Richard, and David Gries
Primer on Structured Programming: Using PL/1, PL/C, and PL/CT

Conway, Richard, and David Gries
An Introduction to Programming: A Structured Approach Using PL/1 and PL/C

Conway, Richard, David Gries, and E. Carl Zimmerman
A Primer on Pascal, Second Edition

Cripps, Martin
An Introduction to Computer Hardware

Easley, Grady M.
Primer for Small Systems Management

Finkenaur, Robert G.
COBOL for Students: A Programming Primer

Freedman, Daniel P., and Gerald M. Weinberg
Handbook of Walkthroughs, Inspections, and Technical Reviews: Evaluating Programs, Projects, and Products

Graybeal, Wayne, and Udo W. Pooch
Simulation: Principles and Methods

Greenfield, S.E.
The Architecture of Microcomputers

Greenwood, Frank
Profitable Small Business Computing

Healy, Martin, and David Hebditch
The Microcomputer in On-Line Systems: Small Computers in Terminal-Based Systems and Distributed Processing Networks

Lias, Edward J.
Future Mind: The Microcomputer—New Medium, New Mental Environment

Lines, M. Vardell, and Boeing Computer Services Company
Minicomputer Systems

Mills, Harlan D.
Software Productivity

Monro, Donald M.
Basic BASIC: An Introduction to Programming

Mosteller, William S.
Systems Programmer's Problem Solver

Nahigian, J. Victor, and William S. Hodges
Computer Games for Businesses, Schools, and Homes

Nahigian, J. Victor, and William S. Hodges
Computer Games for Business, School, and Home for TRS-80 Level II BASIC

Orwig, Gary W., and William S. Hodges
The Computer Tutor: Learning Activities for Homes and Schools

Parikh, Girish
Techniques of Program and System Maintenance

Parkin, Andrew
Data Processing Management

Parkin, Andrew
Systems Analysis

Pizer, Stephen M., with Victor L. Wallace
Numerical Computing: Concepts and Strategies

Pooch, Udo W., William H. Greene, and Gary G. Moss
Telecommunications and Networking

Reingold, Edward M., and Wilfred J. Hansen
Data Structures

Savitch, Walter J.
Abstract Machines and Grammars

Shneiderman, Ben
Software Psychology: Human Factors in Computer and Information Systems

Walker, Henry M.
Problems for Computer Solutions Using FORTRAN

Walker, Henry M.
Problems for Computer Solutions Using BASIC

Weinberg, Gerald M.
Rethinking Systems Analysis and Design

Weinberg, Gerald M.
Understanding the Professional Programmer

Weinberg, Gerald M., Stephen E. Wright, Richard Kauffman, and Martin A. Goetz
High Level COBOL Programming

Contents

Preface xv

Part I Fundamental Concepts 1

1 Introduction 1
1.1 Example of a Computer Program 2
1.2 Analysis of a Problem, Design of a Program 4
1.3 Programming Languages 6
1.4 Compilation and Execution 8
1.5 Program Correctness 9
Exercises 10

2 Variables 11
2.1 Identifiers 12
2.2 Types of Values 13
2.2.1 Decimal Numbers 13
2.2.2 Integers 15
2.2.3 Character Strings 16
2.2.4 Logical Values 19
2.2.5 User-Defined Types 19
2.3 Creation of Variables 19
2.3.1 Implicit Declarations and Default Attributes 21
2.4 Variables with Multiple Values 23
2.4.1 Subscripts 24
2.4.2 Variables with Multiple Subscripts 25
2.5 Initial Values 26
2.5.1 Named Constants 28
2.6 Variables with Structured Values 29
Summary 32

3 Expressions and Assignment of Value 33
3.1 The Assignment Statement 34
3.2 Arithmetic Expressions 39
3.2.1 Arithmetic Operations 40
3.2.2 Precedence of Operations 40
3.2.3 Mixed-Type Arithmetic Expressions 41
3.2.4 Coercion of Values 42
3.2.5 Arithmetic Built-in Functions 43
3.3 String Expressions 45
3.3.1 The Operation of Concatenation 47
3.3.2 The SUBSTR Built-in Function 47
3.3.3 The SUBSTR Pseudo-Variable 48
3.3.4 Numeric-Valued String Functions 49

3.4 Logical Expressions 50
3.4.1 Relational Operators 51
3.4.2 Comparison of String Values 52
3.4.3 Boolean Operators 53
3.5 Conversion of Values 55
3.6 Array Assignment 56
3.7 Structure Assignment 58
3.7.1 BY NAME Assignment 59
Summary 60
Exercises 61

4 Input and Output Statements 62
4.1 The PUT Statement 62
4.1.1 The SKIP Option 63
4.1.2 The LIST Form of PUT 64
4.1.3 The DATA Form of PUT 67
4.1.4 The EDIT Form of PUT 68
4.2 The GET Statement 71
4.2.1 The LIST Form of GET 71
4.2.2 The DATA Form of GET 73
4.2.3 The EDIT Form of GET 74
4.3 The FILE Option 75
4.4 The STRING Option 76
4.5 Array Input and Output 77
4.6 Structure Input and Output 78
Exercises 79

5 Execution of a Sequential Program 80
5.1 Processing of a Program 81
5.2 The Printed Results of Processing 82
5.2.1 PL/CS Output 85
5.3 Tracing Execution 86

6 Conditional Execution 88
6.1 Conditional Execution of a Single Statement 89
6.2 Choice Between Two Statements 90
6.3 Selection From Three or More Statements 91
6.4 Compound Statements 94
6.5 Nesting of Conditional Statements 95
6.6 Simulation of SELECT 98
6.6.1 Label Variables 99
Summary 101
Exercises 102

7 Repetition of Execution 103
7.1 Conditional Repetition 104
7.1.1 The WHILE Loop 104
7.1.2 The UNTIL Loop 106
7.2 The Automatically-Indexed Loop 108
7.3 Nested Loops 113
7.4 Exit From a Loop 114
7.4.1 Simulation of LEAVE 116
7.4.2 Historical Note on GOTO 117
7.4.3 End-of-Data Exit 118
7.5 Tracing Execution of a Loop 123

Summary 127
Exercises 127

8 Program Documentation 134
8.1 Comments 134
8.1.1 Statement-comments 135
8.1.2 Comments in Declarations 137
8.1.3 User Instructions 137
8.1.4 Useless Comments 138
8.2 Special Comments in PL/C and PL/CS 138

Part II Program Structure 141

1 Organization of Declarations 143

2 Statement Organization 147
2.1 Static Versus Dynamic Versions of a Program 147
2.2 Hierarchial Structure and Statement-comments 151
2.2.1 Statement-comments and Abstraction 151
2.2.2 Structuring Larger Program Segments 152
2.3 The Effect of Control-Modifying Statements 156
2.3.1 The Effect of LEAVE 156
2.3.2 The Effect of GOTO 157
2.3.3 The Effect of ENDFILE condition 158
2.4 The Well-Structured Program 158
2.5 A Computer Example 161

3 Sample Programs 165
3.1 A Program to Compute Averages 165
3.1.1 A Minimal Averaging Program 165
3.1.2 A More Useful Averaging Program 167
3.2 A Simplified Statistical System 170
3.3 A Translation Program 175
3.4 Interactive Programs 179
3.4.1 A Game-Playing Program 182
Exercises 187

4 Program Schemata 188

Part III The Development of a Program 195

1 The Phases of Development 195
1.1 Clarification of the Problem 196
1.2 Design of a Solution Strategy 199
1.2.1 Algorithms 199
1.3 Choice of Data Structures 200
1.4 Writing the Program Statements 201

2 Approaches to Program Development 202
2.1 Top-Down Development 203
2.2 Basic Program Units 204
2.3 Similarities Between Programs 206

3 Examples of Program Development 208
3.1 A Listing Program 208
3.2 Searching a List 214
3.2.1 Processing the Inquiries 219
3.3 Ordering a List 222
3.4 An Accounting Problem 226
3.5 Scanning for Symbols 237
3.5.1 Character Strategy 238
3.5.2 Symbol Strategy 239
3.5.3 Line Strategy 241
3.5.4 A Comparison of Strategies 242
3.5.5 Symbols Split on Two Lines 242
Exercises 246

4 General Design Considerations 252
4.1 Top-Down Development 252
4.1.1 Refining a Statement 253
4.1.2 Refining a Data Description 257
4.1.3 Backing Up 259
4.2 Sources of Ideas for Refinements 262
4.2.1 Ideas for Algorithms 263
4.2.2 Solving Simpler Problems 265
4.2.3 Solving Related Problems 270
4.3 Handling Input Errors 271

Part IV Procedures and Blocks 273

1 External Procedures 273
1.1 Procedure to Interchange Values 276
1.2 Definition of a Procedure 280
1.2.1 Parameter Declarations 281
1.2.2 READONLY Parameters 282
1.2.3 Local Variables 283
1.2.4 Labels in a Procedure 284
1.2.5 Statements in the Procedure Body 285
1.3 Procedure Calls 287
1.3.1 Calls and Arguments 287
1.3.2 Details of Call and Execution 289
1.3.3 Arguments with Different Types 293
1.3.4 Expressions and Constants as Arguments 294
1.3.5 Array Names as Arguments and Parameters 295
1.4 Nested Procedure Calls 299
1.5 STATIC Variables 302
1.6 EXTERNAL Variables 303
Summary 307
Exercises 308

2 Functions 314
2.1 Definition of a Function 314
2.1.1 Differences between Functions and Procedures 316
2.2 Execution of a Function 317
2.3 Function "Side-Effects" 318
Summary 321

3 Internal Procedures 322
3.1 Nested Blocks 322
3.2 The Scope of Names 324
3.2.1 The Scope of Labels and Block-Names 325
3.3 Tracing Execution of Blocks 327
3.4 Positioning of Internal Procedures 328
3.5 Uses of Internal Procedures 330
Summary 332

4 Blocks 333
4.1 Dynamic Dimensioning of Arrays 335
4.2 Other Uses of BEGIN Blocks 336

5 The Use of Procedures and Blocks 337
5.1 Subroutines 337
5.2 Control Sections 339
5.3 Sectional Independence 342
5.4 Logical Functions 343
Exercises 344

6 Recursive Use of Procedures 346
6.1 A Simple Example 346
6.2 Exploring Recursion 347
6.2.1 The Recursive Pattern 349
6.2.2 Executing Recursive Procedures 350
6.3 Recursive Procedure Examples 351
6.3.1 The Towers of Hanoi 351
6.3.2 Quicksort 353
6.3.3 The Assignment Problem 354
6.3.4 Procedure to Evaluate Expressions 358
Exercises 362

Part V Program Testing and Correctness 365

1 Errors, Testing and Correctness 365
1.1 The Meaning of Correctness 366
1.2 Types of Errors 368
1.3 Program Testing vs. Program Analysis 369

2 Automatic Diagnostic Services 370
2.1 Detection of Errors 370
2.1.1 Syntax Errors 371
2.1.2 Invalid Operations 372
2.2 Automatic Repair of Errors 373
2.3 Analysis of Identifier Usage 374
2.4 Post-Mortem Dump 374

3 Program Testing 375
3.1 Construction of Test Cases 376
3.2 Diagnosis of Trouble 376
3.2.1 Temporary Output Statements 377
3.2.2 Strategies for Locating Errors 378
3.3 Modular Testing 379
3.3.1 Independent Test of Procedures 380

3.3.2 Testing with Dummy Procedures 382
3.3.3 Top-down Testing 382
3.4 Help from "Consultants" 383
3.5 Testing Habits and Error Patterns 385

4 An Example of Program Testing 386
4.1 Review of Testing History 402

5 Special Diagnostic Facilities 403
5.1 Flow Tracing 403
5.1.1 Limiting the Scope of CHECK 406
5.1.2 FLOW Facilities 406
5.2 Memory Dump 409
5.3 Limitation of Printed Output 409
5.4 Selective Activation of Diagnostic Statements 410
5.4.1 Pseudo-Comments 410
5.4.2 Macro Facility 412
5.5 Assertions 414
Exercises 418

6. Testing in Interactive Systems 423
6.1 Program Entry and Syntax Checking 423
6.2 The "Terminal Procedure" 424
6.2.1 Attention and Error Calls 424
6.2.2 PAUSE and STEP Calls 426
6.2.3 Statements in the Terminal Procedure 428
6.3 Example of Interactive Testing 430

7 Proofs of Correctness 432
7.1 Invariant Relations of a Loop 434
7.1.1 An Example: Sorting 434
7.2 The Invariant Relation Theorem 436
7.3 Simple Examples 439
7.4 More Complicated Examples 441
7.5 Everyday Invariant Relations 444
7.6 Automatic Verification 447
Exercises 449

Part VI Performance Evaluation 453

1 Measuring Storage Space 454

2 Measuring Speed of Execution 457
2.1 Counting Basic Steps 457
2.2 The Order of Execution Time 459
2.3 Worst Case vs Average Case Analysis 461
2.4 Analysis of Binary Search: Logarithms 462
2.5 Analysis of Simple Programs 464
2.5.1 Testing Primeness 464
2.5.2 Generating Unique Numbers 465
2.5.3 Ordering without Duplicates 466
2.6 A More Complicated Example: KWIC Index 468
2.6.1 The Problem and First Refinement 468
2.6.2 The Keyword List 470

2.6.3 The Printing Task 471
2.7 An Example: Heap Sort 473
2.7.1 Binary Trees and Heaps 473
2.7.2 The Basic Algorithm 475
2.7.3 Constructing a Heap 475
2.7.4 Sorting the Heap 477
Exercises 479

3 Problems Impossible to Program 482
3.1 Ill-Defined Problems 482
3.2 Impossibly-Large Problems 483
3.3 "Undecidable" Problems 484

Part VII Data Structures 487

1 Data Structures, Links and Nodes 487
1.1 Representing Nodes and Links using Arrays 489
Exercises 490

2 Stacks, Queues and Deques 491
2.1 Definition of Stack, Queue and Deque 491
2.2 Sequential Allocation of Stacks and Queues 493
2.3 Linked List Allocation of Stacks and Queues 493
2.4 Examples of Stack Implementation 500
Exercises 506

3 Other Forms of Linked Lists 507
3.1 Inserting, Deleting in a Linked List 507
3.2 Stacks and Queues with Headers 508
3.3 Circular Lists 510
3.4 Doubly Linked Lists 512
Exercises 514

4 Trees 516
4.1 Binary Trees 516
4.2 Traversing Binary Trees 519
4.3 Application of Trees 522
4.3.1 Maintaining a List of Values 522
4.3.2 Representing and Evaluating Expressions 525
Exercises 527

Part VIII Database Systems 529

1 Processing with Secondary Storage 532
1.1 Record-at-a-Time Processing 533
1.2 Timing Considerations 533
1.3 Blocking and Buffering 534

2 Logical Structure of a Database 536
2.1 Logical Records 536
2.1.1 Repeating Groups 537
2.2 Logical Files 538
2.2.1 Sequential Files 538

2.2.2 Indexed Files 539
2.3 Relationships Between Records 540

3 Database Processing 543
3.1 Query Processing 543
3.1.1 Information Retrieval Systems 545
3.2 Update Processing 546
3.2.1 Update of a Sequential File 547
3.2.2 Update of a Direct-Access File 548
3.3 Programming Languages for Database Processing 549
3.3.1 COBOL and PL/I 549
3.3.2 Higher-Level Languages 551

Part IX Computer Solution of Mathematical Problems 553
by J. E. Dennis and Jorge J. Moré

1 Floating Point Numbers 554
1.1 Representation of Floating Point Numbers 554
1.2 Roundoff Errors and Significant Decimal Digits 557
1.3 Errors in Floating Point Arithmetic 559
Exercises 562

2 Library Functions (COS and SQRT) 565
2.1 Approximation by Polynomials 565
2.1.1 Horner's Scheme 567
2.2 Approximation by Iteration 569
Exercises 572

3 Algorithms for Two Typical Problems 573
3.1 Simultaneous Linear Equations 573
3.1.1 Gaussian Elimination 574
3.1.2 Efficiency 576
3.1.3 Ill-Conditioned Problems 579
3.2 The Quadrature Problem 580
3.2.1 The Trapezoidal Rule 581
3.2.2 Efficiency 583
3.2.3 Simpson's Rule 587
Exercises 589

4 Suggestions for Further Reading 591

Appendices 593

A. Summary of PL/I 593
A.1 Notation and Basic Definitions 594
A.2 Executable Statements 599
A.2.1 The END Delimiter 618
A.3 Definitions and Declarations 619
A.4 Attributes 626
A.5 Variables, Values and Expressions 635
A.5.1 Scope and Recognition of Names 635

A.5.2 Referencing Variables, Arrays and Structures 636
A.5.3 Expressions 638
A.5.4 Data Conversion 643
A.5.5 Parameter-Argument Correspondence 644
A.6 Conditions and Prefixes 648
A.6.1 Prefixes and Their Use 648
A.6.2 Conditions 649
A.7 Built-in Functions 655
A.8 Formats 662
A.9 Summary of Differences between PL/I and PL/C 666
A.9.1 PL/I(F) Features not in PL/C 666
A.9.2 Additional PL/C Restrictions 667
A.9.3 Incompatible PL/C Features 667
A.9.4 Internal Representation 668
A.9.5 Order of Evaluation in Declarations 668
A.9.6 Dimensional Limits 669
A.10 PL/C Macros 670
A.10.1 Macro Definitions 670
A.10.2 Macro Calls 671
A.10.3 Source Listing 672
A.10.4 Macros with Parameters 673
A.10.5 Uses of Macros 675
A.11 The PL/CT Interactive System 679
A.12 The PL/CS Language 692

B. Operating Procedures for PL/C 697
B.1 Program Deck Structure 697
B.1.1 Examples of PL/C Decks 697
B.2 Program Options 698
B.3 Card Formats 702
B.3.1 Control Cards 702
B.3.2 Program Cards 703
B.3.3 Data Cards 704
B.3.4 Format Control on the Keypunch 704
B.4 Efficient Programming in PL/C 705

References 707

Index 711

Preface

This is the third edition of our Introduction to Programming. The first was written at a time of upheaval in the programming field. The "software crisis" was being discussed, "structured programming" had just been proclaimed, and the advantages and disadvantages of the GOTO were being heatedly debated. The field as a whole was just waking up to the problems of programming notation, style, debugging, and correctness.

At the time, the first edition was radical, for we tried to lessen the typical emphasis on the programming language and its syntax and concentrate instead on how one should develop and organize programs. We tried to discuss programming rather than a programming language.

This approach is no longer radical. Most programming texts have moved in that direction. In revision we found that many points we argued vehemently in the first edition we can now present in a more matter-of-fact manner. But the programming revolution is far from over. Much of the new material and new emphasis in this edition will face the test of general discussion and practice in the coming years.

A key issue concerns approaches to program correctness. A "calculus for the derivation of programs" is beginning to emerge, but it is not yet complete or solid. It is difficult to know how to teach beginners about assertions, preconditions, invariant relations, etc., without getting too mathematical, and we are still experimenting in these areas. Basic ideas on the correctness issue are discussed in this edition, but eventually the whole issue of formal correctness must be integrated into the description of the programming process -- perhaps in the fourth edition.

Some of the more important changes in the third edition are:

1. Recognizing that more and more college students have previous programming knowledge (e.g. they may have learned BASIC in high school) and that our book is often used in a second course, we have raised the level slightly. The book can still be used in an introductory course -- we use it ourselves in such a course -- but the instructor should guide the students in omitting certain sections on the first reading. (Alternatively, our Primer can be used for the first course.)

2. The material in Part I has been reorganized so that it is better for reference and for a reader with some computing background.

3. We have included the new PL/I LEAVE and SELECT statements and the UNTIL loop.

4. Part II on program structure and Part V on testing and correctness have been substantially rewritten.

5. Part VII on data structures has been added, filling a gap that we found when teaching a second course from the book.

6. Material has been added so the book can be used in courses that use the PL/CT or PL/CS dialects as well as PL/I or PL/C.

In every edition we feel obliged to apologize in some fashion for using PL/I and its dialects. We, more so than many others, recognize its inadequacies and its cumbersome notation. Yet we teach it and we write books that use it as a vehicle for discussing programming. While we would rather teach an ALGOL-like language like PASCAL, much of our constituency would rather have us teach FORTRAN, so we compromise on PL/I. This makes neither side really happy, but it does allow a contemporary approach to computing. FORTRAN and PL/I will probably be around for some time, and we must learn to live with them as best as possible.

It is a pleasure to acknowledge our indebtedness to our colleagues John Dennis and Jorge More', who contributed Part IX on the computer solution of mathematical problems. We are also indebted to Ralph Conway and Anselm Soyring who prepared much of the manuscript for computer processing.

This book was produced by an editing program (FORMAT) run on the IBM 370/168 of Cornell's Office of Computer Services.

Ithaca, N.Y.

R. CONWAY
D. GRIES

An Introduction to Programming

Part I Fundamental Concepts

Section 1 Introduction

We are concerned with how a digital computer can be used to aid in solving problems. This involves learning to:

1. Choose problems appropriate to the computer's abilities and describe them clearly and precisely.

2. Design a solution to a problem and describe it in a "programming language" intelligible to a computer. This description is called a "program"; the process of producing it is called "programming". This process transforms a statement of objectives -- what is required -- into a description of an executable procedure -- how the objectives are to be achieved. The process also makes explicit and precise parts of the problem description that are implicit and that rely on intuition, common sense, or technical knowledge, since the computer has none of these virtues.

3. Confirm the correctness of the program; demonstrate that it precisely satisfies the problem requirements.

The selection of appropriate problems is as difficult and important as the analysis and programming, but it is impossible to discuss this issue until one has some understanding of the nature of computing systems. However, two initial observations might be helpful. Firstly, problems for which computer assistance is sought are generally substantial. There is effort involved in obtaining computer assistance, and if the problem is simple, not repetitive, and not likely to recur, it may cost more than it is worth. One must bear this in mind; even though instructional examples are necessarily short and often trivial they are used to develop a competence that will be useful on subsequent real problems.

Secondly, the computer can only help with precisely stated problems for which a precise method of solution can be given. Moreover, while the computer can reliably perform a tremendous number of operations at incredible speed, in principle the operations could be carried out by a human -- if he or she worked long enough. A computer can "play chess" because chess has been described to the computer as an elaborate symbol manipulation task. On the other hand, a computer cannot solve the "vehicle emission problem" because no one has as yet figured out how to describe it strictly in terms of symbol manipulation. As another example, a computer is often asked to "select a date for a person from a set of potential candidates"; its recommendations are often humorous, not because of how it finds a solution but because no one really knows how to precisely and correctly describe the selection process.

1.1 An Example of a Computer Program

We present an example of a simple, complete program. Although you will not understand all the details at this point, you should get a general idea of what the end product of the programming process is going to be.

Suppose one has to determine the maximum of a list of non-negative numbers, which are punched on "IBM cards". The program to do this uses a process that is repeated for each of the numbers. Each repetition causes the computer to "read" a number (by analyzing the pattern of holes punched in the card) and compare it to the greatest number encountered "so far". If the new number is greater than the previous maximum it is retained as the new maximum. The number of numbers is also counted.

This process is straightforward, once it gets started, but some provision is required to initialize it. Secondly, so that the end of the list can be recognized, a dummy number (in this case a -1, which cannot occur in the actual data) is appended to the list. The program will check each value as it is read to see if it is this dummy value.

A program stores values in the "memory" of the computer for later retrieval. Each location for storing a value is called a "variable" and is assigned a name so that the program may refer to it. The names of the variables used in this program are:

```
NUMBER -- the current number being processed
MAXNBR -- the maximum number encountered "so far"
COUNT  -- the number of times the central process has been
          repeated "so far"
```

A complete program for this problem, written in a programming language called PL/C, is given on the next page. The numbers at the beginning of each line are not part of the program but have been added so that the notes following the program can readily reference each line.

```
1)    *PL/C
2)      /* COMPUTE THE MAXIMUM OF NON-NEGATIVE INPUT NUMBERS */
3)      /* DUMMY -1 ADDED AT END OF INPUT FOR STOPPING TEST */
4)      FINDMAX: PROCEDURE OPTIONS(MAIN);
5)
6)      DECLARE (NUMBER,        /* THE CURRENT NUMBER */
7)               MAXNBR,        /* MAXIMUM VALUE SO FAR */
8)               COUNT)         /* NBR OF NUMBERS SO FAR */
9)                   FIXED;
10)
11)     MAXNBR = -10;      /* INITIAL VALUE LESS THAN ALL */
12)                        /* POSSIBLE DATA VALUES */
13)     COUNT = 0;
14)     GET LIST(NUMBER);
15)
16)     DO WHILE (NUMBER ¬= -1);
17)         COUNT = COUNT + 1;
18)         IF NUMBER > MAXNBR
19)             THEN MAXNBR = NUMBER;
20)         GET LIST(NUMBER);
21)         END;
22)     PUT LIST('NUMBER OF VALUES =', COUNT);
23)     PUT SKIP LIST('MAXIMUM VALUE =', MAXNBR);
24)     END FINDMAX;
25)
26)   *DATA
27)    3, 7, 12, 2, 6, -1
```

The printed "output" produced by executing this program with the data on line 27 is:

```
NUMBER OF VALUES = 5
MAXIMUM VALUE =    12
```

The following remarks attempt to explain some of the less obvious aspects of the program:

Line 1 announces that the program is written in a programming language called PL/C. Most computing systems accept programs in many different languages and the user must indicate which one will be used.

Lines 2 and 3 are program comments. These are intended for human readers and have no effect on the execution of the program. In PL/C comments are denoted by /* preceding and */ following the text of the comment. Comments are also included in lines 6, 7, 8, 11 and 12.

Lines 4 and 24 indicate the beginning and end of this program, which is named FINDMAX.

The blank lines 5, 10, 15 and 25 are inserted to visually indicate the separate sections of the program. They have no effect on execution.

Lines 6-9 define the variables used in the program and specify that they may contain integers ("FIXED" means integer).

Lines 11-14 "initialize" the variables so that the central, repeated section operates properly. "MAXNBR = -10;" stores the value of the expression "-10" in the variable MAXNBR. GET LIST(NUMBER); means to "read" the first number on the data card following the *DATA card (line 26) and store it in variable NUMBER.

Lines 16-21 form the central section, which is repeated for each number. The symbol "¬=" in line 16 means "not equal".

Lines 22-23 are the final steps that cause the results to be displayed.

Line 26 indicates that data follow.

Line 27 consists of the data (including a dummy data value of -1) to be processed by this program.

1.2 Analysis of a Problem and Design of a Program

The starting point of the analysis process is a problem statement. This is usually given in English or in a combination of English and the language of the problem area. It generally deals with things -- temperatures, automobiles, colors, voters, dollars, etc. -- that cannot themselves be stored and manipulated by a computer. It is also usually stated in terms of commands that are not intelligible to a computer -- words like "solve", "find", "choose", etc. Typically, an initial problem statement is vague and imprecise, partly because of reliance on the knowledge and common sense of the human reader and partly because the originator has not completely formulated the exact requirements.

The end point of the process is a program -- a procedure that can be executed on a computer and that represents a solution to the problem. This process of transforming a problem description into a program has several different aspects:

1. A translation of language -- from English/mathematics to a programming language (PL/I, FORTRAN, COBOL, etc.)

2. A conversion from a statement of objectives -- <u>what</u> is to be done -- to an executable procedure -- <u>how</u> the task is to be accomplished.

3. The definition of symbols (variables) in a program to represent the real-world objects of the problem. For example, a variable might represent the status of a square of a chess board, the number of dollars in a bank account, or the temperature at a particular point on a rocket nozzle.

4. The elimination of all vagueness, imprecision and ambiguity. There is never vagueness in a computer program -- it always tells the computer or the human <u>precisely</u> what to do. The trick is to construct a program whose execution <u>exactly</u> solves the problem.

Only on very simple problems is there much chance of success if one starts immediately to write the program, no matter how experienced one might be. Typically, a systematic analysis of requirements and a design of the overall program structure precedes any attempt to write program statements. It is convenient to view this process as a "top down" or "level by level" analysis of the problem. The top level is the initial problem statement; the bottom level is a complete program; the number of intervening levels depends on the complexity of the problem.

Generally the second level is just a refinement of the problem statement -- an attempt to make complete and precise exactly what is required. This is often achieved by a dialog between the programmer and the "customer" -- the owner of the problem -- which involves questions like the following:

1. In what form will the data be supplied?

2. Are there reasonable limits on the values of data?

3. How will the end of the data be recognized?

4. What errors in the data should be anticipated? What action should be taken?

5. What form should the output take? What labelling and titling should be provided?

6. What precision (number of significant figures) of results is required?

7. What changes in the problem statement are likely (or possible) to occur during the lifetime of the program?

There may also be discussions of alternative stategies of solution. There might be two approaches -- one more costly to design and program and the other more costly to execute. The customer must provide information to guide such a choice.

While the objective of this dialog is to help the programmer understand exactly what has to be done, often the customer discovers that the problem is not yet well-formulated and that he himself is not sure what he wants done.

The levels occurring after this refinement of the problem statement are generally designed to accomplish two tasks:

1. To break up big problems into little problems, which in turn are attacked by this same approach.

2. To reduce the commands from English to programming terms. That is, "find", "solve", etc. must be reduced to "read", "print", "assign", "repeat", and then eventually to GET, PUT, DO -- the statements of a programming language.

1.3 Programming Languages

The level-by-level transformation of the problem description is complete when the entire description is in a language that is intelligible to a computer. However, there is no single programming language into which all problem descriptions are translated; there are literally hundreds in use today. The choice of language influences the manner in which a problem is solved and may have considerable influence on the difficulty experienced in obtaining a solution. Some languages have been designed for certain classes of problems; they exchange generality for convenience on a particular type of problem. Some exist to serve different makes and models of computers, and many exist just because there are wide differences of opinion as to what a programming language should look like.

Although there are hundreds of languages in use, a handful dominate the field. The most widely used is COBOL, which was designed for business data processing problems. The most widely used language for engineering and scientific computation is FORTRAN. Both of these were developed in the 1950s -- a long time ago in this field. Other important languages are ALGOL, APL, BASIC, LISP, PASCAL, PL/I, and SNOBOL.

PL/I, the language on which this book is based, was developed in the mid-60s in an attempt to serve both the scientific and data processing areas with a single language. The price of this flexibility is complexity, and PL/I is very complicated. It was also designed in something of a hurry, and the design is not as nice as it could be. Nevertheless, PL/I is the most "modern" of the languages in general use. However it has not come close to displacing either FORTRAN or COBOL.

In many places in this book we are critical of PL/I (or at least apologetic). It is far from ideal and we hope that someday it will be replaced by a better language. You should try to keep an open mind on the matter and realize that PL/I represents just one compromise solution to the problem of devising a programming language. Not until you have significant experience in several different languages will you be able to appreciate the relative strengths and weaknesses of PL/I.

Actually, in this book we are concerned with four similar but different languages.

1. PL/I.

2. PL/C: a widely used instructional version of PL/I developed by the Computer Science Department at Cornell. It omits some PL/I features and adds diagnostic features in order to facilitate instruction. PL/C is also a translation program (called a "compiler") that is especially effective and helpful in instruction.

3. PL/CT: an "interactive" version of PL/C designed for running and testing programs in an "interactive mode" with the computer.

4. PL/CS: a new experimental, "disciplined" version of PL/C, which enforces some of the ideas that have come to be regarded as good programming practice. The hope is that it will help to create good habits that will be continued after the programmer graduates to richer but less disciplined languages.

This book can be used in a course where any of these four languages are used. Essentially they are the same, at least for the subset we use, and differences are pointed out at appropriate places in the text.

The main point to remember is that teaching a programmming language is not our main goal; rather we are interested in teaching good programming concepts and principles. We wish to teach problem solving and program methodologies that can be used in dealing with almost any programming language.

For most students, the first programming language learned will be the first of several. This is true both because there are specialized languages available for various different areas of application and because progress in computer science should eventually lead to languages that will replace all those in use today. There is a distinct advantage in learning to program in a language like PL/I or PASCAL rather than FORTRAN or COBOL, even though you might sometime have to use one of the latter. PL/I and PASCAL are more recent, and as such are more representative of current thinking on the subject. Future languages will certainly bear more resemblance to PL/I than FORTRAN. Secondly, PL/I and PASCAL are more general in their capability. All the programming concepts present in FORTRAN and COBOL are present in PL/I and PASCAL, but not conversely. It is easier for a student to first learn PL/I and later FORTRAN or COBOL, rather than vice versa.

1.4 Compilation and Execution of a Program

When the program is complete and data have been prepared, both must be transmitted to the computer. The usual means of communication is the "punched card" or "IBM card". A "keypunch" is used to encode information in a card by punching holes in it. Each different character has a different pattern of holes; each character in the program and data is represented by the pattern in one vertical column of the card.

An alternative method of introducing information into a computing system is by means of a "terminal" directly connected to the computer. The keyboard of such a terminal is like that of the keypunch, but instead of punching holes in a card the terminal transmits its information directly to the computer, essentially as the key is struck. This has the virtue of immediate response -- the user is notified of errors after each line of the program, and sees results as the program is being executed. Although the use of such terminals is increasing, it is still more expensive than using punched cards, and the majority of introductory instruction still uses cards. For our purposes it makes little difference which type of access is used and we will speak of program lines, input lines, and cards almost interchangeably.

The key point in understanding the loading and execution of a program is the timing of the reading of the cards. <u>The card deck consists of two parts</u> -- the <u>program</u> (lines 1 to 25 of the example in Section 1.1) and the <u>data</u> (lines 26 and 27). The cards for the entire program are read initially -- <u>before any execution of the program begins</u>; the data are not. This program is then translated, or <u>compiled</u> by a "compiler", into a language that the computer can directly "understand" or execute. <u>Then</u>, finally, the program is executed. In the course of execution the "card read" statements (such as lines 14 and 20 of 1.1) will cause the data cards to be read.

While the program is being compiled, the compiler checks the program statements for "syntactical" (grammatical) errors and reports these to the user. If any errors are discovered during this process the compiler will halt after loading and refuse to initiate execution of the user-program; a few compilers will effect some repair of minor errors and permit execution to begin. Most users will become aware of the existence of a compiler only through this error checking and will never have occasion to see the strange form their program has assumed in memory.

The printed output for a program can also be divided into two parts, corresponding to the compilation and execution phases described above. During compilation, a copy of the user-program is printed, including announcement of any errors discovered. This much of the printing is automatic -- a service performed by the compiler. Further printing will be done during execution only as called for by the "output" statements (such as lines 22 and 23 of 1.1) of the program. If the user fails to include any such statements there will be no output during execution and the results of the computation will never be known.

1.5 Program Correctness

The task of confirming the correctness of a program is often neglected by writers and teachers, sometimes to an embarrassing degree. In any but the most trivial problem errors will be made, and it is important to systematically plan for the testing phase from the beginning. Typically more than half the total time, effort, and cost of the computing process is devoted to testing and "debugging" the program -- and yet in spite of this effort the process is not often completely successful. This situation is so prevalent and serious that society today has diminishing confidence in the computing process. Computers are thought to be inherently unreliable, but in almost all cases the true fault lies in a program that was poorly designed and/or inadequately tested.

The program in Section 1.1 was constructed to illustrate this point. It works perfectly for the data given, and also for many other sets of data, but line 9 restricts this program so that it can only successfully handle integer values. However, there is nothing in the problem statement that suggests the program will only be used for integer values. As a consequence any time this program is used for noninteger data (i.e., values like 17.3), it is likely to produce incorrect results without even warning the user. The program "works" for some sets of data but it is not correct. Contriving difficult test cases that reveal all errors is something of an art in itself. While testing is listed as a separate phase of the programming process it actually pervades the entire process. It is essential that the necessity of demonstrating correctness be considered when the program is being designed and that provision for testing be incorporated in the program as it is written, rather than as an afterthought.

This issue, and the techniques available to achieve correctness, are discussed in detail in Part V.

Section 1 Exercises

The following all refer to the programming example given in Section 1.1. You cannot be expected to answer all of these questions at this point, but attempting to do so should be interesting and educational.

1. What would have to be done to cause this program to obtain the maximum of the following eight numbers:
   2, 4, 6, 15, 3, 9, 7, 9

2. What would happen if the program were used to find the maximum of the following nine numbers:
   6, 45, -3, 14, 0, 2, -1, 52, 143

3. What would happen if line 27 looked like the following:
   5, 5, 5, -1, -1, -1

4. What would happen if the order of lines 17 and 18 were reversed? Lines 13 and 14? Lines 18 and 19?

5. Suppose the problem definition were broadened to require the program to work for negative as well as positive numbers. What changes would have to be made?

6. How could the program be changed to obtain the minimum rather than the maximum of the numbers?

7. How could the program be changed to produce both the maximum and the minimum of the numbers?

8. What would happen if line 17 were accidentally left out (say the card was dropped) before the program was submitted to the computer? Line 19? Line 23?

9. What would happen if line 22 were replaced by the following line?

```
/* PUT LIST('NUMBER OF VALUES =', COUNT); */
```

10. How could the program be changed to produce the sum of the numbers in addition to the maximum?

11. What would happen if line 2 were replaced by the following line:

```
/* COMPUTE THE PRETTIEST OF THE GREEN NUMBERS */
```

and no other change were made in the program?

12. Construct a set of test data (a replacement for line 27) that would cause the program to produce incorrect results.

Section 2 Variables

The concept of a "variable" is central to programming. It is similar but not identical to the idea of a variable in algebra. In both fields a variable is a symbol that represents a value, and expressions can be written using variables instead of the values they represent. Thus, for example, the value of expression:

X + Y

depends on the values that X and Y currently represent.

In programming, a variable also has a physical interpretation: a variable is a location in the memory of the computer that can be used to contain a value, and the variable name, or "identifier", is used to unambiguously refer to that location and its value. In this book we use the following notational convention to refer to variables:

X 20

The line represents a location in memory, X is the identifier associated with this location, and 20 is the value that location X currently contains.

Literally and physically the expression "X + Y" is evaluated as follows:

> Retrieve a copy of the value currently contained in location X; retrieve a copy of the value currently contained in Y; the value of the expression is the sum of these two values.

2.1 Identifiers

Memory locations actually have permanent identifiers (called "addresses") but these are inconvenient to use directly. Hence the programming language allows the programmer to choose names for locations. Each name chosen is permanently associated with a particular location -- which location doesn't matter to the programmer. This association lasts for the duration of the execution of the program (or more precisely, for the duration of execution of a particular "procedure").

The sequence of characters that forms the name of a variable is called an "identifier". Each programming language has its own rules governing the formation of identifiers. In PL/I an identifier can be any sequence of not more than 31 letters, digits or the special characters "$", "#", "@" and "_", starting with a letter. For example, all the following are valid identifiers:

```
X    Y3    TEMP    STARTING_VALUE

MAX_PRESSURE    QUANTITY@20    SERIAL#

YEAR_TODATE_$SALES
```

●PL/C: The following are "statement keywords" of PL/C and are <u>reserved</u> exclusively for that use. They may not be used as identifiers:

> ALLOCATE BEGIN BY CALL CHECK CLOSE DCL DECLARE DELETE DO ELSE END ENTRY EXIT FLOW FORMAT FREE GET GO GOTO IF NO NOCHECK NOFLOW ON OPEN PROC PROCEDURE PUT READ RETURN REVERT REWRITE SIGNAL STOP THEN TO WHILE WRITE

●PL/CS: The characters "$", "@" and "#" cannot be used in identifiers. (PL/CS itself can generate identifiers using "$" but the programmer cannot.) The following keywords are reserved and cannot be used as identifiers:

> ALL ASSERT BIT BY CALL CHAR CHARACTER DATA DATAEND DCL DECLARE DO EDIT ELSE END ENDFILE EXT EXTERNAL FIXED FLOAT FOR GET GO GOTO IF INIT INITIAL LEAVE LIST MAIN ON OPTIONS OTHER OTHERWISE PROC PROCEDURE PUT READ READONLY RETURN RETURNS SELECT SKIP SOME STATIC THEN TO UNTIL VAR VARYING WHEN WHILE

PL/I permits identifiers to be long enough to allow the choice of variable names that suggest the roles played by the variables in the program. It is also prudent to choose names that are not too similar to each other, in order to reduce confusion in reading the program and to minimize susceptibility to keypunch mistakes. Although PL/I permits identifiers to be identical to keywords it is unwise to choose such names because it makes programs unnecessarily difficult to read.

2.2 Types of Values

Programs in many programming languages can process other kinds of values as well as numbers. Most languages define certain "types" of values and, in effect, provide a sub-language for processing each type. We are concerned with four types of values:

1. decimal number (called "float" in PL/I)

2. integer (called "fixed" in PL/I)

3. character string

4. logical, or bit string.

These are described in the following sections. Additional PL/I types are mentioned in Appendix A.

In PL/I, as in many other programming languages, each variable is restricted to one type of value. Like the name, the type of a variable is permanent. For example, if variable COUNT is declared integer, then at different times it may contain values such as 3, 0, 1501, or -6, but it could never contain a value such as 20.3 (which is a decimal number) or JEWEL (which is a character string).

The notational convention for variables shows the type as follows:

INDEX 6 [fixed]

This indicates a variable named INDEX, restricted to integers, whose current value is 6.

Each variable has a type. When we neglect to specify the type of a variable in a discussion it is only because the type is not relevant to the point at issue, and not because the variable has no type.

2.2.1 Decimal Numbers

"Decimal numbers" or "real numbers" are just the ordinary numbers of everyday usage. They can be positive or negative, big or small (within certain limits), and with or without explicit decimal points and fractional parts. For example, each of the following is a decimal number written as it might appear as a constant in a program:

-20 10365 -0.25 15.125

PL/I converts decimal numbers to a standard exponential form with six significant digits and an exponent of two digits, which specifies the power of ten required to properly scale the number. The number is "normalized" so that the decimal point always follows the leftmost significant digit. For example, the above numbers in this standard form are:

-2.00000E+01   1.03650E+04   -2.50000E-01   1.51250E+01

You can write constants in a program in exponential form, but it is not necessary to use the standard form as shown above. For example, the numbers

3,000,000,000   -.00000001   .000012

could be written as

3E9   -.1E-7   1.2E-5

Regardless of the form used in the program, decimal numbers are stored in float variables in the standard form shown earlier, and appear in that form when the program causes results to be printed.

Exponential form is also called "floating point format" because the real position of the decimal point "floats", depending on the exponent (hence the PL/I designation "float"). It is, of course, limited by the number of significant digits and the digits of the exponent, so results that are too large will "overflow" this representation and results that are too small will "underflow". Also, numbers that are too dissimilar in magnitude cannot be effectively processed. But subject to these limits, arithmetic on numbers of moderate size can be more-or-less automatic.

The number of significant digits in the floating point representation can be changed by the programmer (see Appendix A.5) but we will not use this option. The six digits shown above, and used throughout the book, is the default precision assumed by PL/I in the absence of explicit specification of precision by the programmer.

● PL/CS: The programmer has no control over precision. All floating point numbers are stored internally with 16 significant digits, but only the leftmost 6 digits of these are displayed on output.

One peculiarity of decimal numbers will occasionally be disconcerting. Because the numbers are actually stored in binary rather than decimal form, many fractional numbers cannot be represented exactly -- they are "off" by 1 in the rightmost digit. For example, 1.07 will appear as 1.06999E+00 and .1 as 9.99999E-02. Not all fractions suffer from this approximation -- for example, .5 is exact. These approximations are harmless for ordinary arithmetic purposes -- they give reasonable results when used in calculations -- but they are disconcerting when they appear on output.

When representing variables in this book we often (but not always) indicate their value type. For example, a variable QTY that is restricted to floating point numbers and currently contains the number 25.6, would be shown as:

QTY <u>2.56000E+01 [float]</u>

Moreover, by specifying that the type is "float" we do not always feel obligated to show the value in its actual exponential form. We can write:

QTY <u>25.6 [float]</u>

2.2.2 Integers

When it is known that a variable will always contain an <u>integer</u> it is convenient to use a special type of value called "fixed" in PL/I.

An integer value is stored exactly as written, with the decimal point always assumed to be to the right of the last digit. Arithmetic with fixed operands is simpler than floating point arithmetic (since no preliminary alignment or normalization of the result is required); hence on many computers it is a little faster. For our purpose this gain in efficiency is not significant; nevertheless, it is customary practice to identify those variables that will only contain integers. A corollary benefit of this segregation is that when the values of such variables are displayed they will be in the obvious integer form, rather than the somewhat obscure exponential form.

We show an integer variable as follows:

COUNT <u>7 [fixed]</u>

The maximum number of digits in the integer form we use is 5, but this can be increased to as much as 15 by the programmer (see Appendix A.5).

● PL/CS: The maximum number of digits in an integer is always 5.

2.2.3 Character Strings

A sequence of characters is called a "string value", or often just a "string". The eligible characters consist of the digits, the letters and various special characters. The complete list is shown below:

b̸¢.<(+|&!$*);¬-/,%_>?:#@'="ABCDEFGHIJKLMNOPQRSTUVWXYZ0123456789

The first character of this list is actually the blank character. The blank is a valid character -- in fact, in many ways it is an especially important character. But it is sometimes awkward since it doesn't show on the printed page. Consequently, when necessary, we use the artificial symbol "b̸" to represent the blank character.

Although one initially thinks of "computing" in terms of numbers, the processing of strings is very important. In fact, since business data processing is concerned with values such as names, addresses and descriptions as well as numbers, the world's computers probably process more string data than numbers.

For example, programs called "text editors" take a sequence of words, punctuation marks, and format commands, and format the words and punctuation marks into lines, paragraphs, and pages. They calculate how many blanks to insert in each line so that both margins are aligned. This book was produced using such a program.

String processing is useful as a pedagogical tool, even for programmers who will eventually be primarily concerned with numerical problems. In many respects it is easier to illustrate the key ideas of programming using strings. It is also easier to invent string processing problems of reasonable size and difficulty that still perform interesting and useful tasks.

The number of characters in a string is the length of the string. Perhaps surprisingly, considering the predetermined number of digits in decimal numbers and integers, there is no standard string length. The programmer must explicitly specify the length for each variable that is to contain a string.

● PL/I: The maximum allowable string length is 32,768 characters.

● PL/C: The maximum allowable string length is 256 characters.

PL/I has two different types of character string variables: "fixed length" and "varying length". In both cases the programmer specifies a maximum length for each character string variable (see Section 2.3). For a fixed-length string variable the length is always exactly equal to this specified maximum length, but for a varying-length string the actual length can vary -- from zero up to the specified maximum. In many respects varying-length strings are more convenient and we consider only this type.

● PL/CS: All character strings are "varying length". The maximum allowable string length is 256 chracters.

The following are examples of character string variables. "Char" and "var" are abbreviations of the keywords "character" and "varying", respectively. The number after "char" specifies the maximum length of the value the variable may contain.

```
WORD    AVERAGE [char(12) var]
WORD2   PUT [char(20) var]
SYMB    + [char(1) var]
```

In the case of decimal numbers and integers little had to be said about how to write those values in a program because conventional forms are used. For example, the symbol 37 appearing in a program can only be a numeric value. But several problems arise in writing strings.

First, strings can be equivalent to the symbols used for commands and variable names in the program. For example, consider the variables shown above. The value of WORD could also be a variable name, the value of WORD2 could be a PL/I keyword, and the value of SYMB is also the symbol for addition. Obviously there must be some way of recognizing character string values as such when they are written in a program.

A second problem is that a blank space is ordinarily used to <u>separate</u> the symbols of a program, but since a blank is a valid character in a string it may be <u>included</u> in a string value. For example, the following could be a string of five characters:

Nb̸+b̸3

or it could be three separate symbols ("N", "+" and "3") with an entirely different meaning.

A solution to these problems is to delimit each string value appearing in a program by some special character. PL/I, like many other languages, uses the single <u>quote</u> character for this purpose. (The quote is the character over the "H" on the keypunch.) For example, the sequence

'HALFWAY ROCK'

appearing in a program denotes the twelve character string

HALFWAYb̸ROCK

in the same way that 37 denotes the integer thirty-seven. Note that the quotes are <u>not</u> part of the value; they just delimit it. A string constant like 'HALFWAY ROCK' is called a "literal".

Because the quote character is used as the string delimiter a special convention must be used to denote its occurence inside a string. This convention is to write two quotes for each quote that is part of the value. Thus the thirteen character string

MINOT'Sb̸LIGHT

would be written as a literal as

'MINOT''S LIGHT'

The value itself still consists of thirteen characters -- that is, with a single included quote and without the delimiting quotes. (Note that the repeated quote consists of a repetition of the single quote, which is not the same as the double-quote character.)

To further illustrate the role of blanks and quotes, consider the following examples. Each line shows a value as it would be written as a literal and as it would be stored in a string variable ST:

```
'b̸'        ST b̸ [char(20) var]

'b̸b̸'       ST b̸b̸ [char(20) var]

'b̸''b̸'     ST b̸'b̸ [char(20) var]

''''        ST ' [char(20) var]

'"'         ST " [char(20) var]

''          ST  [char(20) var]
```

The last of these examples is the special value consisting of no characters. It is called the empty string or the null string. This is a legitimate string value and, in fact, an especially important and frequently used value. Note that the empty string is not the same as the string consisting of a single blank.

Note that strings may look like numbers. For example:

NSTRG 2.01000E+02 [char(15) var]

This value looks like a number but is an eleven character string. No string value -- even one that looks like a number -- should be used like a number in arithmetic operations (see Section 3.5).

2.2.4 Logical Values

The final type we consider has only two possible values -- 0 and 1. This type is called "bit", "Boolean", or "logical". PL/I will permit logical strings of any length (either fixed-length or varying-length), but the only form we use has a fixed length of one. These two logical values are written in a program as the literals:

'0'B and '1'B

These values are quoted, like character strings, but are followed by a "B" to indicate a bit string. We show a variable with this type of value as follows:

FLAG 0 [bit(1)]

These bit values 0 and 1 generally represent the truth-values "false" and "true", respectively:

'0'B represents "false"

'1'B represents "true"

They have special uses in the control of a program, as discussed in Section 6.1 and 7.1.

● PL/CS: Single-character, fixed-length bit strings are the only logical variables allowed.

2.2.5 User-Defined Types of Values

In addition to the standard types built into the language, some languages (for example, PASCAL) allow the programmer to define his own types of values, but PL/I does not provide such a facility.

2.3 Creation of Variables

Since variables are not supplied as a fixed part of a programming language, the programmer must describe the variables to be used in each program. This is done with "declarations" at the beginning of the program, which give the name and type of each variable. This causes the variables to be created before the program is executed.

The form of the declaration for a single variable is:

DECLARE variable-name type-attributes ;

The "variable-name" is an identifier chosen by the programmer to identify the variable. The "type-attributes" are language keywords that specify the type of value the variable may contain. Full PL/I offers a bewildering collection of type-attributes (see Appendix A.5) but we use only a small subset of these:

```
FLOAT     for decimal numbers with 6
                significant digits

FIXED     for integers with up to 5 digits

CHARACTER (length) VARYING
                for varying-length character strings

BIT (1)   for single character bit strings.
```

Examples of the declaration of single variables of different types are:

```
DECLARE NBR FLOAT;
DECLARE COUNT FIXED;
DECLARE STR CHARACTER (50) VARYING;
DECLARE FLAG BIT (1);
```

The keywords DECLARE, CHARACTER and VARYING can be <u>abbreviated</u> (but FLOAT, FIXED and BIT cannot). The examples given above could be abbreviated to:

```
DCL NBR FLOAT;
DCL COUNT FIXED;
DCL STR CHAR (50) VAR;
DCL FLAG BIT (1);
```

When FLOAT, FIXED and BIT variables are created they initially have no value. We denote this situation by showing a "?" in place of a value:

```
NBR   ? [float]
COUNT ? [fixed]
FLAG  ? [bit(1)]
```

On the other hand, a newly created varying-length character string contains no characters, but the empty string is a legitimate value for such a variable. We show such a value as follows:

```
STR [char(50) var]
```

<u>Several variables of the same type</u> can be created by a single declaration. For example:

```
DCL (STR1, STR2, WORD) CHAR (40) VAR;
```

is equivalent to:

```
DCL STR1 CHAR (40) VAR;
DCL STR2 CHAR (40) VAR;
DCL WORD CHAR (40) VAR;
```

PL/I declarations can be much more complex, with several different types of variables in the same declaration. Careful "factoring" is then required to indicate which attributes apply to which identifiers. This complexity adds no new capability; it just increases the opportunity to make confusing mistakes. We use only the simple form shown above with a single list of identifiers.

Declarations can be the most perplexing part of PL/I. The punctuation in a declaration is critical -- especially when several variables are included in the same declaration. If the parentheses are not used as shown above, or if too many or too few commas are given, surprising things occur. The result may be a legal PL/I declaration (although not a form we have explained), but its meaning will be quite different from what was intended. Examples and some explanation are given in Section 2.3.1, but basically there are three rules to remember:

1. If more than one variable is included in the declaration, enclose all the variable names in parentheses.

2. Separate the names of the variables with commas.

3. Do not put a comma after the last variable name, or in the attribute portion of the declaration.

4. Terminate the declaration with a semi-colon.

●PL/CS: The parentheses around the variable name or names are required, even if only a single variable is being declared.

2.3.1 Implicit Declarations and Default Attributes

You will soon discover (probably by accident) that PL/I does not really demand explicit declaration of each variable. When you use an identifier in a program without explicitly declaring it, PL/I considers this an "implicit declaration" and automatically creates a variable with the new name. Sometimes this is convenient, but often it is a confusing disservice. You should get in the habit of giving explicit declarations, but nevertheless you will need to know something about this characteristic of PL/I.

The "default" type attributes used in the case of an implicit declaration depend upon the spelling of the identifier:

If the identifier begins with one of the letters I, J,

K, L, M or N then FIXED is assumed. (Type "binary" is also assumed, rather than "decimal", but that is immaterial for our purposes.)

Otherwise FLOAT is assumed.

(This curious distinction is a legacy from an ancient programming language called FORTRAN.)

PL/I does not permit the implicit declaration of either a string or a logical variable, regardless of how the variable may be used in the program.

Unfortunately, an implicit declaration is often an <u>accident</u>. For example, if you misspell the name of a variable a new variable with the misspelled name is created. Since there are then two distinct variables where there should be only one the program is incorrect, but there is little to bring the accident to your attention.

Similarly, many common errors in explicit declarations cause the default attributes to be applied where you did not expect them. For example, suppose you misspelled the attribute FLOAT so that a declaration appeared as follows:

```
DECLARE LIMIT FLAOT;
```

This is taken to be the declaration of two variables LIMIT and FLAOT. (There is also an error, since no comma is given between them.) Since apparently no attributes are given, LIMIT is assumed to be FIXED (since it begins with "L") and FLAOT is of type FLOAT. Or suppose you accidentally place a comma between the variable name and its type-attribute:

```
DECLARE AMT, FIXED;
```

This is taken to be the declaration of two variables AMT and FIXED, both of which are of type FLOAT because of their spelling.

● PL/CS: Explicit declaration is required, and is automatically generated if omitted. The default attribute is always FLOAT regardless of the spelling of the identifier. The attribute keywords are reserved and cannot be mistaken for variable names, regardless of punctuation in the declaration.

The only way to be certain what variables have actually been created in your program is to specify the optional "attribute and cross-reference listing" (see ATR and XREF options in Appendix B.2) at least on the initial runs of your program. Then study this listing very carefully to see that <u>every variable actually created was one that you intended</u>.

2.4 Variables with Multiple Values

The simple variables described so far, called "scalars", provide space for a single value. The value stored in such a variable may be changed from time to time during execution of a program, but at any given instant the variable has only one value.

Suppose it is necessary to store a large amount of data at the same time. For example, we might want to calculate a set of numbers, then sort them into increasing order, and finally print them out in sorted order. If there were 50 numbers, using 50 different variables could be cumbersome. Arrays of subscripted variables provide a more convenient method.

An array is a set of variables with a common identifier and a common type. For example, COUNT could refer to a set of four integer variables:

```
COUNT(1)  20 [fixed]
COUNT(2)  -2 [fixed]
COUNT(3)   0 [fixed]
COUNT(4)   8 [fixed]
```

The individual variables in the set are identified by appending a "subscript" to their common identifier. The usual subscript notation cannot be used since the keypunch lacks the capability of depressing a character below the normal line. Consequently subscripts are identified by enclosing them in parentheses. The parentheses are crucial: COUNT2 would be an entirely different variable, whereas COUNT(2) is a subscripted variable -- an element of the array COUNT.

The array COUNT shown above (without the values shown) would be created by the declaration:

```
DECLARE COUNT(1:4) FIXED;
```

the integers 1 and 4 in the declaration specify the minimum and the maximum subscript values for COUNT, and hence the number of elements in the array.

All the elements of a particular array must have the same type, but that can be any of the types described in Section 2.2. For example:

```
DCL NOR(1:20) FLOAT;

DCL LINE(1:30) CHAR (80) VAR;

DCL (FLAG(1:5), INDICATOR(1:4)) BIT (1);
```

2.4.1 Subscripts

A subscripted variable rarely appears in a program with the subscript actually given as an integer constant, as shown above. Generally the subscript will be written as the name of another variable -- one whose value is an integer. For example, consider the array COUNT declared above. An element of COUNT could be referred to by writing COUNT(I). The value of variable I at the time of this reference must be either 1, 2, 3 or 4. The value of variable I specifies which one of the set of variables named COUNT is being referenced.

In effect, this allows a variable to be used to select a particular element of an array -- or to put it another way, by assigning a value to I the program can determine which element of the array COUNT is to be used. It may not be obvious at this point, but this is an extremely powerful facility in a programming language. Its use is illustrated in Section 7.2.

A subscript value can also be given by an "expression" -- a formula involving variables, constants and arithmetic operators, from which a particular integer value can be computed. For example, subscript values could be specified by expressions such as the following:

```
COUNT(I+2)

COUNT(I-J)

COUNT(K + LIMIT/2)
```

A subscript expression is valid if when evaluated it yields an integer value corresponding to one of the elements of the array.

Subscripts do not have to start with 1. Depending on the problem it may be more natural to start with some other value. For example, to create an array of four variables, with individual names COUNT(0), COUNT(1), COUNT(2) and COUNT(3) the following declaration would be used:

```
DCL COUNT(0:3) FIXED;
```

Other examples are:

```
DCL (TEST(4:7), FLAG(-2:1)) BIT (1);

DCL (SUM(1:4), PROD(2:5)) FLOAT;

DCL CODE(-6:-3) CHAR (10) VAR;
```

Note that each of the arrays created by these declarations has exactly four elements.

PL/I assumes a starting point of 1 if no starting point is explicitly specified. That is, the following are equivalent:

```
DCL COUNT(1:4) FIXED;

DCL COUNT(4) FIXED;
```

2.4.2 Variables with Multiple Subscripts

The singly-subscripted variables described above can be readily visualized as a list (or vector) of variables. But sometimes it is convenient to be able to consider an array as a two-dimensional table (or matrix) of variables. To facilitate this, an array can be declared so that its elements are identified with two subscript values. Each dimension is specified by a separate term in the declaration. For example:

```
DCL SCORE(1:3,1:4) FLOAT;
```

creates an array of twelve variables whose values are decimal numbers. The names of the individual elements of this array are:

```
SCORE(1,1)  SCORE(1,2)  SCORE(1,3)  SCORE(1,4)

SCORE(2,1)  SCORE(2,2)  SCORE(2,3)  SCORE(2,4)

SCORE(3,1)  SCORE(3,2)  SCORE(3,3)  SCORE(3,4)
```

As with singly-subscripted arrays, the subscripts need not start with 1, but 1 is assumed if no starting point is specified. For example, the variables created by:

```
DCL SCORE(0:2,4) FLOAT;
```

would be:

```
SCORE(0,1)  SCORE(0,2)  SCORE(0,3)  SCORE(0,4)

SCORE(1,1)  SCORE(1,2)  SCORE(1,3)  SCORE(1,4)

SCORE(2,1)  SCORE(2,2)  SCORE(2,3)  SCORE(2,4)
```

Singly- and doubly-subscripted variables are the most commonly used, but three or more dimensions are allowed if the problem requires it. For example:

```
DCL ITEM(2,0:3,0:4) FLOAT;
```

2.5 Initial Values

As noted in Section 2.3, FLOAT, FIXED and BIT variables do not automatically have a value when created. The declaration of such variables only creates them. They are capable of containing a value, but the actual assignment of a value is a separate action. You might have assumed that numeric variables would automatically have an initial value of 0 and that logical variables would initially be "false", but PL/I (as well as most other languages) just does not work that way.

However, an initial value can optionally be assigned as part of the creation process. This is done with the INITIAL attribute:

```
INITIAL (initial-value)   or   INIT (initial-value)
```

For example:

```
DECLARE X FLOAT INITIAL (0);

DECLARE COUNT FIXED INIT (5);

DCL IND4 BIT (1) INIT ('0'B);
```

The result of these declarations would be:

```
X      0 [float]

COUNT  5 [fixed]

IND4   0 [bit(1)]
```

The initial value is assigned to each of the variables created by a declaration. For example, the result of

```
DCL (COUNT, LIMIT) FIXED INIT (12);
```

would be

```
COUNT  12 [fixed]

LIMIT  12 [fixed]
```

Although varying length character string variables have the empty string as an automatic initial value, the INITIAL attribute can be used to assign some different initial value. For example:

```
DECLARE DIRECTION CHAR (5) VAR INIT('EAST');
```

```
DECLARE SENTENCE CHAR(100) VAR INIT(' ');
```

The result of these declarations would be:

DIRECTION EAST [char(5) var]

SENTENCE ƀ [char(100) var]

The INITIAL attribute is especially convenient for assigning initial values to arrays. A list of initial values is specified -- usually one value for each element of the array. For example:

```
DECLARE (X(1:4), Y(3:6)) FIXED INIT (5,6,7,8);
```

causes creation of two arrays X and Y with initial values as follows:

X(1) 5   X(2) 6   X(3) 7   X(4) 8

Y(3) 5   Y(4) 6   Y(5) 7   Y(6) 8

The number of values in the INITIAL list need not exactly match the number of elements of the array. If the INITIAL list is shorter, the excess elements of the array will have no initial values; if the INITIAL list is longer, the excess values will simply be ignored. For example:

```
DCL (X(2), Y(3)) FIXED INITIAL (4);

DCL (C, D) FIXED INITIAL (7, 8);
```

would create the following:

X(1) 4   X(2) ?

Y(1) 4   Y(2) ?   Y(3) ?

C 7   D 7

Recall that "?" is used to denote a variable that has no value. Note that the initial value assigned to variable D is 7 (and not 8).

Initial values are assigned to a doubly-subscripted array in "row-major order". That means they are assigned by rows, from left to right, top to bottom. For example:

```
DCL LTR(2,2) CHAR (1) VAR INIT ('A','B','C','D');
```

would create the following:

```
LTR(1,1) A     LTR(1,2) B

LTR(2,1) C     LTR(2,2) D
```

When the same value would appear in consecutive positions on an INITIAL list, the repetition may be avoided by using a "repetition factor". For example, the following are equivalent:

```
INIT (1,(3)0,(2)1)       INIT (1,0,0,0,1,1)
```

This is useful for initializing large arrays. For example:

```
DCL COEF(10,10) FLOAT INIT ((100)0);
```

A repetition factor can also be applied to a list of values, in which case the list of values is also enclosed in parentheses. For example, the following are equivalent:

```
INIT ((3)(0,1),(2)3)       INIT (0,1,0,1,0,1,3,3)
```

2.5.1 Named Constants

Often a particular constant is used in several places in a program. It is convenient, and good practice, to use a variable instead and write the name rather than the value at each point of use. The value can be given in the declaration. For example:

```
DCL INTEREST_RATE FLOAT INIT (.085);
DCL PI FLOAT INIT (3.1416);
DCL START_DATE CHAR(13) VAR INIT ('DEC. 12, 1931');
```

This is especially useful when a value that is a constant throughout the program must occasionally be changed from one run to another. It is easier to change the value once in the declaration than to find all occurrences of the value scattered throughout the program.

Some programming languages (PASCAL, for example) provide a special type for constants, to ensure that they are not accidentally changed in the program. PL/I lacks such a facility, but it is present in PL/CS.

● PL/CS: The READONLY attribute denotes a variable whose value is not to be changed in the body of the program. For example:

```
DCL (INTEREST_RATE) FLOAT INIT (.085) READONLY;
```

2.6 Variables with Structured Values

A "structure" is a special-purpose type of variable which is used in only a few sections of the book (principally in Parts VII and VIII). The description of structures belongs here with the definition of other types of variables, but it should not be studied in detail until you actually need to use this facility. On first reading just note the general nature of structures, and come back to this section later when you need to use them.

● PL/CS: Structures are not allowed.

A PL/I structure is a collection of variables and arrays. For example, suppose four variables are to be used to represent a student's name, age, account balance and marital status:

```
NAME CHAR (30) VARYING
AGE FIXED
ACCOUNT_BALANCE FLOAT
MARRIED_NOW BIT (1)
```

Since these variables are related to each other, and since many processing operations will affect them all, it is convenient to declare them with a common name to indicate their interdependence:

```
DCL 1 STUDENT,
        2 NAME CHAR (30) VARYING,
        2 AGE FIXED,
        2 ACCOUNT_BALANCE FLOAT,
        2 MARRIED_NOW BIT (1);
```

STUDENT is the name of a structure whose components are the variables NAME, AGE, ACCOUNT_BALANCE and MARRIED_NOW. The structure name is recognized as such by the 1 preceding it, and the components by the 2 preceding their identifiers. (Although PL/I allows a structure to be included in a declaration list with other variables, it is clearer and less susceptible to errors if each structure is created by a separate declaration as shown here.)

The structure-name itself is not associated with a value -- note that there are no type-attributes following it. The value of a structure is the value of its individual components. Note also that the individual elements can have any type of value, and in particular that they can have different types of values.

An array can be a component of a structure, as in the example below where CURRENT_COURSES has been added:

```
DCL 1 STUDENT,
        2 NAME CHAR (30) VARYING,
        2 AGE FIXED,
        2 CURRENT_COURSES(10) CHAR (8) VARYING,
        2 ACCOUNT_BALANCE FLOAT,
        2 MARRIED_NOW BIT (1);
```

A component can itself be a "minor structure", such as RESIDENCE in the example below. The preceding 2 indicates that RESIDENCE is a component of STUDENT and the 3's preceding STREET, CITY_STATE and ZIP_CODE indicate these are components of RESIDENCE:

```
DCL 1 STUDENT,
        2 NAME CHAR (30) VARYING,
        2 RESIDENCE,
           3 STREET CHAR (40) VAR,
           3 CITY_STATE CHAR (40) VAR,
           3 ZIP_CODE CHAR (5) VAR,
        2 AGE FIXED,
        2 CURRENT_COURSES(10) CHAR (8) VAR,
        2 ACCOUNT_BALANCE FLOAT,
        2 MARRIED_NOW BIT (1);
```

Minor structures can have multiple values -- that is, there can be "arrays of structures". In the example below the minor structure PAST_COURSES has 100 sets of values -- in effect, equivalent to declaring each of its components COURSE_NBR, CREDIT_HOURS and GRADE as an array with 100 elements.

```
DCL 1 STUDENT,
        2 NAME CHAR (30) VARYING,
        2 RESIDENCE,
           3 STREET CHAR (40) VAR,
           3 CITY_STATE CHAR (40) VAR,
           3 ZIP_CODE CHAR (5) VAR,
        2 AGE FIXED,
        2 CURRENT_COURSES(10) CHAR (8) VAR,
        2 PAST_COURSES(100),
           3 COURSE_NBR CHAR (8) VAR,
           3 CREDIT_HOURS FIXED,
           3 GRADE CHAR (2) VAR,
        2 ACCOUNT_BALANCE FLOAT,
        2 MARRIED_NOW BIT (1);
```

Complete "major" structures can also be arrays. For example: there could be multiple copies of the STUDENT structure:

```
DCL 1 STUDENT(5),
        2 NAME CHAR (30) VARYING,
        etc.
```

For some purposes in a program an entire structure can be treated as a single object and the structure name can be given instead of all the individual component names. However, in other situations it is necessary to refer to an individual component of a structure. The full name of an individual component is called a "qualified name". This is constructed from all of the structure names from the major structure through minor structures, down to the particular component. This must include subscripts for those names that are arrays. For example, the name of the Jth past course of the Ith student would be:

```
STUDENT(I).PAST_COURSE(J).GRADE
```

PL/I permits abbreviations of fully-qualified names when this does not cause ambiguity, but we use only fully-qualified names in the book.

Within a structure the names of identifiers need not be unique. For example:

```
DCL 1 ACCOUNT,
        2 WITHDRAWALS(20),
            3 DATE CHAR (8) VAR,
            3 AMOUNT FIXED,
        2 DEPOSITS(20),
            3 DATE CHAR (8) VAR,
            3 AMOUNT FIXED,
        2 BALANCE FIXED;
```

In spite of the repeated use of the identifiers DATE and AMOUNT the qualified names of the individual components are still unique:

```
ACCOUNT.WITHDRAWALS(J).AMOUNT

ACCOUNT.DEPOSITS(K).DATE
```

Section 2 Summary

1. A variable is a named location in computer memory into which a value may be placed. The name of a variable is an identifier.

2. Each variable is restricted to one type of value: a decimal number, integer, character string, or logical value.

3. Variables are created by declarations specifying their identifier and type attributes. The form is:

```
DECLARE identifier type-attribute ;
```

The only type attributes we use are:

```
FLOAT                       for decimal numbers
FIXED                       for integers
CHARACTER(length) VARYING   for character strings
BIT (1)                     for logical values
```

4. Arrays are variables with multiple values. Individual elements of an array are referenced by subscripted variables.

5. Variables do not automatically have values when created, but initial values may be assigned in their declaration:

```
DECLARE identifier type-attribute INITIAL (value);
```

6. A special collection of variables and arrays to be treated as a single object is called a structure.

Section 3 Expressions and Assignment of Value

Several different kinds of statements are used in the construction of programs. The basic statement types are described in this and the following sections:

- Section 3 - statement to assign values to variables
- Section 4 - statements to read values from external data and to print results
- Section 6 - statements to control selective execution
- Section 7 - statements to control repetition of execution.

In effect, the real work of a program is accomplished by the execution of statements that read data, assign values and print results. The other kinds are "control statements" -- they serve only to <u>control the order</u> in which the working statements are executed.

We face a pedagogical problem in being unable to exhibit realistic programs until we have discussed all these different statement types. Consequently the examples of these next sections are just isolated fragments of programs and are intended to show the form and meaning of the individual statements. In Part II, after all the necessary elements have been introduced, we can display reasonably interesting programs.

3.1 The Assignment Statement

The most important PL/I statement produces a new value and assigns that value to a variable. In fact, this statement characterizes the principal family of programming languages in use today.

This assignment process takes place in two distinct stages:

1. A value is produced by evaluating an expression -- which involves retrieving the value of certain specified variables from memory, and performing specified "operations" on those values.

2. The new value is assigned to some specified variable, replacing whatever value that variable may have had previously.

This process is specified by an assignment statement. The PL/I form for such a statement is:

```
variable-name = expression ;
```

The expression on the right side of the "=" symbol gives the formula to obtain the new value; the variable-name on the left side designates which variable is to receive this value. For example:

```
AMT = BASE + ADJUST;
```

This statement specifies that the following actions are to be performed:

1. Retrieve the current value of the variable named BASE from memory.

2. Retrieve the current value of variable ADJUST from memory.

3. Add these two values (presumably numbers) together to produce the "new value".

4. Assign this new value to variable AMT, replacing whatever value AMT had prior to execution of this statement.

Note that only the value of AMT is changed by the execution of this statement; the values of BASE and ADJUST are copied but doing so does not change their value in memory.

Other programming languages have different forms for an assignment statement. For example:

```
AMT := BASE + ADJUST                    (PASCAL)

AMT = BASE + ADJUST                     (FORTRAN)

AMT <- BASE + ADJUST                    (APL)

LET A1 = B1 + A2                        (BASIC)

COMPUTE AMT = BASE + ADJUST             (COBOL)

ADD BASE TO ADJUST GIVING AMT           (COBOL)
```

Although the form may vary, in each case the idea is the same -- an expression specifies a new value and a target variable receives it.

The PL/I assignment statement looks something like an equation, and this may obscure the true nature of the assignment process. While an equation is a statement of fact, an assignment statement is an imperative command -- a specification of an action to be performed. If you understand this distinction then a statement such as the following is reasonable:

```
COUNT = COUNT + 1;
```

Execution of this statement simply causes the value of the variable named COUNT to be increased by 1.

When assignment to more than one variable is required, the order in which the statements appear can be critical. For example, consider the pair of statements:

```
COUNT = COUNT + 1;
TOTAL = CYCLES + COUNT;
```

The result (the values in memory) of executing the statements in this order would be different from the result of executing them in the opposite order:

```
TOTAL = CYCLES + COUNT;
COUNT = COUNT + 1;
```

The different result occurs because one statement assigns a new value to COUNT and the other statement uses the value of COUNT. Depending on the order in which the statements are executed the new value of TOTAL will reflect either the old or the new value of COUNT. (Presumably only one way or the other is correct, and the programmer must put the statements in the corresponding order.) The point again is that while a pair of assignment statements may look like a set of simultaneous equations, they are actually a description of a sequential process.

In some situations the same value has to be assigned to several variables. For example:

```
NEWBAL = OLDBAL + CHARGES - PAYMENTS;
MONTHBAL = OLDBAL + CHARGES - PAYMENTS;
YEARBAL = OLDBAL + CHARGES - PAYMENTS;
```

The following alternative version produces the same result, but it is easier to write, clearer to read, and faster to execute:

```
NEWBAL = OLDBAL + CHARGES - PAYMENTS;
MONTHBAL = NEWBAL;
YEARBAL = NEWBAL;
```

PL/I also allows such a multiple assignment to be described in a single statement:

```
NEWBAL, MONTHBAL, YEARBAL = OLDBAL + CHARGES - PAYMENTS;
```

The new value is computed first (as before), and then assigned to each of the target variables listed on the left side of the statement. (Although the order of assignment is well-defined -- from left to right -- it is bad practice to write a statement in which this order is significant. If the results would depend on the order in which the target variables are listed, then separate statements should be used so that the order will be obvious to the reader.)

● PL/CS: The assignment statement is limited to a single target variable.

Note that an assignment statement both uses the value of variables and assigns a value to a variable. Whether or not the target variable had a previous value is immaterial -- the new value replaces the old value if one existed, otherwise it becomes the first value for this variable. But a variable whose value is used obviously must have a value. For example, suppose at some point during execution of a program the state of memory is the following:

```
ROWDIFF  16
LIMIT    42
CHANGE   ??
ADJUST    2
```

At this point the following assignment statement could not be correctly executed because variable CHANGE has no value:

```
ROWDIFF = LIMIT - CHANGE;
```

On the other hand the statement shown below could be executed since it does not require CHANGE to have a previous value:

```
CHANGE = ADJUST + 1;
```

This distinction may seem obvious, but nevertheless the attempt to use a variable before it has been assigned a value is one of the most common errors. (It often occurs inadvertently as a result of some other error.) The surprising thing is that PL/I does not detect such errors and treat them as such -- PL/I just uses whatever value happens to have been left in that memory location by the previous program. This introduces an essentially "random" value (depending on whatever happened to precede this program), and it is often an exceedingly difficult error to locate.

● PL/C, PL/CS: An attempt to use a variable before it has been assigned a value is automatically detected and reported as use of an "uninitialized variable".

As an example of the use of assignment statements, consider the task of interchanging the values of two variables. For example, suppose you needed to swap the values of ROWDIFF and LIMIT shown above. The following pair of assignment statements will not accomplish this:

```
ROWDIFF = LIMIT;
LIMIT = ROWDIFF;
```

Starting with the values shown above, after executing these statements the values would be:

```
ROWDIFF 42
LIMIT   42
```

To interchange the values of two variables a third variable is required to temporarily hold one value. For example:

```
TEMP = ROWDIFF;
ROWDIFF = LIMIT;
LIMIT = TEMP;
```

Starting with the same initial values, the result of executing these statements would be:

```
ROWDIFF 42
LIMIT   16
TEMP    16
```

Subscripted variables can be used and assigned values just like simple variables. For example, consider:

```
TALLY(ACTNBR) = BASE(DEPT) + ADJUSTMENT;
```

The value of BASE(DEPT) is obtained in two stages. First the value of variable DEPT is retrieved. This value must be an integer, and in particular one of the integers specified as a valid subscript in the declaration of BASE. The value of DEPT determines which of the multiple values of BASE is to be used. The selected value from BASE is retrieved and added to the value of ADJUSTMENT to produce the new value to be assigned.

Since the target variable is subscripted the assignment must also take place in two stages -- first, determine which element of the array TALLY is to receive the value; second, make the assignment to that element. To determine which element of TALLY is the target, the value of ACTNBR must be retrieved first. This value must be an integer within the range of valid subscripts for TALLY. Using the value of ACTNBR to select a particular element of TALLY the actual assignment then takes place.

For example, suppose these variables had the following values:

TALLY(1)	45
TALLY(2)	63
TALLY(3)	14
BASE(1)	50
BASE(2)	21
ACTNBR	3
DEPT	1
ADJUSTMENT	12

The result of executing the statement

```
TALLY(ACTNBR) = BASE(DEPT) + ADJUSTMENT;
```

would be the following:

TALLY(1)	45
TALLY(2)	63
TALLY(3)	62
BASE(1)	50
BASE(2)	21
ACTNBR	3
DEPT	1
ADJUSTMENT	12

Note that the only value changed is that of TALLY(3) since that is the element of TALLY selected by the value of ACTNBR. Also, the value of BASE(1) was used in the right side expression since this was selected by the value of DEPT.

Note that although the variable ACTNBR appears as part of the name of the target variable it is used in exactly the same sense as the variables in the expression on the right side of the assignment. That is, it supplies a value rather than receives one. Consequently ACTNBR must have been assigned a value by some previous statement before it can be used in this way.

The previous paragraphs have described the proper values for the subscripts DEPT and ACTNBR: integers within the declared range for that particular array. But PL/I does not ordinarily object if these values are invalid; if the value of DEPT is outside the proper range for a subscript for BASE, PL/I simply uses this improper subscript to retrieve some extraneous value that is not even part of array BASE. Somewhat like the use of an uninitialized variable, this introduces a random value into the computation and represents a type of error that is hard to locate.

●PL/C, PL/CS: All subscript values are automatically checked and limited to the proper declared ranges.

To be precise we should note that when the target variable of an assignment statement is subscripted the actual order of events in executing the statement is the following:

1. Evaluate the target variable subscripts.

2. Evaluate the right side expression.

3. Assign the value to the target variable.

The reason why the timing of the evaluation of the target variable subscripts <u>can</u> be significant will not be apparent until Part IV, but even then it is bad practice to write a program where this timing <u>is</u> significant.

3.2 <u>Arithmetic Expressions</u>

The right side of an assignment statement is an "expression", which is evaluated <u>to produce a value</u>. The assignment statement is only one of many contexts in PL/I where expressions are used, but in each case the objective is the same -- to produce a value.

The simplest arithmetic expression is just a numerical constant. The next level of complexity is the name of a single variable whose value is retrieved to provide the expression value. Constants and variables are simply special cases of expressions. More generally, expressions can involve several input values (supplied by constants or variables) and "operations" by which those input values are combined to produce the result. When the values are numbers the operations are the familiar arithmetic ones -- addition, subtraction, etc. -- and the result is a number. An expression that yields a numeric value is called an "arithmetic expression". Other types of expressions are considered in Sections 3.3 and 3.4.

3.2.1 Arithmetic Operations

The PL/I symbols for arithmetic operations are:

+	for addition	
-	for subtraction, or to indicate negation	
/	for division	
*	for multiplication	
**	for exponentiation	(X^2 is written as X**2)

The symbol for an operation is called an "operator". The * operator is used for multiplication in most programming languages, because all the familiar means of indicating multiplication lead to confusion and ambiguity. (For example, a period could get confused with a decimal point -- would 2.34.5 mean 2.34 times 5 or 2 times 34.5?) Similarly, a double asterisk (with _no_ intervening blank) is used to denote exponentiation because there is no way to indicate on a punched card that one symbol is to be elevated.

3.2.2 Precedence of Operations

Some concern must be given to the order in which arithmetic operations are performed. For example, should the expression

```
A + B * C
```

be evaluated as A+(B*C) or (A+B)*C? In any expression, however complicated, a lavish enough use of parentheses will remove any possible ambiguity. However, to avoid too many parentheses, PL/I has conventions corresponding to normal algebra to indicate, for example, that:

	$a + bc$,	$a - b + c$,	$-a^2$
mean	$a + (bc)$,	$(a - b) + c$,	$-(a^2)$
and not	$(a + b)c$,	$a - (b + c)$,	$(-a)^2$.

The PL/I rules for evaluation of an expression are:

1. Expressions in parentheses are evaluated first, from the innermost set of parentheses to the outermost.

2. Subject to rule 1, the order of operations is:
   first: exponentiation (**) and negation (-)
   next: multiplication (*) and division (/)
   last: addition (+) and subtraction (-)

3. Sequences of operations in the same category under rule 2 are evaluated:
   exponentiations and negations - right to left
   multiplications and divisions - left to right
   additions and subtractions - left to right

   For example:

   X**Y**Z is equivalent to X**(Y**Z)

   -X**Y is equivalent to -(X**Y)

   X/Y*Z is equivalent to (X/Y)*Z

   X-Y+Z is equivalent to (X-Y)+Z

It is not necessary to memorize these rules; just use enough parentheses to specify the desired order, and keep a programming language manual handy to look the rules up if necessary. The important thing to note is that PL/I does remember these rules and will always follow them in determining the order of execution.

3.2.3 Mixed-Type Arithmetic Expressions

Both decimal number operands (FLOAT) and integer operands (FIXED) can be used in an arithmetic expression, and these different types of numeric values can be combined by the arithmetic operations. The rules are simple:

1. If both operands are FLOAT the floating version of the operation is used and the result is FLOAT.

2. If both operands are FIXED the fixed version of the operation is used and the result is FIXED.

3. If the operands are of mixed type (one FIXED and the other FLOAT) the FIXED operand is converted to FLOAT form and the floating version of the operation is used. The result is FLOAT. (Note that only the retrieved copy of the FIXED operand is converted -- neither the type of the variable, nor the value in memory is altered.)

This automatic numeric conversion is so unobtrusive that you almost never have to worry about it, but there is one exception. The FIXED division operation can be surprising. For example, the expression 25 + 1/3 is illegal (it causes "overflow") and yields 5.33333 as a result. (This expression is also illegal in PL/C and PL/CS where .333334 is the result.) The reason for this curious definition of integer division involves general integer value types that we are not considering. For our purposes just avoid integer division:

Never write an expression where both operands of a division operation are in FIXED form.

This is easily avoided:

1. Write fractions in decimal form:

   .5 instead of 1/2

2. Write constant operands in a division in floating form:

   COUNT/2E0 instead of COUNT/2

   1E0/INDEX instead of 1/INDEX

3. Force conversion of one operand to floating form by using the FLOAT "built-in function" (see Section 3.2.5):

   if COUNT and INDEX are both FIXED, write
   COUNT/FLOAT(INDEX) instead of COUNT/INDEX

3.2.4 Coercion of Values

In an assignment statement, when the type of value produced by the expression on the right side does not match the type of the target variable the value is said to need "coercion" before it can be assigned. Coercion from FIXED to FLOAT is automatic and generally unsurprising. For example, this means that statements to initialize FLOAT variables to integer values can be written:

```
SUM = 0;
NBR_USED = 1;
```

That is, it is not necessary to write these statements with the constants in floating form:

```
SUM = 0.0;        or   SUM = 0E0;

NBR_USED = 1.0;   or   NBR_USED = 1E0;
```

Similarly, the values on the INITIAL list in the declaration of FLOAT variables can be given as integers:

```
DCL SUM FLOAT INIT (0);
```

Coercion of a FLOAT value to fixed form for assignment to a FIXED variable can cause problems. FLOAT values can exceed the five-digit capacity of the fixed form. This is automatically detected and reported as a "size error", so at least you are warned when it occurs. However a different situation occurs when the FLOAT value has digits to the right of the decimal point. For example, if COUNT is a FIXED variable, execution of the statement

```
COUNT = 17.3;
```

would assign the value 17 to COUNT. This is not considered an error so there is no warning that coercion has resulted in truncation of the value. It is sometimes useful to take advantage of this truncation, but when it happens unexpectedly the difficulty is hard to locate.

3.2.5 Arithmetic Built-in Functions

"Built-in functions" in a programming language are effectively like additional operations, but an entirely different notation is used to specify them. The name of the function is used instead of a special symbol, and the operands (called "arguments" in this case) are given as a parenthesized list following the name. For example, there is a built-in function SQRT to obtain the square root of a value. To obtain the square root of the value of a variable SUM you would write:

```
SQRT(SUM)
```

Since a built-in function produces a value it can be used as an operand in an expression. For example:

```
SUMRTS = SQRT(SUM) + 1/SQRT(CROSSPROD);
```

An expression can be given as an argument to a built-in function. For example:

```
ROOT = (-B + SQRT(B**2 - 4*A*C))/2*A;
```

Combining these two ideas, a built-in function can be an operand in an argument expression of a built-in function:

```
SQRT(1 + SQRT(SUM))
```

Some functions require a list of argument expressions. For example, the MAX function has a list of two or more arguments and yields a value equal to the maximum of the values of its arguments:

```
MAX(COEF, 0)

MAX(LOWLIMIT, SQRT(PRESSURE))

MAX(A, MAX(B,C))  equivalent to  MAX(A,B,C)
```

Which built-in functions are included in a language depends on the problem area for which the language is intended.

FORTRAN, designed primarily for scientific and engineering computation, has a different set of built-in functions from COBOL, which was designed for business data processing. PL/I, which was intended to be used in both of these areas, has a particularly large collection of functions. The more commonly used PL/I functions with numeric arguments are listed below. A complete list of PL/I functions is given in Appendix A.7.

ABS(expr) -- The result is the absolute value of the value of the argument expression "expr".

ATAN(expr) -- The result (FLOAT) is the arctangent, in radians, of expr.

COS(expr) -- The result (FLOAT) is the cosine of expr, where expr is expressed in radians.

EXP(expr) -- The result (FLOAT) is e**expr, where e is the base of the natural logarithm system.

FIXED(expr) -- The result is the FIXED form of the value of expr.

FLOAT(expr) -- The result is the FLOAT form of the value of expr.

FLOOR(expr) -- The result (FIXED) is the largest integer not greater than expr. For example, FLOOR(3.5) is 3; FLOOR(-3.5) is -4.

LOG(expr) -- The result (FLOAT) is the natural logarithm of expr. The value of expr must be greater than 0.

LOG10(expr) -- The result (FLOAT) is the common logarithm of expr (base 10). The value of expr must be greater than 0.

MAX(expr1,expr2,...,exprn) -- The result is the maximum of the values of the arguments expr1, expr2,..., exprn. The result is FLOAT if at least one argument is FLOAT; otherwise the result is FIXED.

MIN(expr1,expr2,...,exprn) -- The result is the minimum of the values of the arguments expr1, expr2,..., exprn. The result is FLOAT if at least one argument is FLOAT; otherwise the result is FIXED.

MOD(expr1,expr2) -- The result (FLOAT if either expr1 or expr2 is FLOAT) is the remainder when dividing expr1 by expr2. If expr1 and expr2 have different signs, the operation is performed on their absolute values, and the result is ABS(expr2)-remainder. For example, MOD(29,6) is 5, while MOD(-29,6) is 1.

SIN(expr) -- The result (FLOAT) is the sine of expr, where expr is expressed in radians.

SQRT(expr) -- The result (FLOAT) is the square root of expr. The value of expr must be greater than or equal to 0.

TAN(expr) -- The result (FLOAT) is the tangent of expr, where expr is expressed in radians.

TAND(expr) -- The result (FLOAT) is the tangent of expr, where expr is expressed in degrees.

The names of built-in functions are <u>not reserved</u> -- it is legal to use MAX, FLOOR, etc. as identifiers. However, when the name of a built-in function is used as an identifier that particular built-in function cannot also be used. In general, avoid the function names when choosing identifiers, but if you happen to choose a function name it should not cause difficulty. (It is hard to remember the names of all the infrequently-used functions. For example, we have used a variable SUM in examples above; there is also a built-in function with that name.)

Note that the implicit declarations described in Section 2.3.1 do not apply if an identifier is also a function name. In the absence of an explicit declaration as an identifier it is assumed that the function is intended.

3.3 <u>String Expressions</u>

An assignment statement for a string variable has the form:

```
string-variable-name = string-valued-expression;
```

A string-valued-expression is an expression that, on evaluation, yields a string value. The components of such an expression are:

1. String constants
2. String variables
3. The concatenation operator
4. The SUBSTR built-in function.

The expression yields a value, which is assigned to the target variable just as in the case of a numeric assignment statement. But there are some additional considerations concerning <u>lengths</u> of values.

The length of a VARYING string variable is the length of its current value -- that is, the length of the most recently assigned value. For example, suppose a variable is declared

```
DECLARE BAY CHAR (10) VARYING;
```

After execution of the statement

```
BAY = 'FUNDY';
```

the value of BAY would be

BAY FUNDY [char(10) var]

and the current length of BAY would be 5 characters. Suppose the next statement executed was

```
BAY = 'PENOBSCOT';
```

Then the value of BAY would be

BAY PENOBSCOT [char(10) var]

and the length would be 9 characters. If this was followed by execution of

```
BAY = 'CAPE COD';
```

the value would become

BAY CAPEƀCOD [char(10) var]

Note that the entire value of BAY is replaced, even though the new value is shorter than the incumbent value.

The declared limit on the length of the variable value may cause a value to be truncated. For example, executing

```
BAY = 'NARRAGANSETT';
```

would result in

BAY NARRAGANSE [char(10) var]

Another significant distinction with varying-length strings is that the empty string -- the string consisting of no characters -- is a legitimate value. For example, the result of executing

```
BAY = '';
```

is to make the value of BAY the empty string. The length of the value is 0, and BAY has been returned to the state that existed immediately after its creation (assuming there was no INITIAL phrase in its declaration). Effectively, there is no "uninitialized state" for a varying-length string. A varying string is initialized to the empty string, and this is a legitimate value.

Note the difference between the null string and a string consisting of one or more blanks. The blank is a proper character, with the same rights and privileges as any other character. This means that execution of each of the three statements below will assign a different value to BAY:

```
BAY = '';

BAY = ' ';

BAY = '  ';
```

3.3.1 The Operation of Concatenation

The *only* operation in string expressions is "concatenation", which simply means to put string operands together, end to end.

The PL/I symbol for concatenation is "||". (The vertical bar is the character above the Y on the keypunch.) Examples are:

```
'A' || 'B'          is equivalent to  'AB'

'A' || ' ' || 'B'   is equivalent to  'A B'

'ST.' || 'JOHNS'    is equivalent to  'ST.JOHNS'
```

Since concatenation is the only operator in string expressions, there is no question of precedence of operations and parentheses are never required. The operands are simply assembled from left to right, in the order written.

3.3.2 The SUBSTR Built-in Function

The SUBSTR function provides the inverse of concatenation; it is used to take string values apart, to extract a portion of the value of a string, and to obtain a "substring". The form is:

SUBSTR(s, f, n)

where

s is a string expression, from which the substring is to be obtained;

f is an integer expression specifying the left most position of the substring (1 specifies the first position)

n is an integer expression specifying the number of characters in the substring.

For example:

```
SUBSTR('ABCDE', 2, 3)   is   'BCD'
```

The third argument, which specifies the length of the substring, can be omitted. When it is, the substring extends from the specified starting position (given by the second argument) to the end of the string. For example:

```
SUBSTR('ABCDE', 2)   is   'BCDE'
```

3.3.3 The SUBSTR Pseudo-Variable

Suppose that a program is required to change only a portion of the value of a string variable. For example, say the current value of variable PORT is:

PORT MARBELHEAD [char(30) var]

and the program is to correct the spelling by replacing the fifth and sixth characters with "L" and "E", respectively. This could be done with an ordinary string assignment statement:

```
PORT = SUBSTR(PORT,1,4) || 'LE' || SUBSTR(PORT,7);
```

Alternatively, PL/I provides a direct way of changing only a portion of the value of a string variable:

```
SUBSTR(PORT,5,2) = 'LE';
```

The left side of this statement is called the "SUBSTR pseudo-variable". This specifies that the substring of PORT consisting of two characters beginning with the fifth is to be replaced by the value of the string expression on the right. The pseudo-variable has the same form as the corresponding built-in function, but in this case it appears on the left and receives a value rather than appearing in an expression and supplying a value. (PL/I has other pseudo-variables but SUBSTR is the only one used in this book.)

The length of the value of the right side expression need not exactly match the length of the substring specified on the left side. If there are extra characters in the right side expression they are ignored (only the required number of left-most characters are used). If there are insufficient characters in the right side expression the value is filled out (at the right end) with blanks. For example, the result of executing

```
SUBSTR(PORT,5,2) = 'LEX';
```

would be

```
PORT MARBLEHEAD
```

The result of executing

```
SUBSTR(PORT,5,2) = 'L';
```

would be

```
PORT MARBLb̸HEAD
```

As is often the case with special features of a programming language, the SUBSTR pseudo-variable does not add any new capability. It simply provides a special construction for a common task that is both more convenient to use and easier to understand when you have to read a program.

3.3.4 Numeric-Valued String Functions

Several built-in functions use string values as arguments but *yield numeric results*. Examples of such functions are LENGTH, INDEX, and VERIFY.

The LENGTH function yields the length of the value of the string expression given as argument. The result is an integer. For example:

```
LENGTH('CAPE COD')    is   8

LENGTH('')            is   0

LENGTH('CA'||'PE')    is   4
```

This is used to determine the current length of a varying string variable. For example, the following expression yields the *last character* of the value of variable BAY (assuming that the value is not the null string):

```
SUBSTR(BAY, LENGTH(BAY), 1)
```

To *delete the last character* of BAY you could write

```
BAY = SUBSTR(BAY, 1, LENGTH(BAY)-1);
```

To *delete the first half* of BAY (including the middle character, if the length is odd) you could write

```
BAY = SUBSTR(BAY, FLOOR(LENGTH(BAY)/2E0) + 1);
```

The INDEX function is used to scan a string value for a particular character pattern. The form is:

```
INDEX(string1, string2)
```

where

string1 is the string expression to be scanned;

string2 is the character pattern that is scanned for.

The result of INDEX is an integer giving the <u>leftmost position</u> in string1 where string2 begins. If string2 does not exist in string1 then the result of INDEX is 0. For example:

```
INDEX('ABCDECD', 'CD')   is  3

INDEX('ABCDECD', 'DC')   is  0
```

The VERIFY function also performs a scanning task over a string expression. The form is:

```
VERIFY(string1, string2)
```

In this case the objective is to find the position of the first character in string1 that is <u>not</u> also in string2. For example:

```
VERIFY('AAABC', 'A')     is  4

VERIFY('JJBCD', 'J')     is  3

VERIFY('TTBC', 'ABCT')   is  0
```

3.4 <u>Logical Expressions</u>

A <u>logical expression</u> has as its value either 1 or 0. Such an expression would appear on the right side of an assignment statement when a logical variable is specified on the left side:

```
logical variable = logical expression;
```

The simplest form of a logical expression is a literal:

```
'1'B    or    '0'B
```

An expression can also consist of a single logical variable. Thus, execution of

```
FLAG = INDICATOR;
```

would simply cause the logical value of INDICATOR to be copied into variable FLAG.

The most common form of logical expression is called a "condition" or "relation", in which two operands are <u>compared</u> to yield a result that is either <u>true</u> ('1'B) or <u>false</u> ('0'B). For example, consider

```
ROWVALUE < 0
```

If the current value of ROWVALUE is less than zero, then the value of this expression is '1'B (true); otherwise the value is '0'B (false). The symbol "<" in this expression is one of eight "relational operators" or "relations". They are described in the next section.

An assignment statement with a logical variable on the left side can have a condition as the expression on the right side. For example:

```
INDICATOR = ROWVALUE < 0;
```

The condition is evaluated (yielding either '1'B or '0'B) and this value is assigned to variable INDICATOR.

"Equals" is another relation that can be used in a condition. For example:

```
INDEX = UPPER_LIMIT

ERROR_COUNT = 0
```

These conditions can also be used on the right side of an assignment statement:

```
STOPPING_FLAG = INDEX = UPPER_LIMIT;
```

This illustrates one of the more confusing constructions in PL/I, since the <u>same symbol</u> "=" is used both for the "equals" relation and the assignment process. It can easily be misinterpreted (by a human reader) as a multiple assignment statement. (Compare this to the correct form for multiple assignment in Section 3.1.) One way to clarify such an assignment is to enclose the <u>logical expression in parentheses</u>:

```
STOPPING_FLAG = (INDEX = UPPER_LIMIT);
```

● PL/CS: Logical expressions <u>must</u> always be given in parentheses.

3.4.1 Relational Operators

A relational operator, or relation, specifies a <u>comparison</u> between two values. The complete list of PL/I relations is the following:

symbol	meaning
=	is equal to
¬=	is not equal to
>	is greater than
¬>	is not greater than
>=	is greater than or equal to
<	is less than
¬<	is not less than
<=	is less than or equal to

If the two values have the specified relationship, the result is *true*, if they do not, the result is *false*.

The values to be compared *should be of the same type*. That is, a number should only be compared to another number and not to a character or bit string.

Comparison of numbers is obvious, but comparison of string values is more complicated and is described in the next section.

3.4.2 Comparison of String Values

The comparison of two string values depends on:

1. an ordering of the individual characters, and

2. rules to handle values of different length.

The ordering of single characters is called the "collating sequence". For PL/I this is the following:

b̸¢.<(+|&!$*);¬-/,%_>?:#@'="ABCDEFGHIJKLMNOPQRSTUVWXYZ0123456789

One character is said to be *less than* another if it appears to its *left* in this sequence. That means that "A" is less than "B", "Z" is less than "5", "," is less than any letter or digit, and "b̸" is less than any other character.

This is a reasonable extension of "alphabetical ordering", with the digits above Z and the special characters below A.

To compare two string values *of equal length* the characters are considered one at a time, from left to right, just as you would in ordinary alphabetization. That is, the leftmost character is dominant, but if two values are "tied" in that position, the second character is considered. If they are tied there, the third is considered, etc. This means that

"AB" is less than "BB"

"BA" is less than "BB"

"BZ" is less than "B7"

" B" is less than "B "

To compare string values of *unequal length* the shorter value is considered to be *extended on the right with blanks* until the two lengths are equal. Then the values can be compared in the manner described above. According to these rules each of the following is *true*:

```
'A'   < 'AA'
' B'  < 'A'
'A A' < 'AA'
'AAA' < 'B'
```

These rules will generally result in orderings consistent with ordinary conventions in ordering words. For example:

'ROCK' is less than 'ROCKPORT'

'HOOD, T.' is less than 'HOOD, TED'

However, PL/I follows these rules absolutely, where a human alphabetizer might not. For example:

'STEPHENS OLIN' is less than 'STEPHENS, JOHN'

' MORISON, S.' is less than 'MORGAN, CHAS.'

3.4.3 *Boolean Operators*

There are three "Boolean" or logical operators with logical values as operands and results. "And" and "or" are "binary" operations involving two operands. "Not" is a "unary" operation involving only one operand. The operations are defined as follows:

operation	*symbol*	*action*
"and"	&	result is '1'B if *both* operands are '1'B result is '0'B if either operand is '0'B
"or"	|	result is '1'B if *either* operand is '1'B result is '0'B if both operands are '0'B
"not"	¬	result is '1'B if operand is '0'B result is '0'B if operand is '1'B

The following table illustrates these operations in terms of all possible combinations of values for logical variables P and Q:

value of P	value of Q	value of P & Q	value of P | Q	value of ¬P
'1'B	'1'B	'1'B	'1'B	'0'B
'1'B	'0'B	'0'B	'1'B	'0'B
'0'B	'1'B	'0'B	'1'B	'1'B
'0'B	'0'B	'0'B	'0'B	'1'B

When the operands of these logical operations are conditions the result is called a "compound condition". Examples are:

```
(I > 56) & (I < 729)
(PRESSURE > PRESSMIN) & (TEMP < TEMPMAX)
(REG_GAP <= 15.2*GAP) | (CASE = 2)
```

Conditions and logical variables can of course be given in the same expression:

```
(PRESSURE > PRESSMIN) | PRESSURE_INDICATOR
```

There are precedence rules for these operations analogous to those for arithmetic operations (Section 3.2.2). "And" is considered before "or". For example, this means that:

```
A=B & C=D | E=F  is equivalent to  (A=B & C=D) | E=F
```

It is a good idea to use parentheses in such expressions to make clear to the reader just what order you intended.

"Not" should be used sparingly, since it tends to make programs harder to understand. When "¬" must be used it helps to enclose its argument in parentheses. In simple cases "not" can often be avoided by choosing the opposite relation. For example:

```
¬(X = Y)   is equivalent to  (X ¬= Y)

¬(X <= Y)  is equivalent to  (X > Y)
```

3.5 Conversion of Values

Quite often, values must be converted from one form to another -- FIXED to FLOAT, bit string to character string, FIXED to character string (for later output), etc. In PL/I, conversion of values is a complicated task, primarily due to the way precision attributes are defined and used. In PL/C, the task is simplified by the fact that as many significant digits as possible are preserved, and it is the PL/C rules that are discussed in Appendix A.5.4 concerning data conversion.

PL/I and PL/C both allow automatic conversion of values from one type to another, although usually with a warning message from PL/C. However, you should be wary of this kindness since misuse can easily lead to errors and mask the effect of other errors. One reason programming languages have different types of values is to be able to separate variables into distinct, disjoint groups which should never implicitly interact. Knowing that they should not interact allows you to view any attempt at interaction as evidence of a program error. Moreover, the use of different types, together with declarations for all variables, gives the reader a good sense of how each variable will be used. The use of automatic, implicit conversion subverts this protection.

There are facilities to *explicitly* convert values from one type to another, and these should be used when conversion is necessary. These are:

FIXED to FLOAT: built-in function FLOAT (see Appendix A.7)

FLOAT to FIXED: built-in functions FIXED, FLOOR and CEIL (see Appendix A.7)

String to numeric or bit string: GET statement with STRING option (see Section 4.4)

Numeric or bit string to string: PUT statement with the STRING option (see Section 4.4)

The automatic conversion from FIXED to FLOAT is so convenient and generally harmless that it merits exemption from these warnings. It is widely used.

3.6 Array Assignment

An entire array may be specified as the target of an assignment. This causes a value to be assigned to each individual element of the array. For example, consider the following declaration:

```
DECLARE (X(1:3), Y(1:3)) FIXED;
```

Then the assignment statement

```
X = 0;
```

is equivalent to

```
X(1) = 0;
X(2) = 0;
X(3) = 0;
```

or to the single statement

```
X(1), X(2), X(3) = 0;
```

Similarly, both sides of the assignment may be arrays:

```
X = Y;
```

is equivalent to

```
X(1) = Y(1);
X(2) = Y(2);
X(3) = Y(3);
```

The right side of an array assignment statement is an "array expression". The examples above show the simplest cases:

1. A scalar constant, which is treated as if it were an array with the same number of elements as the array on the left side, with all values equal to the given constant.

2. An array of exactly the same size as the array specified on the left side. The arrays on the two sides are said to be "conformable".

●PL/CS: The right side of an array assignment statement can only be one of the two cases described above. More general array expressions, described below, are not allowed.

Array expressions can be more complicated, with array operators and built-in functions. The arithmetic operators "+", "-", "*" and "/" can have conformable array operands. Each of these operators specifies an arithmetic operation to be performed on the corresponding elements of the operand arrays. For example:

```
X = X * Y;
```

is equivalent to

```
X(1) = X(1) * Y(1);
X(2) = X(2) * Y(2);
X(3) = X(3) * Y(3);
```

Note that this PL/I array multiplication does not correspond to the usual definition of matrix multiplication.

An example illustrating precedence of operations is:

```
X = (2 + Y) * X;
```

This is equivalent to

```
X(1) = (2 + Y(1)) * X(1);
X(2) = (2 + Y(2)) * X(2);
X(3) = (2 + Y(3)) * X(3);
```

The following illustrates a common misunderstanding of array operations:

```
X = X + X(1);
```

is equivalent to

```
X(1) = X(1) + X(1);
X(2) = X(2) + X(1);
X(3) = X(3) + X(1);
```

This statement does not add the same value of X(1) to each element of the array X, because the value of X(1) is changed in the course of execution of the statement.

Many built-in functions accept an array expression as argument. The function is applied separately to each element of the argument array and the result is an array with the same number of elements as the argument array. For example:

```
X = ABS(X);
```

is equivalent to

```
X(1) = ABS(X(1));
X(2) = ABS(X(2));
X(3) = ABS(X(3));
```

SQRT, FLOOR, CEIL, COS and SIN are other examples of functions that can be used in this way.

A different kind of array function accepts an array as argument but yields a scalar result. For example, function SUM produces the sum of the individual values of a numeric array. A comparable function named PROD yields the product of the individual values of a numeric array.

Two useful functions called ANY and ALL require a bit string array as argument, and return a scalar bit string value as result. ALL yields '1'B if all the values of the argument array are '1'B; otherwise '0'B. ANY yields '1'B if at least one of the values of argument array is '1'B; otherwise '0'B.

3.7 Structure Assignment

Assignment to a structure is comparable to assignment to an array. Each individual component of the structure is assigned a value. For example, consider the following structures:

```
DCL 1 STUDENT
        2 NAME CHAR(30) VAR,
        2 ADDRESS,
            3 STREET CHAR(30) VAR,
            3 CITY CHAR(20) VAR,
            3 STATE CHAR(2) VAR,
            3 ZIP CHAR(5) VAR,
        2 COLLEGE_CODE CHAR(2) VAR;

DCL 1 NEW_ADDRESS,
        2 ADD1 CHAR(30) VAR,
        2 ADD2 CHAR(20) VAR,
        2 ADD3 CHAR(2) VAR,
        2 ADD4 CHAR(5) VAR;
```

The assignment statement

```
ADDRESS = NEW_ADDRESS;
```

would copy values from the components of the structure NEW_ADDRESS into the corresponding components of minor structure ADDRESS. That is, it is equivalent to:

```
STUDENT.ADDRESS.STREET = NEW_ADDRESS.ADD1;
STUDENT.ADDRESS.CITY = NEW_ADDRESS.ADD2;
STUDENT.ADDRESS.STATE = NEW_ADDRESS.ADD3;
STUDENT.ADDRESS.ZIP = NEW_ADDRESS.ADD4;
```

Note that neither the names of the components nor the level numbers are required to match, but the relative structures must match exactly, and the types of value for each corresponding pair of components should match.

3.7.1 BY NAME Assignment

There is an alternative form of structure assignment in which the component names are significant. For example, suppose there was a third structure declared as follows:

```
DCL 1 ADDRESS_CHANGE,
        2 ZIP CHAR(5) VAR,
        2 STREET CHAR(30) VAR,
        2 CITY CHAR(20) VAR,
        2 STATE CHAR(2) VAR;
```

The "BY NAME" assignment statement

```
STUDENT = ADDRESS_CHANGE, BY NAME;
```

would be equivalent to

```
STUDENT.ADDRESS.STREET = ADDRESS_CHANGE.STREET;
STUDENT.ADDRESS.CITY = ADDRESS_CHANGE.CITY;
STUDENT.ADDRESS.STATE = ADDRESS_CHANGE.STATE;
STUDENT.ADDRESS.ZIP = ADDRESS_CHANGE.ZIP;
```

In this case the components are matched by name rather than in declaration order. The matched components should have the same type of value, but the two structures otherwise need not be similar.

Section 3 Summary

1. An assignment statement has the form:

```
variable-name = expression ;
```

The expression is evaluated to obtain a value, which is assigned to the target variable.

2. Arithmetic expressions are composed of numeric variables, numeric constants, arithmetic operators and function references. Parentheses specify the order of performing operations.

3. String expressions are composed of string variables, string constants, the concatenation operator and the SUBSTR function.

4. The SUBSTR pseudo-variable permits assignment to a portion of a string variable.

5. Logical expressions have the form:

```
expr1 relation expr2
```

where expr1 and expr2 are expressions of the same type (arithmetic, string or logical) and the relation compares their values. The result is either true ('1'B) or false ('0'B). A logical variable or literal is also a logical expression.

6. Complete arrays or structures (rather than individual elements) can be assigned values.

Section 3 Exercises

1. In each of the following assignment statements delete all "redundant" parentheses -- that is, parentheses whose deletion does not change the result of the statement:

a) ALT = ALT + (BASE + COL4) + DIV;

b) PRESSURE = (TEMP + ENTROPY) * SPEC22;

c) GRADIENT = (GRADIENT - (HGT-SLOPE));

d) EFF = (EFF + (FULL * (LOSS**H3)));

e) X = -B + SQRT((B*2 -(4*(A*C))));

2. Suppose the following were the values of four variables at a certain point in a program:

BASE	4	[float]
HGT	3	[float]
SIDE	0	[float]
TOP	14.2	[float]

Starting at that point, the following four assignment statements are executed in the order shown below:

```
SIDE = SIDE + BASE/HGT;
SIDE = SIDE + BASE/HGT;
TOP = BASE + HGT + SIDE + TOP;
TOP = TOP/HGT;
```

What are the resulting values of the four variables?

3. The following are all intended to be assignment statements. Which ones contain at least one syntax error?

a) A = B + C

b) A = B, C;

c) A = (B + C);

d) A + B = C;

e) (A = B + C);

f) A = (B) + C;

g) A = B (+) C;

h) A = (B + C;)

Section 4 Input and Output Statements

There are four basic communication statements in PL/I: the GET and READ statements transfer information into memory from devices such as card readers, terminal keyboards, or magnetic tapes or disks; the PUT and WRITE statements copy information from memory onto devices such as printers, display screens or magnetic tapes or disks.

The GET and PUT statements deal with information in "stream" format: the input is a sequence of distinct and separate values. The READ and WRITE statements use "record" format: the input is treated as a continuous sequence of characters, without automatic separation into distinct values. The record format is faster in execution, and consequently it is used for production programs that deal with large volumes of information. The stream format is generally less complicated to understand and use. We consider only the GET and PUT statement, which are adequate for most uses.

The GET and PUT statements both have three different forms: LIST, DATA and EDIT. The LIST and DATA forms involve standard pre-defined data formats. They are easy to use, but somewhat restrictive in that you are limited to these standard formats. The EDIT form gives essentially complete flexibility in choosing the format for data, but you have to work harder to take advantage of it.

4.1 The PUT Statement

Initially, we consider the PUT statement as a means for tranferring data from program variables to the "standard output device". PUT is used to print the results of executing your program, and the standard output device is a printer attached to the computer. Typically, both your program listing and execution output are printed in that order. The standard device might also be a typewriter-terminal if you are using a time-sharing, interactive version of PL/I.

4.1.1 The SKIP Option

All three forms of the PUT statement to be discussed in the next three sections cause data to be printed. The output page is usually considered to be "character oriented" rather than "line oriented". For example, if execution of one PUT statement writes data in columns 1-20 of the first line, then execution of the next PUT statement will write its data beginning in column 21 of the same line.

However, any PUT statement can include the keyword SKIP, which indicates a skip to the beginning of the next line before any data is written. For example, execution of the statements (which will be fully explained in Section 4.1.2)

```
PUT LIST(5);
PUT LIST(6);
```

causes the integers 5 and 6 to be printed on the same line, while execution of

```
PUT LIST(5);
PUT SKIP LIST(6);
```

causes 5 to appear on one line and 6 at the beginning of the next line. SKIP may have an optional expression enclosed within parentheses indicating how many lines to skip. For example, execution of

```
PUT LIST(5);
PUT SKIP(2) LIST(6);
```

causes 5 to be printed on one line, the rest of the line to be skipped, a second line to be skipped, and the 6 to be printed at the beginning of the third line. SKIP is equivalent to SKIP(1).

SKIP can be the only option in a PUT statement, causing lines to be skipped, but no data to be printed:

```
PUT SKIP(expr);
```

This valid statement causes the rest of the current line to be skipped. It is used to end a section of printed output, ensuring separation on the page regardless of the form of the next PUT statement.

4.1.2 The LIST Form of PUT

The simplest output statement in PL/I has the form

```
PUT LIST( variable names, separated by commas );
```

The variables may be simple or subscripted. For example:

```
(4.1.2a)     PUT LIST(TOTAL, I, PLACE(I), MAXPLACE);
```

The standard output format divides the printed page horizontally into six "fields" of 20 columns each. (This is somewhat analogous to the "tab stops" on a typewriter. The width and number of fields is subject to change at each installation.) Each column is one "print position" and will contain one character. Each field is used to display the value of one variable from the list given in the PUT statement. In example (4.1.2a) the value of TOTAL will be printed in the first (leftmost) field; I in the second; PLACE(I) in the third; and MAXPLACE in the fourth. (The particular variable from the array PLACE to appear in the third field will of course depend upon the value of subscript I at the time the statement is executed.) Each value begins at the left of the field and uses as many columns as required. Any unused columns of the field are left blank and the next value begins in the leftmost column of the next field.

FIXED variables are printed in integer form, FLOAT variables in exponential form. The decimal point is always given after the first digit and the power of ten required to properly position the point is given after the digits of the number. For example, if the variables contain:

TOTAL	-.0036	[float]
I	2	[float]
PLACE(1)	-124.3	[float]
PLACE(2)	63.7	[float]
MAXPLACE	806	[float]

the values displayed by PUT statement (4.1.2a) would be as below (the full number of blanks between values is not shown here since the print line in this book is not a full 120 positions):

```
-3.60000E-03   2         6.37000E+01   8.06000E+02
```

A PUT LIST statement does not automatically begin a new line. It begins with the next unused field, wherever that may be. For example, if PUT LIST(J); places J's value in the third field of a line, then the next executed PUT statement will place its first value in the fourth field on that same line. Thus, (4.1.2a) is exactly equivalent to the sequence

```
PUT LIST(TOTAL,I);
PUT LIST(PLACE(I), MAXPLACE);
```

In other words, the variables in consecutively executed PUT statements form one continuous list -- to be assigned to the continuous sequence of fields on the printed page. After the fifth field of one line comes the first field of the next line.

The SKIP option can be used to make output more readable, hence

```
PUT SKIP LIST(TOTAL, I);
PUT SKIP LIST(PLACE(I), MAXPLACE);
```

will cause two new lines to be printed, with values in the first two fields of each line. Note, however, that unless the next PUT statement also specifies SKIP it will begin placing values in the third field of this second line.

4.1.2.1 Titling and Labeling Results

The appearance of printed results can be improved by adding appropriate titles and labels. To a limited extent this can be done with LIST format output by placing a literal in the list of the PUT statement. For example:

```
'TOTAL'
'TEMPERATURE ='
'RESULTS FOR 9/23/72 ARE:'
'*-*-*-*-*-*-*'
' '      (blank is a valid character)
```

The character string is printed exactly as given -- without the quotes. The printing begins in the leftmost column of the "next" field. For example, if TOTAL and SUM have values

```
TOTAL  642.17  [float]
SUM   -1043.7  [float]
```

then execution of the statements

```
PUT SKIP LIST('TOTAL =', TOTAL);
PUT SKIP LIST('SUM =', SUM);
```

would produce the output

```
TOTAL =                   6.42170E+02
SUM =                    -1.04370E+03
```

The appearance of these lines can be improved by including blanks in the literals to displace the words toward the right in the 20 position print field:

```
PUT SKIP LIST('             TOTAL =', TOTAL);
PUT SKIP LIST('               SUM =',SUM);
```

These statements will produce:

```
TOTAL =  6.42170E+02
  SUM = -1.04370E+03
```

Literals are often used to identify different values, using their variable names. For example,

```
PUT SKIP LIST('X', X);
```

will print the name X, in the first field of a line, and the value of X in the second field. Whatever is included in the literal is printed; the content of the literal has no significance to PL/I. For example, execution of the following would cause the deceptive label to be printed, without complaint:

```
PUT SKIP LIST('THE VALUE OF Y IS:', X);
```

Blank literals can be used to control the placement of other values on the printed line. For example, to print the value of X in the second field of a new line, and the value of Y in the fourth field, write:

```
PUT SKIP LIST(' ', X, ' ', Y);
```

PUT statements whose list consists of a single literal are frequently used. For example:

```
PUT SKIP LIST('IMPROPER DATA ENCOUNTERED');
PUT SKIP LIST('UNEXPECTED NEGATIVE VALUE');
```

Such statements announce to the programmer that the flow-of-control has reached a certain point in the program or that an exceptional condition has occurred. Include such statements to help test a new program; remove them after the correctness of the program has been established. This technique is discussed in Section V.3.

If a literal of more than 20 characters is given it will simply continue into the next field on the line. (A literal of exactly 20 characters completely fills one field and causes the next to be skipped.) If a literal reaches the end of a line it will continue in the first field of the next line. This applies to the printed output line -- a different rule applies to the cards on which the PUT statement itself is punched.

PL/C normally forbids a "symbol" to be split between two cards -- to be started on one card and continued on the next. Keywords, variables and constants are all symbols. A literal or a comment, however long, is also considered a single symbol. A statement may be continued onto as many cards as necessary, but an individual symbol cannot be split over a card boundary. (This can be permitted under the NOMONITOR=(BNDRY) option for comments and literals; see Appendix B.2.) Hence, the following would not be valid in PL/C:

```
PUT SKIP LIST(TOTAL,SUM,AVERAGE,MEDIAN,'THESE STATISTICS
   ARE OBTAINED FROM 9/23/72 DATA');
```

This same statement would be valid if it were divided between symbols instead of in the middle of the literal:

```
PUT SKIP LIST(TOTAL, SUM, AVERAGE, MEDIAN,
   'THESE STATISTICS ARE OBTAINED FROM 9/23/72 DATA');
```

Although the statement is now acceptable, the format of the printed output is likely to be disappointing since the long literal will begin in the fifth field of the line and spill over into the first field of the following line. The following sequence would produce more attractive and readable output:

```
PUT SKIP LIST('STATISTICS FROM 9/23/72 DATA:');
   PUT SKIP LIST('             TOTAL =', TOTAL);
   PUT SKIP LIST('             SUM =', SUM);
   PUT SKIP LIST('             AVERAGE =', AVERAGE);
   PUT SKIP LIST('             MEDIAN =', MEDIAN);
```

4.1.2.2 Expressions in LIST Output

Expressions can be included in the list of a PUT LIST statement, but it is not generally a good idea to combine the tasks of computation and display of results in a single statement. While it is legal to write

```
PUT SKIP LIST ((-B + SQRT(B**2 - 4*A*C)) / (2*A));
```

it is clearer to write

```
ROOT = (-B + SQRT(B**2 - 4*A*C)) / (2*A);
PUT SKIP LIST (ROOT);
```

4.1.3 The DATA Form of PUT

The PUT DATA statement has the format

```
PUT SKIP(i) DATA(list of variables, separated by commas);
```

where SKIP(i) is optional. As with PUT LIST, the values are displayed in a fixed format, but in addition the name as well as the value of each variable is displayed. For example, assuming the FIXED variables TOTAL and SUM have values 62 and -3, execution of

```
PUT SKIP DATA(TOTAL, SUM);
```

produces the output line

```
TOTAL= 62          SUM=-3;
```

Note the semicolon that is printed at the end of the output for the statement.

Only variables can be printed with PUT DATA. Neither expressions nor literals can be included in the list of this statement.

PUT DATA is especially useful for debugging purposes; it identifies output values with no extra effort.

4.1.4 The EDIT Form of PUT

More flexible control over the format of output is provided by the PUT EDIT statement. This statement can be very complex; we give only a brief introduction. Nevertheless, even this permits substantial control of printing format in the most common situations. The general form of the statement is:

```
PUT SKIP(i) EDIT(element list)(format list);
```

The "element list" is the list of variables, expressions and literals (separated by commas) to be printed, as with PUT LIST. But with PUT EDIT they are printed under control of the "format list".

The format list is a list of "items", separated by commas. Items are "data-items" (the items A, A(w), F(w,d) and E(w,d) below) or "control-items" (X(i) below). The element list and format list are processed concurrently, from beginning to end. The first data-item controls the printing of the first value, the second data-item controls printing of the second value, and so on. Control-items are "executed" as they are passed over when looking for the next data-item to use to control printing. (Thus, control-items at the end of the format list have no effect.)

Of the twelve items, the following are the most useful for our purposes. (Appendix A.8 has a discussion of all of them.)

A -- print a character string. This can be a literal (or a string-valued expression). The width of the printing field is the length of the string.

A(w) -- print a character string left-justified in a field w positions wide (truncating the string if necessary).

X(i) -- skip i spaces.

F(w) -- print an integer right-justified in a field w positions wide.

F(w,d) -- print a decimal number with d digits to the right of the decimal point, right-justified in a field w positions wide. The width w must include a position for the decimal point and a position for a minus sign, if that can occur. The number is rounded to fit, if necessary.

E(w,d) -- print a number in exponential form, with d digits to the right of the decimal point, right-justified in a field w positions wide. The width w must include positions for the decimal point, the sign, and the exponent. The number is rounded to fit, if necessary.

The F and E format-items can be used for either FIXED or FLOAT values; necessary conversions will be performed automatically.

In EDIT format, fields are not pre-defined (as in LIST format). Each format-item defines its own field-length, which begins immediately after the termination of the preceding field.

We give examples, assuming the following values:

TOTAL 14.3 [float]   COUNT 25   [fixed]

The output produced by various PUT EDIT statements is shown below. (Print position numbers are shown to indicate exact placement. They would not appear on actual output.)

```
PUT SKIP EDIT(COUNT)(F(5));
output:        25
positions: 12345

PUT SKIP EDIT(COUNT)(F(5,1));
output:      25.0
positions: 12345

PUT SKIP EDIT(COUNT)(E(10,2));
output:       2.50E+01
positions: 1234567890

PUT SKIP EDIT(COUNT)(X(4),F(5));
output:            25
positions: 123456789

PUT SKIP EDIT(COUNT, COUNT)(F(5),F(5,2));
output:        2525.00
positions: 1234567890

PUT SKIP EDIT (COUNT, COUNT) (F(5), X(3), F(5,2));
output:        25   25.00
positions: 1234567890123
```

```
PUT SKIP EDIT(TOTAL)(E(10,2));
output:       1.43E+01
positions: 1234567890

PUT SKIP EDIT(TOTAL)(F(6,2));
output:      14.30
positions: 123456

PUT SKIP EDIT(TOTAL)(F(5));
output:         14
positions: 12345

PUT SKIP EDIT('IMPROPER DATA')(A);
output:     IMPROPER DATA
positions: 1234567890123

PUT SKIP EDIT('IMPROPER DATA')(A(8));
output:     IMPROPER
positions: 12345678

PUT SKIP EDIT('COUNT IS:',COUNT,'TOTAL IS:',TOTAL)
       (A,F(4),X(3),A,E(10,2));
output:     COUNT IS:  25   TOTAL IS:  1.43E+01
positions: 12345678901234567890123456789012345
```

Rather than repeat an item in consecutive positions on the format list, a constant or expression enclosed in parentheses may be given as a "repetition factor". For example, if the value of N is 3:

```
PUT SKIP EDIT('VALUES ARE:',X,Y,Z)(A,(N)E(10,1));
```

is equivalent to

```
PUT SKIP EDIT('VALUES ARE:',X,Y,Z)
         (A,E(10,1),E(10,1),E(10,1));
```

Expressions can be given for the parameters w, d, and i in the format-items described above. These expressions are evaluated during execution of the PUT statement to determine the field width or number of digits. This allows the output format to depend on computational results, but this capability is not often used. Generally, the format is predetermined, and w, d, and i are given as constants, as shown in the examples.

4.2 The GET Statement

Initially we consider the GET statement only as a means of entering information into the computer. It will cause information to be transferred from the "standard input device" into the memory of the computer. The standard input device will normally be a card reader, or a terminal keyboard if you are using a "time-sharing" version of PL/I such as PL/CT or the IBM "Checkout-Compiler". The input device is considered the source of a continuous stream of values. A GET statement takes values from this stream and assigns them to variables.

The process is similar to the assignment statement in that new values are assigned to variables. It is different in that instead of the values being generated internally by evaluation of an expression, the values are supplied from outside the computer via an input device.

4.2.1 The LIST Form of GET

The form of the simplest input statement is

```
GET LIST( variable names, separated by commas );
```

An example is:

```
GET LIST(AMOUNT);
```

Its execution causes the next value to be read from the data list given on cards after the program, and assigned to variable AMOUNT. The value is assigned using the same rules as in an assignment statement; if AMOUNT is a FIXED variable the value is truncated to an integer. Execution of the statement

```
GET LIST(X, Y);
```

would cause the next two values to be read (from the data list) and assigned to X and Y, respectively.

Recall (from Section 1.4) that the data cards at the end of the program are not read automatically into memory as the program is being loaded. Loading ends with the last card of the program, and the cards bearing data wait in the card reader, to be read if and when the program calls for them by executing GET statements. The cards supply a list of values; the reading process moves through this list from left-to-right, one card to the next, as demanded by execution of GET statements. Each value is read only once from this list.

Suppose there are three GET statements in a program, where all variables are FLOAT:

```
...
GET LIST(BASE, HEIGHT);
...
GET LIST(WIDTH, TEMP, TIME);
...
GET LIST(LIMIT);
...
```

and the data list for this program is:

```
            *DATA
             17.5
             83.72
(4.2.1a)     23.05
             76
             2314
             964.122
```

When the first GET statement is executed the first two values are read from the data list and 17.5 becomes the value of BASE and 83.72 becomes the value of HEIGHT. When the next GET statement is executed the next three values are read; 23.05 is assigned to WIDTH, 76 to TEMP and 2314 to TIME. When the third GET is executed 964.122 is read and assigned to LIMIT.

A total of six values are read in by the three GET statements and exactly six values are provided in the data list. If more than six had been provided, the extra values would simply have been ignored since the program never calls for them to be read. This could be intentional -- the amount of data processed might depend upon some test the program performs upon the early values. This could also happen by accident if you do not properly coordinate GET statements and the data list.

The opposite condition is more common; a GET statement is executed and an inadequate number of data values remain on the list to satisfy all of the variables in the GET. Different languages react to this situation in different ways. It is essentially an error, but is often considered a legitimate way to stop execution. (PL/I has a special way of handling this situation. See Section 7.4.3.) In order to detect the end of the data from within the program, we often add some marker value at the end of the actual data. This should be a value that is clearly recognizable -- it cannot be a possible data value -- so that the program can test for it after each GET statement. This technique was used in the example of Section 1.1.

The variables listed in the GET statement and the values on the data list must be synchronized with respect to order as well as quantity. The variable to which each value is assigned is entirely determined by the order in which the variable names appear in the GET statements. (For this purpose the order of the GET statements is the order in which they are executed, and not the order in which they are written.) Hence you must know exactly what the order of the variables in the GET lists will be and arrange the data values accordingly.

The data associated with the GET LIST statement is a list of values. No blanks may separate adjacent characters of a value, while adjacent values must be separated by a comma, by one or more blanks, or by both. The entire card may be used, with column 1 considered to come immediately after column 80 of the previous card. (It is generally a good idea to avoid splitting a single value onto two cards. PL/I doesn't mind, but it is hard for humans to follow.) Values can be given in either conventional or exponential form.

In example (4.2.1a) the values were given on six different cards. Each of the following forms is equivalent to (4.2.1a), although (4.2.1e) is the best for humans since the arrangement suggests which values will be read by each GET statement. (4.2.1b) is the least attractive because of the inconsistent (although legal) means of separating values.

(4.2.1b)
```
*DATA
17.5, 83.72,23.05,         76 2314 ,964.122
```

(4.2.1c)
```
*DATA
    17.5, 83.72, 23.05, 76, 2314, 964.122
```

(4.2.1d)
```
*DATA
1.75E1,  8.372E1, 2.305E1, 7.6E1, 2.314E3, 9.64122E2
```

(4.2.1e)
```
*DATA
17.5, 83.72
23.05, 76, 2314
964.122
```

<u>Only values can be given as data</u>. It would not make sense to give a variable as a datum -- each datum will be assigned as the value of a variable, and variables of the kind we are using cannot have another variable as value. Arithmetic operations are not allowed in the data -- .5 cannot be given as 1/2.

4.2.2 <u>The DATA Form of GET</u>

There is a GET DATA counterpart to the PUT DATA statement. Never having used it in 10 years of programming in PL/I, we see no need to discuss it here. See Appendix A.2.

4.2.3 The EDIT Form of GET

Recall the PUT EDIT statement described in Section 4.1.4. Its purpose was to provide complete control over the formatting of output. In the same fashion, the GET EDIT statement allows complete control over the format of the input. With GET EDIT, the input data does not appear in variable format, with a comma between each value; it must appear in fixed, predetermined columns as given by the GET EDIT statement.

The form of the statement is

```
GET SKIP(i) EDIT(element list) (format list);
```

where SKIP(i) is optional and the element and format lists are as described in Section 4.1.4 except that only variables can be given in the element list. The list of "items" in the format list controls the input process in the same way as with PUT EDIT.

As an example, consider execution of

```
GET EDIT(B, C, D) (A(5), X(2), F(3), E(8.2));
```

where the variables are declared as

```
DCL B CHAR(8) VARYING;
DCL C FIXED;
DCL D FLOAT;
```

Suppose the input stream consists of

```
ƀSTUVXY13ƀ820.62   ....
```

Then

(1) A(5) causes the first 5 characters ' STUV' to be assigned to B;

(2) X(2) causes characters 'XY' to be skipped;

(3) F(3) causes '13 ' to be converted to the integer 13 and assigned to C.

(4) E(8.2) causes '820.62 ' to be read, converted to the floating number 820.62E+00, and stored in D.

There are a number of significant differences in GET and PUT with respect to a few items, and you should study the details in the appendix carefully.

One use of GET EDIT is to read a complete card as a sequence of characters and assign it to a string variable. For example:

```
DCL C CHAR(80) VARYING;
```

The execution of the following reads one card into C:

```
GET EDIT(C) (COL(1), A(80));
```

If the input is not positioned at column 1 of a card, the control item COL(1) causes the rest of the input card to be skipped and the input to be positioned at the beginning of the next card. Note that quotes do not have to be placed at the beginning and end of the input card. The contents of the card can then be processed by processing the value of C.

4.3 The FILE Option

Up to this point we have assumed that the source of values for a GET statement is the "standard input device", and the destination of values from a PUT statement is the "standard output device". The "FILE option" in either a GET or PUT allows you to vary this situation by explicitly specifying the source or destination.

Although we have talked in terms of "devices", strictly speaking in PL/I everything outside of main memory is considered a "file". Some file supplies values to the GET statement; some file receives values from a PUT statement. The FILE option is the means by which you specify which file is involved. There is a separate language, outside of PL/I, called "job control language" (JCL), by which files are associated with physical devices. We duck that issue completely and leave you to discover the joys of JCL from some other source.

The standard input file in PL/I is called "SYSIN"; usually it refers to the set of data cards following the *DATA card. A GET statement that explicitly specified the standard input file as the source of values would be written:

```
GET FILE(SYSIN) LIST (...);
```

We have omitted this FILE option from previous GET statements because FILE(SYSIN) is the default -- SYSIN is assumed unless some other file is explicitly specified. (Both PL/I and PL/C issue warning messages to remind you that SYSIN is the assumed source for any GET statements without an explicit FILE option.)

Similarly, the standard output file is called "SYSPRINT". An example of a statement that explicitly directs output to this file is:

```
PUT FILE(SYSPRINT) LIST ('IMPROPER DATA:', X);
```

We have omitted the FILE option from PUT statements because SYSPRINT is the default assumption (with a warning message from PL/I and PL/C).

As your programs become more complicated it will sometimes be convenient to have several parallel streams of input and output. This is easily done in PL/I just by establishing several different files and specifying the appropriate file in GET and PUT statements. For example, suppose you needed to produce two different output lists simultaneously. You could use SYSPRINT for one, and establish a file called ALTPRINT (say) for the other. Some PUT statements would route results to SYSPRINT:

```
PUT FILE(SYSPRINT) ...
```

and others would route results to ALTPRINT:

```
PUT FILE(ALTPRINT) ...
```

Even if the computer you were using actually had only one printer, this would allow the program to behave as if there were two. The files would be produced simultaneously but they would be <u>printed</u> consecutively.

Storage on magnetic tapes and disks is also used by creating files and routing information to and from main memory and tape or disk by means of GET and PUT statements with appropriate file options.

4.4 The STRING Option

The GET statement is usually used to read data from an external file, into program variables. When the "STRING option" is used, GET reads from <u>an internal string variable</u> rather than an external file. This is useful, for example, when you have already read a card into a character variable C (say) and now wish to transfer the data on it into other variables.

The STRING option is an alternative to the FILE option. It has the form:

```
STRING(string variable)
```

As an example, consider the program segment

```
DCL C CHAR(10) VARYING;
DCL I, J, K FIXED;
C = ' -1,3,  5';
GET STRING(C) LIST(I, J);
GET STRING(C) LIST(K);
```

After execution of the assignment, C has the value ' -1,3, 5'. Execution of the first GET reads two values from variable C. Thus after execution I = -1 and J = 3. Execution of the second GET reads a value into K, but again reads from C. But note that it reads from the <u>beginning</u> of C again, and thus after execution K = -1.

The STRING option may be used with GET LIST, GET EDIT or GET DATA; its sole purpose is to designate a string variable instead of an external file as the place from which to get the data.

The STRING option may also be used with PUT statements, in which case the data is <u>stored</u> in the designated string variable instead of an external file. As an example, using string variable C described above, execution of

```
PUT STRING(C) LIST(I, J);
```

assigns C the value

```
'                    -1                    3'
```

Note that the SUBSTR pseudo-variable can also be used; with C having the value just shown, the execution of

```
PUT STRING(SUBSTR(C, 2, 5)) EDIT(J) (F(5));
```

would change C to

```
'     3              -1                    3'
```

4.5 Array Input and Output

The appearance of an array name without a subscript in the list of a PUT statement causes all the variables of the array to be printed, in row-major order. For example, if TAB(1:8) is an array, PUT LIST(TAB); is equivalent to

```
DO I = 1 TO 8 BY 1;
    PUT LIST(TAB(I));
    END;
```

Either form will place values in the next eight fields (starting a new line whenever the last line has been filled). To begin placement with a new line, use either PUT SKIP LIST(TAB); or

```
PUT SKIP;
DO I = 1 TO 8 BY 1;
    PUT LIST(TAB(I));
    END;
```

As another example, for array MATRIX(1:3,1:15), the statement PUT LIST(MATRIX); is equivalent to the following nested loops; either form places values in the next 45 fields.

```
DO I = 1 TO 3 BY 1;
    DO J = 1 TO 15 BY 1;
        PUT LIST(MATRIX(I,J));
        END;
    END;
```

Similarly, appearance of an array name without a subscript in the list of a GET statement causes values to be read in and assigned to the array, in row-major order. For example, execution of

```
GET LIST(TAB, MATRIX);
```

with TAB and MATRIX as defined above would cause 8 values to be read and assigned to TAB(1:8), in order, and 45 values to be read and assigned to MATRIX(1:3,1:15), in row-major order. Note that values for the whole array are always read; it is not possible to use this feature to read in part of an array.

4.6 Structure Input and Output

The appearance of a structure name in the list of a PUT statement causes all the variables of that structure to be printed, in the order in which they appear in the structure declaration. Consider the declaration

```
DCL 1  A,
        2 B CHAR(20) VARYING,
        2 C,
            3 D CHAR(20) VARYING,
            3 E CHAR(20) VARYING,
        2 F,
            3 G FIXED,
            3 H FIXED;
```

Then the statement

```
PUT LIST (A, A.F)
```

is equivalent to

```
PUT LIST(A.B, A.C.D, A.C.E, A.F.G, A.F.H,
         A.F.G, A.F.H);
```

The appearance of a structure name in the list of a GET statement causes all the variables of that structure to recieve input values, in the same order as listed above for PUT.

Section 4 Exercises

1. Write a single PUT statement to produce the same printed output as the following sequence:

```
PUT SKIP LIST(TOTAL);
PUT LIST(MAX);
PUT LIST(MINIMUM, AVG);
```

2. What would the output from the following segment look like?

```
DO I = 1 TO 5 BY 1;
   PUT SKIP LIST(I,I,I,I,I);
   END;
```

3. What is the result of executing the following statement?

```
PUT LIST(' ',' ');
```

4. What is printed by execution of the following statement?

```
PUT SKIP LIST('PUT SKIP LIST(X);');
```

5. Write a sequence of PUT statements to print the pattern shown below (where ƀ indicates a blank):

```
ƀ0ƀ
0ƀ0
ƀ0ƀ
```

6. Write a PUT EDIT statement that will repeatedly display the value of a FIXED variable named K, whose value is 2 to yield exactly the same output as the following statement:

```
PUT SKIP LIST('22222222');
```

7. Assuming that X and Y are FLOAT variables, write a PUT EDIT statement that will produce the same output as:

```
PUT SKIP LIST(X, Y);
```

8. TABLE(1:5,1:5) is a square array of FIXED variables, all of whose values are integers greater than 0 and less than 10. Print the values of this array in rectangular form, on five consecutive lines, with a single blank between the values on each line. For example, if all of the values are 9, the array would be displayed as:

```
9 9 9 9 9
9 9 9 9 9
9 9 9 9 9
9 9 9 9 9
9 9 9 9 9
```

Section 5 Execution of a Sequential Program

We have now introduced enough elements of PL/I to construct a simple but complete program. Although it is neither realistic nor useful we can illustrate the actual execution of a program.

Consider the following trivial task:

1. Read two numbers from a data list,
2. compute the sum of these numbers, and
3. print that sum.

The following is a complete PL/I program to perform that task:

```
SUM2: PROCEDURE OPTIONS(MAIN);
    DECLARE (NBR1, NBR2, SUM) FLOAT;
    GET LIST (NBR1, NBR2);
    SUM = NBR1 + NBR2;
    PUT LIST ('THE SUM OF', NBR1, 'AND', NBR2);
    PUT SKIP (2) LIST ('IS:', SUM);
    END SUM2;
```

This program consists of a single "procedure", called the "main procedure" as indicated by the phrase "OPTIONS(MAIN)". The keywords PROCEDURE and END denote the beginning and end of the text of this procedure. The identifier SUM2 has been chosen as a name for the procedure.

The lines that constitute the text of the procedure -- DECLARE, GET, assignment and PUT -- have been described in the preceding sections. The DECLARE line specifies the variables that are to be created in preparation for the execution of the procedure. The GET, assignment and PUT statements constitute the "body" of the procedure. The procedure is executed by carrying out the actions specified by the statements of the body, in the order in which the statements appear.

To execute this program, the procedure and the corresponding data list are entered into the computer. Together they constitute a "job". A complete job is shown below, with each line representing a separate punched card, or a separate line on a terminal keyboard:

```
*PL/C XREF ATR
 SUM2: PROCEDURE OPTIONS(MAIN);
     DECLARE (NBR1, NBR2, SUM) FLOAT;
     GET LIST (NBR1, NBR2);
     SUM = NBR1 + NBR2;
     PUT LIST ('THE SUM OF', NBR1, 'AND', NBR2);
     PUT SKIP (2) LIST ('IS:' SUM);
     END SUM2;
*DATA
 15.5, 10.2
```

As shown, the data list <u>follows</u> the program. The *PL/C and *DATA lines are "control" lines that are neither program nor data. *PL/C marks the beginning of a new program and indicates that the program is written in the PL/C language. XREF and ATR elect options in the processing. *DATA marks the end of the program and the beginning of the data list. The control lines <u>must begin in column 1</u>. The lines of the program must <u>not</u> begin in column 1. The lines of the data list <u>may</u> begin in column 1, but do not have to.

The program must be preceded and followed by additional control lines that serve to separate this job from its predecessor and successor, and to identify the user to the computer accounting system. However, these additional control lines vary from one computer installation to another. We do not show them and you will have to obtain local instructions.

In this program we have deliberately omitted a comma from the second PUT statement to illustrate what happens in the event of a syntax error.

5.1 <u>Processing of a Program</u>

A PL/I program is processed in two distinct stages:

1. <u>Compilation</u>, during which the program text is read, checked for syntax errors, translated into the "machine language" for the particular computer, and stored in memory.

2. <u>Execution</u> of the stored program.

The execution stage does not begin until the compilation stage is completed. That is, statements are not executed one by one as they are loaded and translated, but rather execution begins with the first statement of the main procedure after the last statement has been translated and stored in memory.

The data portion of the deck is <u>not</u> read during compilation. It is read by the <u>execution of the GET statements</u> in the program. Consider that the compilation stage is terminated by encountering the *DATA card and that the card reader is ready to read the first data card when the first GET is encountered in execution. If too few GETs are executed not all the data will be read; if too many GETs are executed the data list will be exhausted and execution will terminate prematurely. In any event, the data list can only be read <u>once</u> -- the program cannot reread any card a second time.

5.2 The Printed Results of Processing

The PL/C printed output for this program is shown below. There are four sections:

1. <u>Source Listing</u>: a copy of the program.
   a. The control card options are listed at the top of the page.
   b. The first line of the program is used as a title.
   c. The statements are automatically numbered, as shown in the column under STMT. The LEVEL, NEST, BLOCK and MLVL columns are not relevant for this simple program and will be considered later.
   d. Syntax errors are reported by error messages immediately after the illegal statement. This is followed by the repaired form of the statement that is actually used in execution.

2. <u>Cross-Reference and Attribute Listing</u>: an alphabetical listing of all identifiers in the program, showing attributes, where declared, and where used. This is printed only if the XREF and ATR options are effective. If these are not the default options at your installation they should be given explicitly on the *PL/C card for the first run of every program.

2a. <u>Error Messages</u>: for error conditions detected after the source listing has been printed but before execution. Usually they include the message:

    WARNING: NO FILE SPECIFIED. SYSIN/SYSPRINT ASSUMED

    This is a reminder that you are relying on the default files in GET and PUT statements. It is harmless and can be ignored.

3. <u>Execution Output</u>: results printed by the execution of PUT statements. This normally terminates with the message

    IN STMT nnn PROGRAM RETURNS FROM MAIN PROCEDURE

    where nnn is the STMT number of the END of the main procedure.

4. <u>Post-mortem Dump</u>: a final summary of execution giving
   a. The final value of each variable at the end of execution.
   b. The number of times each label and entry-name was encountered in execution (see Section 7.4.1).
   c. Usage statistics for computer time and memory.

   This is only printed if the DUMP option is effective. If this is not the default option it should be given explicitly on the *PL/C card for the early runs of every program.

```
*PL/C XREF ATR

*OPTIONS IN EFFECT*     TIME=(0,15.00),PAGES=30,LINES=2000,ATR,XREF,FLAGW,NOCMNTS,SORMGIN=(2,72,1),ERRORS=(50,50),
*OPTIONS IN EFFECT*     TABSIZE=4132,SOURCE,OPLIST,NOCMPRS,HDRPG,AUXIO=10000,LINECT=60,NOALIST,MONITOR=(UDEF,BNDRY,
*OPTIONS IN EFFECT*     SUBRG,AUTO),MCALL,NOMTEXT,DUMP=(S,F,L,E,U,R),DUMPE=(S,F,L,E,U,R),DUMPT=(S,F,L,E,U,R)

 SUM2: PROCEDURE OPTIONS(MAIN);                                         PL/C-R7.6-003 08/18/78 23:35 PAGE   1

  STMT LEVEL NEST BLOCK MLVL  SOURCE TEXT

     1                           SUM2: PROCEDURE OPTIONS(MAIN);
     2    1          1                 DECLARE (NBR1, NBR2, SUM) FLOAT;
     3    1          1                 GET LIST (NBR1, NBR2);
     4    1          1                 SUM = NBR1 + NBR2;
     5    1          1                 PUT LIST ('THE SUM OF', NBR1, 'AND', NBR2);
     6    1          1                 PUT SKIP (2) LIST ('IS:' SUM);
   ERROR IN STMT     6  MISSING COMMA IN COLUMN 31 (SY06)
         FOR STMT    6 PL/C USES  PUT SKIP (2) LIST ('IS:',SUM);

     7    1          1                 END SUM2;


 SUM2: PROCEDURE OPTIONS(MAIN);                                         PL/C-R7.6-003 08/18/78 23:35 PAGE   2

DCL NO.         IDENTIFIER                              ATTRIBUTES AND REFERENCES

   2             NBR1                                   AUTOMATIC,ALIGNED,DECIMAL,FLOAT(6)
                                                        3,4,5

   2             NBR2                                   AUTOMATIC,ALIGNED,DECIMAL,FLOAT(6)
                                                        3,4,5

   2             SUM                                    AUTOMATIC,ALIGNED,DECIMAL,FLOAT(6)
                                                        4,6

   1             SUM2                                   ENTRY,DECIMAL,FLOAT(6)


ERRORS/WARNINGS DETECTED DURING CODE GENERATION:

     WARNING: NO FILE SPECIFIED. SYSIN/SYSPRINT ASSUMED. (CGOC)
```

```
THE SUM OF              1.55000E+01            AND                     1.01999E+01

IS:                     2.56999E+01


IN STMT    7  PROGRAM RETURNS FROM MAIN PROCEDURE.




 SUM2: PROCEDURE OPTIONS(MAIN);                                                PL/C-R7   POST-MORTEM DUMP   PAGE   1


IN STMT    7  SCALARS AND BLOCK-TRACE:

***** MAIN PROCEDURE SUM2

SUM= 2.56999E+01          NBR2= 1.01999E+01        NBR1= 1.55000E+01


NON-0 PROCEDURE EXECUTION COUNTS:
NAME         STMT COUNT  NAME          STMT COUNT  NAME          STMT COUNT  NAME          STMT COUNT  NAME          STMT COUNT
SUM2         0001 00001


       COMPILATION STATISTICS  (0007 STATEMENTS)      |                    EXECUTION STATISTICS
SECONDS  ERRORS  WARNINGS  PAGES  LINES  CARDS  INCL'S | SECONDS  ERRORS  WARNINGS  PAGES  LINES  CARDS  INCL'S  AUX I/O
  .05       1        1       2     44      9       0 |   .03       0         0      1      7      1      0        0
-------------------------------------------------------+------------------------------------------------------------------
BYTES   SYMBOL TABLE   INTERMEDIATE CODE   OBJECT CODE |   STATIC CORE   AUTOMATIC CORE   DYNAMIC CORE   TOTAL STORAGE
USED       563(  1K)        248(  1K)        222(  1K) |     344(  1K)       231(  1K)        0(  0K)      1359(  2K)
UNUSED   15965( 15K)      15990( 15K)      32436( 31K) |   31925( 31K)     31925( 31K)    15990( 15K)     31925( 31K)

THIS PROGRAM MAY BE RERUN WITHOUT CHANGE IN A REGION  31K BYTES SMALLER USING TABLESIZE=   141
```

5.2.1 Printed Results from PL/CS

If the program is processed by the PL/CS compiler instead of PL/C the execution output and post-mortem dump are the same, but the source listing is significantly different (and the cross-reference/attribute listing does not exist).

The PL/CS source listing for our previous example is shown below:

```
STMT    PROGRAM TEXT                                          COMMENTS/ERRORS/WARNINGS

0101    SUM2: PROCEDURE OPTIONS(MAIN);
0102        DECLARE (NBR1, NBR2, SUM) FLOAT;
0141        GET LIST (NBR1, NBR2);
0142        SUM= NBR1+NBR2;
0143        PUT LIST ('THE SUM OF', NBR1, 'AND', NBR2);
0144        PUT SKIP (2) LIST ('IS:', SUM);
0145        END SUM2;
```

Some differences are apparent:

1. The missing comma in the second PUT statement is not detected as an error. PL/CS is much less demanding with regard to punctuation and simply does not consider this omission worth reporting. Note however, that the statement has in fact been repaired to a syntactically correct form. When more serious errors require messages these appear to the right of the illegal statement rather than below it.

2. The statements are numbered differently. PL/CS begins numbering with 101, reserves numbers 102 to 139 for declarations, and starts numbering the body statements with 141.

3. The LEVEL, NEST, BLOCK and MLVL columns are not provided (or needed) in PL/CS.

There are even more important differences between PL/CS and PL/C that are not apparent in this example:

4. The PL/CS source listing is automatically formatted. That is, the indentation of the lines on the listing reflects the actual structure of the program and is entirely independent of the positions given on the cards.

5. PL/CS prints only the program that is actually executed, rather than the original program received. That is, the source listing shows the repaired program, if any repairs were necessary, without showing the faulty lines that were received. When PL/CS generates statements implied but not given in the input the STMT number is marked with a "G".

5.3 Tracing Execution

You should understand both the meaning of each PL/I statement and the manner in which they are executed, well enough to be able to follow the execution of a program on a statement-by-statement basis. In fact, you should be able to simulate the action of the computer and "trace" the execution of a program on paper. Your action should differ from the computer's only in speed (by a factor of 10^6 or more).

For example, a detailed trace of the loading and execution of SUM2 is given below:

1. The cards, from *PL/C through *DATA are read; a copy of the program (in translated form) is created in memory.

2. Execution begins by entering the main procedure SUM2.

3. As SUM2 is entered three variables are created (recall that ??? is used to indicate that no value yet exists):

```
NBR1 ??? [float]
NBR2 ??? [float]
SUM  ??? [float]
```

4. The first statement in the body of the procedure is GET LIST(NBR1, NBR2);. Execution of this statement reads the next two numbers on the data list and assigns them to variables NBR1 and NBR2. At this point, the variables are:

```
NBR1 15.5 [float]
NBR2 10.2 [float]
SUM  ???  [float]
```

5. Execution of the next statement, SUM = NBR1 + NBR2;, changes the value of SUM. The variables now are:

NBR1	15.5 [float]
NBR2	10.2 [float]
SUM	25.7 [float]

6. Execution of the next statement, PUT LIST(Z);, causes an output line to be printed:

```
2.57000E+01
```

(The actual number printed is 2.56999E+01. Recall Section 2.2.1.)

7. The end of SUM2 is reached; execution of the program is finished.

Having completed SUM2, the computer begins execution of some other program. The next program "overwrites" and destroys the SUM2 program, and its variables NBR1, NBR2 and SUM.

Section 6 Conditional Execution

In "sequential" programs, such as those illustrated in Section 5, statements are executed in the order they appear in the text of the program. But such programs are not very useful and programs are rarely entirely sequential. There are two principal ways in which the execution sequence of statements is caused to be different from the textual sequence:

1. A statement can be made <u>conditional</u> -- that is, the decision as to whether or not it is executed can depend upon a specified condition.

2. The execution of a group of statements can be <u>repeated</u>.

The constructions that make execution conditional are described in this Section; the constructions to repeat execution are described in Section 7.

There are several forms of conditional execution. The simplest allows a statement to be either <u>executed</u> or <u>skipped</u>. The more general form <u>selects</u> one of a group of alternative statements for execution. In both cases the decision is made <u>during execution</u> of the program, based on the value of a logical expression (recall Section 3.4).

6.1 Conditional Execution of a Single Statement

A statement can be written so it may or may not be executed, depending on the value of a logical expression. The form is the following:

```
IF logical expression
    THEN statement
```

The interpretation is suggested by the English meaning of the keywords "IF" and "THEN":

If evaluation of the logical expression yields '1'B ("true") *then* execute the statement. If evaluation yields '0'B ("false") do not execute the statement.

For example, a statement that prints a message could be executed only if a certain value is negative:

```
IF ITEM < 0
    THEN PUT SKIP(2) LIST ('NEGATIVE ITEM:',  ITEM);
```

A statement that adds a value to a sum could be executed only if that value is positive:

```
IF NEWVAL > 0
    THEN SUM = SUM + NEWVAL;
```

A value can be tested to make sure it falls within a certain "range":

```
IF (VALUE < 0) | (VALUE > 10**5)
    THEN PUT SKIP(2) LIST
            ('VALUE OUT OF RANGE:', VALUE);
```

● PL/CS: The logical expression following IF must be enclosed in parentheses.

Conditional execution of a single statement can be shown graphically as follows:

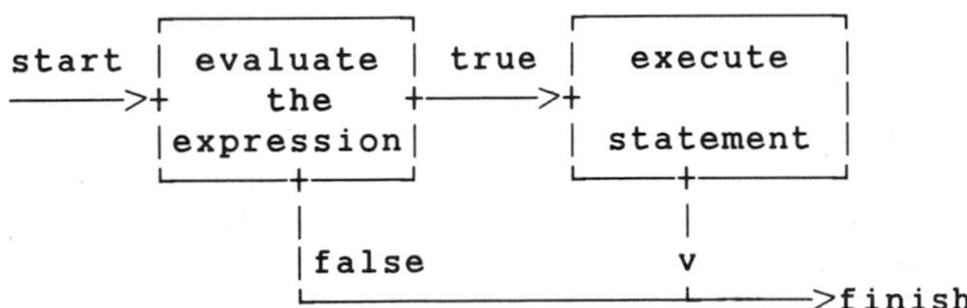

A logical expression can be simply a bit variable. This can be used to separate a test from action that is conditional upon that test. That is, the value of a logical expression can be saved at one point in a program for use at another. For example, the following assignment statement saves the value of the expression ITEM < 0:

```
NEG_DATUM = (ITEM < 0);
```

This result can be used later to control the printing of an error message:

```
IF NEG_DATUM
    THEN PUT SKIP(2) LIST ('NEGATIVE ITEM:',  ITEM);
```

6.2 Choice Between Two Statements

The general form of the IF construction causes one of two statements to be selected for execution. The form is:

```
IF logical expression
    THEN statement1
    ELSE statement2
```

The interpretation of this is:

If the evaluation of the logical expression yields '1'B then execute statement1; if evaluation yields '0'B execute statement2.

This can be shown graphically as follows:

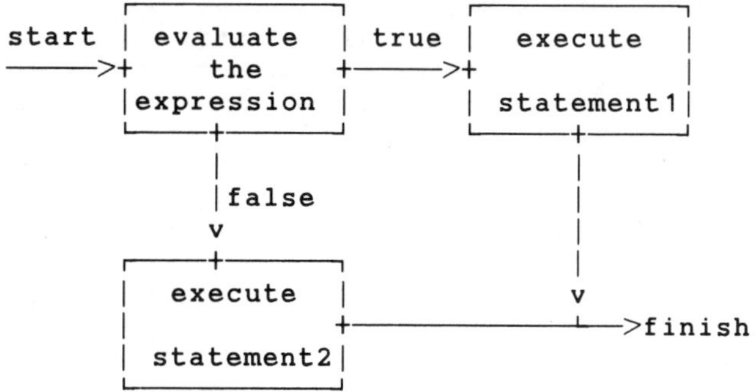

The following are examples:

```
IF DATUM < 0
    THEN NEGSUM = NEGSUM + DATUM;
    ELSE POSSUM = POSSUM + DATUM;

IF (VALUE < 0) | (VALUE > MAXVAL)
    THEN PUT SKIP(2) LIST
            ('IMPROPER DATUM DISCARDED:', VALUE);
    ELSE SUM = SUM + VALUE;

IF (VAL_COUNT < NBR_VALUES) & NEW_VAL_NEEDED
    THEN GET LIST (VALUE);
    ELSE PUT SKIP(3) LIST ('DATA LIST EXHAUSTED');
```

Note there are just two possibilities -- either statement1 or statement2 will be executed.

Comparing the two forms of IF (Sections 6.1 and 6.2) it is apparent that the "ELSE statement" is optional. When ELSE is present its statement is executed if the value of the logical expression is '0'B. When ELSE is omitted no statement is executed if the value is '0'B. In either case the "THEN statement" is executed if the value is '1'B.

There is some ambiguity as to whether the IF construction represents <u>one statement</u> or <u>several statements</u>. It is numbered on the source listing as though the keywords IF, THEN and ELSE each begins a separate statement. However, it is preferable to think of the <u>entire construction as a single unit</u>. Except for the anomaly in numbering it is treated as a single unit in PL/I (see Section 6.5).

6.3 Selection from Three or More Statements

A more general construction to cause execution of exactly <u>one of a group of statements</u> is usually called a "case statement", but in PL/I the keyword "SELECT" is used. The form is:

```
SELECT;
    WHEN (logical-expression)   statement1
    WHEN (logical-expression)   statement2
       ...
    OTHERWISE                   statementN
    END;
```

Effectively, the keywords SELECT and END delimit a <u>list of logical expression-statement pairs</u>. The meaning of the construction is the following:

> Execute the statement corresponding to the <u>first</u> logical expression that yields the value '1'B.
>
> If none of the expressions yields '1'B execute statementN (the "OTHERWISE statement").

This can be shown graphically as follows:

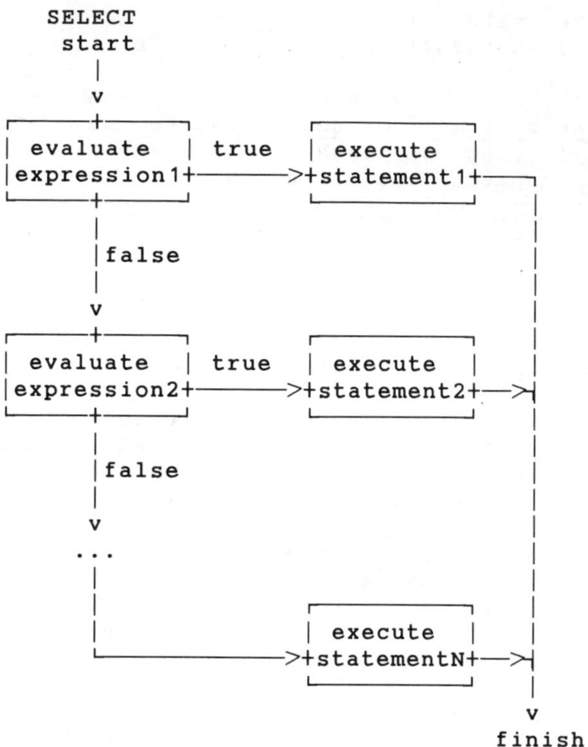

The following are examples:

```
SELECT;
    WHEN (VALUE < 0)  NEGSUM = NEGSUM + VALUE;
    WHEN (VALUE = 0)  ZEROCOUNT = ZEROCOUNT + 1;
    OTHERWISE        POSSUM = POSSUM + VALUE;
    END;

SELECT;
    WHEN (SUBSTR(CARD,1,1) = 'S')
            SPADECOUNT = SPADECOUNT + 1;
    WHEN (SUBSTR(CARD,1,1) = 'H')
            HEARTCOUNT = HEARTCOUNT + 1;
    WHEN (SUBSTR(CARD,1,1) = 'D')
            DIAMCOUNT = DIAMCOUNT + 1;
    WHEN (SUBSTR(CARD,1,1) = 'C')
            CLUBCOUNT = CLUBCOUNT + 1;
    OTHERWISE PUT SKIP (2)
            LIST ('IMPROPER CARD DEALT:', CARD);
    END;
```

Note that the order of the component statements in the SELECT statement is significant since only the first logical expression to yield '1'B will cause the corresponding statement to be executed. SELECT does not cause all the component statements whose expressions have value '1'B to be executed.

Note also that the IF construction is just a special case of SELECT. That is:

```
IF logical expression
    THEN statement1
    ELSE statement2
```

is equivalent to

```
SELECT;
    WHEN (logical expression)   statement1
    OTHERWISE                   statement2
    END;
```

Similarly, IF without the ELSE option:

```
IF logical expression
    THEN statement1
```

is equivalent to SELECT with a "null statement" after OTHERWISE:

```
SELECT;
    WHEN (logical expression)   statement1
    OTHERWISE ;
    END;
```

The IF construction is not really necessary, but it is easier to write and clearer to read than SELECT and should be used wherever applicable. Normal practice is to use SELECT only when there are three or more alternatives.

● PL/C: The current version of PL/C (Release 7.6) does not include SELECT. See Section 6.6.

● PL/CS: SELECT must be <u>labeled</u> by an identifier before SELECT and after END. The form is:

```
select-name: SELECT;
    WHEN (logical expression)    statement1
    WHEN (logical expression)    statement2
        ...
    OTHERWISE                    statementN
    END select-name;
```

6.4 Compound Statements

As discussed thus far one can use the IF or SELECT statement to execute a single statement conditionally. At times, however, one wants to execute a sequence of statements: statement1, statement2, ..., statementN (say) conditionally. This is done with the compound statement, which causes a sequence to be treated as a single statement:

```
DO;
    statement1
    statement2
       ...
    statementN
    END;
```

The sequence of statements statement1 ... statementN is called the body of the compound statement. The use of the delimiters DO; and END; is similar to the use of parentheses in expressions; they unite the statements into a single unit in the same way that the parentheses in (A + B + C) * D serve to indicate that the value of A+B+C is the single unit to be multiplied.

A compound statement may appear wherever any other statement can appear. For example:

```
IF VALUE < 0
    THEN DO;
        PUT SKIP (2) LIST
               ('NEGATIVE DATUM DISCARDED:', VALUE);
        ERROR_COUNT = ERROR_COUNT + 1;
        GET LIST (VALUE);
        END;
```

If the value of the logical expression is '1'B then the entire compound statement is executed: the three individual statements are executed in the order listed.

Another example is:

```
IF QTY < 0
    THEN DO;
        NEG_COUNT = NEG_COUNT + 1;
        NEG_SUM = NEG_SUM + QTY;
        END;
    ELSE DO;
        POS_COUNT = POS_COUNT + 1;
        POS_SUM = POS_SUM + QTY;
        END;
```

Similarly, a compound statement can be given in a SELECT:

```
SELECT;
    WHEN (VAL < GROUP1_LIMIT) DO;
        GROUP1_COUNT = GROUP1_COUNT + 1;
        GROUP1_SUM = GROUP1_SUM + VAL;
        END;
    WHEN (VAL < GROUP2_LIMIT) DO;
        GROUP2_COUNT = GROUP2_COUNT + 1;
        GROUP2_SUM = GROUP2_SUM + VAL;
        END;
    OTHERWISE DO;
        PUT SKIP (2) LIST ('DATUM OUT OF RANGE:',
                VAL);
        ERROR_OCCURRED = '1'B;
        END;
    END;
```

Note in this example that the values of GROUP1_LIMIT and GROUP2_LIMIT should form an <u>increasing</u> sequence (or some of the statements have no chance of being executed).

There is essentially no limit to the number or type of statements that can be included in the body of a compound statement. By this means substantial sequences of statements can be selected or made conditional.

6.5 <u>Nesting of Conditional Statements</u>

When a component statement of an IF or SELECT contains another IF or SELECT the <u>constructions are said to be "nested"</u>. This may be done in several ways. For example, one can include an IF or SELECT as a component of a compound statement:

```
IF expr1
    THEN DO;
        IF expr2
            THEN statement1
        END;
```

This has the following result in execution:

value of expr1	value of expr2	statements executed
'1'B	'1'B	statement1
'1'B	'0'B	none
'0'B	'1'B	none
'0'B	'0'B	none

This particular example would be more easily and clearly written using a "compound condition":

```
IF (expr1) & (expr2)
    THEN statement1
```

However, in more complicated cases the nested construction may be required. For example:

```
IF expr1
    THEN DO;
        statement1
        IF expr2
            THEN statement2
            ELSE statement3
        statement4
        END;
    ELSE statement5
```

This has the following result in execution:

value of expr1	value of expr2	statements executed
'1'B	'1'B	stmt1, stmt2, stmt4
'1'B	'0'B	stmt1, stmt3, stmt4
'0'B	-	statement5

IF and SELECT can be nested without using the compound statement. For this purpose the complete IF or SELECT construction is considered to be a single statement. For example:

```
IF expr1
    THEN IF expr2
        THEN statement1
        ELSE statement2
    ELSE IF expr3
        THEN statement3
        ELSE statement4
```

Execution of this nested construction can be shown graphically as follows:

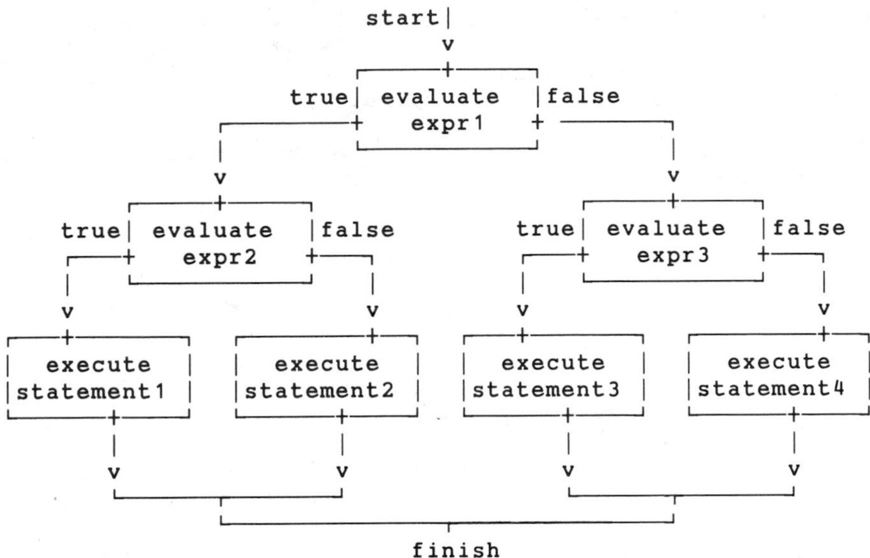

Execution can also be described by the following table:

value of expr1	value of expr2	value of expr3	statement executed
'1'B	'1'B	-	statement1
'1'B	'0'B	-	statement2
'0'B	-	'1'B	statement3
'0'B	-	'0'B	statement4

Interpretation of such a construction is more complicated when not all of the IFs are "complete" -- that is, when one or more lack the ELSE option. For example, compare the following constructions:

```
IF expr1                             IF expr1
    THEN IF expr2                        THEN IF expr2
        THEN statement1                      THEN statement1
        ELSE IF expr3                    ELSE IF expr3
            THEN statement3                  THEN statement3
            ELSE statement4                  ELSE statement4
```

The intention of these two constructions is apparently quite different, but note that in both cases the <u>text is identical</u> -- only the indentation is different. Since indentation is an aid to the human reader and is not significant to PL/I it is obvious that these constructions are in fact the same and that in one of them the indentation is deceptive. The question centers on the first ELSE unit -- should it be associated with the first IF or the second? The answer is that an ELSE belongs to the last preceding IF that lacks an ELSE. Therefore the indentation on the left reflects the actual structure.

To achieve the result implied by the righthand indentation you could write:

```
IF expr1
    THEN DO;
        IF expr2
            THEN statement1
        END;
    ELSE IF expr3
        THEN statement3
        ELSE statement4
```

Conditional constructions can be nested to any depth. PL/I permits greater flexibility in this regard than programmers can prudently use. In complex nests of IFs and SELECTs it is difficult to be sure you wrote what you intended. Therefore it is good practice to try to simplify nested constructions by using compound conditions. That is, write:

```
IF expr1 & expr2
    THEN statement1
```

instead of:

```
IF expr1
    THEN IF expr2
        THEN statement1
```

When complex nesting of conditional statements is unavoidable make generous use of compound statements to make the logical structure clear.

6.6 Simulation of the SELECT Construction

Some versions of PL/I and PL/C do not include SELECT. If you are using one of these dialects the task of selecting one of many alternatives must be achieved with a nested IF construction. Instead of

```
SELECT;
    WHEN (expr1)    statement1
    WHEN (expr2)    statement2
            ...
    OTHERWISE       statementN
    END;
```

you should use the following construction:

```
IF expr1
    THEN statement1
    ELSE IF expr2
        THEN statement2
        ELSE IF ...
                ELSE statementN
```

The usual indentation for IF statements, as shown above, is not the clearest way to indicate that this nest of IFs simulates a SELECT. A preferable presentation would be the following:

```
DO;
    IF expr1
        THEN statement1
    ELSE IF expr2
        THEN statement2
         ...
    ELSE     statementN
    END;
```

The DO and END delimiters are not necessary (execution is the same with or without them), but they help emphasize that all these statements represent one logical unit.

6.6.1 Label Variables

The selection of one of many alternatives can also be achieved with "label variables". A variable can be declared an array of labels. For example:

```
DECLARE L(1:4) LABEL;
```

L is an array of four elements, each of which can contain the label of some statement. For example, if L(1) contains the label INCRX then execution of

```
GOTO L(1);
```

is equivalent to execution of

```
GOTO INCRX;
```

INCRX is a "label constant" which can be assigned as value to a label variable and a GOTO can have either a label constant or a label variable as its argument.

However, in general the use of label variables makes a program difficult to understand. The only form we use and recommend is the special case where subscripted labels are given directly as the labels of statements. That is, L(1), L(2), L(3) and L(4) would be label prefixes at different points in the program. Then GOTO L(I); would branch to one of these four statements, depending on the value of I. For example:

```
/** EXECUTE ONE OF L(I), DEPENDING ON I */
    IF (I < 1) | (I > 4)
        THEN GOTO L_OTHERWISE;
    GOTO L(I);
    L(1): statement1
        GOTO L_END;
    L(2): statement2
        GOTO L_END;
    L(3): statement3
        GOTO L_END;
    L(4): statement4
        GOTO L_END;
    L_OTHERWISE: statement5
    L_END:;
```

This segment is equivalent to:

```
SELECT;
    WHEN (I = 1) statement1
    WHEN (I = 2) statement2
    WHEN (I = 3) statement3
    WHEN (I = 4) statement4
    OTHERWISE    statement5
    END;
```

The label variable form is actually more efficient in execution than the SELECT construction, since it branches directly to the desired statement rather than evaluate a sequence of conditions until one is found to be true. If there are many alternatives the difference can be significant.

●PL/CS: Label variables are not included.

Section 6 Summary

1. The execution of a single statement can be made conditional with the IF statement:

```
IF condition
    THEN statement
```

2. The IF statement can also select between execution of two statements, depending upon a condition:

```
IF condition
    THEN statement1
    ELSE statement2
```

3. The SELECT statement can select between three or more statements:

```
SELECT;
    WHEN (condition1)   statement1
    WHEN (condition2)   statement2
    ...
    OTHERWISE           statementN
    END;
```

The conditions are evaluated in the order listed; the statement corresponding to the first true condition is executed.

4. A compound statement is a sequence of statements, delimited by DO and END, that are treated as a single statement.

Section 6 Exercises

The following exercises are to be written using only conditional statements, assignment statements, and GET and PUT.

1. Write a single conditional statement with only an assignment statement as a substatement, for the following:

```
IF X < 0
    THEN IF Y < 0
        THEN IF Z = 5
            THEN A = X + Y + Z;
```

2. Rewrite the following using a single conditional statement:

```
IF X < 0
    THEN DO;
        IF Y < 0
            THEN A = X + Y + Z;
        END;
    ELSE IF X = 5
        THEN A = X + Y + Z;
```

3. Given are three variables A, B, and C. Write a program segment to interchange the values of A, B and C so that the largest is in A and the smallest is in C.

4. Given three variables X, Y, and Z, write a program to determine if they are the sides of a triangle. (X, Y, and Z are the lengths of the sides of a triangle if all are greater than 0 and if X+Y>Z, X+Z>Y, and Y+Z>X.)

5. Write a program segment to print '1' if X, Y, and Z are the lengths of the sides of an equilateral triangle, and '2' if they are the sides of a non-equilateral triangle. A triangle is equilateral if all its sides are the same.

6. A, B and C are three variables with different values. One of these variables has the "middle value" -- one other is greater, one smaller. Write a program segment that will set variable D to this middle value. Compare this to the program for Exercise 3).

Section 7 Repetition of Execution

The most important way in which the sequence of statements executed differs from the sequence that appears in the program text is that the execution of certain groups of statements will be repeated. This characteristic is present in almost all useful programs and the control of repetition is a key concept in programming.

Two things are required in the control of repetition:

1. Specification of what portion of the program is to be repeated.

2. Specification of how many times the execution is to be repeated.

In PL/I the scope of repetition is always delimited by the keywords DO and END, but there are a variety of ways of specifying the duration. The general form is:

```
DO control-phrase ;
    statement1
    statement2
       ...
    statementN
    END;
```

The complete construction is called a "loop". The statements to be repeated (1 to N) constitute the body of the loop. The control phrase specifies the duration of the repetition of the body. Different forms of control phrase are described in the following sections.

7.1 Conditional Repetition

Continuation of repetition can be made conditional upon the value of a logical expression. For example, suppose you must read the next 500 numbers from the data list and obtain the sum of these numbers. Essentially you must execute a pair of statements such as the following 500 times:

```
GET LIST (DATUM);
SUM = SUM + DATUM;
```

Prior to the first of these 500 repetitions SUM must be set equal to 0. After the last of these 500 repetitions SUM should contain the required sum of the 500 data items.

The idea is to contrive a logical expression whose value is (say) '0'B as long as fewer than 500 repetitions have been performed, and becomes '1'B when the 500th repetition has been completed. This requires the use of an additional variable to keep track of the number of times the body of the loop has been executed. We name this variable NUMBER_REPETITIONS. The next two sections describe two different ways of using this "counting variable" to control the execution of the loop.

7.1.1 The WHILE Loop

The program to read and sum 500 numbers could be written as a WHILE loop as follows:

```
SUM, NUMBER_REPETITIONS = 0;
DO WHILE (NUMBER_REPETITIONS < 500);
    GET LIST (DATUM);
    SUM = SUM + DATUM;
    NUMBER_REPETITIONS = NUMBER_REPETITIONS + 1;
    END;
```

Using the WHILE form of control phrase, the logical expression is evaluated prior to each potential execution of the body. If evaluation yields '1'B the body is executed; if '0'B, execution of the loop has been completed (that is, the body is not executed again).

Initially NUMBER_REPETITIONS contains 0, so the condition is true ('1'B) and the body is executed the first time. The last statement of the body increases NUMBER_REPETITIONS by 1. Then the condition is reevaluated. The condition is still true, so the body is executed again. This continues until the 500th repetition, when NUMBER_REPETITIONS becomes 500. Then, on reevaluation, the value of the condition is false, so execution of the loop has been completed.

The general form of the WHILE loop is:

```
DO WHILE (logical expression);
    statements of the body
    END;
```

This loop is executed as follows:

1. Evaluate the logical expression. If the result is '0'B execution of the loop is completed; if '1'B proceed to step 2.

2. Execute the body of the loop. When the last statement of the body has been executed, return to step 1.

This can be shown graphically as follows:

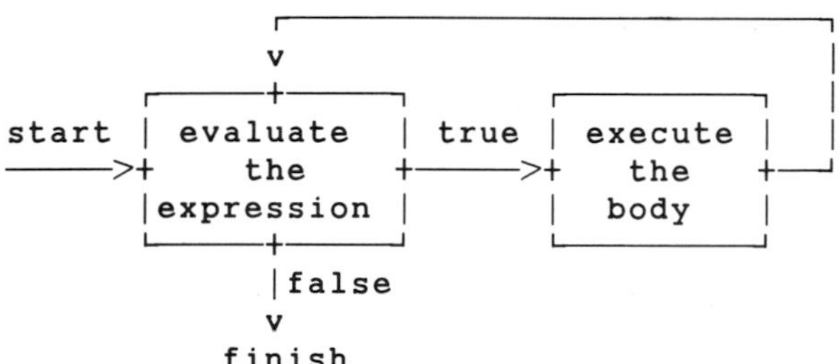

Note that there is no assurance that the body of the loop will be executed even once -- if the initial value of the logical expression is '0'B then the loop is considered to have been "completed" without ever executing the body.

Secondly, note that if the value of the logical expression is initially '1'B then some statement in the body should affect the value of the logical expression. If not, the value of the logical expression will obviously remain '1'B and the repetition of the body will continue forever (or until some time limit on execution is reached).

Thirdly, note that evaluation of the logical expression takes place before each execution of the body. The expression is not continuously monitored during execution of the body. If execution of some statement in the body makes the value of the logical expression '0'B, that fact is not discovered until after the complete body has been executed and the logical expression is being reevaluated prior to the next potential execution.

The parentheses enclosing the logical expression in a WHILE loop are required (unlike the logical expressions in IF and WHEN). This type of inconsistency in the definition of a programming language is unfortunate.

●PL/CS: A loop must be named by an identifier given before DO and after END:

```
loop-name: DO control-phrase;
    body
    END loop-name;
```

7.1.2 The UNTIL Loop

A second type of conditional loop uses an "UNTIL control-phrase":

```
DO UNTIL (logical expression);
    statements of the body
    END;
```

The UNTIL loop differs from the WHILE loop in two important ways:

1. The effect of the logical expression is reversed: repetition continues as long as the result is '0'B; the execution is completed when the result is '1'B.

2. The logical expression is evaluated after execution of the body.

This can be shown graphically as follows:

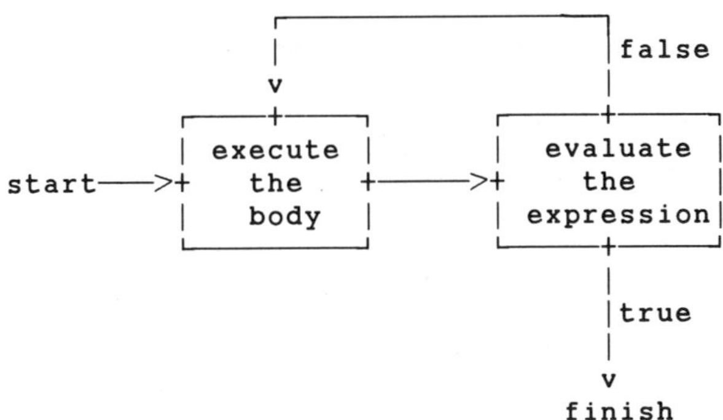

Note that at least one execution of the body of an UNTIL loop is assured.

●PL/C: The current version of PL/C (Release 7.6) does not include the UNTIL loop.

The previous example (in Section 7.1.1) can be rewritten as follows:

```
SUM, NUMBER_REPETITIONS = 0;
DO UNTIL (NUMBER_REPETITIONS = 500);
    GET LIST (DATUM);
    SUM = SUM + DATUM;
    NUMBER_REPETITIONS = NUMBER_REPETITIONS + 1;
    END;
```

For this example the two forms are essentially equivalent and it is not apparent why it is useful to have both WHILE and UNTIL loops in the language. The reason is suggested by the following example. Suppose the task is to read and sum numbers from data, as before, but that it is not known exactly how many data are present. The repetition is to continue until a zero value is encountered in the data list. This can be written as an UNTIL loop as follows:

```
SUM = 0;
DO UNTIL (DATUM = 0);
    GET LIST (DATUM);
    SUM = SUM + DATUM;
    END;
```

This takes advantage of the property that the body of an UNTIL loop is executed at least once. The same task written with a WHILE loop is:

```
SUM = 0;
GET LIST (DATUM);
DO WHILE (DATUM ¬= 0);
    SUM = SUM + DATUM;
    GET LIST (DATUM);
    END;
```

In this case, since the condition is evaluated before execution of the body, DATUM must be supplied an initial value by some statement outside the body. Hence an initializing GET statement is positioned before the loop.

Since in this case the UNTIL loop does not require any extra initializing statements it seems simpler and clearer than the WHILE form, but the advantage does not always lie with UNTIL. There are many ways to write loops and it requires experience and judgment to choose the best form for a given task.

To illustrate, consider a slightly different problem. The task is to read and sum data, but the end of the relevant data is signalled by a <u>negative value</u> (rather than zero) that is <u>not to be included</u> in the sum. The previous UNTIL strategy has to aviod adding in the negative value by making the summing strategy conditional:

```
SUM = 0;
DO UNTIL (DATUM < 0);
    GET LIST (DATUM);
    IF DATUM >= 0
        THEN SUM = SUM + DATUM;
    END;
```

Alternatively, the order of the statements in the body could be reversed and a harmless initial value provided for DATUM:

```
SUM, DATUM = 0;
DO UNTIL (DATUM < 0);
    SUM = SUM + DATUM;
    GET LIST (DATUM);
    END;
```

This is, in effect, similar to the WHILE loop for the previous example. Such a WHILE loop could be used here:

```
SUM = 0;
GET LIST (DATUM);
DO WHILE (DATUM >= 0);
    SUM = SUM + DATUM;
    GET LIST (DATUM);
    END;
```

Still another type of loop for this task is described in Section 7.4.3.

7.2 The Automatically-Indexed Loop

A third type of control phrase specifies an "index variable" whose value is automatically changed for each repetition of the body of the loop. The control phrase specifies an initial value for the index variable, the magnitude of the change for each repetition, and the limiting value that terminates the repetition. The form is:

```
DO index-variable = initial-value TO final-value
                        BY change-value;
    statements of the body
    END;
```

For example, the problem from Section 7.1 to read and sum 500 data items could be written in an "indexed loop" as follows:

```
SUM = 0;
DO NUMBER_REPETITION = 1 TO 500 BY 1;
    GET LIST (DATUM);
    SUM = SUM + DATUM;
    END;
```

Note that no separate assignment statement to assign initial value or to increment the value is required. This tends to make the indexed loop easier to use for those situations in which it is applicable. But it is not as flexible as the conditional loop. For example, the indexed loop cannot be used to read and sum data until a certain stopping value is encountered.

Initial-value, final-value and change-value in the control phrase are arithmetic expressions. The value supplied by change-value can be either positive or negative, causing either an increasing or decreasing sequence of values for the index-variable. If change-value (and the keyword "BY") is omitted a value of +1 is assumed.

It is instructive to precisely define the indexed loop in terms of a WHILE loop since several properties of the indexed loop are not obvious. Consider the following loop:

```
DO index-var = expr1 TO expr2 BY expr3;
    statements of the body
    END;
```

Assuming that the value of expr3 is positive, this loop is exactly equivalent to:

```
index-var = expr1;
TERM_VAL = expr2;
CHG_VAL = expr3;
DO WHILE (index-var <= TERM_VAL);
    statements of the body
    index-var = index-var + CHG_VAL;
    END;
```

If the value of expr3 is negative, the equivalent loop would be the same except that the control phrase would be

```
(index-var >= TERM_VAL)
```

Studied carefully, the equivalent WHILE loop reveals some interesting properties of the indexed loop:

1. A form of assignment is embedded in the control phrase; the value of the index-variable is changed just as if it were the left side variable of an assignment statement.

2. Since the index-variable is incremented and tested after the last execution of the body, the final value of the index-variable is not the same as its value during the last execution of the body.

3. The value of the index-variable in the final repetition of the body need not be exactly equal to the value given in the control phrase. For example, the control phrase

```
DO IND = 1 TO 6 BY 2;
```

would result in three executions of the body -- the first with IND = 1, the second with IND = 3, and the last with IND = 5.

4. It is not necessary to use the index-variable in the body of the loop. Frequently (as in the "read" and "sum" example) it serves only as a "counter variable" to record the number of repetitions of the body.

5. The value of the index-variable can be changed by statements in the body of the loop, but doing so affects the control of repetition. This is a risky practice and makes a loop more difficult to understand.

6. The values of the three control expressions initial-value, final-value and change-value are determined before execution of the loop. Nothing that happens in the body of the loop can affect these control values.

●PL/CS: The indexed loop is further restricted as follows:

1. The "BY phrase" is required.

2. The value of change-value must not be 0.

3. The index-variable as well as all variables that appear in any of the three control expressions are "readonly" in the body of the loop. That is, they cannot be assigned a value in the body of the loop.

4. The index-variable has no value after completion of the loop. It is effectively returned to the state that exists immediately after the creation of a variable.

An indexed loop is often used to perform some task on the elements of an array. Typically, the index variable serves as a subscript so that each repetition of the body is performed on a different element of the array. For example, values from the data list could be assigned to a section of an array X(M:N) by the following loop:

```
DO I = M TO N BY 1;
    GET LIST(X(I));
    END;
```

As another example, suppose you needed to shift the values in an array RING(1:N). That is, the value in element 1 would move to element 2, the value in element 2 would move to element 3, etc., and the value from the last element would move to element 1. This requires one variable in addition to the elements of the array. It could be accomplished as follows:

```
TEMP = RING(N);
DO I = N TO 2 BY -1;
    RING(I) = RING(I-1);
    END;
RING(1) = TEMP;
```

An indexed loop is also useful in performing some task for each position in a character string. For example, suppose WORD and WORDNB are varying length string variables and you need to set WORDNB to the value of WORD with blanks deleted. This could be accomplished by the following:

```
WORDNB = '';
DO C = 1 TO LENGTH(WORD) BY 1;
    IF SUBSTR(WORD,C,1) ¬= ' '
        THEN WORDNB = WORDNB || SUBSTR(WORD,C,1);
    END;
```

In order to use the indexed loop correctly you must understand and respect all its properties, as explained above. To illustrate, let us write a program segment for a slight variation of the previous problem. Consider a varying length string variable WORD that begins with a nonblank character and ends with a nonblank character (see Exercise 1 for an explanation for this restriction). The task is to delete all blanks from WORD itself (without using another variable like WORDNB). Thus, with WORD = 'AƀƀBIGƀCHAIR' upon termination WORD = 'ABIGCHAIR'. In the following attempt at the desired program segment, the assignment statement is used to delete the Cth character from WORD when that character is a blank. Since each character of WORD seems to be processed in turn, on the face of it the loop seems to be alright.

```
DO C = 1 TO LENGTH(WORD) BY 1;
    IF SUBSTR(WORD,C,1) = ' '
        THEN WORD = SUBSTR(WORD,1,C-1) ||
                    SUBSTR(WORD,C+1);
    END;
```

However, this segment is incorrect for two reasons. First, whenever the assignment to WORD is executed the length of WORD is, and hence the number of iterations of the loop should be, reduced by 1. But the number of iterations is determined at the beginning of execution of the loop and is not changed, even though LENGTH(WORD) is changed. Secondly, not all characters are tested; when character C is deleted from WORD the character C+1 becomes the character C and is not tested because C is increased by 1. Thus the second 'ƀ' of 'AƀƀBIGƀCHAIR' would not be deleted.

This task ought to be written using a WHILE loop. To do so, we define variable C to mean the following:

no character before position C of WORD is a blank; that is, SUBSTR(WORD,1,C-1) does not contain a blank.

With this meaning of C, and using the fact that the first and last characters of WORD are nonblank, we write

```
C = 2;
DO WHILE (C < LENGTH(WORD));
    IF SUBSTR(WORD,C,1) = ' '
        THEN WORD = SUBSTR(WORD,1,C-1) ||
                    SUBSTR(WORD,C+1);
        ELSE C = C + 1;
    END;
```

To see that after execution WORD contains no blanks note first that execution of C=2; establishes the truth of the definition of C: SUBSTR(WORD,1,2-1) contains no blanks. Secondly each repetition keeps the definition true: a blank in position C is deleted <u>or</u> C is increased by 1 because SUBSTR(WORD,1,C-1) ¬= ' '. Finally, upon termination C = LENGTH(WORD), SUBSTR(WORD,1,C-1) contains no blanks and the last character is not a blank; hence WORD contains no blanks.

Returning to examples about the indexed loop, the following segment reverses the characters in the value of WORD. That is, "FINISTERRE" becomes "ERRETSINIF". Like shifting the values of an array in a previous example, this requires an extra variable CHR to hold a character during the interchange. We also use a variable L (although it is not strictly necessary) to simplify the task:

```
DCL CHR CHAR(1) VARYING;
DCL L FIXED;
```

The program segment is the following:

```
L = LENGTH(WORD);
DO C = 1 TO L/2E0 BY 1;
    CHR = SUBSTR(WORD,C,1);
    SUBSTR(WORD,C,1) = SUBSTR(WORD,L-C+1,1);
    SUBSTR(WORD,L-C+1,1) = CHR;
    END;
```

Note that in the control phrase the expression for the final value is written to avoid division with two integer operands (recall Section 3.2.3). Trace this program by hand through several examples to see how it works. (Be sure to include an example where the length is odd.)

7.3 Nested Loops

A loop is a "statement", and can be used as such in the body of another loop. In this case one loop is said to be "nested" within the other. For example, suppose you must read strings into an array WD(1:N) and delete blanks from each of these strings. This could be done as follows:

```
READLOOP: DO I = 1 TO N BY 1;
    GET LIST(INPUT_WD);
    WD(I) = '';
    BLANKDELETE:  DO C = 1 TO LENGTH(INPUT_WD) BY 1;
        IF SUBSTR(INPUT_WD,C,1) ¬= ' '
            THEN WD(I) = WD(I) ||
                               SUBSTR(INPUT_WD,C,1);
        END BLANKDELETE;
    END READLOOP;
```

Each repetition of the body of READLOOP consists of three steps:

1. Read the next string input INPUT_WD.

2. Set the next element of WD to the empty string.

3. Move the string from INPUT_WD to an element of WD, eliminating any blanks in the process.

The first two steps are accomplished by single statements, but there is no single PL/I statement to accomplish the third step. It must be performed with the loop BLANKDELETE. But note that with respect to the body of READLOOP, the loop BLANKDELETE behaves as if it were a single statement. Each repetition of the body of READLOOP includes a complete execution of the BLANKDELETE loop involving several repetitions of its body.

When loops are nested it is helpful to give each loop a name, as shown in the example, so there is no uncertainty as to which loop each END belongs to.

Suppose three two-dimensional arrays are declared as follows:

```
DCL (A(N,M), B(N,M), C(N,M)) FLOAT;
```

A program segment to set each element of A to the sum of the corresponding elements of B and C is given below:

```
ROWLOOP: DO I = 1 TO N BY L;
    DO J = 1 TO M BY 1;
        A(I,J) = B(I,J) + C(I,J);
        END;
    END ROWLOOP;
```

This yields exactly the same result as the array assignment

```
A = B + C;
```

The single statement is both easier to write and clearer to read, so it should certainly be used instead of the two-level loop shown above. But you will encounter cases that cannot be written as a single statement and the nested loop is necessary. (Many programming languages do not permit array operations so the loop would always be required.)

A loop can also be nested within a conditional statement -- it can be given as the THEN, ELSE, WHEN or OTHERWISE unit. For example:

```
IF READ_NECESSARY
    THEN DO I = 1 TO N BY 1;
        GET LIST(WD(I));
        END;
```

7.4 Exit From a Loop

An "exit" is a premature termination of the execution of a loop -- that is, termination before that caused by the control phrase of the loop. An exit can be performed anywhere within the body of the loop while normal termination occurs only before or after some complete execution of the body. A loop exit is achieved with the LEAVE statement, which has the form

```
LEAVE loop-name;
```

The loop-name may be omitted, in which case the statement applies to the innermost loop containing the LEAVE.

The LEAVE statement is always used conditionally. For example it often appears in the context

```
IF logical expression
    THEN LEAVE loop-name;
```

If the value of the logical expression is '1'B then the LEAVE statement is executed, and its execution causes immediate termination of the loop indicated. That is, no further statement of the body is executed; execution of the loop has been completed.

For example, recall the task of reading and summing numbers where the process is terminated by encountering a negative number (Section 7.1.2). This could be accomplished as follows:

```
SUM = 0;
DO WHILE ('1'B);
    GET LIST(DATUM);
    IF DATUM < 0
        THEN LEAVE;
    SUM = SUM + DATUM;
    END;
```

This conditional loop is not really conditional. It depends upon a constant that is always true, so repetition would continue indefinitely; termination is entirely dependent upon the LEAVE statement.

A loop may have several means of termination. For example, consider a variation of the problem in Section 7.3 where an array WD(1:N) is to be loaded with "blank-free" strings. Suppose there were three ways to terminate this task:

1. "Normal" termination after loading the Nth string.

2. Encounter the stopping signal 'LAST' (which is not to be included as a string in WD).

3. Encounter a word that includes two or more blanks (only the portion to the left of the second blank is to be included).

The following program segment could be used:

```
READLOOP: DO I = 1 TO N BY 1;
    GET LIST(INPUT_WD);
    IF INPUT_WD = 'LAST'
        THEN LEAVE READLOOP;
    WD = '';
    NBRBLANKS = 0;
    BLANKDELETE:  DO C = 1 TO LENGTH(INPUT_WD) BY 1;
        IF SUBSTR(INPUT_WD,C,1) ¬= ' '
            THEN WD(I) = WD(I) ||
                    SUBSTR(INPUT_WD,C,1);
            ELSE IF NBRBLANKS = 1
                THEN LEAVE READLOOP;
                ELSE NBRBLANKS = 1;
        END BLANKDELETE;
    END READLOOP;
```

Note that the second LEAVE statement (fourth line from the end) is located in the inner loop (BLANKDELETE) but exits the outer loop (READLOOP).

- PL/C: the current version of PL/C (Release 7.6) does not include the LEAVE statement. See Section 7.4.1.

7.4.1 Simulation of the LEAVE Statement

The LEAVE statement is a recent addition to PL/I and is not yet included in some PL/I dialects. In particular, LEAVE is not included in the current version of PL/C. If the LEAVE statement is not available you can simulate its action using the "GOTO statement".

The GOTO statement transfers control to some arbitrary point in the program marked by a "target label". This label can be given as a prefix to many different types of statements, including the null statement. We suggest using it only with the null statement to emphasize the fact that its role is simply to identify a point in the program. The form of the GOTO statement is the following:

```
GOTO label-name;
   ...
label-name :;
```

Note the punctuation in the last line. "Label-name:" labels the statement. Since it is immediately followed by a semi-colon indicating the end of the statement, this is a labelled null statement.

Since the labelled null statement can be positioned anywhere, by placing it immediately after the END of a loop and putting the GOTO where you would have put the LEAVE you can achieve the same result as the LEAVE. The example from Section 7.4 could be rewritten with GOTOs instead of LEAVEs as follows:

```
READLOOP: DO I = 1 TO N BY 1;
    GET LIST (INPUT_WD);
    IF INPUT_WD = 'LAST'
        THEN GOTO LEAVE_READLOOP;
    WD = '';
    NBRBLANKS = 0;
    BLANKDELETE:  DO C = 1 TO LENGTH(INPUT_WD) BY 1;
        IF SUBSTR(INPUT_WD,C,1) ¬= ' '
            THEN WD(I) = WD(I) ||
                     SUBSTR(INPUT_WD,C,1);
            ELSE IF NBRBLANKS = 1
                THEN GOTO LEAVE_READLOOP;
                ELSE NBRBLANKS = 1;
        END BLANKDELETE;
    END READLOOP;
    LEAVE_READLOOP:;
```

We use the LEAVE statement in our examples throughout the book, but wherever it occurs it can be replaced with a GOTO and target label as shown above. Always having the target labels of the form "LEAVE_loop-name" makes clear that the GOTO is being used in lieu of the LEAVE statement.

7.4.2 A Historical Note Concerning the GOTO Statement

The last section used the GOTO in a very limited way -- to simulate the LEAVE statement. It was also used in Section 6.6 to simulate the SELECT statement. But note that the target label of a GOTO can be placed (almost) anywhere in a program. For example, you could write

```
IF logical expression
    THEN DO;
        statement1
        GOTO CONTINUE;
        END;
statement2
CONTINUE:;
```

This has the same effect as

```
IF logical expression
    THEN statement1
    ELSE statement2
```

As another example, you could write

```
STARTLOOP:;
    statement1
        ...
    statementN
    IF ¬(logical expression)
        THEN GOTO STARTLOOP;
```

This has the same effect as

```
DO UNTIL (logical expression);
    statement1
        ...
    statementN
    END;
```

These examples illustrate the fact that you do not actually need the ELSE form of the IF statement or the UNTIL form of a loop -- either construction could be simulated using the GOTO. In fact all control statements can be simulated using IF and GOTO, so only these two are needed to control the sequence of execution. Put another way, the availability of DO WHILE, DO UNTIL, indexed DO, ELSE, SELECT, LEAVE as well as other control statements that will be introduced in Part IV, do not allow you to program anything that you could not program with only IF and GOTO. In fact, early programming languages provided only these two control statements; the others were added later.

Since IF and GOTO can simulate all other control constructs, why do we bother with the others? There are several reasons for this:

1. The alternative control statements are easier to use. That is, control structures designed specifically for a certain task are easier to use for that task than a mechanism "handcrafted" out of the basic IF and GOTO statements. Furthermore, the specialized control statements are less likely to be written incorrectly than the handcrafted variety.

2. Programs using the specialized control forms are easier to read because the intention of the programmer is more obvious. For example, DO WHILE clearly indicates repetition, while the IF and GOTO can be used to denote repetition, termination of a program segment, a case statement, and a host of other constructs.

3. Most importantly, the power and flexibility of the unrestrained GOTO make it impossible to confidently divide a program into small sections that can be completely understood independently, without the need to consider other sections of the program. This crucial point is discussed more fully in Section II.2.

Since 1970 there has been a serious effort to "discipline" the art of programming. The objective has been to improve the practice so as to produce well-structured programs that are clear, easy to read, and capable of being cleanly separated into distinct sections. This campaign has included admonitions against the use of the GOTO. While this constitutes only part of the recommended reform it is often misunderstood as its very essence. Some erroneously believe that any program with GOTOs is necessarily unstructered and conversely, that any program without GOTOs must be well-structured. The GOTO has consequently become the symbol of the reform movement, defended by skeptics and attacked by would-be reformers who don't clearly understand what it represents. The issue is more fully explained in Section II.2. But be warned of the poor GOTO's symbolic and emotional significance. The manner in which you use GOTOs, if indeed you use them at all, is likely to be given a surprising amount of attention by those who read your programs and will have an important bearing on evaluation of your "programming style".

7.4.3 The End-of-Data Exit

A common requirement in programs is to perform some task on each item of data from the external data list. This obviously can be accomplished by a loop in which the body consists of a GET statement and whatever other statements are required to perform the necessary task. The question is how to properly terminate execution of the loop.

Section 7.1.1 illustrated a method to be used when it is known in advance exactly how many data items are present. The task in that example was to compute the sum of the data values:

```
SUM, NUMBER_REPETITIONS = 0;
DO WHILE (NUMBER_REPETITIONS < 500);
    GET LIST (DATUM);
    SUM = SUM + DATUM;
    NUMBER_REPETITIONS = NUMBER_REPETITIONS + 1;
    END;
```

A variation of this method would require inserting a data count in the data list prior to the first item of actual data. The program would then be the following:

```
SUM, NUMBER_REPETITIONS = 0;
GET LIST (DATA_COUNT);
DO WHILE (NUMBER_REPETITIONS < DATA_COUNT);
    GET LIST (DATUM);
    SUM = SUM + DATUM;
    NUMBER_REPETITIONS = NUMBER_REPETITIONS + 1;
    END;
```

An indexed loop could also be used for this purpose:

```
SUM = 0;
GET LIST (DATA_COUNT);
DO NUMBER_REPETITIONS = 1 TO DATA_COUNT BY 1;
    GET LIST (DATUM);
    SUM = SUM + DATUM;
    END;
```

An alternative strategy is to append some special recognizable value to the end of the data list and have the program test for this value. This was illustrated in Section 7.1.2 using a negative number as a "stopping value":

```
SUM = 0;
GET LIST (DATUM);
DO WHILE (DATUM >= 0);
    SUM = SUM + DATUM;
    GET LIST (DATUM);
    END;
```

These strategies require something to be added to the data list to facilitate loop exit -- either a count in front of or a distinctive stopping value after the data. It would be desirable not to have to alter the data list at all.

A natural way to describe the required task is shown below. It is shown as a pseudo-program -- PL/I except that the control phrase of the loop is given in English:

```
SUM = 0;
DO WHILE (there is more data);
    GET LIST (DATUM);
    SUM = SUM + DATUM;
    END;
```

Some languages (PASCAL, for example) provide a mechanism for testing whether or not there is more data waiting to be read. PL/I provides an equivalent capability, but it is part of a more general facility called the "interrupt". This is an unusual feature of PL/I and one not universally admired. We will consider only a very limited form of condition needed to detect the end of the data list.

The loop shown above could be rewritten as an indefinite loop with a conditional exit:

```
SUM = 0;
DO WHILE ('1'B);
    IF there is more data
        THEN GET LIST (DATUM);
        ELSE LEAVE;
    SUM = SUM + DATUM;
    END;
```

This version suggests the intent of the PL/I facility, which we now explain. Typically, when the end of data is detected an <u>endfile interrupt</u> occurs; execution of the program is interrupted and some action is executed. The normal or "default" action is to print a message indicating that an "end of file" occurred in reading the standard data file (called SYSIN) and terminate the program. The programmer can indicate his own action S to perform in case of an endfile interrupt by having his program <u>execute</u> the ON-statement

```
ON ENDFILE(SYSIN) S
```

Here S may be an assignment statement, a GOTO or a BEGIN block (see Section IV.4).

Note that this is an <u>executable statement</u>, not a declaration. Its execution <u>causes S to become the action</u> to be executed when an end of file is detected; its execution does <u>not</u> cause S to be executed.

Below we show the conventional way of using this facility. First, execution of the ON-statement makes GOTO DATAEND; the action to execute in case of an interrupt. SUM=0; is executed, and then the loop executes. When GET LIST (DATUM); is executed and there is no more data, the interrupt occurs and GOTO DATAEND; is executed and the loop is thus terminated. The program follows:

```
...
ON ENDFILE(SYSIN) GOTO DATAEND;
SUM = 0;
DO WHILE('1'B);
    GET LIST (DATUM);
    SUM = SUM + DATUM;
    END;
DATAEND:;
```

To emphasize the executable nature of the ON-statement consider the segment given below. The ON-statement is not executed, so that if an end of file is encountered the default action will be executed, not the GOTO DATAEND;.

```
IF '0'B
    THEN ON ENDFILE(SYSIN) GOTO DATAEND;
DO WHILE ('1'B);
    GET LIST (DATUM);
    END;
DATAEND:;
```

An input statement may, of course, have a list of variables:

```
GET LIST (X1, X2, X3);
```

Should this statement be executed with only one data value, that value will be assigned to X1, the interrupt will occur, and no values will be assigned to X2 and X3. Thus, execution proceeds normally until the end of file is reached and the interrupt occurs.

Another example illustrating the executable nature of the ON-statement uses more than one ON-statement to show a more complicated interrupt action:

```
...
ON ENDFILE(SYSIN)
    BEGIN;
        PUT SKIP LIST
            ('ERROR: FIRST DATA LIST NOT COMLPETE.',
            'ASSUMED TO HAVE', I-1, 'ITEMS');
        N = I-1;
        GOTO DATAEND_FIRST;
        END;
DO I = 1 TO N BY 1;
    GET LIST (A(I));
    END;
DATAEND_FIRST:;

...
ON ENDFILE(SYSIN) GOTO DATAEND_SECOND;
J = 1;
DO WHILE ('1'B);
    GET LIST (B(I));
    END;
DATAEND_SECOND:;
```

Execution of the first ON-statement associates the BEGIN-block BEGIN; ... END; with the end of file interrupt. Execution of the first loop is supposed to read exactly N values. If, however, there are fewer, then the interrupt occurs, a message is printed, N is set to the number of values actually read in (I-1) and processing continues at DATAEND_FIRST. Execution of the second ON-statement then associates the action GOTO DATAEND_SECOND with the end of file interrupt. The last loop then expects to terminate via the end of file interrupt.

In the example above the second ON-statement overrides the effect of the first ON-statement by supplying a different action to be performed when the data is exhausted. Alternatively, the second ON-statement could nullify the effect of the first and <u>restore the normal default action</u> of the "system", which is to issue an error message and terminate execution. This would be achieved by the following statement:

```
ON ENDFILE(SYSIN) SYSTEM;
```

Following this, a GET statement that encounters insufficient data behaves just as it would if there had been no previous ON-statement.

By specifying an ON-statement immediately before, and SYSTEM immediately after a certain segment that reads data, you can specify the end-of-data action for that particular segment without affecting any other part of the program. For example:

```
ON ENDFILE(SYSIN) GOTO DATAEND;
DO I = 1 TO N BY 1;
    GET LIST (A(I));
    END;
DATAEND:;
ON ENDFILE(SYSIN) SYSTEM;
```

This segment reads N items, or to the end of the data -- whichever occurs first. If the data list is already exhausted, it reads nothing at all. But whether or not it exhausts the data list, no error is reported, and execution continues with the next statement. For any subsequent GET statements the normal system action on encountering the end of the data list has been re-established.

● PL/CS: The only ON statement is exactly the following:

```
ON ENDFILE GOTO DATAEND;
```

The particular label "DATAEND" is required, and this target as a labelled null statement must be given at some point after the last GET statement in the procedure. Since there is only one input file in PL/CS the file-name SYSIN need not be specified. Only a single ON statement can be given in a procedure. The SYSTEM option is not allowed.

7.5 Tracing Execution Of A Loop

Tracing was introduced in Section 5.3. To trace execution of a loop, construct a table with a row for each variable, and a column for the execution of each statement that changes the value of at least one variable. For example, consider the following program:

```
 SUMER: PROCEDURE OPTIONS(MAIN);
   DECLARE (N, I) FIXED;
   DECLARE (X, SUM) FLOAT;

   GET LIST(N);
   SUM = 0;
   DO I = 1 TO N BY 1;
       GET LIST(X);
       SUM = SUM + X;
       END;
   PUT SKIP LIST('SUM IS:', SUM);
   END SUMER;
*DATA
   3, 5.6, 42.1, 31.7
```

The first part of the trace table for this program is:

Vari-able	Values as execution proceeds ->										
N	???	3	3	3	3	3	3	3	3	3	3
I	???	???	???	1	1	1	2	2	2	3	3
X	???	???	???	???	5.6	5.6	5.6	42.1	42.1	42.1	31.7
SUM	???	???	0	0	0	5.6	5.6	5.6	47.7	47.7	47.7

It is not necessary to write down each value in each column, but only the <u>value that is being changed</u>. The trace table shown above would then be

Vari-able	Values as execution proceeds ->										
N	???	3									
I	???			1			2			3	
X	???				5.6			42.1			31.7
SUM	???		0			5.6			47.7		

Often, the trace table becomes complicated and messy, and it is difficult to go back and analyze it. To aid in studying it, one often uses an extra row to indicate which statement is being executed, or to indicate the result of evaluating a condition. For example, consider the program segment

```
   START: SUM = 0;
          GET LIST(X);
          DO WHILE (X ¬= 0);
            L: IF X < 0
                 THEN SUM = SUM - X;
                 ELSE SUM = SUM + X;
            GET LIST(X);
            END;
          SUM = SUM+1;
          ...
  *DATA
    8, -5, 0
```

In the trace table below, the top row indicates either the statement executed (by giving its label) or the result of evaluating a condition of a loop or conditional statement.

Vari-able		STA-RT:		loop true	L: X>0			loop true	L: X<0		
SUM	???	0	0	0	0	8	8	8	8	13	13
X	???	???	8	8	8	8	-5	-5	-5	-5	0

The amount of information needed in the trace table varies from program to program, depending on how difficult it is and how much trouble the programmer is having. But get in the habit of putting in as much information as possible.

Tracing is usually done only when you are in difficulty. It must be done with care, one step at a time. While tracing, you must execute the program the way the machine does, without thinking about the task being performed. Too often, a programmer executes what he <u>thinks</u> is there, and not what really <u>is</u> there, which of course doesn't help at all.

Section 7 Summary

1. A loop is a sequence of statements whose execution is to be repeated. The form is:

```
DO control-phrase ;
    Body
    END;
```

2. Control-phrases for loops are:

   WHILE (logical expression)
   : Repeat execution of the body as long as the logical expression remains true.

   UNTIL (logical expression)
   : Repeat execution of the body until the logical expression becomes true (at least one execution is assured).

   DO index-var = init TO final BY increment
   : Repeat execution of the body for each value of index-var from init to final in steps of increment.

3. A loop is a statement and can appear in the body of another loop. The loops are then said to be nested.

4. An exit is the termination of execution of a loop prior to what would be caused by the initial control-phrase. This is accomplished with a LEAVE or GOTO statement.

5. Exit from a loop that reads data can be accomplished with the ENDFILE condition.

Section 7 <u>Exercises</u>

1. Write a separate, complete program to perform each of the following tasks:

a) Read five data values, compute their sum and print the sum.

b) Read three data values, compute the first times the sum of the second and third, and print the result.

c) Without reading any data (no GET statements) compute the sum of the integers from 1 to 8 and print the result.

d) Read four data values, print the maximum of the four values.

2. Write a single program that will perform all four of the tasks listed in Exercise 1, one after another.

3. Trace the execution of the programs in Exercise 1.

4. Keypunch and run the programs in Exercise 1.

5. Trace the execution of the following program segments:

a)
```
TOTAL = 0;
DO WHILE (TOTAL < 5);
   TOTAL = TOTAL + 1;
   END;
```

b)
```
R1, R2, R3 = 0;
ILOOP: DO I = 1 TO 3 BY 1;
   R1 = R1 + 1;
   JLOOP: DO J = 3 TO -1 BY -1;
       R2 = R2 + 1;
       DO K = 3 TO 5 BY 2;
           R3 = R3 + 1;
           END;
       END JLOOP;
   END ILOOP;
```

c)
```
A, X = 2;
B, Y = 5;
Z = 1;
DO WHILE (Y ¬= 0);
     DO WHILE(FLOOR(Y/2E0)*2 = Y);
         Y = Y/2E0;
         X = X*X;
         END;
     Y = Y - 1;
     Z = Z*X;
     END;
```

d) Same as c), but with "A=2; B=5;" replaced by "A=1; B=1;".

e)
```
N = 7;
FIRST = 0;
PUT LIST(FIRST);
SECOND = 1;
PUT LIST(SECOND);
DO I = 3 TO N BY 1;
   THIRD = FIRST + SECOND;
   PUT LIST(THIRD);
   FIRST = SECOND;
   SECOND = THIRD;
   END;
```

f)
```
GET LIST(N);
DO I = 1 TO N BY 1;
    GET LIST(X);
    Y = X + 1;
    Y = X + 1;
    IF X < 0
        THEN PUT LIST(Y);
    END;
  *DATA
    0, 8 , 8, 9, 8 3
```

g) Same as f), but with the data

```
*DATA
  5, -30, 40, 50, -60, -70, -80
```

6. Write a WHILE loop with initialization that is equivalent to:

```
FACT = 1;
DO I = 2 TO N BY 1;
    FACT = FACT*I;
    END;
```

7. Write a program segment to read in a sequence of 50 numbers and print out those numbers that are > 0.

8. Given a variable N with a value greater than 0, write a program segment to print N, N**2, ..., N**N.

9. Given variables N and M, both with values > 0, write a segment to print all powers of N that are less than M. That is, print the value N**i for all i such that N**i < M.

10. The _Fibonacci numbers_ are the numbers 0, 1, 1, 2, 3, 5, 8, 13, 21, ... The first one is 0, the second is 1, and each successive one is the sum of the two preceding ones. (See Excercise 5e.) Given a variable N≥2, write a program segment to print out all Fibonacci numbers which are less than N (_not_ the first N Fibonacci numbers).

11. Write complete programs for the following problems. Most of these use the program segments written in earlier exercises.

a) The input consists of groups of three numbers. The last group is an end-of-list signal consisting of three zero values. Write a program to read each group in, print it out, and print an indication of whether the three numbers represent the sides of a triangle. (See Exercise 4 in Section 6.)

b) The input consists of an integer N ≥ 0, followed by N groups of three numbers. Write a program to read the groups of numbers in, print them out, and then print the middle value of the three. Each group and its middle value should appear on a separate line.

c) The input consists of a single integer N. Write a program to read in N and print the first N Fibonacci numbers. (If N < 1, don't print any out.)

d) The input consists of two positive integers M and N, with M ≥ N. Write a program to print all Fibonacci numbers which lie between M and N.

e) The input consists of a positive integer N. Write a program to read N and to print out the first, second, third and fourth powers of the integers 2, 3, ..., N. The beginning of your output should look like

```
2     4     8     16
3     9     27    81
```

12. Assume there are variables with the following initial values:

B(-3)	20	AGE(1)	1	I	1
B(-2)	25	AGE(2)	13	J	2
B(-1)	42	AGE(3)	21	K	3
B(0)	9	AGE(4)	6	M	4
B(1)	8	AGE(5)	7	SUM	???
B(2)	13	AGE(6)	12	C	???
B(3)	-20	AGE(7)	8	MAX	???
B(4)	-40	AGE(8)	0	MIN	???
B(5)	50				

Trace the execution of the following program segments and show the values that result from their execution.

a)
```
C = J;
SUM = 0;
DO WHILE (C <= M);
    SUM = SUM + AGE(C);
    C = C + 1;
    END;
```

b)
```
MAX = AGE(I);
C = I + 1;
DO WHILE (C <= M);
    IF MAX < AGE(C)
        THEN MAX = AGE(C);
    C = C + 1;
    END;
```

c)
```
C = -3;
DO WHILE (C <= 5);
    B(C) = B(C) + C;
    C = C + 1;
    END;
```

d)
```
AGE(1) = 0;
AGE(2) = 1;
C = 3;
DO WHILE (C <= 8);
    AGE(C) = AGE(C-1) + AGE(C-2);
    C = C + 1;
    END;
```

e)
```
C = 5;
DO WHILE (C >= -3);
    IF B(C) < 0
        THEN B(C) = -B(C);
    C = C - 1;
    END;
```

f)
```
C = 5;
DO WHILE (C > -3);
    B(C) = B(C-1);
    C = C - 1;
    END;
B(-3) = 0;
```

13. Write program segments to accomplish each of the following tasks, using the following variables:

```
DECLARE (A, B) FIXED;

DECLARE AGE(3, 4) FIXED;

DECLARE COST(-3:0) FLOAT;

DECLARE (PAY(0:10),AMOUNT(0:10),I) FLOAT;
```

a) Set all of the variables in the array AGE(1:3,1:4) to zero.

b) Set each variable in the array AGE(1:3,1:4) equal to the sum of its own subscripts -- that is, AGE(I,J) equal to I + J.

c) Set each variable in the array COST(-3:0) equal to whatever is the minimum of the initial values of the variables in COST.

d) Subtract the value of each variable in the array AMOUNT(0:10) from the variable in the corresponding position in the array PAY(0:10).

e) Compute the sum of the values of all of the variables in the array PAY(0:10).

f) Swap the values of PAY(1:10) to put the largest in PAY(10). Thus if initially PAY is

PAY 10 9 8 7 6 5 4 3 2 1

then after execution, the array might be

PAY 9 8 7 6 5 4 3 2 1 10
or PAY 1 9 8 7 6 5 4 3 2 10

14. Suppose array B(1:N) contains a sequence of values, some of which appear more than once. Write a program segment to "delete" duplicates, moving the unique values towards the beginning of the array. Assign to variable M the number of unique values. The order of the values should be preserved. For example, if we have

N 7 B 1 6 1 8 3 7 6

after execution the variables should be as follows (where "-" indicates that the value is immaterial):

N 7 M 5 B 1 6 8 3 7 - -

15. The following segment searches array segment B(1:N) for a value equal to X. When it finds it, it sets J to the index of X in B so that B(J) = X. This is a <u>linear search</u> algorithm.

```
J = 1;
DO WHILE (B(J) ¬= X);
    J = J + 1;
    END;
```

a) What value is in J after execution if X is not in the array?

b) Change the program to set 0 in J if X is not in the array.

c) What happens if N = 0? Change the program segment to store 0 in J if this is the case. (Such a case actually arises in programming, and is not always a mistake.)

16. In Section 7.2 the following segment was given for deleting blanks from WORD providing the first and last characters of WORD were not blank.

```
C = 2;
DO WHILE (C < LENGTH(WORD));
    IF SUBSTR(WORD,C,1) = ' '
        THEN WORD = SUBSTR(WORD,1,C-1) ||
                    SUBSTR(WORD,C+1);
        ELSE C = C + 1;
    END;
```

Why is the restriction on the contents of WORD made? Hint: when is SUBSTR(WORD,i,j) undefined? Rewrite the segment so that it deletes blanks from any varying string variable WORD.

Write programs for the following problems.

17. Read a string of up to 40 characters, reverse the order of the characters, and print it out. For example, 'EVIL' becomes 'LIVE'. You may determine the input form.

18. Read a string of up to 40 characters, using GET LIST; delete all blanks up to the first non-blank; print the result.

19. Read a string of up to 40 characters, delete all characters 'A', and print the result. You may determine the input form.

20. Read in three strings, call them A, PATTERN, and REPLACEBY. Replace every occurrence of PATTERN in A by the string REPLACEBY. Print the result. For example, if we have

A BIG, BIGGER, BIGGEST   PATTERN BIG   REPLACEBY SMALL

the program should print the string

'SMALL, SMALLGER, SMALLGEST'.

Be careful. If we have

A LAST   PATTERN A   REPLACEBY EA

A should not be changed to 'LEAST', then to 'LEEAST', and then to 'LEEEAST', etc. Stop with 'LEAST'.

21. Write a program to perform the equivalent of the functions below (see Appendix A.7 for their definition).

INDEX   VERIFY   TRANSLATE (assume p is always given)

22. Read a three-digit integer and print it in English. For example, print 182 as ONE HUNDRED AND EIGHTY TWO. You will need string arrays to hold the English equivalents of the digits.

23. The input consists of three two-digit numbers representing a date. The first is the day, the second the month, and the third the last two digits of the year. For example: 25, 12, 75. Read the number and print it in English, using the PUT EDIT statement. For example, DECEMBER 25, 1975. Use an array for the names of the months.

24. Read in a list of words and print out (1) the number of words made up of 1 to 6 characters, (2) the number with 6 to 12 characters, and (3) the number of times the word 'THE' appears. The words appear on one card each, left-justified in columns 1 through 12, with no surrounding quotes.

Section 8 Program Documentation

Programs must be read by humans as well as computers. This is required frequently during development and testing of a program, and again if the program must later be modified. The program elements presented in the previous sections have all been instructions to the computer and are read by humans to understand what the computer will do. Now we consider a program element that is ignored by the computer and is used solely for the benefit of the human reader.

8.1 Comments

A "comment" is a string of characters printed in the source listing that has no effect on the execution of the program. In PL/I a comment is delimited by the character pairs "/*" and "*/":

```
/* comment text */
```

The comment text is a string of any length containing any characters except the pair */, which would terminate the comment. A comment can be positioned anywhere a blank could be given and is syntactically equivalent to a blank.

- PL/C: A comment must be on one card unless the NOMONITOR=(BNDRY) option is given.

- PL/CS: A comment must be contained on one card.

Although comments are usually written between statements they can be inserted between symbols within a statement. This is most often done in a declaration to describe the roles of individual variables. For example:

```
DCL (SORTED,  /* =1 IF V(1:N) ARE IN ORDER */
     NEG,     /* =1 IF ANY V(1:N) < 0 */
     EMPTY)   /* =1 IF NO VALUES IN V(1:N) */
       BIT(1); /* =0 OTHERWISE */
```

Some programmers seem to feel that since comments do not affect execution they are unimportant and treat them in a haphazard manner. Student programmers in particular question their value and add them only under duress and often too late to do much good. But comments are a vital part of programming, and careful and consistent use of comments leads to better programs. A program that is well-commented and properly indented is so much easier to read and understand that the prospects of achieving correctness are significantly enhanced.

To use comments effectively is not easy and unless you practice on small programs you will not have the skill when needed on large programs. Since the content of comments is not dictated by the rules of the programming language you have complete freedom to develop your own conventions. Rather than waste this freedom and use comments as random remarks you should develop a consistent and disciplined style. We offer the following sections in this regard. We find these practices useful. You might adopt them until you have sufficient experience to develop your own, or until you program in an environment where strict commenting conventions are imposed on you.

8.1.1 Statement-Comments

The most important use of comments is to <u>specify the action</u> of a certain segment of a program. We write such comments as if they were "statements" in some higher-level programming language and position them before the corresponding PL/I statements. Some examples are:

```
/** READ DATA TO FIRST NEG VALUE INTO X(1:N) */
    DO I = 1 TO N BY 1;
        GET LIST (DATUM);
        IF DATUM < 0
            THEN LEAVE;
        X(I) = DATUM;
        END;


/** ROTATE ELEMENTS OF LINK(A:B) DOWN 1 PLACE */
    TEMP = LINK(A);
    DO I = A+1 TO B BY 1;
        LINK(I-1) = LINK(I);
        END;
    LINK(B) = TEMP;
```

```
/** SET A(1:R,1:T) = B(1:R,1:S) X C(1:S,1:T) */
    ROW: DO I = 1 TO R BY 1;
        COL: DO J = 1 TO T BY 1;
            A(I,J) = 0;
            DO K = 1 TO S BY 1;
                A(I,J) = A(I,J) + B(I,K) * C(K,J);
                END;
            END COL;
        END ROW;
```

We denote such comments with an asterisk as their first character (required by PL/CS -- see Section 8.2) and indent the implementing statements relative to the comment. The statement-comment specifies what is to be done; the indented PL/I statements specify how it is to be accomplished.

In writing statement-comments, observe the following rules:

1. Be precise and complete. For example, consider the following segment:

   ```
   GET LIST (N);
   DO I = 1 TO N BY 1;
       GET LIST (VECT(I));
       END;
   ```

   As heading for this segment, the statement-comment

   ```
   /** LOAD N AND VECT(1:N) FROM DATA */
   ```

   is preferable to alternatives such as

   ```
   /** READ DATA */

   /** LOAD VECT */
   ```

   Always refer to program objects by name.

2. Make statement-comments imperative -- start with a command such as READ, PRINT, SET, FIND, etc.

3. Be concise by omitting detail, but not at the cost of being misleading or inaccurate.

A statement-comment should provide the reader an alternative to reading the indented PL/I statements. Unless he is specifically concerned with how this particular action is performed the statement-comment should provide enough information to understand the role of this segment.

However, recognize that the reader's willingness to read comments as an alternative to the program statements depends entirely on his confidence that they are clear, complete and accurate. Once that trust is damaged the comment becomes a hint rather than an alternative and much of the value is lost.

The use of statement comments is described further in Section II.2.2.

8.1.2 Comments in Declarations

The second vital use of comments is in precisely specifying the role of each variable. Variable names should be chosen to suggest their roles, but in most cases mnemonic names are not sufficient. It is not easy to choose declaration comments that are meaningful, but it is worth the effort. Frequently it forces you to clarify your understanding of the role of each variable and this helps avoid errors.

Declaration comments are discussed in detail in Section II.1.

8.1.3 User Instructions

Most programs require that the user be given some instructions for such things as data formats, options available, limits, restrictions, etc. For flexible programs intended for widescale use such instructions can be voluminous. For example, entire books are required to instruct the users of certain statistical programs (see Section II.3.2).

Such instructions should be regarded as an inherent part of the programming process since the program is not useful without them. The programmer's job is to make a computer perform a task for a user, and he must expect to instruct both parties as to their required actions. Many programmers prefer writing programs and tend to neglect this chore.

Once user instructions are written, they suffer two common kinds of accidents -- they get lost, or become obsolete as the program is changed. Both of these misfortunes are minimized by making user instructions an integral part of the program. It is a good idea to preface a program with a block of comments that describes the manner of its use. This is less likely to be separated from the program, and a subsequent programmer who alters the program is more likely to update the instructions as well.

The programs in this book do not generally illustrate this good advice, but an example is given in Section II.3.2.

8.1.4 Useless Comments

Comments are not always helpful. When poorly written they can be useless or worse. They obviously take some effort on the part of the writer, so unless this is rewarded by a benefit to the reader there is no point to them.

For example, comments should never simply duplicate a PL/I statement that is equally clear and easy to read. Examples of such pointless comments are:

```
/** INITIALIZE SUM TO 0 */
    SUM = 0;

/** EXIT IF ITEM IS NEGATIVE */
    IF ITEM < 0
        THEN LEAVE DATA_LOOP;

/** PUT TWO WORDS TOGETHER */
    LONGWORD = LEFTWORD || RIGHTWORD;
```

These are redundant. The reader should be capable of understanding the PL/I statements and in this case the extra lines obscure rather than clarify.

8.2 Special Comments in PL/C and PL/CS

PL/C and PL/CS have additional uses for certain kinds of comments, distinguished by the first character of the comment text.

If the first character is a colon or an integer (1-7) the rest of the text can optionally be either a comment or part of the program. The use of such "pseudo-comments" is described in Section V.5.4.1.

In PL/CS the first charater of a comment controls <u>indentation</u> on the source listing. An asterisk denotes a statement-comment. A blank line is supplied, the statement-comment is printed and the following lines are indented with respect to the statement-comment in the manner used throughout this book.

With automatic formatting you must also indicate when to terminate indentation relative to a statement-comment. In PL/CS this is done by <u>repeating</u> the statement-comment, or at least giving a statement-comment with the same <u>first symbol</u> as that in the heading comment. For example:

```
/** LOAD N AND A(1:N) FROM DATA */
    GET LIST (N);
    DO I = 1 TO N BY 1;
        GET LIST (A(I));
        END;
    /** LOAD */
```

This comment closure is a nuisance but it is the price paid for automatic formatting. Since this book is not especially oriented to PL/CS we have elected not to show comment closures in our examples.

A PL/CS statement-comment can also be denoted with a "+". This closes the previous statement comment unit, ending indentation, and begins a new statement-comment at the same level. That is, if the last statement-comment was /** r */ then /*+ s */ is equivalent to /** r */ /** s */. For example:

```
/** LOAD A(1:N) FROM DATA */
    GET LIST (N)
    DO I = 1 TO N BY 1;
        GET LIST (A(I));
        END;

/*+ SET AMAX TO MAX OF A(1:N) */
    AMAX = A(1);
    DO I = 2 TO N BY 1;
        AMAX = MAX(A(I), AMAX);
        END;

/*+ PRINT A(1:N), MARKING MAXIMA */
    PUT SKIP(3) LIST('VALUES OF A:');
    PUT SKIP;
    DO I = 1 TO N BY 1;
        PUT SKIP LIST(' ', A(I));
        IF A(I) = AMAX
            THEN PUT LIST('(MAXIMUM)');
        END;
    PUT SKIP(2) LIST('END OF A VALUES');
    /** PRINT */
```

Because of the special significance of the first character of a comment it is generally good practice to start the actual comment text with a blank.

Part II
Program Structure

Part II introduces no new PL/I features. It is entirely concerned with ways in which the statements, declarations and comments presented in Part I should be used to enhance the clarity, readability and understandability of programs.

Programs are not only meant to convey information to a computer; programs are written by people to be read by people, and for many reasons:

1. Except for trivial problems, programs are rarely completed at a single sitting. Programs take several days to over a year to complete, and you must often review what you have done before.

2. Programs are rarely correct on the first try, and the testing process requires that the program be read.

3. A programming task is often divided among several people who must read and understand portions of each other's work, so that their sections communicate properly.

4. Program segments are often reused in contexts other than the one for which originally written. To do so it is necessary to understand exactly what the segment does.

5. Programs often need to be modified to meet changes in problem requirements.

People read programs to understand what the program does when executed by a computer. This does not mean what it will do in one particular execution with one particular set of input data, but what it will do in general, for any possible set of data, any choice of execution options, and any other conditions of context or environment. This is a difficult task at best, and the reader needs all the help he can get.

We must of course understand the precise meaning of each statement type in the programming language so that we can, if necessary, trace or simulate the action of the computer. In theory, we can simulate the entire execution and thereby understand the meaning of any program. In practice this just isn't feasible. Even for programs of modest size we lack the time or patience to read them as if we were a computer. So we are forced to try to read programs in a way that is quite different from a computer. For example, consider the simple program segment:

```
TOTAL = 0;
DO I = 1 TO N BY 1;
    TOTAL = TOTAL + ARR(I);
    END
```

Depending upon the value of N, the computer may execute hundreds or even thousands of statements from this segment. Regardless of the value of N the human reader sees this as a single task:

Compute the sum of the values of ARR(1:N).

In general, being able to understand substantial programs depends on our being able to understand them at a level higher than that of the individual PL/I statements. To facilitate reading a program in this way a programmer should structure the program in terms of higher-level units, and <u>organize</u> and <u>present</u> the program so that its <u>structure is clear and obvious</u>. The organization should make it easy for a reader to study small sections of the program at a time, without having to rely on his knowledge of the rest of the program. The small sections must be made as independent of each other as possible.

In Sections 1 and 2 we discuss the components that make up "well-structured" programs. We describe the use of comments, both for defining the uses of variables and for exposing as much as possible the structure of the program.

In Section 3 we present sample programs, along with commentary. As with English prose, before writing substantial programs yourself it is best to read and study well-written programs. Studying these examples should reinforce the ideas discussed in Sections 1 and 2.

Section 1 Organization of Declarations

Declarations of variables are placed at the beginning of a program for a good reason: they alert the reader to which variables are used and what their attributes are, information that is necessary to understand the statements that follow.

But the reader needs to know more than just the variables and their attributes; he needs to know what the variables are for, or what they mean. The programmer should aid the reader (and himself) by describing this meaning, along with the declarations, in the form of comments. In this way, the declarations serve as a focal point of the whole program. When reading individual statements of a program, the reader can continually refer to the declarations of the variables used in the statements in order to make sure that the use of those variables corresponds to their stated meaning.

In some situations, the description of the meaning of the variables can be so good that the reader doesn't have to study the program statements -- he can tell from the variable meanings themselves what the statements must be. Thus, good descriptions of variables play an important role in making a program understandable.

Generally speaking, a variable by itself doesn't mean much; more important is its relationship to other variables. Thus, variables should be grouped not by their type attributes but by their logical relationship. As an example, consider the variables declared in (1a) as opposed to those declared in (1b).

```
(1a)    DCL (NPR, TP) (50), MAX, MIN) FLOAT;
               /* TABLES OF PRESSURE AND TEMPERATURE */
        DCL (N, M, POSMAX) FIXED;
               /* LENGTHS AND POSITION OF MAX */
```

```
(1b)    DCL PR(50) FLOAT;    /* TABLE OF PRESSURES IS */
        DCL PRTOP FIXED;     /* PR(1:PRTOP) */
        DCL PRMAX FLOAT;     /* MAX VALUE IN PR(1:PRTOP) */
        DCL PRMIN FLOAT;     /* MIN VALUE IN PR(1:PRTOP) */

        DCL TP(50) FLOAT;    /* TABLES OF TEMPERATURES IS */
        DCL TPTOP  FIXED;    /* TP(1:PRTOP) */
        DCL TPPOSMAX FIXED; /* POSTION OF MAX VALUE */
```

The only advantage (1a) enjoys is brevity -- it takes 4 lines instead of 8. But this brevity is obtained at the price of clarity and precision. First, in (1a) variables are grouped by type rather than meaning, which does nothing to explain their interrelationships. Secondly, the comments are vague. We can infer that PR is a table of pressures, but how many are there and where in the array are they stored? Perhaps N or M gives this information, but we can only determine that by analyzing the program statements. Continuing in this fashion, we can ask what is MAX the maximum of? What are N and M the lengths of? POSMAX is the position of some maximum value, but in what array?

The only way to discover the answers is to analyze the program; it is as if the programmer had posed riddles whose answers are hidden in the program statements. The point is, these questions should be answered by the programmer and supplied as documentation. Everything possible should be done to make the program understandable.

Consider the declarations in (1b). First, notice that it is easier to find a particular variable -- something a reader of a program must do often; one simply scans the names in the column following the DCL. Secondly, the grouping by logical relationship, rather than by type, alerts the reader immediately to the related variables. Thus we can see that (PR, PRTOP, PRMAX, PRMIN) and (TP, TPTOP, TPPOSMAX) form two independent groups. The naming convention helps here also.

Next to a variable are its type attributes, and immediately to the right of the type is its meaning, in terms that relate the problem domain to the program. Note that the meaning of the related variables may be expressed by one or more sentences that show their relationship. Thus

```
/* TABLE OF PRESSURES IS PR(1:PRTOP) */
```

indicates (1) that PRTOP is the number of pressure values, (2) that these values are stored in array PR, and (3) that they are actually stored in PR(1), ..., PR(PRTOP). A succinct notation, like PR(1:PRTOP), can express as much information as several sentences, and just as precisely.

As another example, suppose a program is to read cards, one at a time, and process the characters in some fashion, one by one. Consider the declaration

```
DCL C CHAR(81) VARYING; /* THE CHARACTERS READ IN */
                        /* BUT NOT YET PROCESSED, */
                        /* FOLLOWED BY A BLANK */
```

From the meaning of variable C, the reader can infer that as soon as a character is "processed" it will be deleted from C, that the next character to process is always SUBSTR(C,1,1), and that when a new card is read into C a blank will be appended.

On the other hand, the declarations for this task might be the following, which would imply a different processing strategy:

```
DCL CI FIXED;              /* SUBSTR(C,CI) CONTAINS THE */
DCL  C CHAR(80) VARYING;   /* INPUT READ IN BUT NOT YET */
                           /* PROCESSED */
```

Now SUBSTR(C,CI,1) always contains the next character to process, and after it is processed CI must be incremented by 1 (and perhaps a new card must be read).

In both examples, the action to be performed by the program statements are clearly suggested by the declarations, and consequently the reader knows what to expect.

Writing good documentation for variables as in the above examples or in (1b) takes time and effort, but it actually <u>saves</u> time if the programmer writes them <u>before</u> writing the program itself. Indecision and vagueness in the meanings of variables leads to errors when the program statements are being developed.

We prefer the format shown in (1.b), but others can be used as long as variables are precise and clear. Another format for (1.b) is

```
/* TABLE OF PRESSURES IS PR(1:PRTOP), PRMAX */
/* (PRMIN) IS THE MAXIMUM (MINIMUM) PRESSURE VALUE */
    DCL PR(50) FLOAT;
    DCL PRTOP FIXED;
    DCL (PRMAX, PRMIN) FLOAT;

/* TABLE  OF TEMPERATURES IS TP(1:PRTOP). TPPOSMAX IS */
/* POSITION OF THE MAXIMUM TEMPERATURE IN TP(1:PRTOP) */
    DCL TP(50) FLOAT;
    DCL (TPTOP, TPPOSMAX) FIXED;
```

Not all variables need be fully and precisely defined. If a variable is used in a local context only as a "temporary", and if its use is <u>easily</u> determined from that context, then no definition is needed. For example, no definition would be needed for variables I, J and X in the following program segment:

```
/** ADD ARRAYS A AND B TO PRODUCE ARRAY C */
    DO I = 1 TO N BY 1;
        DO J = 1 TO N BY 1;
            X = A(I, J) + B(I, J);
            C(I,J)=X;
            END;
        END;
```

Often, use of words like "counter", "flag", "pointer", and "temporary" in a variable definition is a warning either of an unnecessary definition or of one that is too vague and imprecise; the programmer would do well to analyze and fix the problem.

Section 2 Statement Organization

2.1 Static Versus Dynamic Versions of a Program

The simplest kind of program to understand is a sequence of GET, assignment, and PUT statements. For example

```
GET LIST(X, Y);
Z = X + Y;
PUT LIST(Z, X, Y);
...
```

Such a program is easy to understand, no matter how long, because execution exactly follows the text of the program. The dynamic version -- how it gets executed -- is exactly the same as the static version -- how it is read. We read one statemnt after the other; one statement is executed after the other.

A program is best understood when its static version mirrors the dynamic version as closely as possible. Unfortunately, non-trivial programs all use loops and conditional statements and the dynamic version is much different from the static. Our task, then, is to learn to construct and present a program in such a way that the static version appears to mirror the dynamic. We do this by accepting certain restrictions on the choice of program constructs, and by using indentation to view certain groups of statements as if they were single statements.

For example, conditional statements (IF or SELECT) cause the dynamic and static versions to differ. Consider the following (static) program segment:

```
                ...
                GET LIST (TOOT);
                PUT SKIP LIST (TOOT, 'TOOTS MEAN:');
                DECODE: SELECT;
                    WHEN (TOOT = 1) PUT LIST
                           ('ALTERING COURSE TO STARBOARD');
(2.1a)              WHEN (TOOT = 2) PUT LIST
                           ('ALTERING COURSE TO PORT');
                    WHEN (TOOT = 3) PUT LIST
                           ('ENGINES ARE GOING ASTERN');
                    OTHERWISE PUT LIST ('ALARM -- DANGER');
                    END DECODE;
                ...
```

The corresponding dynamic version of this segment depends on the value of TOOT. There are four possible execution sequences. The one for TOOT=2 is:

```
                GET LIST (TOOT);

                PUT SKIP LIST (TOOT, 'TOOTS MEAN:');
(2.1b)
                test (TOOT = 1)
                test (TOOT = 2)
                PUT LIST ('ALTERING COURSE TO PORT');
```

In this case the dynamic version is <u>shorter</u> because only one alternative of the SELECT statement is actually executed, but all alternatives have to be described in the static version. In a sense, (2.1a) represents four different program segments, each consisting of simple GET, assignment and PUT statements.

We reduce the apparent difference between (2.1a) and (2.1b) by <u>indenting</u> so the whole SELECT construction is viewed as a single statement. If in (2.1a) we consider as statements only those lines that begin in the leftmost column, then the program consists of three sequential statements: GET..., PUT... and DECODE... . In a sense, what we are attempting to do is to abstract out the <u>meaning</u> of the SELECT, which is "Select and print course of action", and thus to view the execution sequence, no matter what the input, as simply

```
GET LIST (TOOT);
PUT SKIP LIST (TOOT, 'TOOTS MEAN:');
Select and print course of action.
```

Loops cause greater differences between static and dynamic versions -- in fact, a single static program text including a loop can evoke an unbounded number of different execution sequences depending on how many times the loop iterates. For example, consider the static text segment

```
PUT LIST ('LIST OF WORDS:');
PUT SKIP;
RPLOOP: DO COUNT = 1 TO N BY 1;
    GET LIST (WORD);
    PUT SKIP LIST (WORD);
    END RPLOOP;
PUT SKIP(2) LIST ('END OF LIST');
```

One <u>dynamic</u> execution sequence, assuming N=3, is:

```
PUT LIST ('LIST OF WORDS:');

PUT SKIP;

RPLOOP: assign 1 to COUNT
compare COUNT to 3
GET LIST (WORD);
PUT SKIP LIST (WORD);
increase COUNT by 1
compare COUNT to 3
GET LIST (WORD);
PUT SKIP LIST (WORD);
increase COUNT by 1
compare COUNT to 3
GET LIST (WORD);
PUT SKIP LIST (WORD);
increase COUNT by 1
compare COUNT to 3

PUT SKIP(2) LIST ('END OF LIST');
```

There is a different execution sequence for each value of N, yet we must comprehend <u>all</u> these sequences just from the program text. It helps to think of the loop as a single statement with a single task to perform, and view the program as four statements to be executed in order.

Notice that the lines of the dynamic version have been carefully grouped into four distinct sections. Now observe that in the static version there are <u>exactly four statements</u> written at the <u>first indentation level</u>, and that there is an obvious one-to-one correspondence between these lines and the execution sections. In effect, what we are pointing out is that if you regard a loop as a single "statement" in both the static and dynamic versions of the program, then the two versions coincide exactly, line for line. This clearly makes it easier to visualize and understand the unseen dynamic version by reading the static version.

Two simple rules allow us to view any program text as a simple sequential program:

1. Begin the statements of any sequence of statements at the same level of indentation.

2. Regard all the components of a DO, SELECT or IF as a single "statement", and indent the subordinate lines with respect to the heading.

This means you can easily envision the execution sequence at some level, just by reading the text lines at the corresponding level.

This is obviously just a trick. The repetition and the selection actions are still there -- we have just hidden them by the artifice of viewing a loop or a selection as a single statement. But this subterfuge is enormously useful. It will enable us to readily comprehend the action of very large programs. It also provides an effective plan for constructing large programs.

Thus we use the following indentation schemes:

```
IF expression          and    IF expression
    THEN statement                THEN statement
                                  ELSE statement

SELECT;
    WHEN (expression)
           statement
    ...
    WHEN (expression)
           statement
    OTHERWISE statement
    END;

DO;                           DO control phrase;
    statement          and        statement
    ...                           ...
    END;                          END;
```

Consistency in indentation is important since it helps the reader know what to expect, but the practice can be tempered with common sense. We occasionally elect to depart from these standards when it seems excessively awkward to adhere to them. Sometimes we depart by accident and since these conventions are not checked by the compiler we do not discover our "error". But you should develop your own indentation conventions and attempt to follow them consistently. We recommend ours as a starting point.

2.2 Hierarchal Structure and Statement-Comments

2.2.1 Statement-Comments and Abstraction

In Section 2.1 we discussed viewing any program segment as a sequence of statements to be executed in order, using indentation to obtain a two-dimensional representation of the program that enforced this view. But this is not always enough. Consider, for example, what the reader must go through to understand the following segment. Although he knows he is supposed to view it simply as three sequential statements, he is still forced into analyzing statement DECODE carefully in order to extract its meaning -- what it does.

```
GET LIST (TOOT);
PUT SKIP LIST (TOOT, 'TOOTS MEAN:');
DECODE: SELECT;
    WHEN (TOOT = 1) PUT LIST
           ('ALTERING COURSE TO STARBOARD');
    WHEN (TOOT = 2) PUT LIST
           ('ALTERING COURSE TO PORT');
    WHEN (TOOT = 3) PUT LIST
           ('ENGINES ARE GOING ASTERN');
    OTHERWISE PUT LIST ('ALARM -- DANGER');
    END DECODE;
```

The programmer can aid the reader by describing the meaning of DECODE with a statement-comment:

```
        GET LIST (TOOT);
        PUT SKIP LIST (TOOT, 'TOOTS MEAN:');
        /** PRINT THE COURSE OF ACTION TAKEN */
            DECODE: SELECT;
                WHEN (TOOT = 1) PUT LIST
(2.2.1a)               ('ALTERING COURSE TO STARBOARD');
                WHEN (TOOT = 2) PUT LIST
                       ('ALTERING COURSE TO PORT');
                WHEN (TOOT = 3) PUT LIST
                       ('ENGINES ARE GOING ASTERN');
                OTHERWISE PUT LIST ('ALARM -- DANGER);
                END DECODE;
```

(2.2.1a) illustrates some important points about program structure and how programs should be read. First, the comment should be viewed as a "high-level" programming language statement. The reader should think of (2.2.1a) as a sequence of the three simple statements that begin in the leftmost column so that the static version at this level corresponds exactly to the dynamic version:

(2.2.1b)
```
GET LIST (TOOT);
PUT SKIP LIST (TOOT, 'TOOTS MEAN:');
Print the course of action TOOT.
```

Secondly, the statement that actually performs "Print the course of action TOOT" appears _indented_ below the statement-comment. The statement-comment indicates as precisely as possible _what_ to do, the indented statements below it show _how_ to do it. The indented statements are sometimes called the _refinement_ of the statement-comment.

(2.2.1a) can be understood in two separate steps:

1. Understand the segment as the simple, three-step process (2.2.1b).

2. Study the refinement of "Print the course of action TOOT" to make sure that it performs as intended. In this case, this means that the message printed in each case corresponds to the number of toots.

In generating the statement-comment we have used an important process called _abstraction_. In order to enhance understanding, we have _extracted one essential quality of the statement_ DECODE _for further study_ at the highest program level: _what_ the statement does. A study of its other qualities (how it works, how long it takes to execute, etc.) has been postponed, so that understanding can be achieved at the highest level. This process of abstraction plays an extremely important role in programming. It allows us to _separate our concerns_ into manageable groups. It allows us to postpone details to a later time, to concentrate on one or two issues at a time.

2.2.2 Structuring Larger Program Segments

We have seen that treating a loop or conditional statement as a single unit and supplying a statement-comment for it allows the reader to view a program segment as a simple sequence of statements, so that, at least at one level of program reading, the static and dynamic versions coincide. This technique can be extended in two ways so that a program of any size can be organized for understanding:

1. Allow a statement-comment for _any_ sequence of statements (not just for a loop or conditional statement). The sequence of statements should perform some logical task, and this task is _precisely_ stated in the statement-comment. The sequence is indented with respect to the statement-comment; it forms the _refinement_ of the statement-comment.

2. The refinement of a statement-comment may itself contain statement-comments (with their refinements). Only

reasonableness and understanding limit the depth of nesting of statement-comments.

The following example illustrates both points.

```
        ...
        /** READ IN A(1:10,1:20), PRINT ROWSUMS, STORE SUM OF */
            /* ALL ELEMENTS IN TOTAL_SUM */
            TOTAL_SUM = 0;
            ROWLOOP: DO I = 1 TO 10 BY 1;
                /** READ IN ROW I OF A, */
                    /* SET ITS SUM IN SUM */
(2.2.2a)            SUM = 0;
                    DO J = 1 TO 20 BY 1;
                        GET LIST(A(I, J));
                        SUM = SUM + A(I,J);
                        END;
                PUT LIST(SUM);
                TOTAL_SUM = TOTAL_SUM + SUM;
                END ROWLOOP;

        ...
```

Assuming that this segment occurs within a larger program, the reader understands this, at the outermost level shown, as a sequential program:

```
...
Read in A(1:10,1:20), print row sums, and store sum of
        all elements in TOTAL_SUM.

...
```

Then, in order to understand how the English statement is implemented, he studies its refinement, which is:

```
TOTAL_SUM = 0;
ROWLOOP: DO I = 1 TO 10 BY 1;
    Read in row I of A and set its sum in SUM
    PUT LIST(SUM);
    TOTAL_SUM = TOTAL_SUM + SUM;
    END ROWLOOP;
```

Finally, if necessary, he studies the refinement of the English statement "Read in row I ...", which is

```
SUM = 0;
DO J = 1 TO 20 BY 1;
    GET LIST(A(I, J));
    SUM = SUM + A(I);
    END;
```

The reader has gained complete understanding of the program by studying it on three levels. The program has been organized to guide him, to direct him to study the program in this manner, on the three levels. And at each level the program segment is viewed as a sequence of statements to execute in order.

Such a program organization is not easy to obtain, especially if it is attempted after the program is written. Statement-comments should be written before and not after their refinements. The whole problem of documentation, of program structure, etc., should guide the programmer while he is programming. This is discussed further in Part III on Program Development.

The purpose of a statement-comment is to allow the reader to concentrate on what a sequence of statements does and to postpone a study of how it works to a later time. This purpose is assured only if the statement-comment is clear, precise and complete. It should be looked upon as a substitute for its refinement.

One way to test the suitability of your own statement-comments is to hide its refinement with a piece of paper and see whether the program still makes sense. If not, then the statement-comment is probably not precise or complete, or it may simply be incorrect.

As a simple but subtle example, consider the refinement of "Read in row I of A and set its sum in SUM" of (2.2.2a). Let us suppose SUM is initialized in its declaration so we have

```
          DCL SUM FIXED INIT(0); /* SUM OF ROW I OF A */
          ...
          ROWLOOP: DO I = 1 TO 10 BY 1;
               ...
               /** READ IN ROW I OF A AND SET ITS SUM IN SUM */
(2.2.2b)            DO J = 1 TO 20 BY 1;
                         GET LIST(A(I, J));
                         SUM = SUM + A(I, J);
                         END;
               ...
               END ROWLOOP;
          ...
```

While the INIT phrase in declarations is sometimes useful, here it has led to an error. For the first row (I=1) SUM is initially zero, but when this part of the program is executed a second time, with I=2, SUM is not zero as it should be. This error occured because the comment does not precisely correspond to its refinement; either the program should have been written as in (2.2.2a) or the segment should be written

```
/** READ ROW I OF A AND SET SUM TO SUM OF A(I,1:20) */
    /* ASSUMING THAT SUM IS INITIALLY ZERO */
    DO J = 1 TO 20 BY 1;
        GET LIST(A(I, J));
        SUM = SUM + A(I, J));
        END;
```

This would have alerted the programmer to the fact that SUM = 0; was needed just beforehand.

This suggests that to be precise a statement-comment must

1. list and describe all variables that it uses as input;

2. list and describe all results that it produces.

Full adherence to this rule is often impractical -- it would lead to such long, detailed statements that their refinements would be completely overshadowed. The programmer's problem, and it is a difficult one, is to word his statement-comments so that they give important details but leave out details that can be <u>easily</u> extracted from the program by the reader. The common type of error in the last example illustrates how easy it is to miss an important point.

One aid in this matter is good documentation of variables, as explained in Section 1. For example, if the program contains the declarations

```
DCL PR(1:50) FLOAT;   /* PR(1:PRTOP) IS A TABLE OF */
DCL PRTOP FIXED;      /* PRESSURE VALUES; PRMAX IS THE */
DCL PRMAX FIXED;      /* MAXIMUM PRESSURE VALUE */
```

Then, instead of having to write the statement-comment

```
/* SET PRMAX TO THE MAXIMUM VALUE IN PR(1:PRTOP) */
```

one could write simply

```
/* SET PRMAX */
```

PRMAX is to be used <u>only</u> for the maximum value of PR(1:PRTOP) and the reader can refer back to the declaration comment to be reminded of that role.

2.3 The Effect of Control-Modifying Statements on Structure

The LEAVE and GOTO statements and the ON unit drastically alter the sequential nature of program execution. These statements are useful, but they must be used with care and with proper documentation.

2.3.1 The Effect of the LEAVE Statement

Suppose we are concerned with some action S that consists of three sequential subactions S1, S2 and S3:

```
/** Perform action S */
    S1
    S2
    S3
```

The static and dynamic versions of the segment are identical -- even if one of the subactions is itself a conditional statement or loop.

But now suppose that one of the subactions -- say S2 -- contains a conditional LEAVE. (This implies that S is part of the body of a loop, but that is not important at the moment.) As a consequence of the presence of the LEAVE there are now <u>two</u> possible <u>execution sequences</u> for this segment:

If the LEAVE is executed: S1, part of S2 up to the LEAVE

If the LEAVE is not executed: S1, S2, S3

This is fundamentally different from the previous conditional examples where the only question was which of several alternatives was executed. We masked that difficulty by considering the entire conditional construct to be a single statement. That won't work here because S3 is involved.

To press the point further, consider a statement at the next higher level, where S is only one step:

```
/** Perform action RST */
    R
    Perform action S
    T
```

We want to understand action RST at this level without having to study the detailed implementation of S. Therefore, not realizing that S contains a LEAVE, we don't understand that there are possible execution sequences for RST in which <u>T is never executed</u>.

The point is that the LEAVE in S2 has substantially changed our ability to describe the execution sequence of every segment that contains S2. The action of S2 is no longer self-contained -- it determines whether or not segments S3, T and perhaps others are ever executed.

The loss of clarity with the LEAVE statement can be minimized in several ways:

1. Limit the depth of exits. The LEAVE statement in a single loop is usually manageable, but when a LEAVE is deeply buried in a nest of loops and exits several levels the program can be very hard to understand.

2. Explicitly name every loop that has a LEAVE exit and specify the loop-name in the LEAVE statement.

3. Warn the reader in the statement-comment when its refinement includes a LEAVE that would affect subsequent segments. (This is an example of making the statement-comment precise and complete.)

These are guidlines rather than rules and must be tempered with common sense. They help when segments are long and complex but, for example, the following segment is clear without them:

```
/** SET XPOS TO POSITION OF FIRST X IN A(1:N) */
    DO XPOS = 1 TO N BY 1;
        IF X = A(XPOS)
            THEN LEAVE;
        END;
```

2.3.2 The Effect of the GOTO Statement

The effect of a conditional forward GOTO is essentially the same as for the conditional LEAVE except that the use is not limited to exiting from a loop. The presence in a segment of a forward GOTO whose target is not in the same segment means that some arbitrary number of subsequent segments may be omitted in execution. Moreover, since the target might not even be at the beginning of a segment the whole idea of partition into segments is less meaningful. Obviously the clear documentation of a program with forward GOTOs is both critical and difficult.

However, the situation is much worse if the GOTO is unrestricted and the target need not follow the GOTO. (This is legal in PL/I and PL/C -- only PL/CS restricts the GOTO to forward branches.) There is no longer anything general or interesting that can be said about the pattern of execution. No matter how carefully you use the other statement types, just the possibility of an unrestricted GOTO means that you can no longer describe the dynamic version in terms of the static version in any simple way. You cannot give any partial ordering to groups of statements. You can no longer confidently consider the program to consist of distinct levels. Programs of this type are sometimes called "spaghetti code" -- they have the same clean logical structure as a plate of spaghetti. The implications for the task of trying to follow and understand the execution path are obvious. The remedy is simple -- the unrestricted (backward) GOTO should be absolutely avoided.

2.3.3 The Effect of the Endfile Condition

The general PL/I ON-conditions are even more destructive of clear program structure than the GOTO. They are unstructured, unclear, unfortunate and almost unexplainable. But the restricted form of the ENDFILE condition described in Section I.7.4.3 is essentially equivalent to a forward GOTO. Moreover, since it is always used for exactly the same purpose the intent is clear, so this convenient facility can be exploited without appreciable penalty.

2.4 The Well-Structured Program

A program is said to be "well-structured" if it is organized as discussed thus far in Part II. This means that the program consists of segments that are readily understandable, perhaps at a level higher than individual PL/I statements, and that the control paths between segments are few in number and simple in form.

Structure and format are actually two different issues, although the preceding sections have treated both together. A program is well-presented if its structure is clearly and quickly apparent to the reader. This means grouping statements in a logical way, and providing statement-comments so the purpose of each group is apparent without having to figure it out from the individual PL/I statements. It also means using indentation in a clear and consistent way to emphasize the grouping and to indicate the flow-of-control during execution.

A program that is both well-structured and well-presented has a high degree of predictability, and this is useful to the reader. For example, suppose you encounter the following line in reading a program:

```
/** SET MINPN TO MIN OF PN FUNCTION */
```

If, at the moment, you are looking for something else in the program and don't need to know how the program actually finds that minimum, you can confidently skip over the lines indented with respect to that statement-comment. The next line below that is left-aligned with this comment will be the next line to consider. Note that it is the commenting and indenting convention that helps you find this next line quickly, but it is the segment structure discipline that allows you to go directly to that line without worrying that the program might have executed a random GOTO somewhere in the SET MINPN segment. Knowing that the SET MINPN segment has a single exit point you know that it will reach that next line, without having to trace through the detail of SET MINPN to make sure.

In a well-structured program the different PL/I statements will always be used in a consistent manner. For example, repetition is always controlled by a DO loop and never with some construction handcrafted from IF, GOTO and a label. This means that when you encounter an IF or a GOTO you do not have to wonder whether it might be part of a homemade DO loop.

You can read and understand a well-structured program more quickly, simply because you actually have <u>less to learn about the program</u>. You know in advance how the program will be organized, how it will be presented, and how each PL/I statement type will be used. If a program <u>doesn't</u> use these conventions, then you must approach it with much less of a headstart. All you have is your knowledge of the meaning of each individual PL/I statement. For example, when you encounter a GOTO in a well-structured program, you know that some segment is being terminated early. The label given as a target of the GOTO helps suggest what segment is being terminated. You know that that label is assigned to some statement further down the page, and when you locate it, its indentation will confirm the level of the segment being terminated. You do not have to figure out what the role of the GOTO is -- you know that in advance. All that has to be determined is which segment is being terminated.

<u>Variation in program style is not desirable</u>. A given programmer, when confronted with similar tasks at different points in a program, should solve those tasks in a similar way. From the point of view of the reader, when he encounters apparently similar tasks that are handled in different ways, he should take this as a warning that he does not fully understand the tasks -- and not just that the programmer got bored with one approach and decided to try another. For example, suppose that in the process of reading a program you encounter the following three segments at three different points:

```
/** MOVE A(1:N) TO B(1:N) */
    DO I = 1 TO N BI 1;
        B(I) = A(I);
        END;

/** REPLACE X(1:N) WITH Y(1:N) */
    DO I = N TO 1 BY -1;
        X(I) = Y(I);
        END;
```

```
/** COPY R(1:N) INTO S(1:N) */
    I = 0;
    DO WHILE (I < N);
        I = I + 1;
        S(I) = R(I);
        END;
```

First you might wonder whether "move", "replace", and "copy" mean exactly the same thing to the writer, or whether there are subtle differences in objective. You should certainly wonder if there is something peculiar about X and Y that makes it necessary to index backward (that is, from N to 1) over their elements. Finally, you should be concerned with why the writer chose to use a WHILE loop for R and S when he has used an indexed loop in other cases. If it turns out that these are in fact exactly comparable tasks, and the writer simply amused himself by seeing how many different ways he could find to write the same task, you will have wasted time looking for differences that don't exist and are entitled to be annoyed -- especially if you were the writer at some earlier time.

Effectively, you are asked to yield some of your freedom of choice in writing a program. It is in <u>your</u> best interest to do this, since you the programmer are the most frequent reader of the program. <u>You</u> must find the errors in it; <u>you</u> must be sure of its correctness.

Another major virtue of the structure recommended above is the <u>limitation of context</u>. This structure makes it possible to understand a particular segment with relatively little knowledge about surrounding segments. Without this type of discipline it may be necessary to examine and understand an entire program before you can understand much about a particular small segment. This same characteristic allows segments of a program to be written, and later modified or replaced, while only considering a carefully circumscribed local environment of that segment. This makes it possible to produce relatively large programs and achieve the same confidence in their correctness as is possible for small programs.

The harmful effect of the unrestricted use of the GOTO statement should be obvious from this discussion. If a segment is allowed to branch arbitrarily to other sections of the program its successor is no longer unique or apparent. The dynamic version of the program is very different from the static text. Similarly, if other segments have the privilege of unrestricted branching then the entry point and entry conditions of the segment under consideration are not easily determined.

This structure is not always the most obvious or natural for a problem. But it is the most desirable structure for a program, and it is worth trying to organize a problem so that it takes this form. It is not always easy to do so and it takes a good deal of practice. For non-trivial programs the effort is clearly worthwhile. The additional time spent in initial planning is more than recovered by a reduction in testing time, and the overall result is a significant improvement in clarity and reliability.

For very small programs a less structured organization may suffice, and a well-structured program does require some extra work in the initial writing. While an experienced programmer who knows how to produce a good program might be permitted to "shortcut" under special circumstances, a beginner trying to learn the art of programming should practice using the proper style at every opportunity. Even for the professional a casual approach is risky since very often little programs reappear later as pieces of big programs.

If there is a "break-even point" with regard to these practices it occurs at a surprisingly small size of program. The extra effort pays off for programs as small as 20 statements just in a reduction in the time required to adequately test the program. This means it will be valuable even for exercises that are encountered in a first programming course.

2.5 A Comparative Example

With this discussion as background we now give another example, presenting the same program in both "well-structured" and "conventional" form. Consider a program that is to read in a 2-dimensional array of integers A(N,N) and then determine the following three values:

1. The largest element on the principal diagonal -- the maximum A(I,I) for I=1,2,...,N. Call this maximum DMAX.

2. The largest element in row I, the row in which DMAX occurs. Calls this RMAX.

3. The largest element in column I, the column in which DMAX occurs. Call this CMAX.

The input consists of a number N, less than 25, followed by the N^2 numbers of the array in row-major order -- that is, the numbers of the top row, left to right, followed by the numbers of the second row, left to right, etc. The required output is a display of the array and the values of DMAX, RMAX and CMAX.

(2.5a) and (2.5b) are alternative programs that are correct and solve the problem. (2.5a) is typical of conventional programming style and format. (Although we are obviously trying to persuade you that (2.5b) is preferable we have tried not to make (2.5a) deliberately obscure.) (2.5b) is written following the recommendations of the preceding sections. As you consider these two programs, realize that they are identical, as far as the computer is concerned. They differ only in the manner in which they are organized and presented for a human reader.

(2.5a)

```
MAXELMT: PROCEDURE OPTIONS(MAIN);
DCL (A(24,24),N,LD,LR,LC,I,J) FIXED;
GET LIST(N); LD=1; LR, LC=1;
IF (N<1)|(N>24) THEN DO; PUT SKIP LIST('WRONG SIZE',N);
GO TO FIN; END;
DO I = 1 TO N BY 1; PUT SKIP;
DO J = 1 TO N BY 1;
GET LIST(A(I,J)); PUT LIST(A(I,J));
END; END;
DO I = 2 TO N BY 1;
IF A(I,I) > A(LD,LD) THEN LD = I; END;
PUT SKIP LIST('DMAX IS:',A(LD,LD),'IN ROW,COL',LD);
DO I = 2 TO N BY 1;
IF A(LD,I) > A(LD,LR) THEN LR=I;
IF A(I,LD) > A(LC,LD) THEN LC=I; END;
PUT SKIP LIST('RMAX IS:',A(LD,LR),'IN COL',LR);
PUT SKIP LIST('CMAX IS:',A(LC,LD),'IN ROW',LC);
FIN: END MAXELMT;
```

(2.5b)

```
/* FIND DMAX, RMAX AND CMAX IN A(N,N).  */
MAXELMT: PROCEDURE OPTIONS(MAIN);
   DCL (A(24,24),
       N,      /* ARRAY IS A(1:N,1:N) */
       LD,     /* ROW, COL OF DMAX */
       LR,     /* COL OF RMAX */
       LC,     /* ROW OF CMAX */
       I,J) FIXED;
   /** READ IN N AND ARRAY A, STOP IF IMPROPER SIZE */
       GET LIST(N);
       IF (N < 1) | (N > 24)
           THEN DO;
               PUT SKIP LIST('SIZE OF ARRAY WRONG:',N);
               GO TO TERM_MAXELMT;
               END;
       DO I = 1 TO N BY 1;
           DO J = 1 TO N BY 1;
               GET LIST(A(I,J));
               END;
           END;
   /** PRINT ARRAY A */
       DO I = 1 TO N BY 1;
           PUT SKIP;
           DO J = 1 TO N BY 1;
               PUT LIST(A(I,J));
               END;
           END;
   /** FIND INDEX LD OF DMAX */
       LD = 1;
       DO I = 2 TO N BY 1;
           IF A(I,I) > A(LD,LD)
               THEN LD = I;
           END;
```

```
/** FIND INDEX LR OF RMAX, LC OF CMAX */
    LR, LC = 1;
    DO I = 2 TO N BY 1;
        IF A(LD,I) > A(LD,LR)
            THEN LR = I;
        IF A(I,LD) > A(LC,LD)
            THEN LC = I;
        END;
/** PRINT RESULTS */
    PUT SKIP LIST('DMAX IS:',A(LD,LD),
            'IN ROW,COL',LD);
    PUT SKIP LIST('RMAX IS:',A(LD,LR),'IN COL',LR);
    PUT SKIP LIST('CMAX IS:',A(LC,LD),'IN ROW',LC);
TERM_MAXELMT:;
END MAXELMT;
```

(2.5b) is more readily understandable than (2.5a) even though it has more lines to read. (2.5b) makes it obvious that the program is a simple sequence of five subtasks:

Read in N and array A and terminate if error
Print array A
Find index LD of DMAX
Find index LR of RMAX and LC of CMAX
Print results.

Each of these subtasks is itself a sequence of subtasks and four of them involve looping, but that does not obscure the fact that there are essentially five steps in executing the program. Within each of the subtasks the extent and purpose of each loop are made clear by labelling and indentation.

It is probably not obvious at this stage of your programming development, but real programs are often modified. That is, after a program is completed and tested, and has been used for awhile, it is not unusual for problem requirements to be slightly changed. Then someone -- not always the original author -- must go back and re-read the program and find the appropriate points at which to make changes. Consider (2.5b) from the point of view of making changes. It is easier to find the place to make the change, easier to write the new statements, and we have greater confidence that the change is correct and does not disturb other sections of the program. In effect, we really have to study (2.5a) in order to find out information that is readily apparent in (2.5b). For example, consider the relative ease and confidence with which (2.5a) and (2.5b) could be modified to make one or more of the following changes:

1. The program is to be run only on "sparse" arrays -- arrays where most of the elements are 0. To make it easier to keypunch the input data, change the program to accept input of the following form, where the user need only specify the non-zero elements:
    a) card 1 contains the integer N

b) each successive card describes one non-zero array element by giving its row number, its column number and its value
c) the last card contains three zero values.

2. Change the program so that DMAX is the largest value on the lower-left-to-upper-right diagonal.

3. Change the output format so the array is printed with 2 stars "**" on either side of the values DMAX, RMAX and CMAX.

Section 3 Sample Programs

3.1 A Program to Compute Averages

A simple but useful task is to compute the average of a list of numbers. We present two programs for this task. The first is a bare-bones minimal program that performs the basic task required and nothing more. The second is more useful and realistic.

3.1.1 A Minimal Averaging Program

The following program computes the average value of a nonempty list of numbers. This version is correct in that it performs the required function, and it is in proper form using language elements in ways recommended in previous sections. Nevertheless it is not entirely adequate in comparison with the second version.

```
/* PRINT AVERAGE OF INPUT NUMBERS */
MEAN: PROCEDURE OPTIONS(MAIN);
    DCL (AVG, NBR) FLOAT;
    DCL SUM FLOAT INIT(0);    /* SUM OF NUMBERS READ SO FAR   */
    DCL COUNT FIXED INIT(0); /* COUNT OF NUMBERS READ SO FAR */

    /** READ, SUM AND COUNT NUMBERS */
        ON ENDFILE(SYSIN) GOTO DATAEND
        DATALOOP: DO WHILE ('1'B);
            GET LIST (NBR);
            SUM = SUM + NBR;
            COUNT = COUNT + 1;
            END DATALOOP;
        DATAEND:;

    /** COMPUTE AND PRINT AVERAGE OF NUMBERS */
        AVG = SUM / COUNT;
        PUT LIST ('AVERAGE IS:', AVG);

    END MEAN;
```

The source listing shows the program divided into three sections:

1. Preparatory section: declaration of variables with initial values.
2. Read, sum and count the numbers given in the data list.
3. Compute and print the average.

Note the following:

1. Variables AVG, NBR, SUM and COUNT have been named to reflect the role each plays in the program. SUM and COUNT have been given more precise meanings with comments. They are used throughout most of the program and it is important to know exactly how they are used. AVG and NBR need no further comment since their values have only a local meaning - from one statement to the very next statement.

2. The program employs a loop with indefinite repetition and an end-of-data exit -- techniques described in Section 7.4.3.

3. The two statements of the final section could be replaced by the single statement:

   ```
   PUT LIST ('AVERAGE IS:', SUM/COUNT);
   ```

   In this case the variable AVG would not be needed.

This program could be written in a more compact form:

```
MEAN: PROC OPTIONS(MAIN);
 DCL NBR FLOAT, (SUM FLOAT, COUNT FIXED) INIT(0);
 ON ENDFILE GOTO DATAEND; DO WHILE ('1'B); GET LIST(NBR);
 SUM=SUM+NBR; COUNT=COUNT+1; END; DATAEND: PUT LIST(SUM/COUNT);
 END;
```

This is equivalent to the previous version in every sense except the ease with which it can be read by a human reader. In this case the program is short and simple enough that you can understand even this compact form, but we will soon present programs for which this would be impossible.

The "user instructions" for this program would be simple. For example:

"This program computes the average of a list of numbers. The numbers should be punched on cards, and placed immediately after the *DATA card at the end of the program. Numbers are punched in ordinary decimal form. For example:

```
*DATA
13.07
-24.345
6
.124
```

There is no limit on the quantity of numbers. The answer is given in exponential form. For example, an answer of 256.3 is printed as 2.563000E+02."

3.1.2 A More Useful Averaging Program

The program shown below performs the same basic task as the last one, but this version was designed with more appreciation of how such a program is likely to be used. Consequently it provides additional information to the user. Consider the following:

1. The averaging program may not be the only program being used, so it is helpful if results are completely self-identifying.

2. A program is often used repeatedly on many different sets of data. It is helpful to identify the results of each individual run so that they can be associated (after the fact) with the corresponding data list. The complete list of data values could be printed for this purpose, but this could involve voluminous printing. This could be offered as an option (see Section 1.2) but for most purposes the identification provided by the program below would be adequate.

3. The program might accidentally be run without any data list. Consequently the program should clearly distinguish between an average of 0 for a nonempty data list and a result of 0 occurring because no data was provided.

4. Separate "user instructions" have a way of getting lost. Therefore they have been incorporated into the heading of the program so that a new copy can be easily obtained.

The point is that certain requirements, while not made explicit in the assignment "write a program to compute an average", are implicit in the experience of a good programmer. In effect, this program and the previous version illustrate the difference between what would be produced by a mediocre (or lazy) programmer and a perceptive and conscientious one.

Note that in spite of the functional enhancement this version of the program still has the same overall structure; it still consists of three sections:

1. Preparation.
2. Read, sum and count data.
3. Compute and print average with additional information.

The program follows:

```
/* COMPUTE THE AVERAGE OF A LIST OF THE NUMBERS THAT APPEAR  */
/* IMMEDIATELY AFTER THE *DATA CARD AT THE END OF THE        */
/* PROGRAM,  IN ORDINARY DECIMAL FORM.  SAMPLE DATA IS:      */
/*          *DATA                                            */
/*              13.07                                        */
/*              -24.345                                      */
/*              6                                            */
/*              .124                                         */
/* THERE IS NO LIMIT ON THE QUANTITY OF NUMBERS. THE ANSWER  */
/* IS GIVEN IN EXPONENTIAL FORM. FOR EXAMPLE, AN ANSWER OF   */
/* 256.3 IS PRINTED AS 2.563000E+02.                         */

MEAN: PROCEDURE OPTIONS(MAIN);
    DCL (AVG, NBR,
         FIRST,                /* FIRST INPUT NUMBER */
         LAST,                 /* LAST INPUT NUMBER */
         SUM)                  /* SUM OF NUMBERS READ SO FAR */
            FLOAT;
    DCL COUNT FIXED INIT(0); /* COUNT OF NUMBERS READ SO FAR */

    /** READ, SUM AND COUNT NUMBERS */
        ON ENDFILE(SYSIN) GOTO DATAEND;
        GET LIST (NBR);
        COUNT = 1;
        SUM, FIRST = NBR;
        DO WHILE ('1'B);
            GET LIST (NBR);
            COUNT = COUNT + 1;
            SUM = SUM + NBR;
            END;
        DATAEND:;
        LAST = NBR;
```

```
/** COMPUTE AVERAGE;  PRINT HEADING AND RESULT */
    PUT LIST ('CG AVERAGING PROGRAM');
    PUT SKIP LIST ('RUN ON:', DATE, 'AT:', TIME);
    PUT SKIP LIST ('FOR LIST OF:', COUNT, 'NUMBERS');
    IF COUNT ¬= 0
        THEN DO;
            PUT SKIP LIST ('FIRST NUMBER IS:', FIRST,
                     'LAST NUMBER IS:', LAST);
            AVG = SUM / COUNT;
            PUT SKIP(2) LIST ('AVERAGE IS:', AVG);
            END;
    PUT SKIP(2) LIST ('END OF AVERAGING RUN');

END MEAN;
```

An example of the execution output of this program is shown below:

```
CG AVERAGING PROGRAM
RUN ON:                 780818                  AT:                     234431250
FOR LIST OF:                 4                  NUMBERS
FIRST NUMBER IS:         1.30699E+01            LAST NUMBER IS:          1.23999E-01

AVERAGE IS:             -1.28774E+00

END OF AVERAGING RUN
```

3.2 A Simplified Statistical System

In addition to computing averages we sometimes need to determine the minimum value, maximum value, range, and standard deviation of a list of numbers, and sometimes need a list of the individual values. Separate programs, each similar to the averaging program, could perform these tasks, but alternatively a single program can offer all these capabilities and the user can select the actions he wants by means of "commands" that precede the numerical data.

For example, the user instructions for such a program might be the following:

```
/* CG STATISTICAL PACKAGE. PROCESS A LIST OF NUMBERS TO        */
/* TO PRODUCE ANY OF THE FOLLOWING:                             */
/*      1. COMPLETE LIST OF VALUES (SPECIFY 'LIST)              */
/*      2. AVERAGE OR MEAN VALUE (SPECIFY 'MEAN)                */
/*      3. MAXIMUM VALUE (SPECIFY 'MAX')                        */
/*      4. MINIMUM VALUE (SPECIFY 'MIN')                        */
/*      5. RANGE OF VALUES (SPECIFY 'RANGE')                    */
/*      6. STANDARD DEVIATION (SPECIFY 'STDDEV')                */
/*      7. 95 PERCENT CONFIDENCE LIMITS ON THE MEAN             */
/*                               (SPECIFY 'LIMITS)              */
/* ONLY THE FIRST THREE LETTERS OF THE ABOVE DATA COMMANDS      */
/* MUST BE CORRECT;  OTHER MISPELLINGS ARE IGNORED.             */
/* THE DESIRED ACTIONS ARE SPECIFIED FIRST (IN ANY ORDER),      */
/* FOLLOWED BY THE COMMAND: 'DATA', FOLLOWED BY THE LIST OF     */
/* NUMBERS.  FOR EXAMPLE:                                       */
/*      *DATA                                                   */
/*          'MEAN' 'LIMITS' 'RANGE' 'DATA'                      */
/*                  13.07 -24.345 6 .124                        */
/* THERE IS NO LIMIT ON THE QUANTITY OF NUMBERS.                */
/* RESULTS ARE GIVEN IN EXPONENTIAL FORM.  FOR EXAMPLE, A       */
/* RESULT OF 256.3 IS PRINTED AS 2.563000E+02.                  */
```

Such a program is called a "statistical system" or "statistical package". In fact, elaborate systems of this type, such as SPSS and SAS (see References), are widely used. The program shown below is a simplified version of such a system.

```
/* CG STATISTICAL PACKAGE */
STAT: PROCEDURE OPTIONS(MAIN);
    DCL COMMAND  CHAR(6) VARYING;
    DCL ACTION(7) BIT(1) INIT ((7)'0'B);
            /* BIT(1) MEANS 'LIST OPTION ACTIVE' */
            /* BIT(2) MEANS 'MEAN OPTION ACTIVE' */
            /* BIT(3) MEANS 'MAX OPTION ACTIVE' */
            /* BIT(4) MEANS 'MIN OPTION ACTIVE' */
            /* BIT(5) MEANS 'RANGE OPTION ACTIVE' */
            /* BIT(6) MEANS 'STDDEV OPTION ACTIVE' */
            /* BIT(7) MEANS 'LIMITS OPTION ACTIVE' */
    DCL (SUM, SUMSQ) FLOAT INIT (0);
    DCL (NBR, HALFINT, AVG, SUMSQDEV, STDDEV) FLOAT;
    DCL (SMALLEST, LARGEST) FLOAT;
    DCL COUNT FIXED INIT (0);

    /** READ COMMANDS AND SET ACTION FLAGS */
        COMMAND_LOOP: DO WHILE(COMMAND ¬= 'DATA');
            GET LIST (COMMAND);
            SELECT;
                WHEN (LENGTH(COMMAND) < 3)
                    PUT SKIP LIST ('INVALID ACTION:', COMMAND);
                WHEN (SUBSTR(COMMAND,1,3) = 'LIS')
                    ACTION(1) = '1'B;
                WHEN (SUBSTR(COMMAND,1,3) = 'MEA')
                    ACTION(2) = '1'B;
                WHEN (SUBSTR(COMMAND,1,3) = 'MAX')
                    ACTION(3) = '1'B;
                WHEN (SUBSTR(COMMAND,1,3) = 'MIN')
                    ACTION(4) = '1'B;
                WHEN (SUBSTR(COMMAND,1,3) = 'RAN')
                    ACTION(5) = '1'B;
                WHEN (SUBSTR(COMMAND,1,3) = 'STD')
                    ACTION(6) = '1'B;
                WHEN (SUBSTR(COMMAND,1,3) = 'LIM')
                    ACTION(7) = '1'B;
                OTHERWISE
                    PUT SKIP LIST ('INVALID ACTION:', COMMAND);
                END;
            END COMMAND_LOOP;

    /** TITLE THE RESULTS */
        PUT LIST ('CG STATISTICAL PACKAGE');
        PUT SKIP(2) LIST ('RUN ON', DATE, 'AT', TIME);
        IF ACTION(1)
            THEN PUT SKIP(3) LIST ('LIST OF DATA VALUES:');

    /** READ, PRINT SUM AND COUNT THE NUMBERS */
        ON ENDFILE(SYSIN) GOTO DATAEND;
        GET LIST (NBR);
        SMALLEST, LARGEST = NBR;
        NUMBERLOOP: DO WHILE ('1'B);
            SUM = SUM + NBR;
            SUMSQ = SUMSQ + (NBR * NBR);
            COUNT = COUNT + 1;
```

```
            LARGEST = MAX(NBR, LARGEST);
            SMALLEST = MIN(NBR, SMALLEST);
            IF ACTION(1)
                THEN PUT SKIP LIST (COUNT, NBR);
                ELSE IF COUNT = 1
                    THEN PUT SKIP LIST ('FIRST VALUE IS:',
                            NBR);
            GET LIST (NBR);
            END NUMBERLOOP;
        DATAEND:;

    /** COMPUTE AND PRINT FINAL RESULTS */
        IF ACTION(1)
            THEN PUT SKIP(2) LIST ('END OF DATA LIST');
        PUT SKIP(3) LIST ('SUMMARY OF RESULTS');
        PUT SKIP(2) LIST ('NUMBER OF DATA ITEMS:', COUNT);
        IF COUNT = 0
            THEN GOTO END_COMPUTE_AND_PRINT;
        PUT SKIP;
        AVG = SUM / COUNT;
        IF ACTION(2)
            THEN PUT SKIP LIST ('AVERAGE IS:', AVG);
        IF ACTION(3)
            THEN PUT SKIP LIST ('MAXIMUM IS:', LARGEST);
        IF ACTION(4)
            THEN PUT SKIP LIST ('MINIMUM IS:', SMALLEST);
        IF ACTION(5)
            THEN PUT SKIP LIST ('RANGE IS:',
                    LARGEST - SMALLEST);
        IF COUNT = 1
            THEN GOTO END_COMPUTE_AND_PRINT;
        SUMSQDEV = SUMSQ - ((SUM*SUM) / COUNT);
        STDDEV = SQRT(SUMSQDEV / (COUNT-1));
        IF ACTION(6)
            THEN PUT SKIP LIST ('STD DEV IS:', STDDEV);
        IF ACTION(7)
            THEN DO;
                HALFINT = 1.96 * (STDDEV/SQRT(COUNT));
                PUT SKIP LIST ('95 PERCENT',
                        'CONFIDENCE LIMITS ON THE MEAN:');
                PUT SKIP LIST (' ', 'LOWER LIMIT IS:',
                        AVG - HALFINT);
                PUT SKIP LIST (' ', 'UPPER LIMIT IS:',
                        AVG + HALFINT);
                END;
        END_COMPUTE_AND_PRINT:;

    PUT SKIP(2) LIST ('END OF SUMMARY');

    END STAT;
```

Two examples of the use of this program are given below. Suppose the following data were presented:

```
'MEAN', 'LIST', 'RANGE', 'DATA'
    23.4
    16.9
    25.05
    19.7
    20.4
```

The resulting output would be:

```
CG STATISTICAL PACKAGE

RUN ON                  780822                  AT                  092541960


LIST OF DATA VALUES:
       1                 2.33999E+01
       2                 1.68999E+01
       3                 2.50499E+01
       4                 1.96999E+01
       5                 2.03999E+01

END OF DATA LIST


SUMMARY OF RESULTS

NUMBER OF DATA ITEMS:          5

AVERAGE IS:              2.10899E+01
RANGE IS:                8.14999E+00

END OF SUMMARY
```

Suppose the same list of numbers was preceded by a different selection of commands:

```
'MEAN', 'STD DEV', 'LIMITS', 'DATA'
```

The resulting output would be:

```
CG STATISTICAL PACKAGE

RUN ON                      780821                  AT                          170226080
FIRST VALUE IS:              2.33999E+01

SUMMARY OF RESULTS

NUMBER OF DATA ITEMS:              5

AVERAGE IS:                  2.10899E+01
STD DEV IS:                  3.20085E+00
95 PERCENT                  CONFIDENCE LIMITS ON THE MEAN:
                            LOWER LIMIT IS:          1.82843E+01
                            UPPER LIMIT IS:          2.38956E+01

END OF SUMMARY
```

This program exhibits several interesting points. Note that the separate loops to process commands and numbers employ different types of exits. The number loop uses an end-of-data exit, like the programs in 3.1. But the command loop cannot use such an exit since it must terminate before the physical end of the data list is reached. That is, it must terminate with the last command and must not read the numerical data. To facilitate exit from the command loop the user is required to separate commands and numbers by a terminal command 'DATA'.

You should conclude from this discussion that problem requirements are seldom stated so completely and precisely that programming is entirely a task of translation. Usually there is much left to the programmer's judgment and ingenuity. (This is one reason some people find programming interesting and others find it totally frustrating.) A good programmer attempts to anticipate the way in which a program will be used and to make the program as convenient as possible. He also trys to anticipate the shortcomings of the user, and designs the program to perform "reasonably" in the face of such shortcomings.

This program suggests an interesting point about the use of computed results. Unless you have had training in statistics you won't appreciate the meaning of "95 percent confidence limits on the mean". However any user, whether or not he understands and can interpret this, has only to specify 'LIMITS' to secure these results. This invites abuse -- the use of statistical procedures without concern for inherent assumptions and limitations. The following observation is made in the user's guide to a widely-used statistical system called SPSS:

> "The wide dissemination of statistical packages such as SPSS, containing large numbers of complex statistical procedures, have, almost overnight, made these techniques available to the social science community. There is little doubt that social scientists are using them, and there is equally little doubt that in many instances statistical techniques are being utilized by both students and researchers who understand neither the assumptions of the methods nor their statistical or mathematical bases. There also can be little doubt that this situation leads to some "garbage-in, garbage-out" research. The statistical procedures in SPSS have little ability to distinguish between proper and improper applications of the statistical techniques. They are basically blind computational algorithms that apply their formulas to whatever data the user enters. (Nie, et al; page 3)"

You as a programmer can do little to prevent uninformed and abusive use of a program, but it is nevertheless a significant aspect of the computing scene and you should be aware of it.

3.3 A Translation Program

A simple form of translation can be accomplished by replacing each word in a passage of text by the comparable word from an alternate vocabulary. For example, given the two parallel vocabularies:

```
boat          bateau
overloaded    surcharge'
large         grand
the           le
is            est
```

word replacement in

"The large boat is overloaded."

would yield

"Le grand bateau est surcharge'."

As another example, assuming that unmatched words are not replaced, the vocabularies

```
LIST        LINE
SKIP        NEW
PUT         PRINT
```

could be used to translate

```
PUT SKIP LIST ('RESULT IS:', AVG);
PUT LIST (COUNT);
```

into statements of some other programming language:

```
PRINT NEW LINE ('RESULT IS:', AVG);
PRINT LINE (COUNT);
```

In general, given two vocabulary lists, say the "left list" and the "right list", this translation requires searching the left list for each word. If it is found in the left list the word is replaced by the corresponding word from the right list.

A program to do this consists of three sections:

1. Preparatory.
2. Read vocabulary lists.
3. Translate input text.

Assuming the input text is divided into sentences, the third section could be described in more detail as follows:

```
3.  For each sentence of the input text:
    3.1 Print the given sentence.
    3.2 Replace each word in the sentence.
    3.3 Print the translated sentence.
```

The major task is, of course, "replace each word". This can be described in more detail:

```
3.2 For each word in the sentence:
    3.2.1 Isolate the word.
    3.2.2 Search the left list for the word.
          If found, replace it with corresponding
             word from right list.
    3.2.3 Append word (with or without
             replacement) to output sentence.
```

Initially we simplify the task by eliminating step 3.2.1. That is, we shift the burden of word isolation to the user by requiring that the input text be given as individual (quoted) words. With this change, it is also convenient to defer printing the given sentence (step 3.1) until after the word replacement (step 3.2).

The program follows:

```
/* CG TRANSLATION PROGRAM. USER INSTRUCTIONS:                        */
/* SUPPLY 2 VOCABULARIES, CALLED "LEFT" AND "RIGHT", IN THE          */
/* FORM OF N <= 30 PAIRS OF WORDS AS FOLLOWS:                        */
/*      N, 'LEFT WORD 1', 'RIGHT WORD 1', 'LEFT WORD 2',             */
/*      ... , 'LEFT WORD N', 'RIGHT WORD N'                          */
/* THE LENGTH OF INDIVIDUAL WORDS CANNOT EXCEED 20 CHARS.            */
/* FOLLOW VOCABULARIES WITH SENTENCES TO BE TRANSLATED. EACH         */
/* SENTENCE CONSISTS OF A SEQUENCE OF INDIVIDUAL WORDS               */
/* FOLLOWED BY THE SPECIAL WORD '*S*'.  THE LAST SENTENCE            */
/* IS FOLLOWED BY THE SPECIAL WORD '*T*'.  FOR EXAMPLE:              */
/*         'WORD 1', 'WORD 2', '*S*',                                */
/*         'WORD 3', ... , '*S*',                                    */
/*         '*T*'                                                     */
/* SENTENCES OF LENGTH GREATER THAN 100 CHARACTERS ARE               */
/* DIVIDED AT CONVENIENT POINTS                                      */

TRANS: PROCEDURE OPTIONS(MAIN);
    DCL VL FIXED;              /* SIZE OF VOCABULARIES */
    DCL (LEFT(31),             /* LEFT(I), RIGHT(I) ARE THE ITH */
        RIGHT(31))             /* WORD AND ITS TRANSLATION. POS */
         CHAR(20) VARYING;     /* 31 IS FOR A "SENTINEL".       */
    DCL (GSENT,                /* PART OF SENTENCE, AND ITS     */
        TSENT)                 /* TRANSLATION,  THAT IS READ    */
         CHAR(120) VARYING;    /* IN BUT NOT YET PRINTED.       */
    DCL WORD CHAR(20) VARYING;
    DCL I FIXED;
    PUT LIST ('CG TRANSLATION PROGRAM', DATE);
    PUT SKIP(2) LIST (
            'TRANSLATION BASED ON FOLLOWING VOCABULARIES:');
    PUT SKIP LIST (' ', 'INPUT', 'OUTPUT');

    /** LOAD VOCABULARY LISTS */
        GET LIST (VL);
        IF (VL < 1) | (VL > 30)
            THEN PUT SKIP LIST ('IMPROPER VOCABULARY LENGTH:',
                    VL);
        DO I = 1 TO VL BY 1;
            GET LIST (LEFT(I), RIGHT(I));
            PUT SKIP LIST (' ', LEFT(I), RIGHT(I));
            END;
```

```
/** READ WORDS, TRANSLATE, PRINT SENTENCES */
    GET LIST (WORD);
    SENTENCES: DO WHILE (WORD ¬= '*T*');
        GSENT, TSENT = '';
        SENTENCE: DO WHILE (WORD ¬= '*S*' &
                MAX(LENGTH(GSENT), LENGTH(TSENT)) <= 100 );
            GSENT = GSENT || WORD || ' ';
            /** REPLACE LEFT WORD WITH RIGHT */
                LEFT(VL+1), RIGHT(VL+1) = WORD;
                I = 1;
                DO WHILE (LEFT(I) ¬= WORD);
                    I = I + 1;
                    END;
                WORD = RIGHT(I);
            TSENT ...
            GET LIST (WORD);
            END SENTENCE;
        IF LENGTH(GSENT) ¬= 0
            THEN DO;
                PUT SKIP(3) LIST ('SENTENCE:', GSENT);
                PUT SKIP(2) LIST ('TRANSLATION:', TSENT);
                GSENT, TSENT = '';
                END;
        IF WORD = '*S*'
            THEN GET LIST (WORD);
        END SENTENCES;

PUT SKIP(4) LIST ('END OF TRANSLATION');
END TRANS;
```

An example of the use of this program is shown below. Suppose the following data is presented to the program:

```
8,
'BOAT',          'BATEAU',
'OVERLOADED',    'SURCHARGE''',
'LARGE',         'GRAND',
'THE',           'LE',
'IS',            'EST',
'LIST',          'LINE',
'SKIP',          'NEW',
'PUT',           'PRINT',

'THE', 'LARGE', 'BOAT', 'IS', 'OVERLOADED', '*S*',

'PUT', 'SKIP', 'LIST', '(''RESULT IS:'',', 'AVG);', '*S*',
'PUT', 'LIST', '(COUNT);', '*S*',

'*T*'
```

The resulting output would be:

```
CG TRANSLATION PROGRAM  780821

TRANSLATION BASED ON FOLLOWING VOCABULARIES:
                            INPUT                   OUTPUT
                            BOAT                    BATEAU
                            OVERLOADED              SURCHARGE'
                            LARGE                   GRAND
                            THE                     LE
                            IS                      EST
                            LIST                    LINE
                            SKIP                    NEW
                            PUT                     PRINT

SENTENCE:                   THE LARGE BOAT IS OVERLOADED

TRANSLATION:                LE GRAND BATEAU EST SURCHARGE'

SENTENCE:                   PUT SKIP LIST ('RESULT IS:', AVG);

TRANSLATION:                PRINT NEW LINE ('RESULT IS:', AVG);

SENTENCE:                   PUT LIST (COUNT);

TRANSLATION:                PRINT LINE (COUNT);


END OF TRANSLATION
```

An interesting feature of this program is the strategy used to search the left vocabulary list. The search is initialized by inserting the word being sought as a "sentinel" at the end of both lists. This ensures that the search of the left list will always be successful, and that replacement of left with right can always take place -- even when the word is actually not in the given left vocabulary.

3.4 Interactive Programs

The distinctive characteristic of an "interactive" computing system is, as the name implies, the opportunity for the user to interact with the program during its execution. He does this by supplying data to be read by the GET statements as they are executed in the program. The key point is that he does not have to supply all the data at once and in advance of execution. Up to this point we have been describing computer systems where the data are prepared and submitted as a unit with the program for processing. When processing is completed all the output is returned in one batch to the user. These are often called "batch" processing systems.

Now we are talking about a system in which the user employs a "terminal" -- usually a device like an electric typewriter, although sometimes equippped with a TV-like screen on which characters are displayed rather than a printing mechanism. The terminal is connected directly to the computer while the program is being executed. Execution output -- the result of executing PUT statements -- appears on the terminal, and the data requested by the execution of GET statements is entered from the terminal. The crucial point is that the input and output are interleaved on this same device, corresponding to the order in which GETs and PUTs are encountered in execution of the program. This means that the data are not entered all at once, but just as needed for each execution of a GET statement. In deciding what data to supply in response to a particular request the user has before him all of the execution output produced up to that point in the program. The user interacts with the program by examining output and deciding on the basis of this information what data to supply in response to the next request. This in turn may influence the next output to appear, which affects future input, etc.

This mode of operation opens up some interesting new possibilities. The user and the program can cooperate or they can compete. For example, a problem could be attacked by a "trial and error" strategy in which the user supplies a trial value and the program obtains a solution based on this estimate and reports it to the terminal. The user then supplies the next trial value based somehow on the results of the previous trials. If the user can precisely describe the algorithm by which new trial values are determined from previous results then it can be incorporated into the program and the entire process can be run in the conventional batch mode. But there are some problems where the selection of new trial values is largely intuitive and the user cannot readily reduce his thought process to an algorithm. An interactive system allows some part of the process to remain intuitive while part is described algorithmically in the program. If done cleverly this makes it possible to combine the best features of human intelligence and computer processing, and allows an attack on problems that are not susceptible to a completely intuitive or completely algorithmic approach.

Another opportunity arises in programs in which the user is the adversary of the program. These are called "game-playing" problems, although the objective may in fact be serious business rather than pure entertainment. In such programs the user makes a "move" and describes it in input data to the program. The program operates on these data to determine its own "move", and reports this to the user. The program is usually performing two roles. It implements the mechanics of operating the game, as well as the implementation of the strategy of the opponent. (The user must trust that these roles are fairly separated and that his automated opponent is not in programmed collusion with the referee.)

In principle, an interactive system could be used for any problem a batch system could execute, in addition to those interactive problems for which it is uniquely qualified. However, interactive execution is generally more costly than batch execution, and the terminal is a relatively slow device for input and output. Hence programs with voluminous input and/or output may be painfully slow on an interactive system, and it may be somewhat extravagant to use an interactive system where its unique capabilities are not required. This issue is the subject of impassioned argument, with the apostles of interaction maintaining that a good, flexible interactive system is uniformly preferable and that eventually all computing will be done in this mode. Their arguments are quite persuasive.

The principal differences in programming technique appropriate for an interactive system are concerned with obtaining input from the terminal. There are two key issues: <u>prompting</u> and <u>persistence</u> in the face of errors.

Prompting is the process of providing instructions to the user at each point that input is required. Each GET in an interactive program will ordinarily be immediately preceded by a PUT which displays at the terminal sufficient instructions to tell the user what is expected of him. This is unique to an interactive system since in a batch system nothing printed by a particular execution of a program can be seen by the user in time to be of any help to him in preparing input. Once you understand the opportunity to prompt, and the need for it, it is not difficult to compose appropriate messages. However, unless your system uses a display screen you must remember that these messages will be printed on a printer that is painfully slow. It takes practice to develop skill in composing messages that are concise without being cryptic.

Long descriptive messages that are initially very helpful to the user will eventually become unnecessary, and finally become very annoying. It is often desirable to have several levels of prompting and to be able to switch to an abbreviated form as execution continues. For example, a Checker-playing program might initially prompt the user:

```
ENTER YOUR MOVE ON THE TERMINAL.  GIVE RANK AND FILE  OF
PIECE TO BE MOVED, AND THEN RANK AND FILE WHERE IT IS TO
BE MOVED.  THAT IS, GIVE MOVE AS 4 INTEGERS.
```

After the first move this could be reduced to:

```
YOUR MOVE.
```

An interactive program has the same responsibility as a batch program for testing its input for errors, but the interactive program can respond to errors in a very different way. Since the batch program cannot communicate with the user until after execution is completed it has only two options when an error is encountered: either <u>abort execution</u>, or effect some form of <u>repair</u> so execution can continue. The interactive program has the additional possibility of going back to the user and asking him to <u>try again</u>. This is so much more effective than either of the batch strategies that it is almost always used. The interactive program should <u>persistently return to the user</u> until it elicits the required input. For example, a program segment to print instructions for a Checker game could be programmed as follows:

```
/** PRINT OPTIONAL INSTRUCTIONS */
   PUT SKIP LIST ('DO YOU WANT INSTRUCTIONS?');
   ANSWER = ' ';
   DO WHILE ((ANSWER ¬= 'YES') | (ANSWER ¬= 'NO'));
       PUT LIST ('ANSWER ''YES'' OR ''NO''');
       GET LIST (ANSWER);
       END;
   IF ANSWER = 'YES'
       THEN DO;
           /** PRINT RULES OF CHECKERS */
               PUT SKIP LIST (...
```

The loop in this segment will not terminate until a valid answer -- in this case either 'YES' or 'NO' -- is obtained from the terminal.

A segment such as this should be the standard technique for every request for input in an interactive system -- that is, a prompting message followed by a persistent loop that will not terminate until an acceptable response has been obtained.

A more sophisticated version of this approach would be to produce <u>more</u> detailed information as the user shows less ability to provide reasonable answers. A very short prompting message would be used initially, with provision for additional and more detailed information to be printed if the user does not respond successfully on his first try. Some interactive programs are written so they will accept some word such as "help" as input to any request -- and the program responds by describing what the user's options are at that point.

3.4.1 A Game-Playing Program

We will illustrate a complete program for an interactive system using a simple variation of a venerable game called NIM. This variation is just complex enough to be interesting, yet is simple enough to describe and program.

We call the game "Match-Snatch". There are two players. Our program will represent one player and the user at the terminal will be the other player, but we will initially describe the game as it would be played by two people.

Some number of matchsticks are placed in a pile between the two players. A "move" is for a player to remove some number of matches from those remaining in the pile. To be a valid move, he must take at least one match, and not more than some number agreed upon as a move-limit before the game begins. The players alternate moves and the object of the game is to avoid being the player who has to take the last match. (Obviously, without the move-limit the game would be trivial since faced with a pile of n matches the first player would immediately take n-1 and the second player would lose on his first move.) A typical game might start with a pile of fifteen matches and have a move-limit of three. In the computer version of Match-Snatch there will, of course, not actually be any physical pile of matches. A variable, say MATCHES, will represent the number of matches in the imagined pile. The removal of matches from the pile will be simulated by announcing an integer representing the number to be removed. This number will be subtracted from MATCHES and the game will terminate when the value of MATCHES becomes zero.

There is an algorithm for playing this game that will allow the first player to assure himself victory if he unfailingly follows the algorithm. If he lapses on even one move, then this same algorithm becomes available to his opponent and allows him to guarantee victory -- if he is more careful. It is not difficult to discover what this algorithm is. Suppose the move-limit is k matches. If you can take enough matches to leave just one in the pile your opponent will lose on his next move. So obviously, if the pile presented to you on some move contains n matches, where 2 <= n <= k+1, you will simply take n-1 matches and leave your opponent with 1. But if n > k+1 it is not that simple since you cannot take enough matches to leave only 1. However, if you manage to leave k+2 matches in the pile after your move, no matter how many matches your opponent takes in his next move he cannot leave you with 1, and you will be able to leave him with 1 on your next move. By repeating this reasoning, you will discover that if you leave 2k+3 matches after some move you will surely be able to leave k+2 after the next move and leave 1 on the move after that. In general, if you can arrange to leave m(k+1)+1 matches in the pile after your move, for m=0,1,2,..., you will be able to win the game in m more moves. But if you ever fail to leave m(k+1)+1 matches after your move then your opponent can move to leave you m(k+1)+1 and he is in the driver's seat unless he gets careless (or doesn't understand the game).

Our Match-Snatch program uses this algorithm for the computer's moves, so that if the user grants the computer the first move the user will always lose (unless the user has been clever and chosen initial values for the number of matches and the move-limit so that the number of matches is m(k+1)+1 when the program makes its first move.) If the user claims the first move he can win, but if he slips up just once the computer will seize the opportunity and win.

In addition to acting as one player the Match-Snatch program also operates the game. It negotiates the initial conditions with the user, keeps track of the number of matches and announces the outcome. A high-level comment outline would be the following:

```
/* MATCH-SNATCH GAME */
   /** INITIALIZATION */
       /** GET GAME PARAMETERS */
       /** DETERMINE WHO MOVES FIRST */
   /** ALTERNATE MOVES -- USER & PROGRAM */
   /** REPORT OUTCOME */
```

A complete program to play Match-Snatch on an interactive system is given below. The format shown is PL/CT, which is based on PL/C.

```
/* MATCH-SNATCH GAME */
MATCH_SNATCH: PROCEDURE OPTIONS(MAIN);
   DCL (MATCHES,        /* NUMBER OF MATCHES LEFT */
        MOVE_LIMIT,     /* LIMIT ON EACH MOVE */
        MOVE)           /* CURRENT MOVE */
        FIXED;
   DCL (WHOSE_MOVE) CHAR(3) VAR; /* 'YOU'=PROG; 'ME'=USER */

   /** INITIALIZATION */
       /** GET GAME PARAMETERS */
           PUT SKIP LIST('WELCOME TO MATCH-SNATCH');
           PUT SKIP;
           MATCHES = 0;
           DO WHILE(MATCHES < 1);
               PUT SKIP LIST
                  ('HOW MANY MATCHES TO START?');
               GET LIST (MATCHES);
               IF MATCHES < 1
                   THEN PUT SKIP LIST
                       ('MUST BE AT LEAST 1');
               END;
           MOVE_LIMIT = 0;
           DO WHILE((MOVE_LIMIT < 1) |
                   (MOVE_LIMIT > MATCHES));
               PUT SKIP LIST
                  ('HOW MANY IN 1 MOVE?');
               GET LIST (MOVE_LIMIT);
               IF MOVE_LIMIT < 1
                   THEN PUT SKIP LIST
                           ('MUST BE AT LEAST 1');
               IF MOVE_LIMIT > MATCHES
                   THEN PUT SKIP LIST
                           ('NOT THAT MANY MATCHES');
               END;

       /** DETERMINE WHO MOVES FIRST */
           WHOSE_MOVE = ' ';
           DO WHILE((WHOSE_MOVE ¬= 'ME') &
                    (WHOSE_MOVE ¬= 'YOU'));
               PUT SKIP LIST ('WHO MOVES FIRST?',
                       '''YOU'' OR ''ME''');
               GET LIST (WHOSE_MOVE);
               END;
```

```
        PUT SKIP;
/** ALTERNATE MOVES -- USER & PROGRAM */
    MOVE_LOOP: DO WHILE(MATCHES > 0);
      IF WHOSE_MOVE = 'ME'
       THEN DO; /* USER'S MOVE */
        MOVE = 0;
        USER_LOOP: DO WHILE((MOVE < 1) |
                (MOVE > MATCHES) | (MOVE > MOVE_LIMIT));
          PUT SKIP LIST
            ('HOW MANY DO YOU TAKE?');
          GET LIST (MOVE);
          IF MOVE < 1
            THEN PUT SKIP LIST
                ('MUST TAKE AT LEAST 1');
          IF MOVE > MOVE_LIMIT
            THEN PUT SKIP LIST
                ('THAT''S MORE THAN WE AGREED ON');
          IF MOVE > MATCHES
            THEN PUT SKIP LIST
                ('THERE AREN''T THAT MANY');
          END USER_LOOP;
        MATCHES = MATCHES - MOVE;
        PUT SKIP LIST ('THERE ARE', MATCHES, 'LEFT');
        WHOSE_MOVE = 'YOU';
        END;
       ELSE DO; /* PROGRAM'S MOVE */
        MOVE = MOD(MATCHES -1, MOVE_LIMIT + 1);
        IF MOVE = 0
            THEN MOVE = 1;
        PUT SKIP LIST ('I TAKE', MOVE, 'MATCHES');
        MATCHES = MATCHES - MOVE;
        PUT SKIP LIST ('THERE ARE', MATCHES, 'LEFT');
        WHOSE_MOVE = 'ME';
        END;
      END MOVE_LOOP;

/** REPORT OUTCOME */
        /* PLAYER WHO MADE LAST MOVE LOST */
    IF WHOSE_MOVE = 'ME'
        THEN PUT SKIP(2) LIST
            ('YOU WON, NICE GOING.');
        ELSE PUT SKIP(2) LIST
            ('I WON, TOUGH LUCK.');

END MATCH_SNATCH;
```

Playing Match-Snatch by executing this program on an interactive system would produce output similar to the lines shown below. We have indented the lines that represent input from the terminal to distinguish them from output printed by the program. We have also slightly modified the format of some of the output lines relative to that actually produced by the program.

```
WELCOME TO MATCH-SNATCH

HOW MANY MATCHES TO START?
    10
HOW MANY IN 1 MOVE?
    0
MUST BE AT LEAST 1
HOW MANY IN 1 MOVE?
    15
NOT THAT MANY MATCHES
HOW MANY IN 1 MOVE?
    4
WHO MOVES FIRST?  'YOU' OR 'ME'
    'I DO'
WHO MOVES FIRST?  'YOU' OR 'ME'
    'ME'

HOW MANY DO YOU TAKE?
    9
THAT'S MORE THAN WE AGREED ON
HOW MANY DO YOU TAKE?
    2
THERE ARE 8 LEFT
I TAKE 2 MATCHES
THERE ARE 6 LEFT
HOW MANY DO YOU TAKE?
    2
THERE ARE 4 LEFT
I TAKE 3 MATCHES
THERE ARE 1 LEFT
HOW MANY DO YOU TAKE?
    0
MUST TAKE AT LEAST 1
HOW MANY DO YOU TAKE?
    2
THERE AREN'T THAT MANY
HOW MANY DO YOU TAKE?
    1

I WON, TOUGH LUCK.
```

Section 3 <u>Exercises</u>

1. The user instructions for the program of Section 3.2 specify the command 'DATA' should separate the commands from the list of numbers. Based on the program given, what are the <u>actual</u> requirements for the command to denote the beginning of the list of numbers?

2. Given the program and user-instructions in Section 3.3, what are some errors that are likely to be frequently made by users? How will the program react to each of these errors?

3. How would the translation program of Section 3.3 have to be modified to make leading blanks irrelevant. That is, if 'X' was in the left list and 'b̸X' was given in a sentence, these two words would be considered equivalent. The program should also ensure that no word in either vocabulary list has any leading blanks.

Section 4 Program Schemata

When we introduced the IF construction in Section I.4.3 we gave the model of the construction as

```
IF condition
   THEN statement
```

This gave the form or "schema" of that conditional statement in PL/I. The symbol "statement" in the schema stands for any simple or compound PL/I statement. The symbol "condition" stands for any simple or compound condition. Written in this form, before some particular statement and particular condition is specified, the schema is said to be "uninterpreted". We defined the action of the IF construction in terms of an uninterpreted schema; that is, we described its action independent of what particular statement and particular condition might be given in a specific example.

This seems like a complicated way of explaining something that was fairly obvious on first encounter, but we would like to extend this argument to larger program constructions. For example, (4a) is a schema for a particular kind of repetition unit, one in which the body is to be repeated a definite number of times:

```
        /** Comment describing action of the unit */
           i = 0;
           DO WHILE ( i < n );
               i = i + 1;
(4a)           Body
               END;
```

This schema is uninterpreted with respect to the body, the index variable i, the stopping value n, the loop-name and the statement-comment -- the elements given in lower-case letters. A particular example or interpretation of this schema would have these lower-case elements replaced by specific PL/I elements. For example, the following are specific interpretations of (4a):

```
/** MOVE A(1:K) TO B(1:K) */
    J = 0;
    DO WHILE (J < K);
         J = J + 1;
         B(J) = A(J);
         END;

/** PRINT 12 LINES OF 10 *'S EACH */
    I = 0;
    DO WHILE (I < 12);
         I = I + 1;
         PUT SKIP LIST('**********');
         END;


/** CLEAR X(1:K) TO ZERO */
    M = 0;
    DO WHILE (M < K);
         M = M + 1;
         X(M) = 0;
         END;


/** CLEAR A(1:K,2:M) IF < A(1:K,1) */
    I = 0;
    CLRK_LOOP: DO WHILE (I < K);
         I = I + 1;
         /** CLEAR ITH ROW */
              DO J = 2 TO M BY 1;
                   IF A(I,J) < A(I,1)
                        THEN A(I,J) = 0;
                   END;
         END CLRK_LOOP;
```

Although these examples perform very different tasks, in each case the basic structure is the same -- some task is repeated a definite number of times. That subtask may be a single statement or a substantial program segment, but the statements that control its repetition are the same (except for the particular names used). Each of these examples follows the pattern shown in (4a) with the lower-case elements of (4a) replaced by particular PL/I elements. These different interpretations of (4a) <u>differ</u> from each other <u>only in the choices of specific elements to replace the lower-case elements of (4a)</u>.

Definite repetition is a common task, and (4a) can be regarded as a schema for a "statement" to accomplish this task. You can learn this schema and use it more-or-less automatically each time that you need to repeat some action a definite number of times. It means that you will not have to "re-invent" a mechanism for definite repetition each time it is required.

There are many other common tasks and corresponding schemata. For example, suppose some action is to be performed on each item of a data list, where the end of the list is recognized by the presence of some distinctive value. (4b) gives an appropriate schema:

```
        /** Comment describing task and stopping flag */
            Initialize
            GET LIST(item);
            DO WHILE(item ¬= stopping flag);
(4b)           Perform action on item
                GET LIST(item);
                END;
```

Each of the following is an example (or interpretation) of (4b):

```
        /** FIND MAX X, STOPPING AT FIRST 0 */
            XMAX = 0;
            GET LIST(X);
            DO WHILE (X ¬= 0);
                IF X > XMAX
                    THEN XMAX = X;
                GET LIST(X);
                END;

        /** PRINT, SUM AND COUNT DATA UNTIL -999 */
            PUT SKIP(2) LIST('LIST OF INPUT DATA:');
            PUT SKIP;
            SUM = 0;
            COUNT = 0;
            GET LIST(ITEM);
                DO WHILE(ITEM ¬= -999);
                PUT SKIP LIST(ITEM);
                SUM = SUM + ITEM;
                COUNT = COUNT + 1;
                GET LIST(ITEM);
                END;
```

An especially common task in programs is to perform some action on each element of an array, or on some portion of an array. (4c) gives a schema for this task:

```
        /** Perform action on each element of a(j:k) */
            Initialize
            DO i = j TO k BY 1;
(4c)           Perform action on a(i)
                END;
```

The following are examples of interpretations of (4c):

```
        /** DISPLAY VALUES OF AR(A:B) */
            PUT SKIP(3) LIST('VALUES OF AR(A:B)');
            PUT SKIP LIST('A =', A, 'B =', B);
            PUT SKIP;
            DO I = 1 TO A BY 1;
                PUT SKIP LIST(AR(I));
                END;
```

```
/** LOAD X(1:N) FROM DATA */
    DO I = 1 TO N BY 1;
        GET LIST(X(I));
        END;


/** MOVE X(1:N) TO Y(1:N) */
    DO J = 1 TO N BY 1;
        Y(J) = X(J);
        END;
```

Sometimes a task can be viewed in several different ways. For example, suppose you are required to read data values into an array X(1:N), but not past the first -1 in the data list. That is, the reading process will read N values, or up to the first -1, whichever occurs first. This could be written as an interpretation of (4c):

```
/** LOAD X(1:N), UP TO FIRST -1 */
    DO I = 1 TO N BY 1;
        GET LIST(X(I));
        IF X(I) = -1
            THEN LEAVE;
        END;
```

Alternatively, the same task could be written as an interpretation of (4b):

```
/** LOAD X(1:N), UP TO FIRST -1 */
    I = 1;
    GET LIST(X(I));
    DO WHILE (X(I) ¬= -1);
        I = I + 1;
        IF I > N
            THEN LEAVE;
        GET LIST(X(I));
        END;
```

These segments are quite comparable and there is no strong reason to prefer one over the other. However, you might note that it is <u>possible that neither is correct</u>, depending upon the precise requirements of the problem. Both will include the stopping flag value (-1) as an element of X if it occurs within the first N items on the data list. This may well not be a valid element for X and probably should not be included. Also note that for either example the only way of knowing how many items were actually loaded is the value of I after finishing the loop, and this value is <u>1 too large</u>. That is, the final value is I is either N+1 or the subscript of the element containing -1. Either version could be written to avoid this flaw. For example:

```
/** LOAD X(1:N), UP TO FIRST -1 */
    I = 0;
    GET LIST(Y);
    DO WHILE (Y ¬= -1);
        IF I = N
            THEN LEAVE;
        I = I + 1;
        X(I) = Y;
        GET LIST(Y);
        END;
```

As a final example of a schema, another common task is to perform some action on each element of a data list, when the list is preceded by an integer specifying the number of items on the list. An appropriate schema is given in (4d).

```
        /** Read n, and perform action on n following items */
            Initialize
            GET LIST(n);
            DO WHILE (n > 0);
                GET LIST(item);
(4d)            Perform action on item
                n = n - 1;
                END;
```

An interpretation of (4d) is the following:

```
/** LOAD M ELEMENTS INTO A(1:N) */
    I = 0;
    GET LIST(M);
    LOADLOOP: DO WHILE (M > 0);
        IF I > N
            THEN DO;
                PUT SKIP(2) LIST('EXCESS DATA');
                LEAVE LOADLOOP;
                END;
        I = I + 1;
        GET LIST(A(I));
        M = M - 1;
        END LOADLOOP;
```

We cannot catalog all common program tasks for you and give schemata for them. We are just trying to make you aware that certain patterns recur frequently, and that you should learn to recognize them. You should develop your own repertoire of schemata, and apply them whenever a familiar task appears. This will save you the time and effort of re-inventing solutions to these problems, and make your programs more consistent and predictable.

Notice that it is the <u>control structure</u> of the segment that recurs more often than the specific action. The action will vary from problem to problem, but the manner in which it is repeated is often familiar. There are infinitely many different problems to be solved -- you will rarely meet one that is identical to one you have solved before. But any problem can be broken down into sections, and many of the sections may be recognizable as some action to be repeated in some familiar way. Viewed in this way, even large problems are not quite so formidable.

Part III
The Development of a Program

Section 1 The Phases of Development

Our task is to write a program to solve some problem. Given an initial problem description, we have to plan a way in which a computer can be used to solve the problem, and then describe this plan very precisely in some programming language. This process has four distinct phases:

1. Clarify the problem requirements.

2. Design a program strategy.

3. Specify critical data structures.

4. Write the program statements.

Although these phases should occur roughly in the order listed, there is generally a good deal of overlap and backtracking, and particularly for small problems the phases are difficult to separate. Nevertheless they each represent a distinct function that must be performed.

At least initially, while you are struggling to learn the details of a programming language, phase four may look the most formidable. With practice and experience you will discover that if the other three phases are properly done then writing the program statements is quite straightforward. It may still be time-consuming but it will not be the critical phase.

1.1 Clarification of the Problem

Surprisingly, clarification of the problem is a major phase of the process. It would seem reasonable that a clear and precise statement of the problem would be given, but in fact this is rarely the case and more programming disasters can be blamed on failure in this regard than on any other. It is easy to slightly misunderstand the exact requirements and therefore to write a program that solves the wrong problem. This phase is hard enough even in a programming course where the problem is stated by someone who (presumably) understands what can be programmed and chooses problems to be only interestingly difficult. Real problems are usually posed by someone who isn't sure exactly what he wants done, much less how the computer is going to contribute to a solution, and the problem definition usually becomes precise only in response to persistent and pointed questions on the part of the programmer.

A substantial fraction of the clarification dialog is concentrated on three key issues:

1. Input. What is its format and order? What are the limits of volume and how will the end of the input be recognized? What are the limits on input values?

2. Output. What is the content, format and order of output? What titling is appropriate? What limits on volume may be expected?

3. Errors. What types of errors (both in input and in processing) must the program guard against and what action should be taken when they are encountered? Which specifications can be taken as guaranteed and which only as good intentions -- to be checked by the program?

For example, suppose you are given the following problem:

(1.1a) Write a program to compute the sum of a list of numbers.

This statement gives only a general idea of the objective of the program; more detailed information is required before you can begin to design the program. For example:

1a. Can the data be presented on punched cards in a format acceptable to the PL/I GET LIST statement?

b. How many values can there be? How can the end of the list of values be recognized?

c. What types and sizes of values might be expected?

2a. In what form should the sum be displayed?

b. What identifying title should be provided?

3a. What action should be taken for values that violate the specifications of 1c?

b. What action should be taken if the quantity of values violates instructions given in 1b?

After obtaining specific answers to these questions you might have the following refinement of (1.1a):

(1.1b) Write a program to compute the sum of a list of positive integers given in PL/I LIST format. The end of the data list will be denoted by two consecutive values of -999. Improper values on the list should be rejected (excluded from the sum) and printed on a list titled "REJECTED VALUES:". Any irregularity in termination should result in a warning message. The result should be given in three lines, after the list of rejects (if any):

```
SUM OF POSITIVE INTEGERS

    n VALUES INCLUDED

    SUM IS s
```

As a second example, consider a simple text-processing problem:

(1.1c) Write a program to delete duplicates from a word list.

Clarification of (1.1c) might result in something like the following:

(1.1d) Write a program to print a list of words, one per line, in the order given, but excluding any word that has appeared earlier in the list. The data will be given as an integer n ($0 \leq n \leq 100$) followed by n words, each a quoted character string in LIST format. A word must contain from one to twenty characters. Each word should consist only of letters A-Z; no digits, blanks or special characters are allowed. The output should be given as follows:

```
WORD LIST WITHOUT DUPLICATES:
    m ENTRIES

    first word
    second word
    ...
```

The value m given in the title indicates the length of the final list, after duplicates and improper words have been rejected. Report any difficulties with the length of the list, but produce some list if at all possible.

(1.1b) and (1.1d) anticipate many of the difficulties the programmer must face. Given a description in this form and this much detail, the program is well specified and not difficult to write. But, in general, (1.1a) and (1.1c) are examples of what you can *expect to be given* as an initial problem statement, while (1.1b) and (1.1d) are examples of what *you must produce* by asking the right questions. In a programming course your assignments may look more like (1.1b) and (1.1d), but some day you will face problems like (1.1a) and (1.1c).

Whenever possible, obtain *samples of input* and *corresponding output*. English is disappointingly ambiguous, and a concrete example often clarifies (or obviates) a voluminous description.

When beginning on a problem don't initially think too much about the *program* you are to write; concentrate on the *problem* until the detailed requirements are absolutely clear. Make up several sets of input data, and figure out the corresponding output results. This sample data should be designed to test and increase your understanding of the *details* of the problem, and not just its general nature. It might seem a waste of time to make up input data and perform hand calculations, but in doing so you are actually executing an algorithm to solve the problem. Thus while concentrating on understanding the problem, you are also working toward designing the solution.

While studying the problem you should ask questions like "What is to be done if the input number is incorrect?", "What happens if this particular number is 0? Is it correct or incorrect and what should I do with it?", and "What should I do here -- the problem statement seems to be ambiguous?" It is important that these questions be raised and answered *before* any programming is done. Proper understanding of the problem before programming is crucial. Without this understanding, the program can never be correct.

Clarification of a significant problem is rarely completed as the first step in development. Often you will discover the omission of some necessary detail in the problem requirements only after you are engaged in the detailed execution of a later phase. For example, you may discover the lack of some detail about the volume of data only when you are attempting to specify the data structures and need a specific value to give as the size of an array. Or you may discover that you don't know how to process a particular error when actually writing the statements to check for that error. In either case, you have discovered that the first phase is not quite completed and needs more work.

1.2 Design of a Solution Strategy

This is certainly the hardest part of the process for which to give general advice. Much of the creativity in programming is concentrated in this phase. We can give suggestions as to where you may get ideas, and describe some helpful procedures for developing ideas once you have them -- but we recognize that we are helping you least where you need it most. We recommend you read Polya's classic book How to Solve It.

One useful tactic is to initially ignore the computer, and figure out how you would solve the problem by hand. Assume you are presented with the input data on cards in such a way that you can see each item only once, and only in the order given. Assume further that the only "scratch paper" available to you is a number of small cards (one number or string apiece) on which you can write, erase and rewrite numbers. If you can solve the problem by hand under these restrictions, you can describe that method in a program.

The important thing is to separate the process of planning a solution from the task of describing that solution in a programming language. Once you make this separation, the challenging and difficult part of the process will be the planning. For example, if you cannot write a program to "sort" a list of numbers into increasing order, it is probably because you cannot figure out how to do it systematically by hand, and not because you don't know PL/I. Conversely, if your sort program is efficient it is because you devised a clever plan, and not because a mediocre plan was cleverly described in PL/I.

1.2.1 Algorithms

The plan for a program is generally called an "algorithm". An algorithm is a sequence of steps, whose execution solves a problem.

Algorithms are written in whatever language and notation will make them understandable to the reader. Often we assume a certain background and knowledge on the part of the reader and adopt technical vocabulary that makes the algorithm more precise and compact. Algorithms are written for people to read, rather than for computers and are therefore generally not written in a programming language. We adopt or invent whatever language seems best for the particular problem. Often this is a combination of English, mathematics and whatever technical vocabulary is peculiar to the problem area.

A program is an algorithm that has been translated into a programming language. We regard a program as a specific implementation of an algorithm. The point is that the algorithm is written first, in an informal (but still precise) English-like language. The program comes later, by a process of translation rather than creation.

An algorithm can be translated into different programming languages. However, since we often know in advance what language we will use, we tend to bias the algorithm toward convenient operations of that language. In our case, knowing that we are headed for a PL/I program, we start with a mixture of English and PL/I, using PL/I terms where convenient but inventing terms whenever that seems more convenient. Generally the invented terms are at a "higher level" than PL/I statements. For example, we might say "Swap A and B". Since PL/I has no single statement to "swap", this will later have to be translated into three assignment statements:

```
T = A;
A = B;
B = T;
```

In algorithms we can use terms like "find", "solve", and "search" that are at a much higher level than program statements and that will eventually have to be expressed as a substantial segment of program. In our examples, as we illustrate the gradual and systematic conversion of an algorithm into a program, we use upper case (capital) letters for phrases in PL/I and lower case letters for phrases that have not yet been translated into PL/I.

We will sometimes simply replace the English phrase with its PL/I equivalent, but usually we will use the English phrase in the program as a statement-comment, to be followed by the indented PL/I statements that perform the task described by the comment.

1.3 Choice of Data Structures

Key decisions must be made with regard to what elements of the problem will require storage. Variables have to be specified, with names, dimensions, type attributes, and descriptions of the logical relationship between variables. Much of this information obviously comes from the clarification of the problem, but the choice of data structures depends equally importantly on the program strategy.

The specification of data structures takes place after the program strategy has been chosen, and sometimes the final decisions can be delayed until after most of the actual program statements are written. In general, postpone the final specification of data structures as long as possible. This will reduce the backtracking that is required. Often, details don't become clear until much of the program has been written.

Relationships between variables are important, and you should emphasize these relationships by the order of declarations.

Reread Section II.1. It helps to write these relationships <u>precisely</u> before writing the final program statements.

1.4 Writing the Actual Program Statements

Relatively little needs to be said about the detailed programming phase. If phase two has been adequately done you have a <u>detailed comment outline</u> describing the action of each segment of the program. Phase three has defined the objects upon which those units must act. All that remains is to translate these detailed specifications into statements of PL/I (or whatever programming language is being employed).

However, as suggested earlier, as you write the detailed program statements you often discover that the data structures are not quite right, so you have to return to phase three. You may also find it necessary to return to phase two to alter the organization of the program. Rarely can you complete the detailed translation without having to return at least once to phase one to clarify some aspect of the problem definition, which in turn may require changes in the program organization or data structures. Backing up and making changes can be a tricky business. The difficulty lies in making sure that you have identified <u>all</u> the implications of the change and have made all the necessary adjustments.

Few people compose well at a keypunch or terminal. The usual practice is to write the program statements by hand, and then to key-enter from this handwritten copy. The accuracy of the keying depends, to a considerable extent, upon the legibility of the handwritten copy. We often see students keying from a barely-legible copy. This inevitably introduces errors into the program. I's get mistaken for 1's, 2's for Z's, and O's for zeros. Variables get misspelled, statements get omitted, and inserts get inserted in the wrong place. Considering how hard it is to detect and remove errors once they are in a program it is worth spending time and effort keeping them out in the first place.

Section 2 Approaches to Program Development

The hardest part of the process is unquestionably the planning and design of the program, rather than the translation of that design into the statements of a programming language. Students who have difficulty in programming often believe their problem is unfamiliarity with the language, when actually it is inability to find a suitable design for the program. Programming is not unusual in this regard. For example, it is easier to learn the "moves" of the various pieces in chess than it is to learn how to use the moves to play an effective game. It is easier to learn the axioms and some theorems in geometry than it is to learn how to construct proofs from these components. These are all examples of a process called "synthesis", which is one of the most demanding kinds of intellectual activity. In any form, it requires a certain amount of insight and inventiveness and, as far as we know, no one has been enormously successful in describing exactly how to go about inventing something.

On the other hand, several general approaches seem to be useful. They are little more than systematic ways of thinking about programming, and they certainly do not reduce the process to a routine series of steps guaranteed to lead to a correct and efficient program. These approaches may initially seem to be of little help, but reread this section after you have written some medium-sized programs. With that background, this may make more sense and may help you discipline your approach to more difficult problems.

We briefly describe three general ideas about program development and then illustrate them with several examples in Section 3. The ideas are the following:

Systematic "top-down development" from problem statement to finished program.

Viewing a program in terms of units larger than individual PL/I statements.

Exploiting similarities between different programs.

Each of these ideas has been introduced in previous sections, so this is really just a review and summary.

2.1 Top-Down Development

We first introduced the "top-down" approach in Section I.7.3 where we talked about nested loops. The idea, simply stated, is to approach the development of a program level by level, from the top level down to the lowest level. Each level is viewed as a separate task, and essentially the same thought process is repeated at each level.

In Section II.2 we analyzed the structure of a program in terms of different levels, and showed why it is useful to design each level as a sequential, or "almost sequential", program. Now we can restate these ideas in terms of a definite sequence of steps to be followed in developing a program -- in effect, a "program" for developing programs:

1. Plan the top level of the program by determining a simple sequence of steps, whose execution in order will provide a solution to the given problem. Each step is to be one of the following:

   Statement written in English
   Loop
   Selection from among alternatives (SELECT or IF)
   Assignment statement
   GET or PUT statement

2. Consider each one of the "compound" steps at that top level as a separate problem and repeat the process. That is, develop a plan for the body of each compound step as if it had initially been assigned as a problem.

3. Continue this process, level by level, until you reach a level where there are no further compound steps.

4. Throughout this process, keep track (on a separate sheet) of each variable used, noting its type of value and role in the program. After the lowest level has been developed into non-compound steps go back and fill in the required declarations for the variables.

5. Finally, write the enclosing PROCEDURE and END lines and provide the necessary control cards -- such as *PL/C, *DATA, etc.

Because of steps 2 and 3 above, in which each compound step of the program is expanded into greater detail at the next lower level, this process is sometimes called "program development by step-wise refinement".

We will try to convince you by example in Section 3 that this is an effective way of breaking down a formidable problem into manageable and recognizable sub problems.

As a practical matter, the subcomponents of a loop or alternative statement may be PL/I statements and therefore will need no further refinement. For example:

```
IF VALUE < 0
    THEN PUT SKIP (2) LIST
            ('IMPROPER NEGATIVE VALUE');
```

On the other hand, when the construction after THEN is compound:

```
IF condition
    THEN DO;
        body
        END;
```

then it is useful to treat the body as a separate level that needs further refinement.

2.2 Basic Program Units

As your programming experience accumulates, you should develop the facility to think in terms of much larger functional units than individual PL/I statements. For example, a common function performed by many programs is to load the individual elements of an array by reading values from the data list. We have described four different methods of doing this. Three involve loops (Section I.7.4.3) and one requires only a single statement (Section I.4.5). But before you worry about which method is appropriate in a particular case, you should think of this as a single task:

```
Load A(1:N) from data.
```

It is often useful to actually describe it as a single task with a statement-comment:

```
/** LOAD A(1:N) FROM DATA */
```

Then later you can decide exactly how this particular "load" has to be performed, and write the detailed PL/I statements indented under the statement-comment. For example:

```
/** LOAD A(1:N) FROM DATA */
    GET LIST (N);
    DO I = 1 TO N BY 1;
        GET LIST (A(I));
        END;
```

Another common task is to find the maximum value in an array. You should think in terms of a "step" such as

```
/** SET AMAX TO MAX VALUE OF A(1:N) */
```

and worry later about how to actually perform the task. In fact, this is such a common task that a programming language might well have a single statement to perform it. PL/I does not, and you will have to write it as follows:

```
/** SET AMAX TO MAX VALUE OF A(1:N) */
    AMAX = A(1);
    DO I = 2 TO N BY 1;
        AMAX = MAX(AMAX, A(I));
        END;
```

(In Part IV we describe "procedures" with which you can, in effect, add operations to the language, so you could have a single statement for this task.) But the point here is that regardless of the details of exactly how this is going to be done you should initially think of it as a single high-level step.

By learning to think in terms of larger elements than individual PL/I statements, you proportionally increase the size of the problem you are capable of programming. This is a natural process, and it tends to happen anyway. It occurs in learning any skill. For example, when you first learn to drive an automobile with a manual transmission you are concerned with detailed elemental steps such as:

1. Disengage the clutch while simultaneously backing off the throttle.

2. Move the gear shift lever from position i to position j.

3. Open the throttle to synchronize engine and shaft speed.

4. Engage the clutch.

Soon these steps become integrated and automatic, and you think in terms of an action:

Change from gear i to gear j.

At this higher level you can concentrate on learning the functions of the various gears, and how they are used to achieve different purposes. Eventually you come to think at an even higher level, which emphasizes objectives rather than methods:

Accelerate from rest to a speed of n miles per hour.

At this level you ignore details such as whether the vehicle is equipped with a manual or an automatic transmission; you concentrate on what you want to accomplish, rather than on the mechanics of operation.

Learning to program is similar. The individual PL/I statements correspond to the details of pushing the clutch pedal and moving the shift lever. Until those details become second-nature and you are comfortable with steps such as "load array" and "find maximum", it is not feasible to program a non-trivial problem.

2.3 Similarities Between Programs

A third characteristic of programming, which makes the task of invention manageable, is the fact that programs are rarely entirely original. In fact, only your very first program is completely original. After that, every new program borrows from its predecessors. Sometimes the borrowing is literal -- you use (or copy) a group of statements used in some other program. ("Procedures" described in Part IV considerably enhance this interchangeability of program segments.) Sometimes the borrowing is only conceptual -- you reuse an idea from a previous program.

There are two different kinds of similarities between programs. Programs can be similar in structure, although different in the task performed. For example, consider the following two program segments:

```
DCL SUM FLOAT INIT(0);
DCL ITEM FLOAT;
DCL (NBROFITEMS, ITEMNUMBER) FIXED;
GET LIST (NBROFITEMS);
DO ITEMNUMBER = 1 TO NBROFITEMS BY 1;
    GET LIST (ITEM);
    SUM = SUM + ITEM;
    END;
PUT DATA (SUM);
```

```
DCL LINE CHAR(100) VAR;
DCL ITEM CHAR(20) VAR;
DCL (NBROFITEMS, ITEMNUMBER) FIXED;
GET LIST (NUMBEROFITEMS);
DO ITEMNUMBER = 1 TO NBROFITEMS BY 1;
    GET LIST (ITEM);
    LINE = LINE || ITEM;
    END;
PUT DATA (LINE);
```

The first program sums numbers, while the second constructs lines from words, but their structure is the same.

The second kind of similarity is the existence of common subtasks. Even though two programs serve different objectives and have a different organization, they may still have many subtasks in common. The units described in Section 2.2 -- such as loading an array, or finding the maximum value in an array -- are examples of small tasks that are frequently encountered. The existence of such common subtasks may not be apparent in the brief examples used so far, but it should be evident in the examples given in Section 3.

Hence as your programming experience increases, you not only develop a technique that allows you to approach brand new problems, you also accumulate a repertoire of programs and program segments that makes it unnecessary for you to view each new program as absolutely original. This reliance on previous programs can be overdone, of course. You should not distort the algorithm for a new problem just to cannibalize a previous program. Just be aware that your previous programs are a valuable resource, and recognize that there is no reason to start from scratch with every new problem.

Section 3 Examples of Program Development

The following sections present the development of five different examples in varying degrees of completeness. Although we are primarily concerned with the development process rather than the particular problems, three of these examples -- searching, sorting and scanning for symbols -- are in fact important problems with which you should become familiar.

We describe the development process in detail, identifying each phase and presenting alternative choices. For short examples this seems laborious since you obviously can produce a satisfactory program by a much less studied and formal process. However, the process described is indispensable for larger and more complicated problems. Since it is not entirely natural or intuitively obvious, it must be studied and practiced on small problems where it is not absolutely necessary.

3.1 A Listing Program

A simple program to read and print a list of items is shown below:

```
/* PROGRAM TO READ AND PRINT NUMBERS */
RPNBRS: PROCEDURE OPTIONS(MAIN);
    DECLARE NBR FLOAT;
    ON ENDFILE(SYSIN) GOTO DATAEND;
    DO WHILE ('1'B);
        GET LIST (NBR);
        PUT SKIP LIST (NBR);
        END;
    DATAEND:;
    END RPNBRS;
```

This program consists of a single "data-driven" loop. (Recall Section I.7.4.3.) That is, the top level of the program is a loop, iterated once for each item of the data list. We could perform complex processing of each item of data, and still have a program whose top level had the same simple form. The body of the loop would be expanded, but the mechanism controlling repetition would be similar.

Now consider a listing problem that sounds similar to the one above but does not quite fit the data-driven model, and hence that leads to a different type of program:

> Given a list of numbers, print the numbers (one per line) in the order given, but terminate the printing after the number which is the maximum of all the numbers on the list.

For example, suppose the following is given:

```
*DATA
 1, 7, 3, 9, 5, 0
```

The required output is:

```
1
7
3
9
```

The catch is that we don't know when to terminate printing until we know which number is the maximum on the list, and we can't know which number is the maximum until we have seen the entire list. Consequently, a single loop that both reads and prints is no longer possible.

Obviously, reading must be separated from printing. The problem apparently has three stages:

1. Read the list from data.
2. Find the maximum value.
3. Print from first to the maximum.

It is important to realize you can make only one pass over the data list. That is, a program cannot read all the numbers on the data list to determine which is the maximum, and then read the whole list again to print the values up to the maximum. Thus the program must save the entire list internally, so the values will be available for later printing. This requires a data structure to hold a list of numbers -- obviously, an array.

Suppose we call the array NBRLIST. What type of value should the elements of NBRLIST have? The example above uses only integers, but this is a common characteristic of simple illustrative samples and should be regarded skeptically. Since nothing in the problem description restricts the numbers to integers, the type should be FLOAT. How many elements should NBRLIST have? That depends upon the maximum length of the list the program might be expected to process. For the previous listing program the length of the list is immaterial, but now, because the list must be stored internally, an upper limit on its length is needed. This requires a clarification of the problem requirements. Suppose whoever posed the problem is willing to specify that the length will never exceed 80. Then you have the information required for the necessary data structure:

```
DECLARE NBRLIST(80) FLOAT;
```

But observe that the initial problem specification didn't mention the length of the list, because whoever posed the problem didn't realize that the information was necessary to write the program. Similarly, we didn't know it was necessary until we had analyzed the problem sufficiently to realize the list had to be stored internally.

Now the three steps of the problem can be restated in terms of the internal list:

1. Read the data list into NBRLIST.
2. Find the maximum value in NBRLIST.
3. Print the values in NBRLIST, from the first to the maximum.

Note that, while NBRLIST has 80 elements, in general not all 80 will be used. So we need a variable to describe how many of the elements of NBRLIST are actually being used. Call it LASTNBR. We need another variable to record the position of the maximum value -- call it MAXPOSN. Now the three steps can be restated:

1. Read the data list into NBRLIST and set LASTNBR.
2. Find the maximum value in NBRLIST(1:LASTNBR) and store its position in MAXPOSN.
3. Print the values in NBRLIST(1:MAXPOSN).

Examining these steps, we realize that 1 and 2 could be combined. That is, the loop that reads can also check for the maximum value. Thus the algorithm becomes:

1. Load NBRLIST and set MAXPOSN to position of maximum value in NBRLIST.
2. Print NBRLIST(1:MAXPOSN).

These steps could be specified in statement-comments that will head actual sections of the program:

```
/** LOAD NBRLIST AND SET MAXPOSN */

/** PRINT NBRLIST(1:MAXPOSN) */
```

The first step is a loop whose body stores the next datum into the next element of NBRLIST and determines the position of the maximum value thus far. A program segment for this step is the following:

```
DECLARE NBRLIST(80)  FLOAT; /* NBRLIST(1:LASTNBR) */
DECLARE LASTNBR FIXED;      /* ARE THE NUMBERS */
                            /* READ SO FAR */
DECLARE MAXPOSN FIXED;/* NBRLIST(MAXPOSN)=MAXNBR, */
DECLARE MAXNBR FLOAT; /* THE LARGEST THUS FAR */

/** LOAD NBRLIST AND SET MAXPOSN */
    ON ENDFILE(SYSIN) GOTO DATAEND;
    MAXNBR = -1E75;
    DO LASTNBR = 1 TO 80 BY 1;
        GET LIST (NBRLIST(LASTNBR));
        IF NBRLIST(LASTNBR) > MAXNBR
            THEN DO;
               MAXNBR = NBRLIST(LASTNBR);
               MAXPOSN = LASTNBR;
               END;
        END;
    DATAEND:;
```

Note that (approximately) the smallest number representable in PL/I floating-point form is assigned to MAXNBR as an initial value to ensure that the first data value read will become the incumbent maximum. This initial value <u>could</u> have been set with the INITIAL attribute in the declaration of MAXNBR, but it is better done with an assignment statement because this is logically part of the task described by

```
/** LOAD NBRLIST AND SET MAXPOSN */
```

Hence it should be included in the statements that perform this task. Otherwise, the heading comment should be corrected to say

```
/** LOAD NBRLIST AND SET MAXPOSN (ASSUMING MAXPOSN */
        /* IS INITIALLY -10**75) */
```

The difference is not critical for a short program like this, but you should get in the habit of writing heading comments as precisely as possible, and having them agree exactly with their refinements. Many errors in large programs originate in imprecise descriptions such as illustrated here.

An even better practice is to create a variable to contain this smallest possible number:

```
DCL SMALLEST_FNBR FLOAT INIT(-1E75);
    /* READONLY: SMALLEST FLOAT NUMBER */
```

PL/I has no special provision for variables such as this whose value is never changed (some programming languages do), so we note our intention as "readonly" in the comment. The initializing assignment statement would be written

```
MAXNBR = SMALLEST_FNBR;
```

On another point, it is good practice not to write control values as constants in the program. For example, this program is to process a list of up to 80 values, and the constant 80 appears both in the declaration of NBRLIST and in the control of the loop. If you ever wanted to use this program for a list of some other length it would be easy to overlook the second occurrence of 80. It would be better to create a variable to specify the maximum list length:

```
DECLARE LISTLENGTH FIXED INIT(80);
        /* READONLY: LENGTH OF NBRLIST */
```

The loop control would then be written

```
DO LASTNBR = 1 TO LISTLENGTH BY 1;
```

Finally, if this program is ever used as a section of a larger program its use of ENDFILE may have unfortunate side-effects. The default action performed on encountering the end of data is replaced by a branch to DATAEND. If some subsequent program section reads and runs out of data the program will still branch to DATAEND, probably with disastrous results. Consequently it is good practice to restore the normal system action as an integral part of the segment that alters it.

Once the position of the maximum value is known, printing the partial list is straightforward:

```
/** PRINT NBRLIST(1:MAXPOSN) */
    DO I = 1 TO MAXPOSN BY 1;
        PUT SKIP LIST (NBRLIST(I));
        END;
```

Putting these sections together, with the changes suggested above, the complete program is:

```
/* READ AND LIST TO MAXIMUM */
RPMAX: PROCEDURE OPTIONS(MAIN);
    DECLARE NBRLIST(80)  FLOAT; /* NBRLIST(1:LASTNBR) */
    DECLARE LASTNBR FIXED;      /* ARE THE NUMBERS */
                                /* READ SO FAR */
    DECLARE LISTLENGTH FIXED INIT(80);
           /* READONLY: LENGTH OF NBRLIST */
    DECLARE MAXPOSN FIXED;/* NBRLIST(MAXPOSN)=MAXNBR, */
    DECLARE MAXNBR FLOAT; /* THE LARGEST THUS FAR */
    DECLARE SMALLEST_FNBR FLOAT INIT(-1E75);
           /* READONLY: SMALLEST FLOAT NUMBER */
    DECLARE I FIXED;
```

```
/** LOAD NBRLIST AND SET MAXPOSN */
    ON ENDFILE(SYSIN) GOTO DATAEND;
    MAXNBR = SMALLEST_FNBR;
    DO LASTNBR = 1 TO LISTLENGTH BY 1;
        GET LIST (NBRLIST(LASTNBR));
        IF NBRLIST(LASTNBR) > MAXNBR
            THEN DO;
               MAXNBR = NBRLIST(LASTNBR);
               MAXPOSN = LASTNBR;
               END;
        END;
    DATAEND: ON ENDFILE(SYSIN) SYSTEM;

/** PRINT NBRLIST(1:MAXPOSN) */
    DO I = 1 TO MAXPOSN BY 1;
        PUT SKIP LIST (NBRLIST(I));
        END;

END RPMAX;
```

Before pronouncing this draft program "ready for testing", check to see if it will behave reasonably for various extreme situations. For example:

1. What would happen if some (or all) of the data were negative numbers?

2. What would happen if the actual length of the data list exceeds 80? (That can easily happen.)

3. What would happen if the program is run with a data list of length 0?

The answers to these concerns are the following:

1. The program performs properly for positive numbers, negative numbers, or mixed values -- as long as at least <u>one number is greater than -1E75</u>. If all values are less than -1E75 then PL/C will give an error message, since MAXPOSN is used in the final loop but will never have been assigned a value.

2. With too much data, the program reads <u>only the first 80 numbers</u>. PL/C indicates the surplus of data in the postmortem dump, but this message is easily overlooked (and the program may be used with the dump option turned off). It would be better to change the first loop heading to:

   ```
   DO LASTNBR = 1 TO LISTLENGTH + 1 BY 1;
   ```

   Then if an 81st repetition is attempted an improper subscript is used for NBRLIST and a noticeable error message will be given by PL/C.

3. If no data is provided, the ENDFILE termination of LOAD_LOOP occurs on the first iteration. This leaves MAXPOSN without a value, and the final loop, which uses MAXPOSN, will generate an error message (reporting an uninitialized variable). However, in this case the program should actually print nothing. This could be remedied just by initially assigning MAXPOSN the number 0. This will be accepted by the final loop without any message, and since this "final value" is less than the "initial value" in that indexed loop, the body of the loop will not be executed. That is exactly what is required.

   But note that we were counting on the uninitialized state of MAXPOSN under point 1 above, and obviously cannot have it both ways at once. It would be better to initialize MAXPOSN to 0 to protect the empty-data-list case, and rely on a sufficiently small value of MAXNBR to guard against a list of very small numbers.

These undoubtedly seem like picky details concerned with unlikely events. But unlikely events have a way of happening sooner or later, and a reliable program must behave reasonably no matter what happens. One distinguishing characteristic of a good programmer is the careful provisions for all possible circumstances the program might encounter.

3.2 The Problem of Searching a List

Consider the following "list-searching" problem:

> Given is a "list" of numbers, in a particular order, and a set of "inquiries" -- numbers that may or may not be in the list. For each inquiry determine whether or not it is in the list. If it is, indicate what position it occupies; if it is not, report that fact.

For example, with the list (9, -4.5, 16) an inquiry "16" should be reported to be in position 3; the inquiries "12" and "4.5" should be reported not in the list.

Clarifying the problem will lead to detail about the quantity and the form of the input. This might result in the following specification:

> The input will consist of:
> a) an integer specifying the length of the list;
> b) the list values, in order;
> c) the inquiries.
>
> The list will have no more than 100 values, which can be positive, negative or zero, and in integer, decimal or exponential form.

This means that the example above could be:

```
*DATA
 4, 9, -4.5, 16, 5,
 16, 12, 4.5
```

Specification of required output might be the following:

> For each inquiry print a line (double-spaced) that gives the value and either its position on the list or the fact that it does not appear on the list.

The exact format and wording of the output is left to your discretion. Presumably lines such as the following would be acceptable (but it is worth checking in advance to make sure):

```
16 IS IN POSITION 3

12 IS NOT ON THE LIST

4.5 IS NOT ON THE LIST
```

Now consider possible data errors that might occur. For example, the first value, specifying the length of the list list, might be improper. You must decide what tests to perform and what action to take. This might result in the following refinement of the problem specification:

> The list length may be anything from 0 to 100; if not, terminate execution with an appropriate warning. The number of inquiries is arbitrary.

Specifying list length with a control value is not particularly good. Miscounting can easily occur and the program can do little against it. For example, if the list length is specified as 90 but 91 values are actually given, then the 91st will be interpreted as the first inquiry. If only 89 list values are actually given then the first inquiry will be taken to be the last item on the list.

On the other hand, the specification that the program should work for a list of length zero or for no inquiries is not unreasonable. Posed as a separate problem, it would be foolish for anyone to run the program with no list or inquiries, but such programs are often later incorporated into larger programs. The ability to operate properly for extreme values -- in particular, the ability to do nothing, gracefully, is very valuable.

Suppose there is an error in one of the list values (not the list length value). Say that a 9 was punched as an 8. There is no way for a program to discover such an error. Conceivably , a number could serve as an upper bound on the values of the list, so that any larger value would be rejected, but this would not help much.

Let us assume the problem statement is augmented as follows to specify the treatment of data errors:

> List values must lie between -30 and +30; any value outside this range should be rejected with an appropriate message.

Now consider the question of processing strategy. Note that the data list is, in fact, two separate data lists. This obviously means that the main structure of the program cannot be a single loop. The key point in the design of the program strategy is to recognize that this problem must be handled in two distinct steps:

1. Load the complete list into memory.

2. Process the inquiries, one at a time.

These are the steps in the top level description of the program. Note that at this level we have a strictly sequential program -- we perform step 1, then step 2, and the process is finished. Each will internally involve a loop, but at this top level they are single steps.

Now we have two simpler problems:

Problem 1: Given a number followed by a list of numbers load the list into memory.

Problem 2: Given a list of numbers in memory and another data list, report the position in the list in memory of each value on the data list.

The only relationship between these two problems is the list of numbers in memory -- problem 1 produces the list, and problem 2 uses the list. But other than the fact that the list is common, these problems can be analyzed independently.

The key data structure is obviously the list of numbers that links the two steps. The issues are the length of the list, and the type of value of its elements. The type is obviously numeric, and since there is no assurance that the values will only be integers, the type must be FLOAT. The length can be as much as 100, so we create an array of 100 elements. Let's choose the name NBRLIST for this array. We will also need a variable to denote the length of the list. Call it LISTLENGTH. Its type can be FIXED.

These are the only data structure decisions required to get started on subproblems 1 and 2. We will certainly need other variables, but we will keep track of them as we develop the program rather than try to anticipate them now.

Now we can restate problems 1 and 2 in terms of our data structure decisions:

Problem 1: Load LISTLENGTH and NBRLIST(1:LISTLENGTH).

Problem 2: For each inquiry, report its position in NBRLIST(1:LISTLENGTH).

Statement-comments can be written as headings for the corresponding sections of the program:

```
/** LOAD LISTLENGTH AND NBRLIST(1:LISTLENGTH) */

/** REPORT POSITION OF EACH INPUT DATUM */
       /* IN NBRLIST(1:LISTLENGTH) */
```

The LOAD step of the program is trivial. Initially ignoring the issue of error checking, the program would be:

```
/** LOAD LISTLENGTH AND NBRLIST(1:LISTLENGTH) */
    GET LIST (LISTLENGTH);
    DO I = 1 TO LISTLENGTH BY 1;
        GET LIST (NBRLIST(I));
        END;
```

Make a note that we need a variable I.

Both LISTLENGTH and the values in the first list must be checked to make sure they lie in the specified ranges. The statements to do this will have the form:

```
IF value is improper
    THEN take appropriate action;
```

In the case of LISTLENGTH, the condition must detect values outside the range (0:100), and the appropriate action is to issue an error message and terminate the program. The actual statements would be the following:

```
IF (LISTLENGTH < 0) | (LISTLENGTH > 100)
    THEN DO;
        PUT SKIP(2) LIST
                ('IMPROPER LENGTH OF LIST',
                 'VALUE GIVEN WAS:', LISTLENGTH);
        GOTO TERM_PROGRAM;
        END;
```

Note that the PUT statement specifies SKIP(2). Although this is apparently the first line to be printed and SKIP is not necessary, it doesn't hurt and it is prudent to write it this way. Later if title lines are added to the output, this error routine will not have to be changed in order to maintain the visual separation of the error message from other output.

Note that the error message is not written in terms of the variable name LISTLENGTH; it is written for the benefit of a <u>user</u> who need not know how the program works.

Note down that the final program must have a target-label TERM_PROGRAM at its end so this branch can immediately abort execution.

Error checking of the elements of NBRLIST is more interesting. The test is easy:

```
IF ABS(NBRLIST(I)) > 30 ...
```

The "appropriate action" is less obvious. The problem statement says extreme values should be "rejected with an appropriate message". "Reject" means they shouldn't go on the list NBRLIST. This means the list read from the data and the internal list are not identical. In particular, their lengths differ, and LISTLENGTH cannot describe the length of both. Thus we revise the meaning of LISTLENGTH and add a new variable, as follows:

```
DCL DATACOUNT FIXED;  /* LENGTH OF DATA LIST */
DCL LISTLENGTH FIXED; /* NUMBER OF GOOD VALUES */
```

Note how necessary error processing required a revision in the preliminary version of the program. This is not uncommon -- in fact, an optimist has been defined as "someone who programs in ink". The revised program segment is:

```
/** LOAD DATACOUNT, NBRLIST(1:LISTLENGTH) */
    GET LIST (DATACOUNT);
    LISTLENGTH = 0;
    IF (DATACOUNT < 0) | (DATACOUNT > 100)
        THEN DO;
            PUT SKIP(2) LIST
                   ('IMPROPER LENGTH OF LIST',
                   'VALUE GIVEN WAS:', DATACOUNT);
            GOTO TERM_PROGRAM;
            END;
    DO I = 1 TO DATACOUNT BY 1;
        GET LIST (NUMBER);
        IF ABS(NUMBER) > 30
            THEN PUT SKIP(2) LIST
                   ('IMPROPER VALUE:', NUMBER);
            ELSE DO;
               LISTLENGTH = LISTLENGTH + 1;
               NBRLIST(LISTLENGTH) = NUMBER;
               END;
        END;
```

3.2.1 Processing the Inquiries

Now consider subproblem 2, processing the inquiries. First observe that each inquiry is independent of the others. The inquiries can be read and processed, one at a time, and only one inquiry need be in memory at any time. Hence an array to store all the inquiries at once is not needed. Subproblem 2 is just another data-driven loop.

Since the inquiries are at the end of the data ENDFILE can be used to detect the end of the list. At its top level, subproblem 2 is:

```
/** PRINT POSITION OF EACH INQ IN */
    /* NBRLIST(1:LISTLENGTH) */
    ON ENDFILE(SYSIN) GOTO DATAEND;
    INQ_LOOP: DO WHILE ('1'B);
        GET LIST (INQ);
        process the inquiry
        END INQ_LOOP;
    DATAEND: ON ENDFILE(SYSIN) SYSTEM;
```

This controls the repetition for each inquiry on the data list. All that remains is to refine the task "process the inquiry".

Consider "process the inquiry" as if it were a separate problem. That is, concentrate on one particular inquiry. Don't worry about the fact that this task will be repeated, and don't worry about how this inquiry or the list got into memory. The problem statement is the following:

> Given an internal list NBRLIST(1:LISTLENGTH) and a single number INQ, if INQ is on the list, report its position; otherwise, announce its absence.

This obviously requires a loop to compare each element of NBRLIST(1:LISTLENGTH) with INQ. An indexed loop could be used but there is the complication of two types of exit: one for a successful search, and one for a failure. The program could be written as follows:

```
FOUND = '0'B;
SEARCH: DO I = 1 TO LISTLENGTH BY 1;
    IF INQ = NBRLIST(I)
        THEN DO;
            POSN = I;
            FOUND = '1'B;
            END;
    END SEARCH;
IF FOUND
    THEN PUT SKIP(2) LIST (INQ,
            'IS IN POSITION', POSN);
    ELSE PUT SKIP(2) LIST (INQ,
            'IS NOT ON THE LIST');
```

The efficiency of this segment could be improved by realizing that once the value of INQ is found on the list, it is not necessary to complete the search over the rest of the list. So the body of the conditional statement in the loop could include a LEAVE statement:

```
IF INQ = NBRLIST(I)
    THEN DO;
        POSN = I;
        FOUND = '1'B;
        LEAVE SEARCH;
        END;
```

A simpler segment is possible if it is known that the search will always be successful, and this can be ensured by inserting the value INQ at the end of the list. This is the sentinel strategy discussed in Section II.3.3. Note that it requires NBRLIST to have an additional element to hold INQ.

```
NBRLIST(LISTLENGTH + 1) = INQ;
INQPOSN = 1;
DO WHILE (NBRLIST(INQPOSN) ¬= INQ);
    INQPOSN = INQPOSN + 1;
    END;
IF INQPOSN = LISTLENGTH + 1
    THEN PUT SKIP(2) LIST (INQ,
            'IS NOT ON THE LIST');
    ELSE PUT SKIP(2) LIST (INQ,
            'IS IN POSITION', INQPOSN);
```

Assembling the pieces and adding the necessary declarations, etc., we have the following program:

```
/* PRINT POSITION OF NUMBERS ON A LIST */
FINDPOS: PROCEDURE OPTIONS(MAIN);
    DCL  DATACOUNT FIXED;       /* LENGTH OF DATA LIST */
    DCL  LISTLENGTH FIXED;      /* NBRLIST(1:LISTLENGTH) ARE */
    DCL  NBRLIST(101) FLOAT;    /* GOOD VALUES INCLUDED SO FAR */
                                /* NBRLIST(101) IS A SENTINEL */
    DCL  NUMBER FLOAT;          /* CANDIDATE VALUE FOR NBRLIST */
    DCL  INQ FLOAT;             /* NUMBER TO BE FOUND */
    DCL  INQPOSN FIXED;         /* POSITION OF INQ IN NBRLIST */
    DCL  I FIXED;
```

```
/** LOAD DATACOUNT, NBRLIST(1:LISTLENGTH) */
    LISTLENGTH = 0;
    GET LIST (DATACOUNT);
    IF  (DATACOUNT < 0) | (DATACOUNT > 100)
        THEN DO;
            PUT SKIP(2) LIST
                   ('IMPROPER LENGTH OF LIST',
                   'VALUE GIVEN WAS:', DATACOUNT);
            GOTO TERM_PROGRAM;
            END;
    DO I = 1 TO DATACOUNT BY 1;
        GET LIST (NUMBER);
        IF  ABS(NUMBER) > 30
            THEN PUT SKIP(2) LIST ('IMPROPER VALUE:',
                    NUMBER);
            ELSE DO;
                LISTLENGTH = LISTLENGTH + 1;
                NBRLIST(LISTLENGTH) = NUMBER;
                END;
        END;

/** PRINT POSITION OF EACH INQ IN NBRLIST(1:LISTLENGTH) */
    ON ENDFILE(SYSIN) GOTO DATAEND;
    INQ_LOOP: DO WHILE ('1'B);
        GET LIST (INQ);
        /** PROCESS INQUIRY INQ */
            NBRLIST(LISTLENGTH + 1) = INQ;
            INQPOSN = 1;
            DO WHILE (NBRLIST(INQPOSN) ¬= INQ);
                INQPOSN = INQPOSN + 1;
                END;
            IF INQPOSN = LISTLENGTH + 1
                THEN PUT SKIP(2) LIST (INQ,
                        'IS NOT ON THE LIST');
                ELSE PUT SKIP(2) LIST (INQ,
                        'IS IN POSITION', INQPOSN);
        END INQ_LOOP;
    DATAEND: ON ENDFILE(SYSIN) SYSTEM;

TERM_PROGRAM:;
END FINDPOS;
```

Although this is a larger program than previous examples, by breaking it down, level by level, we reduced it to more-or-less familiar problems of manageable size.

3.3 The Problem of Ordering a List

A common task is to reorder the elements of a list so that their values are "in order". For numeric variables this is usually "algebraic order", either increasing or decreasing; for character variables it is usually according to the collating sequence, which implies both alphabetical and algebraic order. The process of rearranging values so they satisfy some order relationship is called "sorting". A simple form of sorting problem is:

> Given a list of numbers, sort them into order of increasing value. Display the list before and after sorting.

For example, from the list 5, 0, -7, 6.2, 1 the list -7, 0, 1, 5, 6.2 would be produced. One possible clarification of the problem is:

> Given data consisting of an integer n (not greater than 50) followed by a list of n numbers, sort these n numbers into increasing order. Display the list in original order in a single column, followed by the sorted list in single column. Provide appropriate titles.

Obviously we need <u>all the data available at once</u>, so the program is not a single data-driven loop. The numbers must be loaded before they can be sorted, and they must be sorted before they can be printed in sorted order. This suggests that the top level of the program should consist of three steps:

1. Read list.
2. Sort list.
3. Print sorted list.

This does not indicate when the display of the initial (unsorted) list takes place. There are two possibilities -- before or after sorting. The most obvious is to display the initial order before it is changed. This could be done separately:

1. Read list.
2. Print unsorted list.
3. Sort list.
4. Print sorted list.

It could also be combined with the "read" step:

1. Read and print list.
2. Sort list.
3. Print sorted list.

The first choice results in two separate loops and the second in a single loop with both GET and PUT statements in the body. There seems to be no advantage in separation and we decide, at least tentatively, in favor of the single loop.

If we wanted to have all printing done in one section of the program we could make an extra copy of the list, so we could sort one copy and keep the other in initial order. The top level in this case would be:

1. Read list into 2 copies.
2. Sort 1 copy.
3. Print both copies.

This two-copy strategy is unnecessary for the problem as stated, but note that only a slight variation in the original problem statement -- requiring display in side-by-side columns -- would make this strategy necessary.

We have separated off two minor tasks "read and print" and "print", each obviously implementable with a straightforward indexed loop. By now the programming of tasks like these should be familiar and almost automatic. It is also clear that the principal data structure will be an array to hold the list and a variable to specify how much of that array is used. The array has to be FLOAT since no restriction on values is implied by the problem statement. What remains is the following task:

Given L(1:N), reorder its elements into increasing order.

To figure out a method for reordering, suppose you had n cards, each bearing a number, laid out in a row. How could you go about rearranging the cards so the numbers were in increasing order? One way would be to scan the cards and find the one with the largest value. This card could be interchanged with the one at the end of the row. Now, ignoring that card, which has been properly positioned, repeat the process for the remaining n-1 cards. That is, locate the card with the second largest value (the largest of the remaining n-1) and interchange it with the second from last (the last of the n-1). Now with the last two cards in proper position, work on the remaining n-2 cards in the same way. If this is continued until the first and second cards are put in order, the entire row will have been sorted. Let us transform this idea into an algorithm:

Repeat for lists of diminishing length m=n,n-1,n-2,...,2:
1. Find the maximum value of L(1:m).
2. Interchange the maximum with L(m).

Both "find maximum" and "interchange" are familiar tasks -- problems you have seen before. This version differs from previous "find maximum" problems only in that the numbers are already in an array (rather than being in an external data list) and in that we need to find the <u>position</u> as well as the value of the maximum. A program segment to do this is

```
/** SET MAXPOS TO POSITION OF MAX IN L(1:M) */
    MAXVAL = L(1);
    MAXPOS = 1;
    DO I = 2 TO M BY 1;
        IF L(I) > MAXVAL
            THEN DO;
                MAXVAL = L(I);
                MAXPOS = I;
                END;
        END;
```

Given that MAXPOS points to the maximum value in L(1:M) the interchange is simply

```
/** INTERCHANGE L(MAXPOS) AND L(M) */
    TEMP = L(M);
    L(M) = L(MAXPOS);
    L(MAXPOS) = TEMP;
```

These two segments must be repeated for lists whose lengths M vary from N down to 2:

```
/** SORT L(1:N) */
    SUBLIST_LOOP: DO M = N TO 2 BY -1;
        /** SET MAXPOS TO POSITION OF MAX IN L(1:M) */
            MAXVAL = L(1);
            MAXPOS = 1;
            DO I = 2 TO M BY 1;
                IF L(I) > MAXVAL
                    THEN DO;
                        MAXVAL = L(I);
                        MAXPOS = I;
                        END;
                END;
        /** INTERCHANGE L(MAXPOS) AND L(M) */
            TEMP = L(M);
            L(M) = L(MAXPOS);
            L(MAXPOS) = TEMP;

        END SUBLIST_LOOP;
```

The complete program is shown below:

```
/* SORT AND DISPLAY A LIST OF NUMBERS */
SORT: PROCEDURE OPTIONS(MAIN);
    DCL L(50) FLOAT; /* L(1:N) IS THE LIST TO BE SORTED */
    DCL N FIXED;     /* ACTUAL LENGTH OF LIST IN L */
    DCL M FIXED;     /* LENGTH OF SUB-LIST */
    DCL I FIXED;
    DCL TEMP FLOAT;
```

```
/** READ AND DISPLAY INITIAL LIST */
    GET LIST (N);
    IF (N < 0) | (N > 50)
        THEN DO;
            PUT SKIP(3) LIST ('IMPROPER LENGTH;', N);
            GOTO TERM_SORT;
            END;
    PUT SKIP LIST ('LIST IN INITIAL ORDER');
    PUT SKIP;
    DO I = 1 TO N BY 1;
        GET LIST (L(I));
        PUT SKIP LIST (L(I));
        END;

/** SORT L(1:N) */
    SUBLIST_LOOP: DO M = N TO 2 BY -1;
        /** SET MAXPOS TO POSITION OF MAX IN L(1:M) */
            MAXVAL = L(1);
            MAXPOS = 1;
            DO I = 2 TO M BY 1;
                IF L(I) > MAXVAL
                    THEN DO;
                        MAXVAL = L(I);
                        MAXPOS = I;
                        END;
                END;
        /** INTERCHANGE L(MAXPOS) AND L(M) */
            TEMP = L(M);
            L(M) = L(MAXPOS);
            L(MAXPOS) = TEMP;
        END SUBLIST_LOOP;

/** DISPLAY L(1:M) */
    PUT SKIP(3) LIST ('SORTED LIST');
    PUT SKIP;
    DO I = 1 TO N BY 1;
        PUT SKIP LIST (L(I));
        END;

TERM_SORT:;
END SORT;
```

Sorting is an important problem in practice and a convenient problem to illustrate points in programming. We refer back to this often in future sections and it will help if you thoroughly understand this simple version.

3.4 An Accounting Problem

A bank would like to produce records of the transactions during an accounting period in connection with their checking accounts. For each account the bank wants a list showing the balance at the beginning of the period, the number of deposits and withdrawals, and the final balance. (This is a simplified version of a very common and important type of computer application.)

The accounts and transactions for an accounting period will be given on punched cards as follows:

1. First will be a sequence of cards describing the accounts. Each account is described by two numbers: the account number (greater than 0), and the account balance at the beginning of the period, in dollars and cents. The last account is followed by a "dummy" account consisting of two zero values to indicate the end of the list. There will be at most 200 accounts.

2. Following the accounts are the transactions. Each transaction is given by three numbers: the account number, a 1 or -1 (indicating a deposit or withdrawal, respectively), and the transaction amount, in dollars and cents. The last real transaction is followed by a dummy transaction consisting of three zero values.

The following sample input has been supplied, where the words at the right are not part of the input, but explanatory notes.

input numbers			meaning
1025	61.50		(account 1025 contains $61.50)
1028	103		(account 1028 contains $103)
1026	100		(account 1026 contains $100)
0	0		(end of accounts)
1025	1	500	(deposit $500 in account 1025)
1028	-1	20	(withdraw $20 from account 1028)
1025	-1	400	(withdraw $400 from account 1025)
1025	+1	50	(deposit $50 in account 1025)
0	0	0	(end of transactions)

For this input, the output should be:

ACCOUNT	PREV BAL	WITHDRAWALS	DEPOSITS	FINAL BAL
1025	61.50	1	2	211.50
1028	103	1	0	83
1026	100	0	0	100

Some of the errors that could occur in the data are:

1. An account is listed two or more times.

2. The end-of-account signal is missing or incorrect.

3. A transaction number is not in the list of accounts.

4. The withdrawal-deposit number is not 1 or -1.

5. The transaction amount is negative.

6. The end-of-transaction signal is wrong or missing.

All these errors could be detected by the program. Detecting other situations such as overdrafts (which are not really input errors) would probably make the program more valuable. Of course, not all errors can be detected by the program. For example, a withdrawal keypunched as a deposit or an error in a transaction amount can not be detected. To keep our program development to manageable size we will largely neglect the question of data errors. In the real world this is clearly unrealistic, and the program would have to detect and process these errors.

The following stages give a reasonable chronological record of the development of a program for this problem.

Stage 1. Discovering the overall structure of the algorithm.

Looking at the problem description, note that the account data precedes the transactions. Thus all accounts must be read and stored internally, before the transactions can be read and "processed". Moreover, while processing the transactions we must be able to access any account at any time, since no ordering of the transactions by account number is mentioned in the description of the problem. The sample data confirm this lack of ordering. Also, since the last transaction may apply to any account, no result may be printed for an account until all transactions have been processed. This analysis indicates that the top level of the program will consist of the following steps:

1. Read in and set up the accounts in a "table".
2. Read in and process the transactions.
3. Print the results.

It should already be apparent that this is just a more complicated version of the problem described in Section 3.2. The initial "read" step is similar, but in this case the "table of accounts" is a more complicated data structure than the list of values in 3.2. In the second step, there must be a search for a particular value in the table, but instead of just reporting the position of the value, the program will modify that entry in the table. The "print" step is extra -- it has no counterpart in the program in 3.2.

There are now three separate, smaller problems, but they are obviously not entirely independent of each other. All three share the data structures used to contain the accounts and the information connected with them. Whenever we split a problem into several smaller parts, it is important to look at the "interface" or connections between them. Often, several strategies exist for implementing each one, but implementing one in a particular way may reduce the flexibility in designing the others. We must weigh carefully the benefits and disadvantages, including effects on other modules, in choosing a strategy for a given module.

Stage 2. The data structures representing the accounts.

We must keep the accounts accessible in a table until all transactions have been processed and the results have been reported. This can be done using an array ACCT (say) to hold the ACCounT numbers and an array IBAL to hold the corresponding Initial BALances. We also need a variable N (say) to hold the number of accounts. Thus, if i is an integer between 1 and N, ACCT(i) contains an account number and IBAL(i) contains the corresponding initial balance. Other alternatives for storing the data exist of course, but this is probably the simplest and easiest.

Now review the problem statement to make sure the accounts have been described completely and accurately. Certainly this is all we need initially, but look at the sample output. After processing the transactions, in addition to the initial balance we must report the number of deposits and withdrawals and also the final balance. This will require three more arrays; we need two arrays to contain the number of withdrawals and deposits, and a third to contain the balances. The arrays holding the number of withdrawals and deposits will be initially set to 0, and will be increased to count the number of withdrawals and deposits that are processed for each account. Similarly, the array holding the final balances will be initialized to the initial balances and will be updated as transactions are processed.

To summarize, we write down the names of the variables which describe the accounts and define as precisely as possible how they will be used:

1. Variable N contains the number of accounts.

2. Five arrays describe the accounts: ACCT, IBAL, WITH, DEP and CBAL (meaning Current BALance). If i is an integer between 1 and N, then during execution

   ACCT(i) is an ACCounT number,
   IBAL(i) is the corresponding Initial BALance,
   WITH(i) is the number of WITHdrawals processed so far,
   DEP(i) is the number of DEPosits processed so far,
   CBAL(i) is the Current BALance in the account.

CBAL(i) depends of course on the withdrawals and deposits processed so far. In order to fix these definitions more clearly in our minds, consider some examples. Just after reading in all the accounts in the sample input, the arrays are:

	ACCT	IBAL	WITH	DEP	CBAL
(1)	1025	61.50	0	0	61.50
(2)	1028	103	0	0	103
(3)	1026	100	0	0	100

Note that each CBAL(i) is the same as IBAL(i), since no transactions have been processed. After processing the first transaction, the arrays are:

	ACCT	IBAL	WITH	DEP	CBAL
(1)	1025	61.50	0	1	561.50
(2)	1028	103	0	0	103
(3)	1026	100	0	0	100

At this point we could write declarations for these data structures, but it is better to wait. These structures should be considered tentative, and may have to be revised as the detailed design of the program unfolds.

We have looked at the data structures that contain the accounts from the viewpoint of the information that must be available as the program executes. Now consider *how* this information is accessed and changed -- how the three steps at the top level of the program use the information.

The second step, "Read in and process the transactions", requires us to locate in the table of accounts the account associated with each transaction. This means a search in array ACCT of account numbers for each transaction account number. That is, given a transaction like (1028, 1, 100), we have to find an integer i such that ACCT(i) = 1028. Assuming a search algorithm such as the one used in Section 3.2 on the average we must look at half of the accounts in order to find the right one. If there are only a few hundred accounts this may be feasible. But if there are 5000 or more accounts the time to search would be in seconds for each transaction, and we could not afford to structure the table of accounts as we have done.

This search time can be drastically reduced if the accounts are rearranged so that the account numbers are in ascending order: ACCT(1) $\le$ ACCT(2) $\le$ ... $\le$ ACCT(N). If we sort the array of accounts as we read them in, we can process the transactions more efficiently. But sorting takes time too, and we must carefully weigh the sorting time against the efficiency gained in processing, before we decide which approach to take. This depends on the number of accounts relative to the number of transactions, and we now realize that we lack such information. The problem description is not complete, and without such information we cannot design the best program.

An even better solution would be for the bank to *keep* their accounts in ascending order, so that neither sorting nor a slow search would be required.

This discussion should illustrate the need for thinking about the various ways of implementing each succesive statement of an algorithm, and considering the effects of each. For now, assume that the accounts cannot be kept sorted because of other considerations, and that the simple search algorithm of Section 3.2 is adequate.

Stage 3. Refining the statement "Read and set up the accounts."

The refinement of this statement will obviously involve a loop. Each execution of the body will set up one individual account. Iteration of the loop will continue until the final dummy account is encountered. In other words, this will be a data-driven loop with termination based on the "stopping value" strategy (see Section I.7.4.3).

There are various ways of managing such a loop. You could test for the stopping value in a WHILE or an UNTIL condition, or construct the loop to repeat indefinitely and make termination depend upon a conditional LEAVE statement. These tactics were compared in Section I.7.4. In that example, the LEAVE tactic seemed clearest, so we will try that for the present problem.

We have not yet discussed what it means to "set up an account". So far we are just concerned with creating the mechanism that will repeat that set up action the proper number of times. So the refinement at this level suggests something like the following:

```
/** READ AND SET UP THE ACCOUNTS */
    K = 0;
    SETUP: DO WHILE ('1'B);
        Read value pairs into temporary locations
        IF dummy account
            THEN LEAVE SETUP;
        K = K + 1;
        Set up the Kth account
        END SETUP;
```

Alternatively, suppose we read the data values directly into the account, instead of using a temporary location, as shown above. One segment to do this is the following:

```
/** READ AND SET UP THE ACCOUNTS */
    K = 0;
    SETUP: DO WHILE ('1'B);
        K = K + 1;
        Read Kth account
        IF Kth account is dummy
            THEN LEAVE SETUP;
        Finish setting up Kth account
        END SETUP;
    K = K - 1;
```

This has two undesirable characteristics. First, it requires that there actually be a dummy account along with the real accounts in the table, since the dummy will be read into the table before it is known to be the dummy. Second, the value of K must be "corrected" after termination of the loop so that it does not include the dummy in the count of real accounts. On balance, in this case it seems clearer and simpler to read the account into a temporary location, and to not move it into the table until it is known that it is not the dummy account.

So we create two temporary variables to receive data values:

```
GET LIST (TEMPACCT, TEMPIBAL);
```

Now refinement of the statement "set up the Kth account" is:

```
ACCT(K) = TEMPACCT;
IBAL(K) = TEMPIBAL;
WITH(K) = 0;
DEP(K)  = 0;
CBAL(K) = IBAL(K);
```

Note when we declare arrays for the table of accounts, we must specify the number of elements in each array. If the data contains too many accounts, eventually K will become too large to be a valid subscript for these arrays. PL/C will automatically detect this situation and produce an error message (but PL/I will just quietly overflow the table).

Stage 4. <u>Refining "Read and process the transactions."</u>

Consider the task of processing the transactions, keeping in mind that the table of accounts is not ordered by account number. Two actions are required -- <u>reading</u> and <u>processing</u> the transactions -- and there may be several ways of performing them. Two possibilities come to mind:

1. First read and store all the transactions, then process the transactions.

2. Read and process the first transaction, read and process the second transaction, etc.

The first possibility requires arrays in which to store all the transactions. How big should the arrays be? We don't know, since we have no idea how many transactions there may be. To use this method, we would have to determine the maximum number of transactions in any one run.

The question with the second method is feasibility. Is it possible to process a single transaction without having access to the others? The answer in this case is yes.

This is not really such a pointless question to ask as it might seem. For example, consider the task "Read in a list of transactions and print them out in order of the account number." We cannot "Read one and print, read one and print, etc.", so we <u>must</u> read all of them before we can begin printing.

With the second method, hold the transactions, since we need only keep track of one transaction at a time. This second method seems to have no disadvantages compared to the first, and should be used. An array is not needed to

Note that without a change in the problem definition, we are forced to use the second method. Since we don't know how many transactions might appear, we cannot use the first method. Quite often, a careful examination of the problem will answer a question for us. We should be continually asking ourselves questions like: "Have I used everything that was given to me?" "Could the problem definition be changed to make the solution easier, clearer, or more efficient?" "Have I assumed something that is not explicitly stated to be true?"

A second point concerns efficiency. For example, we use the second possibility rather than the first, because it uses less computer storage space but otherwise is essentially the same. We may strive for efficiency with respect to execution time, storage space, or with respect to the time it takes to write the program. There is generally a "trade-off" when trying to gain efficiency; usually what executes faster will take more space, or what is easier to program and understand may be slower. A programmer must know what the value criterion is for each program he is to design.

In this case we decide to process the transactions as they are read -- that is, to use the following algorithm:

```
Repeat for each transaction:
    Read the transaction.
    Process the transaction.
```

Once again, the question is how best to test for the presence of the dummy transaction. Since this is essentially the same problem as the one in reading and setting up the accounts, it should be solved by the <u>same tactics</u>. Although there may be several equivalently good ways of performing a certain task, in a particular program we should <u>strive for consistency</u>. That is, if two tasks at different points in the program are essentially similar, they should be implemented by essentially the same method. So this suggests that the transactions should be handled by the following kind of loop:

```
/** PROCESS TRANSACTIONS */
    TRAN_LOOP: DO WHILE ('1'B);
        Read transaction.
        IF transaction is dummy
            THEN LEAVE TRAN_LOOP;
        Process the transaction
        END TRAN_LOOP;
```

Further refinement requires a decision as to how the transactions are to be stored. It might be useful to question the format of the input transactions. For example, if we allow a negative amount to specify a withdrawal, then the withdrawal-deposit code is not necessary. But let us assume that the bank says the given form is indeed necessary, and continue with the development.

Since only one transaction need be accessed at any time, only three simple variables are needed:

```
TACCT   contains the Transaction ACCounT number.
DEPWITH contains the action code:
            1 means DEPosit, -1 means WITHdrawal.
AMT     contains the AMounT of the transaction.
```

The final task is to determine just what it means to "process" an individual non-dummy transaction. Processing a transaction requires finding the corresponding account in ACCT. Suppose that while searching ACCT we store in a new variable J an integer so that TACCT = ACCT(J). Then account ACCT(J) is to be changed as follows: If DEPWITH(J) = 1 then add 1 to DEP(J) and add AMT to CBAL(J); if DEPWITH(J) = -1 then add 1 to WITH(J) and subtract AMT from CBAL(J).

The search algorithm can be based on the search step of the program in Section 3.2. (This requires us to allow for one extra element in array ACCT.) If the search is successful (the account is found) then that account is changed; if unsuccessful then an error message is printed. The program is as follows:

```
/** PROCESS THE TRANSACTION */
    ACCT(K+1) = TACCT;
    J = 1;
    DO WHILE(TACCT ¬= ACCT(J));
        J = J + 1;
        END;
    IF J <= K
        THEN
            POST: SELECT;
               WHEN (DEPWITH = 1) DO;
                    DEP(J) = DEP(J) + 1;
                    CBAL(J) = CBAL(J) + AMT;
                    END;
               WHEN (DEPWITH = -1) DO;
                    WITH(J) = WITH(J) + 1;
                    CBAL(J) = CBAL(J) - AMT;
                    END;
               OTHERWISE PUT SKIP(2) LIST
                    ('IMPROPER CODE',
                    'ACCT NUM:', TACCT,
                    'CODE:', DEPWITH);
               END POST;
        ELSE DO;
            PUT  SKIP(2) LIST ('NO ACCOUNT EXISTS');
            PUT SKIP LIST ('ACCT NUM:', TACCT);
            END;
```

Stage 5. Refining "Print the results."

The "print" step is relatively straightforward. Since order was not specified by the problem description, we print the accounts in the easiest order possible -- the order in which they were read in. Realistically, very precise format specifications would be given for such a problem and the EDIT form of PUT would have to be used. However, we will just provide a rough form of output using the standard LIST format. In practice, this crude form of output might be used in order to test the rest of the program. When you are satisfied the rest of the program is correct, you would replace this temporary output step with a more precise version. Note that only the output step would be affected by this replacement.

The LIST format version of the output step is shown below:

```
/** PRINT THE RESULTS */
    PUT SKIP LIST ('ACCOUNT', 'PREV BAL',
            'WITHDRAWALS', 'DEPOSITS', 'FINAL BAL');
    PUT SKIP;
    DO I = 1 TO K BY 1;
        PUT SKIP LIST (ACCT(I), IBAL(I), WITH(I),
                DEP(I), CBAL(I));
        END;
```

Stage 6. <u>Assembling the complete program</u>.

The final task is to gather together the refinements for the three top-level statements to produce a complete program. We also produce declarations from the descriptions of variables produced in stages 2 and 4. We end up with the program below.

```
/* SIMPLIFIED BANK ACCOUNTING PROBLEM */
BANK: PROCEDURE OPTIONS(MAIN);
    DCL (ACCT(201),      /* ACCOUNT NUMBERS */
        WITH(200),       /* NBR OF WITHDRAWALS */
        DEP(200))        /* NBR OF DEPOSITS */
            FIXED;
    DCL (IBAL(200),      /* INITIAL BALANCES */
        CBAL(200))       /* CURRENT BALANCES */
            FLOAT;
    DCL TEMPACCT FIXED: /* TEMPORARY BUFFER FOR ACCT */
    DCL TEMPIBAL FLOAT; /* TEMPORARY BUFFER FOR IBAL */
    DCL (TACCT,          /* TRANSACTION ACCOUNT NUMBER */
        DEPWITH)         /* TRANSACTION DEP/WITH CODE */
            FIXED;       /* 1 = DEPOSIT, -1 = WITHDRAWAL */
    DCL AMT FLOAT;       /* TRANSACTION AMOUNT */
    DCL K FIXED;         /* NUMBER OF ACCOUNTS */
    DCL (I, J) FIXED;

    /** READ AND SET UP THE ACCOUNTS */
        K = 0;
        SETUP: DO WHILE ('1'B);
            GET LIST (TEMPACCT, TEMPIBAL);
            IF TEMPACCT = 0
                THEN LEAVE SETUP;
            K = K + 1;
            ACCT(K) = TEMPACCT;
            IBAL(K) = TEMPIBAL;
            WITH(K) = 0;
            DEP(K) = 0;
            CBAL(K) = IBAL(K);
            END SETUP;
```

```
/** PROCESS TRANSACTIONS */
    TRAN_LOOP: DO WHILE ('1'B);
        GET LIST (TACCT, DEPWITH, AMT);
        IF TACCT = 0
            THEN LEAVE TRAN_LOOP;
        /** PROCESS THE TRANSACTION */
            ACCT(K+1) = TACCT;
            J = 1;
            DO WHILE(TACCT ¬ = ACCT(J));
                J = J + 1;
                END;
            IF J ≤ K
                THEN
                    POST: SELECT;
                        WHEN (DEPWITH = 1) DO;
                            DEP(J) = DEP(J) + 1;
                            CBAL(J) = CBAL(J) + AMT;
                            END;
                        WHEN (DEPWITH = -1) DO;
                            WITH(J) = WITH(J) + 1;
                            CBAL(J) = CBAL(J) - AMT;
                            END;
                        OTHERWISE PUT SKIP(2) LIST
                                ('IMPROPER CODE',
                                'ACCT NUM:', TACCT,
                                'CODE', DEPWITH);
                        END POST;
                ELSE DO;
                    PUT SKIP(2) LIST ('NO ACCOUNT EXISTS');
                    PUT SKIP LIST ('ACCT NUM:', TACCT);
                    END;
        END TRAN_LOOP;

/** PRINT THE RESULTS */
    PUT SKIP LIST ('ACCOUNT', 'PREV BAL', 'WITHDRAWALS',
            'DEPOSITS', 'FINAL BAL');
    PUT SKIP;
    DO I = 1 TO K BY 1;
        PUT SKIP LIST (ACCT(I), IBAL(I), WITH(I),
                DEP(I), CBAL(I));
        END;

END BANK;
```

3.5 Scanning for Symbols

Many programs process "text". Two examples are the PL/C translator and the "text-editing" program used to produce this book. Such programs have the common subproblem of reading lines of text and dividing them into separate "symbols". We define a symbol, for the purpose of this example, to be simply a sequence of consecutive, non-blank characters. For example, the following line consists of five separate symbols:

```
PUT SKIP (2) LIST (A);
```

Alternatively, the same line could be presented so that it contains only three symbols:

```
PUT SKIP(2) LIST(A);
```

Actually, in PL/C, punctuation marks and operators are considered separate symbols, but this simplified version in which only blanks are significant in defining symbols gives a reasonable introduction to the problem.

Initially, we consider symbol scanning as if it were a separate problem, although it would have little purpose used separately. The problem can be stated as follows:

> Read a list of lines (or punched cards) and print a list of the symbols each line contains, in order.
>
> A symbol is any substring of a line consisting of consecutive non-blank characters.
>
> The input format will be quoted character strings.
>
> The output format is to be one symbol per line, single-spaced, left-justified.

We use this example to show the development of three alternative stategies. Each is reasonable in that it solves the required task, but the three programs are quite different. They differ on whether the character, symbol or line is viewed as the driving force behind the problem.

One problem is solved in a similar fashion in all three versions, and it is perhaps best to explain it here. Note that any symbol must be contained on one line -- it may not begin on one line and end on the next. This means that it may be terminated either by a blank or by the end of the line. One principle in programming is to reduce the number of cases to a minimum, and we can do this here by adding a blank to each line as it is read in. Then, every symbol is terminated by a blank character.

3.5.1 Character Strategy

In this section, the top level of the algorithm is based on processing character by character. As a first attempt, it looks like

```
For each character of the input, in order:
   Process the character.
```

How do we process a character? If it is part of a symbol, it should be added to the symbol under construction. If it is a blank, then it either signals the termination of a symbol that must be printed, or it is simply an extra blank that can be deleted. We obviously need a variable in which to build a symbol, and so we use

```
DCL SYMBOL CHAR(80) VARYING;
        /* SYMBOL UNDER CONSTRUCTION */
```

Processing a character then falls into three cases:

```
Character is nonblank: add it to SYMBOL.
Character is blank and SYMBOL = '': do nothing.
Character is blank and SYMBOL ¬= '': Print SYMBOL and set
    SYMBOL = ''.
```

This can be written using a SELECT statement as

```
SELECT;
    WHEN (character ¬= ' ')
            SYMBOL = SYMBOL || character;
    WHEN (character = ' ' & SYMBOL ¬= '')
            DO; Print SYMBOL;
               SYMBOL = '';
               END;
    WHEN (character = ' ' & SYMBOL = '')    ;
    OTHERWISE;
    END;
```

In the final program given below we have taken advantage of the order in which the WHEN conditions are tested (first to last) in order to reduce the content of the conditions. (Compare this with the version above.) This must be done carefully since the SELECT used in the program would <u>not</u> be equivalent if the order of the WHEN statements was reversed.

The body of the loop should be understood in terms of the definitions of variables SYMBOL, LINE, and POS.

```
/* PRINT LIST OF SYMBOLS */
SYM: PROCEDURE OPTIONS(MAIN);
    DCL SYMBOL CHAR(80) VAR; /* SYMBOL UNDER CONSTRUCTION */
    DCL LINE CHAR(81) VAR;   /* INPUT LINE FOLLOWED BY ' ' */
    DCL POS FIXED;           /* POSITION IN CHARACTER LINE */
                             /* BEING PROCESSED */
    SYMBOL = '';
    LINE = ' ';
    POS = 1;
    ON ENDFILE(SYSIN) GOTO DATAEND;

    CHAR_LOOP: DO WHILE ('1'B);
        SELECT;
            WHEN (SUBSTR(LINE,POS,1) ¬= ' ')
                    SYMBOL = SYMBOL || SUBSTR(LINE,POS,1);
            WHEN (SYMBOL ¬= '') DO;
                    PUT SKIP LIST (SYMBOL);
                    SYMBOL = '';
                    END;
            OTHERWISE ;
            END;
        /** SET POS TO POINT TO NEXT CHARACTER */
            POS = POS + 1;
            IF LENGTH(LINE) < POS
                THEN DO;
                    GET LIST (LINE);
                    LINE = LINE || ' ';
                    POS = 1;
                    END;
        END CHAR_LOOP;

    DATAEND: ON ENDFILE(SYSIN) SYSTEM;
    END SYM;
```

3.5.2 Symbol Strategy

The purpose of the program is to find and print symbols, and it makes sense to write the top level algorithm as

```
Repeat for each symbol:
   Find the next symbol.
   Print the next symbol.
```

Thus in this version the symbol is the driving force, and not the character; the main loop iterates once for each symbol instead of once for each character. Note that, in both the character and symbol strategy, reading lines is incidental and is not even mentioned at the top level. In both cases, however, reading lines does provide the exit mechanism for the main loop using the ENDFILE condition.

In finding the next symbol, we have the choice of moving one character at a time from LINE to SYMBOL (as in Section 3.5.1) or locating the ends of the symbol and moving the entire symbol as a single unit. Choosing the latter, the top level algorithm becomes

```
    Repeat for each symbol:
        Locate first non-blank character (LEND).
        Locate the following blank character (REND).
        Print the symbol.
```

The complete program appears below. Note the loop that makes sure that LINE actually does contain a symbol. This is necessary because completely blank input lines are not excluded. In this version, we also use a different definition for LINE. The complete LINE is not saved -- only that portion that has not yet been processed.

```
 /* PRINT LIST OF SYMBOLS */
 MOVESYM: PROCEDURE OPTIONS(MAIN);
     DCL LINE CHAR(81) VAR;  /* THAT PART OF THE INPUT LINE */
                             /* (FOLLOWED BY A BLANK) THAT HAS*/
                             /* NOT YET BEEN PROCESSED */
     DCL (LEND,              /* POSN OF FIRST CHAR OF SYMBOL */
         REND) FIXED;        /* POSN OF BLANK FOLLOWING SYMBOL*/
     ON ENDFILE(SYSIN) GOTO DATAEND;

     SYMBOL_LOOP: DO WHILE ('1'B);
         /** SET LEND TO POSITION OF FIRST NON-BLANK */
             DO WHILE (LINE = ' ');
                 GET LIST (LINE);
                 LINE = LINE || ' ';
                 END;
             LEND = 1;
             DO WHILE (SUBSTR(LINE,LEND,1) = ' ');
                 LEND = LEND + 1;
                 END;
         /** SET REND TO POSITION OF FOLLOWING BLANK */
             REND = LEND + 1;
             DO WHILE (SUBSTR(LINE,REND,1) ¬= ' ');
                 REND = REND + 1;
                 END;
         PUT SKIP LIST (SUBSTR(LINE,LEND,REND-LEND));
         LINE = SUBSTR(LINE,REND);
         END SYMBOL_LOOP;

     DATAEND: ON ENDFILE(SYSIN) SYSTEM;
     END MOVESYM;
```

3.5.3 Line Strategy

If we consider the main task to be decomposing input lines (rather than finding symbols) the top level of the algorithm would be:

> Repeat for each input line:
> > Remove and print symbols of line, one at a time.

Here, the construction and printing of the symbol is incidental, and processing lines is considered to be the driving force. We are then led to the problem of removing and printing symbols of a line, and in doing so we find that we can process a line using either the character or symbol stategy. Choosing the former would yield a program similar to the following:

```
/* PRINT LIST OF SYMBOLS */
DECLINE: PROCEDURE OPTIONS(MAIN);
    DCL LINE CHAR(81) VAR;  /* INPUT LINE FOLLOWED BY A BLANK*/
    DCL POS FIXED;          /* POSITION IN CHARACTER LINE */
                            /* BEING PROCESSED */
    DCL SYMBOL CHAR(80) VAR;/* SYMBOL UNDER CONSTRUCTION */
    ON ENDFILE(SYSIN) GOTO DATAEND;

    LINE_LOOP: DO WHILE ('1'B);
        GET LIST (LINE);
        LINE = LINE || ' ';
        SYMBOL = '';
        DO POS = 1 TO LENGTH(LINE) BY 1;
            SELECT;
                WHEN (SUBSTR(LINE,POS,1) ¬= ' ')
                    SYMBOL = SYMBOL || SUBSTR(LINE,POS,1);
                WHEN (SYMBOL ¬= '') DO;
                        PUT SKIP LIST (SYMBOL);
                        SYMBOL = '';
                        END;
                OTHERWISE ;
                END;
            END;
        END LINE_LOOP;

    DATAEND: ON ENDFILE(SYSIN) SYSTEM;
    END DECLINE;
```

3.5.4 A Comparison of Strategies

All three solutions are reasonable in that they solve the problem fairly efficiently. The symbol stategy is perhaps the best, for it solves the problem at the level in which the problem is described, which makes it easier to modify the program if the problem requirements are changed (which happens very often). For example, you might want to allow a single symbol to be split over two input lines (see Section 3.5.5).

The line decomposition strategy is the hardest to understand. The concept of a line appears in the specification of the problem only because of the physical constraints of the input medium. Logically, we would rather consider the input to be a continuous sequence of symbols, but we are forced to consider it in terms of lines just because of a characteristic of the physical input medium. Consequently, making the line the central concept of the algorithm is awkward and leads to a comparatively clumsy program. This is more apparent in Section 3.5.5 where a line end need not terminate a symbol.

The character strategy is more natural than the line strategy, but it treats the problem at an unnecessarily low level. Contrast the character program with the line program. The former has a single loop, and within the loop one character is processed and the next character obtained in a straightforward manner. On the other hand, the line program requires two nested loops. The outer loop iterates once for each line, but needs an interior loop to process the characters of that line. In general, a program with fewer levels of nested loops is easier to understand and therefore preferable. In comparing these two strategies, note that processing a character is exactly the same in both cases; only the method of proceeding to the next character is different.

We should also point out that none of these programs takes full advantage of the character-processing built-in functions provided by PL/I. See Exercise 15 at the end of this section.

3.5.5 Symbols Divided over Two Input Lines

Let us now develop a program that processes symbols as before, but with the complication that a symbol may be split onto more than one input line. For example, with the symbol "THE", the letter "T" could appear in column 80 of one line (or card) and "HE" could appear in columns 1 and 2 of the next. One difficulty that arises is that now a symbol can be longer than a single input line, so we have to put some limit on the length of a symbol.

Let us also modify the task to require complete 80-character card images to be processed (to avoid having to quote the lines of input).

With these modifications, the problem is as follows:

> The input consists of a sequence of "symbols" on cards. Each symbol consists of 1 to 60 nonblank characters, and each adjacent pair of symbols is separated by one or more blanks. The last symbol is also followed by at least one blank. A symbol may be split onto two cards.
>
> Write a program segment that, when executed, will read in and print the symbols, one per line. If a symbol is more than 60 characters long, it may be split into two or more symbols without giving an error message.

Let us look at the problem of constructing the next symbol. We use a symbol strategy (Section 3.5.2). Assume a CHAR VARYING variable named LINE will always contain that part of the input that has been read but not yet "processed". Initially, then, we have LINE = ''. The process of getting the next symbol into a SYMBOL for printing consists of deleting blanks preceding the next symbol, moving it to SYMBOL, and finally, deleting the symbol from LINE. Thus we write down the following algorithm:

```
S1: Delete blanks preceding the first nonblank in LINE
    and the rest of the input.
S2: Find the first blank in LINE and the input.
S3: Put the symbol into SYMBOL.
S4: Delete the symbol from LINE.
```

Step 1. Refinement of S1, Deleting the Blanks

There are two difficulties with S1. First, LINE may contain nothing but blanks, and secondly it might even contain nothing (as it does the first time this segment is executed). Either case should cause us to read in more input. The following program segment serves the purpose:

```
/** DELETE BLANKS BEFORE SYMBOL.  */
    /** PUT INTO I THE POSITION OF FIRST NONBLANK */
        FIND: DO WHILE ('1'B);
            /** SEARCH LINE, TERMINATE IF */
                /* NONBLANK FOUND */
                DO I = 1 TO LENGTH(LINE) BY 1;
                   IF SUBSTR(LINE,I,1) ¬= ' '
                       THEN LEAVE FIND;
                   END;
            /** NO NONBLANKS - GET MORE INPUT */
                GET EDIT (LINE) (A(80));
            END FIND;

    /** DELETE THE BLANKS IN POSITIONS 1:I-1 */
        LINE = SUBSTR(LINE,I);
```

Step 2. Refinement of S2, Finding the End of the Symbol

The only difficulty with S2 is that the symbol may be split on two lines. We must also watch out for the length of the symbol. We should stop when the length is 60. The program uses a CHAR(80) variable named LINE1 as a temporary location to hold a card just read.

```
/** AFTER EXECUTION OF THIS SEGMENT, THE SYMBOL IS */
    /* IN SUBSTR(LINE,1,I-1); */
    FD: DO I = 1 TO 60 BY 1;
        IF I > LENGTH(LINE)
            THEN DO;
                GET EDIT (LINE1) (A(80));
                LINE = LINE || LINE1;
                END;
        IF SUBSTR(LINE,I,1) = ' '
            THEN LEAVE FD;
    END FD;
```

Step 3. The Final Program

Statements S3 and S4 of the original algorithm are simple statements, so the development is finished. We assemble the various segments below, adding the necessary declarations.

```
/* PRINT LIST OF SYMBOLS */
SYM: PROC OPTIONS (MAIN);
    DCL LINE CHAR(139) VAR;   /* INPUT READ */
                              /* BUT NOT YET PROCESSED */
    DCL LINE1 CHAR(80) VAR;   /* TEMPORARY TO HOLD CARD */
    DCL SYMBOL CHAR(60) VAR;  /* CONSTRUCTED SYMBOL */
    DCL I FIXED;

    LINE = '';
    SYMBOL = '';
    ON ENDFILE (SYSIN) GOTO DATAEND;

    DO WHILE ('1'B);
        /** PUT NEXT INPUT SYMBOL INTO "SYMBOL". */
           /** DELETE BLANKS BEFORE SYMBOL */
              /** PUT POSITION OF FIRST NONBLANK INTO I*/
                 FIND: DO WHILE ('1'B);
                    /** SEARCH LINE AND TERMINATE */
                       /* IF NONBLANK FOUND */
                       DO I = 1 TO LENGTH(LINE) BY 1;
                          IF SUBSTR (LINE,I,1) ¬= ' '
                             THEN LEAVE FIND;
                          END;
                    /* NO NONBLANKS - GET MORE INPUT */
                       GET EDIT (LINE) (A(80));
                    END FIND;
              /** DELETE THE BLANKS IN POSITIONS 1:I-1 */
                 LINE = SUBSTR(LINE,I);
```

```
        /** AFTER EXECUTION OF THIS SEGMENT,  THE */
           /* SYMBOL IS IN SUBSTR(LINE,1,I-1) */
           FD: DO I = 1 TO 60 BY 1;
              IF I > LENGTH(LINE)
                 THEN DO;
                    GET EDIT (LINE1) (A(80));
                    LINE = LINE || LINE1;
                    END;
              IF SUBSTR(LINE,I,1) = ' '
                 THEN LEAVE FD;
              END FD;

        /** PUT SYMBOL INTO "SYMBOL" */
           SYMBOL = SUBSTR(LINE,1,I-1);

        /** DELETE SYMBOL FROM INPUT */
           LINE = SUBSTR(LINE,I);

     PUT SKIP LIST (SYMBOL);
     END;

 DATAEND: ON ENDFILE (SYSIN) SYSTEM;
 END SYM;
```

Section 3 Exercises

Exercises 1 to 7 refer to the accounting problem of Section 3.4.

1. Suppose the alternative strategy for Stage 3 was chosen. How would the data structures (and the declarations) have to be altered?

2. For each of the 6 errors discussed in the first part of Section 3.4, indicate whether the program should stop or whether it may be reasonable to continue.

3. Change the program to consider these 6 errors. These changes should not be made by trying to revise the final program. Instead, go back to the proper stage (3, 4, or 5) and perform the complete analysis and program creation once more, this time with the view of checking and documenting possible input errors.

4. Suppose the signal ending the accounts is a single 0 instead of two 0's. Change the program to reflect this. In making the changes, repeat the program analysis and development from the beginning; don't attempt to just change the final program. Which signal is better and why?

5. Suppose we wish to change the end-of-transaction signal to a single 0 instead of three. Change the program to reflect this.

6. Suppose the account numbers were limited to three digits. Can you think of a way to sort the accounts efficiently? What modifications would you have to make in the program? What are the relative merits of your solution and the one developed here in terms of time and space?

7. In Stage 4, develop an alternative loop to process the transactions that does not use "indefinite repetition". That is, have a WHILE or UNTIL condition that actually terminates the loop when the dummy transaction has been read. Compare your program segment to the one given in the text. Which is more efficient? Which is easier to understand? Which would be easier to modify if problem requirements were slightly changed?

8. Below are several problem statements. For each, develop an algorithm (in English) to solve it. This algorithm should contain no details about arrays used, variables used, etc. It should just be a description of the program strategy.

   a) The input consists of two lists X and Y of numbers. Print out the number of times each number in list Y occurs in the first list X.

   b) The input consists of a list of bank accounts and transactions concerning these accounts. Print out the number of transactions for each account.

c) The input consists of the text of a book, punched on cards, followed by a list of words. Print out the number of times each word on the list is used in the book.

d) The input consists of a list of student records (name, address, grades in each course, etc.), followed by a list of a few student names. Print the average, highest, and lowest grade point average for the students in the second list.

9. Below are several problem statements. For each, develop an algorithm that shows the overall structure of the final program.

a) The input consists of a list of integers. Print the even integers.

b) The input consists of a list of integers. Print the primes. (An integer is prime if it is greater than 1 and divisible only by 1 and itself. The integers 2, 3, 5, 7, 11, 59 are prime; the integers -2, 0, 1, 4, 9, 100 are not.)

c) The input consists of a list of names of people. Print the names that contain the letter A.

10. "Comment outlines" for the top level of development of several programs are given below. Complete the programs by adding the actual PL/I statements that will perform what is specified by the heading comments. The problem requirements given in these comments are sketchy; assume whatever detail is necessary to write the programs. Document all such assumptions.

10a.
```
/* DETERMINE POSITIVE ROW AVERAGES, AND NBR OF ZEROES */
POSROW: PROCEDURE OPTIONS(MAIN);
   DCL TAB(10,10) FLOAT; /* GIVEN ARRAY IS */
   DCL (NR, NC) FIXED;   /* TAB(1:NR,1:NC) */
   DCL (SUM(10), AVG(10)) FLOAT;
          /* SUM(1:NR) ARE ROW SUMS OF TAB */
          /* AVG(1:NR) ARE ROW AVERAGES OF TAB */
   DCL ZEROS(10) FIXED;
          /* ZEROS(1:NR) ARE NBR OF ZEROS IN ROWS */
   DCL (I, J) FIXED;

   /** READ AND TEST: NR AND NC */

   /** LOAD TAB(1:NR,1:NC) IN ROW MAJOR ORDER */

   /** REPLACE NEGATIVE ENTRIES OF TAB(1:NR,1:NC) WITH */
       /* 0, AND COUNT ALL ZEROS IN EACH ROW */

   /** COMPUTE ROW AVERAGES FOR NON-ZERO ENTRIES */

   /** DISPLAY AVG AND NBR ZEROS FOR EACH ROW */

   END POSROW;
```

```
10b. /* READ 7X9 ARRAY, REVERSE ODD ROWS */
     /* FIND COLUMN MAXIMA, AND DISPLAY */
     INVMAX: PROCEDURE OPTIONS(MAIN);
        DCL TAB(7, 9) FLOAT;
        DCL COLMAX(9) FLOAT; /* COLUMN MAXIMA */
        DCL (I, J) FIXED;

        /** LOAD TAB IN ROW MAJOR ORDER */

        /** REVERSE ORDER OF ELEMENTS IN ODD ROWS OF TAB */

        /** FIND MAXIMUM VALUE IN EACH COLUMN OF TAB */

        /** DISPLAY COLUMN MAXIMA */

        END INVMAX;

10c. /* REVERSE STRINGS AND TEST FOR "A" BEFORE "B" */
     REVTEST: PROCEDURE OPTIONS(MAIN);
        DCL STR(50) CHAR (20) VAR; /* TABLE OF STRINGS IS: */
        DCL N FIXED;               /* STR(1:N) */
        DCL L FIXED;               /* L CHARS IN EACH STR */
        DCL (I, J) FIXED;

        /** READ  NBR AND LENGTH OF STRINGS FROM INITIAL DATA */

        /** LOAD STR(1:N) */

        /** REVERSE EACH STRING S(I) FOR 1≤I≤N */

        /** PRINT A LIST OF REVERSED STRINGS S(I) IN WHICH AN */
           /* "A" APPEARS TO THE LEFT OF THE FIRST "B" */

        END REVTEST;

10d. /* ROTATE SQUARE ARRAY QUARTER-TURN CLOCKWISE */
     ROTATE: PROCEDURE OPTIONS(MAIN);
        DCL (AR(40, 40), AR2(40, 40)) FLOAT; /* ARRAYS ARE */
        DCL N FIXED; /* AR(N,N), AR2(N,N) */
        DCL (I, J) FIXED;

        /** READ NBR OF ROWS N, AND LOAD AR BY ROWS */

        /** COPY EACH COLUMN OF AR, LEFT TO RIGHT, */
           /* INTO ROW OF AR2, TOP TO BOTTOM */

        /**  DISPLAY ROTATED ARRAY AR2 BY ROWS, TOP TO BOTTOM */

        END ROTATE;
```

11. For each of the following problems, develop a program to the point of having a "comment outline", such as those illustrated in Exercise 10.

11a. Given a list of non-zero numbers (with zero added to the end as a stopping flag) determine which numbers in the list are not unique (that is, which appear more than once). The list may be long but it will not contain more than 40 different numbers.

11b. Given a list of not more than 100 non-negative numbers (with -1 added as a stopping flag) either:

1. Print a list of the numbers that are greater than the final value on the list <u>and</u> that are not repeated in the list, or

2. Print a list of the numbers greater than the average of all the numbers on the original list.

Let V be the first value. Do 1 if there are more numbers on the list <u>greater</u> than V than there are numbers <u>less</u> than V; otherwise do 2. There will be at least one value besides the stopping flag.

11c. Given three lists of numbers, each n numbers long, produce another list called the "merged list" with the following properties:

1. It contains all the non-zero values from the 3 lists.

2. Values on the merged list are in the same order they appeared in the given lists.

3. If a value was in position i in one of the given lists, it will appear in the merged list before any number that was in a position later than i in any one of the given lists.

The 3 given lists are preceded by an integer n (less than 50) specifying the length of each of the 3 given lists. Print the merged list first, 3 values per line. Then print the given lists in 3 column format. For example, if the data are:

```
   4,    7,0,3,9,    0,4,5,0,    1,2,0,0
```

the output would be:

```
MERGED LIST
   7   1   4
   2   3   5
   9

GIVEN LISTS
   7   0   1
   0   4   2
   3   5   0
   9   0   0
```

12. Rewrite the following program so that it has the same function but is properly structured and well-presented with appropriate labels, comments and indentation.

```
TEST: PROCEDURE OPTIONS(MAIN);
DCL (J, N, K) FIXED;
DCL LIM FLOAT;
J = 1;
LOOP:; IF J = N+1 THEN GOTO BODY;
J = 1;
LOOP2:; IF J = K THEN GOTO OUT;
IF X(J) < LIM THEN PUT SKIP LIST (J, X(J));
J = J+1;
GOTO LOOP2;
DCL X(50) FLOAT;
BODY:; GET LIST (X(J));
X(J) = X(J) + J;
J = J+1;
GOTO LOOP;
OUT:; END TEST;
```

13. The game of NIM is similar to the Match-Snatch game described in Section II.3.4. The differences are that there are several piles of matches in NIM instead of one, and in each move a player may take as many matches as he wishes (at least one), but only from one pile. The object of NIM may be either to take the last match, or to avoid having to take the last match, at the option of the players and decided upon in advance.

Write an interactive program to play NIM. The parameters of the game are

1. How many piles there are;
2. How many matches there are in each pile;
3. Whether the winner takes the last match or avoids doing so;
4. Who plays first.

As for Match-Snatch there is an algorithm for playing NIM such that the player to go first can win under all but some very special conditions. However it is not a trivial exercise to determine this algorithm. But even without an "optimal" algorithm you should be able to write a program that will be a "good" NIM player. In fact, if several students write NIM-playing programs, you could have a "NIM tournament"! This is actually done with programs that play Chess. Every year there is a tournament among the World's Chess-playing programs. Some of the programs play good Chess but so far they can all be beaten by any really excellent human Chess player.

14. Suppose the requirements of the symbol scanning problem of Section 3.5 were changed to consider either a left or right parenthesis to be a separate symbol. Parentheses also serve to separate symbols. With this change each of the following lines is equivalent, and consists of the same four symbols:

```
SKIP(2)
SKIP (2)
SKIP ( 2 )
```

Modify any one of the three programs given in Section 3.5 to achieve this expanded requirement.

15. Rewrite one of the symbol-scanning programs of Sections 3.5.1 - 3.5.3 to take advantage of the character-processing built-in functions INDEX, TRANSLATE and/or VERIFY.

16. Suppose that the list to be ordered by the program in Section 3.3 consisted of <u>words</u> rather than numbers, and they were to be put into alphabetical order. How would the program have to be changed?

Section 4 General Design Considerations

The preceding sections have described the basic idea of program development in several different ways:

1. Break a problem into a sequence of subproblems.

2. Refine a statement into several finer statements with increasing detail.

3. Expand a statement of what has to be done into a specification of how it is to be done.

4. Expand "high-level" commands such as "solve", "find" or "compute" into lower-level statements of a programming language.

5. Translate a problem description from English to PL/I.

These are different aspects of the same general process: the systematic transformation of a statement of requirements in English to a detailed specification of actions in PL/I.

We outlined the phases of the process in Section 1, suggested general approaches in Section 2, and gave examples in Section 3. In Section 4 we review the process and describe several of the key issues in more detail.

4.1 Top-Down Development

In general, development decisions should be made in "outside-in", "top-down" order -- in order of increasing detail. In the bank problem of 3.4, initially a number of questions could have been raised and answered -- how accounts should be stored, how the transactions should be processed, how the transactions should be stored, etc. Out of all these, we chose the one that helped determine the overall structure and that led to a correct program with just more detail: what were the main subproblems and in which order should they be executed?

This is not to say that your thoughts shouldn't skip to various parts of the program in varying amounts of detail. (They will whether you want them to or not.) There is nothing wrong in beginning by looking at various possibilities for the representation of data and subalgorithms to process them. Sometimes this is necessary in order to obtain a better understanding of the problem and possible solutions. Sometimes this is necessary in order to come up with any idea at all. But this should just be considered a side trip. Any ideas discovered on it should not be accepted as final, and the main program development should then proceed top-down. It may be necessary to develop several alternatives to some depth before it is clear which one is best.

This top-down process is not as easy and straightforward as it may seem from the examples given in Section 3. Programming, like any problem solving, is a trial and error process. Mistakes will be made, or just the wrong avenue explored, which will cause the programmer to undo several levels of refinements and to repeat the process in a different manner. This "backing up" is discussed in more detail in Section 4.1.3.

Programming in top-down fashion may seem foreign and difficult, especially to beginners. Yet for most problems it is the best approach, because it will lead to efficient, understandable, and correct programs. Attempt right from the beginning to develop programs in a top-down, outside-in, general-statement-to-fine-detail, manner.

In programming in this fashion we attempt to make one clear decision at a time. A decision leads to a refinement of part of the program. The two types of refinement are:

1. A statement is refined.

2. The method of storing data is refined, by describing the variables used to store the data.

We discuss these separately in the next two subsections.

4.1.1 Refining a Statement

4.1.1.1 Concentrating on "What" Rather than "How"

One of the advantages of top-down programming is that it helps us concentrate initially on what is to be done, and then systematically becomes concerned with how. For example, in developing the overall structure of the accounting problem in Section 3.4, in Stage 1 we refined "Solve the problem" into an algorithm with three steps:

1. Read and set up the accounts.
2. Read in and process the transactions.
3. Print the results.

Here, we were not primarily interested in how the accounts and transactions were to be stored or processed, but only in what was to be done, so that we could concentrate on the order in which the various functions were to be performed.

As another example, consider the sorting problem of 3.3. Sorting is refined in terms of

"move the maximum element to the end of the list".

This states what is to be done, but not how. There are several methods that could be used. "Move..." is refined into

"find the position of the maximum"
"interchange maximum and last".

This suggests what could be done to accomplish "move..." without specifying how either "find..." or "interchange..." will be performed.

4.1.1.2 Limiting Ourselves to Understandable Refinements

When refining a statement we replace a statement of what to do by an algorithm that indicates how to do it. In making such a refinement it is important to limit ourselves to refinements we can easily understand and communicate to others.

Given a statement, what possibilities exist? The most general possibility is a sequence of statements to be executed in order. Thus we should attempt to break the original statement into successive parts to be executed in order. Other possibilities for a refinement are:

1. Use a conditional statement to break the problem into two subcases.

2. Break it into several (instead of two) subcases.

3. Replace it by a loop (perhaps with initialization statements).

Faced with these limited possibilities for refining a statement, we can focus attention on the following questions:

1. How can it be broken up into successive parts?

2. Does it break up easily into two or more subcases?

3. Is it an iteration problem -- can a loop be used?

These methods of refinement lead naturally to the program units described in Section II.2.

The symbol scanning problem of Section 3.5.5 is a good example. Given an "unprocessed" string in LINE, we want to "process" the left-most "symbol" of that string into SYMBOL. We might refine this into a sequence of four steps:

```
S1: Delete blanks preceding the first nonblank in LINE
     and the rest of the input;
S2: Find the first blank in LINE and the input;
S3: Put the symbol into SYMBOL;
S4: Delete the symbol from LINE.
```

We now have four simpler problems to refine. The problems of an empty line or a word split onto two lines have been postponed -- in fact, we didn't even have to mention them.

4.1.1.3 Using Suitable Notation for Statements

Whatever language and notation suits the problem at hand should be used in order to aid in an orderly development and to make the final program as lucid as possible. Usually the initial notation consists of English commands like "Sort the list", "Process the transactions" and "Generate a value to ...". _Any_ imperative statement can be used, provided its meaning is sufficiently clear.

In particular, it is often convenient to _invent_ control mechanisms that do not exist in PL/I (and perhaps not in any real programming language). For example, the loop exit is a convenient mechanism, but until the recent addition of the LEAVE there was no exit in PL/I. Nevertheless, in previous editions of this book we invented an "exit statement" and used it in program development. If you are currently using a PL/I dialect without the LEAVE statement, you should still use it in developing your programs and then, at the final stage, implement the exit with a GOTO.

As other examples, the meaning of the following two algorithms should be clear without any formal definition of how the "for each" statement is to be executed:

```
For each account in the list:
    IF the account balance < 0
        THEN Print a message.
```

```
For each position of the chessboard:
    IF the position is occupied by a white piece
        THEN DO;
            IF the white piece can capture the black
                king
              THEN Print "check".
            IF the white piece can capture the black
                queen
              THEN Print "watch out!".
            END;
```

Using such statements helps postpone decisions about the order in which the accounts or positions on the chessboard should be processed. These can wait, and will probably depend on how the list and chessboard are stored as variables. Once we decide on an order, translating the "for each" segments into PL/I loops should not be difficult.

As another example, consider a program to simulate a baseball game. We have variables that keep track of the inning, number of outs, men on base, etc., and we have a way of generating an integer PITCH to represent what happens next. A partial list of the values of PITCH and the corresponding actions are given below:

value of PITCH	action after pitch
1	ball
2	strike
3	foul ball
4	single
5	double
etc.	

We need a program section that will select one of these alternatives depending on the value of PITCH. A convenient notation during program development might be something like:

```
Do one of following, depending on value of PITCH:
    1: Process ball;
    2: Process strike;
    3: Process foul ball;
    4: Process single;
    5: Process double;
     etc.
```

There are several ways this can be translated into PL/I (recall Section I.6.3) but during development it is clearer to have it in the form shown here.

4.1.2 Refining a Data Description

Data refinements are just as important as statement refinements. You will gradually learn that there are many different ways of keeping data in variables. For example, the list of accounts in the bank problem of 3.4 can be kept in unsorted form in an array, or sorted in ascending or descending order. There are also more sophisticated storage structures such as hash tables, singly linked lists, doubly linked lists, circular lists, deques, stacks and trees. Each method has advantages and disadvantages, depending on the nature and form of the operations to be performed. In order to intelligently choose a method for data representation, it is necessary to wait until the operations to be performed on the data are well understood.

The method of storing transactions in the bank problem is a good illustration. We could have initially decided to use an array, since there were many transactions. But waiting and later deciding based on what was to be done with the transactions led to the discovery that only one transaction had to be stored at any time.

Whenever you decide upon variables, write down their names with their exact meanings immediately. Don't wait until you write the declaration for them. Every variable is important (or else it shouldn't be in the program) and you must know exactly why it is there. Don't trust these exact meanings to your memory; write them down.

A recent incident will illustrate the importance of this. A student came in with a two-page program, the relevant parts of which are given in (4.1.2a). The program was a simplified "text editor"; it read text -- a sequence of words interspersed with symbols for commands like "begin a new line" and "begin a new paragraph" -- and printed out the text as formatted by the commands. Each output line was "right justified", which means that not only were the left margins lined up, but also the right margins. (Right justification is performed by inserting extra blanks between words, as in the lines you are now reading.)

There was obviously an error, since occasionally a blank at the end of a word was missing -- "the big black fox" might come out as "thebig black fox". The problem was found by examining the exact role of the variables. Looking at the program, it was surmised that OUTLINE would contain the current line to be written out and LENGTHLINE would contain its length. The student was asked what N meant, since its meaning was not written down. After some uncertainty he said "Oh, it's just the length of the word being added to the current line OUTLINE." ("It's just" is used often when one doesn't really know. It seems to belittle the variable, making it all right not to know exactly why it is there.)

The program was then examined to find if N was always assigned and used in this way. The error was exposed when it was discovered that in one place, N was the length of the word, while in the other it was the length plus one, to take into account the blank character following it.

(4.1.2a)

```
            ...
            IF ...
                THEN DO;
                    ...
                    WORD = SUBSTR(LINE,M,N);
                    WORD = WORD || ' ';
                    ...
                    END;
                ELSE DO;
                    ...
                    WORD = WORD || ' ';
                    N = LENGTH(WORD);
                    ...
                    END;
            ...
            LENGTHLINE = LENGTH(OUTLINE) + N;
            OUTLINE = ...
            ...
```

The importance of clearly understanding and having an exact written description of each variable cannot be overemphasized.

4.1.2.1 Using Suitable Notation for Data

We used notation outside PL/I in Section 3.4 during development of the bank program, programming in terms of a "table of accounts" and a "transaction" as long as possible before describing how these quantities were to be represented in the PL/I program. In effect, we talked as if the whole table of accounts were contained as a value in a variable. Data can often be represented using variables in many ways, and it is important to talk in general terms about the "list" or the "records" until more is known about the operations to be performed on them. For example, see the "KWIC index" development in Section VI.2.6.

Some algorithms just cannot be described coherently without resorting to notation outside of PL/I. A good example of this is the "heap sort" algorithm developed in Section VI.2.7.

Using high-level notation for data structures is just as important as for statements. However it is difficult to give good examples of this until you have more programming experience and are familiar with a variety of different data structures. This is discussed in more detail in Part VII.

4.1.3 Backing Up

Program development is a trial and error process. We make refinements and try some subalgorithms, and if they don't serve our purpose we redo them. Redoing one subalgorithm may require us to change other parts of the algorithm, both in data structures and in statements, and it is important that all these changes be made in a systematic way. This should usually be done by "backing up" to a previous level of the algorithm that the changes don't affect, and then proceeding to redo all the top-down refinements taking the changes into account.

For example, suppose a top-down analysis has produced the comment outline shown in (4.1.3a), where each Si represents a statement-comment. This outline was produced level by level by successive refinement. That is, statement S2 was refined to consist of four steps S4, S5, S6 and S7. Then S5 was refined to consist of S11, S12, S13, S14 and S15. Now suppose while attempting to refine statement S19 we discover a mistake, or recognize that a change in data structures designed earlier will make S19 more efficient. In order to make the change, we must back up to a point where the change has no effect. Suppose this point is S2. Then we must proceed forward again from there, redoing all refinements (in the example, S4-S7, S11-S15, S18 and S19) to make sure that every refinement leads to a correct program.

```
(4.1.3a)    Problem statement

                  S1
                  S2
                      S4
                      S5
                          S11
                          S12
                          S13
                              S18
                              S19
                          S14
                          S15
                      S6
                      S7
                  S3
                      S8
                      S9
                          S16
                          S17
                      S10
```

The portion of the outline that must be considered in the light of the change required for S19 is shown in (4.1.3b):

```
(4.1.3b)     S2
                  S4
                  S5
                       S11
                       S12
                       S13
                            S18
                            S19
                       S14
                       S15
                  S6
                  S7
```

Backing up in this manner is extremely important if a correct program is desired. There is a limit to how much we can keep in our heads, and the only way to extend this limit is to keep things well organized on paper. The more complicated the program, the more important it is to back up systematically.

If instead of using such a systematic procedure, we just "looked around" and tried to figure out what to change, the chances are that we would miss at least one place to change or would change some segment incorrectly. Backing up with a detailed outline as a guide indicates not only what has to be changed, but also what doesn't have to be changed. For example, in the above illustration, once we decide that the change affects only S2 and its refinements, we need not worry about changing anything else in the outline.

To illustrate this process on a real problem, consider again the sorting problem of Section 3.3. The algorithm used is:

```
(4.1.3c)     /** SORT L(1:N) */
                  DO M = N TO 2 BY -1;
                       Find position of maximum in L(1:M)
                       Interchange maximum and L(M)
                       END;
```

Now consider a different way of performing the same task. Instead of finding the largest value and then making one interchange at the end, compare successive values and interchange immediately if out of order:

```
(4.1.3d)     /** SWAP VALUES OF L(1:M) TO PUT MAX IN L(M) */
                  DO I = 2 TO M BY 1;
                       IF L(I-1) > L(I)
                            THEN Swap L(I-1) and L(I)
                       END;
```

We notice that this refinement has a property that may be of some use. It looks at successive pairs of L(1:M) and swaps any pair that is out of order. If no swaps occur during an execution of this subalgorithm, then no adjacent pair is out of order and the array is already sorted. Hence, if no swaps occur the algorithm can be terminated.

How will we stop execution? We have a new idea now, but we must fit it in at the right program level. Part of the change must occur not only in (4.1.3d), but also in the higher level algorithm (4.1.3c) since it must terminate. Thus we should back up to the statement "Sort L(1:N)" and refine anew. This new refinement will be a modification of (4.1.3c).

Looking at (4.1.3c) we see that we now have two stopping conditions:

1. M < 2, and

2. "no swaps performed during one execution of the loop body".

We introduce a new variable SORTED with the following meaning:

SORTED = '1'B means the array is known to be sorted.

SORTED = '0'B means it is uncertain whether or not the array is sorted.

Now modify (4.1.3c) into (4.1.3e):

```
(4.1.3e)     /** SORT L(1:N) */
                 SORTED = '0'B;
                 M = N;
                 DO WHILE (¬SORTED & (M >= 2));
                     Swap values of L(1:M) to put largest in
                         L(M), and also set SORTED as necessary
                     M = M - 1;
                     END;
```

Now proceed down to the next level, refining the English substatement:

```
             /** SWAP L(1:M) TO PUT MAX IN L(M) AND SET SORTED */
                 SORTED = '1'B;      /* ASSUME L(1:M) IS SORTED */
                 DO I = 2 TO M BY 1;
                     IF L(I-1) > L(I)
                         THEN DO;
                             Swap L(I-1) and L(I)
                             SORTED = '0'B;
                             END;
                     END;
```

This yields the final program known as "bubble-sort":

```
(4.1.3f)     /** SORT ARRAY L(1:N) USING BUBBLE SORT */
                 SORTED = '0'B;
                 M = N;
                 BUBBLE: DO WHILE (¬SORTED & (M >= 2));
                     /** SWAP L(1:M) TO PUT MAX IN L(M), */
                         /* ALSO SET SORTED */
                         SORTED = '1'B; /* ASSUME IT IS SORTED */
                         DO I = 2 TO M BY 1;
                              IF L(I-1) > L(I)
                                 THEN DO;
                                      T = L(I-1);
                                      L(I-1) = L(I);
                                      L(I) = T;
                                      SORTED = '0'B;
                                      END;
                             END;
                     M = M - 1;
                     END BUBBLE;
```

The important point in the example is to note how we <u>backed up to a higher program level</u> in order to incorporate changes in a systematic manner. One <u>can</u> just look around and try to find all necessary places to change in a haphazard manner, but doing it in a systematic manner is actually easier and more reliable.

This systematic backing up process is particularly useful during testing. If an error is located during testing, it should be corrected by backing up as we have described here, and then proceeding down again, taking into account whatever changes are necessary. The discovery of an error during testing may well occur several days after that section of the program is written and your recollection may be less than perfect. Unless you proceed very systematically in the repair process there is a good chance you will introduce new errors while trying to eliminate old ones.

4.2 <u>Sources of Ideas for Refinements</u>

"How to invent something" is difficult to describe, and it is not clear that creativity can be effectively taught. Fortunately, the typical programmer is rarely asked to develop something radically different, and the type of creativity required is modest. Greater amounts of determination, logical thinking, hard work, attention to detail, and patience are involved. We attempt in this section to give some insight into how and where program ideas originate.

4.2.1 Sources of Ideas for Algorithms

A programmer has two main sources of ideas:

1. Programs previously written or studied;

2. Familiar algorithms from everyday life.

For the beginner, the first source is practically non-existent. One obvious way to expand this source is to read and study good programs written by others. Besides expanding the set of algorithms one has at his disposal, it helps teach and emphasize good style and programming practices. Surprisingly, studying other people's programs is not a common practice, even among professional programmers.

The second source of ideas is almost unlimited. Every day we use algorithms or see others use them. Often, of course, they are informal and not too well defined, and describing them precisely may be difficult. But the ideas are there.

The bank problem is a good example of this. How did we know what to do? Perhaps we imagined what a clerk would do to manually perform this task. In order to write a program for it, we needed only to be able to write down an exact description of the process the clerk performs, taking into account the format of the input (which the clerk need not worry about) and the fact that all data must be stored in variables. The top-down method of development was used only to aid us in writing the algorithm correctly and precisely.

As a second example, suppose we have an array B(1:N) whose values are in ascending order. We want to find the position J of another variable X in the list. That is, search B for X and store in variable J an integer such that B(J) = X. If no such integer exists, store 0 in J. If the list were not sorted we would use a simple search as in Section 3.2:

```
DO J = 1 TO N BY 1;
    IF B(J) = X
        THEN GOTO END_SEARCH;
    END;
J = 0;
END_SEARCH:;
```

However, the additional information that B is sorted may permit a more efficient algorithm.

Everyday situations in which something is sought in an ordered list are numerous, and in general a more efficient search method is used. A good example is looking for a name in the telephone book. To find a name, say "Smith", we look at some entry in the book rather randomly, but as near to the S's as we can get. The entry serves to divide the book into two parts -- "before" the entry and "after" the entry. If this entry is less than Smith (alphabetically), then Smith is in the second part, after the entry. So we "discard" the first part and repeat the process using only the last part. If the entry is greater than Smith, we discard the second part and repeat the process using the first part.

Thus we can repeat a process over and over until we find the desired entry or until we have discarded the whole list (in which case the desired value is not in the list). This repetition suggests the use of a WHILE loop, and after some work we arrive at the following algorithm:

```
Let the list to be searched be B(1:N)
DO WHILE (the list to be searched is not empty);
    J  = index of some entry B(J) still in list, near X;
    SELECT:
        WHEN B(J) < X
            Discard  first half of list, including B(J);
        WHEN B(J) = X GOTO END_OF_SEARCH;
        WHEN B(J) > X
            Discard last half of list, including B(J);
        END;
    END;
J = 0; /* X IS NOT IN THE LIST */
END_OF_SEARCH:;
```

The statement

```
"J = index of some entry B(J) still in list, near X;"
```

is not precise enough. How do we compute "near"? To simplify this, let us just use

```
J = index of middle entry of the list;
```

which is easier to compute. It may not be as good an algorithm as we use with the telephone book, but this change does make it easier to program. When searching the telephone book, we have common sense information that is not ordinarily available to the program. For example, we know there are lots of S's and T's, but few W's and X's. This certainly affects the way we perform the search. The main problem in developing a program based on our experiences is to be able to formalize how we do something, to ferret out the essential details.

This is the beginning of the development of a well-known algorithm called <u>binary search</u>. It is a vast improvement over the algorithm used in 3.2. For example, if there are 32,768 entries, the 3.2 algorithm may have to look at <u>all</u> the entries, while binary search will <u>never</u> look at more than 16 of them! This algorithm is discussed further in Section VI.2.4. The key point here is that the idea for this algorithm comes from the prosaic task of using a directory.

4.2.2 Solving Simpler Problems

Since we have not previously seen every problem we are asked to solve and program, somehow we must be able to find connections between the problems at hand and problems whose solutions we already know (or at least whose solutions are easier). Two obvious methods are to simplify the problem and to find related problems.

It is often useful to explore a problem similar in structure to the one assigned but simpler in detail. One can explore alternative strategies and algorithms in this simpler context, and choose which strategy to pursue for the real problem.

To illustrate consider the sorting problem again. We have all done this -- sorted mailing lists, books on shelves, and so on. The problem and its solution are not unfamiliar, but explaining precisely how to sort is not easy if we haven't seen an algorithm for it before. Let us attack the problem as if we had not seen it earlier, and look for simpler problems within the sort.

What must happen for the list L(1:N) to be sorted? For one thing, the largest value must eventually appear in L(N). This is a simpler problem, which we know how to handle (Section I.7, Exercise 13f).

(4.2.2a)

```
DO I = 1 TO N-1 BY 1;
    IF L(I) > L(N)
        THEN Swap L(I) and L(N);
    END;
```

What else must be done? The second largest value must appear in L(N-1). If the largest has already been put into L(N) by the above algorithm, then this means we want to put the largest of L(1:N-1) into L(N-1). This is roughly the same as (4.2.2a):

```
DO I = 1 TO N-2 BY 1;
    IF L(I) > L(N-1)
        THEN Swap L(I) and L(N-1);
    END;
```

Continuing, we should recognize that we are performing essentially the same process a number of times. Getting back to the original problem, we can write it as

```
Swap values of L(1:N)   to put largest in L(N);
Swap values of L(1:N-1) to put largest in L(N-1);
Swap values of L(1:N-2) to put largest in L(N-2);
                  ...
Swap values of L(1:2)   to put larger  in L(2);
```

or

```
        /** SORT L(1:N) BY SUCCESSIVE MAXIMA */
            DO M = N TO 2 BY 1;
(4.2.2b)        Swap values of L(1:M) to put largest in L(M)
                END;
```

One way of refining the English substatement of (4.2.2b) is

```
        /** SWAP VALUES OF L(1:M) TO PUT LARGEST IN L(M) */
            DO I = 1 TO M-1 BY 1;
(4.2.2c)        IF L(I) > L(M)
                    THEN Swap L(I) and L(M)
                END;
```

Note that we got the idea for the program by tackling smaller simpler ones and noticing that we had to repeat essentially the same process many times. We then returned to the original level and wrote the program (4.2.2b). At this point, we _knew_ how to write the segment for "Swap values of L(1:M) to put largest in L(M)", and yet we still wrote this statement in English in (4.2.2b). This was because we wanted to make _one_ decision at a time, the decision turning out to be the order in which the values were placed in their final positions (first L(N), then L(N-1), and so on). _How_ the values get in their positions is not a problem of (4.2.2b), but the order in which they get there is. We can even design different algorithms for swapping the values, different from the one in (4.2.2a) that helped us find the solution. Sometimes tackling a simpler problem or a subproblem is the only way we can proceed. But once the process of solving the simpler problem has led to an idea, set the solution to the simpler problem aside, at least temporarily, and concentrate again on the top-down analysis.

One way to _find_ a simpler problem is to temporarily _make_ the problem definition simpler. Set aside all inessential details (perhaps even some of the essential ones), until a simple, understandable problem emerges. Once this has been solved, the original problem can be attacked with more understanding. This deletion of material must of course be done with care to make sure that the remaining problem is instructive and not trivial.

To illustrate this, consider the following problem:

(4.2.2d) _A Text Editor_. Input to the program consists of normal words, on cards, each adjacent pair being separated by one or more blanks. A word may be split onto two cards (the end of one and the beginning of the next). The words are to be read in and written out in 60-character lines. Each line is to be both right and left justified (as are the lines of this book). A word may not be split onto two lines, unless it is more than 60 characters long or unless otherwise there will be only one word on a line (these are probably errors, but the program must handle them).

Interspersed between words (and separated from them by one or more blanks) may be _commands_ to be executed by the program, at the time they are read. These are:

command	meaning
)L	Begin a new output line;
)P	Begin a new paragraph (indent 3 spaces);
)E	End of input.

When processing a command, if a partially filled line must be written out, do not right-justify that line. For example, the last line of a paragraph is never right-justified. Commands may not appear as words in the input; only as commands.

Below is some sample input, with the corresponding output shown at the right, using 14-character (instead of 60-character) lines:

Sample input	Sample output
)P One way to find a simpler	| One way to
problem is to make the)L)L	|find a simpler
problem	|problem is to
definition simpler.	|make the
Throw out all	|
inessential details.)E	|problem defini
	|tion simpler.
	|Throw out all
	|inessential de
	|tails.

This description is full of details, and it is difficult to know where to start, so begin by temporarily setting details aside to make it simpler:

1. Any number of blanks may separate a pair of words, and a word can be split on two cards. This may be difficult, so initially consider the input to be just a series of words and commands. That seems to be the essential point.

2. Why are lines 60 characters, and not 61 or 62? Perhaps the line length should be part of the input to the program. For now, since we need some length, use 60.

3. Justifying a line looks relatively complicated, but does not seem important relative to the overall structure of the program. Set it aside.

4. The problem of words of 60 characters or more and the problem of only one word on the line do not seem essential. Set them aside.

5. The commands are essential, and yet probably difficult to work with. Try setting them aside, and if that doesn't work out, bring them back.

This leads to the following problem description:

(4.2.2e) *Simplified Text Editor*. Read in a sequence of "words" and print them out on 60-character lines. Put as many as possible on one line, but separate each pair by a blank. Don't split words across two lines.

This simpler problem is much easier to understand and work with. A variable L (say) will hold the line currently being built. It will be written out when the next word to be inserted causes it to be longer than 60 characters. The following algorithm could be designed fairly quickly:

```
            L = '';         /* NOTHING IS IN THE CURRENT LINE */
            DO WHILE (there is another input word);
                Read the next word into WORD
                IF LENGTH(L) + LENGTH(WORD) > 60
                    THEN DO;
                        Print L
                        L = '';
(4.2.2f)                END;
                Concatenate WORD onto L
                IF LENGTH(L) < 60
                    THEN Concatenate 'b̸' onto L
                END;
            Remove blank from end of L, if it has one
            Print L if nonempty
```

The most important part of the original problem left out of (4.2.2e) is the commands, so now reinsert them. This will complicate the algorithm (4.2.2f), so we first should hide some of its details. (4.2.2f) can be rewritten as

```
        L = '';         /* NOTHING IS IN THE CURRENT LINE */
        DO WHILE (there is more input);
(4.2.2g)    Read the next word into WORD
            Process the word in WORD
            END;
        Remove blank from end of L, if it has one
        Print L if nonempty
```

In adding commands, we see we must process *either a word or a command*. We also know when to stop the loop -- when the command ")E" is read. Rewriting (4.2.2g) with this information yields

```
              L = '';         /* NOTHING IS IN THE CURRENT LINE */
              WORD = '';      /* NO WORD OR COMMAND READ YET */
              DO WHILE (WORD ¬= ')E');
                 Read the next word or command into WORD
(4.2.2h)         IF WORD is a command
                       THEN Process WORD as a command
                       ELSE Process WORD as a word
                 END;
              Remove blank from end of L, if it has one
              Print L if nonempty
```

where "process WORD as a word" is

```
/** PROCESS WORD AS A WORD */
    IF LENGTH(L) + LENGTH(WORD) > 60
        THEN DO;
            Print L
            L = '';
            END;
    Concatenate WORD onto L
    IF LENGTH(L) < 60
        THEN Add 'b̸' onto L
```

We now have a reasonable solution to the simpler problem (4.2.2e) plus commands. At this point the original problem should be reread and programmed in top-down fashion, using (4.2.2h) as a model.

On the text editor problem just described, the most common "mistake" is to write the main part of the program as a loop:

```
DO WHILE (there exists a card);
   Read a card
   Process the card
   END;
```

This then requires a second loop in processing the card, and the whole program is unnecessarily complicated because a word could be split across card boundaries. If the problem is first simplified, we realize that the card boundary problem is just a detail to be handled at a later time, and is not an essential point in understanding the general flow of the program.

4.2.3 Solving Related Problems

Consider writing a program segment to sort an array C(1:N) in descending order: C(1) ≥ C(2) ≥ ... ≥ C(N). You might recall having developed an ascending sort in the previous section (program (4.2.2b)). The new sorting program could just be a modification of the previous one.

Related problems, both in programming and in the everyday world, are a rich source of ideas. If we can find something related that we know how to handle, then the problem becomes much simpler.

In the previous section, we discussed solving simpler problems, which are of course related to the original problem. By a "related problem" in this section we mean one that is roughly the same order of magnitude in size or complexity. One that with some work, can be transformed into the desired one. Everybody uses related problems all the time, and in effect we are just saying the obvious here. The point is that you should become aware of the fact that you are using related problems; this will increase your ability to find solutions and design programs. Learning consists not only of doing something, but also of learning why and how one does it.

In programming, related problems occur more often than one might think. For example, consider the four parts of Exercise 8 of Section 3. Although these look quite different, at the highest level they all have the same algorithmic solution:

```
Read in a list of values.
Read and process a second list of values.
Print results.
```

In fact, they are equivalent at this level to the algorithm of the accounting problem of 3.4 and differ only in the meaning of "values", "read", "process", and "results". Similarly, all the problems of Exercise 9 of Section 3 have the solution

```
DO WHILE (there exists input);
    Read a value
    Process the value
    END;
```

Each of these is an interpretation of schema (4b) of Section II.4. In order to see that problems are related, we must be able to recognize the important elements of a problem. All four problems in Exercise 8 of Section 3 look different on first inspection, until we state them in a more general manner.

Most programs include a number of simple subalgorithms, many of which seem to occur over and over again (with perhaps slight variations). Examples are algorithms to:

Search a list.
Search a sorted list.
Find the maximum or the average of a set of values.
Delete duplicate values from a list.
Read in a list of values which ends with some signal.

Many of these will become part of your "repertoire of algorithms" and you will find that programming consists in part in determining how these standard subalgorithms should be combined into a larger program. In order to do this, however, you must be able to recognize familiar problems in the mass of detail of the overall problem, and work on modifying them to fit the current problem.

4.3 Handling Input Errors

Programs are written to be used in the real world -- which means that they must not assume that input data will always conform exactly to the problem specifications. In general, programs must check all input for errors, and when errors are detected provide informative output that will help the user to find and correct the mistake. When a data error is not detected, the best that can happen is that the program will "blow up" -- an infinite loop will be executed, an array subscript will be checked and found to be out of range, or some similar indication will be given. The worst that can happen is that the program processes the erroneous input as if it were correct, giving no indication that anything is wrong. If and when the error is eventually detected, it can be embarrassing and costly to correct.

With some errors the program should stop and print a message. For example, in the accounting problem of 3.4 if the end-of-account signal is missing, then all transactions have been read as accounts, and there is no hope of proceeding usefully. With other errors the program should just print a message and continue. For example, if a transaction gives a non-existant account number, that transaction can be rejected and a message can be printed.

Many programs process data that actually consists of sections that are quite independent. For example, in 3.4 the data pertaining to each account is independent of the data preceding and following. An error in a particular item of data may well make processing for that account meaningless until the error is corrected, but it does not affect processing of the other accounts. This suggests that a well-designed program would reject the erroneous data with an informative error message, skip over that account, but resume processing with the next account. Error rates of several percent in hand-prepared data are not unusual and programs that have to process thousands of data cards are also not unusual. If these programs were to stop as soon as any error is encountered and insist that it be repaired before proceeding they would be impractical to use. On the other hand there are cases where the data are all logically related and the effects of errors are cumulative. In such cases it is pointless to continue processing. It requires both knowledge of the problem and good judgement to decide whether an error should terminate processing or whether some action will permit useful continuation.

One could conceivably overdo error checking. The programmer must weigh each type of input error and the damage its occurrence might cause against the amount of programming necessary to detect it. But at least the programmer should think of all the possible errors and come to a rational decision on each one. If necessary the manager should be questioned about them. Very often the person in charge may not have thought about all the possibilities and will be delighted to hear they can be detected. On the other hand, he may say that a particular error will never occur because, for example, the data is produced by another program of known reliability.

In some cases error processing is so important that it dominates the program. For example, there are programs whose sole purpose is to screen data for errors so that these can be corrected prior to submitting the data for actual processing. In general, error processing should be considered an important and integral part of the problem. Error processing is usually more successful when it is developed along with other requirements rather than added on after the program is otherwise finished.

Part IV
Procedures and Blocks

Section 1 External Procedures

The language features presented in Part I are adequate to write small programs, but something more is required if we are to effectively write and test significant programs. We need some means of organizing things so that

1. different sections of the program can be made relatively independent, so they can be written and tested separately;

2. program segments can be written in one place and executed "remotely" from some other point in the program;

3. program segments can be reused in different contexts without having to be rewritten; and

4. large programs can be easily constructed from smaller ones already written and checked out.

These capabilities are provided by "procedures" in PL/I. One defines a procedure in one place in a program. This procedure can then be "called" or "invoked" into action from other places within the program. In executing the procedure, it behaves as if it were copied into each position from which it is invoked.

This technique is not peculiar to programming. For instance, when baking a cake we might be instructed to "make chocolate icing, page 56". The icing recipe is a separate procedure, with its own set of instructions. To execute this command, we postpone further action on the cake, turn to the icing recipe, and execute it. When finished, we return to the cake recipe and continue where we left off.

The following program is a simple example of the use of PL/I procedures. Its execution prints the following three lines:

```
FIRST LINE
SECOND LINE
FIRST LINE
```

The program is given below:

```
*PL/C
 /* PRINT 3 LINES */                             ┐
 P3LINES: PROCEDURE OPTIONS(MAIN);              |main
     CALL FIRST;                                |procedure
     CALL SECOND;                               | P3LINES
     CALL FIRST;                                |
     END P3LINES;                               ┘

*PROCESS
 /* PRINT FIRST LINE */                          ┐
 FIRST: PROCEDURE;                              |
     PUT SKIP LIST('FIRST LINE');               |procedure
     RETURN;                                    | FIRST
     END FIRST;                                 ┘

*PROCESS
 /* PRINT SECOND LINE */                         ┐
 SECOND: PROCEDURE;                             |
     PUT SKIP LIST('SECOND LINE');              |procedure
     RETURN;                                    | SECOND
     END SECOND;                                ┘
```

While all previous programs have consisted of a single procedure, this program consists of <u>three separate procedures</u>:

> P3LINES is the <u>main procedure</u> because "OPTIONS(MAIN)" is given in its heading. A program <u>must have exactly one main procedure</u>.
>
> FIRST is an <u>external procedure</u>. It is essentially an independent program that is executed by being "called" from the main procedure. When executed it causes the literal 'FIRST LINE' to be printed.
>
> SECOND is another external procedure. When executed it causes the literal 'SECOND LINE' to be printed.

The *PROCESS cards are control cards (which must start in column 1) that denote the start of an external procedure much as the *PL/C card denotes the start of the main procedure.

Execution of any PL/I program always starts at the <u>first statement</u> of the <u>main procedure</u>, and continues until the main procedure is completed. In this case the first statement in P3LINES is

```
CALL FIRST;
```

Execution of a CALL statement is accomplished by executing the procedure that it references -- in this case, the procedure named FIRST. You may think of execution of the main procedure as having been suspended temporarily while FIRST is being executed, and resumed when FIRST is completed. It is probably better to think of execution of FIRST *as being* the execution of the CALL FIRST statement.

P3LINES consists of three statements. Since there is no loop or selection its execution consists simply of the execution of these statements in order. But effectively, this means execute procedure FIRST, then execute procedure SECOND, and then execute procedure FIRST again. It doesn't matter that the last statement requires the re-execution of a procedure that has already been executed once -- the same external procedure can be executed any number of times in the course of executing a program.

Now consider in more detail what it means to execute procedure FIRST. The first statment in FIRST is

```
PUT SKIP LIST ('FIRST LINE');
```

which causes the literal 'FIRST LINE' to be printed. The next statement is

```
RETURN;
```

which means that execution of FIRST is completed, and therefore execution of CALL FIRST has been completed. So, in effect, the result of executing

```
CALL FIRST;
```

is to execute the statement

```
PUT SKIP LIST ('FIRST LINE');
```

since that is the only executable statement in FIRST. Overall, the result of executing P3LINES would be to produce the same printed output as the following program:

```
*PL/C
 /* PROGRAM TO PRINT 3 SIMPLE LINES */
 PRINT3: PROCEDURE OPTIONS(MAIN);
     PUT SKIP LIST ('FIRST LINE');
     PUT SKIP LIST ('SECOND LINE');
     PUT SKIP LIST ('FIRST LINE');
     END PRINT3;
```

This second form is obviously simpler and no one would actually use the first form -- but then no one would use a computer to write these three lines anyway. However, if the body of FIRST were a substantial program segment, it would be useful to be able to execute this segment from different points in the program without having to rewrite the segment.

We illustrate the idea of procedures by another example in Section 1.1, and then explore the definition and use of procedures in more detail in the following sections.

1.1 A Procedure to Interchange Values

Consider the task of exchanging the values of two variables X and Y. We can do this with the three assignment statements shown in (1.1a). These statements use a third variable T in addition to X and Y.

```
(1.1a) T = X;
       X = Y;
       Y = T;
```

Alternatively, we can write a procedure to do this:

```
       *PROCESS
        /* SWAP VALUES OF X AND Y */
        SWAP: PROCEDURE(X, Y);
            DECLARE (X, Y) FIXED;
(1.1b)      DECLARE T FIXED;
            T = X;
            X = Y;
            Y = T;
            RETURN;
            END SWAP;
```

This procedure definition would be placed at the end of the program, out of the way. Then, wherever we wanted to swap the values of X and Y, instead of writing the three statements of (1.1a) we would instead write the single statement

```
CALL SWAP(X, Y);
```

Executing this statement is <u>equivalent to executing all the statements in the body of procedure SWAP</u>.

For example, a complete program using procedure SWAP of (1.1b) is given in (1.1c). During each repetition of the body of SWAP_LOOP in (1.1c) the GET statement obtains the next two values from the data list and assigns them to X and Y. Then if those values are out of order the CALL statement "passes" X and Y to procedure SWAP. The next statement to be executed is the first assignment statement in SWAP, that is, T=X;. That and the two following assignment statements interchange the values. Execution of the RETURN statement terminates procedure SWAP and hence completes execution of the CALL SWAP(X, Y); statement. The next statement executed is the PUT. This cycle is repeated

N times, which completes execution of the loop. A final PUT statement completes execution of the main procedure ORDER2 so execution of the program is finished. Execution does not continue on into the SWAP procedure; SWAP is not a main procedure and is executed only by means of a CALL.

```
        *PL/C
         /* ORDER N DATA PAIRS */
         ORDER2: PROCEDURE OPTIONS(MAIN);
             DCL (X, Y, I, N) FIXED;
             PUT LIST ('ORDERED PAIRS:');
             PUT SKIP;
             GET LIST (N);
             SWAP_LOOP: DO I = 1 TO N BY 1;
                 GET LIST (X, Y);
                 IF X > Y
                     THEN CALL SWAP(X, Y);
(1.1c)           PUT SKIP LIST (X, Y);
                 END SWAP_LOOP;
             PUT SKIP(2) LIST ('END OF LIST');
             END ORDER2;

        *PROCESS
         /* SWAP VALUES OF X AND Y */
         SWAP: PROCEDURE(X, Y);
             DECLARE (X, Y) FIXED;
             DECLARE T FIXED;
             T = X;
             X = Y;
             Y = T;
             RETURN;
             END SWAP;
        *DATA
            3,
            9, 8,    5, 0,    1, 15
```

Execution of (1.1c) with the data shown would print the following lines:

```
ORDERED PAIRS:

    8           9
    0           5
    1          15

END OF LIST
```

Now go one step further. Suppose we wanted to swap the values of some pair of variables whose names were not X and Y. More generally, suppose we wanted to swap the value of one pair of variables at some point in the program and to swap the values of a different pair of variables at some other point. It would be convenient not to need two different swap routines just because the variables to be swapped happen to have different names. For example, suppose a data list consists of values in groups of three, and each group is to be rearranged so that its values are in non-decreasing order. Each group could be assigned as values to a set of three variables, say A, B and C. Then by comparing A and B and swapping their values if they are out of order; comparing B and C and swapping their values if out of order; and finally comparing A and B again and swapping their values if out of order, the three values would be put in non-decreasing order. (This is, of course, just a special case of the sorting algorithm of Section III.3.3) The point is that we would need to swap A and B, then B and C, and then A and B again. It may surprise you to learn that the SWAP procedure of (1.1b) is capable of doing this, <u>without any change whatever</u>. This is illustrated in (1.1d).

(1.1d)

```
*PL/C
 /* ORDER N DATA TRIPLES */
 ORDER3: PROCEDURE OPTIONS(MAIN);
     DCL (A, B, C, I, N) FIXED;
     PUT LIST ('ORDERED TRIPLES:');
     PUT SKIP;
     GET LIST (N);
     DO I = 1 TO N BY 1;
         GET LIST (A, B, C);
         IF A > B
             THEN CALL SWAP(A, B);
         IF B > C
             THEN CALL SWAP(C, B);
         IF A > B
             THEN CALL SWAP(A, B);
         PUT SKIP LIST (A, B, C);
         END;
     PUT SKIP (2) LIST ('END OF LIST');
     END ORDER3;

*PROCESS
 /* SWAP VALUES OF X AND Y */
 SWAP: PROCEDURE(X, Y);
     DECLARE (X, Y) FIXED;
     DECLARE T FIXED;
     T = X;
     X = Y;
     Y = T;
     RETURN;
     END SWAP;
*DATA
 4,
 17, 23, 15,
 9, 56, 1,
 105, 0, -2,
 42, 43, 44
```

Execution of (1.1d) with the data shown would print the following lines:

```
ORDERED TRIPLES:

      15          17          23
       1           9          56
      -2           0         105
      42          43          44

END OF LIST
```

In each repetition of the body of the loop in (1.1d) the GET obtains the next three values from the data list and assigns them to A, B and C, respectively. If the values of A and B are out of order they need to be swapped. Execution of

```
CALL SWAP(A, B);
```

calls procedure SWAP and directs it to swap the values of A and B. Variable A takes the place of X in SWAP; variable B takes the place of Y. Execution of this CALL statement is equivalent to executing SWAP as if its assignment statements had been written as

```
T = A;
A = B;
B = T;
```

After execution of SWAP is completed, the next statement to be executed is another conditional CALL of SWAP. This time if the values of B and C are out of order SWAP is called to interchange their values. This time B takes the place of X in SWAP and C takes the place of Y. SWAP is now executed as if its assignment statements had been written as

```
T = B;
B = C;
C = T;
```

After completion of this execution of SWAP the next statement is a third conditional CALL of SWAP. This again checks the ordering of A and B (which may have been upset by the interchange of B and C). After execution of these three conditional calls the values of A, B and C will be in non-decreasing order.

The point is that each execution of SWAP interchanges the values of whatever variables are specified in the CALL statement that causes that execution. The fact that SWAP is written in terms of X and Y is immaterial. In fact, X and Y in SWAP are not variables at all -- they are parameters. A parameter is used in place of a variable in writing a procedure because it is not known until the procedure is called what particular variable it will be. The specific variables to be used by the procedure are given in the call, and are known as the arguments of the call. A and B are the arguments of the first call of SWAP in (1.1d); B and C are the arguments of the second call; and A and

B are the arguments of the third call. Before executing a procedure the parameters are replaced by the corresponding arguments of that particular call.

The replacement of parameters with arguments is exactly the same in (1.1c), but in that case the arguments happened to have the same names as the parameters -- which allowed us to postpone explaining what really happened until (1.1d). But actually, even in (1.1c) the parameter X in SWAP and the argument X in the call are different -- they just happen to have the same name. Execution of CALL SWAP(X, Y) passes arguments X and Y to SWAP to have their values interchanged. The first parameter X of SWAP is replaced by the first argument X of the call; the second parameter Y by the second argument Y. It is just a coincidence that the names happen to be the same. Any pair of variables could be passed as arguments to SWAP to have their values interchanged.

However, the attributes of the arguments must exactly match those of the corresponding parameter. For example, if variables A, B and C in (1.1d) had been declared to be FLOAT this program would not work properly, simply because the attributes of the arguments would not match the FIXED attributes of the parameters of SWAP.

Note that exactly the same procedure SWAP is used in both (1.1c) and (1.1d). This reuse of a procedure is a common occurrence in programming. It means that after you have some experience and have accumulated a repertoire of commonly used program segments you will not have to write each new program entirely from scratch. A procedure is a particularly convenient way to package a program segment so that it can be used in different programs.

1.2 Definition of a Procedure

Initially we consider "external" procedures -- that is, procedures whose definitions are positioned so that they are not within the body of any other procedure. ("Internal" procedures are described in Section 3.) Programs (1.1c) and (1.1d) show the proper position for a procedure definition. The general form of the definition of an external procedure is

```
*PROCESS
 /* Comment summarizing what the procedure does */
 procedure-name: PROCEDURE(list of parameters);
     Declarations to specify parameters
     Declarations to create variables
     Statements
     END procedure-name;
```

The *PROCESS card is a control card, similar to the *PL/C or *DATA card. Like all control cards it must begin in column 1, whereas all other program cards should leave column 1 blank. On most systems *PROCESS will cause the source listing to skip to a new page so that the listing of each external procedure begins at the top of a new page. (At some installations PL/C is modified so that only a few lines are skipped rather than the rest of the page.) Any number of external procedures may be included in a program.

The procedure-name is like other PL/I identifiers. (If the procedure-name is longer than seven characters a warning message will be given by PL/C, but this is irrelevant for our purposes and may be ignored.) This is the name by which the procedure will be called to be executed. Names should be chosen to suggest the action that the procedure performs, like SWAP in (1.1c).

The list of parameters is a sequence of names, separated by commas. These names are associated with this particular procedure and have no connection with the names used in other procedures.

The comment at the beginning of the procedure should precisely define what the procedure does, in terms of its parameters, but should say little about <u>how</u> it works. The purpose of the comment is to free the reader from having to read the statements of the procedure each time he needs to know what the procedure does. The programmer or reader, when writing a CALL on the procedure or attempting to understand a CALL, should have to read only (1) the comment, (2) the procedure name and list of parameters, and (3) the specification of parameters.

1.2.1 Parameter Declarations

There are now two different sets of declarations -- for <u>parameters</u> and for <u>variables</u>. The first set specifies the type attributes of the parameters. The form of parameter declarations is almost like that of variable declarations. For example

```
*PROCESS
 /* SET Z TO SOLUTION OF HEAT EQUATION IN (X, Y) */
 HEAT: PROCEDURE(X, Y, Z);
     DECLARE (X, Y) FLOAT;
     DECLARE Z FIXED;
     ...
```

The INITIAL attribute must not be given in a parameter declaration. Since a parameter is not a variable, it does not have a value and hence cannot have an initial value. (A parameter is <u>replaced</u> by a variable when the procedure is called.)

The form of the declaration of parameters also differs for character-string and array parameters. The length of a string parameter must be left unspecified. This is indicated by giving "*" for the length -- that is, by writing CHARACTER(*). For example

```
       *PROCESS
        /* DELETE OCCURRENCES OF STR2 IN STR1 */
        DEL_STRG: PROCEDURE(STR1, STR2);
(1.2.1a)   DECLARE (STR1, STR2) CHARACTER(*) VARYING;
           ...
```

When executing the procedure, the length of a string parameter is always the length of the argument associated with it.

The declaration of array parameters is discussed in Section 1.3.5.

Except for this use of the "*" you cannot tell from the declaration alone whether a parameter or a variable is being declared. The distinction depends entirely upon whether or not the name appears in the parameter list in the procedure heading. If the name is on that list it is the name of a parameter; if the name is not on that list it is the name of a variable.

All parameters should be declared and their type attributes given explicitly. PL/I does not absolutely insist on this, but if you do not give a complete declaration of each parameter PL/I will supply default attributes and these usually will not match the attributes of the corresponding arguments. The result of unmatched attributes will surely surprise you. Without complete declarations your program will sometimes work, and sometimes not. The explanation is given below in Section 1.3.3.

Some procedures do not need any parameters. In such cases there are no parameter lists and no declarations of parameters. Examples of parameterless procedures are given in (1.2.5a) and (1.2.5b).

1.2.2 READONLY Parameters

A parameter may serve as an "input parameter", an "output parameter", or both. For example, in (1.1b) parameters X and Y of SWAP are input and output parameters, since the arguments associated with the parameters supply values to SWAP and are assigned values by SWAP. In (1.2.1a) parameter STR1 of DEL_STRG is similarly both input and output, but parameter STR2 is input only.

If a parameter is used only in an input role it is useful to designate the parameter as "readonly". This can be done in a comment after the declaration:

```
*PROCESS
 /* SET X TO THE MOST WRINKLED OF Y AND Z */
 WRINKLE: PROCEDURE (X, Y, Z);
     DECLARE (Y, Z) FLOAT; /* READONLY */
     DECLARE X FLOAT;
     ...
```

When a parameter is designated READONLY, it should not be used:

1. as the left-side of an assignment statement

2. in the list of a GET statement

3. as the index variable of a loop

4. as an argument for a parameter that is not READONLY.

The first three of these uses would certainly assign a value to the parameter, so they are excluded. Usage as an argument of a procedure call could result in a value being assigned, so this usage is excluded as well.

● PL/CS: READONLY can be given as an attribute rather than as a comment. For example

```
DECLARE (X, Z) FLOAT READONLY;
```

Violations of restrictions 1-3 given above are automatically detected. A stronger version of 4 is enforced: a READONLY parameter can not appear in any CALL.

1.2.3 Local Variables

The second group of declarations in a procedure create variables. You can recognize that these declarations create variables rather than parameters simply because they declare names that do not appear on the parameter list. For example

```
*PROCESS
 /* SET MAXFN TO MAX FUNCTION VALUE */
 SAVEMAX: PROCEDURE(MAXFN, NEWVAL);
     DECLARE MAXFN FLOAT;
     DECLARE NEWVAL FLOAT; /* READONLY */
     DECLARE (TEMP, SQVAL) FLOAT;
     ...
```

TEMP and SQVAL are variables and not parameters because they do not appear in the parameter list with MAXFN and NEWVAL.

Now that we are concerned with more than one procedure we must note that variables are "local" to the procedure in which they are declared. This means that they can be used by name only in that procedure. Their names are not known outside that procedure. Each procedure has its own set of variables, independent of those of every other procedure, and it is immaterial if some of the names happen to coincide. For example

```
*PL/C
 /* EDIT TEXT BY SKIPPING LINES WITH DUPLICATES */
 CONTROL: PROCEDURE OPTIONS(MAIN);
      DECLARE FL BIT(1);
      ...
      END CONTROL;

*PROCESS
 /* SET F TO 0|1 IF LINE HAS NO DUPLICATES */
 SETF: PROCEDURE(F, LINE);
      DECLARE F BIT (*);
      DECLARE LINE CHAR (*) VAR; /* READONLY */
      DECLARE FL FIXED;
      ...
      END SETF;
```

The two variables FL in CONTROL and FL in SETF are _entirely different objects_ that just happen to have the same name. Also note that the variables of a procedure are _created as the procedure is entered_, and then _destroyed when that execution of the procedure is completed_. This is discussed further in Sections 1.3 and 1.5.

1.2.4 _Labels in a Procedure_

Labels are also "local" to the procedure in which they are declared. (The declaration or definition of a label is just its use as a prefix to a statement.) "Label" in this sense applies not only to the target labels for the GOTO statement, but also to the _names_ of loops and SELECT constructions. The label names in one external procedure have nothing to do with names in any other procedure. Therefore the same name can be used in two different procedures.

The target label of a GOTO should be located _in the same procedure_ as the GOTO statement. For example:

```
*PL/C
 /* TEST INPUT AND OUTPUT FORMATS */
 TEST: PROCEDURE OPTIONS(MAIN);
     ...
     IF ITEM = 'LAST'
         THEN GOTO TERM_DATA;
     ...
     TERM_DATA:;
     ...
     END TEST;

*PROCESS
 /* CONVERT EDIT FORMAT */
 CONVERT: PROCEDURE(X, D);
     ...
     TERM_DATA: DO ...
     ...
     RETURN;
     END CONVERT;
```

The GOTO in TEST refers to label TERM_DATA in TEST. The fact that the same name is used in CONVERT is irrelevant. Moreover, a GOTO in one external procedure can never branch to a target label in another external procedure. Hence one can neither enter into nor exit from an external procedure by means of a GOTO statement.

1.2.5 Statements in the Procedure Body

The procedure body consists of a sequence of statements, which are executed whenever the procedure is called. Any statement may appear within the procedure body -- an assignment, conditional, GET, PUT, compound statement, a loop, or a call on another procedure (as explained in Section 1.4). Note however that these statements may contain parameters as well as variables. This means that the body cannot be executed unless it is properly called, with variables as arguments to replace the parameters. We write the procedure as if the parameters were variables or arrays, knowing that they will be replaced by actual variables or arrays when the procedure is called. In effect, the procedure is a way of describing a specified action on unspecified variables.

The procedure body should include a RETURN statement to indicate when execution of the procedure is to be terminated (and hence when execution of the calling statement is completed). If RETURN is omitted, it is implied when execution reaches the END of the procedure.

Execution of a PL/I program consists of one execution of the main procedure. In effect, PL/I executes a single implied call (without arguments) of the main procedure. Execution of the program is finished whenever that single execution of the main procedure is completed -- regardless of whether or not other external procedures happen to follow the main procedure. Procedures are executed only if they are called; you cannot "run into" a procedure and execute it as you might with a DO loop. For example, the execution output of (1.2.5a) would be

```
LINE 1
LINE 3
```

Note that "LINE 2" will <u>never be printed</u> because L2 is never called.

```
            *PL/C
             /* PRINT 2 LINES */
             PRT2: PROCEDURE OPTIONS(MAIN);
                  PUT LIST ('LINE 1');
(1.2.5a)          PUT SKIP LIST ('LINE 3');
                  END PRT2;

            *PROCESS
             /* PRINT 'LINE 2' */
             L2: PROCEDURE;
                  PUT SKIP LIST ('LINE 2');
                  RETURN;
                  END L2;
```

As another example, the execution output of (1.2.5b) is

```
LINE 1
LINE 2
LINE 2
LINE 2
LINE 3
```

Note that "LINE 2" is printed three times <u>before</u> "LINE 3" as a result of three calls of L2, but "LINE 2" does not appear after "LINE 3".

```
            *PL/C
             PPL: PROCEDURE OPTIONS(MAIN);
                  DCL I FIXED;
                  PUT LIST ('LINE 1');
                  DO I = 1 TO 3 BY 1;
(1.2.5b)              CALL L2;
                      END;
                  PUT SKIP LIST ('LINE 3');
                  END PPL;

            *PROCESS
             /* PRINT 'LINE 2' */
             L2: PROCEDURE;
                  PUT SKIP LIST ('LINE 2');
                  RETURN;
                  END L2;
```

Note that neither (1.2.5a) nor (1.2.5b) involves parameters and arguments since procedure L2 neither requires nor returns any information. These examples are unrealistically simple, and one would not actually write procedures that are this short and simple. But some procedures need no parameters.

1.3 Procedure Calls

1.3.1 Calls and Arguments

There are two forms of procedure call, corresponding to procedures with and without parameters (as in (1.2.5a)):

```
CALL procedure-name(list of arguments);

CALL procedure-name;
```

The procedure-name given in the CALL must be the name of a procedure whose definition is included in this program.

The arguments in the list are separated by commas. Each argument may be a reference to a variable, an expression, a constant (see Section 1.3.4), or the name of an array (see Section 1.3.5). The first argument corresponds to (replaces) the first parameter of the procedure, the second argument corresponds to the second parameter, and so on. The _number of arguments_ given in the call of a procedure must _exactly match the number of parameters_ given in the definition of that procedure.

A procedure call is a PL/I statement and can be placed anywhere in a program that a statement may appear. For example, it can be executed conditionally:

```
IF B < 0
    THEN CALL FIX(B);
```

It can be in the body of a loop:

```
DO WHILE (X > 10**5);
    CALL NEXT(X);
    END;
```

Execution of a procedure call includes replacing parameters by arguments. We have described this replacement as a sort of "textual" substitution of one name for another. However, this replacement can be interpreted in several different ways, and we must therefore define more carefully what we mean by replacement, or parameter-argument correspondence. In order to do this, we must adopt a notation for describing which variables can be referenced at each point in a program.

Consider the program shown in (1.3.1a). We can show the variables and parameters of this program in boxes associated with their procedures as in (1.3.1b). Array A and variables I, J, X and T are declared in the main procedure, so they are shown in the box for that procedure. Variable T declared in SWAP is shown in the box for SWAP; it has not yet been assigned a value. The parameters X and Y of SWAP are shown in the box for SWAP, but note that they do not have lines for their values. When SWAP is called these parameters will be associated with the arguments of the call, as described in detail in Section 1.3.2.

```
        *PL/C
         /* PROGRAM TO ROTATE AXES */
         AXES: PROCEDURE OPTIONS(MAIN);
             DCL A(2) FIXED;
             DCL (I, J, X, T) FIXED;
             ...
             CALL SWAP(I, J);
(1.3.1a)     ...
             END AXES;

        *PROCESS
         /* SWAP VALUES OF X AND Y */
         SWAP: PROCEDURE(X, Y);
             DCL (X, Y) FIXED;
             DCL T FIXED;
             T = X;
             X = Y;
             Y = T;
             RETURN;
             END SWAP;
```

```
           ┌──────────┐   ┌──────┐
           |A(1)->3   |   |      |
           |A(2)->8   |   |      |
           |I---->2   |   |X     |
(1.3.1b)   |J---->1   |   |Y     |
           |X---->6   |   |T->?  |
           |T---->4   |   |      |
           └──────────┘   └──────┘
              AXES          SWAP
```

Note that we have drawn an arrow from each variable name to the line representing its storage location. We will see that parameters are also attached to lines at the time parameter-argument correspondence is made. But in (1.3.1b) no arrows are attached to parameters X and Y because SWAP has not been called yet.

When executing a statement, to determine which variable a name references, we look <u>only</u> in the box of variables for the procedure in which that statement occurs.

1.3.2 Details of Procedure Call and Execution

Let us examine in detail how execution of the statement CALL SWAP(I, J); in the main procedure of (1.3.1a) actually works. Execution of a procedure call takes place as follows:

1. Draw a box to contain the variables and parameters of the procedure (Fig. 1b below).

2. Within the box write the parameters (Fig. 1c).

3. Make the parameter-argument correspondence as follows: Each argument name has an arrow leading from it. For each parameter, draw an arrow from it to the same line to which the corresponding argument points (Fig. 1d). The first parameter corresponds to the first argument; the second parameter to the second argument, etc.

4. Within the box, write the variables declared locally within the procedure, using "?" to indicate where a value has not yet been assigned (Fig. 1e).

5. Execute the procedure body. Whenever a parameter is referenced, use the line to which it is attached. (The results of executing statements T=X; X=Y; Y=T; are shown in Figs. 1f, 1g, and 1h.)

6. Erase the procedure's box and any arrows leading from it; execution of the procedure call is now finished (Fig. 1i).

Study these steps carefully. Understanding this simple case of parameter-argument correspondence is necessary for understanding the more complicated situations that will arise later.

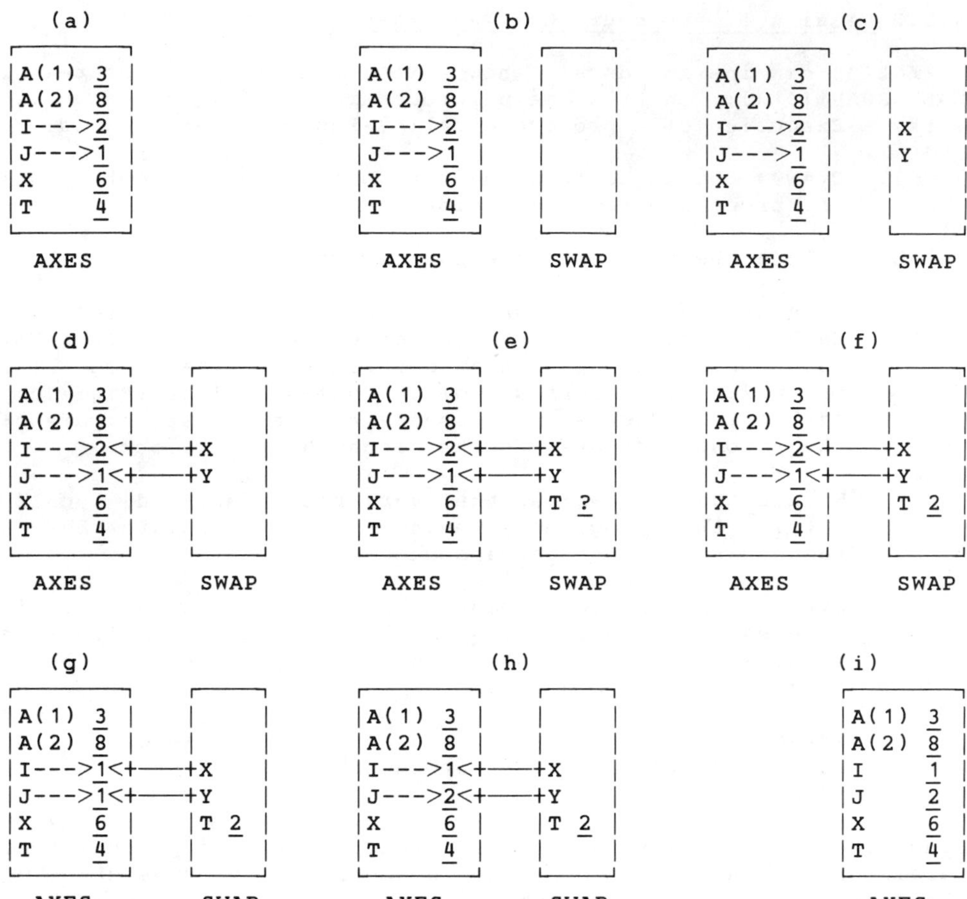

Figure 1. Example of Execution of a Procedure Call

Let us call a procedure *active* from the time it is initially called until the time that its execution terminates. As can be seen by the above rules for procedure execution, a procedure is active when its box exists, since the first step of execution is to create the box and the last is to erase the box. During execution on a computer, the equivalent of these boxes and arrows are effectively "drawn" as depicted. Storage locations are set aside to hold the variables and "parameter arrows" of the procedure. The parameter arrow locations contain references to the locations where the arguments reside.

Figure 1 illustrates several important points. First, note that the local variables of the procedure (in this case, T) *exist only when the procedure is active*. The local variables are *created* when the procedure is called and *destroyed* when the procedure execution terminates. This means that the local variables do *not* retain their values from one invocation of the procedure to the next. In the current example of procedure SWAP, T is initially undefined each time the procedure is called.

Secondly, the names used in one external procedure have nothing to do with names used in others. Both AXES and SWAP happen to have a variable named T, but these are two different variables, which, by coincidence, happen to have the same name. Any reference to T in AXES is assumed to mean the variable T declared in AXES; any reference to T in SWAP refers to the T declared in SWAP. Don't go out of your way to use common names like this, but on the other hand there is no reason to avoid it. If T is the natural and suggestive name for the variable in both cases, then it should be used in both cases. PL/I gives you the freedom of choosing the best name for a variable in each procedure without worrying about whether that name happens to be used in another procedure.

Thirdly, arguments and parameters are matched strictly <u>according to the order</u> in which they appear in their respective lists -- their names are irrelevant in this matching. Figure 1 is drawn for the particular call shown in (1.3.1a), matching parameter X with argument I and parameter Y with argument J. Matching for various other possible calls is shown in Figure 2. (In Figures 2g, 2i and 2j the values for the subscripts I and J are taken from Figure 1a.)

Fourthly, the correspondence between parameters and arguments is determined <u>before</u> execution of the body of the procedure begins, and <u>is not changed</u> throughout the particular execution. This means that if a subscripted variable is given as an argument, the subscript is evaluated before execution of the procedure begins, and the correspondence between parameter and argument is based on this initial value. Although the value of the subscript may change during execution of the procedure the argument-parameter correspondence is <u>not</u> revised. For example in Figure 2j, A(I) is given as the second argument. The value of I (from Figure 1a) is 2 so A(2) is associated with the second parameter Y. The value of I will be changed by SWAP, but this will not alter the association of Y with A(2). Thus, according to the values in Figure 1a, after execution of CALL SWAP(I,A(I)), I will be 8 and A(2) will be 2.

Fifthly, whenever an assignment X= ... is executed where X is a parameter, the corresponding argument variable has its value changed <u>immediately</u>. The change to the argument does not occur after the procedure terminates, but at the time the assignment is executed.

```
                                     Argument<----Parameter
(a) CALL SWAP(J,I);                  J<----X,     I<----Y

(b) CALL SWAP(X,J);                  X<----X,     J<----Y

(c) CALL SWAP(J,X);                  J<----X,     X<----Y

(d) CALL SWAP(T,X);                  T<----X,     X<----Y

(e) CALL SWAP(A(1),J);               A(1)<----X,  J<----Y

(f) CALL SWAP(A(1),A(2));            A(1)<----X,  A(2)<----Y

(g) CALL SWAP(A(J),A(I));            A(1)<----X,  A(2)<----Y

(h) CALL SWAP(J,J);                  J<----X,     J<----Y

(i) CALL SWAP(A(2),A(I));            A(2)<----X,  A(2)<----Y

(j) CALL SWAP(I,A(I));               I<----X,     A(2)<----Y
```

Figure 2. Matching Arguments and Parameters for (1.3.1a)

Finally, and most importantly, execution of a call statement works as described above only if the attributes of each argument exactly match those of the corresponding parameter. That is, if a parameter is declared FIXED then it must be associated with an argument that is also FIXED. If the parameter is FLOAT then the argument must also be FLOAT. If the parameter is CHARACTER VARYING then the argument must also be CHARACTER VARYING.

If attributes do not match exactly, the association of parameters to arguments values works differently. This is discussed in Section 1.3.3. But until you thoroughly understand this make sure that the attributes of arguments and parameters match.

The only exception to this type matching requirement is that a parameter cannot have the INITIAL or STATIC attribute (see Section 1.5), so they are not considered in the matching of argument and parameter attributes.

● PL/CS: A parameter may have the READONLY attribute and this is not considered in the type matching.

1.3.3 Arguments with Different Types

The rule for parameter-argument correspondence is this:

(1.3.3a) During execution, the arrow leading from a parameter X (say) which is not an array must point to a *variable with exactly the same attributes* as specified for X.

If the argument whose attributes differ from those of the parameter, then the argument is *automatically* evaluated to yield a value; a new variable with the correct attributes, called a *dummy argument*, is generated and initialized to this value; and the parameter arrow is drawn to this dummy argument. This dummy argument will never be referenced by name, so it doesn't matter what name we give it. We indicate such automatically generated variables by using lower case letters for their names.

Consider CALL SWAP(I,J); of the procedure defined in (1.3.1a). Suppose I is FLOAT and J is FIXED. The values of I and J are given by Fig. 3a. Since I is FLOAT and the corresponding parameter is FIXED, the value 2E0 of I is converted to 2 and stored in a new dummy argument which we have arbitrarily named "d". Parameter X corresponds to this dummy argument as shown in Fig. 3b. Fig. 3c shows the state of affairs after execution of the procedure body, while Fig. 3d shows the situation after the call has been completed. Note that the dummy argument was deleted since it couldn't be referred to any more.

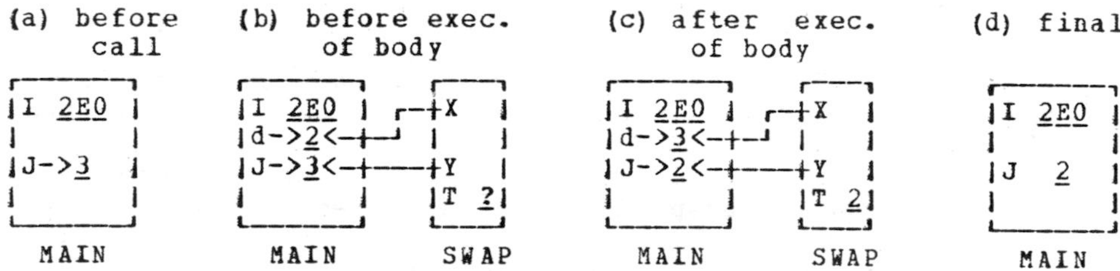

Figure 3. Execution of CALL SWAP(I,J);

This example illustrates an important implication of rule (1.3.3a). If we want an argument to be used as an "output" argument -- that is, if we want the procedure to store a value in it -- then *the type attributes of the argument must match those of the parameter exactly*. Procedure SWAP could not store a value in I because it had no way of referencing I. In this example, the effect of the procedure call was to store I's value in J, but *not* J's value in I.

Because of the hidden effects that may occur, as in the above example, PL/C gives a warning message before program execution for each argument which doesn't match its parameter. *Look at* these warnings carefully. For READONLY input arguments they probably don't matter. For output arguments they indicate an error on your part. Actually, PL/I doesn't allow nonmatching arguments unless an "entry declaration" is also given (see Section IV.2.2).

1.3.4 Expressions and Constants as Arguments

Consider the following procedure:

```
            /* STORE IN ANS THE LARGER OF A AND B */
            LARGE: PROCEDURE (A, B, ANS);
(1.3.4a)         DECLARE (A, B, ANS) FIXED;
                 IF A > B
                      THEN ANS = A;
                      ELSE ANS = B;
                 END LARGE;
```

Suppose we wish to store in L the larger of 3 and F+G, where F, G and L are FIXED variables. We can do this using:

```
(1.3.4b)    CALL LARGE (3, F+G, L);
```

This is equivalent to using the following sequence of statements (where T1 and T2 are FIXED variables not used elsewhere):

```
(1.3.4c)    T1 = 3;
            T2 = F+G;
            CALL LARGE(T1, T2, L);
```

Expressions and constants as arguments thus do not add "power" to the language, they just provide convenience and readability.

When an expression or constant is used as an argument, the parameter-argument correspondence is performed in three steps:

1. Create a new dummy argument with attributes of the parameter.

2. Evaluate the expression or constant and assign the result to the dummy argument.

3. Draw the arrow from the parameter to the dummy argument.

Fig. 4 illustrates this for (1.3.4b). The dummy variables are designated as p and q, but these names are wholly for the purpose of explanation -- they cannot be used in the program.

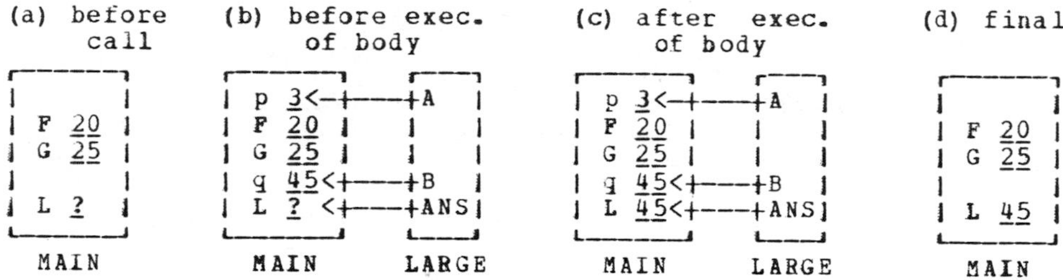

Figure 4. Execution of CALL LARGE(3, F+G, L);

The creation of a dummy argument whenever an expression is given can be exploited to <u>protect variables</u> from the action of a procedure. For example, suppose a procedure P requires three arguments -- the first two to supply input to P and the third to return the result. Say your program uses P to obtain Z from X and Y:

```
CALL P(X, Y, Z);
```

Suppose you want to ensure that P is "readonly" with respect to X and Y. If you simply enclose the arguments in parentheses they become expressions:

```
CALL P((X), (Y), Z);
```

Two dummy arguments are created and given the values of X and Y, respectively. P may change the value of these dummy arguments (although perhaps it was not supposed to) but it cannot affect the original variables X and Y.

1.3.5 Array Names as Arguments and Parameters

Individual elements of an array may be passed as arguments to a procedure that is expecting to receive a simple variable, as for example in Figure 2. But it is often convenient to pass an entire array as a single argument. This can be done if

1. both the parameter and the argument are declared as arrays,

2. both have the same number of dimensions, and

3. both have the same type attributes (FIXED, FLOAT, CHARACTER VARYING or BIT).

The parameter is declared to be an array, but only the number of dimensions and not the size is given in the declaration. This is done by giving an asterisk where the size would normally appear:

```
DECLARE ROW(*) FLOAT;
DECLARE TABLE(*,*) FIXED;
DECLARE WORDS(*) CHARACTER(*) VARYING;
DECLARE FLAG(*) BIT(*);
```

The size of a parameter array is the size of the argument array with which it is associated. This may vary from one call to the next, but the number of dimensions must be the same. That is, a parameter array of one dimension (a column array) cannot be associated with an argument array of two dimensions (a table array). As with simple variables, the type attributes of the parameter array should exactly match those of the argument array. A simple example is shown in (1.3.5a).

```
        *PL/C
         /* PROGRAM TO SUM ITEMS OF A DATA LIST */
         SUMER: PROCEDURE OPTIONS(MAIN);
              DCL ITEM(50) FLOAT;
              DCL N FIXED; /* DATA LIST IS ITEM(1:N) */
              DCL SUM FLOAT;
              DCL I FIXED;
              GET LIST (N);
              IF (N < 1) | (N > 50)
                   THEN PUT LIST ('IMPROPER DATA LENGTH', N);
              DO I = 1 TO N BY 1;
                   GET LIST (ITEM(I));
                   END;
              CALL COMPSUM(ITEM, N, SUM);
(1.3.5a)      PUT SKIP LIST ('SUM OF', N, 'ITEMS IS:', SUM);
              END SUMER;

        *PROCESS
         /* SET SUM TO SUM OF VECT(1:M) */
         COMPSUM: PROCEDURE(VECT, M, SUM);
              DCL VECT(*) FLOAT; /* READONLY */
              DCL M FIXED; /* READONLY */
              DCL SUM FLOAT;
              DCL J FIXED;
              SUM = 0;
              DO I = 1 TO N BY 1;
                   SUM = SUM + VECT(J);
                   END;
              RETURN;
              END COMPSUM;
        *DATA
         5
         49.3, 4E2, -42, 17, 263.15
```

Another example is the procedure SEARCH in (1.3.5b). SEARCH has four parameters:

Parameter A: the array to be searched
Parameter N: the index of the last element to be searched
Parameter X: the value being searched for
Parameter J: the index of the element found (or 0).

Figure 5 illustrates execution of

```
CALL SEARCH(B, M, X, K);
```

where the arguments in the calling procedure CALP (say) have been declared:

```
DECLARE B(0:4) FIXED;
DECLARE (M, X, K) FIXED;
```

The values of the arguments before the call are shown in Figure 5a. The parameter-argument correspondence is depicted in Figure 5b. Note that parameter A refers to the whole array B(0:4), even though the procedure does not reference every element. Since M is 2, only B(1:2) is searched and the result of execution is a 0 in K.

```
          *PROCESS
           /* SEARCH A(1:N) FOR VALUE X, SET J SO THAT A(J)=X */
           /* STORE 0 IN J IF NO SUCH INTEGER EXISTS */
           SEARCH: PROCEDURE(A, N, X, J);
               DECLARE (A(*), N, X) FIXED; /* READONLY */
               DECLARE J FIXED;
(1.3.5b)       DO J = 1 TO N BY 1;
                   IF A(J) = X
                       THEN RETURN;
                   END;
               J = 0;     /* INDICATES VALUE NOT FOUND */
               RETURN;
               END SEARCH;
```

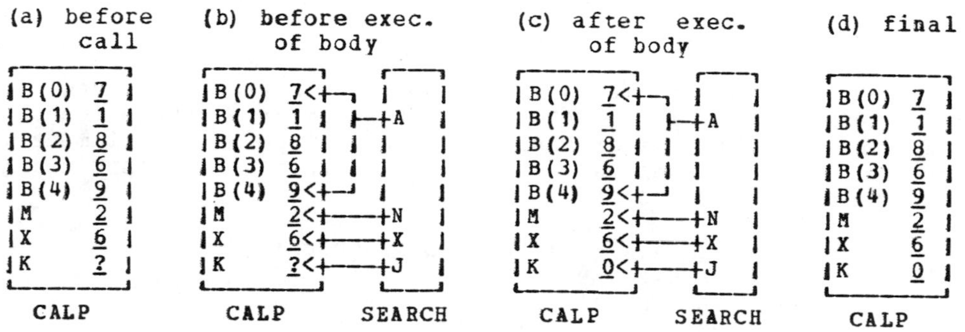

```
(a) before     (b) before exec.      (c) after exec.       (d) final
    call           of body               of body

|B(0) 7|       |B(0) 7<+-+  | |      |B(0) 7<+-+  | |      |B(0) 7|
|B(1) 1|       |B(1) 1 | +-+A |      |B(1) 1 | +-+A |      |B(1) 1|
|B(2) 8|       |B(2) 8 | |  | |      |B(2) 8 | |  | |      |B(2) 8|
|B(3) 6|       |B(3) 6 | |  | |      |B(3) 6 | |  | |      |B(3) 6|
|B(4) 9|       |B(4) 9<+-+  | |      |B(4) 9<+-+  | |      |B(4) 9|
|M    2|       |M    2<+----+N|      |M    2<+----+N|      |M    2|
|X    6|       |X    6<+----+X|      |X    6<+----+X|      |X    6|
|K    ?|       |K    ?<+----+J|      |K    0<+----+J|      |K    0|

 CALP           CALP    SEARCH        CALP    SEARCH        CALP
```

Figure 5. Execution of CALL SEARCH(B, M, X, K);

Notice that the program in (1.3.5b) has *two* RETURN statements. One is a conditional RETURN in the body of the loop. This statement simultaneously provides an *exit from the loop* and a *return from the procedure*.

Note that SEARCH cannot conveniently employ the "sentinel strategy" described in Section III.3.2 since that requires an extra element in the array to receive the search argument. In this case SEARCH cannot count on the availability of an extra element in the argument array. Moreover, SEARCH should treat its arguments as readonly values and not employ a strategy that requires it to change the array.

The type-matching considerations of Section 1.3.3 also apply to array arguments. If the type attributes of the argument do *not* match those of the parameter, then the whole array is copied into a new "dummy" array, and the arrow is drawn to this new array. This of course takes time proportional to the size of the array. Note that the *whole* array is copied, and not just those parts of it that the procedure is going to actually use.

For example, suppose we executed CALL SEARCH(D,M,X,K); where D is FLOAT and the values are as given in Fig. 6a. After parameter-argument correspondence, the boxes are as shown in Fig. 6b.

```
(a) before          (b) after correspondence
┌────────────┐      ┌─────────────────────────────────────┐  ┌───┐
│D(1)  1E0   │      │D(1)  1E0      d(1)  1  <+─┐         │  │   │
│D(2)  5E0   │      │D(2)  5E0      d(2)  5   │ ├─────────┼──+A │
│D(3)  4E1   │      │D(3)  4E1      d(3)  40  │ │         │  │   │
│D(4)  8E1   │      │D(4)  8E1      d(4)  80  │ │         │  │   │
│D(5)  3E0   │      │D(5)  3E0      d(5)  3  <+─┘         │  │   │
│M       3   │      │M       3 <──────────────────────────+──+N │
│X       4   │      │X       4 <──────────────────────────+──+X │
│K       ?   │      │K       ? <──────────────────────────+──+J │
└────────────┘      └─────────────────────────────────────┘  └───┘
    MAIN                       MAIN                          SEARCH
```

Figure 6. Partial Execution of CALL SEARCH(D, M, X, K);

Nonmatching array arguments work properly (in PL/C) as long as the argument array is a READONLY input argument -- the procedure uses the values but never assigns values to the array elements. However, suppose we wanted to sort a FLOAT array TABLE using procedure SORT defined as follows:

```
/* SORT VECT(1:N) INTO ASCENDING ORDER*/
SORT: PROCEDURE(NAME, N);
    DECLARE VECT(*) FIXED;
    DECLARE N       FIXED;
    ...
    END SORT;
```

Execution of CALL SORT(TABLE,50); causes array TABLE to be copied into a new dummy array and this new array will be sorted. It will look as if the procedure had not done its job, but the problem is simply that the result was lost when the dummy argument was destroyed.

1.4 Nested Procedure Calls

Thus far we have been considering only procedure calls in the main procedure. Actually, since a procedure call may appear anywhere that a statement may appear, this includes the body of *any* procedure. A call is simply placed wherever the action of the procedure is required, with the call designating the particular arguments upon which the procedure is to be executed.

(1.4a) illustrates a complete program consisting of a main procedure and three external procedures. The main procedure SRTG reads in a list of integers, calls procedure SORT to sort the list, and then prints the list. This SORT uses a successive-minima algorithm, a fairly obvious variation of the one used in Section III.2.x. It calls two other procedures: FINDMIN to determine the array element with minimum value, and SWAP to interchange the values of two variables. The ordering of the four procedure definitions in (1.4a) is not significant; any ordering could have been used. (Although it is customary to give the main procedure first it is not necessary to do so.)

● PL/CS: The main procedure *must* be given first.

The program consists of four separate sections, each of which performs some logically independent task, each written as a separate procedure. Each can be understood by itself, without having to understand how the others work. In actual practice one would rarely write such short procedures as are shown here; this program would have been just as readable had we written just a main program and a SORT procedure, performing the FINDMIN and SWAP commands within the sort procedure itself. We have written (1.4a) this way just to illustrate the use of nested calls.

```
*PL/C
 /* READ IN 3 INTEGERS, PRINT IN SORTED ORDER */
 SRTG: PROCEDURE OPTIONS(MAIN);
     DECLARE (A(3), I, M) FIXED;
     DO I = 1 TO 3 BY 1;
         GET LIST (A(I));
         END;
     M = 3;
     CALL SORT(A, M);
     DO I = 1 TO 3 BY 1;
         PUT LIST (A(I));
(1.4a)   END;
     END SRTG;
```

```
*PROCESS
 /* SORT ARRAY X(1:N) USING SUCCESSIVE MINIMA */
 SORT: PROCEDURE(X, N);
     DECLARE (X(*), N) FIXED;
     DECLARE (I, J) FIXED;
     DO I = 1 TO N-1 BY 1;
         CALL FINDMIN(X, I, N, J);
         CALL SWAP(X(I), X(J));
         END;
     RETURN;
     END SORT;

*PROCESS
 /* SET J TO INDEX OF MINIMUM OF X(I:N) */
 FINDMIN: PROCEDURE(X, I, N, J);
     DECLARE (X(*), I, N) FIXED; /* READONLY */
     DECLARE J FIXED;
     DECLARE K FIXED;
     J = I;
     DO K = I+1 TO N BY 1;
         IF X(K) < X(J)
             THEN J = K;
         END;
     RETURN;
     END FINDMIN;

*PROCESS
 /* SWAP VALUES OF X AND Y */
 SWAP: PROCEDURE(X, Y);
     DECLARE (X, Y) FIXED;
     DECLARE T FIXED;
     T = X;
     X = Y;
     Y = T;
     RETURN;
     END SWAP;
*DATA
    2, 8, 1
```

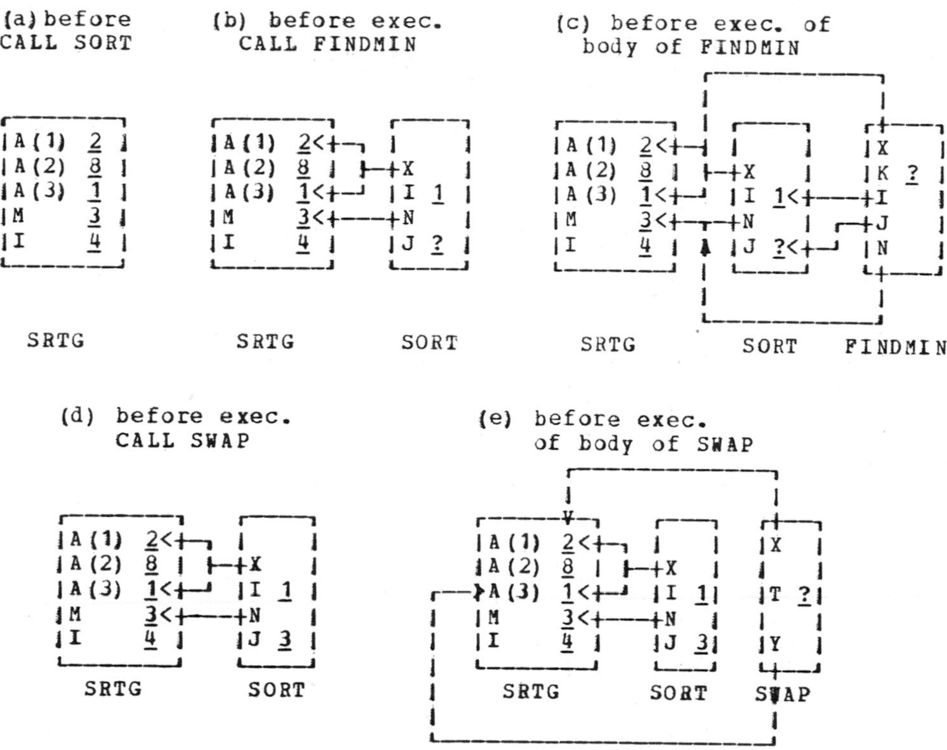

Figure 7. Partial Execution of Program (1.4a)

Let us now execute program (1.4a). Fig. 7a shows the variables after the list of values has been read, and just before execution of the first CALL statement. Fig. 7b shows the state of affairs after the SORT procedure body execution has begun, and just before the CALL FINDMIN statement is executed for the first time. Thus I (within SORT) has the value 1. J still has no value.

CALL FINDMIN is now executed. A box for procedure FINDMIN is drawn, the parameter correspondences are made, and local variable K is created. Fig. 7c shows the boxes at this stage, just before execution of the procedure body. Note that the arrow for argument X of SORT has been copied over to parameter X of FINDMIN. Similarly parameter N of FINDMIN points where parameter N of SORT does.

Now procedure body FINDMIN executes and terminates. We show the boxes just after the completion of the call of FINDMIN and before execution of CALL SWAP in Fig. 7d. J is now 3 since A(3) contains the minimum value of A(1:3). We now execute CALL SWAP. Fig. 7e shows the state of affairs just before execution of the body of SWAP. Note carefully where parameters X and Y point. Parameter X corresponds to the argument X(I) in SORT. Since X in SORT is A and I has the value 1, this is A(1). Similarly, Y refers to A(3). Thus SWAP will exchange the values of A(1) and A(3).

When SWAP finishes, its box will be deleted and we will return to the point following CALL SWAP in SORT. The values of A(1) and A(3) will have been interchanged.

Note that when procedure SWAP is called from within SORT, the box for SORT remains in existence. Although execution of SORT is temporarily suspended while SWAP is being executed, SORT is still active because its execution has not terminated.

1.5 STATIC Variables

Section 1.3.2 described execution of a procedure call. The creation and erasure of the boxes in Figure 1 accurately reflect what actually takes place during each execution of a call. In particular the local variables, such as T of SWAP in figure 1, exist only when their procedures are active. This process is called "dynamic storage management" and in PL/I variables that are treated in this way are said to be AUTOMATIC.

Dynamic storage management permits efficient use of storage space. Since variables are assigned storage space only when their procedures are active, the same space can be used at different times for different variables. However, it also means that information about AUTOMATIC variables is not preserved from one execution of a procedure to the next. For example, a procedure could not even keep a cumulative count of the number of times it had been called.

To permit retention of information a variable can be declared STATIC. A static variable is created just before execution of the main procedure begins, and remains around during all of execution; a static variable exists exactly when the main procedure is active. It is not destroyed on return from a procedure; it retains whatever value exists at the time of return.

If a static variable is declared with the INITIAL attribute the initial value is assigned only once as the variable is created and not each time the procedure is entered. Note, however, that a static variable is still local to the procedure in which it is declared. Although it exists throughout execution of the program (and not just when its procedure is being executed) it cannot be accessed from any other procedure.

For example, the values of J printed by repeated calls of INCR in (1.5a) are always 1 because J is recreated with initial value 0 on each call. By contrast the values of K are 1, 2 and

3 since this static variable retains its value from one call to the next. It is created and assigned initial value zero only once, just before execution of the main program begins.

```
            ...
            CALLCOUNT = 0;
            DO WHILE (CALLCOUNT < 3);
               CALLCOUNT = CALLCOUNT + 1;
               CALL INCR;
               END;
            ...
(1.5a)
        *PROCESS
         /* INCREASE J & K BY 1, AND PRINT */
         INCR: PROCEDURE;
            DCL J FIXED INIT(0);
            DCL K FIXED INIT(0) STATIC;
            J = J + 1;
            K = K + 1;
            PUT SKIP LIST (J, K);
            RETURN;
            END INCR;
```

As another example, COUNT in (1.5b) has the simple task of counting the number of times that it has been called and reporting this count to the calling procedure. This could be used to count the occurrences of some particular event in various places in a program -- say, the occurrences of negative numbers in a set of data arrays.

```
        *PROCESS
         /* SET N TO CUMULATIVE NUMBER OF CALLS */
         COUNT: PROCEDURE(N);
            DECLARE N FIXED;
(1.5b)      DECLARE CT FIXED INIT(0) STATIC;
            CT = CT + 1;
            N = CT;
            RETURN;
            END COUNT;
```

As a third example, NEXTLET in (1.5c) serves to divide input words of ten characters each into individual letters. Each time NEXTLET is called it returns the next letter of the input data stream to the calling procedure. On the first call, and every tenth call thereafter, NEXTLET obtains a new word from the external data list.

```
        *PROCESS
         /* SET L TO NEXT LETTER OF 10 LETTER INPUT WORD */
         NEXTLET: PROCEDURE(L);
            DCL L CHAR(*) VAR;
            DCL WORD CHAR(10) VAR STATIC;
            DCL COUNT FIXED INIT(10) STATIC;
            IF COUNT = 10
                THEN DO;
(1.5c)                  GET LIST (WORD);
                        COUNT = 0;
                        END;
            COUNT = COUNT + 1;
            L = SUBSTR(WORD, COUNT, 1);
            RETURN;
            END NEXTLET;
```

Local variable WORD in NEXTLET must be STATIC because it must get a value from the data list on the first call and retain this value for nine more calls. If it were not declared STATIC the value would be lost on return from the first call. COUNT is similarly declared STATIC so that NEXTLET can keep track of the position in WORD of the "next" letter, and so it will know when the data word is exhausted and a new value must be obtained from the data list.

Note that STATIC applies only to <u>variables</u>. A <u>parameter</u> in a procedure <u>cannot be declared STATIC</u>. It would not make any sense to do so since parameters are associated with arguments each time a procedure is called.

1.6 EXTERNAL Variables

In addition to the parameter-argument path described above, communication between procedures can be achieved using an "external" variable. A simple variable or array of any type can be made external just by adding the attribute EXTERNAL (or EXT) to its declaration.

External variables are "global" variables -- they do not belong to any one procedure of the program. Any procedure can <u>obtain access</u> to an external variable, just by <u>repeating its declaration</u> in that procedure. For example:

```
*PL/C
 /* DETRANSIFY A PASSAGE OF TEXT */
 DETRAN: PROCEDURE OPTIONS(MAIN);
     DECLARE LINES(200) CHAR(100) VAR EXTERNAL;
     ...
     END DETRAN;

*PROCESS
 /* LOAD LINES(1:200) FROM DATA */
 LOAD: PROCEDURE;
     DECLARE LINES(200) CHAR(100) VAR EXT;
     DECLARE LINECOUNT FIXED;
     ON ENDFILE GOTO DATAEND;
     DO LINECOUNT = 1 TO 220 BY 1;
         GET LIST (LINES(LINECOUNT));
         END;
     DATAEND:;
     RETURN;
     END LOAD;

*PROCESS
 /*  SET PTR TO FIRST VALUE IN LINES THAT CONTAIN WORD */
 SEARCH: PROCEDURE (PTR, WORD);
     DECLARE WORD CHAR(*) VAR; /* READONLY */
     DECLARE PTR FIXED;
     DECLARE LINES(200) CHAR(100) VAR EXT; /* READONLY */
     ...
     END SEARCH;
```

In this example LINES is the basic data structure that is processed by the program. Each of the procedures obtains direct access to this array by including an EXTERNAL declaration. Other procedures (not shown) that do not need access to LINES would not have this declaration. Procedure LOAD has no parameters, and its sole communication with other procedures is through LINES. On the other hand, SEARCH uses both communication mechanisms. It searches for a particular line in LINES, and reports the result by means of arguments.

Note that all the declarations of LINES must be the same.

An EXTERNAL variable is always STATIC -- this attribute is automatically assumed -- so that the variable is created before execution of the <u>main program</u> and it exists throughout execution of the entire program.

When should you use external variable communication rather than the argument-parameter method? Generally, external variables are used for data structures that logically seem to be the <u>common property</u> of several procedures, as in the example above. If the data structure logically <u>belongs to one particular procedure</u> then it should be made local to that procedure, with other procedures being granted access only through the argument-parameter route. Note that the external variable route does not permit "renaming", like the argument-parameter method does. That is, the SEARCH procedure above will only search LINES, whereas it can be called many times with different variables as arguments to specify the nature of the search.

Notice that regardless of which communication method is employed, the declarations in a procedure provide a complete list of the ways that the procedure can communicate with its neighbors. If a variable is neither external nor presented to a procedure as the argument of a call, the variable simply cannot be referenced or changed by another procedure.

Section 1 Summary

1. An external procedure is a subprogram that performs some distinct, clearly specified task.

2. The definition (or declaration) of an external procedure (excluding the main procedure) has the form:

```
*PROCESS
 /* Comment describing function of procedure */
 procedure-name: PROCEDURE(list of parameters);
   Declarations of parameters
   Declarations of local variables
   Statements (including RETURN)
   END procedure-name;
```

3. External procedures are placed (in any order) after the main procedure and before the *DATA card.

4. External procedures are executed by CALLing them by name. There can be many calls of a particular procedure, located anywhere in the main procedure or in any external procedure.

5. Execution of an external procedure is terminated by executing a RETURN statement. This completes execution of the particular CALL statement that caused this particular execution of the procedure.

6. An external procedure has its own local variables, independent of the variables of any other procedure. Normally these local variables exist only when the procedure is *active*; they are created each time execution of the procedure begins and are destroyed when that execution terminates. Local variables can be made "permanent" by declaring them to be STATIC.

7. An external procedure has its own local statement labels, accessible only to GOTOs within that procedure. You can neither enter a procedure nor exit from a procedure by means of a GOTO.

8. Communication between external procedures is by means of the parameters of the procedure declaration and the arguments of the CALL. Parameters and arguments are matched in the order listed (independent of their names). The attributes of parameters should exactly match those of the corresponding arguments.

9. An alternative form of communication is by means of EXTERNAL variables. These are global variables accessible to any procedure in which their declaration is given.

Section 1 Exercises

1. For each sequence of statements below, write a procedure with that sequence as the body, complete with declarations. The parameters are those variables and arrays described in the comment. Other variables should be local to the procedure. All variables are FIXED.

```
a) /** STORE THE MAXIMUM OF A AND B IN C */
     IF A >= B
          THEN C = A;
          ELSE C = B;

b) /** SET SUM TO SUM OF A(1:N) */
     SUM = 0;
     DO I = 1 TO N BY 1;
          SUM = SUM + A(I);
          END;

c) /** REVERSE THE ELEMENTS OF X(1:N) USING T */
     FIRST = 1;
     LAST = N;
     DO WHILE (FIRST < LAST);
          T = X(FIRST);
          X(FIRST) = X(LAST);
          X(LAST) = T;
          FIRST = FIRST + 1;
          LAST = LAST - 1;
          END;
```

2. Make the program segments of Exercise 2, Section I.5, into procedures. Only the variables described in the comment of each program segment should be parameters.

3. Execute the following procedure calls by hand, drawing all necessary boxes. Procedure SWAP is given in (1.1b). Assume all variables are FIXED.

```
a) CALL SWAP(A,B); where    A 5    B 6
b) CALL SWAP(T,X); where    T 3    X 4
c) CALL SWAP(Y,X); where    Y 1    X 8
d) CALL SWAP(V,V); where    V 3
```

4. Rewrite the program given in Exercise 3 of Section I.8 as an external procedure so it can be called from another procedure.

5. Write a procedure MEAN that, given an array segment X(1:N) calculates the mean of the values. The mean is the sum of the elements divided by N.

6. Execute the following procedure calls by hand, drawing all the boxes. Procedure SEARCH is given in (1.3.3c). The variables used are given below.

```
T(0) 6        N0 0        F 8
T(1) 8        N1 1        G 5
T(2) 4        N2 2        H 6
T(3) 9        N3 3        I 3
```

a) CALL SEARCH(T, N0, H, I);
b) CALL SEARCH(T, N1, H, I);
c) CALL SEARCH(T, N3, H, I);
d) CALL SEARCH(T, N3, G, I);
e) CALL SEARCH(T, N3, F, I);

7. Write a procedure with five parameters that will set the fifth parameter equal to the sum of the first four.

8. Write a procedure MEDIAN that, given an array segment X(1:N), calculates the median of the values. The median is the value such that half the numbers are greater than that value and half are less. One way to do this is to first sort the array and then pick the middle value. If you use this method, use a previously written sort procedure to do the sorting. But be careful; MEDIAN should <u>not</u> change the order of the values in its argument array -- a procedure should never modify the arguments unless its specific task is to modify them.

9. Write a program to read a list of values and to print out the mean and the median. Your program should use the procedures written in Exercises 5 and 8.

10. Write a procedure that calculates sin(x) using the formula

$$\sin(x) = x/1! - x^3/3! + x^5/5! - x^7/7! + \ldots$$

The number of terms of the series to be used should be a parameter of the procedure. Next, write a program to compare the values of sin(x) calculated using the built-in SIN function against those values calculated by your procedure. Run the program with various values of x and various values of the number of terms used in the series.

11. Write a procedure to calculate the product of two n by n matrices A(1:N,1:N) and B(1:N,1:N). Each element C(i,k) of the resulting matrix C(1:N,1:N) is defined as the sum of the values

A(i,j) * B(j,k)   for j = 1, ..., N.

12. Assume you are given the subroutine FLP shown below and told only that IN is an input parameter, that OUT is an output parameter, and that the routine neither reads any data nor prints any lines. Write a program that will allow FLP to be tested by repeatedly calling it with different input values and displaying the results. Your program will include FLP but not change it in any way.

```
*PROCESS
 /* SET OUT TO ...  */
 FLP: PROCEDURE(IN, OUT);
    DCL IN CHAR(*) VAR; /* READONLY */
    DCL OUT FIXED;
    ...
    RETURN;
    END FLP;
```

13. What is the <u>execution</u> output from the program shown below?

```
*PL/C
 /* SQUARE-DUPLICATE AND PRINT EACH OF J DATA PAIRS */
 LST: PROCEDURE OPTIONS(MAIN);
    DCL L CHAR(8) VAR;
    DCL (N, J, K) FIXED;
    GET LIST (J);
    DO K = 1 TO J BY 1;
        GET LIST (L, N);
        CALL EDITOR(N, L);
        PUT SKIP LIST (L, N);
        END;
    END LST;

*PROCESS
 /* SQUARE NBR AND DUPLICATE FIRST CHAR OF CHR */
 EDITOR: PROCEDURE(NBR,CHR);
    DCL NBR FIXED;
    DCL CHR CHAR(*) VAR;
    IF NBR ¬= 0
        THEN CALL SQUARE(NBR);
    IF CHR ¬= ' '
        THEN CALL DUP(CHR);
    RETURN;
    END EDITOR;

*PROCESS
 /* DUPLICATE FIRST CHARACTER OF STR */
 DUP: PROCEDURE(STR);
    DCL STR CHAR(*) VAR;
    STR = SUBSTR(STR,1,1) || STR;
    RETURN;
    END DUP;

*PROCESS
 /* SET VALUE = SQUARE OF VALUE */
 SQUARE: PROCEDURE(VALUE);
    DCL VALUE FIXED;
    VALUE = VALUE * VALUE;
    RETURN;
    END SQUARE;
*DATA
 4, 'X', 4, 'YY', -3, 'XYX', 0, '4',
 4, 'ABC', 567.9032
```

14. Write a procedure that will read a list of words (quoted strings of characters) whose lengths may be anywhere from 1 to 15 characters, and will print a list of any words that occur more than once in this data list. The end of the data list is indicated by the string '<*>', which is not itself considered an item on the list. Title the output appropriately.

15. Write a body for the procedure REPTEST, started below, so it will perform the task described in the heading comment. That is, it should check for repetitions of each character in the argument word. Any repetition of a character should be replaced by an asterisk. For example, 'AAABCDDBE' would become 'A**BCD**E'.

```
*PROCESS
 /* REPLACE ALL REPEATED OCCURRENCES (EXCEPT THE FIRST)*/
 /* OF ANY CHARACTERS IN WORD BY '*' */
 REPTEST: PROCEDURE(WORD);
    DCL WORD CHAR(*) VAR;
    ...
    END REPTEST;
```

16. What is the <u>execution</u> output from the following program?

```
*PL/C
 /* PROBLEM IV.1.16.  */
 PROB: PROCEDURE OPTIONS(MAIN);
    DCL M FIXED;
    DCL N FIXED INIT(4);
    DO M = 1 TO 3 BY 1F
        CALL SUB(M);
        PUT SKIP LIST('RESULT IS:', M, N);
        END;
    PUT SKIP LIST('AFTER LAST CALL',M,N);
    END PROB;

*PROCESS
 /* PRINT N AND M+2 */
 SUB: PROCEDURE(N);
    DCL N FIXED; /* READONLY */
    DCL M FIXED INIT(5);
    M = M + 2;
    PUT SKIP LIST ('INSIDE', M, N);
    RETURN;
    PUT SKIP LIST('STILL INSIDE',M,N);
    RETURN;
    END SUB;
```

17. Write a procedure DEBLANK to serve as a subroutine to eliminate all blanks from a character string given as argument.

18. Modify the subroutine DEBLANK of Exercise 17 so that it has a second parameter, which is FIXED. If the second argument has a non-zero value then DEBLANK is to return as the value of the second argument the cumulative number of blanks that have been eliminated in all calls so far (including the current call). If the value of the second argument is zero then it is to remain unchanged by DEBLANK.

19. Complete procedure FINDMAX started below. This is a procedure to recieve positive numbers and report the largest of the numbers received. Its action when called is the following:

-if ACT=1 the value given in VAL is to be saved -- that is, it is to be stored in some available slot in the array VALS. If this can be done, indicate success by returning with RES='1'B; if no space is available, indicate failure by returning with RES='0'B.

-if ACT=2 then the maximum of the values currently in VALS is to be returned in VAL. This maximum value is to be removed from VALS and the space it occupied made available for a new arrival. Indicate success by returning with RES='1'B and failure (if VALS is empty) by returning with RES='0'B.

```
*PROCESS
 /* SAVE VAL IF ACT=1; RETURN MAX VAL IF ACT=2; */
 /* RES = 1,0 FOR SUCCESS,FAILURE */
 FINDMAX: PROCEDURE(VAL,ACT,RES);
    DCL VAL FLOAT; /* READONLY */
    DCL ACT FIXED; /* READONLY */
    DCL RES BIT(*);
    DCL VALS(5) FLOAT INIT((5)-1) STATIC;
    ...
    END FINDMAX;
```

20. Write a procedure GETMAX: PROCEDURE(VAL,ACT,RES); that has exactly the same action from the caller's point of view as FINDMAX of Exercise 19. GETMAX is to work by calling FINDMAX, except that by keeping track of the kinds of calls GETMAX knows when FINDMAX would fail (return with RES='0'B) so in these cases GETMAX doesn't bother to call FINDMAX. It simulates FINDMAX's action and returns directly. Do not change FINDMAX.

21. Write a procedure that can be used to sum all the elements in a set of adjacent rows in a two-dimensional array. The parameters (all FIXED) are to be the following (in the order listed below):

Parameter 1: the array
Parameter 2: the number of columns in the array
Parameter 3: the first row to be included
Parameter 4: the last row to be included
Parameter 5: the sum of the required elements (the result).

22. Write a main procedure that can be used to test the summing procedure of Exercise 21. That is, this main procedure should

a) read a set of values that will serve as arguments
b) print the argument values (appropriately titled)
c) call the summing procedure
d) print the sum value returned.

23. Complete the procedure SEARCH given in the example in Section 1.6.

24. Rewrite procedure LOAD in the example in Section 1.6 to use an array input statement (see Section I.4.5) instead of the loop as shown. This change should be <u>invisible</u> to the calling procedure. That is, the revised procedure should act the same way as the version shown, as far as the calling procedure is concerned.

25. Rewrite procedure SEARCH in the example in Section 1.6 so that it uses only argument-parameter communication and has no direct access to the external array LINES.

Section 2 Functions

An alternative form of procedure, called a "function procedure" or simply a "function", offers some useful properties. It is also subject to some significant limitations. Functions are comparable to the built-in functions of the language and, in effect, provide a means by which you can augment the list of functions provided with the language.

Recall the properties of a built-in function, and note how these differ from the properties of the procedures described in Section 1:

1. The arguments of a function supply input to the function. A function cannot change the value of any argument.

2. The result of a function is the value of the function itself -- not a value assigned to some argument.

3. The arguments of a function can be simple variables, expressions or arrays, but the result is always a single value (never an array).

4. A function is used just by writing its name as a term in an expression, and not by writing a separate CALL statement.

These characteristics hold for user-defined functions as well.

2.1 Definition of a Function

Suppose we have a program that requires the computation of the average of the first n elements of an array. Suppose this must be done in several places, and to several different arrays, so obviously it should be written as a separate procedure. Written as an ordinary procedure, like those of Section 1, it would look something like the following:

```
/* SET ANS TO AVERAGE OF A(1:N) */
AVERAGE: PROCEDURE (A, N, ANS);
    DCL A(*) FLOAT; /* READONLY */
    DCL N FIXED;    /* READONLY */
    DCL ANS FLOAT;
    DCL SUM FLOAT INIT (0);
    DCL I FIXED;
    DO I = 1 TO N BY 1;
        SUM = SUM + A(I);
        END;
    ANS = SUM/N;
    RETURN;
    END AVERAGE;
```

To use this procedure to find the average of, say, B(1:M) and assign it to AVG, we would write

```
CALL AVERAGE(B, M, AVG);
```

Alternatively, this summing routine could be written as a function:

```
/* AVERAGE -- RESULT IS AVERAGE OF A(1:N) */
AVERAGE: PROCEDURE (A, N) RETURNS (FLOAT);
    DCL A(*) FLOAT; /* READONLY */
    DCL N FIXED;    /* READONLY */
    DCL SUM FLOAT INIT (0);
    DCL I FIXED;
    DO I = 1 TO N BY 1;
        SUM = SUM + A(I);
        END;
    RETURN (SUM/N);
    END AVERAGE;
```

To use this function to assign the average of B(1:M) to AVG we would write:

```
AVG = AVERAGE(B, M);
```

Suppose we needed the sum of three different averages. The function could be used as follows:

```
SUMAVG  = AVERAGE(B, M) + AVERAGE(C, L) + AVERAGE(X, N);
```

Using the averaging procedure, this would have to be written as:

```
CALL AVERAGE(B, M, AVG1);
CALL AVERAGE(C, L, AVG2);
CALL AVERAGE(X, N, AVG3);
SUMAVG = AVG1 + AVG2 + AVG3;
```

The function insertion <u>results</u> <u>in</u> <u>a</u> <u>value</u>, so it can be used wherever a value can appear. For example:

```
PUT SKIP (3) LIST ('AVERAGE OF B(1:M) IS:',
      AVERAGE(B, M));
```

The general form of a function definition is:

```
/* comment summarizing what the function returns */
function-name: PROCEDURE( list of parameters )
               RETURNS( attributes );
   Declarations to specify parameters
   Declarations to create local variables
   Function body (including RETURN(expr);)
   END function-name ;
```

2.1.1 Differences Between Functions and Procedures

Compare the forms of a function definition and a procedure definition, as shown by the example in Section 2.1:

1. There must be a phrase in the heading of a function definition to specify the type of value returned by the function. This should be one of the following:

   ```
   RETURNS (FLOAT)
   RETURNS (FIXED)
   RETURNS (CHARACTER (256) VARYING)
       (the maximum string length is always specified)
   RETURNS (BIT (1))
   ```

   Note that the keyword is RETURNS and not RETURN.

2. The RETURN statement in a function must have an expression (enclosed in parentheses) to specify the value to be returned. This value must be of the type specified in the RETURNS phrase of the heading. Note that this implies that the RETURN statement must be explicitly executed in a function (whereas in a procedure RETURN is implied by the procedure END.)

Except for these restrictions, the definition of a function is like the definition of a procedure, so all the material in Sections 1.2, 1.5, and 1.6 applies to functions as well as procedures.

2.2 Execution of a Function

Execution of a function is like execution of a procedure, as described in Section 1.3 and 1.4. In particular, association of arguments and parameters and creation of local variables are performed in exactly the same way. The only difference lies in the form by which the execution is invoked: a procedure is CALLed, but a function is invoked by writing its name as a term in an expression. This distinction must be strictly observed -- a function cannot be executed using a CALL and a procedure cannot be executed by giving its name in an expression.

Invoking a function in an expression is convenient, but it can lead to dangerous programming practices. This issue is discussed in Section 2.3.

In procedures in which the function is going to be used, an ENTRY declaration must be given to indicate that the name is a function (and not a subscripted variable). The declaration gives the attributes of each argument (in order) and the attributes of the returned value. (If this declaration is omitted PL/C will execute properly but give a warning message.) The general form of the declaration is:

```
        DCL function-name
            ENTRY ( list of attributes for each parameter )
            RETURNS( attributes of returned value );
```

For example, the declaration in procedures in which AVERAGE is to be used would be:

```
            DCL AVERAGE
                    ENTRY((*) FLOAT, FIXED)
                    RETURNS(FLOAT);
```

● PL/CS: the ENTRY declaration is not required.

As an example, consider two different programs that read in two values and print their maximum. The first uses a procedure, the second a function. Note the ENTRY declaration for MAXI in the main procedure of the second example.

```
  *PL/C
   /* READ TWO VALUES AND PRINT THEIR MAXIMUM */
   M: PROCEDURE OPTIONS(MAIN);
       DCL (A, B, C) FLOAT;
       GET LIST(A, B);
       CALL MAXI(A, B, C);
       PUT LIST(A, B, C);
       END M;
```

```
*PROCESS
 /* STORE IN C THE MAXIMUM OF A AND B */
 MAXI: PROCEDURE(A, B, C);
     DCL (A, B, C) FLOAT;
     IF A > B
         THEN C = A;
         ELSE C = B;
     END MAXI;
```

```
*PL/C
 /* READ TWO VALUES AND PRINT THEIR MAXIMUM */
 M: PROCEDURE OPTIONS(MAIN);
     DCL (A, B, C) FLOAT;
     DCL MAXI ENTRY(FLOAT, FLOAT)
              RETURNS(FLOAT);
     GET LIST (A, B);
     C = MAXI(A, B);
     PUT LIST(A, B, C);
     END M;

*PROCESS
 /* RETURN MAXIMUM OF A AND B */
 MAXI: PROCEDURE(A, B) RETURNS(FLOAT);
     DCL (A, B) FLOAT;
     IF A > B
         THEN RETURN(A);
         ELSE RETURN(B);
     END MAXI;
```

2.3 The Question of Function "Side-Effects"

A function is obviously *intended* to compute a value and return this value to the expression in which the function invocation appears. However, the question is whether that is *all* that a function *can* do.

There is, in fact, *absolutely no limit* on what a function can perform, and hence there is no limit to what can take place *in the evaluation of any expression*.

To examine the consequences of this flexibility, consider a simple statement intended to skip F(2) lines in the printed output, where F is a function:

```
PUT SKIP (F(2));
```

What is the precise meaning of this statement? That depends on function F. Suppose F were defined as

```
*PROCESS
 F: PROC(I) RETURNS(FIXED);
     DCL I FIXED;
     PUT SKIP LIST('******');
     RETURN(2);
     END F;
```

Then execution of PUT SKIP(F(2)); would cause a line of 6 asterisks to be printed and then 2 lines to be skipped. In fact, F could be altered to read 50 items of data, or to print 100 lines, or to cause almost any other action. PUT SKIP(F(2)); can be subverted by so-called "side-effects" of function F.

Consider another example. Suppose the following variables exist in a procedure:

```
DCL X FLOAT;
DCL Z(10) FLOAT EXTERNAL;
```

Now consider an assignment statement of the form:

```
X = Z(expression);
```

Presumably such a statement is intended to assign the value of one of the elements of Z to X. But realize that if there is a function reference in the subscript expression (which is allowed) then the effect might be quite different. In fact, this statement could assign the value of X to some element of Z.

These examples are deliberately exaggerated to underscore the point that with unrestricted functions any statement that includes an expression is essentially unpredictable in its action. The rule to use is that a function should only return a value to the expression in which it is used. Specifically:

1. A function should not change the value of any object that could be used by some other section of the program.

2. The insertion or removal of a particular use of a function should have absolutely no effect on the execution of any other statement of the program.

3. The value returned by a function should depend only on the values of the arguments provided and not on the context in which the function is used. Stated in another way, a particular function reference with certain argument values should return exactly the same value from any point in the program.

To achieve these objectives the body of the function should be restricted in the following ways:

1. All parameters of the function should be readonly; no parameter should appear as the target of an assignment.

2. EXTERNAL variables should be readonly -- that is, used only as input and never changed. (EXTERNAL variables are essentially additional input arguments.)

3. STATIC local variables should not be used.

4. A function can reference other functions (since they are presumably subject to the same restrictions) but a function cannot call any non-function procedure (since procedures are not similarly restricted). That is, the CALL statement should not be used in the body of a function.

5. A function should neither read nor write since altering the state of either the input data list or the output stream will affect the results of other statements outside the function. This means that neither GET nor PUT statements should be used in the body of a function.

These restrictions are matters of recommended style in PL/I and PL/C; the proscribed actions are actually legal according to the rules of the language. The restrictions are nevertheless important and strict adherence to them makes a program significantly easier to understand.

● PL/CS: these restrictions on the function body are mandatory.

These restrictions are severe, but they are essentially the weakest set that will guarantee that functions, and therefore expressions, have no side-effects whatever. With these restrictions a function can do nothing but return a value. Given that assurance it is possible to confidently and precisely state the meaning of each statement in the language.

Section 2 Summary

1. A function is an alternative form of procedure.

2. The differences are in the form of the definition:

   a. There must be a phrase in the PROCEDURE heading that specifies the type of value returned by the function -- one of the following:

   ```
   RETURNS (FLOAT)
   RETURNS (FIXED)
   RETURNS (CHARACTER (256) VARYING)
   RETURNS (BIT (1))
   ```

   b. Every RETURN statement in the function body must include a parenthesized expression specifying the value to be returned.

   c. There must be at least one parameter.

3. Recommended restrictions on the body of a function to eliminate side-effects are the following:

   a. CALL, GET and PUT cannot be used.

   b. All parameters must be READONLY.

   c. EXTERNAL and STATIC variables must be READONLY.

4. A function is executed by writing its name as a term in an expression. (It cannot be executed by means of a CALL.) Each procedure in which a function is used must have an ENTRY declaration for the function name.

5. Except for the differences noted above, functions and procedures are comparable.

Section 3 Internal Procedures

Up to this point we have considered programs that consist of one or more external procedures, one of which is the main procedure. Each external procedure constitutes an independent environment whose variables are separate and distinct from those of other external procedures. The only communication is through parameters and EXTERNAL variables. We now introduce a variation of the procedure concept in which the definition of one procedure is placed within the body of another procedure.

● PL/CS: There are no internal procedures or blocks in PL/CS.

3.1 Nested Blocks

Basic to this topic is the concept of an independent environment, which in PL/I is called a "block". A procedure is one type of block; another type is described in Section 4. The significance of blocks is related to their use in restricting the "scope" of a variable, that is, the parts of the program that can refer to the variable. For example, in Section 1 we saw that a variable within an external procedure, which is a block, can be referenced only from within that procedure; its scope is that procedure.

Note that the property of the scope of a variable is different from the property of when that variable is in existence. Scope has to do with where it can be used; the attribute STATIC or AUTOMATIC with when it exists.

As with procedures, we call a block active from the time its execution is begun until the time its execution is completed. Then, as described in Section IV.1.5, an AUTOMATIC variable is created at the time the block in which it is declared becomes active and is destroyed when the block becomes inactive. A STATIC variable, on the other hand, exists when the main procedure is active -- it is created just before execution of the whole program begins and is destroyed upon termination of the program.

With only external blocks (or procedures) each block is a separate, independent entity that is disjoint from other blocks. Each block has its own set of variables and the scope of a variable is the block in which it is declared. We now break this rule of independence and introduce <u>nesting of blocks</u>. Consider Fig. 1a. It shows five blocks named A, B, C, D, and E. Blocks A and E are <u>external</u>; their defining statements are not contained in any other block. B and C are immediately <u>internal</u> to A; their defining statements occur within block A. We also say that block A <u>surrounds</u> blocks B and C. Similarly, D is internal to C and C surrounds D.

Nesting of blocks is similar to nesting of loops. The nesting can continue to any depth and no overlap is possible; either two blocks are completely disjoint or one is completely internal to the other.

The <u>position</u> of a block relative to others determines which variables, labels, and procedures it may reference, as discussed in the next section.

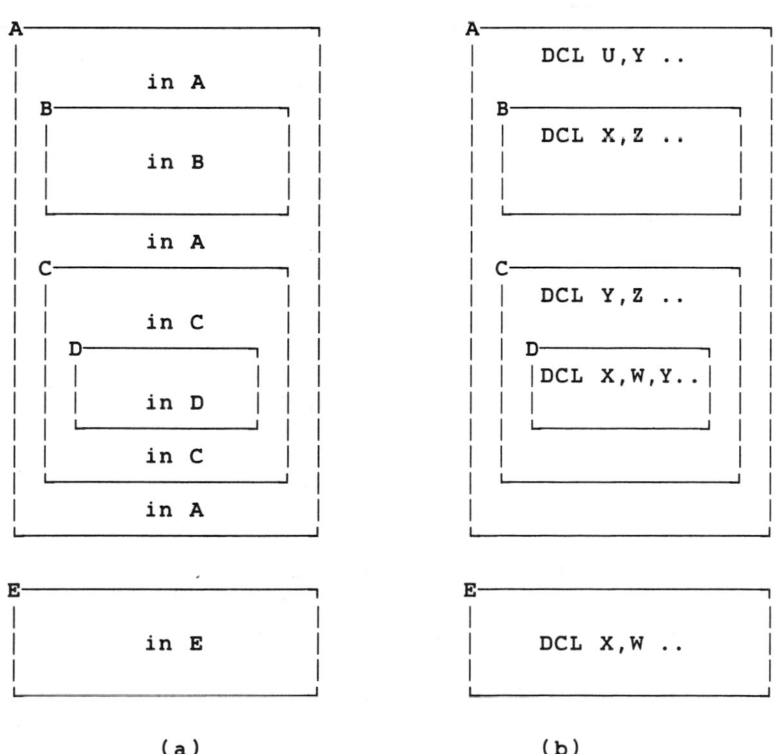

Figure 1. Nested Blocks

3.2 The Scope of Names

A *local variable of a block* is a variable that is declared immediately within that block. In Fig. 1b, variables U and Y declared within block A are local to A. Similarly, variables X and Z declared in block B are local to B. Note that block C has two local variables Y and Z; these are *not* the same variables as Y of A and Z of B. In PL/I programs different objects may have the same name but the language is designed so that with each use of a name one can (easily) determine which object that name refers to.

Clearly, the scope of a variable includes the block to which it is local; this rule was used in defining which variables could be used in an external procedure. With nested blocks the definition of scope becomes more complicated, and rather than define where a particular variable can be used it is easier to define which variables can be used in a particular block. This is done with two rules:

1. The names declared local to a block may be used within that block.

2. *Except* for the names determined by rule 1, a block inherits the use of all names, and the objects they represent, that can be used in the immediately surrounding block. These are called *global variables of the block*.

To illustrate, the variables that can be used in the blocks shown in Fig. 1b are:

1. Within block A: U of A, Y of A.

2. Within block B: X of B, Z of B, U of A, Y of A.

3. Within block C: Y of C, Z of C, U of A.

4. Within block D: X of D, W of D, Y of D, Z of C, U of A.

5. Within block E: X of E, W of E.

Let us substantiate this. Within block A local variables U and Y may be used, by rule 1. Block A is not contained in any other block, so rule 2 can not be used to increase the number of names to be used in A. Similarly block E can refer only to its local variables X and W.

Within block B of Fig. 1b, by rule 1 the local variables X and Z can be used. By rule 2, any variables useable in A (that are not named X or Z) can also be used; these are U and Y of block A. Hence B can refer to the four variables listed above.

Block C can refer to its local variables Y and Z. By rule 2 it can refer to global U of A since A surrounds C, but *not* to Y of A since C has a local name Y.

The determination in a similar fashion of the variables that can be used in block D is left to the reader.

Consider Fig. 1b where each block is a procedure. Suppose variable U of A is used in block D, which is legal. Suppose now that the programmer decides he needs to declare a local variable U in procedure C. Then use of U within D no longer refers to U of A; it has been changed to the local U of C. The point is that the meaning of a name in block D has been changed without any line in the definition of D being changed. The meaning of an internal block can be altered by a change in a surrounding block. Since the change may be several pages away the result can be very mystifying. A common dialog goes something like this:

> A: "The computer is fouled up. This program worked last time, but now it won't and I didn't change a thing."
>
> B: "Nothing?"
>
> A: "Well, nothing in the part we're talking about."

Internal blocks are more complicated than external blocks, and therefore riskier. They should be used only when the additional risk is outweighed by the advantages (see Section 3.5).

3.2.1 The Scope of Labels and Block-Names

The rules for determining where labels and block (procedure) names can be used are exactly the same as for variables. A label is defined (declared) where it appears as a statement label. Writing LA:...; defines label LA. Writing GOTO LA; references or uses the label.

To show the use of procedure or block names let us rewrite Fig. 1b as a program where each block is a procedure:

```
*PL/C
 A: PROC;
      DCL U,Y ...
      ...
      B: PROC;
           DCL X,Z ...
           ...
           END B;
      C: PROC;
           DCL Y,Z ...
           ...
           D: PROC;
                DCL X,W,Y ...
                ...
                END D;
           END C;
      END A;

*PROCESS
 E: PROC;
      DCL X,W ...
      ...
      END E;
```

The names A and E are "external". They are considered to belong to an imaginary block that surrounds the whole program. In fact, one considers the built-in functions to be declared in this imaginary block also. The names B and C are <u>local to block</u> A, so these two procedures may be called from A. The full list of block-use names is given below:

1. Within A: U, Y, B, C (local); A, E.

2. Within B: X, Z (local); U, Y, B, C of A; A, E.

3. Within C: Y, Z, D (local); U, B, C of A; A, E.

4. Within D: X, W, Y (local); Z, D of C; U, B, C of A. A, E.

5. Within E: X, W of E; A, E.

Note that the list for each block includes the name of that block. This means that a procedure can be called from within itself. This useful feature, called <u>recursion</u>, is described in Section IV.6.

3.3 Tracing Execution of Blocks

Consider the following program outline:

```
         A: PROCEDURE OPTIONS(MAIN);
              DCL X, Y
              ...
              RETURN;
              B: PROC
                   DCL X, Z
(3.3a)                  ...
                   RETURN;
                   E: PROC
                        DCL Y, W
                        ...
                        END E;
                   F: PROC
                        DCL X, Z
                        ...
                        END F;
                   END B;
              C: PROC
                   DCL X, W
                   ...
                   END C;
              END A;
```

The meaning of the variable names in the different blocks is shown in (3.3b):

	In block:	Name:	
	A	X	X local to A
		Y	Y local to A
	B	X	X local to B
		Y	Y declared in A
		Z	Z local to B
(3.3b)			
	E	X	X declared in B
		Y	Y local to E
		Z	Z declared in B
		W	W local to E
	F	X	X local to F
		Y	Y declared in A
		Z	Z local to F
	C	X	X local to C
		Y	Y declared in A
		W	W local to C

During execution of (3.3a) variables will be created as the block in which they are declared becomes active and then destroyed when it becomes inactive. We trace this process by drawing boxes for each block showing the variables created as that block becomes active. If a block is internal we draw its box inside that of the containing block.

Figure 2 illustrates this for various points in the execution of (3.3a). Fig. 2a shows the variables just after beginning execution of procedure A. During execution of procedure B, Figure 2b is in force. Note that there are two variables named X. While executing in procedure B, we look first in B's box for a variable. If we don't find it there we look in the surrounding box, and then the box surrounding that one, and so on. Thus while in B, X refers to the local variable of B. Figure 2c shows the variables while executing in procedure E. When procedure E is finished executing, its box is deleted and we return to the state shown in Fig. 2b. When procedure F is entered, a box for it is drawn as in Fig. 2d. When execution of both F and B is finished, we are back to Fig. 2a.

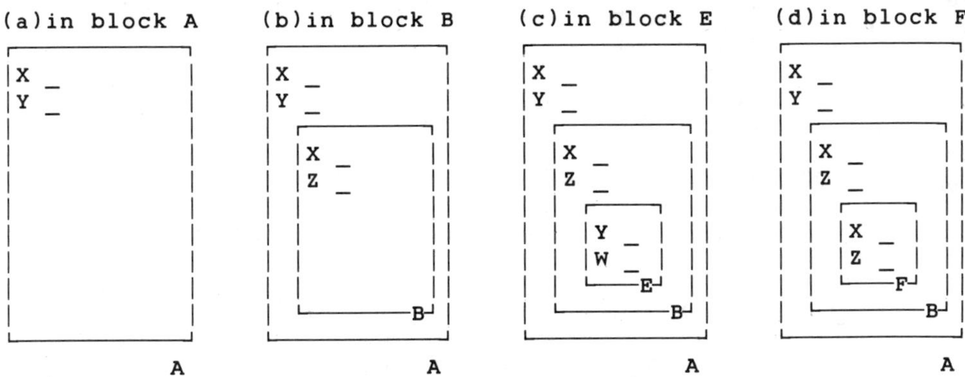

Figure 2. Various Stages of Execution of (1.3a)

3.4 Positioning of Internal Procedures

Internal procedures are similar to the external procedures described in Section 1. The differences are the following:

1. The definition of an internal procedure is positioned within another block, as for example, B or C in Figure 1. The definition is not preceded by a *PROCESS card.

2. An internal procedure may be called only from blocks that are within the scope of the procedure-name. That is, in Figure 1 neither B nor C can be called from within E. An external procedure can be called from anywhere in the program (actually, from anywhere where the name has not been declared for some other purpose).

3. Communication with an internal procedure, in addition to

the arguments of the call and EXTERNAL variables, includes variables useable in the surrounding block (as long as the names have not been declared for another purpose in the internal procedure).

Except for these points, the form definition and call, the use of parameters and arguments, and the creation and destruction of local variables is exactly as described in Section 1.2.3. Internal procedures may have STATIC variables (Section 1.5) and may be defined as function procedures (Section 2).

Since the definition of an internal procedure is placed within another block you should wonder what happens when one "runs into" the definition of a procedure in the course of executing the containing block. The answer is that the procedure definition is invisible to normal execution of the containing block. Execution skips immediately to the statement following the END of the internal procedure definition. You cannot "run into" a procedure to execute it; the only way to execute it is to invoke it with a CALL (or functionally, if it is a function procedure). Therefore, it does not matter as far as execution is concerned exactly where within the surrounding block a procedure definition is placed. However, it is clearer to a human reader if definitions are placed at the end of the surrounding block. It is also good practice to precede such definitions with a RETURN statement so that the reader does not have to scan past the internal definitions to see if there are further executable statements in the surrounding block. For example, if B and C are internal to A their definitions should be positioned as follows:

```
A: PROCEDURE
      ...
      RETURN;
      B: PROCEDURE
            ...
            END B;
      C: PROCEDURE
            ...
            END C;
      END A;
```

(3.4a) below is a nonsense program segment that illustrates the key points concerning internal procedures. You should be sure you understand why the first execution of CALL P1; produces the following output:

```
P2    8    2    7    2
P1    8    7    5
P2    9    2    8    3
P1    9    8    5
```

```
(3.4a)  P1: PROCEDURE;
            DCL I FIXED;
            DCL J FIXED INIT(6);
            DCL K FIXED INIT(5);
            DO I = 8 TO 9 BY 1;
                CALL P2(I);
                PUT SKIP LIST('P1',I,J,K);
                END;
            RETURN;

            P2: PROCEDURE(H);
                DCL H FIXED;
                DCL I FIXED INIT(1);
                DCL K FIXED STATIC INIT(1);
                I = I + 1;
                J = J + 1;
                K = K + 1;
                PUT SKIP LIST('P2', H, I, J, K);
                RETURN;
                END P2;

            END P1;
```

3.5 Uses of Internal Procedures

There are two reasons to position a procedure definition internal to another block:

1. To take advantage of the internal procedure's access to names of the surrounding block without having to pass those names as arguments.

2. To make the procedure inaccessible to other sections of the program.

The price paid to obtain these characteristics is substantial: the internal procedure and the containing block are no longer independent programs. While two external procedures can affect each other only through their arguments and parameters -- a limited and well-specified interface -- two nested procedures must always be mutually suspicious since their opportunities for mutual interference are considerable. For example, just by accidentally omitting a declaration, the internal procedure can inadvertently alter the value of _any_ of the variables of the containing block.

The following are useful guidelines as to circumstances when internal placement of a procedure is reasonable:

1. The action of the procedure is so specialized that it is very unlikely ever to be used in any other context.

2. The procedure is to be written by the same person, and

at the same time, as the containing block.

3. The procedure has so many arguments that it is inconvenient to enumerate them on each call.

4. The arguments of the procedure would be identically the same on each call.

5. The procedure must be kept private -- inaccessible to some other section of the program.

External placement is always safer; it should be normal practice except when there are convincing arguments for internal placement. Internal placement often seems easier (because of the simplified call) but this minor saving is usually offset by increased difficulty in testing and increased risk of error in future modifications.

Since the interface with an internal procedure is not entirely specified by its parameters, it should be carefully detailed in comments. These should enumerate each of the global names that is used in the procedure.

The procedure SWIMMER in the recursive program of Section 6.3.3 is a good example of the use of an internal procedure.

Section 3 Summary

1. A "block" establishes a separate environment. In PL/I, procedures are one form of block.

2. A block can be nested within another block; one block is said to be internal to the surrounding block.

3. Each block has a set of variables, labels and procedure names that can be referenced from within that block. For an internal block this set is not necessarily distinct from that of the surrounding block.

4. The "scope" of a variable, label or procedure name is the set of blocks within which that object can be referenced. The scope of an EXTERNAL variable or procedure name is all blocks. The scope of other variables, labels or procedure names is determined by the rules:

    1. The names declared local to a block may be used within that block.

    2. Except for the names determined by rule 1, a block inherits the use of all names that can be used in the immediately surrounding block.

5. An internal procedure is executed only by an explicit call, or reference (for a function procedure). It cannot be executed by "running into" the definition during execution of the surrounding block.

Section 4 Blocks

A second type of block in PL/I is called a "BEGIN block". The general form of the definition is:

```
block-name: BEGIN;
     Declarations to create local variables
     Block body
     END block-name;
```

BEGIN blocks are like procedures in that they establish a separate environment. The discussion of Sections 3.1 and 3.2 about nesting and scope applies equally to blocks of both types. The two types of blocks differ in the following ways:

1. BEGIN blocks cannot be external -- they must be internal to some other block.

2. BEGIN blocks cannot have parameters -- their only communication is through access to the names of the surrounding block.

3. BEGIN blocks cannot be called. They can only be executed by "running into" them in the course of executing the surrounding block. The BEGIN block is a statement to be executed.

● PL/CS: BEGIN blocks are not included.

As far as execution is concerned, the BEGIN block acts much like a compound statement. The following are equivalent except that the BEGIN block causes certain local variables to be created as its execution begins and then destroyed as it is completed:

```
DO;                         BEGIN;
 S1                              DCL local variables ;
 ...                             S1
 Sn                              ...
 END;                            Sn
                                 END;
```

The purpose of a BEGIN block is to establish a separate environment for a section of a program. A block in which every referenced variable is declared locally is independent of what goes on outside that environment; it cannot affect outside variables, nor can actions outside affect the values of local variables.

For example, suppose a large, complicated segment must be repeated N times. The segment could become the body of a loop:

```
I = 0;
DO WHILE (I < N);
    I = I + 1;
    body
    END;
```

This will do the job, unless a variable named I or N is used in the body. Then the control and the action interfere and the program will fail. However, interference can be avoided by creating a separate environment for the body:

```
I = 0;
DO WHILE (I < N);
    I = I +1;
    BEGIN;
        declarations
        body
        END;
    END;
```

If the declarations in the BEGIN block include every variable used in the body, then action and control are independent regardless of whether or not I or N are used in the body -- the control-I and the action-I would be different variables. Alternatively, just declaring I and N in the BEGIN block, regardless of whether they are used in the block, ensures isolation of the control variables.

At this point, this concern may seem artificial and unnecessary. You could just scan the body to see what variables it uses and choose two others for control variables. But eventually you will face the task of combining two program segments written by different people. It will be inconvenient (and risky) to change variable names in one segment to avoid conflict with the other, yet you need assurance that there is no conflict. The separate environment established by a block provides exactly this assurance.

4.1 Dynamic Dimensioning of Arrays

A BEGIN block can be used to allow the dimensions of an array to depend upon values determined during execution of a program, rather than having them specified as constants when the program is written. We have frequently given examples in which the dimensions of an array were overspecified when the program was written. Then a value obtained from data specifies how much of the array is actually going to be used. For example:

```
          DCL L(50) FLOAT;
          DCL N FIXED; /* ONLY L(1:N) ARE USED */
          DCL I FIXED;
          GET LIST(N);
          IF N<0 | N>50
(4.1a)       THEN DO;
             PUT SKIP LIST ('IMPROPER SIZE', N);
             N = 50;
             END;
          DO I = 1 TO N BY 1;
              GET LIST (L(I));
              END;
          ...
```

The use of a BEGIN block in (4.1b) is a better way to handle this common task:

```
          DCL N FIXED; /* LENGTH OF LIST */
          GET LIST(N);
          B: BEGIN;
              DCL L(N) FLOAT;
              DCL I FIXED;
              DO I = 1 TO N BY 1;
(4.1b)            GET LIST (L(I));
                  END;
              ...
              END B;
```

Since block B in (4.1b) has no declaration of a local N it has access to the N of the surrounding block. As B is entered the local array L is created, using whatever value N currently contains as the required number of elements. Except for DCL N and GET LIST(N) the entire segment is written as the body of block B. The whole purpose of B is to postpone creation of L until after N has been given a value. This strategy makes it unnecessary to estimate how large the array needs to be or to test to make sure that estimate was adequate. It also means that no more space than necessary is allocated to hold this array.

Our previous rule for array bounds was that they must be integer constants. We now relax this restriction; array bounds may be integer expressions, as long as the values of all variables used in the expressions are known when the space for the array is created -- that is, when the block in which the array is declared is entered.

An array takes space proportional to the number of variables in it. The programmer can control the use of memory to some extent by using blocks. Suppose that in two different parts of a program two arrays A(1:1000) and B(-500:0,1:20) are to be used. First array A is used and then later array B, but not both together. The programmer could structure his program as shown in (4.1c). The two arrays would automatically share the same space, since neither exists when the other does. This reduces the total amount of storage space needed by the program.

```
         X: PROCEDURE OPTIONS(MAIN);
                ...
                Y: BEGIN;
                     DECLARE A(1:1000) FIXED;
                     ...
                     END Y;
(4.1c)
                Z: BEGIN;
                     DECLARE B(-500:0,1:20) FLOAT;
                     ...
                     END Z;
                ...
                END X;
```

One could perform the same task for simple variables, but the memory space saved is generally not worth the effort.

4.2 Other Uses of BEGIN Blocks

We briefly note several other sections that refer to the use of BEGIN blocks. Recall Section I.7.4.3 concerning "ON conditions". An action was specified to be performed when a certain event occurs -- for example, reaching the end of the data list or the end of a printed page. When the action consists of more than a single statement the action is specified as a BEGIN block:

```
ON condition-name BEGIN;
    body
    END;
```

Section V.5.1 describes the PL/I "CHECK facility" used in program testing. This facility is applied to a particular block, so BEGIN blocks can be temporarily introduced to control the scope of the diagnostic facility. Note that BEGIN and END can be inserted into a program and if no declarations are added the action of the program is unaffected. Consequently BEGIN blocks can be temporarily introduced for diagnostic purposes without altering the action of the program under test.

Section 5 The Uses of Procedures and Blocks

Procedures provide essentially three different capabilities:

1. The ability to write a section of program in one place and have it executed as if it were written in another -- and consequently, the ability to have it executed from two or more different locations.

2. The ability to write a section in terms of parameters so that it can be used for different variables at different times. This is effectively defining a new operation to be used in a program, like SORT(A,N) or SWAP(X,Y).

3. The ability to create an independent environment whose names are distinct from those of the rest of the program, and for which the total communication is clearly and completely specified.

4. The ability to determine array bounds at runtime. (BEGIN blocks also provide this facility. See Section 4.1.)

5.1 Subroutines

The term "subroutine" is often used in programming to identify a sequence of statements that is needed in more than one place in a program. It is convenient to be able to write the common statements only once and use them as often as and wherever necessary. If a subroutine is written in a general way, without commitment to particular variable names, its opportunity for use is clearly increased. This obvious use of procedures in PL/I was suggested by the examples of the preceding sections.

There is generally a sense of both permanence and portability in subroutines. That is, they are written so that they can be used in more than one program. There are various "libraries" of subroutines that are quite permanent and widely used. In effect, the built-in functions of PL/I -- SQRT, MAX, MIN, MOD, etc. -- constitute such a library.

Subroutines can be considered a means of <u>extending</u> a programming language: of adding whatever operators or statements the user needs that the language doesn't happen to offer. For example, in Section 1.1 we developed a procedure to interchange the values of two variables. With this procedure appended to any program the "swap" operation is effectively added to the language. Procedure SEARCH in Section 1.3.3 is another, more complex, example.

In Part III we often wrote a statement in English and then translated or refined it into PL/I. By writing a subroutine to perform that task we effectively add that high-level statement to the language (at least temporarily). For example, in Section II.4.3 we developed a program to order the elements of an array. If this were written as an external procedure with the array as argument then one could regard

```
CALL SORT(A);
```

as part of the language. Moreover, the procedure could be saved and reused in future programs whenever needed. For all practical purposes we could now think of "sort" as an operation available in our private augmented-PL/I. In the development of future programs, once we reached a point where the algorithm required something to be sorted, we would not have to worry about that particular step any longer.

Either the procedure or the function form can be used for a subroutine, depending upon:

1. The nature of the task -- certain things (like reading and printing) should not be done in a function.

2. The context in which it is to be used -- a procedure can only be invoked by a separate CALL statement, while a function can be used as a term in an expression.

3. The communication requirements -- a function can only return a single value (not an array) and should not change the value of its parameters.

Subroutines exploit all three capabilities of external procedures. The first two are obvious, but it is the third -- the independent environment -- that allows a subroutine to be moved freely from one program to another without any concern for whether the variables in the subroutine happen to coincide with names in the host program.

5.2 Control Sections

The techniques described in Part II to make small programs clear and understandable don't always work well when applied directly to large programs. For example, if the steps at the top level are so long that it is impossible to comprehend them as a single unit, then their role and relationship to other units is less clear.

The indentation convention, which makes vertical left-alignment significant in understanding a program, clearly works best if successive statements with the same alignment appear on the same page. If the successor to a particular step is several pages away, then vertical alignment is much less effective.

Procedures can be used to alleviate these problems by reducing the apparent size of programs. Simply take some logically convenient section of program, write it in a remote position as an external procedure, and provide a CALL in its original location. For example, suppose one has to perform some task on each element of a 3-dimensional array:

```
/** GRIMBLE ARRAY AR */
    PLANE: DO I = 1 TO R BY 1;
       ROW: DO J = 1 TO S BY 1;
           COL: DO K = 1 TO T BY 1;
               /* GRIMBLE AN ELEMENT */
                   ...
               END COL;
           END ROW;
       END PLANE;
```

This segment is reasonably clear as long as the body of the "grimble an element" task is not too large. If it is large, or if it involves many levels of nesting, it is worthwhile writing it as a separate procedure:

```
     ...
     /** GRIMBLE ARRAY AR */
         PLANE: DO I = 1 TO R BY 1;
            ROW: DO J = 1 TO S BY 1;
                COL: DO K = 1 TO T BY 1;
                    CALL GRIMBLE(AR(I,J,K));
                    END COL;
                END ROW;
            END PLANE;
     ...
*PROCESS
 /* PERFORM GRIMBLE PROCESS UPON G */
 GRIMBLE: PROCEDURE(G);
    DECLARE G FLOAT;
    ...
    END GRIMBLE;
```

The following are some reasonable limits on the size of

individual steps in a program:

1. The body of a step should be no more than 50 lines (1 page) in length.

2. Nesting should not exceed 3 or at most 4 levels.

To maintain these limits, use procedures so that a CALL can replace some section of program, thereby reducing the size or apparent nesting level of the main program.

Procedures should be routinely used in this way. In fact, any program of more than one or two pages should be entirely written in this manner. At the top level, the program should consist primarily of CALL statements. The main procedure, doing nothing but calling other procedures, serves as a control section of the program. It is short and shows clearly how the program is organized and the major steps in its action.

For example, the sorting program in Section 1.4 is essentially written in this manner. The actual sorting is done by a procedure SORT called from the main procedure. This allows the main procedure to be short and clear: it simply reads the data, calls SORT, and prints the sorted results. The details of how the sorting is actually done do not obscure the simple sequence of tasks in the main procedure.

The accounting problem of Section III.3.4 would be a good candidate for this type of organization. This program has three sections:

```
/** READ AND SET UP THE ACCOUNTS */
/** PROCESS THE TRANSACTIONS */
/** PRINT THE RESULTS */
```

Since the problem presented in III.3.4 is highly simplified, compared to the real task, the program all fits on one page and is not too difficult to follow. However, a useful program for a realistic version of this problem, including adequate error checking, would be many pages long. It might still consist of three sections, but if each section were long and complicated the overall structure would not be clear to the reader. To preserve clarity of structure the main procedure of this program should be a control section, with each of the subtasks written as a separate procedure:

```
/** READ AND SET UP THE ACCOUNTS */
    CALL ACCTRD(N, ACCT, WITH, DEP, IBAL, CBAL);
/** PROCESS THE TRANSACTIONS */
    CALL PTRAN(N, ACCT, WITH, DEP, IBAL, CBAL);
/** PRINT THE RESULTS */
    CALL PRINT(N, ACCT, WITH, DEP, IBAL, CBAL);
```

With this organization the accounts are declared in the main procedure and passed as arguments to each of the processing procedures. The extra variables needed to process the transactions -- TACCT, DEPWITH, AMT -- are needed only by PTRAN so they are declared in PTRAN rather than the main procedure.

As another example, the index for this book was produced by a sizable program. Nevertheless, its high level structure is clear from its control section:

```
/* PRODUCE INDEX */
INDEX: PROCEDURE OPTIONS(MAIN);
   DCL LN(3000) CHAR (50) VAR; /* TABLE OF LINES */
   DCL TOPLINE FIXED INIT (0); /* TOP LINE IN LN */
   /** READ TOPIC/PG-NBR PAIRS INTO LN */
       CALL LOAD(LN,TOPLINE);
   /** SORT REFERENCES INTO ALPHABETICAL ORDER */
       CALL SORT(LN,TOPLINE);
   /** CONDENSE MULTIPLE REFERENCES TO A SINGLE LINE */
       CALL CONDENSE(LN,TOPLINE);
   /** CONVERT LINES TO FORMAT REQ'D BY TEXT-EDITOR */
       CALL CONVERT(LN,TOPLINE);
   /** PUNCH CARD FOR EACH LINE */
       CALL PUNCH(LN,TOPLINE);
   END INDEX;
```

In general, a good way to organize and present a large program is to have four sections:

1. A block of comments that fully and precisely describe the function of the program.

2. A control section of not more than one page that calls various procedures to do the work.

3. A block of comments serving as a "table of contents" for the following procedures.

4. A set of external procedures, called by the control section.

Of course, some of the individual procedures may be so large that they would also benefit from the same treatment. Entry to such a procedure would encounter another control section, which would call other procedures. There is no limit to how large a program can become and still be understandable, if procedures are used to keep the apparent size down to where the techniques of Part III are effective.

5.3 Sectional Independence

An external procedure is a relatively independent section of a program, and this independence is very useful. Communication between different procedures is strictly limited and completely described. A given procedure's only communication with other procedures is through its parameters, and possibly through EXTERNAL variables. But in either case, the communication possibilities are completely described in the declarations of the procedure. Separate procedures have no other effects on each other. When reading a program you can analyze each external procedure separately, with complete confidence that no action (or mistake) elsewhere in the program will have the slightest effect on this procedure, except possibly in the way that it affects the values of arguments.

When writing an external procedure you simply have less environment to worry about. You can be entirely concerned with how to perform the required action. You have no concern that other sections of program will interfere with this one, or that this section may have unexpected side-effects elsewhere. You need not remember what variable names have been used elsewhere in the program; you can use whatever names are most natural for this local use.

This independence of sections is particularly useful when a program is to be produced by a team of programmers. If each programmer (or group) is assigned a separate external procedure the communication problems are minimized. Joint planning will concern only the function of each procedure and its parameter communication. Given this "problem specification" the design and development of the procedure can proceed as described in Part III, just as if this were an independent problem. It should also be tested as if it were an independent problem, as described in Section V.3.3. The procedures should be integrated into a final program only after there is great confidence in their individual performance.

For example, suppose a program is required to perform some task upon an array of words that are in alphabetical order. Suppose the input consists of lines in which the words are not in alphabetical order. Obviously the program will be required to scan lines and break them up into individual words, and then sort the resulting list of words. It is useful to design a program with these "scan" and "sort" tasks as separate procedures. As far as the principal program is concerned all that has to be specified for these tasks is the action to be performed and the manner in which arguments are to be given. This specification is called the "interface" between the procedures. Once the interfaces have been specified the design, writing and testing of the scan procedure, the sort procedure and the rest of the program could proceed independently. All three could be done by one person (working in any order), by three separate programmers, or parts could be drawn from a library of existing subroutines. The programmers of the different procedures do not have to discuss with each other what names they plan to use in their particular procedure.

One particularly important aspect of interface specification is the identification of each parameter as being input, output, or both input and output. The independence of procedures protects the variables of one procedure from the actions of other procedures -- except for those variables that are given as arguments in a call -- so the calling and called procedure must have a clear understanding as to how arguments are to be treated. For example, a procedure should change the value of the argument associated with a particular parameter only if it is explicitly agreed that it is an output parameter.

5.4 Logical Functions

Conditions (expressions that are either true or false) can often have a simple high-level, English description that requires a rather involved, complicated implementation in PL/I. A logical function -- one that returns a BIT(1) value -- can be used to hide the complicated implementation. The body of the function is this implementation and returns the BIT(1) value, while the user or caller of the function need only remember what the function does.

For example, suppose it is necessary to decide whether two one-dimensional arrays are identical -- element by element. The following function could be used:

```
/* IDENTICAL RETURNS THE RESULT "A = B" */
/* (THE BOUNDS OF A AND B MAY DIFFER) */
IDENTICAL: PROCEDURE (A, B) RETURNS (BIT(1));
    DCL (A(*), B(*)) FLOAT; /* READONLY */
    DCL I FIXED;
    DCL SDIF FIXED; /* DIFFERENCE IN SUBSCRIPTS */
    IF (HBOUND(A,1)-LBOUND(A,1)) ¬=
            (HBOUND(B,1)-LBOUND(B,1))
        THEN RETURN ('0'B);
    SDIF = LBOUND(A,1) - LBOUND(B,1);
    DO I = LBOUND(A,1) TO HBOUND(A,1) BY 1;
        IF A(I) ¬= B(I-SDIF)
            THEN RETURN ('0'B);
        END;
    RETURN ('1'B);
    END IDENTICAL;
```

Now suppose a loop is to iterate as long as two lists LEFT and RIGHT are identical. The loop can be controlled by the following:

```
    DO WHILE (IDENTICAL(LEFT, RIGHT));
```

Section 5 Exercises

1. Suppose there were no ABS built-in function in PL/I to find the absolute value of an argument. Design and write a function that would provide this "extension" to the language.

2. Write a procedure to add two matrices, producing a third matrix. A matrix C is the sum of two matrices A and B if each element of C is the sum of the elements in the corresponding positions in A and B. That is

$$C(i,j) = A(i,j) + B(i,j)$$

All three matrices must have the same number of rows and columns. The procedure should have five parameters:

Parameter 1: first input matrix
Parameter 2: second input matrix
Parameter 3: output matrix
Parameter 4: number of rows in each matrix
Parameter 5: number of columns in each matrix.

3. Write a procedure to "rotate" a square matrix (one with the same number of rows as columns) 90^0 clockwise. That is, the element initially in the upper left corner will become the element in the upper right corner, etc. The procedure should have two parameters:

Parameter 1: matrix to be rotated
Parameter 2: number of rows (or columns).

4. Write a procedure to format print lines from individual words supplied as arguments. The procedure should have a single parameter that is a character string. On each call the procedure is presented with a "word". It builds a print line with these words, adding each new word to the right end of the line (with an intervening blank between words). The line length is at most 60 positions. When a new word cannot be added to the line without exceeding this length, the old line is printed and a new line is begun starting with the word that wouldn't fit on the old line.

5. Convert the symbol-scanning program of Section III.4.5.3 into a procedure to deliver individual symbols when the input consists of test lines.

6. Write the programs described in Exercise 10 of Section III.3 in the form described in IV.5.2. That is, write them with a short control section calling external procedures to perform the actual subtasks.

7. Write a dummy version of the "list-inquiry" program developed in Section III.3.2 that could be used to test a larger program of which list-inquiry was to be a part.

8. Repeat exercise 7 for the sorting program developed in Section III.3.3.

9. Consider the procedure SORT in Section IV.1.4.

   a. Make a list of the potential problems, special cases, extreme values, etc. that ought to be tested before this procedure is pronounced "correct".

   b. Devise a set of test data that will reveal a flaw (if one exists) for each of the problems listed in 9.a.

   c. Devise a "test driver" that will allow the SORT procedure to be tested independently of the rest of that program. The driver should permit several of the test cases developed in 9.b to be combined in a single run.

   d. Devise a dummy version of SORT that will allow the main procedure SRTG to be tested without using the actual SORT procedure.

10. Write a function named TESTORDER with a parameter consisting of a one-dimensional array of FLOAT numbers. TESTORDER should return '1'B if the values of the elements of the array given as argument are in non-decreasing order, that is, if

```
element(i) <= element(i+1) <= element(i+2) <= ...
```

Otherwise return '0'b. (See Section 5.5.)

11. Show how the list searching program of Section III.3.2 would be rewritten to take advantage of the dynamic dimensioning technique described in Section 5.5.

Section 6 Recursive Use of Procedures

A recursive procedure is one which calls itself -- a call of the procedure occurs within the body of the procedure itself, or in another procedure called by the original one. Recursion can be used quite extensively in programming, and in some cases can make difficult problems look easy. In fact, for some problems recursion is the natural way to describe the task.

6.1 A Simple Example

The term recursive is derived from mathematics where some formulas are written using recursive definition - something is defined in terms of itself. For example, consider the function N! which for N > 0 is defined as

(6.1a) $$N! = N * (N-1) * (N-2) * \ldots * 2 * 1$$

This can also be defined recursively (in terms of itself) as

(6.1b) $$N! = \begin{cases} 1 & \text{if } N = 1 \\ N * (N-1)! & \text{if } N > 1 \end{cases}$$

We can write a recursive PL/I procedure to calculate N! for any positive integer N directly from this recursive definition:

(6.1c)

```
/* STORE N! IN ANS*/
FACT: PROCEDURE(N, ANS) RECURSIVE;
        DECLARE (N, ANS) FIXED;
        DECLARE TEMP FIXED;
        IF N = 1
           THEN ANS = 1;
           ELSE DO;
                F: CALL FACT(N-1, TEMP);
                ANS = N*TEMP;
                END;
        END FACT;
```

The keyword RECURSIVE must appear between the parameters and the semicolon in the heading of any recursive procedure, as shown above.

● PL/CS: The keyword RECURSIVE is not required.

Consider the body of procedure FACT of (6.1c). If N is 1, the procedure stores 1 in ANS and returns, as required by definition (6.1b). If N > 1, then FACT is called a second time to store (N-1)! in TEMP (at label F). This value is then multiplied by N and the result is stored in ANS. This again satisfies definition (6.1b). Note that while discussing the call F: CALL FACT(N-1,TEMP); we don't worry about <u>how</u> FACT will work; we just assume that the procedure FACT will do its job -- will store (N-1)! in TEMP for us. That FACT also happens to be the procedure currently being executed should not disturb us; just think of it as two different procedures which just <u>look</u> the same.

This particular function N! is not a good example of a useful, efficient recursive procedure, since it can be written more easily and efficiently using definition (6.1a) as

```
/* STORE N! IN ANS*/
FACT: PROCEDURE(N, ANS);
       DECLARE (N, ANS) FIXED;
       DECLARE I FIXED;
       ANS = 1;
       DO I = 2 TO N BY 1;
           ANS = ANS * I;
           END;
       END FACT;
```

However the recursive procedure for N! is short and simple enough to illustrate how recursion works and how we should deal with it, and we will use it extensively in the next section.

6.2 <u>Exploring Recursion</u>

Recursion may seem strange at first; it seems odd to be executing the same procedure two or more times at the same time. Let us motivate recursion as follows. Below we have written four procedures. (We have left out the declarations to save space). FACT1 will store in ANS the value N!, but only if N = 1. FACT2 produces N! if N≤2, by calling FACT1 to evaluate 1!. Similarly, FACT3 and FACT4 produce N! if N≤3 and N≤4, respectively, by calling on the other procedures. Thus we have written four different procedures, each of which calculates N! for a certain range of values of N.

These procedures are easy to understand, and obviously perform the required action. However, to be able to calculate 5! we must write a procedure FACT5, and for 6! a procedure FACT6, and so on. This is inconvenient.

Now note that all the procedures (except for the first) are similar, save for the name of the procedure being called. It would be useful to be able to have one procedure which we can call many times instead of many procedures once. Thus, we write the procedure FACT of (6.1c), with the same body as FACT2, FACT3 and FACT4 except for the name of the procedure being called. In effect, we can consider FACT to be as many procedures as we want. Each time it is called recursively, a new "copy" of the procedure is made and used for that call, and we can think of these different copies as having names FACT1, FACT2, FACT3, and so on.

```
FACT1: PROCEDURE(N, ANS); /* ANS = N! IF N=1*/
     IF N = 1
          THEN ANS = 1;
          ELSE Give error message;
     END FACT1;

FACT2: PROCEDURE(N, ANS); /* ANS = N! IF N≤2*/
     IF N = 1
          THEN ANS = 1;
          ELSE DO;
               CALL FACT(N-1,TEMP);
               ANS = N*TEMP;
               END;
     END FACT2;

FACT3: PROCEDURE(N, ANS); /* ANS = N! IF N≤3*/
     IF N = 1
          THEN ANS = 1;
          ELSE DO;
               CALL FACT2(N-1,TEMP);
               ANS = N*TEMP;
               END;
     END FACT3;

FACT4: PROCEDURE(N, ANS); /* ANS = N! IF N≤4*/
     IF N = 1
          THEN ANS = 1;
          ELSE DO;
               CALL FACT3(N-1,TEMP);
               ANS = N*TEMP;
               END;
     END FACT4;
```

6.2.1 The Recursive Pattern

Most recursive definitions and recursive procedures have the same pattern or flavor as does N!. For one or two values of the argument, the result is defined nonrecursively, usually in a quite simple manner. Thus, if N = 1, N! = 1. For all other argument values, the result is defined recursively. This recursive definition is arranged so that it is easy to see that the recursion will terminate. For example for N!, if N > 1 we have N! = N*(N-1)!. Here we see that the result for N! is defined in terms of (N-1)! -- 5! is defined in terms of 4! which is defined in terms of 3! and so on. Thus we must eventually get to 1 and the process terminates.

As another example, we can define multiplication of two positive, nonzero integers X and Y in terms of addition and subtraction as follows:

$$X*Y = \begin{cases} X & \text{if } Y = 1 \\ X + X*(Y-1) & \text{if } Y > 1 \end{cases}$$

Y = 1 is the simple, nonrecursive case, while the second case is recursive. The second argument Y decreases by one at each step of the recursion, so that the process must terminate when Y = 1.

In general, any recursive procedure can be transformed into one which is not recursive. The question then is why use recursion? The answer is threefold:

1. A recursive procedure is often easier to understand and prove correct.

2. Thinking recursively often leads to simpler algorithms, even though they may finally end up in a nonrecursive form.

3. Recursive procedures tend to divide the problem into smaller but similar ones which can be solved the same way, and this often increases efficiency.

Once we understand the basic idea behind recursion, we find that recursive procedures are much easier to understand than the conventional iterative loops. Loops are hard because the way they look is so different from the way they execute. The body of the loop appears only once, but it may be executed any number of times. This is also true of recursive procedures, but they are easier to understand because of the way we read them. When we see a call like CALL FACT(N-1,ANS); we can concentrate on <u>what</u> FACT is doing, and leave until later <u>how</u> it does it. This is much more difficult to do with iteration, and we have to resort to invariant relations, as described in Section V.7.1.

6.2.2 Executing Recursive Procedures by Hand

Executing recursive calls by hand is no more difficult than executing regular nested procedure calls. The only problem is that several boxes will exist for a procedure called recursively, one for each invocation which has not finished executing. To illustrate this, consider a call M: CALL FACT(3,X); in the main program, where the main program variables are as shown in Fig. 1a. We will now execute this call, assuming that FACT is an external procedure, and show how the boxes are drawn at each point of execution. In order to keep track of which box for FACT to use at each point, we will put a superscript after the procedure name. Thus Fig. 1b shows the boxes just after the box for FACT is drawn for the main procedure call M: CALL FACT(3,X); but before the procedure body is executed. The superscript indicates the "level" of recursion.

In order to keep track of the place from where each procedure activation was called, the label of the call is written at the bottom right of the box for the activation.

The procedure body of FACT is now executed. Since $N \neq 1$, the call at label F of FACT is executed. Another box is drawn for this second call of FACT, labeled $FACT^2$ as in Fig. 1c. When executing the procedure body for this second call of FACT, refer to the box labeled $FACT^2$ for names used within the procedure body.

Now execute the procedure body for $FACT^2$. Since $N \neq 1$ (it is 2), execute the call F: FACT(N-1,TEMP); again. Drawing the box and making the parameter-argument correspondence for this call yields Fig. 1d.

For the third time, begin executing the procedure body for FACT. This time N = 1. The value 1 is stored in ANS (which changes TEMP within $FACT^2$ to 1), and execution of the procedure body is finished. The call labeled F in the second invocation of FACT has been completed and the boxes look like Fig. 1e.

Now execute ANS=N*TEMP; of the second invocation of FACT, which stores 2 in TEMP of $FACT^1$. The result of this is shown in Fig. 1f. Fig. 1g shows the boxes after deletion of the box $FACT^2$ and thus completion of the call labeled F in the first invocation of FACT. Now execute ANS=N*TEMP; once more, which stores the value 6 in the main program variable X. Execution of the procedure body has ended, so delete the box for $FACT^1$. Execution of the procedure call labeled M in the main program is finished, and the boxes look like Fig. 1h.

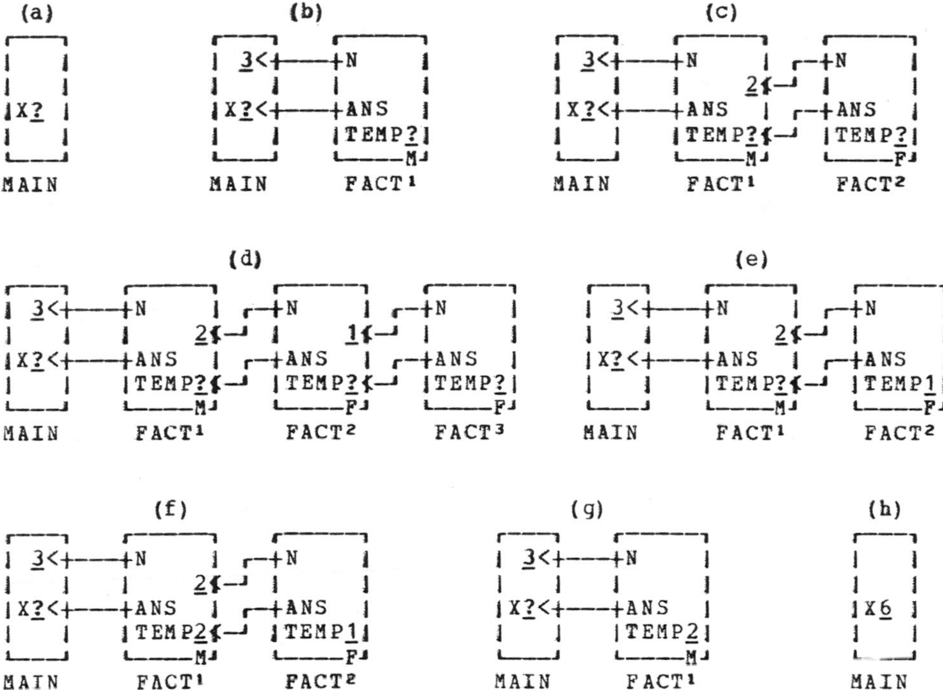

Figure 1. Various stages of execution of CALL FACT(X,3);

6.3 Recursive Procedure Examples

6.3.1 The Towers of Hanoi

The following legend is told about a temple in Hanoi. When the temple was built, three large towers or poles were placed in the ground, and 64 disks of different diameters were placed on the first pole, in order of decreasing diameter (with the smallest on the top and the largest on the bottom -- see (6.3.1a)). The monks at the temple were to move the disks from pole 1 to pole 3, following these two rules: Only one disk could be moved at a time, and no disk was to be placed on top of a smaller disk. When they finished their task, the world would come to an end.

(6.3.1a)

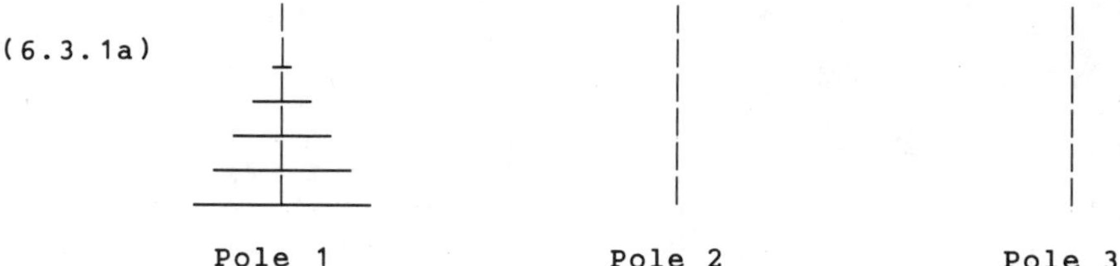

How do the monks perform their task, and how long will it actually take? The task seems difficult (because of the rule that no disk may be placed on a smaller one), but if viewed recursively it is quite easy (although still long). A recursive procedure could print out a list of moves for the monks, like

```
MOVE DISK FROM 1 TO 2
```

One way of performing the task is to

1) Move 63 disks from pole 1 to pole 2;
2) Move 1 disk from pole 1 to pole 3;
3) Move 63 disks from pole 2 to pole 3;

Note that the largest disk is always at the bottom of pole 1 or 3, so that it is never placed on top of a smaller one. This assumes of course that we know how to move 63 disks. How is this done? Again, use the same technique:

1) Move 62 disks from pole 1 to pole 3;
2) Move 1 disk from pole 1 to pole 2;
3) Move 62 disks from pole 3 to pole 2;

A pattern emerges; at each step move a number of disks by moving all but the last to one pole, then moving the last to its proper pole, and then moving the other disks back on top of it. This pattern forms the basis for the body of the following recursive procedure:

```
/* MOVE N DISKS FROM POLE X TO POLE Y.  USE POLE Z TO */
/* STORE DISKS IF NECESSARY */
HANOI: PROCEDURE(X, Y, Z, N) RECURSIVE;
   DECLARE (X, Y, Z, N) FIXED;
   IF N = 1
        THEN PUT SKIP LIST('MOVE DISK FROM',X,'TO',Y);
        ELSE DO;
             CALL HANOI(X, Z, Y, N-1);
             PUT SKIP LIST ('MOVE DISK FROM', X, 'TO', Y);
             CALL HANOI(Z, Y, X, N-1);
             END;
   END HANOI;
```

If you run this procedure on the computer, make sure N is not more than 6 or 7. To show why, consider the number of moves M(N) if pole 1 originally contains N disks. For N = 1, M(1) = 1. For N > 1 the number of moves is

M(N) = M(N-1) + 1 + M(N-1) = 2*M(N-1) + 1.

(Note that this is a recursive definition.) If you draw a table of moves for N = 1, 2, 3, 4, etc., you will see that in general M(N) = 2**N - 1.

Now suppose there are 64 disks. Then the above algorithm will generate M(64) = 2^{64}-1 moves. This is a tremendous number. Assuming that the monks can move one disk per second, if they work continuously it will take them well over a trillion (10^{12}) years. The computer is of course faster, and can print about 1000 moves per minute. Still, to print all the moves will take over 30 billion years. This is a good example of a problem with a simple algorithmic solution, but for which no computer is fast enough. The problem is impossibly large (see Section VI.3.2).

6.3.2 Quicksort

The Tower of Hanoi problem is interesting but perhaps not practical. Sorting is practical, and we show here a recursive variation of a useful sorting algorithm.

Given an array segment A(M:N), suppose it can be partitioned so that it looks like

```
                A(M)       A(K-1) A(K) A(K+1)      A(N)
               ┌──────────────────┬────┬──────────────────┐
(6.3.2a)       │      ≤ A(K)      │    │      > A(K)      │
               └──────────────────┴────┴──────────────────┘
```

Then the segment A(M:N) will be sorted when the two separate segments A(M:K-1) and A(K+1:N) are sorted. Thus the original sorting problem has been broken up into two separate smaller problems. These smaller problems can be sorted by the same technique.

The procedure is given below; it uses a Partition algorithm which is given in Section V.7.4. It is not necessary to know <u>how</u> Partition works, but just <u>what</u> it does. The quicksort algorithm is also given in Section V.7.4 in a non-recursive version. Compare the two versions and note how much simpler the recursive version seems.

```
QUICKSORT: PROCEDURE(A, M, N) RECURSIVE;
/* SORT SEGMENT A(M:N) */
   DECLARE (A(*), M, N) FIXED;
   DECLARE K FIXED;
   IF N <= M
        THEN RETURN; /* 0 OR 1 ELEMENTS IN SEGMENT */
   IF N = M+1
        THEN DO; /* SEGMENT HAS 2 ELEMENTS.  SORT */
             IF A(M) > A(N)
                  THEN swap A(M) and A(N);
             RETURN;
             END;

   /* A(M:N) HAS 3 OR MORE ELEMENTS.  PARTITION AND SORT*/
        Partition A(M:N) as in (6.3.2a) and set variable K;
        CALL QUICKSORT(A, M, K-1);
        CALL QUICKSORT(A, K+1, N);
   END QUICKSORT;
```

6.3.3 The Assignment Problem

Suppose a swimming coach has ten swimmers to enter in a meet consisting of ten events, and the rules specify that each swimmer may compete in only one event. The coach writes down his estimate of how many points each swimmer would earn in each event in a table of ten rows (one for each swimmer) and ten columns (one for each event). Now he wants to determine the assignment of swimmers to events to maximize the team's score.

We could try every possible assignment, add up the total score for each one, and select the assignment that gives the highest score. A conventional, non-recursive program to do this is given below. It is for four swimmers and four events, but it should be obvious how to change array sizes and add levels of loops to accommodate more swimmers and events.

```
/* PROGRAM TO DETERMINE MAXIMUM POSSIBLE TEAM SCORE */
/* ONE SWIMMER ASSIGNED TO EACH EVENT */
ASSIGN: PROCEDURE OPTIONS(MAIN);
   DCL PT(4,4) FLOAT;          /* PTS FOR SWIMMER I IN EVENT J  */
                               /* (ROW/SWIMMER, COL/EVENT)      */
   DCL EV(4) FIXED;            /* EVENT ASSIGNMENTS -- EV(I) IS */
                               /* EVENT ASSIGNED TO SWIMMER I   */
   DCL MAXEV(4) FIXED;         /* EVENT ASSIGNMENT FOR MAX PTS  */
   DCL NS(4) FIXED;            /* NO. SWIMMERS ASSIGNED TO EV.  */
   DCL MAXNS FIXED;            /* MAX NBR ASSIGNED TO ANY EVENT */
   DCL PTSUM FLOAT;            /* SUM OF PTS FOR ASSIGNMENT     */
   DCL MAXPTSUM FLOAT;         /* MAXIMUM TEAM SCORE            */
   DCL (ROW, COL) FIXED;
```

```
/** LOAD AND INITIALIZE */
  MAXPTSUM = 0;
  DO COL = 1 TO 4 BY 1;
    NS(COL) = 0;
    END;
  DO ROW = 1 TO 4 BY 1;
    DO COL = 1 TO 4 BY 1;
        GET LIST(PT(ROW,COL));
        END;
    END;

/** FOR SWIMMER 1, TRY EACH EVENT */
  ROW1: DO EV(1) = 1 TO 4 BY 1;
    NS(EV(1)) = NS(EV(1)) + 1;
    /** FOR SWIMMER 2, TRY EACH EVENT */
      ROW2: DO EV(2) = 1 TO 4 BY 1;
        NS(EV(2)) = NS(EV(2)) + 1;
        /** FOR SWIMMER 3, TRY EACH EVENT */
          ROW3: DO EV(3) = 1 TO 4 BY 1;
            NS(EV(3)) = NS(EV(3)) + 1;
            /** FOR SWIMMER 4, TRY EACH EVENT */
              ROW4: DO EV(4) = 1 TO 4 BY 1;
                NS(EV(4)) = NS(EV(4)) + 1;
                /** CONSIDER ONLY 1 TO 1 ASSIGNMENTS */
                  MAXNS = MAX(NS(1), NS(2), NS(3), NS(4));
                  IF MAXNS = 1
                   THEN DO;
                    /** COMPUTE TEAM SCORE */
                      PTSUM = 0;
                      DO ROW = 1 TO 4 BY 1;
                        PTSUM = PTSUM + PT(ROW,EV(ROW));
                        END;
                    /** SAVE NEW MAX IF FOUND */
                      IF PTSUM > MAXPTSUM
                        THEN DO;
                          MAXPTSUM = PTSUM;
                          DO COL = 1 TO 4 BY 1;
                              MAXEV(COL) = EV(COL);
                              END;
                          END;
                    END;
                NS(EV(4)) = NS(EV(4)) - 1;
                END ROW4;
            NS(EV(3)) = NS(EV(3)) - 1;
            END ROW3;
        NS(EV(2)) = NS(EV(2)) - 1;
        END ROW2;
    NS(EV(1)) = NS(EV(1)) - 1;
    END ROW1;
```

```
/** DISPLAY ASSIGNMENTS AND SCORE */
  PUT SKIP LIST('SWIMMER ASSIGNMENTS');
  PUT SKIP(3) LIST('SWIMMER', 'EVENT', 'POINTS');
  DO ROW = 1 TO 4 BY 1;
    PUT SKIP LIST(ROW, MAXEV(ROW), PT(ROW,MAXEV(ROW)));
    END;
  PUT SKIP(2) LIST(' ', 'TOTAL TEAM SCORE', MAXPTSUM);

END ASSIGN;
```

This program is logically simple but is not easy to read or use. Since it involves a nest of DO groups with one level for each swimmer the program would have to be changed if there were more or less than four swimmers. However, since each level in this nest (except the innermost) performs a very similar action, the algorithm can be easily rewritten using a recursive procedure.

In the recursive version the dimensions of the problem are specified in the data, and not in the program. It also uses array assignments (see Section I.3.6), the INITIAL attribute in declarations (see Section I.2.5), and global variables. The procedure SWIMMER must be internal, so it can reference the arrays describing swimmers and events.

While this recursive program is clearer and more flexible, neither version is useful since the execution time is enormous. This is discussed further in Section VI.2. It is nevertheless a good illustration of the difference between an iterative and a recursive program.

```
/* PROGRAM TO DETERMINE MAXIMUM POSSIBLE TEAM SCORE */
/* ONE SWIMMER ASSIGNED TO EACH EVENT */
ASSIGN: PROCEDURE OPTIONS(MAIN);
 DCL (N, M) FIXED;            /* N IS THE NUMBER OF SWIMMERS */
                              /* M IS THE NUMBER OF EVENTS */
 GET LIST(N, M);
 ASSIGN2: BEGIN;
  DCL PT(N, M) FLOAT;         /* ESTIMATED POINTS FOR ITH */
                              /* SWIMMER IN JTH EVENT */
                              /* EACH ROW IS ONE SWIMMER */
                              /* EACH COLUMN IS ONE EVENT */
  DCL SW(N) FIXED;            /* SW(I) IS SWIMMER ASSIGNED */
                              /* EVENT I */
  DCL SWMAX(N) FIXED;         /* SWIMMERS FOR MAXIMUM SCORE. */
  DCL MAXPTSUM FLOAT INIT(-1); /* MAXIMUM TEAM SCORE */
  DCL (ROW, EV) FIXED;

  /** INITIALIZE ASSIGNMENTS */
      SW = 0;
      GET LIST(PT);
      CALL SWIMMER(1);

  /** DISPLAY ASSIGNMENTS AND SCORE*/
   PUT SKIP LIST('SWIMMER ASSIGNMENTS');
   PUT SKIP(3) LIST('SWIMMER', 'EVENT', 'POINTS');
   PRINT_SWIMMER_LOOP:  DO ROW = 1 TO N BY 1;
     FIND_EVENT:  DO EV = 1 TO M BY 1;
        IF SWMAX(EV) = ROW
          THEN DO;
             PUT SKIP LIST(ROW, EV, PT(ROW, EV) );
             LEAVE FIND_EVENT;
             END;
        END FIND_EVENT;
     END PRINT_SWIMMER_LOOP;
     PUT SKIP(2) LIST(' ','TOTAL TEAM SCORE', MAXPTSUM);
```

```
  /* DETERMINE ALL POSSIBLE ASSIGNMENTS FOR SWIMMERS I, I+1,  */
  /* ..., N, ASSUMING 1, ..., I-1 ARE ASSIGNED. SAVE BEST ONE.*/
  /* USES GLOBALS N, M, PT */
  /* CHANGES GLOBALS SW, SWMAX AND MAXPTSUM */
   SWIMMER: PROCEDURE(I) RECURSIVE;
     DCL I FIXED;               /* SWIMMER (ROW) NUMBER */
     DCL PTSUM FLOAT INIT(0); /* SUM OF PTS FOR ASSIGNMENT */
     DCL EV FIXED;
     IF I <= N
       THEN DO EV = 1 TO M BY 1;
         IF SW(EV) = 0
           THEN DO;
             SW(EV) = I;
             CALL SWIMMER(I+1);
             SW(EV) = 0;
             END;
         END;
       ELSE DO;/* ALL SWIMMERS ASSIGNED. */
               /** FIND PTSUM, CHECK AGAINST MAXPTSUM */
                 DO EV = 1 TO M BY 1;
                   IF SW(EV)¬=0
                     THEN PTSUM = PTSUM + PT(SW(EV),EV);
                   END;
                 IF PTSUM > MAXPTSUM
                   THEN DO;
                     MAXPTSUM = PTSUM;
                     SWMAX = SW;
                     END;
               END;
     END SWIMMER;

  END ASSIGN2;

 END ASSIGN;
```

6.3.4 A Procedure to Evaluate Expressions

We want to write a set of procedures to evaluate any expression consisting of additions +, multiplications *, parentheses (and), and integer constants. For example, the expressions

```
    1 + 3 * 10                   (20 + 30) * (5 + 6)
    (1 + 3) * 10                 (10 + (20 + (30 * (4))))
```

An expression will be stored in two arrays, a character array SYMBOL that will contain the expression but with the character C representing each constant, and a fixed array VALUE that will contain the actual constant. The character E will mark the end of the expression. SIZE will contain the number of symbols. For example, the expression (1+3)*10 will be stored as

SYMBOL(1)	(	VALUE(1)	0	SIZE	8
SYMBOL(2)	C	VALUE(2)	1		
SYMBOL(3)	+	VALUE(3)	0		
SYMBOL(4)	C	VALUE(4)	3		
SYMBOL(5)	)	VALUE(5)	0		
SYMBOL(6)	*	VALUE(6)	0		
SYMBOL(7)	C	VALUE(7)	10		
SYMBOL(8)	E	VALUE(8)	0		

We assume no mistakes will be made in storing an expression in the arrays, and our procedures have not been designed to handle errors.

To evaluate an expression stored in SYMBOL(1:SIZE) and VALUE(1:SIZE) we execute

```
NUMBER = 1;
CALL EVALEXP(NUMBER, ANSWER);
```

NUMBER indicates where the expression to be evaluated begins -- in SYMBOL(1). The arrays themselves will be communicated as global variables. Execution of this call will store the value of the expression in ANSWER, and will also put into NUMBER the number of the symbol _following_ the expression evaluated (8 in this case).

How does EVALEXP work? To see this, note that _any_ expression is made up of a series of additions; the expression looks like

(6.3.4a) operand + operand + ... + operand

For example the expression (3*5) consists of one operand, and no additions; it is a degenerate case of (4.3.4a). The expression 1+3+(2+4)*3 consists of the addition of three operands: 1, 3, and (2+4)*3. Let us assume we can write a procedure PLUSOP to evaluate an operand for an addition. Just how PLUSOP works we leave until later. For now, let us just state _what_ it should do. Execution of CALL PLUSOP(NUMBER,ANS); performs the following:

1. The operand for an addition beginning at SYMBOL(NUMBER) is evaluated and the result is stored in ANS.

2. NUMBER is changed to contain the number of the symbol _following_ the operand evaluated.

We can now easily write procedure EVALEXP to evaluate any expression, using this new procedure PLUSOP:

```
/* STORE IN ANS THE VALUE OF THE EXPRESSION BEGINNING*/
/* AT SYMBOL(NUMBER).  CHANGE NUMBER TO POINT TO SYMBOL */
/* FOLLOWING THE EXPRESSION.*/
EVALEXP: PROCEDURE(NUMBER, ANS);
   DECLARE (NUMBER, ANS) FIXED;
   DECLARE ANS2 FIXED;
   /** EVALUATE FIRST OPERAND (THERE MUST BE ONE)*/
     CALL PLUSOP(NUMBER, ANS);

   /** EACH ITERATION OF LOOP EVALUATES ANOTHER OPERAND*/
     /* AND ADDS ITS RESULT TO ANS.*/
     DO WHILE (SYMBOL(NUMBER) = '+');
        NUMBER = NUMBER + 1;        /* SKIP OVER THE '+' */
        CALL PLUSOP(NUMBER, ANS2); /* EVAL. OPERAND*/
        ANS = ANS + ANS2;
        END;
   END EVALEXP;
```

How does PLUSOP work? An operand for an addition has the form

    simple-operand * simple-operand * ... * simple-operand

where a simple-operand is either a constant or a parenthesized expression. For example,

    1 * 2 * (3+5) * (82)

has the simple operands 1, 2, (3+5) and (82). This is quite similar to the form of an expression consisting of a sequence of additions, and you might suspect that the routine PLUSOP will be similar to EVALEXP. It looks for * instead of + and it calls a procedure SIMPLOP instead of PLUSOP to evaluate its operands.

Procedure SIMPLOP also takes two arguments: where its expression begins and the variable in which to store the result. It works as follows. If the expression is just a constant, then it stores that constant in the answer. The other alternative is to have a parenthesized expression as the operand. In this case, SIMPLOP <u>calls the original procedure EVALEXP to evaluate the expression within the parentheses</u>. Thus we have a system of three recursive procedures, each calling the other.

```
/* STORE IN ANS THE VALUE OF THE EXPRESSION BEGINNING AT */
/* SYMBOL(NUMBER). CHANGE NUMBER SO THAT IT POINTS AT*/
/* THE SYMBOL FOLLOWING THE EXPRESSION*/
EVALEXP: PROCEDURE(NUMBER, ANS) RECURSIVE;
   DECLARE (NUMBER, ANS) FIXED;
   DECLARE ANS2 FIXED;
   CALL PLUSOP(NUMBER, ANS);
   DO WHILE (SYMBOL(NUMBER) = '+');
     NUMBER = NUMBER + 1;
     CALL PLUSOP(NUMBER, ANS2);
     ANS = ANS + ANS2;
     END;
   END EVALEXP;

/* EVALUATE AN OPERAND FOR + AND STORE RESULT IN ANS.*/
/* CHANGE NUMBER TO POINT TO JUST AFTER THE OPERAND.*/
PLUSOP: PROCEDURE(NUMBER, ANS) RECURSIVE;
   DECLARE (NUMBER, ANS) FIXED;
   DECLARE ANS2 FIXED;
   CALL SIMPLOP(NUMBER, ANS);
   DO WHILE (SYMBOL(NUMBER) = '*');
     NUMBER = NUMBER + 1;
     CALL SIMPLOP(NUMBER, ANS2);
     ANS = ANS * ANS2;
     END;
   END PLUSOP;

/* EVALUATE A SIMPLE-OPERAND AND STORE RESULT IN ANS.*/
/* CHANGE NUMBER TO POINT TO JUST AFTER THE OPERAND.*/
SIMPLOP: PROCEDURE(NUMBER, ANS) RECURSIVE;
   DECLARE (NUMBER, ANS) FIXED;
   IF SYMBOL(NUMBER) = 'C'
     THEN DO;
          ANS = VALUE(NUMBER);
          NUMBER = NUMBER + 1;
          END;
     ELSE DO;
          NUMBER = NUMBER + 1;
          CALL EVALEXP(NUMBER, ANS);
          NUMBER = NUMBER + 1;
          END;
   END SIMPLOP;
```

Section 6 Exercises

1. Write recursive procedures for the following recursively-defined functions. These could all be written more efficiently using iteration; they are intended only to get you used to recursion.

a) Greatest common divisor GCD(A,B) of two integers greater than 0:

```
           ┌B if MOD(A,B) = 0
GCD(A,B) = |
           └GCD(B, r) if MOD(A,B) = r, r > 0
```

b) nth Fibonacci number, where n ≥ 0 is an integer

```
         ┌0 if n = 0
Fib(n) = |1 if n = 1
         └Fib(n-1) + Fib(n-2)    if n > 1
```

c) Reverse(S) where S is a string variable:

```
             ┌S if LENGTH(S) ≤ 1
Reverse(S) = |Reverse(SUBSTR(S,2)) || SUBSTR(S,1,1)
             └otherwise
```

d) Ackermann's function, where M, N are integers ≥ 0

```
         ┌N + 1     if M = 0
A(M,N) = |A(M-1,1) if M ≠ 0 and N = 0
         └A(M-1, A(M,N-1)) if M ≠ 0 and N ≠ 0
```

2. Write a non-recursive procedure, using iteration, for each of the problems in Exercise 1. (Ackermann's function will be difficult to write without recursion.)

3. Prove that the recursive Towers of Hanoi procedure satisfies the rule that no disk be placed on top of a smaller one.

4. Execute CALL WITHIN('ABCD','BD',ANS); of the following procedure by hand. State exactly what the procedure does. (In PL/I, execution will produce an error message when SUBSTR(Y,2) is evaluated and Y has only one character. This should however be allowed; the result should be the empty string.)

```
WITHIN: PROCEDURE(X, Y, ANSWER) RECURSIVE;
   DECLARE (X, Y) CHAR(*) VAR;
   DECLARE ANSWER FIXED;
   DECLARE I FIXED;
   ANSWER = 1;
   IF LENGTH(Y) = 0
     THEN RETURN;
   DO I = 1 TO LENGTH(X) BY 1;
     IF SUBSTR(X,I,1) = SUBSTR(Y,1,1)
        THEN DO;
             CALL WITHIN(SUBSTR(X,I+1), SUBSTR(Y,2),
                        ANSWER);
             RETURN;
             END;
     END;
   ANSWER = 0;
   RETURN;
   END WITHIN;
```

5. Execute by hand the call CALL QUICKSORT(A,1,5);, drawing all the boxes. See Section 6.3.2 for the procedure definition. Use the array A where A(1)=1, A(2)=3, A(3)=2, A(4)=5, and A(5)=0. When executing the Partition command, always choose the value in A(1) for the pivot value -- it will end up in A(K). You do not need to refer back to the Partition algorithm of Section VIII.2.4; just perform the command without using a formal algorithm.

6. Merge Sort. One way of sorting an array segment A(M:N) is to

    1. Let K = FLOOR((M+N)/2);
    2. Sort segment A(M:K);
    3. Sort segment A(K+1:N);
    4. Merge the two sorted segments into one sorted list.

Write a recursive procedure to do this. The merge operation should be performed in linear time -- in time proportional to the number of elements to be merged. You may use an extra array of size A(M:K) if you wish.

7. Study the following solution to the Towers of Hanoi problem and satisfy yourself that it works. It assumes the three pegs are positioned in a circle.

```
Move the smallest disk one peg clockwise;
DO WHILE
    (A disk (besides the smallest) can be moved);
    Move that disk /* why is this move unique?  */
    Move the smallest disk one peg clockwise
    END;
```

Part V Program Testing and Correctness

Section 1 Errors, Testing and Correctness

An error-free program is almost never obtained on the first try. Programming is just too complicated a process for that to happen often. For a careful and competent programmer the probability of each possible error is very small, but there are so many opportunities that the probability of avoiding all errors is also very small. Prudence demands that we assume each new program is incorrect until we can demonstrate otherwise. We must accept the fact that testing is an integral part of the programming process -- and that a program is not really "finished" until we have demonstrated its correctness.

The magnitude of the testing effort required for large problems might surprise you. Often at least half the manpower, cost and elapsed time of the total programming process is consumed in testing. In spite of this, the results are often not entirely satisfactory. Consequently, computers are not held in high public esteem for their reliability, when in fact they are exceedingly reliable machines -- handicapped by inadequate programs.

Few beginning programmers take the trouble to learn to test programs efficiently. To plan testing in advance seems to be admitting inadequacy, so most beginners assume an ostrich-like, head-in-the-sand attitude. When it is obvious that something is wrong, they test in a haphazard manner. But testing does not have to be as time-consuming and unpleasant as many make it seem; effective testing is a skill that must be studied and learned.

Before describing techniques and tools that can be used to demonstrate that a program is correct, consider the meaning of "correctness".

1.1 The Meaning of Correctness

"Program correctness" is not easily defined. The programmer and user of a program may interpret "correctness" quite differently and hence have different expectations of program performance. Various interpretations of correctness are listed below in order of increasing difficulty of achievement:

1. The program contains no syntax errors that can be detected during translation by the language processor.

2. The program contains no errors, either of syntax or invalid operation, that can be automatically detected during translation or execution of the program.

3. There exists some set of test data for which the program will yield the correct answer.

4. For a typical (reasonable or random) set of test data the program will yield the correct answer.

5. For deliberately difficult sets of test data the program will yield the correct answers.

6. For all possible sets of data that are valid with respect to the problem specification, the program yields the correct answers.

7. For all possible sets of valid test data, and for all likely conditions of erroneous input, the program gives a correct (or at least reasonable) answer.

8. For all possible input, the program gives correct or reasonable answers.

In the early stages of your programming experience you will feel harassed by error messages and feel a sense of relief and accomplishment when none appear. Later you will understand that the real work of testing starts after the error messages have been eliminated. The absence of error messages is only a necessary and not a sufficient condition for reasonable correctness.

Some programmers never mature beyond level 3 in their attitude toward correctness. Considering, however, the higher levels (say 4, 5 or 6), it is clear that satisfactory performance on any single set of test data is not sufficient grounds for an assertion of correctness. Moreover, failure on a single test is sufficient to demonstrate that the program is not correct. No matter how many tests the program may have passed successfully, just one test on which it fails is enough to show that it is not correct. This is not inherently a democratic process, and a program that works "most of the time" is a dangerous tool.

From the user's point of view a reasonable definition of correctness is certainly not less than level 6. Level 7 is better and level 8 is what he would really like. The programmer may maintain that a literal interpretation of problem specifications cannot demand more than level 6, while the user will maintain that certain implied requirements do not have to be explicitly stated. In effect, this corresponds to the "implied warranty of merchantability" that accompanies a manufactured product. A consumer is entitled to assume that a product is "suitable for the purpose for which it is intended". A car buyer, for example, can rightfully assume that the wheels will remain firmly attached to the car, without a written guarantee from the dealer. In the same way, much is assumed about a computer program, without its having been explicitly detailed in the problem requirements. The user of a program is entitled to consider it incorrect if it fails to satisfy implicit as well as explicit requirements.

Unfortunately this often leads to heated discussions between programmer and user, the object being to assign blame for a program found to be incorrect. The programmer takes the position that there is no such thing as implicit requirements; the user maintains that, in retrospect, anything he neglected to specify is covered by implicit commonsense requirements. Both parties should realize that implicit requirements are an inherent part of most problem descriptions, and that it is a _mutual_ responsibility to explore this subject to ensure mutual understanding.

However, the _primary responsibility rests with the programmer_. A program is _incorrect if it does not serve the user's purposes_. This can occur because the programmer failed to elicit an adequate description, because he failed to recognize implicit requirements, or because he made mistakes in designing or translating the algorithm into a programming language. Most programmers admit responsibility for only the last two sources of error, but the distinction between different types of failure is not interesting to a user with an unsolved problem.

In summary, the situation is the following. The user would like to have level 8 correctness -- but this is often unrealistic. Level 7 is a reasonable compromise, which is obviously going to lead to arguments since it leaves critical questions open to varying interpretations. The programmer's dilemma is that level 5 is the highest that can be achieved by purely empirical means -- by running the program on test cases -- so he must thoughtfully design test cases that permit a plausible assertion that level 6 has been achieved. To achieve level 7 the programmer must know enough about the intended use of the program to estimate what errors are likely to be encountered, and what response is appropriate.

1.2 Types of Errors

There are four distinct types of errors:

1. Errors in understanding the problem requirements.

2. Errors in understanding the programming language. For example, errors could result from not understanding the rules for default attributes.

3. Failure of the algorithm underlying the program.

4. Accidents. Errors where you knew better but simply slipped up.

Type 1 errors tend to increase as problems become larger, more varied, and less precisely stated. Although you can learn from experience, human communication is difficult, English is surprisingly ambiguous, and programming demands unfailing precision. Some errors of type 1 seem inevitable but there are ways to reduce the number:

1. Show the user sample input and output. (If you don't he will surely want to change them as soon as you are finished.)

2. Discuss what should be done for extreme cases, and for various kinds of errors in the data.

3. Discuss the general program strategy (at the algorithmic level) with the user, and make sure he agrees that it does represent a <u>solution</u> to the problem.

Type 2 errors will diminish with experience, but unfortunately PL/I is a rich language with many curious and unexpected properties, so the opportunities for this type of error are numerous.

Type 3 errors can be minimized by systematic development and careful structuring of programs. Errors that remain are in fairly predictable places -- often just entry and exit problems -- and can be systematically sought using the diagnostic tools described in the following sections. These kinds of errors <u>must</u> be kept to a minimum. They are the hardest to correct later on. One purpose of a programming course is to get you to think carefully, methodically, and in a structured manner so these errors don't often occur.

Type 4 errors -- accidents -- occur everywhere in the process, to experienced as well as beginning programmers. They range from syntax errors detected by the translator to subtle errors with intermittent effect that elude competent and persistent testing. The only general defense is a skeptical attitude that regards every program segment as a potential haven for accidental errors.

Accept the fact that all errors in the program are your responsibility. Much time is wasted trying to blame the computer, the programming language, or the problem description. True machine errors are exceedingly rare, so every time you become convinced a machine error is responsible for your trouble, you are postponing the eventual necessity of discovering what really happened. Blaming errors on the programming language is a similar delusion. Every programming language has its surprises -- things that are done in an unexpected way. (PL/I is especially culpable in this regard.) While the language may be unreasonable, it is not wrong. It is your responsibility to learn what the language actually means, rather than assume it means what you think it should.

1.3 Program Testing vs Program Analysis

There are two fundamentally different approaches to determining the correctness of a program. The most obvious one is to actually try the program and evaluate the results produced. Assuming that you can distinguish between correct and incorrect results (not always an easy task), the question becomes how to infer the correctness of a program from the correctness of sample results from that program. This is essentially the difference between level 3 and higher levels of correctness. Each test execution of the program actually confirms correctness for only that one set of input data. Since obviously the program cannot be actually executed for all possible sets of input data, you must infer the program's correctness from its behavior on a few sample inputs. The catch is that appropriate rules of inference are not clear.

This empirical approach is both difficult to perform and inherently unsatisfactory in results -- even when conscientiously carried out by a competent person. There is simply no effective way of knowing when the process is complete; that is, when the last error has been detected and removed and the program is really correct. Consequently, this dependence on the skill and diligence of the programmer makes the outcome highly variable.

It would be better to have a more systematic process that provided a credible guarantee of correctness. For example, it is possible to consider a program to be a mathemetical theorem and rigorously prove that it is correct. When done from the program text, without involving execution, the proof holds for all possible sets of input to the program -- hence assuring level 8 correctness. This is currently the subject of much computer science research, but the goal has not yet been fully achieved. For all practical purposes empirical testing is still a necessity, and Sections 2 to 6 of Part V are concerned with that approach. Section 7 introduces some of the ideas about proving correctness.

Section 2 Automatic Diagnostic Services

Some diagnostic information is available without significant effort by the programmer. Some is automatic. For example, language processors check for violations of syntax rules and report discrepancies (Section 2.1). Other facilities must be requested, but once requested are automatic. For example, a "cross-reference listing" (Section 2.3) summarizes where each identifier is used.

However, except for the automatic repair of certain errors (Section 2.2) these diagnostic facilities just supply information. The use of that information to detect, locate and eliminate errors still involves skill and effort on the part of the programmer.

2.1 Detection of Errors

Only certain limited kinds of errors can be automatically detected. A "syntax error" occurs when a statement is not well-formed according to the rules of the language. These errors are detected as the program is compiled, and are normally reported in the source listing of the program. An "execution error" occurs when a statement that is syntactically legal requests the performance of an operation that for some reason is invalid. These errors cannot be detected until the program is executed, so error messages of this kind appear in the execution output of the program.

2.1.1 Syntax Errors

Every violation of the syntax rules of the programming language should be detected during compiling of the program. The manner in which detection is announced and the amount of explanation provided depends upon the language used. Ordinarily some form of error message is printed.

In many cases the error and correction are obvious. However, in some situations the actual error may be far removed from the point of detection. In these cases the messages provided are not always helpful. For example

```
Y = X(I);
```

might trigger a message about an improper subscript not because it is improperly formed, but because a missing or faulty declaration has failed to declare array X. However mystifying an error messages may be, it indicates that something related to this statement is wrong somewhere, and the cause must be tracked down.

There is little redundancy in programming languages and many mistakes yield statements that are still syntactically legal. For example, suppose an assignment statement should be given as

```
COUNT = COUNT + 1;
```

Each of the following variations might somehow appear in place of the correct statement:

```
(a) COUNT = COUNT + .1;
(b) COUNT = COUNT - 1;
(c) CONUT = COUNT + 1;
(d) COUNT = CONUT + 1;
(e) COUNT = COUNT + 1
```

None of these is correct, but only (e) is syntactically improper. (Alternative (d) will be detected as an execution error (by PL/C or PL/CS, not PL/I) since it uses a variable to which no value has been assigned.)

Simple syntactic errors in PL/I declarations often lead to syntactically valid but semantically incorrect programs. For example, suppose you intend to write:

```
DECLARE X FIXED;
```

but accidentally insert a comma:

```
DECLARE X, FIXED;
```

This is still a valid declaration so no syntax error is reported, but the variables created are quite different from what you intended. (Two FLOAT variables -- X and FIXED -- are created.)

Error messages cannot always be taken at face value. For example, suppose you erroneously thought that VARY was a valid abbreviation for VARYING and wrote:

```
DECLARE WORD CHAR(40) VARY;
```

The error reported is the omission of a comma and not the misspelling of a keyword. (The result will be the creation of a non-varying string WORD and a FLOAT variable VARY.)

The cross-reference and attribute listing described in Section 2.3 can be helpful in discovering errors concerning the use of identifiers.

2.1.2 Invalid Operations

Just what constitutes an invalid operation depends on the language and computer being used. Generally these include such operations as:

a) dividing by zero,
b) taking the square root of a negative number, and
c) adding two numbers whose sum exceeds the largest number the computer can handle.

Invalid operations are often caused by an action in some statement other than the one accused in the error message. For example, if STMT 69 attempts to take the square root of X, which is negative, the problem lies not in STMT 69 but in the statement that assigned the negative value to X. Execution error messages announce the <u>point at which the result of an error causes an invalid operation</u> to be executed, but give little indication of what actually caused the error.

The use of a variable before it has been assigned a value is a common error. For example, consider a loop to sum the elements of X(1:N):

```
DO I = 1 TO N BY 1;
     SUM = SUM + X(I);
     END;
```

If SUM is not initialized to 0 before executing the loop, the first iteration will encounter an invalid operation in attempting to obtain the value of SUM. PL/C and PL/CS report an error in the assignment statement, which alerts you that something is wrong, but the actual error is of course the omission of another statement. Curiously, PL/I does not recognize this as an invalid operation. It just uses whatever value happens to have been left in the memory location assigned to SUM.

Another common execution error is the construction of an invalid subscript. For example, in the summing loop above, suppose the array X had been declared X(1:40) and the value of N was 50. On the 41st iteration of the body the reference X(I) will be invalid. PL/C and PL/CS will detect the invalid operation, although they will not explain that the source of the difficulty is the incompatiblity between the declaration of X and the value of N. PL/I does not recognize this as an error and will continue to retrieve values of other variables as if they were X(41), X(42), etc.

2.2 PL/C and PL/CS Automatic Repair of Errors

After reporting an error, PL/C repairs it. It would be nice to make a correction, but PL/C can only effect a repair. Sometimes a repair happens to be a correction and achieves what the programmer intended, but the real purpose of the repair is to allow translation and execution to continue in order to obtain maximum information from each run.

The repaired statement is displayed so you know precisely what statement is used in execution of the program:

```
STMT 8                    X = Y * (X+Z ;
ERROR IN STMT 8           MISSING ) IN COLUMN 10 (SY04)
FOR STMT 8 PL/C USES X = Y * (X + Z);
```

Even when the repair happens to achieve what you intended, you should correct the fault and not rely on PL/C's repair.

When errors are numerous or serious, PL/C's repairs can be confusing, or even amusing. For example, suppose the following single line were presented as a complete program:

```
PTU FILE(OUTPUT A+1 'CORRECTION.
```

PL/C produces the following:

```
$L001$: PROCEDURE OPTIONS(MAIN);
   PUT FILE(OUTPUT) LIST(A+1,'CORRECTION.');
   END;
```

As a last resort, when an erroneous statement is beyond PL/C's repair capability, it is replaced with a null statement. This preserves syntactic correctness and permits the program to be executed, but the prospects of useful output are much diminished. A warning message appears during execution of a program whenever one of these null statements is encountered.

Error repair also takes place during execution. For example, if a subscript references a non-existent array element, an error message is given and some valid subscript value is provided so that execution can continue. As another example, if a variable without a value is used, an error message is given and an initial value is provided (0 for a numeric and blank for a character variable).

2.3 PL/I and PL/C Analysis of Identifier Usage

The "cross-reference and attribute listing" produced by the XREF and ATR options is a useful diagnostic service. If this listing is not produced automatically as the default option at your computer installation then you should specify XREF and ATR options on at least the early runs of each program.

Two of the most common errors in programming are keypunch spelling mistakes and errors in the punctuation of declarations. The XREF/ATR listing is a powerful weapon against both of these errors. Any identifier in this listing without a declaration number should be investigated. It represents an implicit declaration, which is either bad practice or the result of a spelling mistake.

The attribute listing should be carefully compared to your declarations to see if you actually achieved what you intended. Remember that punctuation in PL/I declarations is critical, and mistakes often are not detected as syntax errors. A high proportion of the most mystifying PL/I errors are eventually traced back to flaws in declarations, and many of these could be detected and eliminated at the outset by a conscientious examination of the XREF/ATR listing.

2.4 PL/C and PL/CS Post-Mortem Dump

After completion of execution PL/C and PL/CS automatically print a "post-mortem dump". (If the dump is not the default option at your computer installation specify the DUMP or DUMPE option.)

The dump provides two different types of diagnostic information:

1. The final state reached by execution is shown by displaying the final values of all variables. The final values of arrays are included if DUMP=(ARRAYS) is specified.

2. The number of times each label and entry-name was encountered during execution. This is especially useful information, enabling you to reconstruct how execution progressed. Its utility can be enhanced by including labelled null statements at key points in the program, just so the number of times execution reached each of these points will be reported in the dump.

Section 3 Program Testing

No matter how carefully a program is constructed and analyzed, it must still be subjected to the test of actual execution. The testing process is the following:

1. Run the program on a sequence of test cases that range from the gentlest possible to the most demanding and exhaustive you can contrive. Each test case should be chosen so that you can reasonably infer that the program works on a set of similar ones. From <u>all</u> test cases, one should be able to infer correctness on <u>all input data</u>.

2. Pursue each deviation from expected performance until you are sure you understand what occurred, and why, and then make a suitable repair.

3. For any nontrivial program, this process is applied piece-wise, level by level, from the bottom up to the top. In particular, each procedure is separately tested.

Although the idea is simple its application is not. Specifically, two different skills are involved:

1. The ability to develop sufficiently demanding and exhaustive test cases so that satisfactory performance on these cases gives some real basis for confidence in the correctness of the program.

2. The ability to systematically track down and identify the problem whenever the program fails to perform as expected.

3.1 The Construction of Test Cases

It is usually easy to generate an initial test case and to determine what the results should be. It can have a limited quantity of undemanding data, without errors or other complications. It is enormously encouraging when a new program is finally able to process such a gentle test but you cannot quit at that point. You have just reached level 3 correctness and have more work to do.

Contriving difficult test cases is an art that has to be learned. It requires that you forget that it is your own creation you are attacking and try to make the program fail. Draw upon your knowledge and experience in programming to anticipate the kinds of errors likely to occur. For example, you know that declarations, initializations, and timely exits from loops are common trouble spots. Consequently, test cases should be carefully designed to reveal errors in these aspects of your program. In general, test cases should exhibit the following properties:

a. Extremes of volume: the legal minimum and maximum, as well as too little and too much. In particular, test null cases.

b. Extreme values: the legal minimum and maximum as well as excessive values -- too big, too small.

c. Special values: zero, blank, one, etc., depending on the problem.

d. Non-integer values, where allowed.

e. Values falling on and near stated limits.

f. Repeated values and ties of various sorts.

3.2 The Diagnosis of Trouble

When execution does not exactly achieve what was expected you must find out where the discrepancy arises, and why.

A complete, statement-by-statement trace of program execution should provide all the information needed to understand that execution. Unfortunately, the length of a complete trace makes it impractical. For example, the complete trace of one second of execution would be several thousand pages long. Thus, in printing output whose purpose is to help locate an error, the idea is to be selective and print no more than is needed. Selectivity in this regard means two things:

1. Only print information in the immediate neighborhood of the difficulty.

2. Don't print information about things that do not change.

For example, you should not need confirmation that in the absence of control statements such as IF, DO, CALL, SELECT, RETURN, execution proceeded sequentially from one statement to the next. You should only need sequencing information in the neighborhood of such control statements. Similarly, you should not need to observe every assignment to every variable; display of assignment to certain key variables whose values serve to control the program is usually sufficient.

3.2.1 Temporary Output Statements

The normal output specified as part of the problem requirements is rarely sufficient to diagnose or repair errors in a program. Printing a wrong answer for a test case indicates that the program is incorrect, but does not indicate why and is not helpful in locating the error(s).

More information is required -- essentially, some carefully selected fraction of the total trace information described above. This information is obtained by inserting additional PUT statements in the program -- statements that will eventually be removed when the program is thought to be correct. (Alternatively, these statements can be inserted using the macro facility (Section 5.4.2) or can be sheltered in pseudo-comments so they can be physically left in the deck, and selectively activated or de-activated by the CMNTS option -- see Section I.8.2.)

These additional temporary PUT statements do two things:

1. Report the arrival of execution at a key point in the program -- a "checkpoint".

2. Report the value of key variables at that point.

Each diagnostic display should include the position in the source program from which it originated. For example:

```
PUT SKIP(2)  LIST ('CHECKPOINT 14. COUNT =', COUNT);
PUT SKIP (2);

PUT SKIP(2) LIST ('BEFORE SUM_LOOP. TOTAL=', TOTAL);
PUT SKIP (2);
```

(The two SKIPs ensure that this diagnostic message will be visually separated from normal program output.) Note that the insertion of temporary output statements may disturb the format (but not the values) of normal output. If a diagnostic output statement is inserted between two other PUT statements that contribute to the same printed line, then the format of that normal line will obviously be altered. The DATA format is convenient for this purpose:

```
PUT SKIP (2) LIST
     ('CHECKPOINT 12 BEFORE OPR_SELECT');
PUT SKIP DATA (OPR, DATUM, LEVEL, PAREN_FLAG);
PUT SKIP (2);
```

This undoubtedly looks like extra work, and for your first programs you will try to get along without it. Unsystematic testing may be adequate for trivial problems and you will get the wrong impression of the nature of the task. Substantial programs do not readily succumb to brute force testing and you will have to learn to discipline your approach to testing.

3.2.2 Strategies For Locating Errors

The basic idea underlying the search for an error is suggested by an analogy. Suppose you were asked to identify a particular number between 1 and 100, by asking a limited number of questions. Consider the following strategies:

1. Guess numbers at random: "Is it 37?", "Is it 9?", ...

2. Guess every number in order: "Is it 1?", "Is it 2?", ...

3. Examine equal intervals: "Is it in the first 10?", "Is it in the second 10?", ...

4. Repeatedly divide the region of uncertainty in half:
   "Is it less than 50?" (yes),
   "Is it less than 25?" (no),
   "Is it less than 37?" (yes), ...

Roughly speaking, the numbers correspond to the statements in a program, and the questions correspond to the placement of temporary PUT statements. Obviously, if repeated runs of the program are convenient, the fourth strategy (a form of "binary search") will pin down the offending statement with the fewest runs and the fewest temporary PUTs. To get the most information out of a single run, the third strategy is better. It is hard to imagine circumstances under which the first or second strategies are appropriate, but some programmers still seem to use them.

In this numbers game, all numbers are similar and presumably each has an equal chance of being the goal. This is not the case in program testing, and the strategies should be modified accordingly. There are certain positions where temporary PUT statements are especially helpful:

1. After each GET statement, to display the values just read in. In fact, these statements are so helpful that it is good practice to routinely provide such temporary statements after <u>every GET</u> statement, and to do this <u>as you are writing the initial program</u>.

2. Before a CALL statement, to display the values given as arguments. Alternatively, place the PUT at the beginning of the body of the procedure, to report the values of its input parameters.

3. After a CALL statement, to display the results of the procedure execution. Alternatively, the PUT can be placed as the last statement of the procedure body.

4. Before a loop, to display the initial values.

5. After a loop, to display the results.

6. As the last statement in a loop body, to display the values used in the controlling condition.

7. Before a SELECT or IF statement, to indicate which alternative will be selected.

3.3 Modular Testing

Testing a large program can be difficult (if not impossible) if performed in an undisciplined manner, simply because there are too many combinations of things to be tested. To test a large program one must make use of the same "abstraction" principals that were used in program development. In this book we have generally advocated a top-down, stepwise refinement method of program development. At each step, an English statement, which says <u>what</u> to do, is refined into a sequence of statements which say <u>how</u> to do it. This idea is reinforced by using the procedure concept of the language; at a call we deal only with <u>what</u> the procedure is to do, and only those interested in <u>how</u> the procedure works need study the procedure body.

We use these same ideas in testing, as follows. Suppose we have a program segment

```
...
/** Perform process X */
    S1
    S2
    .
    .
    .
    Sn
...
```

which may be written as a procedure

```
...
CALL PERFORMX;
...

/* Perform process X */
PERFORMX: PROCEDURE;
    S1
    .
    .
    .
    Sn
    END PERFORMX;
```

Then testing the program involves two things:

1. Testing the sequence S1, ..., Sn to make sure that it does actually perform process X (test procedure PERFORMX),

2. Testing to make sure that the statement "Perform process X" (or CALL PERFORMX) is used correctly within the larger program. In this step, we _assume that_ "Perform process X" is correctly implemented -- we deal with the _what_ rather than the _how_. Thus, we do not worry about interaction of the larger program with the _individual_ statements S1, ..., Sn.

This is simply an application of the _divide and conquer_ rule. By testing program segments independently the number of combinations of interactions is considerably reduced. This process can be reapplied at each level of a large program. Thus, if S1 above is itself an English statement or procedure call, it is treated similarly.

3.3.1 Bottom-up, Independent Test of Procedures

In the traditional way of testing large programs, the lower-level procedures -- those that contain no calls of other procedures -- are tested first. Then, at each successive testing phase, a new procedure is tested whose only calls are calls on already-tested procedures. It can be assumed that already-tested procedures are correct, and thus one can concentrate completely on the new procedure being tested.

This bottom-up testing is the reverse of the top-down program design; in the extreme case the _last procedure written is the first tested_ and _all programming precedes all testing_. However, this method is seldom that strictly observed except for very small programs.

Testing a procedure independently requires the construction of a program whose sole purpose is to call the procedure to be tested, supply it with arguments, and display its results. Extra effort is required to write such "drivers" but it is comparatively modest once you have written one or two of them and the effort is generously rewarded by a reduction of test time when you put the program together.

For example, suppose a program must be protected against a number of special conditions that might occur in its data, and the testing provisions are isolated in a procedure:

```
/* DETECT AND CORRECT EACH CATACHRESIS IN ARRAY */
DATATEST: PROCEDURE(A);
   DCL A(*) FLOAT;
       ...
   END DATATEST;
```

This subroutine can be tested by the following driving routine:

```
/* TESTING DRIVER FOR DATATEST */
DTDRIVER: PROCEDURE OPTIONS(MAIN);
   DCL X(10) FLOAT;
   DCL N FIXED INIT(10);
   DCL I FIXED;
   /** LOAD AND PRINT */
       PUT SKIP LIST('ARRAY SIZE IS', N);
       DO I = 1 TO N BY 1;
           GET LIST(X(I));
           PUT SKIP LIST(X(I));
           END;
   CALL DATATEST(X);
   PUT SKIP(2) LIST('CORRECTED ARRAY AFTER DATATEST');
   DO I = 1 TO N BY 1;
       PUT SKIP LIST(X(I));
       END;
   END DTDRIVER;

*PROCESS
 /* DETECT AND CORRECT EACH CATACHRESIS IN ARRAY */
 DATATEST: PROCEDURE(A);
    ...
    END DATATEST;
```

3.3.2 Testing with Dummy Procedures

It is often useful to replace actual procedures with highly simplified versions during program development and testing. The simplest replacement is just a dummy procedure that returns immediately upon entry without doing anything at all.

For example, in Section 3.3.1 certain error-checking provisions of a program are isolated in a procedure DATATEST. For initial test of the main program, using carefully prepared error-free data, these provisions are not needed and the program could be run with the following version of DATATEST:

```
/* DUMMY VERSION OF INPUT ERROR-CHECKING ROUTINE */
DATATEST: PROCEDURE(A);
   DCL A(*) FLOAT;
   END DATATEST;
```

Such dummy procedures are sometimes called "stubs".

3.3.3 Top-down Testing

Recently there have been some experiments with a different approach to testing. "Top-down testing" allows some testing of large programs to be done concurrently with programming. In a simplistic version it works as follows. Suppose one has written the main procedure of a large program, with calls on two procedures X and Y. Exactly what X and Y are to do has been precisely defined, but how they are to do it is not yet certain. The following is therefore written with stubs for X and Y.

```
        M: PROCEDURE OPTIONS (MAIN);
              .
              .
              .
              .
              CALL X(...);
              .
              .
              .
              CALL Y(...);
              .
              .
              .
              END M;

    *PROCESS
        /* Precise description of what X does */
        X: PROCEDURE(...);

              END X;
```

```
*PROCESS
    /* Precise description of what Y does */
    Y: PROCEDURE(...);

        END Y;
```

In parallel with programming the body of X and Y, the main procedure can be partially tested, using perhaps some extremely simple version of X and Y as mentioned in Section 3.3.2. Then, when X and Y have been written (note they may also contain calls on stubs), they can be tested using the main program M as the driver routine. Secondly, M itself can be tested more completely. If X and Y contain calls on stubs, the process is repeated.

This scheme has three major advantages over traditional bottom-up testing. First, programming and testing can proceed in parallel, thus reducing the total elapsed time. There are cases where large programs (representing more than a year of development) were completely tested just a few weeks after the last line of code was written; this is unheard of in bottom-up testing. Secondly, driver routines need not be written. Thirdly, the precise specification of a procedure -- the interface -- is tested much earlier in the process. Too often in bottom-up testing one programmer programs and tests his procedure independently, and is confident that it is correct. Months later, when an attempt is made to integrate it into the rest of the program, it is discovered that <u>his</u> version of the interface specification differs from those of the programmers who <u>use</u> the procedure. This can necessitate a major redesign. With top-down testing it is much less likely to happen.

Top-down testing requires a competent, experienced programming team, and beginners should stick to bottom-up testing. Top-down testing does <u>not</u> mean that testing can begin two weeks after beginning a large 1-2 year project (say). Generally, a large project has a long design phase, in which the overall structure of the system is planned, data structures are designed, etc. The actual programming doesn't begin until the major design strategy has been laid out in sufficient detail to give confidence in the program that will result.

3.4 Help From "Consultants"

Your programming course and/or your computing center probably offer help in the form of "programming consulting". There are also numerous informal consultants in the dorm, the union, etc. The quality of advice may be somewhat variable, but in general, experienced programmers provide a valuable resource for beginners.

Unfortunately, beginners tend to use this resource in such a way as to ensure that they will continue to be dependent on it.

Consultants are usually asked:

> "Why doesn't my program work?"

The proper answer is:

> "Why don't you run it again with temporary PUT statements at key places and find out what is going on?"

But most consultants are not hard-hearted enough to give this valuable advice (especially after the supplicant has waited in line to reach the oracle) and instead, proceed to try to do the programmer's work for him. Thus he may point out that you failed to properly initialize the WHILE loop starting in statement 63. This may help you get <u>this</u> program to run but it postpones your learning how to test a program on your own.

A consultant ought to be presented with questions like:

> "I am having trouble with execution of procedure SQUEEZE. This is supposed to squeeze all blanks out of a word given as argument. I have inserted diagnostic PUT statements before the call, in the procedure, and immediately after the call. The correct value seems to be obtained in SQUEEZE, but it never gets back to the calling procedure since the value of WORD after the call is exactly the same as before."

Then the consultant can reply:

> "It sounds like the attributes of the argument do not exactly match those of the corresponding parameter. Have you compared them in the XREF/ATR listing?"

It is difficult to spot our own mistakes. We can go over a troublesome section many times and be unable to spot an obvious error. Often a fresh view will help to find an error quickly. A programming consultant may spot an error not because he knows more, but because he has no preconceptions about what the program is supposed to do. He reads what <u>is</u> there, and not what he wants to be there. Often we see the error ourselves while explaining the program to someone else.

In this connection <u>distrust every source of assistance except the computer</u>. Programming language reference manuals and textbooks (including this one) contain errors. Teachers and consultants have their own misconceptions. If you want to be <u>certain</u> what will happen if ..., then <u>try it</u> on the computer, with enough PUT statements to be sure you have adequate information to understand the result.

In general, you are probably better off going to your own desk for some thought <u>first</u>, to the <u>machine second</u>, and <u>then</u> to the consultant with more information in hand and a more specific problem.

3.5 Testing Habits and Error Patterns

It is a good idea to critically analyze your own testing habits by reviewing the course of the battle after testing is completed. For example, how many times have you written a program that ran perfectly on the first try? How many times have you submitted a new program for its first run just to see if it might happen to "work", before giving serious thought to the information you will need to find out why it doesn't work? Once in a great while you may be lucky, but the odds are that you consistently waste the first few computer runs just discovering that something is wrong.

After you have finally tracked down an error, review the strategy of your attack. Knowing what the error is, and where it is, determine what sort of attack would have been most effective. It is good practice to save every output until testing is completed. Then go back and evaluate each test run to see which runs actually provided useful information and which runs were a waste of time. The next error will, of course, be different, but in the long run a pattern will emerge. You can learn what sort of information is generally useful, at what points in the program to seek information, and how to systematically eliminate possibilities.

Admittedly it is difficult to force yourself to do this. By the time you finish testing a program you are usually sick of looking at it and thinking about it. But unless you learn from this experience you are doomed to repeat it -- and as your assignments become more complex the burden of testing becomes overwhelming.

Section 4 An Example of Program Testing

This section consists of a single example illustrating how testing of a modest-sized program progresses using repeated execution. We have deliberately inserted errors in this program to show how they can be "discovered". You are entitled to be suspicious of such a rigged game, but we have tried to be realistic both in the nature of the errors and the manner of their detection.

The problem is John Conway's "Game of Life":

> Consider a population that lives on a rectangular grid. Each square in the grid either contains a member of the population or is vacant. Each square has eight adjacent squares that may contain a "neighbor".
>
> This population evolves from generation n to generation n+1 by the following algorithm:
>
> > If a square in generation n contains a member, that square in generation n+1:
> > contains a member if it had 2 or 3 neighbors in n;
> > otherwise it is vacant.
> > If a square in generation n is vacant, that square in generation n+1:
> > contains a member if it had 3 neighbors in n;
> > otherwise it is vacant.

This is a remarkably interesting game, considering the simplicity of the birth and death rules. You specify an initial configuration for a population, apply the rules to produce succeeding generations, and observe whether the population dies out, continually expands, stabilizes, migrates, alternates between two stable states, etc.

Our program plays on a 10 by 10 grid -- too small for many interesting configurations, but appropriate to limit the volume of output during testing. We assume that we have been given the procedure DISP to format and display a population so presumably DISP is correct and we are only concerned with testing the main procedure.

The deck submitted for the initial run is the following. Note that options specify XREF and ATR and suppress printing of the second procedure. The test data specifies:

1 population
5 generations
2 initial members at (3,4) and (4,4).

```
*PL/C XREF ATR
 /* GAME OF LIFE */
 LIFE: PROCEDURE OPTIONS(MAIN);
     DECLARE (ROWS, COLS) FIXED INIT(10);
     DECLARE (R(10,10), S(10,10)) FIXED;
     DECLARE (POPRQD,         /* NBR OF POP'NS REQUIRED */
              POPNBR,         /* NBR OF CURRENT POPULATION */
              GENRQD,         /* NBR OF GENERATIONS REQUIRED */
              GENNBR) FIXED;  /* NUMBER OF THIS GENERATION */
     DECLARE CHANGE BIT(1);   /* HAS BEEN CHANGE IN NEW GEN */
     DECLARE (NPOP,           /* NBR MEMBERS ON INIT POP'N */
              NBOR) FIXED;    /* NBR OF NEIGHBORS */
     DECLARE ENBR FIXDE;      /* NBR OF INITIAL ELEMENT */
     DECLARE (I, J) FIXED;    /* COORDINATES OF ELEMENT */

     PUT LIST ('GAME OF LIFE');
     PUT SKIP(2);

     /** PROCESS POPRQD DIFFERENT POPULATIONS */
         GET LIST (POPRQD);
         POP_LOOP: DO POPNBR = 1 TO P0PRQD BY 1;
             PUT SKIP(3) LIST ('POPULATION NUMBER', POPNBR);
             PUT SKIP(2);
             GET LIST (GENRQD);
             /** LOAD R WITH INITIAL GENERATION */
                 GENNBR = 0;
                 R = 0;
                 GET LIST (NPOP);
                 DO ENBR = 1 TO NPOP BY 1;
                     GET LIST (I,J);
                     R(I,J) = 1;
                     END;
             PUT SKIP LIST ('INITIAL POPULATION CONFIGURATION');
             CALL DISP(R);
```

```
                /** CREATE, DISPLAY NEW GENERATION, GENRQD TIMES */
                    CHANGE = '1'B;
                    GEN_LOOP: DO WHILE ((GENRQD > 0) & (CHANGE));
                        CHANGE = '0'B;
                        S = 0;
                        DO I = 2 TO ROWS-1 BY 1;
                            DO J = 2 TO COLS-1 BY 1;
                                NBOR = R(I-1,J-1) + R(I-1,J) +
                                       R(I-1,J+1) + R(I,J-1) +
                                       R(I,J+1) + R(I+1,J-1) +
                                       R(I+1,J) + R(I+1,J-1);
                                IF NBOR = 3
                                    THEN S(I,J) = 1;
                                IF (NBOR = 2) & (R(I,J) = 1)
                                    THEN S(I,J) = 1;
                                IF R(I,J) ¬= S(I,J)
                                    THEN CHANGE = '1'B;
                            END;
                        GENNBR = GENNBR + 1;
                        S = R;
                        PUT SKIP(3) LIST ('GENERATION NUMBER:',
                                GENNBR);
                        CALL DISP(R);
                        GENRQD = GENRQD - 1;
                        END GEN_LOOP;
                END POP_LOOP;

        PUT SKIP(4) LIST ('END OF GAME OF LIFE');
        END LIFE;
*PROCESS NOSOURCE
 /* FORMAT AND DISPLAY GENERATION G */
 DISP: PROCEDURE(G);
        DECLARE G(*,*) FIXED;
        DECLARE LINE CHAR(19) VAR;
        DECLARE LINEINIT CHAR(19) VAR INIT('. . . . . . . . . .');
        DECLARE (I, J) FIXED;

        PUT SKIP;
        ON ENDPAGE(SYSPRINT) BEGIN; END;
        ROW: DO I = 1 TO DIM(G,1) BY 1;
            LINE = LINEINIT;
            COL: DO J = 1 TO DIM(G,2) BY 1;
                IF G(I,J) = 1
                    THEN SUBSTR(LINE,2*J-1,1) = 'X';
                END COL;
            PUT SKIP LIST (LINE);
            END ROW;
        RETURN;
        END DISP;
*DATA
 1, 5, 2,  3,4,  4,4
```

The result of executing this program is shown on the following three pages.

```
*PLC XREF ATR

*OPTIONS IN EFFECT*     TIME=(0,15.00),PAGES=30,LINES=2000,ATR,XREF,FLAGW,NOCMNTS,SORMGIN=(2,72,1),ERRORS=(50,50),
*OPTIONS IN EFFECT*     TABSIZE=4132,SOURCE,OPLIST,NOCMPRS,HDRPG,AUXIO=10000,LINECT=60,NOALIST,MONITOR=(UDEF,BNDRY,
*OPTIONS IN EFFECT*     SUBRG,AUTO),MCALL,NOMTEXT,DUMP=(S,F,L,E,U,R),DUMPE=(S,F,L,E,U,R),DUMPT=(S,F,L,E,U,R)

 /* GAME OF LIFE */                                                              PL/C-R7.6-003 07/09/78 17:26 PAGE    1

  STMT LEVEL NEST BLOCK MLVL  SOURCE TEXT

                                   /* GAME OF LIFE */
    1                              LIFE: PROCEDURE OPTIONS(MAIN);
    2    1          1                  DECLARE (ROWS, COLS) FIXED INIT(10);
    3    1          1                  DECLARE (R(10,10), S(10,10)) FIXED;
    4    1          1                  DECLARE (POPRQD,        /* NBR OF POP'NS REQUIRED */
                                                POPNBR,        /* NBR OF CURRENT POPULATION */
                                                GENRQD,        /* NBR OF GENERATIONS REQUIRED */
                                                GENNBR) FIXED; /* NUMBER OF THIS GENERATION */
    5    1          1                  DECLARE CHANGE BIT(1);  /* HAS BEEN CHANGE IN NEW GEN */
    6    1          1                  DECLARE (NPOP,          /* NBR MEMBERS ON INIT POP'N */
                                                NBOR) FIXED;   /* NBR OF NEIGHBORS */
    7    1          1                  DECLARE ENBR FIXDE;     /* NBR OF INITIAL ELEMENT */
   ERROR IN STMT    7  MISSING COMMA IN COLUMN 19 (SY06)
         FOR STMT   7 PL/C USES  DECLARE ENBR,FIXDE;

    8    1          1                  DECLARE (I, J) FIXED;   /* COORDINATES OF ELEMENT */

    9    1          1                  PUT LIST ('GAME OF LIFE');
   10    1          1                  PUT SKIP(2);

                                       /** PROCESS POPRQD DIFFERENT POPULATIONS */
   11    1          1                      GET LIST (POPRQD);
   12    1          1                      POP_LOOP: DO POPNBR = 1 TO POPRQD BY 1;
   13    1    1     1                          PUT SKIP(3) LIST ('POPULATION NUMBER', POPNBR);
   14    1    1     1                          PUT SKIP(2);
   15    1    1     1                          GET LIST (GENRQD);
                                               /** LOAD R WITH INITIAL GENERATION */
   16    1    1     1                              GENNBR = 0;
   17    1    1     1                              R = 0;
   18    1    1     1                              GET LIST (NPOP);
   19    1    1     1                              DO ENBR = 1 TO NPOP BY 1;
   20    1    2     1                                  GET LIST (I,J);
   21    1    2     1                                  R(I,J) = 1;
   22    1    2     1                                  END;
   23    1    1     1                          PUT SKIP LIST ('INITIAL POPULATION CONFIGURATION');
   24    1    1     1                          CALL DISP(R);
                                               /** CREATE, DISPLAY NEW GENERATION, GENRQD TIMES */
   25    1    1     1                              CHANGE = '1'B;
   26    1    1     1                              GEN_LOOP: DO WHILE ((GENRQD > 0) & (CHANGE));
   27    1    2     1                                  CHANGE = '0'B;
   28    1    2     1                                  S = 0;
   29    1    2     1                                  DO I = 2 TO ROWS-1 BY 1;
   30    1    3     1                                      DO J = 2 TO COLS-1 BY 1;
   31    1    4     1                                          NBOR = R(I-1,J-1) + R(I-1,J) +
                                                                      R(I-1,J+1) + R(I,J-1) +
                                                                      R(I,J+1) + R(I+1,J-1) +
                                                                      R(I+1,J) + R(I+1,J-1);


   32    1    4     1                                          IF NBOR = 3
   33    1    4     1                                              THEN S(I,J) = 1;
   34    1    4     1                                          IF (NBOR = 2) & (R(I,J) = 1)
   35    1    4     1                                              THEN S(I,J) = 1;
   36    1    4     1                                          IF R(I,J) ¬= S(I,J)
   37    1    4     1                                              THEN CHANGE = '1'B;
   38    1    4     1                                      END;
   39    1    3     1                                  GENNBR = GENNBR + 1;
   40    1    3     1                                  S = R;
   41    1    3     1                                  PUT SKIP(3) LIST ('GENERATION NUMBER:',
                                                                  GENNBR);
   42    1    3     1                                  CALL DISP(R);
   43    1    3     1                                  GENRQD = GENRQD - 1;
   44    1    3     1                                  END GEN_LOOP;

   45    1    1     1                          END POP_LOOP;

   46    1          1                  PUT SKIP(4) LIST ('END OF GAME OF LIFE');
   47    1          1                  END LIFE;
```

```
/* GAME OF LIFE */                                          PL/C-R7.6-003 07/09/78 17:26 PAGE   3

DCL NO.   IDENTIFIER                   ATTRIBUTES AND REFERENCES

   5      CHANGE                       AUTOMATIC,UNALIGNED,BIT,STRING
                                       25,26,27,37

  59      COL                          STATEMENT LABEL CONSTANT

   2      COLS                         AUTOMATIC,INITIAL,ALIGNED,DECIMAL,FIXED(5,0)
                                       30

          DIM                          BUILT-IN FUNCTION
                                       57,59

  48      DISP                         ENTRY,DECIMAL,FLOAT(6)
                                       24,42

   7      ENBR                         AUTOMATIC,ALIGNED,DECIMAL,FLOAT(6)
                                       19

   7      FIXDE                        AUTOMATIC,ALIGNED,DECIMAL,FLOAT(6)

  49      G                            (*,*)PARAMETER,ALIGNED,DECIMAL,FIXED(5,0)
                                       48,57,59,60

  26      GEN_LOOP                     STATEMENT LABEL CONSTANT

   4      GENNBR                       AUTOMATIC,ALIGNED,DECIMAL,FIXED(5,0)
                                       16,39,39,41

   4      GENRQD                       AUTOMATIC,ALIGNED,DECIMAL,FIXED(5,0)
                                       15,26,43,43

  52      I                            AUTOMATIC,ALIGNED,DECIMAL,FIXED(5,0)
                                       57,60

   8      I                            AUTOMATIC,ALIGNED,DECIMAL,FIXED(5,0)
                                       20,21,29,31,31,31,31,31,31,31,31,33,34,35,36,36

  52      J                            AUTOMATIC,ALIGNED,DECIMAL,FIXED(5,0)
                                       59,60,61

   8      J                            AUTOMATIC,ALIGNED,DECIMAL,FIXED(5,0)
                                       20,21,30,31,31,31,31,31,31,31,31,33,34,35,36,36

   1      LIFE                         ENTRY,BINARY,FIXED(15,0)

  50      LINE                         AUTOMATIC,UNALIGNED,VARYING,CHARACTER,STRING
                                       58,61,63

  51      LINEINIT                     AUTOMATIC,INITIAL,UNALIGNED,VARYING,CHARACTER,STRING
                                       58

   6      NBOR                         AUTOMATIC,ALIGNED,DECIMAL,FIXED(5,0)
                                       31,32,34

   6      NPOP                         AUTOMATIC,ALIGNED,DECIMAL,FIXED(5,0)
                                       18,19

  12      POP_LOOP                     STATEMENT LABEL CONSTANT

   4      POPNBR                       AUTOMATIC,ALIGNED,DECIMAL,FIXED(5,0)
                                       12,13

   4      POPRQD                       AUTOMATIC,ALIGNED,DECIMAL,FIXED(5,0)
                                       11

          POPRQD                       AUTOMATIC,ALIGNED,DECIMAL,FLOAT(6)
                                       12

   3      R                            (*,*)AUTOMATIC,ALIGNED,DECIMAL,FIXED(5,0)
                                       17,21,24,31,31,31,31,31,31,31,31,34,36,40,42

  57      ROW                          STATEMENT LABEL CONSTANT

   2      ROWS                         AUTOMATIC,INITIAL,ALIGNED,DECIMAL,FIXED(5,0)
                                       29

   3      S                            (*,*)AUTOMATIC,ALIGNED,DECIMAL,FIXED(5,0)
                                       28,33,35,36,40

          SUBSTR                       BUILT-IN FUNCTION

          SYSPRINT                     FILE,STREAM,OUTPUT,PRINT,EXTERNAL
                                       54


ERRORS/WARNINGS DETECTED DURING CODE GENERATION:

     WARNING: NO FILE SPECIFIED. SYSIN/SYSPRINT ASSUMED. (CGOC)
```

```
GAME OF LIFE

***** ERROR IN STMT   12  POPRQD  HAS NOT BEEN INITIALIZED.  IT IS SET TO ZERO. (EX5D)


END OF GAME OF LIFE


IN STMT   47  PROGRAM RETURNS FROM MAIN PROCEDURE.
```

```
 /* GAME OF LIFE */                                                         PL/C-R7   POST-MORTEM DUMP    PAGE   1


IN STMT   47  SCALARS AND BLOCK-TRACE:

***** MAIN PROCEDURE LIFE

POPRQD= 0.00000E+00    J=         ?           I=        ?           FIXDE= ?.?????E+??     ENBR= ?.?????E+??
NBOR=        ?         NPOP=          ?       CHANGE='?'B           GENNBR=        ?       GENRQD=         ?
POPNBR=        1       POPRQD=          1     COLS=         10      ROWS=        10


NON-0 PROCEDURE EXECUTION COUNTS:
NAME         STMT COUNT  NAME         STMT COUNT  NAME         STMT COUNT  NAME         STMT COUNT  NAME         STMT COUNT
LIFE         0001 00001

LABEL EXECUTION COUNTS:
NAME         STMT COUNT  NAME         STMT COUNT  NAME         STMT COUNT  NAME         STMT COUNT  NAME         STMT COUNT
COL          0059 00000  ROW          0057 00000  GEN_LOOP     0026 00000  POP_LOOP     0012 00001


       COMPILATION STATISTICS  (0066 STATEMENTS)       |                         EXECUTION STATISTICS
SECONDS  ERRORS  WARNINGS  PAGES  LINES  CARDS  INCL'S | SECONDS  ERRORS  WARNINGS  PAGES  LINES  CARDS  INCL'S  AUX I/O
   .20       1         1      4    182     85       0 |     .04       1         0      1     12      1       0        0
-------------------------------------------------------+-----------------------------------------------------------------
BYTES    SYMBOL TABLE   INTERMEDIATE CODE   OBJECT CODE |   STATIC CORE   AUTOMATIC CORE    DYNAMIC CORE   TOTAL STORAGE
USED       4982(  5K)        1976(  2K)     3690(  4K) |     364(  1K)      2258(  3K)        0(  0K)      9138(  9K)
UNUSED    11546( 11K)       14310( 13K)    26760( 26K) |   24146( 23K)     24146( 23K)    14310( 13K)     24146( 23K)

THIS PROGRAM MAY BE RERUN WITHOUT CHANGE IN A REGION  23K BYTES SMALLER USING TABLESIZE=  1246
```

As is usually the case, our optimism that the program might work on the first try is unwarranted; this is obvious since no display of the grid appears. An error message in the source listing reports that STMT 7 is missing a comma. STMT 7 has been repaired by supplying a comma, but note in the XREF-ATR listing that the result of this declaration is two FLOAT variables ENBR and FIXDE. The problem was not a missing comma, but rather that the letters of the keyword FIXED were transposed so FIXDE was taken as another variable.

Another error message appears in the execution output, reporting that POPRQD is uninitialized when used in STMT 12. This is curious since STMT 11 clearly reads a data value and assigns it to POPRQD. Again, the answer to the mystery is found in the XREF-ATR listing where there are two distinct variables named POPRQD, the second of which is used in STMT 12 and not explicitly declared. With this much information you should discover that the second is spelled with a zero instead of the letter O, so the problem is a keypunch mistake in STMT 12. If the XREF-ATR listing had not been printed this misspelling might still have been detected by noting that the post-mortem dump contained two different POPRQDs.

Execution apparently reached the end of the program, since the closing message is printed and the program returns from STMT 47, as expected. But it doesn't appear to have accomplished much. Note in the PM dump that POPRQD and POPNBR have the values you would expect, so STMTs 11 and 12 were executed, but GENRQD has no value so STMT 15 was never executed. This is a consequence of the misspelling of POPRQD in STMT 12. A value of zero was supplied for the upper limit of iteration so the loop was executed from 1 TO 0 BY 1 -- that is, the body was never executed.

After correcting the keypunching mistakes in STMTs 7 and 12 and dropping the XREF-ATR options the next run produces the following:

```
*PLC

*OPTIONS IN EFFECT*     TIME=(0,15.00),PAGES=30,LINES=2000,NOATR,NOXREF,FLAGW,NOCMNTS,SORMGIN=(2,72,1),ERRORS=(50,50),
*OPTIONS IN EFFECT*     TABSIZE=4132,SOURCE,OPLIST,NOCMPRS,HDRPG,AUXIO=10000,LINECT=60,NOALIST,MONITOR=(UDEF,BNDRY,
*OPTIONS IN EFFECT*     SUBRG,AUTO),MCALL,NOMTEXT,DUMP=(S,F,L,E,U,R),DUMPE=(S,F,L,E,U,R),DUMPT=(S,F,L,E,U,R)

 /* GAME OF LIFE */                                                        PL/C-R7.6-003 07/09/78 17:26 PAGE   1

  STMT LEVEL NEST BLOCK MLVL  SOURCE TEXT

                                  /* GAME OF LIFE */
    1                             LIFE: PROCEDURE OPTIONS(MAIN);
    2    1          1                 DECLARE (ROWS, COLS) FIXED INIT(10);
    3    1          1                 DECLARE (R(10,10), S(10,10)) FIXED;
    4    1          1                 DECLARE (POPRQD,        /* NBR OF POP'NS REQUIRED */
                                               POPNBR,        /* NBR OF CURRENT POPULATION */
                                               GENRQD,        /* NBR OF GENERATIONS REQUIRED */
                                               GENNBR) FIXED; /* NUMBER OF THIS GENERATION */
    5    1          1                 DECLARE CHANGE BIT(1);  /* HAS BEEN CHANGE IN NEW GEN */
    6    1          1                 DECLARE (NPOP,          /* NBR MEMBERS ON INIT POP'N */
                                               NBOR) FIXED;   /* NBR OF NEIGHBORS */
    7    1          1                 DECLARE ENBR FIXED;     /* NBR OF INITIAL ELEMENT */
    8    1          1                 DECLARE (I, J) FIXED;   /* COORDINATES OF ELEMENT */

    9    1          1                 PUT LIST ('GAME OF LIFE');
   10    1          1                 PUT SKIP(2);

                                      /** PROCESS POPRQD DIFFERENT POPULATIONS */
   11    1          1                     GET LIST (POPRQD);
   12    1          1                     POP_LOOP: DO POPNBR = 1 TO POPRQD BY 1;
   13    1    1     1                         PUT SKIP(3) LIST ('POPULATION NUMBER', POPNBR);
   14    1    1     1                         PUT SKIP(2);
   15    1    1     1                         GET LIST (GENRQD);
                                              /** LOAD R WITH INITIAL GENERATION */
   16    1    1     1                             GENNBR = 0;
   17    1    1     1                             R = 0;
   18    1    1     1                             GET LIST (NPOP);
   19    1    1     1                             DO ENBR = 1 TO NPOP BY 1;
   20    1    2     1                                 GET LIST (I,J);
   21    1    2     1                                 R(I,J) = 1;
   22    1    2     1                                 END;
   23    1    1     1                         PUT SKIP LIST ('INITIAL POPULATION CONFIGURATION');
   24    1    1     1                         CALL DISP(R);

                                              /** CREATE, DISPLAY NEW GENERATION, GENRQD TIMES */
   25    1    1     1                             CHANGE = '1'B;
   26    1    1     1                             GEN_LOOP: DO WHILE ((GENRQD > 0) & (CHANGE));
   27    1    2     1                                 CHANGE = '0'B;
   28    1    2     1                                 S = 0;
   29    1    2     1                                 DO I = 2 TO ROWS-1 BY 1;
   30    1    3     1                                     DO J = 2 TO COLS-1 BY 1;
   31    1    4     1                                         NBOR = R(I-1,J-1) + R(I-1,J) +
                                                                     R(I-1,J+1) + R(I,J-1) +
                                                                     R(I,J+1) + R(I+1,J-1) +
                                                                     R(I+1,J) + R(I+1,J-1);
   32    1    4     1                                         IF NBOR = 3
   33    1    4     1                                             THEN S(I,J) = 1;
   34    1    4     1                                         IF (NBOR = 2) & (R(I,J) = 1)
   35    1    4     1                                             THEN S(I,J) = 1;
   36    1    4     1                                         IF R(I,J) ¬= S(I,J)
   37    1    4     1                                             THEN CHANGE = '1'B;
   38    1    4     1                                     END;
   39    1    3     1                                 GENNBR = GENNBR + 1;
   40    1    3     1                                 S = R;
   41    1    3     1                                 PUT SKIP(3) LIST ('GENERATION NUMBER:',
                                                                         GENNBR);
   42    1    3     1                                 CALL DISP(R);
   43    1    3     1                                 GENRQD = GENRQD - 1;
   44    1    3     1                                 END GEN_LOOP;
   45    1    1     1                         END POP_LOOP;

   46    1          1                 PUT SKIP(4) LIST ('END OF GAME OF LIFE');
   47    1          1                 END LIFE;

ERRORS/WARNINGS DETECTED DURING CODE GENERATION:

      WARNING: NO FILE SPECIFIED. SYSIN/SYSPRINT ASSUMED. (CGOC)
```

```
GAME OF LIFE


POPULATION NUMBER                1

INITIAL POPULATION CONFIGURATION

. . . . . . . . . .
. . . X . . . . . .
. . . X . . . . . .
. . . . . . . . . .
. . . . . . . . . .
. . . . . . . . . .
. . . . . . . . . .
. . . . . . . . . .
. . . . . . . . . .

GENERATION NUMBER:               1

. . . . . . . . . .
. . . X . . . . . .
. . . X . . . . . .
. . . . . . . . . .
. . . . . . . . . .
. . . . . . . . . .
. . . . . . . . . .
. . . . . . . . . .
. . . . . . . . . .

GENERATION NUMBER:               2

. . . . . . . . . .
. . . X . . . . . .
. . . X . . . . . .
. . . . . . . . . .
. . . . . . . . . .
. . . . . . . . . .
. . . . . . . . . .
. . . . . . . . . .
. . . . . . . . . .

GENERATION NUMBER:               3

. . . . . . . . . .
. . . X . . . . . .
. . . X . . . . . .
. . . . . . . . . .
. . . . . . . . . .
. . . . . . . . . .
. . . . . . . . . .
. . . . . . . . . .
. . . . . . . . . .

GENERATION NUMBER:               4

. . . . . . . . . .
. . . X . . . . . .
. . . X . . . . . .
. . . . . . . . . .
. . . . . . . . . .
. . . . . . . . . .
. . . . . . . . . .
. . . . . . . . . .
. . . . . . . . . .

GENERATION NUMBER:               5

. . . . . . . . . .
. . . X . . . . . .
. . . X . . . . . .
. . . . . . . . . .
. . . . . . . . . .
. . . . . . . . . .
. . . . . . . . . .
. . . . . . . . . .
. . . . . . . . . .
```

```
GENERATION NUMBER:              6

. . . . . . . . . .
. . . . . . . . . .
. . . X . . . . . .
. . . X . . . . . .
. . . . . . . . . .
. . . . . . . . . .
. . . . . . . . . .
. . . . . . . . . .
. . . . . . . . . .
. . . . . . . . . .

GENERATION NUMBER:              7

. . . . . . . . . .
. . . . . . . . . .
. . . X . . . . . .
. . . X . . . . . .
. . . . . . . . . .
. . . . . . . . . .
. . . . . . . . . .
. . . . . . . . . .
. . . . . . . . . .
. . . . . . . . . .

GENERATION NUMBER:              8

. . . . . . . . . .
. . . . . . . . . .
. . . X . . . . . .
. . . X . . . . . .
. . . . . . . . . .
. . . . . . . . . .
. . . . . . . . . .
. . . . . . . . . .
. . . . . . . . . .
. . . . . . . . . .

END OF GAME OF LIFE

IN STMT    47   PROGRAM RETURNS FROM MAIN PROCEDURE.



 /* GAME OF LIFE */                                                   PL/C-R7    POST-MORTEM DUMP    PAGE    1

IN STMT    47   SCALARS AND BLOCK-TRACE:

***** MAIN PROCEDURE LIFE

J=        10              I=        10             ENBR=        3             NBOR=        0              NPOP=        2
CHANGE='1'B               GENNBR=         8        GENRQD=       -3           POPNBR=        2            POPRQD=        1
COLS=       10            ROWS=       10

NON-0 PROCEDURE EXECUTION COUNTS:
NAME         STMT COUNT  NAME          STMT COUNT  NAME          STMT COUNT  NAME          STMT COUNT  NAME          STMT COUNT
DISP         0048 00009  LIFE          0001 00001

LABEL EXECUTION COUNTS:
NAME         STMT COUNT  NAME          STMT COUNT  NAME          STMT COUNT  NAME          STMT COUNT  NAME          STMT COUNT
COL          0059 00090  ROW           0057 00009  GEN_LOOP      0026 00001  POP_LOOP      0012 00001


      COMPILATION STATISTICS  (0066 STATEMENTS)        |                     EXECUTION STATISTICS
SECONDS  ERRORS  WARNINGS  PAGES  LINES  CARDS  INCL'S | SECONDS  ERRORS  WARNINGS  PAGES  LINES  CARDS   INCL'S  AUX I/O
   .16       0         1      2     85     84       0  |    .15       0         0      1    140      1        0       . 0
-------------------------------------------------------+-----------------------------------------------------------------
BYTES   SYMBOL TABLE   INTERMEDIATE CODE   OBJECT CODE |  STATIC CORE   AUTOMATIC CORE   DYNAMIC CORE   TOTAL STORAGE
USED      4840(   5K)      1974(   2K)     3704(   4K) |    366(   1K)    3034(    3K)       0(   0K)     9794(  10K)
UNUSED   11688(  11K)     14312(  13K)    26880(  26K) |  23490(  22K)   23490(   22K)   14312(  13K)    23490(  22K)

THIS PROGRAM MAY BE RERUN WITHOUT CHANGE IN A REGION  22K BYTES SMALLER USING TABLESIZE=  1210
```

This output is encouraging, but something is obviously still wrong since there are more generations than expected and they are all identical. Since we neglected to include any diagnostic PUT statements the only information that might help is in the PM dump.

One problem is that the body of GEN_LOOP is executed too many times. This is not because the loop itself is executed too often -- note the execution count for GEN_LOOP is 1. Iteration of the loop is controlled by either GENRQD or CHANGE. GENRQD presumably starts at 5 (STMT 15); presumably is decreased by 1 in each iteration (STMT 43); and presumably the loop will terminate when it becomes 0. But the final value is -3 so one of these presumptions is not correct.

The first depends upon the assumption that 5 was the next data value when STMT 15 was executed. Since 5 is the second item on the data list you should check to be sure that exactly one GET statement with a single variable on its list was executed prior to STMT 15. This is STMT 11 and everything looks fine, but you could check it on the next execution by inserting the following line after STMT 15:

```
PUT SKIP(2) DATA(GENRQD);
```

But before making another run to test presumption 1 it is worth considering the second and third presumptions to see if useful information about them could be obtained in the same run.

Presumption 2 centers on STMT 43. If GENRQD started at 5, then STMT 43 was executed 8 times (to give a final value of -3), which checks with the amount of output produced by the neighboring STMTs 41 and 42. But after the fifth execution of STMT 43, why didn't the loop terminate? A first suspicion would be the compound condition in the loop control, since these are notoriously susceptible to error -- even experienced programmers occasionally interchange "and" and "or". Perhaps iteration is being continued because of the value of CHANGE. But that is not the case here; the condition seems correct so the trouble must lie elsewhere. Having eliminated these other possibilities we must eventually conclude that STMT 43 is not being executed exactly once per iteration of the body of GEN_LOOP -- somehow it is being executed more often than that. The only clue available is the column headed NEST at the left of the source listing. This column indicates the depth of loop nesting. Notice that STMT 44, END GEN_LOOP;, reduces the nesting depth by 2 rather than 1. The reason is that when a named END is encountered in PL/I any necessary implied ENDs are supplied but do not appear on the source listing. Only the NEST column reveals this misguided charity. This means that STMT 43 is not the last statement in the body of GEN LOOP but, in fact, is the last statement in the body of the loop that begins in STMT 29. The problem is actually the omission of an END to close the loop that starts in STMT 30. The STMT 38 END was intended to close the 29-loop, but since the 30-loop was still open the END was applied to it and the 29-loop remained open. This caused STMTs 39 to 43 to be included in the body of the 29-loop. The named END in STMT 44 then closed both the 29-loop and GEN_LOOP.

Unfortunately, one tends to believe that the structure of the program is reflected by the indentation of the lines. The END in STMT 38 was indented as if it closed the 29-loop, but PL/I ignores indentation and closed the 30-loop instead. Indentation is helpful to the human reader, but you must remember that it is not considered by PL/I in determining the actual structure of the program.

The obvious correction in this case is to insert another END, but recognizing that if we had followed the practice of naming all nested DOs and ENDs the error would have been less likely in the first place, we belatedly add names to the loops within GEN_LOOP.

However, this still doesn't explain why each succeeding generation is the same as the original. So we make another run with diagnostic PUT statements inserted as STMTs 32 and 41:

```
 /* GAME OF LIFE */                                       PL/C-R7.6-003 07/09/78 17:26 PAGE   1

  STMT LEVEL NEST BLOCK MLVL   SOURCE TEXT

                                /* GAME OF LIFE */
     1                          LIFE: PROCEDURE OPTIONS(MAIN);
     2    1          1              DECLARE (ROWS, COLS) FIXED INIT(10);
     3    1          1              DECLARE (R(10,10), S(10,10)) FIXED;
     4    1          1              DECLARE (POPRQD,          /* NBR OF POP'NS REQUIRED */
                                             POPNBR,          /* NBR OF CURRENT POPULATION */
                                             GENRQD,          /* NBR OF GENERATIONS REQUIRED */
                                             GENNBR) FIXED;   /* NUMBER OF THIS GENERATION */
     5    1          1              DECLARE CHANGE BIT(1);    /* HAS BEEN CHANGE IN NEW GEN */
     6    1          1              DECLARE (NPOP,            /* NBR MEMBERS ON INIT POP'N */
                                             NBOR) FIXED;     /* NBR OF NEIGHBORS */
     7    1          1              DECLARE ENBR FIXED;       /* NBR OF INITIAL ELEMENT */
     8    1          1              DECLARE (I, J) FIXED;     /* COORDINATES OF ELEMENT */

     9    1          1              PUT LIST ('GAME OF LIFE');
    10    1          1              PUT SKIP(2);

                                    /** PROCESS POPRQD DIFFERENT POPULATIONS */
    11    1          1                  GET LIST (POPRQD);
    12    1          1                  POP_LOOP: DO POPNBR = 1 TO POPRQD BY 1;
    13    1     1    1                      PUT SKIP(3) LIST ('POPULATION NUMBER', POPNBR);
    14    1     1    1                      PUT SKIP(2);
    15    1     1    1                      GET LIST (GENRQD);
                                            /** LOAD R WITH INITIAL GENERATION */
    16    1     1    1                          GENNBR = 0;
    17    1     1    1                          R = 0;
    18    1     1    1                          GET LIST (NPOP);
    19    1     1    1                          DO ENBR = 1 TO NPOP BY 1;
    20    1     2    1                              GET LIST (I,J);
    21    1     2    1                              R(I,J) = 1;
    22    1     2    1                              END;
    23    1     1    1                      PUT SKIP LIST ('INITIAL POPULATION CONFIGURATION');
    24    1     1    1                      CALL DISP(R);
                                            /** CREATE, DISPLAY NEW GENERATION, GENRQD TIMES */
    25    1     1    1                          CHANGE = '1'B;
    26    1     1    1                          GEN_LOOP: DO WHILE ((GENRQD > 0) & (CHANGE));
    27    1     2    1                              CHANGE = '0'B;
    28    1     2    1                              S = 0;
    29    1     2    1                              G1: DO I = 2 TO ROWS-1 BY 1;
    30    1     3    1                                  G2: DO J = 2 TO COLS-1 BY 1;
    31    1     4    1                                      NBOR = R(I-1,J-1) + R(I-1,J) +
                                                                   R(I-1,J+1) + R(I,J-1) +
                                                                   R(I,J+1) + R(I+1,J-1) +
                                                                   R(I+1,J) + R(I+1,J-1);
    32    1     4    1                                      PUT SKIP DATA(I,J,NBOR);
    33    1     4    1                                      IF NBOR = 3
    34    1     4    1                                          THEN S(I,J) = 1;
```

```
/* GAME OF LIFE */                                          PL/C-R7.6-003 07/09/78 17:26 PAGE   2

 STMT LEVEL NEST BLOCK MLVL  SOURCE TEXT

   35    1    4     1                                      IF (NBOR = 2) & (R(I,J) = 1)
   36    1    4     1                                         THEN S(I,J) = 1;
   37    1    4     1                                      IF R(I,J) ¬= S(I,J)
   38    1    4     1                                         THEN CHANGE = '1'B;
   39    1    4     1                                      END G2;
   40    1    3     1                                   END G1;
   41    1    2     1                                PUT SKIP(2) DATA(S);
   42    1    2     1                                GENNBR = GENNBR + 1;
   43    1    2     1                                S = R;
   44    1    2     1                                PUT SKIP(3) LIST ('GENERATION NUMBER:',
                                                          GENNBR);
   45    1    2     1                                CALL DISP(R);
   46    1    2     1                                GENRQD = GENRQD - 1;
   47    1    2     1                                END GEN_LOOP;

   48    1    1     1                          END POP_LOOP;

   49    1          1                    PUT SKIP(4) LIST ('END OF GAME OF LIFE');
   50    1          1                    END LIFE;

ERRORS/WARNINGS DETECTED DURING CODE GENERATION:

     WARNING: NO FILE SPECIFIED. SYSIN/SYSPRINT ASSUMED. (CGOC)


GAME OF LIFE



POPULATION NUMBER               1


INITIAL POPULATION CONFIGURATION

. . . . . . . . . .
. . . . . . . . . .
. . . X . . . . . .
. . . X . . . . . .
. . . . . . . . . .
. . . . . . . . . .
. . . . . . . . . .
. . . . . . . . . .
. . . . . . . . . .
. . . . . . . . . .
I=        2              J=        2              NBOR=        0;
I=        2              J=        3              NBOR=        0;
I=        2              J=        4              NBOR=        1;
I=        2              J=        5              NBOR=        2;
I=        2              J=        6              NBOR=        0;
I=        2              J=        7              NBOR=        0;
I=        2              J=        8              NBOR=        0;
I=        2              J=        9              NBOR=        0;
I=        3              J=        2              NBOR=        0;
I=        3              J=        3              NBOR=        1;
I=        3              J=        4              NBOR=        1;
I=        3              J=        5              NBOR=        3;
I=        3              J=        6              NBOR=        0;
I=        3              J=        7              NBOR=        0;
I=        3              J=        8              NBOR=        0;
I=        3              J=        9              NBOR=        0;
I=        4              J=        2              NBOR=        0;
I=        4              J=        3              NBOR=        2;
I=        4              J=        4              NBOR=        1;
I=        4              J=        5              NBOR=        2;
I=        4              J=        6              NBOR=        0;
I=        4              J=        7              NBOR=        0;
I=        4              J=        8              NBOR=        0;
I=        4              J=        9              NBOR=        0;
I=        5              J=        2              NBOR=        0;
I=        5              J=        3              NBOR=        1;
I=        5              J=        4              NBOR=        1;
I=        5              J=        5              NBOR=        1;
I=        5              J=        6              NBOR=        0;
I=        5              J=        7              NBOR=        0;
I=        5              J=        8              NBOR=        0;
I=        5              J=        9              NBOR=        0;
I=        6              J=        2              NBOR=        0;
I=        6              J=        3              NBOR=        0;
I=        6              J=        4              NBOR=        0;
I=        6              J=        5              NBOR=        0;
I=        6              J=        6              NBOR=        0;
I=        6              J=        7              NBOR=        0;
I=        6              J=        8              NBOR=        0;
I=        6              J=        9              NBOR=        0;
```

```
I=      7        J=      2        NBOR=      0;
I=      7        J=      3        NBOR=      0;
I=      7        J=      4        NBOR=      0;
I=      7        J=      5        NBOR=      0;
I=      7        J=      6        NBOR=      0;
I=      7        J=      7        NBOR=      0;
I=      7        J=      8        NBOR=      0;
I=      7        J=      9        NBOR=      0;
I=      8        J=      2        NBOR=      0;
I=      8        J=      3        NBOR=      0;
I=      8        J=      4        NBOR=      0;
I=      8        J=      5        NBOR=      0;
I=      8        J=      6        NBOR=      0;
I=      8        J=      7        NBOR=      0;
I=      8        J=      8        NBOR=      0;
I=      8        J=      9        NBOR=      0;
I=      9        J=      2        NBOR=      0;
I=      9        J=      3        NBOR=      0;
I=      9        J=      4        NBOR=      0;
I=      9        J=      5        NBOR=      0;
I=      9        J=      6        NBOR=      0;
I=      9        J=      7        NBOR=      0;
I=      9        J=      8        NBOR=      0;
I=      9        J=      9        NBOR=      0;

S(1,1)=     0    S(1,2)=     0    S(1,3)=     0    S(1,4)=     0    S(1,5)=     0
S(1,6)=     0    S(1,7)=     0    S(1,8)=     0    S(1,9)=     0    S(1,10)=     0
S(2,1)=     0    S(2,2)=     0    S(2,3)=     0    S(2,4)=     0    S(2,5)=     0
S(2,6)=     0    S(2,7)=     0    S(2,8)=     0    S(2,9)=     0    S(2,10)=     0
S(3,1)=     0    S(3,2)=     0    S(3,3)=     0    S(3,4)=     0    S(3,5)=     1
S(3,6)=     0    S(3,7)=     0    S(3,8)=     0    S(3,9)=     0    S(3,10)=     0
S(4,1)=     0    S(4,2)=     0    S(4,3)=     0    S(4,4)=     0    S(4,5)=     0
S(4,6)=     0    S(4,7)=     0    S(4,8)=     0    S(4,9)=     0    S(4,10)=     0
S(5,1)=     0    S(5,2)=     0    S(5,3)=     0    S(5,4)=     0    S(5,5)=     0
S(5,6)=     0    S(5,7)=     0    S(5,8)=     0    S(5,9)=     0    S(5,10)=     0
S(6,1)=     0    S(6,2)=     0    S(6,3)=     0    S(6,4)=     0    S(6,5)=     0
S(6,6)=     0    S(6,7)=     0    S(6,8)=     0    S(6,9)=     0    S(6,10)=     0
S(7,1)=     0    S(7,2)=     0    S(7,3)=     0    S(7,4)=     0    S(7,5)=     0
S(7,6)=     0    S(7,7)=     0    S(7,8)=     0    S(7,9)=     0    S(7,10)=     0
S(8,1)=     0    S(8,2)=     0    S(8,3)=     0    S(8,4)=     0    S(8,5)=     0
S(8,6)=     0    S(8,7)=     0    S(8,8)=     0    S(8,9)=     0    S(8,10)=     0
S(9,1)=     0    S(9,2)=     0    S(9,3)=     0    S(9,4)=     0    S(9,5)=     0
S(9,6)=     0    S(9,7)=     0    S(9,8)=     0    S(9,9)=     0    S(9,10)=     0
S(10,1)=     0   S(10,2)=     0   S(10,3)=     0   S(10,4)=     0   S(10,5)=     0
S(10,6)=     0   S(10,7)=     0   S(10,8)=     0   S(10,9)=     0   S(10,10)=     0;

GENERATION NUMBER:        1

. . . . . . . . . .
. . . . . . . . . .
. . . X . . . . . .
. . . X . . . . . .
. . . . . . . . . .
. . . . . . . . . .
. . . . . . . . . .
. . . . . . . . . .
. . . . . . . . . .
. . . . . . . . . .
I=      2        J=      2        NBOR=      0;
```

STMT 32 produces useful but voluminous output (100 lines per generation) and reveals that the computation of the number of neighbors is not always correct. For example, cell (2,5) is reported to have 2 neighbors in the initial configuration rather than 1. This should lead you to discover that the last term in assignment statement 31 has an incorrect subscript -- it should be R(I+1, J+1).

The output from STMT 41 confirms that generation S is, in fact, different from R. But when the next generation is displayed by STMT 45 it has somehow reverted to the earlier configuration. Eventually you will notice that the replacement in STMT 43 is reversed and the new generation is being destroyed. This is the kind of silly mistake that is often difficult to discover. You can overlook it for a long time, and feel quite foolish when someone with a fresh perspective points it out.

Correcting statements 31 and 43, and removing diagnostic STMTs 32 and 41, the output from the next execution is:

```
GAME OF LIFE


POPULATION NUMBER                1

INITIAL POPULATION CONFIGURATION

. . . . . . . . . .
. . . . . . . . . .
. . . X . . . . . .
. . . X . . . . . .
. . . . . . . . . .
. . . . . . . . . .
. . . . . . . . . .
. . . . . . . . . .
. . . . . . . . . .
. . . . . . . . . .


GENERATION NUMBER:               1

. . . . . . . . . .
. . . . . . . . . .
. . . . . . . . . .
. . . . . . . . . .
. . . . . . . . . .
. . . . . . . . . .
. . . . . . . . . .
. . . . . . . . . .
. . . . . . . . . .
. . . . . . . . . .


GENERATION NUMBER:               2

. . . . . . . . . .
. . . . . . . . . .
. . . . . . . . . .
. . . . . . . . . .
. . . . . . . . . .
. . . . . . . . . .
. . . . . . . . . .
. . . . . . . . . .
. . . . . . . . . .
. . . . . . . . . .


END OF GAME OF LIFE

IN STMT    48  PROGRAM RETURNS FROM MAIN PROCEDURE.
```

```
/* GAME OF LIFE */                                                       PL/C-R7   POST-MORTEM DUMP   PAGE   1


IN STMT   48  SCALARS AND BLOCK-TRACE:

***** MAIN PROCEDURE LIFE

J=        10            I=        10            ENBR=        3           NBOR=        0          NPOP=        2
CHANGE='0'B             GENNBR=        2        GENRQD=        3         POPNBR=        2        POPRQD=        1
COLS=       10          ROWS=       10


NON-0 PROCEDURE EXECUTION COUNTS:
NAME        STMT COUNT  NAME         STMT COUNT  NAME         STMT COUNT  NAME         STMT COUNT  NAME         STMT COUNT
DISP        0049 00003  LIFE         0001 00001

LABEL EXECUTION COUNTS:
NAME        STMT COUNT  NAME         STMT COUNT  NAME         STMT COUNT  NAME         STMT COUNT  NAME         STMT COUNT
COL         0060 00030  ROW          0058 00003  G2           0030 00016  G1           0029 00002  GEN_LOOP     0026 00001
POP_LOOP    0012 00001


      COMPILATION STATISTICS  (0067 STATEMENTS)         |                    EXECUTION STATISTICS
SECONDS  ERRORS  WARNINGS  PAGES  LINES  CARDS  INCL'S  | SECONDS  ERRORS  WARNINGS  PAGES  LINES  CARDS  INCL'S  AUX I/O
  .16       0        1       2      86     85       0   |   .10       0        0       1      56     1       0        0
--------------------------------------------------------+-----------------------------------------------------------------
BYTES   SYMBOL TABLE   INTERMEDIATE CODE   OBJECT CODE  |  STATIC CORE   AUTOMATIC CORE   DYNAMIC CORE   TOTAL STORAGE
USED      4974(  5K)       1990(  2K)       3728(  4K)  |     366(  1K)      2284(  3K)        0(  0K)      9196(  9K)
UNUSED   11554( 11K)      14296( 13K)      26728( 26K)  |   24088( 23K)     24088( 23K)    14296( 13K)    24088( 23K)

THIS PROGRAM MAY BE RERUN WITHOUT CHANGE IN A REGION  23K BYTES SMALLER USING TABLESIZE=  1244
```

This is correct output for this test case, so there is no longer any evidence of errors. But we should not quit yet. This is only a "gentle first test" and we have reached only level 3 correctness. Many aspects of the program have not yet been exercised, much less punished by difficult test cases.

4.1 Review of Testing History

Reviewing the effectiveness of this testing, we performed 4 runs with the following results:

Run 1 with XREF-ATR
  Discovered 2 keypunch spelling mistakes.

Run 2
  Using PM dump and NEST values, discovered missing END.

Run 3 with diagnostic PUTs
  Discovered 2 faulty assignment statements.

Run 4
  Correct results; no evidence of errors.

If our first run had been made without the XREF-ATR option it is likely that it would have been wasted and another run would have been required to get that information. Therefore:

<u>Lesson 1</u>: Always specify XREF-ATR on the first run.

The structural flaw discovered in run 2 would have been less likely if we had either named all nested loops (and ENDs) in our original program, or had checked the NEST column in run 1. Consequently:

<u>Lesson 2</u>: Name your loops (both DOs and ENDs) if there is any nesting.

<u>Lesson 3</u>: Check the nest column against your indentation on the first run.

Delaying insertion of diagnostic PUTs until run 3 was wasteful. If they had been present in run 2 it would have been easier to detect the missing END, and would probably have indicated the flawed assignment statements as well. So:

<u>Lesson 4</u>: Expect to need diagnostic PUTs and include them on the first run.

It would seem that one more run was used in this case than should have been required.

Section 5 Special Diagnostic Facilities

Although in principle only the basic output statement is needed to obtain information it is nevertheless convenient to have more specialized and powerful facilities. Diagnostic facilities vary widely among languages and compilers. The PL/I family is particularly well-endowed in this regard. PL/I itself includes better diagnostic facilities than other major languages (FORTRAN, COBOL, ALGOL, PASCAL) and the Cornell dialects (PL/C, PL/CT and PL/CS) have extended this capability substantially.

The situation is confusing since each dialect offers a different set of facilities. The convention employed elsewhere in the book of describing concepts in common to all dialects and then noting exceptions is impractical here, so we have indicated the relevant dialect in the title of each section.

5.1 PL/I and PL/C Flow Tracing

We have referred to hand execution of programs as "tracing". The same word is used to describe computer execution when detailed information about the flow of execution is obtained. This can be done by placing output statements at strategic points in the program, but PL/I provides a more convenient way. In order to "check" all values that are assigned to certain key variables, one can list these variables in a "CHECK prefix" given before a procedure:

```
(CHECK( list )):
procedure-name: PROCEDURE ...
```

This CHECK prefix should be given on a separate line so that it can be conveniently removed when testing is completed. Note that the list of variables is enclosed in one set of parentheses and the entire prefix in another.

Each time a variable on the CHECK list is assigned a value a message is automatically printed. For example:

```
    /* PROCEDURE TO COMPUTE THE QUADRATIC SUM OF DATA */
    (CHECK(POINT,I,QUADSUM)):
    QUADSUMMER: PROCEDURE OPTIONS(MAIN);
        ...
(5.1a)  GET LIST(POINT);
        QUADSUM = 0;
        DO I = 1 TO POINT BY 1;
            ...
            END;
        ...
```

The CHECK output from (5.1a) is similar to what would be produced by (5.1b):

```
    /* PROCEDURE TO COMPUTE THE QUADRATIC SUM OF DATA */
    QUADSUMMER: PROCEDURE OPTIONS(MAIN);
        ...
(5.1b)  GET LIST(POINT);
        PUT SKIP DATA(POINT);
        QUADSUM = 0;
        PUT SKIP DATA(QUADSUM);
        DO I = 1 TO POINT BY 1;
            PUT SKIP DATA(I);
            ...
            END;
        PUT SKIP DATA(I);
        ...
```

Labels can also be checked. For example

```
            (CHECK(MAINLOOP)):
            SOLVE: PROCEDURE OPTIONS(MAIN);
               ...
               MAINLOOP: DO WHILE ...
```

is equivalent to writing

```
            SOLVE: PROCEDURE OPTIONS(MAIN);
               ...
               MAINLOOP: PUT SKIP LIST('MAINLOOP;');
               DO WHILE ...
```

(5.1c) illustrates checking both labels and variables:

```
     /* SUM INTEGERS FROM 1 TO ABSOLUTE VALUE OF DATUM */
     /* STOP ON FIRST ZERO DATUM */
     (CHECK(VALUE, INVERT, SUM)):
     ABS_SUM: PROCEDURE OPTIONS(MAIN);
        DCL (VALUE, /* NEW VALUE READ IN */
             SUM,   /* SUM OF INTEGERS */
             I)  FIXED;
(5.1c)  GET LIST(VALUE);
        DO WHILE(VALUE ¬= 0);
            IF VALUE < 0
                THEN INVERT: VALUE = -VALUE;
            /** SET SUM TO SUM OF 1 TO VALUE */
                SUM = 0;
                DO I = 1 TO VALUE BY 1;
                    SUM = SUM +I;
                    END;
            PUT SKIP LIST('VALUE IS:',VALUE,'SUM IS:',SUM);
            GET LIST(VALUE);
            END;
        END ABS_SUM;
    *DATA
     2, -3, 0
```

<u>Without</u> the CHECK prefix, execution output would be:

```
     VALUE IS:        2        SUM IS:        3
     VALUE IS:        3        SUM IS:        6
```

<u>With</u> the CHECK prefix, PL/C execution produces the following output (PL/I execution is slightly different):

```
     CHECK IN STMT 0003:      VALUE=         2;
     CHECK IN STMT 0007:      SUM=        0;
     CHECK IN STMT 0009:      SUM=        1;
     CHECK IN STMT 0009:      SUM=        3;
     VALUE IS:        2      SUM IS:      3
     CHECK IN STMT 0012:      VALUE=        -3;
     CHECK IN STMT 0006:      INVERT;
     CHECK IN STMT 0006:      VALUE=         3;
     CHECK IN STMT 0007:      SUM=        0;
     CHECK IN STMT 0009:      SUM=        1;
     CHECK IN STMT 0009:      SUM=        3;
     CHECK IN STMT 0009:      SUM=        6;
     VALUE IS:        3      SUM IS:      6
     CHECK IN STMT 0012:      VALUE=         0;
```

PL/I and PL/C differ in CHECK printing of an array. PL/I prints the <u>entire</u> array upon completion of execution of any statement that assigns a value to one or more elements of the array. PL/C prints only the particular element(s) assigned.

The CHECK prefix applies only to the statements written within the particular procedure -- not to statements in other external procedures that may be called. For example, in (5.1d) the statements in PR1 will be checked, but not those in PR2:

```
         (CHECK(X, Y)):
         PR1: PROCEDURE OPTIONS(MAIN);
             ...
             CALL PR2(X);
(5.1d)       ...
             END PR1;

        *PROCESS
         PR2: PROCEDURE(A);
             ...
             END PR2;
```

A separate CHECK prefix could be assigned to PR2, and in PL/C the CHECK list can include parameters:

```
        *PROCESS
         (CHECK(A, K)):
         PR2: PROCEDURE(A);
             ...
             END PR2;
```

5.1.1 PL/C Limiting the Scope of CHECK

The volume of output resulting from CHECK can be overwhelming and it is generally necessary to restrict the CHECK action to small sections of a program. This can be done in PL/I with a BEGIN block (see Section IV.4) but PL/C offers an easier way: CHECK and NOCHECK statements. When NOCHECK; is executed, all printing generated by the CHECK prefix is suppressed. When CHECK; is executed, CHECK printing is resumed (if it has been suppressed). These statements can be positioned to make the action of the CHECK prefix effective in only a small section of the procedure.

These statements can be used in many ways. They can limit output to a few iterations of a loop:

```
     (CHECK(I,SUM,VALUE)):
     X: PROCEDURE ...
        ...
        DO I = 1 TO N BY 1;
            IF I = 5
                THEN NOCHECK;
(5.1.1a)    ...
            END;
        CHECK;
        ...
```

They can deactivate the CHECK mechanism until trouble arises:

```
(CHECK(WIDTH, BASE)):
AREA_CALC: PROCEDURE OPTIONS(MAIN);
   NOCHECK;
   ...
   IF WIDTH < 0
       THEN CHECK;
   ...
```

An expression is optional in the CHECK statement:

```
CHECK(expression);
```

To execute this statement, the expression is evaluated to provide an integer that specifies the number of CHECK actions to be printed. After this many messages, the NOCHECK suppression is automatically invoked. Printing can be resumed by execution of another CHECK; statement. For example, CHECK(10); permits ten CHECK messages to be printed, and then no more until another CHECK statement is executed. Using this "limited quantity CHECK" (5.1.1a) could be written as:

```
(CHECK(I,SUM,VALUE)):
X: PROCEDURE ...
   ...
   CHECK(5);
   DO I = 1 TO N BY 1;
       ...
       END;
   CHECK;
   ...
```

5.1.2 PL/C FLOW Facilities

PL/C offers another method of tracing the flow-of-control. The information provided is roughly comparable to that obtained by CHECKing labels but is obtained automatically, without attaching labels to statements or listing the labels in a prefix. When PL/C FLOW tracing is invoked, any time the program departs from normal sequential execution a message of the following form is printed:

```
mmmm->nnnn
```

where mmmm and nnnn are STMT numbers as shown on the source listing. DO, CALL, functional procedure reference, IF, GOTO, END and RETURN will trigger these messages.

The FLOW mechanism is established by prefixing a statement with a FLOW prefix. This prefix should be placed on a separate line so it can be easily removed when testing is completed. Message printing is controlled by execution of the FLOW and

NOFLOW statements, which are comparable to the CHECK and NOCHECK statements except that CHECK prints unless explicitly suppressed while FLOW prints only when explicitly activated.

The program of (5.1c) is shown below, with FLOW tracing rather than CHECKing:

```
STMT
     /* SUM INTEGERS FROM 1 TO ABSOLUTE VALUE OF DATUM */
     /* STOP ON FIRST ZERO DATUM */
  1  (FLOW):
     ABS_SUM: PROCEDURE OPTIONS(MAIN);
  2      DCL (VALUE, /* NEW DATUM READ IN */
              SUM,   /* SUM OF INTEGERS */
              I) FIXED;
  3      FLOW;
  4      GET LIST(VALUE);
  5      DO WHILE(VALUE ¬= 0);
  6           IF VALUE < 0
  7              THEN VALUE = -VALUE;
             /** SET SUM TO SUM OF 1 TO VALUE */
  8              SUM = 0;
  9              DO I = 1 TO VALUE BY 1;
 10                 SUM = SUM + I;
 11                 END;
 12           PUT SKIP LIST('VALUE IS:',VALUE,'SUM IS:',SUM);
 13           GET LIST(VALUE); END;
 15      END ABS_SUM;
    *DATA
     2, -3, 0
```

Execution produces the following output:

```
*FLOW*       06->08    2*(11->09)      09->12
VALUE IS:       2        SUM IS:      3
*FLOW*       14->05      06->07    3*(11->09)       09->12
VALUE IS:       3        SUM IS:      6
*FLOW*       14->05      05->15
```

As with the CHECK statement, FLOW may have an argument that specifies the maximum number of FLOW messages to be printed. For example, FLOW(24); prints at most twenty-four FLOW messages. Printing is then suppressed until another FLOW statement is executed.

The rules and usage of the PL/C FLOW prefix are almost the same as those given above for CHECK. A (NOFLOW): prefix can be used to exclude an internal block from the effect of a (FLOW): prefix on a containing block, but it is generally simpler to use the NOFLOW and FLOW statements. Unlike the CHECK and NOCHECK prefixes, (FLOW): and (NOFLOW): can be specified on individual simple statements, compound statements, or loops as well as procedures and BEGIN blocks.

5.2 PL/C Memory Dump

An alternative to tracing is to periodically display the values of key variables. This is called "dumping memory". It does not provide as complete information, but for just that reason it is useful in a preliminary search to determine the neighborhood of an error. By displaying values at different key points (usually section interfaces) during execution, one can determine which intervals need to be traced in detail.

It is important that each dump contain enough identification to relate it to the proper point in the program. For example, statements like the following should be used:

```
PUT SKIP LIST('DUMP 3',I,X(I),TOTAL);
```

Without the identifying literal, the line produced by execution of this statement might be indistinguishable from other output lines.

PL/C provides two useful PUT options for dumping:

```
PUT ALL;     and     PUT ARRAY;
```

PUT ALL; displays the current values of all simple variables in the active procedures, while PUT ARRAY; displays arrays as well as simple variables. This automatically gives the name and value of each variable, plus an indication of which procedures and BEGIN blocks are active.

5.3 PL/C Limitation of Printed Output

The preceding sections are concerned with facilities for producing extra printed output for diagnostic purposes. It is also important to know how to limit the amount of printed output, both to reduce the cost of the testing process and to make it easier to find relevant information in the output. One can, of course, alternately insert and remove the statements that generate the output, but this is both inconvenient and risky; each change involves the possibility of introducing new errors into the program. PL/C has various facilities to make it possible to control printing with much less manipulation of the program. There are three principal kinds of printed output to control:

1. The listing of the source program.

2. "Normal" execution output -- that is, output generated by PUT statements.

3. Diagnostic output generated by the CHECK and FLOW facilities, and by the PL/C diagnostic PUT options.

The PL/C CHECK, NOCHECK, FLOW and NOFLOW statements to control diagnostic output were described in Sections 5.1.1 and 5.1.2. PL/C methods of controlling the other kinds of output are described below.

The source listing is controlled by the SOURCE and NOSOURCE options given on * control cards. NOSOURCE on a *PROCESS or *OPTIONS card suspends printing of the source listing; SOURCE resumes printing. However, NOSOURCE on the *PL/C card supresses printing for the entire program.

Normal execution printing may be controlled by PUT options

PUT OFF; and PUT ON;

Execution of PUT OFF; renders normal PUT statements ineffective. They are still executed, but the actual printing is suppressed until a PUT ON; is executed. (Strictly speaking, only PUT to the default file SYSPRINT is affected.) This suppression does not affect error messages generated by PL/C, or output generated by CHECK, FLOW, PUT ALL or PUT ARRAY.

Note that PUT OFF; and PUT ON; are statements whose execution causes supression of printed output, while SOURCE and NOSOURCE are options whose position in the program text affects printing during compilation of the program.

5.4 PL/C Selective Activation of Diagnostic Statements

Once the correctness of a program has been established the statements and prefixes added to generate diagnostic information must be removed. This must be done carefully so that the correct program is not accidentally damaged in this process. This is more complicated than it might seem, since it is often not clear when testing is really finished -- so diagnostic statements may have to be repeatedly inserted and removed.

Two PL/C facilities, "pseudo-comments" and "macros", permit segments to be rendered ineffective without requiring physical removal.

5.4.1 PL/C and PL/CS Pseudo-Comments

Segments can be written so that they can be considered either a comment or program text. "Pseudo-comments" are written as normal PL/I comments but with either a colon or an integer 1,2,3,4,5,6,7 as its first character. The CMNTS option on the *PL/C, *PROCESS or *OPTIONS card specifies which pseudo-comments are considered program text. For example:

```
/*4 PUT SKIP(3) LIST('TEST POINT 23', XMIN); */
```

Under the CMNTS=(4) option the contents of this pseudo-comment are considered program text. The delimiters /*4 and */ are ignored and the effect is the same as if one had written

```
PUT SKIP(3) LIST('TEST POINT 23', XMIN);
```

Without the CMNTS=(4) option the pseudo-comment is treated as an ordinary comment, and its contents have no effect on the program.

There are eight "classes" of pseudo-comments: those beginning with :, those beginning with 1, with 2, etc. The CMNTS option selects entire classes. Pseudo-comments beginning with a colon are considered program text if the option CMNTS is given, or if any of the numeric classes is specified. For example, CMNTS=(1,5) means all pseudo-comments beginning with either a 1, a 5, or : are read as program text.

The program of (5.1c) is rewritten below with the diagnostic statements given as pseudo-comments. Instructions for this program are:

1. NOCMNTS (the normal default option) suppresses diagnostic output.

2. CMNTS=(3) provides full diagnostic output.

3. CMNTS=(3,4) provides at most ten lines of diagnostic output.

```
/* SUM INTEGERS FROM 1 TO ABSOLUTE VALUE OF DATUM */
/* STOP ON FIRST ZERO DATUM */
/*3 (CHECK(VALUE, INVERT, SUM)): */
ABS_SUM: PROCEDURE OPTIONS(MAIN);
   DCL (VALUE, /* NEW DATUM READ IN */
        SUM,    /* SUM OF INTEGERS */
        I) FIXED;
   /*4 CHECK(10); */
   GET LIST(VALUE);
   DO WHILE(VALUE ¬= 0);
        IF VALUE < 0
             THEN INVERT: VALUE = -VALUE;
        /** SUM INTEGERS FROM 1 TO VALUE */
             SUM = 0;
             DO I = 1 TO VALUE BY 1;
                  SUM = SUM + I;
                  END;
        PUT SKIP LIST('VALUE IS:', VALUE,'SUM IS:',SUM);
        GET LIST(VALUE);
        END;
   END ABS_SUM;
```

A pseudo-comment can appear anywhere a normal comment can. It can contain one or more distinct symbols. These can represent part of a statement, an entire statement or several statements. However, be careful that the program is syntactically correct both with and without the inclusion of the comment text. Examples are:

```
/*3 TESTPOINT26: */
/*1 (CHECK(TOTAL,I,SUMQ)): */
/*4 ELSE CALL ERRORPROCESS(VAL); */
PUT SKIP LIST(A, B /*4 ,'CHKPT 4', C */ );
/*: PUT ALL; */
/*: PUT SKIP LIST('CHKPT A4',AMAX); AMAX=36; */
```

Pseudo-comments can be confusing since they appear on the source listing just as given on the card, without any clear indication as to whether the contents were treated as comment or program text in that particular run. You can check the *OPTIONS IN EFFECT* lines to be sure just which comments were scanned as program text. In most cases the statement numbering at the left of the source listing will help to distinguish between comments and program text. Comments do not have STMT numbers. If STMT numbers appear, then the content was scanned as source text and the delimiters /*n and */ were ignored.

Pseudo-comments can also be used to preserve compatibility between PL/C and PL/I. If all special PL/C features used in testing are written as pseudo-comments the program can be run in PL/I after its correctness is established. In this way you can take advantage of the fast compilation and diagnostic facilities of PL/C during development and testing, and the increased execution efficiency of PL/I for production.

5.4.2 PL/C Macro Facility

PL/C provides a facility for adding new constructions to the language. These new constructions, called "macros", are defined at the beginning of a program in the following way:

```
*MACRO
   Macro-name = macro-body %;
   ...
   Macro-name = macro-body %;
*MEND
```

The *MACRO and *MEND control cards (the * must be in column 1) indicate the beginning and end of the macro definitions -- one or more definitions may be included. Each definition has the form shown: a name followed by "=", and a body followed by "%;".

As the program is loaded, each occurrence of a macro-name is textually replaced by its corresponding macro-body. For example, memory dump facilities could be provided by a set of macros:

```
*MACRO
   DUMP = PUT ALL %;
   DUMPARRAYS = PUT ARRAY %;
   DUMPX = PUT SKIP DATA(X) %;
*MEND
```

Writing DUMP; in the program would have the same effect as writing PUT ALL;. In effect, for this particular program three new statement types have been added to PL/C. Like other statement keywords the macro names are "reserved" and cannot be used for any other purpose in this program. The point is not that it is easier to write DUMP than PUT ALL in the program, but rather that one can easily change the meaning of DUMP. When testing is complete these diagnostic facilities can be deactivated without removing them from the program just by changing their definition. This can be done by replacing the previous definition with

```
*MACRO
   DUMP = %;
   DUMPARRAYS = %;
   DUMPX = %;
*MEND
```

This defines each name to be equivalent to a blank -- so the semi-colon that follows each is a null statement. To reactivate the facility, restore the initial definition; to modify the facility, supply some other definition.

Like procedures, macros can have parameters. For example, DUMPX would be more flexible if defined as

```
*MACRO
   DUMP(X) = PUT SKIP DATA(X) %;
*MEND
```

In this definition X is a parameter rather than a specific variable and the DUMP(-) macro may be used for any variable:

```
DUMP(VAL);    is equivalent to    PUT SKIP DATA(VAL);
```

Another example provides diagnostic information at entry and exit of procedures:

```
*MACRO
  ENTER(PROC_NAME, KEY_PARAM) =
   PUT SKIP(2) LIST('EXECUTING PROC', PROC_NAME, 'WITH');
   PUT DATA(KEY_PARAM);
   PUT SKIP(2) %;
  DEPART(PROC_NAME, RESULT) =
   PUT SKIP(2) LIST('TERMINATING', PROC_NAME, 'WITH');
   PUT DATA(RESULT);
   PUT SKIP(2);
   RETURN %;
*MEND
```

ENTER and DEPART macro calls could be inserted at the beginning and end of each procedure:

```
INVERT: PROCEDURE(VALUE, LIMIT);
   DCL (VALUE, LIMIT) FLOAT;
   ENTER('INVERT', VALUE);
      ...
   DEPART('INVERT', VALUE);
   END INVERT;
```

During testing ENTER and DEPART provide a useful "procedure trace". When testing is completed the macro calls can be left in place but deactivated by redefining ENTER to be a blank and DEPART to be a simple RETURN.

The control of diagnostic facilities is only one possible use of macros. A more thorough explanation and other examples are given in Appendix A.10.

5.5 PL/CS Assertions

PL/CS allows assertions about what you expect to be true at a certain point in the program. There are three different forms:

```
ASSERT (logical expression);

ASSERT (logical expression)
    FOR ALL index-var = exp1 TO exp2 BY exp3;

ASSERT (logical expression)
    FOR SOME index-var = exp1 TO exp2 BY exp3;
```

Execution of an assertion either:

generates an appropriate message if the assertion is not true, or

has no effect if the assertion is true.

There are two principal uses:

1. As a post-assertion -- to confirm the result obtained by a certain section of the program.

2. As a pre-assertion -- to verify an assumption that is necessary for the correct execution of a certain section of the program.

The following are examples of the use of post-assertions. (The examples use PL/CS syntax.)

Example 1. Suppose a procedure FIND(X,VAL,POS) is to return in POS the position in array X of value VAL. The body of FIND might be something like the program developed in Section III.3.2. But in the procedure that uses FIND you don't care how FIND works, you just want to ensure that, in fact, it accomplishes the promised result. To do this you could write the following:

```
...
CALL FIND(A, VAL, LOCNVAL);
ASSERT (A(LOCNVAL) = VAL);
...
```

If the condition cited in the assertion is true, then execution of the assertion has no effect. If the condition is false, an error message identifying the failed assertion is automatically printed. In effect, it is equivalent to writing the following:

```
IF (A(LOCNVAL) ¬= VAL)
    THEN PUT SKIP (2) LIST
            ('ASSERTION STMT 54 NOT SATISFIED');
```

Example 2. Suppose procedure SORT is to order a portion of an array. Its action could be partially confined by an assertion:

```
...
CALL SORT(VLIST, J, K);
ASSERT (VLIST(I) <= VLIST(I+1))
    FOR ALL I = J TO K-1 BY 1;
...
```

Example 3. Suppose procedure FINDMAX returns the maximum value in part of an array. Its action could be confirmed by an assertion:

```
...
CALL FINDMAX(A, J, K, AMAX);
ASSERT (AMAX >= A(I))
    FOR ALL I = J TO K BY 1;
...
```

Note this assertion does not really establish that AMAX is the maximum value in A(J:K) -- it only ensures that it is greater than or equal to that maximum value. A stronger test would be provided by a pair of assertions:

```
...
CALL FINDMAX(A, J, K, AMAX);
ASSERT (AMAX >= A(I))
    FOR ALL I = J TO K BY 1;
ASSERT (AMAX = A(I))
    FOR SOME I = J TO K BY 1;
...
```

Even this does not absolutely guarantee the correctness of FINDMAX. For example, consider the following implementation of FINDMAX:

```
/* SET XMAX TO MAXIMUM TO X(A:B) */
FINDMAX: PROCEDURE (X, A, B, XMAX);
    DECLARE (X(*)) FLOAT;
    DECLARE (A, B) FIXED READONLY;
    DECLARE (XMAX) FLOAT;
    DECLARE (I) FIXED;
    MAX_LOOP: DO I = A+1 TO B BY 1;
        X(I) = X(A);
        END MAX_LOOP;
    XMAX = X(A);
    RETURN;
    END FINDMAX;
```

This version of FINDMAX is incorrect, but it would still satisfy the assertions that were supposed to establish the correctness of its result. The point is that often assertions do not absolutely guarantee the correctness of the result they address. From a practical point-of-view they are nevertheless useful in detecting the types of errors one tends to make unintentionally. But they are not always strong enough to police the program against deliberate subversion.

As an example of a pre-assertion, suppose a word-processing procedure COMPRESS assumes (without checking) that the string array it receives has no null elements. The procedure could be protected against errors in preceding sections of the program by writing:

```
...
ASSERT (LENGTH(WLIST(I)) ¬= 0)
    FOR ALL I = 1 TO LASTWORD BY 1;
CALL COMPRESS(WLIST, LASTWORD);
...
```

Alternatively, and perhaps better, the assertation could be put as the first statement of the procedure body, rather than before each call. Of course, a pre-assertion is, in effect, just a post-assertion for the entire preceding program, but it is nevertheless useful to think of it as related to the segment that follows.

Assertations add no new capability to the language, since everything they do could be accomplished with the conditional and PUT statements. The advantage is that their purpose is made clear to the reader. They are also easier to write and provide less opportunity to make errors.

Assertions can optionally be "turned off" without physically removing them from the program (see the MONITOR ASSERT option in Appendix A.4). Thus they can be left in the program as documentation for the reader without affecting execution speed.

Some judgement is required to decide when a condition should be tested by an assertion and when the normal IF statement should be used. The choice depends upon the nature of the condition, and the presumed origin of the fault. Assertions are intended (1) as program documentation and (2) as program diagnostic facilities intended to detect program errors. They should not be used for testing and processing of data errors. For example, suppose a particular data value is required to be non-negative. This should be tested with an ordinary IF statement:

```
...
GET LIST (RATE);
IF (RATE < 0)
    THEN DO;
        PUT SKIP (2) LIST
                ('IMPROPER RATE:', RATE);
        PUT SKIP LIST ('RATE = 1 ASSUMED');
        RATE = 1;
        END;
...
```

Section 5 Exercises

1. Rewrite the program given in Section I.1.1 as it should be for an initial testing run
   a) using additional PUT statements,

   b) using the PL/I CHECK feature,

   c) using the PL/C CHECK prefix, CHECK and NOCHECK statements, and pseudo-comments,

   d) with a test control procedure similar to (V.2.2b) that permits the program to be repeated with several data sets.

2. For the program given below
   a) What execution output is produced if the program is run with the option NOCMNTS?

   b) What is the execution output if the program is run with the CMNTS=(3) option?

```
/* MOVE MINIMUM TO HEAD OF LIST */
(CHECK(MINPOS)):
MINMOVE: PROCEDURE OPTIONS(MAIN);
   DCL L(50) FLOAT;
   DCL MINVAL FLOAT; /* MIN VALUE SO FAR */
   DCL MINPOS FIXED; /* POSITION OF MINVAL IN LIST */
   DCL N FIXED;      /* EFFECTIVE LENGTH OF LIST */
   DCL I FIXED;

   /** LOAD N AND L(1:N) */
       GET LIST(N);
       IF (N<1)|(N>50)
           THEN DO;
               PUT SKIP(4) LIST('IMPROPER LENGTH');
               GO TO TERM_MINMOVE;
               END;
       DO I = 1 TO N BY 1;
           GET LIST(L(I));
           END;

/** SET MINVAL = MINIMUM OF L(1:N); */
       /* MINPOS TO ITS POSITION */
       MINVAL = L(1);
       MINPOS = 1;
       DO I = 1 TO N BY 1;
           IF L(I) < MINVAL
               THEN DO;
                   MINVAL = L(I);
                   MINPOS = I;
                   END;
           /*3 IF I = 4 THEN NOCHECK; */
           END;
       CHECK;
```

```
    /** MOVE MIN TO HEAD POSITION AND REPORT */
        L(MINPOS) = L(1);
        L(1) = MINVAL;
        PUT SKIP LIST('MIN VALUE IS', L(1));
        PUT SKIP LIST('ORIG POSN OF MIN IS',MINPOS);
    TERM_MINMOVE:;
    END MINMOVE;

*DATA
    8, 7, 6, 9, 8, 5, 4, 6, 4, 3
```

3. Rewrite the following program to give essentially the same diagnostic output, but without using the CHECK facility.

```
/* COMPUTE BOUNDED INTEGER SUMS */
(CHECK(LOW, HIGH, INT, SUM)):
SUMER: PROCEDURE OPTIONS(MAIN);
   DCL (LOW, HIGH) FIXED; /* RANGE LIMITS */
   DCL INT FIXED;         /* CURRENT INTEGER */
   DCL SUM FIXED;         /* SUM OF INTEGERS */

   GET LIST(LOW, HIGH);
   IF LOW > HIGH
       THEN PUT SKIP LIST('IMPROPER BOUNDS');

   /** COMPUTE SUM FROM LOW TO HIGH */
       SUM = 0;
       DO INT = LOW TO HIGH BY 1;
           SUM = SUM + INT;
           END;

   PUT SKIP LIST(LOW, HIGH, SUM);
   END SUMER;
```

4. Rewrite the following program segment to give essentially the same diagnostic output, but without using the CHECK facility.

```
(CHECK(L1, L2, L3)):
X: PROCEDURE ...;
   ...
   L1: IF X + Y < Z
       THEN L2: Y = 2*Z;
       ELSE L3: Y = 0;
   ...
```

5. For the program given below how many lines of execution output would be produced running under option

a) CMNTS=(3)?
b) CMNTS=(4)?
c) CMNTS=(5)?
d) CMNTS=(4,5)?

```
/* COUNT OCCURENCES OF SPECIFIED CHARACTER */
   /*3 (CHECK(TESTCHAR)): */
   /*4 (CHECK(WORDNUM, CHARNUM)): */
   /*5 (CHECK(COUNT)): */
CTCHAR: PROCEDURE OPTIONS(MAIN);
   DCL WORD CHAR(30) VARYING; /* WORD TO BE TESTED */
   DCL TESTCHAR CHAR(1) VAR;  /* CHAR TO BE COUNTED */
   DCL NBR FIXED INIT(0);     /*NO.  OF OCCURENCES */
   DCL (WORDNUM, CHARNUM) FIXED;

   /** READ IN CHARACTER TO TEST FOR */
       GET LIST(TESTCHAR);

   /** PROCESS EACH INPUT WORD UNTIL 'END' */
       GET LIST(WORD);
       WORDNUM = 1;
       DO WHILE(WORD ¬= 'END');
           /** COUNT OCCUR. OF TESTCHAR IN WORD */
               DO CHARNUM = 1 TO LENGTH(WORD) BY 1;
                   IF SUBSTR(WORD,CHARNUM,1)=TESTCHAR
                       THEN COUNT: NBR = NBR + 1;
                   END;
           GET LIST(WORD);
           WORDNUM = WORDNUM + 1;
           END;
       WORDNUM = WORDNUM-1; /* DON'T COUNT END MARKER*/

   /** DISPLAY RESULTS */
       PUT SKIP LIST('TEST CHAR IS:',TESTCHAR);
       PUT SKIP LIST('TOTAL OCCURENCES:',NBR);
       PUT SKIP LIST('NBR WORDS TESTED:',WORDNUM);

   END CTCHAR;

*DATA
 'P',
 '1P2P3P4P5P6P7P', '123P123P123P',
 'PPPPPPP', 'M', 'MP', '12345678P', 'END'
```

6. Rewrite the program given below so that its action is unchanged except for the following:

a) If run under CMNTS=(6) it will print a copy of the list in initial order.

b) If run under CMNTS=(5) it will omit printing the display of the final sorted list.

c) If run under CMNTS=(2) it will announce the beginning of each pass.

d) If run under CMNTS=(3) it will report each interchange.

e) If run under CMNTS=(3,4) it will report only the first 5 interchanges.

```
/* SORT LIST INTO ASCENDING ORDER */
SORT: PROCEDURE OPTIONS(MAIN);
   DCL L(50) FLOAT; /* LIST TO BE SORTED */
   DCL N FIXED;       /* EFFECTIVE LENGTH */
   DCL TEMP FLOAT;
   DCL (I,J) FIXED;

   /** LOAD N AND L(1:N) */
       GET LIST(N);
       IF N>50
           THEN PUT SKIP LIST('LIST TOO LONG');
       DO I = 1 TO N BY 1;
           GET LIST(L(I));
           END;

   /** SORT L(1:N) BY BUBBLE SORT, "BUBBLING" THE */
       /* LARGEST TO THE TOP AT EACH STEP */
       DO J = N TO 2 BY -1;
         /** CARRY MAX VALUE TO END OF L(1:J) */
           DO I = 1 TO J-1 BY 1;
             /** INTERCHANGE IF OUT OF ORDER */
               IF L(I) > L(I+1)
                   THEN DO;
                       TEMP = L(I);
                       L(I) = L(I+1);
                       L(I+1) = TEMP;
                       END;
             END;
         END;

   /** DISPLAY SORTED LIST */
       PUT SKIP(2) LIST('SORTED LIST');
       PUT SKIP(2);
       DO I = 1 TO N BY 1;
           PUT SKIP LIST(L(I));
           END;

   END SORT;
```

7. Rewrite the program given below adding suitable diagnostic facilities, enclosed in pseudo-comments.

```
/* CHANGE DUPLICATE CHARACTERS IN INPUT WORDS TO '*'.  */
/* END OF WORD LIST IS INDICATED BY WORD 'END'.  */
DELDUP: PROCEDURE OPTIONS(MAIN);
   DCL WORD CHAR(78) VARYING;
   DCL (CHR,TEST) FIXED;

   /** READ IN AND PROCESS THE WORDS */
       GET LIST(WORD);
       DO WHILE (WORD ¬= 'END');
         PUT SKIP LIST(WORD,'IS CHANGED TO');
         /** REPLACE DUPLICATE CHARACTERS IN WORD BY * */
           DO CHR=1 TO LENGTH(WORD)-1 BY 1;
             DO TEST=CHR+1 TO LENGTH(WORD) BY 1;
               IF SUBSTR(WORD,TEST,1) =
                       SUBSTR(WORD,CHR,1)
                   THEN SUBSTR(WORD,TEST,1) = '*';
               END;
             END;
         PUT LIST(WORD);
         GET LIST(WORD);
         END;

   END DELDUP;
```

Section 6 Testing in Interactive Systems

Section II.3.4 identified the distinguishing characteristic of an interactive system as the ability to communicate with a program during its execution. This provides the opportunity to defer supplying data until the program is actually being executed, and hence allows you to see output up to that point in execution before having to decide what data to supply. Section II.3.4 showed how this could be used to write interactive programs in which the user and the computer cooperate in the solution of a problem.

An interactive system is also valuable during testing. The ability to see intermediate results before supplying further test data can be very helpful. It allows you to accomplish in a single run what would require several runs in a batch system. Thus, a common mode of operation where both interactive and batch systems are available is to test each new program interactively and then, when testing has been completed, to run the program in the more economical batch mode if it does not really require interactive execution.

This ability to postpone the supply of test data would in itself be sufficient justification for the use of an interactive system during testing, but there are two further advantages; these are discussed in the following sections.

6.1 Program Entry and Syntax Checking

When program statements are entered on the terminal of an interactive system syntax checking takes place on a statement-by-statement basis, and any errors detected are reported to the user at the terminal <u>immediately</u> after entry of the invalid statement. PL/CT, like PL/CS and PL/C, not only reports the errors but also proposes a repaired form of the statement. In PL/C the repaired statement is what is actually used in execution of the program -- since the user does not see the repair until after execution has been completed he has no chance to object to it. However, in PL/CT the user sees the proposed repair as soon as it is made and can accept it (by doing nothing) or type in a proper correction himself.

In its present form, PL/CT does not allow the simple replacement of a single statement -- the altered program must be reentered from the beginning. However, PL/CT is usually used in conjunction with some "text-editing" system, so that this alteration and resubmission is not difficult. But the text editing system used depends on the computing installation and you must get instructions for its use from your own installation.

6.2 The "Terminal Procedure" of PL/CT

During execution of a program, in addition to its role as an input and output device for GET and PUT statements, the terminal (and the user) can act as if it were part of the program. That is, execution can be interrupted and statements can be entered from the terminal for immediate execution. Upon termination, execution of the original program can be resumed. Because of the analogy with executing a CALL statement, we refer to this role of the terminal as the "terminal procedure".

There are several ways to "call" this terminal procedure; that is, ways in which you can interrupt program execution so you can execute statements from the terminal:

1. Striking the "attention key" on the terminal.

2. Encountering an execution error in the program.

3. Encountering a "breakpoint" that you have established in the program specifically for this purpose.

4. Completing execution of a specified number of statements in the normal program.

Initially we explain just the first two to give a general idea of what is happening, and then give a more complete explanation involving all four methods.

6.2.1 Attention and Error Calls of the Terminal Procedure

Imagine that your program contains two external BIT(1) variables ATTN_FLAG and ERROR_FLAG, each with initial value '0'B. Suppose that the effect of striking the attention key is to instantaneously assign '1'B to ATTN_FLAG and that the "execution error routine" of PL/C assigns '1'B to ERROR_FLAG (in addition to its chores of issuing messages and making repairs).

Remark We have used the word "statement" throughout the book to mean an executable statement, loop, conditional statement. PL/I uses the word "statement" differently, calling, for example, DO a statement and "IF expression" a statement. On the source listing, PL/I calls these things <u>STMTs</u>, and numbers them successively. Throughout this section, then, "STMT" will be used to refer to the PL/I "statements" that are numbered on the source program listing.

Now suppose that a conditional call like the one shown below has been automatically inserted <u>before each STMT</u> of your original program:

```
IF ((ATTN_FLAG) | (ERROR_FLAG))
    THEN CALL TERMINAL_PROCEDURE;
```

These inserted statements are invisible (do not appear on the source listing) and unnumbered (do not affect the numbering of the original STMTs).

Suppose also that an internal procedure is automatically added (in the block or procedure where the interrupt occurs):

```
TERMINAL_PROCEDURE: PROCEDURE;
    ATTN_FLAG = '0'B;
    ERROR_FLAG = '0'B;
    statements to be entered from terminal
    END TERMINAL_PROCEDURE;
```

Thus when your program encountered an execution error it would complete processing of the STMT containing the error, including printing the error message and making the usual PL/C repair, and then it would give you the opportunity to enter statements from the terminal. For example, you might want to display certain variables to see why the error occurred or change variables. When you have completed action from the terminal, execution of the original program is resumed.

Similarly, if you strike the attention key the program will complete the STMT currently being executed and call the terminal procedure before proceeding.

Unlike real procedures, this imaginary terminal procedure does not consist of a fixed sequence of statements. Except for the initial statements that reset the flags, it consists of whatever statements you enter from the terminal. These are executed immediately when typed, and are not saved. In general, the terminal procedure will be different each time it is called since you will enter different statements from the terminal. The particular statements that can be entered are described in Section 6.2.3.

Note that the input-output and procedure roles of the terminal are completely distinct. During testing you use both. Once testing is completed the procedure role is not needed and the terminal serves only as an input and output device for GET and PUT statements in the original program. But during testing it is important that you understand the two roles and know which one you are using at each instant.

PL/CT clarifies the roles by printing a distinctive message each time the terminal procedure is called. For example, if you strike the attention key while the program happens to be executing STMT 162, PL/CT will enter terminal procedure mode with the message

```
ATTN AT STMT  163.  DBC:
```

If an execution error occurs in STMT 513 PL/CT will enter terminal procedure mode with the message

```
AFTER EXEC ERROR; NOW AT STMT  514.  DBC:
```

Every PL/CT message ending "DBC:" means the system is in terminal procedure mode and is waiting for a DeBug Command.

No automatic message is printed on the terminal when the system asks for data to satisfy execution of a GET statement. However, as noted in Section II.1.4, it is a good idea to precede each GET statement in the program with a PUT that will cause a suitable "prompting message" to be printed on the terminal before each request for data.

6.2.2 PAUSE and STEP Calls of the Terminal Procedure

It is useful to be able to enter terminal procedure mode at specified places in the program, or after executing some specified number of statements, to trace execution. This can be done by establishing "breakpoints" in the program -- called "pauses" in PL/CT -- and by "stepping" the program through execution. These facilities in PL/CT can be explained by extending the description of the last section.

Suppose that, in addition to ATTN_FLAG and ERROR_FLAG, the following external variables have been added:

```
STEP          FIXED INITIAL(c)
STEP_RESET    FIXED INITIAL(c)
IGNORE        FIXED INITIAL(0)
IGNORE_RESET  FIXED INITIAL(0)
PAUSE(1:n)    BIT(1) INITIAL((n)'0'B)
```

Here, c is a large integer, like 2^{16}, and n is the number of STMTs in the program. Now suppose each STMT i in the original program is surrounded by invisible unnumbered statements as shown below:

```
    IF ((PAUSE(i)) | (STEP = 0) |
            (ATTN_FLAG) | (ERROR_FLAG))
        THEN CALL TERMINAL_PROCEDURE;
    STMT i
    STEP = STEP - 1;
```

This is analogous to the conditional call inserted in Section 6.2.1 except that there are now four ways of activating the call instead of only two, and that a "step-counter" is reduced by 1 after each STMT is executed. The corresponding version of the terminal procedure would be:

```
TERMINAL_PROCEDURE: PROCEDURE;
    IF (IGNORE ¬= 0)
        THEN DO;
            IGNORE = IGNORE - 1;
            RETURN;
            END;
    IGNORE = IGNORE_RESET;
    STEP = STEP_RESET;
    ATTN_FLAG = '0'B;
    ERROR_FLAG = '0'B;
    statements to be entered from terminal
    END TERMINAL_PROCEDURE;
```

Now assume that ATTN_FLAG and ERROR_FLAG will be assigned '1'B by the attention key and execution error routine, as before. Assume that STEP_RESET is assigned a value specifying the number of program statements to be executed before coming back to terminal procedure mode. Assume that PAUSE(i) is '1'B if you want to enter terminal procedure mode before executing STMT i, and is '0'B otherwise. Finally, assume IGNORE_RESET contains an integer specifying the number of pauses to be ignored before coming back to the terminal. The STMTs that assign to STEP_RESET, PAUSE(i), and IGNORE_RESET are described in the next section.

With these assumptions the program can be interrupted to enter statements from the terminal in each of the four ways described in the beginning of Section 6.2. You can interrupt at will by striking the attention key, but it is impossible to time this so as to have any real control over where you are in the program, so it is less useful than it might seem. The program will be interrupted after an execution error is detected, which is useful but, as noted in previous sections, the serious testing really begins after all errors that can be detected by PL/C have been eliminated. Hence you will primarily use the pause and step interrupts to trace the program and make certain it is executing as you intended.

6.2.3 Statements in the Terminal Procedure

The statements entered and executed from the terminal in PL/CT are called "debug commands" because they are primarily used for debugging or testing a program. They are executed immediately upon entry at the terminal. They are not saved and do not become part of the program. To be executed a second time they must be entered again from the terminal.

A debug command that corresponds to a PL/C statement has the same effect as if that statement had been encountered in the original program. These statements are the following:

PUT SKIP LIST(list of variables);

PUT SKIP DATA(list of variables);

assignment statement
: The right-side of the assignment must be a constant.

RETURN;
: End execution of the terminal procedure and resume execution of the original program.

GOTO label;
: End execution of the terminal procedure and resume execution of the original program beginning with the statement whose label is given. Note that in PL/C, and hence in PL/CT, a loop-name can be a target for a GOTO, and unlike PL/CS you can branch backward in the program to re-execute a section.

CHECK;

NOCHECK;

PUT ALL;

PUT ARRAY;

The following debug commands are not PL/C statements. They are used to control the values of the hypothetical variables STEP_RESET, IGNORE_RESET and PAUSE described in Section 6.2.2.

STEP m;
: Assign constant m to STEP_RESET. This causes the terminal procedure to be executed every m program STMTs. This interval will be used until another STEP command is given. That is, each time execution of the original program is resumed, at most m STMTs will be executed before coming back to the terminal.

PAUSE AT s;
: Assign '1'B to PAUSE(s), the element of the PAUSE array

corresponding to STMT s. A particular STMT is specified either by its number or a label or procedure-name that labels the statement. That is, both of the following are legal:

```
PAUSE AT 45;

PAUSE AT SUM_LOOP;
```

NOPAUSE AT s;
Assign '0'B to PAUSE(s).

IGNORE m;
Assign constant m to IGNORE_RESET. This causes the program to ignore the next m pauses encountered, and call the terminal procedure on pause m+1.

PUT s, m; or PUT s;
Execution displays the contents of one or more lines from the source listing (since the original source listing may not be available at the terminal). PUT s, m; means display m lines beginning with the line on which s begins. If m is not given, 1 is assumed.

The identifiers (variables, labels and procedure names) known in the terminal procedure, and hence useable in the debug commands described above, are exactly those known in the block in which the interrupt occurs. That is, the terminal procedure can be viewed as an internal procedure, without declarations of its own, whose definition is positioned within the block in which the interrupt occurs.

For example, suppose you are testing the following program:

```
         P1: PROCEDURE
             DCL (X, Y, Z) FLOAT;
             ...
             P2: PROCEDURE;
                 DCL X FLOAT;
                 ...
>>>interrupt>>>
                 ...
                 Z:;
                 RETURN;
                 END P2;
             END P1;
```

Consider the debug commands that could be executed if the program was interrupted at the point indicated:

1. PUT SKIP LIST (Y); is valid; it refers to the Y in P1 (since there is no declaration of a local Y in P2).

2. PUT SKIP LIST (X); is valid; it refers to the local X declared in P2.

3. PUT SKIP LIST (Z); is invalid because the only Z known in P2 is a label and labels are not valid objects in a PUT list.

4. GOTO Z; is valid since the Z known in P2 is a label.

6.3 An Example of Interactive Testing

Suppose you wanted to test procedure FINDMIN of Section IV.1.4 on a PL/CT terminal. After entering the entire program you would give a PL/C command to begin execution. By specifying the PAUSE option on this command the program pauses immediately after it begins execution of the main procedure. It enters terminal procedure mode with the prompting message

```
PAUSED AT STMT    2.  DBC:
```

You can use this opportunity to set a pause at MIN_LOOP in SORT, but since you are effectively in procedure SRTG you cannot refer directly to a name in SORT. However you can refer to STMTs by <u>number</u> anywhere in the program, so give the command

```
PAUSE AT 15;
```

PL/CT will indicate that this has been done and request another command by prompting

```
DBC:
```

Enter the command

```
RETURN;
```

Execution will resume and continue until just before execution of STMT 15. PL/CT then enters terminal mode with the prompting message

```
PAUSED AT STMT   15.  DBC:
```

To make sure you have the right statement give the command

```
PUT 15;
```

and PL/CT would reply

```
DO I = 1 TO N-1 BY 1;
DBC:
```

Now assign values to the input arguments of FINDMIN:

```
I = 1;
DBC:
N = 2;
DBC:
```

If no assignment is made to X from the terminal the values will remain as read in SRTG before the call of SORT. You could check these values with a PUT command. Now you could execute procedure FINDMIN by giving the commands

```
STEP 2; RETURN;
```

This sets the "step interval to 2" and resumes execution. The program will return to the terminal after every 2 STMTs of execution. The first such return will be announced by:

```
STEPPED TO STMT   17.  DBC:
```

To see what FINDMIN found to be the minimum of X(1:2) you could now enter the command

```
PUT SKIP LIST(J);
```

You could then reassign to I, J, and X and repeat execution of FINDMIN until you are satisfied that it is correct. There would be several ways to do this. You could change the step interval to 4 by giving the command:

```
STEP 4;
```

Then the program will return to the terminal on each iteration of the loop:

```
STEPPED TO   17.  DBC:
```

Alternatively, if STMT 15 had a label MIN_LOOP you could enter:

```
GOTO MIN_LOOP;
```

This would start the loop over again from the beginning.

In effect, with PAUSE, STEP, and GOTO, you can precisely control the flow of execution. You can set trial values and examine results until you completely understand what is taking place during execution.

Section 7 Proofs of Correctness

We have argued in Parts II and III that the systematic development of a program, using only certain restricted structures, will reduce the frequency and severity of errors. Realistically we know that we cannot eliminate them entirely. Conceding this fallibility we have presented strategies and tools for testing programs -- for trying to detect the existence of errors and for locating and identifying them. But this process is not guaranteed either. When testing reveals no further errors, it may be that no errors are present, but it could also mean only that the testing is not sufficiently rigorous. You can disprove the correctness of a program -- by exhibiting an incorrect action -- but _failing to disprove correctness_ is _not_ the same thing as _proving correctness_. The absence of evidence of errors is not equivalent to evidence of their absence.

It would be nice to be able to _prove_ the correctness of a program, much as one proves a mathematical theorem, in a way that does not depend importantly upon the skill of the individual programmer.

There are two aspects to a program. First, a program is a _static object_. It exists on paper and we read it in this form, usually from left-to-right and top-to-bottom. Second, a program is _dynamic_, in that it is _executed_ to produce a result. The order of execution of statements is quite different from the static order, and yet we attempt to understand the order of events that take place during execution just from the static, top-to-bottom description. This is further complicated by the fact that the order of events changes from one execution to another, depending on the input data. Thus, when reading a program, we are attempting to understand a multitude of _different_ executions. From the static description, we would like to understand the program enough to _prove_ that _all possible_ executions are correct.

If we would be satisfied to prove properties about the static version of a program things would not be so difficult, but about all that one could prove about a static program is that it is syntactically correct. The proof of syntactic correctness is sufficiently straightforward that it can be mechanized. This is considered a standard part of the task of translating a programming language and many translators do an adequate job in this regard. However, as noted in Section V.1.1, a reasonable meaning of correctness implies much more than the absence of syntactic errors.

The fundamental difficulty is that we would like to prove properties of the dynamic aspect of a program using characteristics of its static version. The process is clearly aided if we make the static and dynamic aspects of a program as much alike as possible. This is really what the concept of program units in Section II.1 is all about. For a single, simple statement the static and dynamic aspects are identical. To say that we understand what a written statement means is essentially equivalent to saying that we understand what the results of executing it are. If we can make a sequence of statements behave as a single statement, then this property of static-dynamic identity is preserved for a compound statement. The compound statement will have component steps, but as long as they are in strictly sequential order this poses no great difficulty. For example, to say that the meaning (or execution) of a compound statement S is

1. perform S1,
2. then perform S2,
3. finally perform S3,

is not inherently different or more difficult than to say that the meaning of an assignment statement is

1. evaluate the expression on the right side,
2. and assign its value to the variable on the left.

If one of the components Si of a compound statement is itself compound this does not change the situation. After all, the evaluation of the expression in the assignment statement may have involved the execution of a built-in function like SIN or SQRT which is actually a substantial segment of program. It may have involved a user-supplied function procedure (Section IV.1.6) and there is no limit to the size or complexity of program that could be included in that procedure. In understanding the assignment statement we regard these functions as elemental tasks -- performing some action in a clearly specified order with respect to other tasks. Each component of the compound statement is regarded in the same way.

In these terms we have some chance of making a convincing argument that a certain algorithm is correct for a particular problem. We may be able to argue that

P1 then P2 then P3 is equivalent to P

and then that

P21 then P22 is equivalent to P2.

Eventually, at some low level, we could show that program segment Si is equivalent to algorithm step Pi.

Alternative steps in the algorithm don't greatly complicate the argument:

Pi1 then (IF e THEN Pi2 ELSE Pi3) then Pi4 ...

But <u>repetition</u> does complicate things. The following type of sequence is relatively hard to understand:

P1 P2 P3 P2 P3 ... P2 P3 P4

It is hard to summarize this sequence with a statement that is true for any number of repetitions of the pair (P2,P3). This is the situation in which the static and dynamic aspects of a program differ most widely. There are two basic difficulties with repetition:

1. We must be able to show that the loop will halt -- that is, that the condition that allows repetition will eventually terminate it.

2. Provided the loop does halt, we must be able to show that the loop performs its intended function, <u>no matter how many times the loop iterates</u>.

We discuss this problem in the next section.

7.1 <u>Invariant Relations of a Loop</u>

The dynamic execution of a loop is quite different from its static description, and we need some technique to connect the two. This will turn out to be a <u>relation about the values of the variables used in the loop</u> -- a statement about them which is either true or false. We illustrate first with a familiar sorting algorithm.

7.1.1 <u>An Example: Sorting</u>

Consider the successive-minima algorithm to sort an array A(1:N) where N≥0.

```
          I = 1;
          DO WHILE (I <= N);
(7.1a)       Swap values of A(I:N) to put smallest in A(I)
             I = I+1;
             END;
```

This algorithm halts with I = N+1, since I is increased by 1 each time the loop body is executed. Initially, the array A looks like the left diagram of (7.1b), while upon termination we want it to look like the right diagram of (7.1b). We want to be able to "prove" that it looks like the right diagram, but not just by mentally executing one or two cases.

```
            A(1)                 A(N)     A(1)            A(N)
           ┌──────────────────────────┐  ┌──────────────────┐
  (7.1b)   │ values may be unsorted   │  │ values are sorted│
           └──────────────────────────┘  └──────────────────┘
```

We first draw a picture of array A that will describe A <u>at any point</u> during execution:

```
            A(1)     A(I-1) A(I)                          A(N)
           ┌───────────────┬─────────────────────────────────┐
  (7.1c)   │    sorted     │ each value in this partition    │
           │               │ ≥ each value in A(1:I-1)        │
           └───────────────┴─────────────────────────────────┘
```

We now prove several points that lead to the conclusion that algorithm (7.1a) does indeed sort the array.

1. (7.1c) describes the array just before execution of the loop -- after execution of I=1. (This is true because the array segment A(1:I-1) has no elements -- I-1=0. Thus <u>all</u> values are in A(I:N).)

2. Each iteration of the loop leaves the array as described by (7.1c) (but of course with I increased by 1). We show this below.

3. Because of point 2, (7.1c) describes the array after the last iteration, and after the loop has halted.

4. The loop halts with I=N+1 and (7.1c) describing the array. Since I=N+1 the segment A(I:N) contains no values. Thus the first partition A(1:I-1), which is A(1:N), contains all the values. Since this partition is always in sorted order, the array is sorted.

We have to show that each iteration of the loop leaves the array as described by (7.1c), that is, that point 2 above is true. Only execution of the loop body might change this picture, so let us consider <u>one</u> execution of the loop body with (7.1c) describing the array beforehand and with I≤N. Executing the first statement "Swap values" changes the picture to

```
 A(1)     A(I-1)       A(I)              A(I+1)            A(N)
┌────────────────┬───────────────────┬──────────────────────┐
│    sorted      │ a value ≥ each    │ each value in this   │
│                │ value in A(1:I-1) │ partition ≥ A(I)     │
└────────────────┴───────────────────┴──────────────────────┘
```

This must be so since the smallest of A(I:N) is put into A(I). Note that now the segment A(1:I) is sorted. Thus executing the second statement I=I+1 of the body yields the picture

```
A(1)                          A(I-1) A(I)          A(N)
┌───────────────────────────────────┬──────────────────────┐
|   sorted                          | each value in this   |
|                                   | partition ≥ A(I-1)   |
└───────────────────────────────────┴──────────────────────┘
```

But if this holds after execution of the body, then so does (7.1c). Thus executing the body of the loop has not changed the picture.

This may seem like a lot of intricate detail to go through just to show the algorithm works. Why, it's obvious from just looking at the algorithm that it works! This may be true for this simple example, but we have illustrated a powerful technique that can be used with any loop. We discuss this in more general terms in the next section.

Note how (7.1c) connects the static description of the algorithm with the dynamic execution. (7.1c) is always true, no matter how many times the loop iterates, and we have shown this by considering only one execution of the loop body. In effect, (7.1c) is a picture of what is not changing during execution. Dynamic execution is hard to understand because the values of variables continually change, and the way they change depends on the input data. What the picture gives is an invariant relation about the variables -- a relation that is always true no matter what the input values are.

(7.1c) can also be put into words:

(7.1d) The array A(1:N) is partitioned into A(1:I-1) and A(I:N). A(1:I-1) is sorted. Each value in A(I:N) is not less than each value in A(1:I-1).

7.2 The Invariant Relation Theorem

We develop a simple but powerful theorem that can be useful in understanding any WHILE loop. First we must introduce some notation. Let P and Q be relations concerning the values of variables used in a sequence of statements S. The notation

{P} S {Q}

means:

If P is true before execution of the sequence of statements S, then Q is true after execution of S.

For example, suppose I and N are FIXED variables and that

```
P       is the relation    I < N
S       is the statement   I = I+1;
Q       is the relation    I ≤ N
```

Then |P| S |Q| is the statement

```
|I < N| I = I + 1 |I ≤ N |
```

Note that |I < N| I = I + 1 |I < N| is not true.

This notation is important to the proper understanding of what follows. (It is suggested that you do Exercise 1 at this point, before proceeding.)

Now consider a loop

```
        DO WHILE ( c );
(7.2a)     Body
           END;
```

where c is a condition and Body is a sequence of statements, and suppose

(7.2b) |P & c| Body |P|

where P is a relation about the variables used in the loop. That is, execution of the Body with condition c true leaves relation P true. Then, provided the loop halts, we know that

```
|P| DO WHILE(c); Body END; |P & ¬c|
```

Why? During execution of the loop only execution of the Body may change the relation P. But by (7.2b) execution of the Body does not change the relation P. Thus P remains true after the loops halts. Relation c must be false when the loop halts, because that is the only way the loop may halt.

We have quite simply proved a very powerful theorem:

(7.2c) Invariant Relation Theorem

Provided the loop halts, |P & c| Body |P| implies

```
|P| DO WHILE(c); Body END; |P & ¬c|
```

P is called an invariant relation of the loop. It is a relation concerning the variables of the program -- a statement about them that is either true or false. It is invariant in that it remains true after the loop halts if it is true before execution of the loop begins.

This theorem only applies if the loop halts because c becomes false. If we terminate the loop by using a LEAVE or GOTO, we have to use other means to check correctness. Such exits are of course very useful at times, and we illustrate in later examples how to handle them.

Consider again the successive-minima algorithm of Section 7.1. We have:

condition c: $I \le N$

relation P: (7.1c) or (7.1d)

Body: Swap values of A(I:N) to put smallest in A(I)
I = I+1;

upon halt: P & ¬c imply the array is sorted.

It is sometimes difficult to find the right relation P. There are an infinite number of invariant relations that satisfy the hypothesis of the theorem. For example, the relations

array A(1:N) <u>may</u> be sorted

I*0 = 0

are always true, but they are not useful in understanding any loop. We must look for the <u>one</u> relation P that, together with ¬c, implies the intended result.

Let us summarize by stating how the invariant relation helps us, how it connects the dynamic and static aspects of the loop. The loop has the form

```
DO WHILE ( c );
    Body
    END;
```

To understand the loop and prove it correct, we need to do the following four things (five if exits occur in the loop):

1. Find a relation P such that P & ¬c imply the intended result.

2. Prove that P is true just before execution of the loop.

3. Prove that {P & c} Body {P}.

4. Prove that the loop halts.

5. If the loop contains exits (LEAVEs, GOTOs, STOPs, or RETURNs that terminate the loop) the correctness of the results upon exit must be ascertained by other means.

We have to prove that execution of the body with c true leaves P true. We do <u>not</u> have to worry about how many times the loop will be iterated, and we do not have to worry about the dynamic execution of the loop; just about <u>one</u> dynamic execution of the <u>loop body</u>. This is very important.

7.3 Simple Examples of Invariant Relations

Each of the following examples is a simple loop together with initialization statements. With each, we give the invariant relation that can be used to understand the loop. For each, you should show that:

1. The relation P is true before execution of the loop.

2. P and ¬c imply the desired result.

3. {P & c} Body {P}.

4. The loop halts.

This is enough to show that the loop is correct. From points 1 and 2 you should get the main idea behind the algorithm; from 3 and 4, how the idea is carried out.

```
1. /* STORE IN X THE MAXIMUM OF A(1:N). N >= 1 */
   /* THE INVARIANT RELATION OF THE LOOP IS: */
   /* X CONTAINS THE MAXIMUM VALUE OF A(1:I) */
   /* AND 1 ≤ I ≤ N */
       I = 1;
       X = A(1);
       DO WHILE ( I ¬= N );
           I = I + 1;
           IF A(I) > X
               THEN X = A(I);
           END;
```

```
2. /* SWAP VALUES OF A(I:N) TO PUT SMALLEST IN A(I).  */
   /* 1<=I<=N.  THE INVARIANT RELATION OF THE LOOP IS: */
   /* A(I:J) CONTAINS ITS ORIGINAL VALUES, BUT WITH */
   /* THE SMALLEST IN A(I), AND I ≤ J ≤ N */
       J = I;
       DO WHILE (J ¬= N);
           J = J+1;
           IF A(J) < A(I)
               THEN Swap A(J) and A(I)
           END;
```

3.
```
/* STORE IN SUM THE SUM OF VALUES IN A(1:N).  N >= 1 */
/* THE INVARIANT RELATION OF THE LOOP IS:*/
/* SUM CONTAINS THE SUM OF VALUES IN A(1:I) */
/* AND 1 ≤ I ≤ N */
    I = 1;
    SUM = A(1);
    DO WHILE (I ¬= N);
        I = I + 1;
        SUM = SUM + A(I);
        END;
```

4.
```
/* SORT-BY-INSERTION.  SORT ARRAY A(1:N)*/
/* THE INVARIANT RELATION OF THE LOOP IS: */
/* THE ARRAY LOOKS LIKE                   */

/* A(1)          A(I)                    A(N) */
/* ┌──────────┬────────────────────────────┐*/
/* | SORTED   | UNSORTED, NOT "LOOKED AT"  |*/
/* └──────────┴────────────────────────────┘*/

    I = 2;
    DO WHILE (I <= N);
        Swap values of A(1:I) so that A(1:I) is sorted
        I = I + 1;
        END;
```

5. In PL/I, the following program may produce a runtime error message. Discover why and fix the program.

```
/* SWAP VALUES OF A(1:I) SO THAT A(1:I) IS SORTED,*/
/* ASSUMING THAT A(1:I-1) IS ALREADY SORTED.*/
/* THE INVARIANT RELATION FOR THIS LOOP IS:*/
/* A(1:J-1) IS SORTED & A(J:I) IS SORTED & */
/* IF 1 < J < I THEN A(J-1) <= A(J+1)*/
    J = I;
    DO WHILE ((J¬=1) & (A(J) < A(J-1)));
        Swap A(J) and A(J-1)
        J = J-1;
        END;
```

6. This is the binary search algorithm of Section VI.2.4. It searches the array A(1:N) for a value X. The invariant relation theorem helps us in proving that if the loop terminates normally, then X is not in the list. If X is in the list, then the program stops by executing a GO TO out of the loop.

```
/* BINARY SEARCH.  GIVEN A(1:N) AND X, STORE IN J A VALUE*/
/* SUCH THAT A(J) = X.  STORE 0 IN J IF X NOT IN LIST*/
/* THE INVARIANT RELATION OF THE LOOP IS:*/
/* IF X IS IN A(1:N), IT IS IN A(FIRST:LAST).*/
    FIRST = 1;
    LAST = N;
    DO WHILE (FIRST <= LAST);
        J = FLOOR((FIRST+LAST)/2E0);
        IF A(J) = X
            THEN GOTO ENDSEARCH;
        IF A(J) < X
            THEN FIRST = J + 1;
            ELSE LAST = J - 1;
        END;
    J = 0;
    ENDSEARCH:;
```

7.4 More Complicated Examples

The last section showed several familiar algorithms to help gain facility with invariant relations. Here we present new algorithms. Remember, it is not necessary to execute the algorithm with a set of initial values in order to understand it; indeed this sometimes tends to confuse the issue. It is only necessary to go through the four points discussed at the beginning of Section 7.3.

Some of these algorithms contain nested loops. We have only written the invariant relations where they indeed help. We have also sometimes written a comment describing <u>what</u> the body of a loop does, and written the statements to perform that function underneath. When trying to understand the loops, read the comment as the loop body. Later, you can read the statements to make sure the statements do what the comment says.

1.
```
/* CALCULATE Z = A**B WHERE A AND B ARE INTEGERS > 0*/
/* WITHOUT USING EXPONENTIATION*/
/* THE OUTER LOOP HAS THE INVARIANT RELATION*/
/*    Z*(X**Y) = A**B    AND 0 ≤ Y */
    Z = 1;
    X = A;
    Y = B;
    DO WHILE (Y ¬= 0);
        /** DECREASE Y, KEEPING Y>=0 AND RELATION INVARIANT*/
            DO WHILE (MOD(Y,2) = 0);
                Y = Y/2E0;
                X = X*X;
                END;
            Y = Y - 1;
            Z = Z*X;
        END;
```

2. Quicksort This algorithm sorts an array A(1:N). The expected runtime is proportional to N*LOG2(N) although the worst case is proportional to N^2. (See Section VI.2.)

The algorithm uses a command "Partition A(L:U)..." which is given as algorithm 3 below. To understand Quicksort itself, it is not necessary to understand how Partition works, but only what it does.

Quicksort uses two additional arrays LOWER and UPPER and a simple variable M. Their definition is actually the invariant relation of the loop:

> A(LOWER(1):UPPER(1)), A(LOWER(2):UPPER(2)), ..., A(LOWER(M):UPPER(M)) are disjoint segments of the array A such that, if these M segments are sorted then the whole array is sorted.

Originally then, we have M=1, LOWER(1) = 1, UPPER(1) = N, and at the end, when M=0 there are no segments in this list, and hence the array must be sorted.

```
LOWER(1) = 1;
UPPER(1) = N;
M = 1;
ST: DO WHILE (M ¬= 0);
   /* EITHER SORT SEGMENT A(LOWER(M):UPPER(M)) AND DELETE IT */
   /*      FROM LIST IF IT IS SMALL ENOUGH,*/
   /* OR SPLIT IT INTO SMALLER SEGMENTS TO BE SORTED. IN THIS*/
   /*      CASE REPLACE SEGMENT ON LIST BY THESE SMALLER ONES.*/
       L = LOWER(M);
       U = UPPER(M);
       M = M - 1;
       IF U = L + 1 /* A(L:U) HAS TWO MEMBERS.  SORT*/
            THEN IF A(L) > A(U)
                 THEN Swap A(L) and A(U)
       IF U > L + 1 /* A(L:U) HAS OVER TWO ELEMENTS*/
            THEN PARTIT: DO;
                 Partition A(L:U) into three segments
```

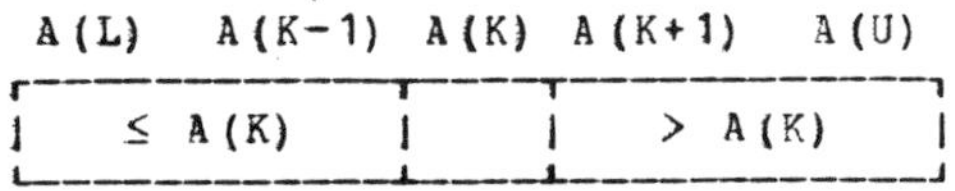


```
                 and set K.
```

```
            /* A(L:U) WILL BE SORTED WHEN A(L:K-1) AND */
            /* A(K+1:U) ARE.  ADD THEM TO LIST TO SORT.*/
            /* PUT THE LARGER OF THE TWO SEGMENTS ON*/
            /* LIST FIRST; REDUCES SIZE OF LOWER, UPPER*/
               IF U - K > K - L
                  THEN DO;
                     M = M + 1;
                     LOWER(M) = K + 1;
                     UPPER(M) = U;
                     END;
               M = M + 1;
               LOWER(M) = L;
               UPPER(M) = K - 1;
               IF U - K <= K - L
                  THEN DO;
                     M = M + 1;
                     LOWER(M) = K + 1;
                     UPPER(M) = U;
                     END;
            END PARTIT;
   END ST;
```

3. Partition algorithm. This algorithm is given an array segment A(L:U) as input. It rearranges the values of the array segment and stores an integer in variable K so that the array looks like

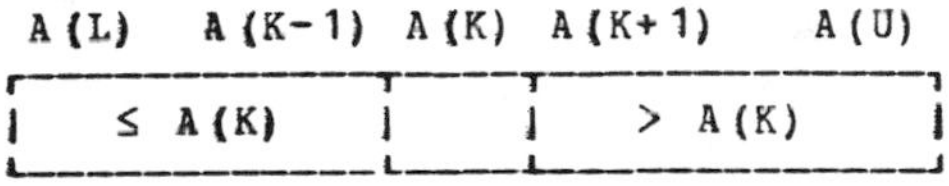

```
 A(L)   A(K-1) A(K) A(K+1)    A(U)
┌──────────────┬────┬──────────────┐
│   ≤ A(K)     │    │   > A(K)     │
└──────────────┴────┴──────────────┘
```

The value initially in A(L) will end up in A(K); this is used as the "pivot" value. The main loop has the invariant relation:

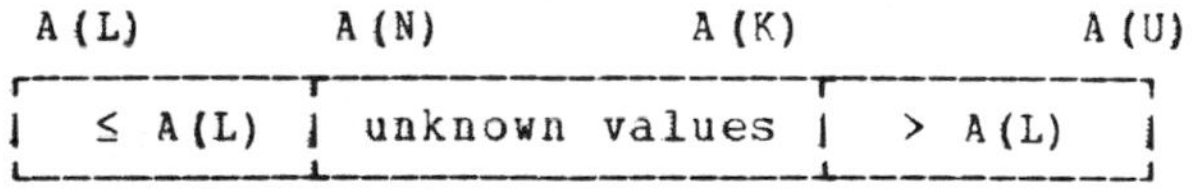

```
 A(L)        A(N)            A(K)          A(U)
┌──────────┬───────────────────┬───────────┐
│  ≤ A(L)  │  unknown values   │  > A(L)   │
└──────────┴───────────────────┴───────────┘
```

When the loop halts the array looks like

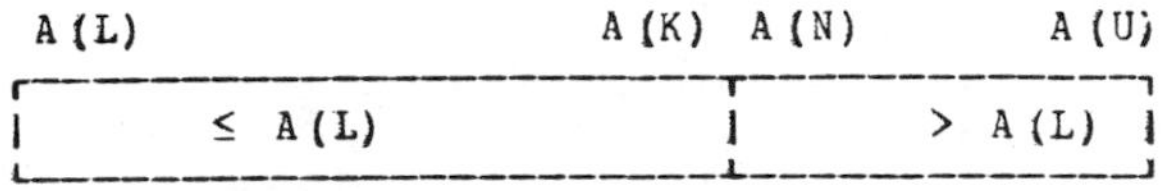

```
 A(L)                      A(K) A(N)        A(U)
┌────────────────────────────┬──────────────┐
│         ≤ A(L)             │      > A(L)  │
└────────────────────────────┴──────────────┘
```

and we need only swap values of A(L) and A(K) to yield the desired result.

```
N = L + 1;
K = U;
NLEQK: DO WHILE (N <= K);
   /** DECREASE K OR INCREASE N, KEEPING RELATION INVARIANT*/
       IF A(N) <= A(L)
           THEN N = N + 1;
           ELSE DO;
               DO WHILE (A(K) > A(L));
                   K = K - 1;
                   END;
               IF N < K
                   THEN DO;
                       Swap A(N) and A(K)
                       N = N + 1;
                       K = K - 1;
                       END;
               END;
   END NLEQK;
Swap A(L) and A(K);
```

7.5 Invariant Relations in Everyday Programming

Invariant relations should also be used in *developing* loops; in getting ideas about how an algorithm should work. Often, the use of an invariant relation can lead to a more efficient algorithm. Using an invariant relation gets us away from thinking about how values change, which is hard to comprehend, and instead gets us to think about how relations about values remain the same, which is easier.

Suppose we have a problem that we feel will be solved by some sort of loop. We have some idea of how the loop will work, but the details are not clear. One good way of developing the loop is the following:

1. Write down a statement or picture of what the loop should do -- of the result assertion.

2. Write down a statement or picture of what is known initially.

3. Tie the above two statements together with a more general statement that has these two as extreme cases. This should turn out to be the necessary invariant relation.

4. Now develop the initialization, the loop condition, and the body of the loop from the invariant relation.

Of course, it is a trial and error process and these four steps will be repeated, in various orders, until the final loop emerges. But there is a significant difference between this and the typical way of developing a loop.

The typical loop is programmed by test cases. The programmer makes up some sample data and develops the program for it. He then makes up another set of sample data and modifies his algorithm to fit it. This process is repeated until the programmer finally "feels" his program is correct. The chances are it is not, because he has developed it from a finite number of test cases.

The method outlined above has nothing to do with isolated test cases. It is more general because it works with relations about the variables, and not the values of the variables themselves. Thus, any set of data that satisfies the initial relations should be executed correctly.

The following example is due to E. W. Dijkstra:

> Problem. An array A(1:N), N≥1, containing only values 1, 2, and 3, is to be sorted. Values of the array may be changed only by using the command "Swap A(I) and A(J)".

We could of course use a general sort algorithm, but we may be able to take advantage of the restricted values of A to develop a more efficient algorithm.

Initially the array looks like the left diagram below. When the algorithm has finished, it must look like the right diagram. These two are the statements spoken of in the first two steps of the development process. In the diagram, "U" represents an unknown value.

```
A(1)  A(N)          A(1)                A(N)
┌──────────┐       ┌────────┬────────┬────────┐
|   U's    |       |   1's  |  2's   |  3's   |
└──────────┘       └────────┴────────┴────────┘
```

It seems logical to have a WHILE loop that at each iteration puts one value into its correct partition, and a possible candidate for the general picture is:

```
A(1)            A(N1)           A(N2)           A(U)     A(N)
┌───────────────┬───────────────┬───────────────┬──────────────┐
|      1's      |      2's      |      3's      |     U's      |
└───────────────┴───────────────┴───────────────┴──────────────┘
```

where N1 is the index of the first value that is not a 1,
N2 is the index of the first value that is not a 1 or a 2,
U is the index of the first unknown value.

This yields the simple algorithm:

```
N1, N2, U = 1;
DO WHILE (U <= N);
    Determine partition for A(U) and put A(U) into it;
    END;
```

Moving A(U) into its partition may require two swaps. For example, if A(U) is 1, we must first swap A(U) with A(N2) and then swap A(N2) with A(N1). How can we reduce the number of swaps to at most 1 at each iteration? Let us change the general picture to the following, where the partition of unknowns now appears between the 2's and 3's:

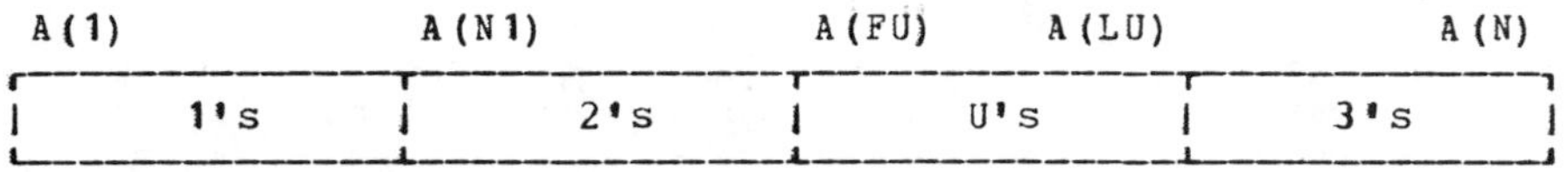

```
A(1)             A(N1)            A(FU)     A(LU)            A(N)
┌────────────────┬────────────────┬────────────────┬────────────────┐
│      1's       │      2's       │      U's       │      3's       │
└────────────────┴────────────────┴────────────────┴────────────────┘
```

where N1 is the index of the first non-1,
FU is the index of the first unknown,
LU is the index of the last unknown.

Using this relation we end up with the following algorithm.

```
N1, FU = 1;
LU = N;
DIJK: DO WHILE (FU <= LU);
    /** DETERMINE PARTITION FOR A(FU) AND PUT IN PLACE; */
        SELECT;
            WHEN A(FU) = 1 DO;
                Swap A(N1) and A(FU)
                FU = FU + 1;
                N1 = N1 + 1;
                END;
            WHEN A(FU) = 2
                FU = FU + 1;
            WHEN A(FU) = 3 DO;
                Sway A(FU) and A(LU)
                LU = LU - 1;
                END;
            OTHERWISE;
            END;
    END DIJK;
```

This is much more efficient than general sorting algorithms. In terms that are developed in Section VI.2 this is said to be a "linear" algorithm. The loop is iterated N times, and each iteration requires at most two comparisons and one interchange.

A subtle point should be noted about the definition of the variables. N1 was defined as the index of the first non-1, and was therefore initialized to 1. If we had defined N1 to be the index of the first 2, we would have had to initialize N1 to 0 since there are no 2's initially, just U's. The algorithm would have been more complicated. From the picture, we cannot tell whether N1 is the first 2 or the first non-1, and we must be careful to write down exactly what we mean.

7.6 Automatic Verification of Correctness

Empirical testing is such an inadequate way of positively establishing the correctness of a program that there is considerable research in process seeking a viable alternative. Essentially what is sought is some way of treating the text of a program as a mathematical argument, from which certain conclusions can be drawn without resorting to any actual execution of the program. These conclusions would ideally establish properties of a program that do not depend upon any particular set of data, hence would hold for all possible executions of the program.

The most desirable property to establish for a program is obviously "correctness". But as we pointed out in Section 1.1, correctness is not even easy to define, let alone prove. Except in the limited sense of syntactic correctness one cannot say that a program is correct without knowing precisely what the program is supposed to do. Essentially the issue comes down to the following:

1. The task is formally specified. This is usually done by giving precise, detailed relations P and R that describe the input and output -- in the notation of Section 7.5, the program must satisfy ¦P¦ program ¦R¦.

2. The program is judged correct if and only if it is formally proven that ¦P¦ program ¦R¦ does indeed hold.

Several approaches are being explored. They have in common reliance upon the computer to aid in the proof process. Most approaches involve some scheme for automatically generating a proof. A more modest approach is to use the computer only to verify a proof that is supplied by the programmer. The hypothesis is that verification of a given proof may be just within the limits of current capability, while the automatic generation of a proof may well be just beyond the current state of the art. This approach does require the programmer to generate a formal proof for his program.

Such a verification effort has been a part of the PL/CS project from the start. One of the principal objectives in defining the PL/CS language was to provide a hospitable language vehicle for practical verification. This was of paramount concern in deciding upon the various restrictions upon the use of PL/CS constructions (relative to the corresponding PL/I form). These restrictions materially simplify the task of an automatic verifier. A prototype Verifier has been written and is being used experimentally in computer science classes at Cornell. It does not yet handle the entire PL/CS language, and the "proof language" is such that writing the proof is more difficult than writing the program. The proof language is in the form of generalizations of the PL/CS assertions described in Section 5.5.

By the time the Verifier accepts a program and proof as equivalent (usually the proof, as well as the program, needs some corrections to achieve this) a fairly strong statement of correctness can be made. But it is not yet clear whether this is just a pedagogical device to give a student deeper understanding of programming or a practical tool that could someday be used routinely to verify the correctness of real programs. The Verifier's power is gradually being increased, and the proof language is being simplified.

The PL/CS Verifier is described in detail in <u>A Programming Logic</u> by Constable and O'Donnell.

Section 7 Exercises

1. Indicate whether the following statements are true or false. All variables are assumed to be FIXED.

a) |I is even| I = FLOOR(I/2E0); |I is even|

b) |I is negative| I = I*I; |I is non-negative|

c) |Z = A**B & A and B are integers| B = B/2E0; A = A*A;
|Z = A**B & A and B are integers|

d) |true| DO WHILE(I is even); I = I/2E0; END; |I is odd|

e) |I > 0| I = FLOOR(I/2E0); I = I-1; |I ≥ 0|

f) |N > 0| SUM=1; DO I = 2 TO N BY 1; SUM = SUM*I; END;
|SUM=N!|

g) |N ≥ 0 & SUM = N!| N = N+1; SUM = SUM*N; |SUM = N!|

2. Consider the following program segment written to search A(1:N) for a value X and set J accordingly. The only difference between this segment and the binary search segment of Section 7.3 is in the statement that throws away half of the list. Prove whether the program segment is correct or incorrect, and if incorrect, indicate for what initial values it will not work.

```
FIRST = 1;
LAST = N;
DO WHILE (FIRST <= LAST);
     J = FLOOR((FIRST+LAST)/2E0);
     IF A(J) = X
        THEN GOTO TERM_SEARCH;
     IF A(J) < X
        THEN FIRST = J;
        ELSE LAST = J;
     END;
J = 0;
TERM_SEARCH:;
```

3. For each of the following algorithms, write down what the result of execution of each loop is, and then write down the invariant relation that together with ¬c indicates that the loop executes correctly.

a)
```
/** REVERSE THE VALUES OF A(1:N).  N >= 1.  */
    LOWER = 1;
    UPPER = N;
    DO WHILE (LOWER < UPPER);
        Swap values of A(LOWER) and A(UPPER);
        LOWER = LOWER + 1;
        UPPER = UPPER - 1;
        END;
```

b)
```
/** I > 2 AND I IS ODD.  */
/** STORE 1 IN P IF I IS PRIME; 0 OTHERWISE.  */
    S = SQRT(I);
    J = 3;
    DO WHILE(J <= S & MOD(I,J) ¬= 0);
        J = J + 2;
        END;
    IF MOD(I,J) ¬= 0
        THEN P = 1;
        ELSE P = 0;
```

4. A game is played by two players on a grid of points (of any size) as shown below.

```
.  .  .  .  .  .  .  .  .
.  .  .  .  .  .  .  .  .
.  .  .  .  .  .  .  .  .
.  .  .  .  .  .  .  .  .
```

Player A first draws a horizontal or a vertical solid line between any two adjacent points. Then player B draws a dotted horizontal or vertical line. This process continues until there are no more lines to fill in. The game can thus be pictured as execution of the loop

```
DO WHILE (there exists another move );
   Player A draws | or - ;
   Player B draws : or .. ;
   END;
```

The object of the game is for player A to draw a closed curve consisting of only solid lines, while B wins if he can prevent A from drawing a closed curve.

Does there exist an algorithm for player B's move so that he can always win? If so, give it. This problem is most easily solved by considering an invariant relation of the loop that implies that A has not drawn his closed curve.

5. Write algorithms for the following problems. Each will be a simple loop, together with some initialization statements and the like. This loop should be developed from an invariant relation. That is, try to discover the relation first, then write the loop, not the other way around.

a) The GCD of two positive integers A and B, written GCD(A,B), is the greatest positive integer that divides them both evenly. Write a program to calculate the GCD of A and B. You may use the MOD function. The following facts about GCDs should help. First, GCD(A,B) = GCD(B,A). Second, if A = p·B where p is an integer greater than 0, then of course B is the GCD of A and B. Third, if

$$A = p \cdot B + r \qquad \text{where } p \geq 0 \text{ and } 0 < r < B,$$

and p and r are integers, then GCD(A,B) = GCD(B,r). This follows easily by noting that any divisor of A and B must also divide r.

Hint: Note that GCD(A,B) = GCD(B,r). Suppose we initialize variables X and Y to A and B respectively. Then GCD(X,Y) = GCD(A,B). Then making the assignments X=Y; Y=r; does not change this relation GCD(X,Y) = GCD(A,B).

b) A(1:K) and A(K+1:N) are each sorted in ascending order. Write an algorithm that sorts the whole array in linear time. (It will probably be a single loop.) You may use an extra array which has no more than K elements.

c) An array TEM(1:100) contains 100 temperatures. Print the number of temperatures above 100 and the number below 32.

Part VI
Performance Evaluation

We provide an overview of the criteria by which algorithms can be evaluated and compared, and explain in some detail how to measure both the speed and space needs of a program.

Programs can be judged on various grounds, and a programmer must know what criteria are appropriate for each program he writes. Among possible measures of comparison are:

1. Execution speed
2. Space (in computer memory during execution)
3. Readability and documentation
4. Ease of subsequent modification
5. Time needed to complete the project.

Note that neither <u>correctness</u> nor <u>reliability</u> is on the list. The list is concerned with comparing programs that are both correct and reliable. Those criteria are dominatingly important.

The criteria usually mentioned as important are execution speed and space, and we discuss these in detail. Quite often, however, readability and ease of modification are the main factors. This happens in industry, for example, where programs are routinely modified after completion, usually by someone other than the original programmer.

Comments, indenting rules, naming conventions, and the like should concern the programmer <u>during</u> program development, and not just after the program is "checked out". A programmer who documents his program after it is written rarely documents well.

Some programmers feel that documentation is a waste of time, and would rather spend their time in trying to make a program faster. They feel their job is to write the fastest program they can contrive. This often leads to the use of obscure programming tricks, which turn out to be counter-productive because of the time necessary for somebody else to understand them when modifying the program later. Local cleverness is not the dominant source of execution speed; usually a good logical strategy will outperform a collection of tricky tactics.

Section 1 Measuring Storage Space

On most current computers, memory consists of entities called "bytes". Each byte consists of 8 bits, where a bit is a binary digit -- 0 or 1. Each byte stores one character of information. (Some computers consider memory to consist of "words", where each word consists of a fixed number of bytes -- usually 1, 2 or 4.)

Memory sizes today range from 1000 to more than ten million bytes. Memories are usually described in terms of kilobytes (thousands of bytes) or megabytes (millions of bytes). Thus a "128K" computer is one with 128,000 bytes of main memory.

The main memory of most computers is supplemented by some form of secondary memory -- usually magnetic discs or tapes. Secondary memory is much larger, but a computer does not operate directly in secondary memory. Information must be copied into main memory before it can be used, so our immediate concern is for the main memory requirements of a program. (See Part VIII for further consideration of secondary memory.)

A program being executed resides in main memory, and main memory is also required for the variables, arrays and structures for that program. The space required depends somewhat on the programming language being used, and varies significantly with the compiler being used. As a specific example, consider the memory requirements for PL/C. Space for the program itself is divided into two areas:

1. An area of fixed size (approximately 70K) for the library of built-in functions, routines to service input and output, and error monitoring and repair routines.

2. An area of variable size to hold the compiled program. The space required to hold each statement depends on the statement type and length, but an average of 100 bytes per statement is a reasonable estimate.

This means that a program of 200 statements needs approximately 90K.

Space for scalar variables in PL/C is allocated as follows:

a FLOAT variable	requires 8 bytes
a FIXED variable	requires 8 bytes
a CHAR (m) VARYING variable	requires 8+m bytes
a BIT (1) variable	requires 9 bytes.

An array with n elements requires n times as much space as a scalar variable of the same type. Space for a structure is simply the sum of the space required for the individual scalars and arrays that constitute the structure.

From these numbers it should be obvious that the space requirement for scalar variables is trivial -- even for large programs. It makes no sense to economize on the number of such variables by reusing the same local variable in different sections of a program. This just makes the role of each variable less clear and makes the program harder to read.

On the other hand, space for arrays is a concern. You can easily declare arrays that require more space than is available. For example:

```
DECLARE (DECK(100)) CHAR (80) VARYING;
```

Each element of the array requires 88 bytes, so the entire array is almost 9K of memory. Or suppose you are solving large sets of simultaneous equations and want two copies of a matrix of coefficients:

```
DECLARE (CF1(200, 200), CF2(200, 200)) FLOAT;
```

This requires more than a half-million bytes of memory.

The conclusion is that you must be concerned with <u>total array space</u>, and this concern must be exercised when you are choosing an algorithm for the problem. For example, consider the list searching problem described in Section III.3.2. The data list consisted of an initial list of numbers, followed by a list of inquiries. The initial list <u>had</u> to be loaded into an array, so the space available established a limit on the length of the initial list that could be handled. The inquiries <u>could</u> have been loaded into an array before processing, but didn't need to be. The problem requirements were such that inquiries could be read and processed <u>one at a time</u>. Hence, if we had chosen an algorithm that loaded the inquiries into an array before processing, we could have produced a program that was correct, clear, and all other good things, but because the algorithm was unnecessarily inefficient in its use of memory space, the program would have an unnecessary limit on the number of inquiries that it could handle.

For a large program with several procedures, PL/I is automatically efficient in its management of space for variables and arrays. Except for EXTERNAL and STATIC variables, space is allocated for the variables of a particular procedure <u>only while that procedure is being executed</u>. In other words, the variable space for all procedures of the program does not need to exist simultaneously. The same space is automatically reused for different variables, depending upon which procedure is being executed. Moreover, the "dynamic dimensioning" technique (Section IV.4.1) allows arrays to be allocated <u>exactly the required space</u>, without wasting space by having to "over-dimension".

Section 2 Measuring Speed of Execution

2.1 Counting Basic Steps

One way to compare the speed of two programs is to run them with the same data and compare the resulting execution times. This is often done for large programs. For example, we usually judge a compiler (which is just a program) by how many cards or statements it compiles per second. Students often compare output to see whose program compiled faster and whose executed faster.

However, it is often necessary to compare algorithms with respect to speed even before they have been programmed. We need to do this to choose between alternative algorithms during program development. Moreover, these measures of speed should be as independent as possible of the particular machine the algorithm will be run on; they should be attributed only to the algorithm itself.

The usual method is to count the number of basic steps the algorithm executes, as a function of the "size of the input". A basic step is a step whose execution time does not depend on the values of the variables used in it; one whose execution time is essentially the same for any input. For example, execution time of the statement A = 3+B; is the same no matter what the value of simple variable B. Basic steps in PL/I are (but see exercise 12):

1. Assignment statement,
2. PUT and GET statements (with a list of simple and subscripted variables),
3. Procedure call (not the execution of the procedure itself, but the act of calling it),
4. Termination statement (RETURN, LEAVE, or a GOTO used to terminate a subalgorithm),
5. Null statement,
6. The test in a WHILE loop or conditional statement.

In addition,

7. A "DO I = ..." loop is considered as the WHILE loop by which it is defined (see Section I.7.2.1).

As a first illustration, consider the following two loops:

```
        I = 1;                         For N >= 1, 4*N+2 basic
(2.1a)  DO WHILE(I <= N);              steps are executed (the test
            X = X + A(I);              I<=N N+1 times and the 3
            X = X + B(I);              statements in the body
            I = I + 1;                 N times)
            END;


(2.1b)  I = 1;                         For N >= 1, 3*N+2 basic steps
        DO WHILE (I <= N);             are executed (the test I<=N
            X = X + A(I) + B(I);       N+1 times; the two statements
            I = I+1;                   in the body N times)
            END;
```

Certainly, different basic steps take different times to execute, and by only counting basic steps we make some errors in estimating the execution time of programs. Segments (2.1a) and (2.1b) clearly perform the same task in essentially the same way, and yet we say that one uses 4*N+2 basic steps and the other 3*N+2. We would <u>like</u> to say that the two perform essentially the same, and will subsequently extend our terminology to that effect. But first let us look at more important differences that might occur in execution times.

Suppose we want to process an array A(1:N) in some manner. We have seven different algorithms to carry out that process. (2.1c) gives the number of basic steps executed in each as a function of N, the size of the array.

	Algorithm	Number of basic steps executed
	A1	SQRT(N)
	A2	N+5
(2.1c)	A3	2*N
	A4	N^2
	A5	N^2+N
	A6	N^3
	A7	2**N

We notice immediately that for "very small" N any of these algorithms can be used. If we assume each basic step takes roughly .0001 seconds to execute, for N=10 the fastest algorithm A1 takes .0003 seconds while the slowest takes .1024. Typically, when comparing the speeds of algorithms, we are not interested in execution times for small inputs, but only for large inputs. With small amounts of data almost any algorithm will do. As the amount or size of the data increases, we have to be more careful about which algorithm we use. Figure 1 illustrates this well.

Algorithm A1 is clearly the best (with respect to time), but any of the first three seem reasonable. For large values of N, A2 and A3 aren't too different (one is twice as fast as the other), and we might use other criteria besides time to choose between them. Algorithms A4 and A5 seem all right for "moderately sized" input, but as N increases past 1000 they become useless. Algorithms A6 and A7 clearly cannot be used for moderate values of N.

algorithm	N = 20	N = 50	N = 100	N = 1000
A1	.0004 sec	.0007 sec	.0010 sec	.0032 sec
A2	.0025 sec	.0055 sec	.0105 sec	.1005 sec
A3	.0040 sec	.0100 sec	.0200 sec	.2000 sec
A4	.0400 sec	.2500 sec	1.000 sec	100 sec
A5	.0420 sec	.2550 sec	1.010 sec	100.1 sec
A6	.8 sec	12.5 sec	100 sec	28 hrs
A7	105 sec	3570 yrs	$4*10^{10}$ yrs	-----

Figure 1. Amount of Time Required as a Function of N

Consider A4 and A5. For large N they perform essentially the same; the term N in N^2+N has little effect when N is large. We next introduce terminology that puts A4 and A5 in the same category.

2.2 The Order of Execution Time

Let f(n) and g(n) be functions. We say that

(2.2a) f(n) is of order g(n), written O(g(n)), if there is a constant c > 0 such that, for all (except possibly a finite number of) positive values of n,

$$f(n) <= c*g(n).$$

Example 1. Let f(n) = n+5 and g(n)=n. Let c=5. Then n+5 = f(n) <= 5*g(n) = 5*n for n=1,2,3,... Hence n+5 is O(n).

Example 2. Let f(n) = 2*n+5 and g(n) = n. Let c = 7. Then 2*n+5 <= 7*n for n=1,2,3,... Hence 2*n+5 is O(n).

Example 3. Let f(n) = $(1/2)*n^2+n$ and g(n) = n^2. Let c = 2. Then $(1/2)*n^2+n <= 2*n^2$, for n = 1,2,3,... Hence $(1/2)*n^2+n$ is $O(n^2)$.

If f(N) is the number of basic steps executed for a program with "input size" N, and if g(N) satisfies the above definition, then the following are equivalent:

1. The running time is order g(N),

2. The running time is O(g(N)),

3. It's an order g(N) algorithm.

We give below a table of typical execution time orders that seem to crop up in programming, in increasing size. (Other orders occur, but not so often.) When we compare two programs, with respect to time, that have different orders, all other things being equal we choose the one with smaller order. Only when comparing algorithms with the same order should we worry about the constant involved. When comparing 4*N with $1/2*N^2$, we choose the 4*N algorithm; when choosing between 4*N and 1/2*N we choose the 1/2*N algorithm.

Order	term used
constant	fixed time (it contains only basic steps)
LOG2(N)	logarithmic algorithm (see Section 2.4)
SQRT(N)	
N	linear algorithm
N*LOG2(N)	
N*SQRT(N)	
N^2	quadratic (or N^2) algorithm
N^3	cubic (or N^3) algorithm
2**N	exponential algorithm
N!	factorial algorithm

Figure 2. Typical Execution Time Orders

Two other phrases used often are

1. The algorithm runs in time proportional to g(N),

2. Execution takes time proportional to g(N).

The meaning of "f(N) is proportional to g(N)" is that f(N) is of order g(N) <u>and</u> g(N) is of order f(N). The difference between "f(N) is of order g(N)" and "f(N) is proportional to g(N)" is a fine one, which we will largely ignore. As an example, we know that

f(n) = n+5 is of order g(n) = n

and

g(n) = n is of order f(n) = n+5.

Hence

f(n) = n+5 is proportional to g(n) = n.

But

f(n) = n+5 is also of order $g(n) = n^2$

while

$g(n) = n^2$ is <u>not</u> of order f(n) = n+5.

2.3 Worst Case Versus Average Case Analysis

Consider the problem of finding a value X in an array B(1:N), with N ≥ 1. We want to store in J an integer so that B(J) = X, and if no such integer exists, we want to store 0 in J:

```
J = 1;
DO WHILE (J <= N);
    IF B(J) = X
       THEN GOTO TERM_LINEAR_SEARCH;
    J = J + 1;
    END;
J = 0;
TERM_LINEAR_SEARCH:;
```

If X is not in array B(1:N), then the algorithm executes at most 3*N+4 basic steps. If X is in the array, the algorithm executes fewer basic steps. Thus in the worst case linear search is an order N, or linear algorithm.

Sometimes we would rather know the average number of basic steps executed if we ran the algorithm a large number of times with different data. This average is also called the "expected" number, but the word "expected" is used in a special statistical sense (meaning average) and not with the usual English meaning. Consider linear search, assuming that X is in the list. If the values of B(1:N) are assumed to be "randomly" chosen, then X has an equal probability of appearing in any of the elements B(I). On the average then, we may expect to look halfway through the list before finding X, executing roughly 3*(N/2) basic steps, which is still linear.

If X may not be in the list, we can expect more than 3*(N/2) basic steps -- how many more depends on the probability that X doesn't appear. However, the algorithm is still linear on the average, since it is linear for the worst case. This is in fact why the algorithm is called "linear" search.

For linear search then, both a worst case and average case analysis show that the algorithm is linear in the size of the input. This is not always the case, and frequently the average speed is much better than the worst speed. Which analysis should we choose? This depends in part on how easy it is for us to compute. In general, average case analysis is much harder because it requires estimates of various probabilities, and involves more complex calculations. Worst case analysis is often quite easy; we need just identify the worst case data and count how many operations the algorithm executes with that data. It may however not be a realistic estimate, since the worst case may never arise with "real" input.

2.4 Analysis of Binary Search: Logarithms

We can perform a search for a value X more efficiently than linear search if the array B(1:N) is already sorted into ascending or descending order. We do this ourselves whenever we look up a name in the telephone book. We don't begin at the beginning of the telephone book, but we turn roughly to where the name we want is, and decide by that entry which half of the book to continue looking in. Then we repeat the process with just this half of the telephone book.

We can write down this algorithm as follows, where at each iteration we actually look in the middle of the list where we expect to find the name:

```
         /* LOOK FOR X IN B(1:N), SET J TO ITS INDEX */
         /* IF X IS NOT IN B(1:N), SET J TO 0.  */
            Let the list to be searched be B(1:N);
            DO WHILE (the list to be searched is not empty);
                 J = index of middle entry of list;
                 IF B(J) = X
(2.4a)                THEN GOTO TERM_SEARCH;
                 IF B(J) < X
                      THEN discard first half of list, including B(J);
                      ELSE discard second half of list, including B(J);
                 END;
            J = 0; /* X IS NOT IN THE LIST */
            TERM_SEARCH:;
```

To describe the list to be searched we use two variables FIRST and LAST. At any time during execution, the list still to be searched is B(FIRST:LAST). Thus the list is not empty if FIRST <= LAST. With this data refinement, (2.4a) is easily translated into the following PL/I algorithm:

```
              FIRST = 1;      /* SEARCH WHOLE LIST B(1:N) */
              LAST = N;
              DO  WHILE (FIRST <= LAST); /* DO WHILE LIST NOT EMPTY */
                  J = FLOOR((FIRST+LAST)/2); /* J = MIDDLE ENTRY */
(2.4b)            IF B(J) = X
                     THEN GOTO TERM_SEARCH;
                  /** DISCARD HALF OF LIST NOT CONTAINING X */
                       IF B(J) < X
                          THEN FIRST = J+1;
                          ELSE LAST = J-1;
                  END;
              J = 0; /* X IS NOT IN LIST */
              TERM_SEARCH:;
```

Let us perform a worst case analysis of (2.4b). Clearly the worst case arises when the loop iterates as often as possible, and this is the case when X is not in the list B(1:N). In this case, 5*i+5 basic steps are executed, where i is the number of times the loop body is executed.

If N = 1, the loop body is executed once, because the whole list B(1:1) is discarded if B(1) ¬= X. If N = 2, the first execution of the loop body discards at least half the list, leaving at most one element in it. Since we know that the loop body executes only once if N = 1, we see that for N = 2 the loop body is executed at most twice. Similarly, if 2<N≤4 the loop body is executed at most 3 times, and if 4<N≤8 the loop body is executed at most 4 times.

Table (2.4c) gives a list of possible values of N, all powers of 2, and the corresponding number of loop iterations that can occur. We see that if N is between 2**(n-1) and 2**n for an integer n, then the loop iterates <u>at most</u> <u>n+1</u> times. Hence the number of basic steps executed is no more than 5+5*(n+1).

(2.4c)

N	number of iterations
1 = 2^0	1
2 = 2^1	2
4 = 2^2	3
8 = 2^3	4
16 = 2^4	5
32 = 2^5	6
64 = 2^6	7

If N = 2**n, then n is called <u>the logarithm to the base 2 of N</u>. It is written <u>LOG2(N)</u>. (LOG2 is also a built-in function in PL/I and is written this way.) Table (2.4d) contains some values of N and corresponding logarithms.

What is LOG2(9)? It lies somewhere between 3 and 4, as you can see from table (2.4d). Exactly where it is doesn't really matter from our point of view, and we will never ask you to compute it. We just don't need to. What <u>is</u> important is to note that the function LOG2(N) "grows much more slowly" than N itself. When N = 1, LOG2(N) is quite close to it, but as N grows to 1024, LOG2(N) only grows to 10. Thus an algorithm that performs only LOG2(N) operations for input of size N is far superior in speed to an equivalent linear algorithm.

(2.4d)

N	LOG2(N)	reason
1	0	1 = 2^0
2	1	2 = 2^1
4	2	4 = 2^2
8	3	8 = 2^3
16	4	16 = 2^4
256	8	256 = 2^8
1024	10	1024 = 2^{10}
32768	15	32768 = 2^{15}

The binary search algorithm runs in time proportional to LOG2(N). This yields a tremendous saving over the linear search. For example, if N = 32,768, linear search executes <u>on the average</u> over 49,152 basic steps, while binary search executes <u>at most</u> 85 steps! If a list is sorted, and if it contains over 20 elements, say, then the crucial difference here is that linear search is a linear algorithm while binary search is logarithmic.

2.5 Analysis of Simple Program Segments

2.5.1 A Program Segment to Test Primeness

An integer greater than 1 is <u>prime</u> if it is exactly divisible only by 1 and itself. The first few primes are 2, 3, 5, 7, 11, 13, 17, 19, 23, 29, 31. Segment (2.5a) tests whether a positive integer > 2 is prime. Assuming the loop condition can be implemented by a basic step (which it can), we see that the algorithm performs at most 4+2*(N-2) basic steps to test the primeness of N, and is thus linear.

(2.5a)

```
/* N CONTAINS AN INTEGER > 2. STORE 1 IN ANS IF N IS A*/
/* PRIME NUMBER, 0 OTHERWISE. ALGORITHM TAKES AT MOST */
/* 4 + 2*(N-2) STEPS, AND IS THUS LINEAR */
    I = 2;
    DO WHILE ((I < N) & (I does not divide N));
        I = I+1;
        END;
    IF I = N
       THEN ANS = 1;
       ELSE ANS = 0;
```

We see two ways to improve this algorithm. First note that the program tests whether 2, 4, 6, 8, ... all divide N. Obviously, if 2 does not divide N, then no even number will. This inefficiency is eliminated in algorithm (2.5b). Secondly, suppose a number J greater than SQRT(N) divides N. Then so does the number

N / J

which is <u>less than</u> SQRT(N). Hence it is not necessary to test integers greater than SQRT(N) to see if they divide N. This change is made in (2.5c).

Which algorithm is better, (2.5b) or (2.5c)? (2.5b) cuts the worst case execution time in half, but note that it is still <u>linear</u>. Algorithm (2.5c) executes at most 4+2*(SQRT(N)-2) basic steps and is thus an O(SQRT(N)) algorithm. Now if N>10,000 and prime, (2.5b) executes over 10,000 basic steps, while (2.5c) executes around 200.

```
        /* N CONTAINS AN INTEGER > 2. STORE 1 IN ANS IF N IS A*/
        /* PRIME NUMBER, 0 OTHERWISE. ALGORITHM TAKES AT MOST */
        /* 5 + 2*(N/2 - 2) STEPS AND IS THUS LINEAR. */
        IF 2 divides N
            THEN ANS = 0;
            ELSE DO;
                I = 3;
(2.5b)          DO WHILE((I<N)&(I does not divide N));
                    I = I+2;
                    END;
                IF I = N
                    THEN ANS = 1;
                    ELSE ANS = 0;
                END;
```

```
        /* N CONTAINS AN INTEGER > 2. STORE 1 IN ANS IF N IS A*/
        /* PRIME NUMBER, 0 OTHERWISE. ALGORITHM TAKES AT MOST */
        /* 4+2*(SQRT(N)-2) STEPS AND IS THUS 0(SQRT(N)).  */
            I = 2;
            SQRTN = SQRT(N);
            DO WHILE ((I < SQRTN) & (I does not divide N));
(2.5c)          I = I+1;
                END;
            IF I divides N
                THEN ANS = 1;
                ELSE ANS = 0;
```

2.5.2 Generating a List of Unique Numbers

Supppose the input consists of a list of N integers (N is already initialized), and we want to store these integers in an array B but with each unique integer appearing only once. Thus if N = 8 and the list is

3 8 12 8 6 5 8 3

then upon termination of the algorithm B should contain

3 8 12 6 5 - - -

where "-" indicates that the value in that position is immaterial. Let us also assume that a variable M should contain the number of unique integers in B upon termination. A simple program segment to do this is

```
        M = 0;          /* NO INTEGERS IN B YET */
        DO I = 1 TO N BY 1;
            GET LIST (INT);
(2.5d)      Search B(1:M) for INT and set J to 1 if found,
                   to 0 otherwise;
            IF J = 0
                THEN DO;
                    M = M + 1;
                    B(M) = INT;
                    END;
            END;
```

The operation Search B(1:M) will probably be done by linear search, since the array is not sorted. (Be careful in writing this search, however, since it must work when M = 0.) Thus each execution of "Search" takes time proportional to the current value of M.

Execution of each of the other statements in the loop body takes essentially a constant time, so that, for M sufficiently large, execution of the loop body alone is proportional to M.

The worst case arises when the search is as slow as possible at each iteration of the loop, and this occurs when the value being searched for is not in the list. Hence the worst case arises when all N input numbers are different. For I=1 the search takes time proportional to 0; for I=2 it takes time proportional to 1, for I=3, 2 and so on. Thus the total search time is proportional to

$$0 + 1 + 2 + \ldots + (N-1) \quad = \quad N(N-1)/2 \quad = \quad N^2/2 - N/2$$

In the worst case, execution time is proportional to N^2.

Now suppose that there are only M different integers in the original list of N integers. We leave it to the reader to show that the worst case running time is O(N*M).

2.5.3 <u>Printing Names in Alphabetical Order, Without Duplicates</u>

Consider the following problem:

> The input is a list of roughly 5000 names of people. Some names, say about 30% of them, are duplicates. The program should read in these names and print them out in alphabetical order, with each different name appearing only once. (This problem occurs frequently. For example the list might be a mailing list, a list of alumni and their addresses, a list of students and their courses, where each student's name appears once for each course, and so on.)

Recall that the last example (2.5d) was somewhat similar. One solution to this problem consists of first making up the list of unduplicated names as in (2.5d), then sorting the list, and then printing it. The algorithm is:

```
        S1: Read in list and delete
             duplicates (algorithm (2.5d)).
(2.5e)  S2: Sort the list.
        S3: Print the list.
```

This would probably be our first thought, since it is related to a problem just studied. However, we know that S1 runs in time proportional to M*N (if there are M unique names and N total names), which is roughly .70N since about 30 percent of the names are duplicates. Let us assume we can sort the list in time proportional to N*LOG2(N). This can be done by several algorithms, for example heap sort of Section 2.7 and Quicksort in Section V.7.4. We show below the statements of (2.5e) together with their execution time orders as functions of the size of the input. Clearly the most time is spent in executing S1 and we should look for a more efficient way of performing it.

<u>Statement</u>	S1	S2	S3
<u>Time</u>	M*N	M*LOG2(M)	M

Suppose we leave all names in the list, including duplicates, then sort using the N*LOG2(N) heap sort, and then print:

```
       Read names into list B.
(2.5f) Sort B.
       Print B, but avoid printing duplicates.
```

Reading names into the list is now of order N, the number of names; sorting is of order N*LOG2(N); and we should be able to print B as stated in linear time (with respect to N), since all duplicates of one name now appear together in the sorted list. Hence sorting dominates and the whole algorithm runs in time N*LOG2(N). This is much faster than (2.5e).

A third possibility exists. Suppose after reading each new name we immediately sort B:

```
M = 0;
DO I = 1 TO N BY 1;
    Read one name into NAME
    Search sorted list B(1:M) for NAME
    IF NAME not in list
        THEN insert NAME into proper place in B(1:M);
    END;
Print B
```

This may seem like a good idea, but we leave it to you to show that the total time spent inserting names into their proper places will be of order M^2 and thus not very attractive. The <u>searching</u> can be performed by binary search, but the <u>insertion</u> will be too slow. This algorithm is called "insertion sort".

2.6 A More Complicated Example: KWIC Index

We will discuss the development of a program to produce a "KWIC Index" as we did with other examples in Section III.2 but now we can pay more attention to the choice of an efficient algorithm. It is also a good example of several points discussed in III.4:

1. Using notation to fit the problem,
2. The importance of analyzing all possibilities for a refinement, and
3. The importance of knowing which operations are to be performed on a data structure before deciding on its representation.

Without a top-down development, or at least a clear description of the program at a high level, it would be difficult to even *see* that there are so many choices to choose from.

2.6.1 The Problem and a First Refinement

(2.6.1a) *KWIC Index*. KWIC stands for "KeyWord In Context". Its meaning is as follows: suppose we have a list of titles of books, research articles, etc. For example,

```
THE RENTED STOLE
MYSTERY OF THE STOLEN RENT
RENTED HOUSE MYSTERY
STOLEN HOUSE
RENT A MYSTERY RENT HOUSE
```

A KWIC index is a list of the titles arranged so that it is easy to find out which of the titles contain each "key" word. The KWIC index for the above list would be:

```
                         ┌──keyword column
                         |
               RENTED HOUSE MYSTERY
               STOLEN HOUSE
   RENT A MYSTERY RENT HOUSE
                      MYSTERY OF THE STOLEN RENT
         RENTED HOUSE MYSTERY
               RENT A MYSTERY RENT HOUSE
        RENT A MYSTERY RENT HOUSE
MYSTERY OF THE STOLEN RENT
                      RENT A MYSTERY RENT HOUSE
                  THE RENTED STOLE
                      RENTED HOUSE MYSTERY
           THE RENTED STOLE
                      STOLEN HOUSE
        MYSTERY OF THE STOLEN RENT
```

> In each title, words that are <u>not</u> articles, prepositions, and the like are called <u>keywords</u>. In the index, each title occurs once in the list for each keyword in the title, and the titles are so aligned that the keywords all occur in the same column. The titles are printed in alphabetical order of the keywords. Note that if a keyword appears two or more times in a title (e.g. RENT in "RENT A MYSTERY RENT HOUSE"), the title appears two or more times under that keyword in the final list.

Such a KWIC index is an invaluable aid to researchers in finding books and articles. To find them, one just has to search the list for relevant keywords and note down the corresponding titles. A typical index may contain 1000 to 5000 different titles.

A program to produce a KWIC index is given the titles and the list of "non-keywords" as input. The program must read the titles and non-keywords, make up a list of possible keywords, sort the list of keywords, and then print the titles according to the list of keywords. Often, it will take several "runs" of the program to get the index in shape. The list of non-keywords may be changed from run to run to add more words than just prepositions and articles. For example, the word "computer" appears in many titles in computer science, and it may be irrelevant to have a listing of 300 titles each with the keyword "computer". Such cases may not be detected until after the list is first printed.

The general outline (first refinement) for the KWIC index program can be easily created from the above description. It uses three "lists": TITLES is the list of titles, NONKEY the list of non-keywords, and KEYWORDS the list of keywords. Although they will probably be implemented in standard fashion using arrays, we will not make that decision now, but just talk in terms of lists. The first attempt at a program is:

```
                S1: Read titles into list TITLES.
                S2: Read non-keywords into list NONKEY.
(2.6.1b)        S3: Make up list KEYWORDS from the titles
                     and non-keywords.
                S4: Sort the list KEYWORDS.
                S5: Print the titles according to list KEYWORDS.
```

Refinements of statements S1 and S2 will depend on the input format and we will not discuss them further. We are mainly interested in statements S3, S4 and S5. Speed of execution will be important since there can be so many titles (up to, say, 5000). First, note that a sort is involved. We will use an N*LOG2(N) algorithm like heap sort (see Section 2.7) instead of an N^2 algorithm like bubble sort. We hope to also refine S3 and S5 into algorithms no worse than N*LOG2(N).

In order to intelligently talk about speed, we must have some estimate of the size of the lists. Suppose that

```
                1.  There are T titles.  T <= 5000.
(2.6.1c)        2.  On the average there are 5 keywords per title.
                3.  Each keyword appears about 5 different times.
                    Thus there are roughly T different keywords.
                4.  There are a maximum of 10 words per title.
```

We don't know there are 5 keywords per title, or that there are T different keywords, but these estimates are close enough in order to make reasonable time estimates.

2.6.2 Analyzing and Refining Statement S3

To save space, first consider keeping only the different keywords in KEYWORDS. No matter how many times a word appears in titles, it appears only once in the list. Thus, for the sample input, the list KEYWORDS would be

HOUSE MYSTERY RENT RENTED STOLE STOLEN

Statement S3 must perform as follows:

```
          /* MAKE UP LIST OF KEYWORDS */
              Set list of KEYWORDS to empty
              For each word in title:
(2.6.2a)            IF that word is not in NONKEY
                       THEN DO;
                            Search KEYWORDS for the word
                            IF the word isn't in KEYWORDS
                               THEN add word to KEYWORDS
                            END;
```

This looks similar to a problem discussed at the end of Section 2.5. There, the problem was to read a list of values and put them in an array, but include each duplicated value only once. Here, we get the words from the titles, but that is the only essential difference. In Section 2.5, we saw that the approach we just took led to an N^2 algorithm. Looking at (2.6.2a), we see that a search of the keyword list is performed in time T. This leads to a T^2 algorithm, as in the last section.

To have the algorithm run in time no worse than T*LOG2(T) we must revise it along the lines suggested by the related problem of Section 2.5. We must first put all the keywords in KEYWORDS, whether they are duplicates or not, then sort, and then delete the duplicates:

```
              S1: Read titles into list TITLES
              S2: Read non-keywords into list NONKEY
(2.6.2b)      S3: Make up list KEYWORDS from the titles
                  and non-keywords
              S4: Sort list KEYWORDS
              S4A:Delete duplicates from KEYWORDS
              S5: Print the titles according to list KEYWORDS.
```

S3 is now

```
/** S3: MAKE UP LIST KEYWORDS FROM TITLES */
    Set list KEYWORDS to empty
    For each word in each title:
        IF that word is not in NONKEY
            THEN put that word in list KEYWORDS
```

We have lost the space advantage we were looking for in the beginning of this section, but we have satisfied our speed requirement. Indeed, statement S3 runs in time proportional to the number of titles T, while the sort is still T*LOG2(T). Statement S4A can also obviously be done in time proportional to the number of keywords, which is roughly 5*T. The only statement to take care of now is statement S5.

2.6.3 Analyzing and Refining Statement S5 to Print the Titles

Our first attempt at statement S5 is

```
        For each keyword in KEYWORDS:
(2.6.3a)    Search the titles and print those containing the
                keyword (if a keyword appears i times in
                a title, print the title i times)
```

Searching the titles will take time proportional to the number of titles T. Since this must be done T times (once for each keyword), this is a T^2 algorithm, which is above our hoped-for upper bound of T*LOG2(T).

We have to process each keyword, so the only way of reducing the time in executing (2.6.3a) is to somehow get rid of the search through the titles each time. How can we do that? One possible way would be to keep with each keyword a list of the titles to be printed for that keyword, or better still, to keep a list of the positions of the titles in TITLES, to be printed.

Keeping such a list may be quite messy, but notice that if we don't delete duplicate keywords, then for each keyword in KEYWORDS we need only keep track of which title it appeared in and its character position in the title. For example, with the sample input, the keyword list could be represented by three arrays KEYWORDS, TITLENO, and CHARPOS, as follows:

	KEYWORDS	TITLENO	CHARPOS		KEYWORDS	TITLENO	CHARPOS
(1)	RENTED	1	5	(8)	MYSTERY	3	14
(2)	STOLE	1	12	(9)	STOLEN	4	1
(3)	MYSTERY	2	1	(10)	HOUSE	4	8
(4)	STOLEN	2	16	(11)	RENT	5	1
(5)	RENT	2	23	(12)	MYSTERY	5	8
(6)	RENTED	3	1	(13)	RENT	5	16
(7)	HOUSE	3	8	(14)	HOUSE	5	21

Statement S5 will then look something like

```
DO I = 1 TO number of keywords;
    N = TITLENO(I);
    POS = CHARPOS(I);
    Print the Nth title in TITLES, with the POSth
            character in the keyword column
    END;
```

This requires several changes in the higher level algorithm (2.6.2b). For example, we must remove S4A, which deletes duplicate keywords. At this point we must back up to this algorithm, change it, and then proceed in top-down fashion to refine its statements once more. We leave this to you.

Now we can specify in detail the data structures to be used:

1. The list of titles is kept in an array TITLES. TITLES(1) is the first title, TITLES(2) the second, and so on. There are T titles in the array.

2. The list of non-keywords is kept in an array NONKEY. NONKEY(1) is the first, NONKEY(2) the second, and so on.

3. The keywords are kept in <u>three</u> arrays KEYWORDS, TITLENO, and CHARPOS. The Ith keyword is in KEYWORD(I), and was added to the array because it was found in title TITLENO(I), beginning at character position CHARPOS(I). At any point, there are K keywords in the list.

In terms of these structures the algorithm is:

```
S1: Read titles into TITLES
S2: Read non-keywords into NONKEY
S3: Make up keyword list in arrays KEYWORDS, TITLENO, and
     CHARPOS
S4: Sort array KEYWORDS. Whenever a swap of KEYWORDS(I)
     and KEYWORDS(J) (say) occurs, also swap TITLENO(I)
     and TITLENO(J), and CHARPOS(I) and CHARPOS(J)
S5: Print the titles according to the keywords
```

We have the following refinements of S3 and S5:

```
/* S3: MAKE UP LIST OF KEYWORDS, */
/* ASSUMING NONKEY IS SORTED.  */
/* IF BINARY SEARCH IS USED TIME IS PROPORTIONAL */
/* TO T*LOG2(NO. OF NON-KEYWORDS). */
    K = 0;      /* KEYWORD LIST IS EMPTY */
    MAKE_UP: DO I = 1 TO T BY 1;
        For each word in TITLES(I):
            IF the word is not in NONKEY
                THEN DO;
                    K = K + 1;
                    KEYWORD(K) = the word;
                    TITLENO(K) = I;
                    CHARPOS(K) = pos. of keyword in
                                 title;
                    END;
        END MAKE_UP;

/* S5: PRINT  TITLES.  TIME PROPORTIONAL TO NUMBER OF */
/* KEYWORDS K. */
    DO I = 1 TO K BY 1;
        Print out TITLES(TITLENO(I)), with character
            CHARPOS(I) appearing in the keyword column
        END;
```

2.7 An Example: Heap Sort

Problem: Sort the array B(1:N) into ascending order.
(Assume B and N are already initialized.)

A number of sorting algorithms have already been given, but all have run in time proportional to N^2 in the worst case. The algorithm developed here runs in time proportional to N*LOG2(N). However, understanding this algorithm requires a knowledge of "trees" and "heaps".

2.7.1 Binary Trees and Heaps

Binary trees are discussed in Section VII.4; we briefly give the definition here. A binary tree is a finite set of nodes (the underlined values in the trees of (2.7.1a)) that is either empty or consists of a root node and two disjoint binary trees, called the left and right subtrees, respectively. In tree 1 of (2.7.1a) the root node contains the value 8, the left subtree the values 7,6,1,0,3 and the right subtree the values 5,4,2. Those subtrees consisting of a root node and two empty binary trees are called leaves, or end nodes. One sometimes calls the lines in the trees of (2.7.1a) that connect a root node to the roots of its subtrees branches.

Each node is labeled with an integer to its right. If i labels a node, we use the notation NODE(i) to refer to the node itself. In tree 1 of (2.7.1a) NODE(1)=8, NODE(2)=7, and NODE(3)=5.

Any node is called the *father* of the nodes on branches emanating downward from it. Similarly, they are called his sons. Since each father can have at most two sons, we designate them the *left son* and the *right son*. The position of a node is important. A father can have only a left son, or only a right son, or both. In tree 1 of (2.7.1a), node 1's sons are nodes 2 and 3, node 3's sons are 6 and 7. 7's father is 3.

A father's sons, his sons' sons, etc., are called his *descendants*. Similarly, we talk of a node's *ancestors* -- his father, father's father, etc. In tree 1 of (2.7.1a) node 2's descendants are nodes 4, 5, 8, and 9; 9's ancestors are nodes 4, 2, and 1.

The root node is on *level 1*, his sons are on *level 2*, their sons are on *level 3*, and so on.

We label the nodes in a very systematic manner. The root node is node 1. If a node is labeled i, his sons are always labeled 2i (the left son) and 2i+1 (the right son). Thus node 4's sons are nodes 8 and 9. Finally, we restrict our trees so that if node i exists, then so do nodes 1, 2, ..., i-1. Thus there are no "holes" in the tree. Tree 2 of (2.7.1a) does not satisfy this restriction and we will not use this tree further. This restriction is made so that a later implementation of trees in PL/I arrays is simple and efficient.

The following property will be useful: a binary tree is a *heap* if for every node i with a father,

NODE(father of i) ≥ NODE(i)

Tree 1 of (2.7.1a) is a heap, as you can see by inspection. Tree 1 of (2.7.1b) is not, since NODE(4) < NODE(9).

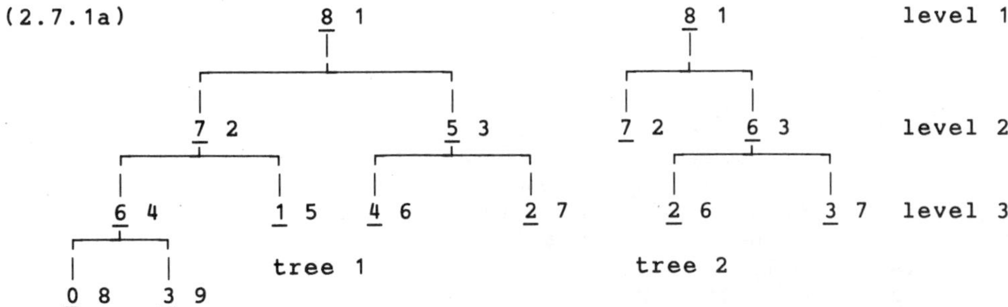

(2.7.1b)

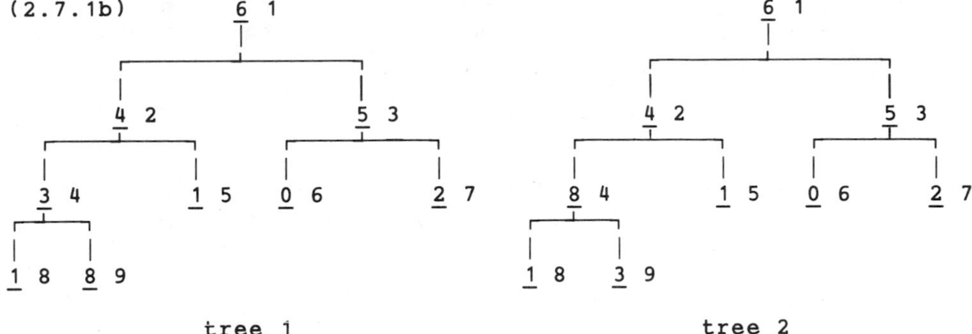

2.7.2 The Basic Heap Sort Algorithm

We now outline the algorithm for sorting B(1:N). First, consider B to be a binary tree; the value in B(i) is NODE(i) for any i. It is easy to calculate fathers and sons:

```
father(B(i))      is    B(FLOOR(i/2))
leftson(B(i))     is    B(2i)
rightson(B(i))    is    B(2i+1)
```

We shall use terms like "father(i)" when referring to B because we must think of it as a binary tree in order to understand the algorithm. The sorting algorithm consists of two steps:

S1: Make B(1:N) into a heap
S2: Sort the heap so that B(i) ≤ B(i+1) for i=1,...,n-1.

As we will see, each step can be done in time proportional to N*LOG2(N) so that the whole algorithm runs in time proportional to N*LOG2(N).

2.7.3 Making B(1:N) into a Heap

The algorithm is:

```
            DO I = 1 TO N BY 1;
(2.7.3a)        Make B(1:I) into a heap, assuming B(1:I-1) is
                        already a heap;
                END;
```

Thus we make the tree into a heap one node at a time, in the order the nodes are labeled. For example, consider tree 1 of (2.7.1b). The nodes 1 through 8 already form a heap. If we add node 9 (value 8), we no longer have a heap since NODE(4) < NODE(9). To make it into a heap we need only "bubble" the offending value 8 up to its father, and to its father's father, etc. until it has reached the root node or until it is finally not greater than its father. Tree 2 of (2.7.1b) shows the first step of this bubbling process, in which NODE(4) is exchanged with NODE(9).

There is one important property necessary to follow the subalgorithm given here. This is:

> Suppose a tree would be a heap except for <u>one</u> node j where NODE(father of j) < NODE(j). If we exchange the values of NODE(father of j) and NODE(j) (as in the transformation of tree 1 to tree 2 in (2.7.1b)), then the <u>only</u> offending relations can be between NODE(father of j) and <u>his</u> father.

Work with examples, and then <u>prove</u> this for yourself.

With this property in mind, we give the following algorithm for the English statement of (2.7.3a):

```
J = I;
DO WHILE (node J has a father);
    IF B(father of J) ≥ B(J)
        THEN LEAVE;
    Swap B(father of J) and B(J)
    J = father of J;
    END;
```

Incorporating this into (2.7.3a) and translating into PL/I (except for the Swap) yields the following:

```
        /** MAKE B(1:N) INTO A HEAP.  */
            HP: DO I = 1 TO N BY 1;
                /** MAKE B(1:I) INTO A HEAP */
                       /* ASSUMING B(1:I-1) IS A HEAP */
                    J = I;
                    /** BUBBLE B(J) UP AS FAR AS IT WILL GO */
                        DO WHILE (J > 1);
(2.7.3b)                       /* WHILE J HAS A FATHER */
                           FATHER_OF_J = FLOOR(J/2E0);
                           IF B(FATHER_OF_J) >= B(J)
                               THEN LEAVE;
                           Swap B(FATHER_OF_J) and B(J);
                           J = FATHER_OF_J;
                           END;
                END HP;
```

Let us see why this is an N*LOG2(N) algorithm. Consider a value of I, and see how many times the body of the WHILE loop is executed. Each iteration of the loop "bubbles" the offending value up one level in the tree. Hence the maximum number of times the body can be executed is the number of levels in the tree, minus one.

If the tree has 2 nodes the level is 2, if 4 nodes the level is 3, if 8 nodes the level is 4, and so on. The level is exactly FLOOR(LOG2(I))+1. Thus for a given value of I, the loop body is executed at most LOG2(I) times.

Hence the total number of times the inner loop body is executed is <u>at most</u>

LOG2(1) + LOG2(2) + LOG2(3) + ... + LOG2(N)

and this is bounded above by N*LOG2(N). The total number of basic steps executed is bounded above by the sum of the following, and this sum is of the order N*LOG2(N):

3*N	(basic steps in executing DO I = 1 TO N loop)
N	(J=I is executed N times)
5*N*LOG2(N)	(steps executed in inner loop)

Exercise 13 introduces a <u>linear</u> algorithm for this problem.

2.7.4 Sorting the Heap

The heap B satisfies the property B(father(i)) ≥ B(i). We want to change B so it satisfies the property B(i) ≤ B(i+1), since then the array will be sorted. Note that for any heap, the largest value is in the root node, and that if the heap is to look like a sorted array, that largest value must be put in the <u>last</u> node of the tree.

Algorithm (2.7.4a) has the following property which holds just before each execution of the loop body.

> B(1:I) is a heap. Every value in B(1:I) ≤ every value in B(I+1:N). The array segment B(I+1:N) is sorted in ascending order:

```
 B(1)                              B(I)  B(I+1)              B(N)
 -------------------------------------------------------------------
| These form a heap and are not | These are sorted:    |
|greater than values in B(I+1:N)|  B(I+1)≤B(I+2),etc. |
 -------------------------------------------------------------------
```

Thus each execution of the loop body takes the largest number out of the heap B(1:I) and puts it in the correct position of the array.

```
           I = N;
           DO WHILE (I > 1);
(2.7.4a)      Swap B(1) and B(I);
              I = I-1;
              Make B(1:I) into a heap
              END;
```

The only thing left is to show how to make B(1:I) back into a heap. It is <u>not</u> a heap only because the new value in B(1) is too small (probably); this value just came from the previous last node of the heap. In order to make the tree back into a heap, then, we bubble this small value down as far as it can go, the opposite of what we did in the last section. However, the process is quite similar; we need only make sure we exchange it (if necessary) with its larger son.

```
        /** MAKE B(1:I) INTO A HEAP */
            J = 1;
            DO WHILE (J has a son);
                K = left son of J;
                IF J has a right son
(2.7.4b)           THEN IF B(K) < B(right son of J)
                        THEN K = right son of J;
                IF B(J) >= B(K)
                    THEN LEAVE;
                Swap B(J) and B(K)
                J = K;
                END;
```

Incorporating this into (2.7.4a) yields the following program; we leave it to you to show that it is also of order N*LOG2(N).

```
        /** SORT THE HEAP B(1:N) */
            I = N;
            SP: DO WHILE (I > 1);
                Swap B(1) and B(I);
                I = I-1;
                /** MAKE B(1:I) INTO A HEAP */
                    J = 1; /* K WILL BE J'S LARGER SON */
                    K = 2*J;
                    DO WHILE (K <= I); /* WHILE J HAS A SON */
                        IF K < I
                           THEN IF B(K) < B(K+1);
                               THEN K = K+1;
                        IF B(J) ≤ B(K)
                           THEN LEAVE;
                        Swap B(J) and B(K);
                        J = K;
                        K = 2*J;
                        END;
                END SP;
```

Section 2 Exercises

1. Show that the function

$$f(N) = c1 + c2 \cdot N$$

is order O(N), where c1 and c2 are constants. Any such function is said to be linear in N.

2. Show that the function

$$f(N) = c1 + c2 \cdot N + c3 \cdot N^2$$

is $O(N^2)$, where c1, c2 and c3 are any constants. F(N) is a quadratic function.

3. Show that the function

$$f(N) = c1 + c2 \cdot N + c3 \cdot LOG2(N) + c4 \cdot N \cdot LOG2(N)$$

is O(N*LOG2(N)), where c1, c2, c3 and c4 are any constants.

4. Show that the function N + SQRT(N) is O(N). Show that it is not O(SQRT(N)).

5. Show that the function N+LOG2(N) is O(N) but not O(LOG2(N)).

6. Determine the order of execution time for each program segment of Exercise 2, Section I.5, in the worst case.

7. Consider the binary search algorithm of (2.4b). Suppose N = 16 and B = 1, 3, 5, 7, 9, 11, 13, 15, 17, 19, 21, 23, 25, 27, 29, 99.

   a) Execute algorithm (2.4b) by hand with X = 99.
   b) Execute algorithm (2.4b) by hand with X = 1.
   c) Execute algorithm (2.4b) by hand with X = 17.
   d) Execute algorithm (2.4b) by hand with X = 18.

8. Will binary search (2.4b) work correctly if, when discarding half the list, B(J) is not also discarded?

9. Binary search (2.4b) makes two array-element comparisons for each iteration of the loop, while the likelihood that the condition B(J) = X is true early during execution is quite low. Change the program to make only one comparison within the loop, say B(J) <= X. Then after the loop make a few comparisons to set J correctly.

10. The following algorithm, the <u>successive</u> <u>maxima</u> sorting algorithm, sorts array B(1:N) into ascending order. Find the order of the worst case execution time as a function of N.

```
/** SORT ARRAY B(1:N) */
    DO J = N TO 2 BY -1;
        /** Swap B(1:J) to put largest in B(J) */
            DO I = 1 TO J-1 BY 1;
                IF B(I) > B(J)
                   THEN Swap B(I) and B(J);
                END;
        END;
```

11. Below are two program segments to calculate the <u>mode</u> of an array A(1:N), where it is assumed that A is already sorted in ascending order. The mode is the most frequently occurring value; the mode of an empty array is arbitrarily taken as 0. Find an upper bound for the number of basic steps executed and the worst case order of execution time, for each. The second program may contain an execution error, due to the way PL/I evaluates a condition like (J<N)&(A(J)=A(J+1)). Fix the error.

```
/* FIND A MODE M OF SORTED ARRAY A(1:N), N>=1.  */
/* BEFORE AND AFTER EACH EXECUTION OF THE LOOP BODY, */
    /* M IS THE MODE OF A(1:I), */
    /* MCT = NUMBER OF TIMES M OCCURS IN A(1:I), */
        I,MCT = 1;
        M = A(1);
        DO WHILE (I < N);
            I = I+1;
            IF A(I) = A(I-MCT)
                THEN DO;
                    MCT = MCT + 1;
                    M = A(I);
                    END;
            END;
```

```
/* CALCULATE A MODE M OF SORTED ARRAY A(1:N).  */
/* BEFORE AND AFTER EACH EXECUTION OF THE MAIN LOOP BODY,*/
    /* M = MODE(A(1:I)), */
    /* MCT IS THE NUMBER OF TIMES M OCCURS IN A(1:I),*/
    /* A(I) ¬= A(I+1)  (IF THEY BOTH EXIST).  */
        I,M,MCT = 0;
        DO WHILE (I < N);
            J = I+1;
            DO WHILE ((J < N) & (A(J) = A(J+1)));
                J = J+1;
                END;
            IF J - I > MCT
                THEN DO;
                    M = A(J);
                    MCT = J - I;
                    END;
            I = J;
            END;
```

12. Let A(1:N,1:N) be an array. What is the execution time order of each of the following statements?

```
   a) PUT LIST(A);

   b) A = 0;

   c) DO I = 1 TO N BY 1;
          DO J = 1 TO N BY 1;
              A(I,J) = 0;
              END;
          END;
```

13. Algorithm (2.7.3b) makes B(1:N) into a heap by successively bubbling up the values B(1), B(2), ..., B(N). The following algorithm instead bubbles values <u>downward</u>, as in (2.7.4b). Refine the algorithm so that it is entirely in PL/I. Then prove that it is a <u>linear</u> algorithm; its execution time is proportional to N and not to N*LOG2(N) (this requires some mathematical knowledge). Note that only N/2 node values must be bubbled down, since the other N/2 values are already in "leaves" of the tree and can't be bubbled any further.

```
            DO I = FLOOR(N/2E0) TO 1 BY -1;
                Bubble B(I) down as far as possible, as
                    B(1) is bubbled down in (2.7.4b)
                END;
```

Section 3 Problems Impossible to Program

This section discusses three types of problems that are impossible to program -- no approach will yield an effective program. Sections 3.1 and 3.2 concern problems that are too vague or too large. Such problems occur frequently and the programmer must be wary of them. Section 3.3 introduces the existence of problems for which it can be proved that no effective program can be written.

3.1 Ill-Defined Problems

Many problems are just not understood well enough to program. We have suggested that in program development one use English commands and phrases, such as "solve", "find", "create", etc. This is useful, but it can lead to unwarranted optimism about the kinds of problems that can be programmed. Eventually, each of these commands must be refined or developed into the statements of a programming language. The process breaks down if, at any point in the development, one encounters a command that cannot be refined into program statements. For example, it is easy to write "solve", but it is sometimes difficult to figure out "how to solve". One can write "find" and not even be sure where to look.

It is often easy to disguise the inability to refine such a command. For example, in developing a program to select potential companions for an applicant to a computer dating service, one must at some point define the meaning of "appropriate date". No algorithm capable of doing this has yet been discovered. Nevertheless, scores of people have written programs to perform this task. Unfortunately, the use of a computer sometimes lends respectability or authenticity to an algorithm that would be laughable if performed by a human.

While it is often necessary to obtain approximate solutions to difficult or impossible problems, programming ethics demand that the approximation be clearly identified, and that the program not be used to obscure the dubiousness of the algorithm.

3.2 Impossibly-Large Problems

Most beginners are somewhat awed by the computer's speed. Programs that take hours to write are executed in seconds, and one begins to regard its speed as essentially infinite. Therefore, it is surprising and a bit disillusioning to discover problems that are clearly and precisely stated, easily programmed, but that require so much execution time that they are effectively impossible.

The following program makes the point. It does nothing, but takes at least hours to do so on the fastest computer. If a third level of loops were added to the nest it would become impossibly long for the fastest computers that exist.

```
/* TWO LEVEL EMPTY DO NEST */
FUTILE: PROCEDURE OPTIONS(MAIN);
    DCL (I,J) FIXED;
    DO I = 1 TO 10000 BY 1;
        DO J = 1 TO 10000 BY 1;
            END;
        END;
    END FUTILE;
```

As a more reasonable example, consider the problem of assigning swimmers described in IV.6.3.3. Two versions of the program are given -- but either one takes surprisingly long to execute. To understand why, note that in the non-recursive version the DO loop for the fourth swimmer (labelled ROW4) will be executed 4^4 = 256 times. For ten swimmers and ten events (not an unreasonably large number) the innermost group would be executed 10^{10} times. Since a computer will execute several thousand PL/I statements per second, and there are approximately $3x10^7$ seconds in a year, this problem would take <u>at least months</u>, <u>and perhaps years</u> to execute (depending on the computer used). If that is not sufficiently discouraging, consider a problem with twelve swimmers and twelve events.

This algorithm involves "complete enumeration" -- it examines every possible solution in order to select the best. This brute force solution relies on the computer's speed, which is inadequate for the task. Fortunately, a more efficient algorithm is known that will easily obtain solutions for hundreds of swimmers and events. This so-called "assignment algorithm" is described in most operations research texts. (For example, see Section III.2 in Ford and Fulkerson, <u>Flows in Networks</u>, Princeton Press, 1962.) This particular problem can be programmed and solved on a computer, because a clever and efficient algorithm happens to be available. Unfortunately, there are many problems, as simple in form as this one, where no algorithm except complete enumeration is known, and in some cases it can be proved that no algorithm except complete enumeration exists.

In general, these problems have the characteristic that their computation time grows very rapidly with increases in size of the problem. If n is some key dimension of the problem, the computing time may depend upon n**n, 2**n, e**n or some similar function of n. Such problems grow so rapidly with n that, while small problems (n = 3 or 4 or 5) can often be solved by hand, problems only two or three times as large (in terms of n) cannot be solved by the most powerful computers.

3.3 "Undecidable" Problems

For certain problems it can be proved that no effective program can be written. It is not just a matter of not having yet found an efficient algorithm, or not yet having computers that are fast enough; it can be rigorously proved that no program is possible. One important branch of computer science is concerned with classifying problems according to degree of difficulty (rate at which execution time increases with increasing values of n) and, in particular, identifying such non-computable problems. In most cases rather sophisticated mathematical arguments are involved, but the following example will suggest the general nature of the problems and proofs.

Suppose one is asked to write a program TRUTHTEST that will be able to determine the truth or falsity of a certain restricted class of English statements. Assume that each such statement is given an identifying label prefix. For example:

STATEMENT_23: ROSES ARE RED.

After processing such a statement, TRUTHTEST would produce one of two possible outputs:

STATEMENT_23 IS FALSE. or STATEMENT_23 IS TRUE.

Suppose TRUTHTEST were presented with the following statement as data:

STATEMENT_9: STATEMENT_9 IS FALSE.

If TRUTHTEST reports

STATEMENT_9 IS FALSE.

it will be confirming the truth of the statement it is declaring to be false. This is a contradiction. If TRUTHTEST reports

STATEMENT_9 IS TRUE.

it will be contradicting a statement that it claims is true. The only resolution of this paradox is to conclude that it is <u>impossible to produce a program to do what TRUTHTEST is supposed to do</u>.

This difficulty does not lie in the definition of truth and falsity; this is not an example of an "ill-defined" problem, as discussed in Section 3.1. The following example should clarify the distinction. It is similar to the TRUTHTEST problem, but the task is more precisely defined. Nevertheless, it leads to the same type of paradox and conclusion of impossibility.

Suppose we want a program to test other programs for the presence of an error called an "infinite iterative loop". If a program contains an infinite iterative loop (abbreviate this as "iil") it will never complete execution, and it would be useful to have a diagnostic program that would detect such errors before large amounts of computer time are wasted. Note that one cannot empirically test for such errors just by running the suspect program, because one could not distinguish between programs that would <u>never</u> terminate, and those that are just <u>impossibly long</u> (as in Section 3.2).

The testing program TESTIIL loads a program P and data D into character arrays. TESTILL then determines whether P processing D contains an iil. If it does, the value 'NOHALT' is assigned to variable RESULT; if it does not contain an iil the value 'HALT' is assigned. That is:

```
/* TEST FOR PRESENCE OF IIL */
TESTIIL: PROCEDURE OPTIONS(MAIN);
    Declarations
    Load program P and data D
    IF P processing D contains an iil
        THEN RESULT = 'NOHALT';
        ELSE RESULT = 'HALT';
    PUT SKIP LIST (RESULT);
    END TESTIIL;
```

For example, suppose P is

```
XLOOP: PROCEDURE OPTIONS(MAIN);
    DECLARE X FLOAT;
    GET LIST (X);
    DO WHILE (X = 3);
        END;
    END XLOOP;
```

If D is 4, XLOOP processing D does not contain an iil, and TESTIIL should report HALT. If D is 3, then TESTIIL should detect an iil in XLOOP processing D and report NOHALT.

If TESTIIL can be written, it would be trivial to write another program REPEAT that is very similar but contains an extra WHILE loop. Furthermore, where TESTIIL will test any program P processing any data D, REPEAT considers only the special case where a program P processes a copy of itself. That is, data D is a copy of program P. (It is not unusual for one program to be read as data by another program. For example, this is what occurs during compilation of a PL/C program.)

```
/* REPEAT IF IIL NOT PRESENT WHEN P PROCESSES P */
REPEAT: PROCEDURE OPTIONS(MAIN);
    Declarations from TESTIIL
    Load program P
    Copy program P to be used as data D
    /** REPEAT TESTIIL UNTIL RESULT IS 'NOHALT' */
        RESULT = 'HALT';
        DO WHILE (RESULT = 'HALT');
            IF P processing D contains an iil
                THEN RESULT = 'NOHALT';
                ELSE RESULT = 'HALT';
            END;
    END REPEAT;
*DATA
    Program P
```

Observe that REPEAT is designed so that

a) REPEAT processing data P halts only if P processing data P does not halt, and

b) REPEAT processing data P does not halt only if P processing data P does halt.

Since program P can be <u>any</u> program, it can be the program REPEAT. That is, write another copy of REPEAT after the *DATA so that REPEAT processes itself. Now rewrite the observations a) and b) with P = REPEAT:

a) REPEAT processing data REPEAT halts only if REPEAT processing data REPEAT does not halt, and

b) REPEAT processing data REPEAT does not halt only if REPEAT processing data REPEAT does halt.

Hence, assuming REPEAT halts leads to a contradiction, and assuming it does not halt also leads to a contradiction. But REPEAT <u>must</u> either halt or not halt. The only flaw in the argument is our initial assumption that a program TESTIIL could be produced. Therefore <u>TESTIIL cannot be written</u>. No matter what computer language is used, it is impossible to write a program that will test any arbitrary program and set of data to determine whether or not that program will halt.

This is an example of a phenomenon called "undecidability". The problem of determining whether program P processing data D will ever halt is said to be "undecidable". This particular problem was first proved undecidable by a British mathematician Alan Turing in 1936 (ten years before the first modern computer). A readable contemporary exposition of the idea is Chapter 8 of Minsky's <u>Computation</u> (Prentice-Hall, 1967).

Part VII
Data Structures

Section 1 Data Structures, Links and Nodes

Suppose you are writing a program to play a card game like poker. The game involves a "deck", several "hands", and a "discard pile". There are also actions such as "shuffling" and "dealing". In programming this game it would be convenient to have a single variable represent the deck, another variable represent the discard pile, and a separate variable represent each hand. It would also be helpful to have operations that correspond to shuffling and dealing.

Or suppose you want to write a program that simulates a supermarket in order to determine how many cashiers and baggers are needed. It would be convenient to think and program in terms of a queue of customers, baskets of groceries, bags of groceries, and operations bagging and adding up the prices.

The point is that it is generally advantageous to think and program in terms of the natural entities and actions of the problem, and these are often complex objects. So it is useful to be able to construct correspondingly complex data representations so that a single data object can represent a natural entity -- a player's hand of cards or a queue of customers. Part VII describes how to use PL/I structures for this purpose and how to write procedures to perform operations on these structures -- such as dealing or shuffling.

In particular, certain complex structures of data have been found to be useful in a wide variety of different problems. So we begin by introducing some common structures -- "stacks", "queues" and "linked lists". These involve basic concepts and techniques with which you should become familiar.

By a <u>data structure</u> we mean a table of data including structural relationships. For example, if a data structure describes a deck of playing cards, the relationships concern the order of the cards in the deck -- which card is on top, which is underneath the top card, etc.

The structural relationships can of course be more complicated; if the deck is being used to play a game like poker or gin rummy, then the data structure includes a description of the cards each player holds, the discard pile, and so on. As another example, the structural relationships of an administrative organization include the order of command: who reports to whom and who supervises whom.

If we want to program in terms of a certain data structure then we must implement it in PL/I. That is, we must decide how the data is to be represented in PL/I variables, arrays, etc., and how the structural relationships are to be recorded or calculated. An important point in this regard is the following: when implementing a data structure in a program we must consider not only the data structure but also the operations to be performed on that data structure. The wise programmer delays his decision about the implementation of a data structure until he knows more about these operations.

To illustrate this point, consider the important data structure called a (finite) sequence (or linear list). This is a set of n elements (X1, X2, ..., Xn) where $n \geq 0$. If $n > 0$ the structural relationships are: X1 is the first element, Xn is the last element, Xi precedes (is the predecessor of) X(i+1) for $1 \leq i < n$, and X(i+1) succeeds (is the successor of) Xi for $1 \leq i < n$. If n=0 the sequence is empty; this is denoted by ().

The following operations might be used on sequences:

1. Insert a new element y before X1.

2. Insert a new element y after some Xi. (We sometimes allow insertion only at the end of the sequence.)

3. Delete an element Xi from the sequence. (We sometimes restrict deletions to the beginning of the sequence.)

4. Delete all elements Xi having the value y.

5. Determine the predecessor of some Xi.

6. Determine the successor of some Xi.

7. Merge two sequences into one.

It is easy to choose a representation for sequences so that any one of these operations can be efficiently executed; it is very difficult to represent sequences so that all are efficient. Thus, the programmer must determine which operations should be efficient before deciding on the representation to use in his program.

We now introduce terminology that will be used throughout this Part. Generally, the value of an element Xi of a sequence (or other structure) consists of several parts. These parts together with any explicitly written structural relationships constitute a record or node. Consider for example a deck of three playing cards. Each card can be described pictorially as a node with three named fields:

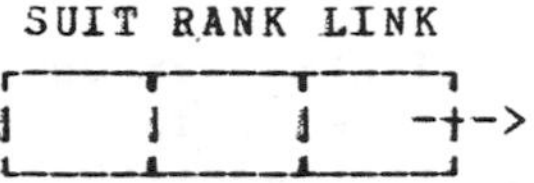

where the field named SUIT contains a representation for the suit (e.g. 0=diamonds, 1=clubs, 2=hearts, 3=spades), the field named RANK contains an integer from 1 to 13 (with 1=ACE, 11=JACK, 12=QUEEN, 13=KING) and field LINK is a link or pointer to the next card. Thus the pile (ace of hearts, two of spades, jack of clubs) is represented as

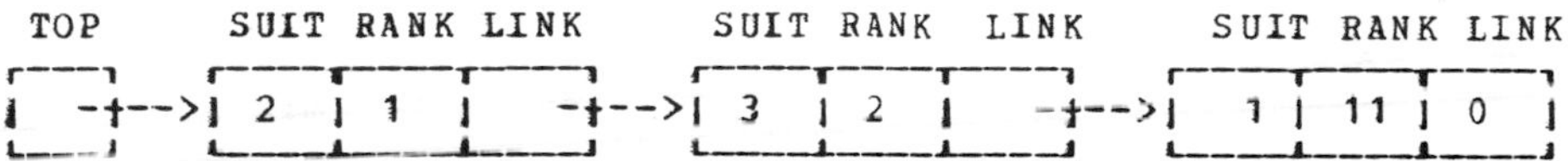

The LINK field is used to describe the successor relationship; its value is a link or pointer to the card underneath. The bottom card has no card underneath it, and we represent this with the nil link 0. Just how a link is implemented in PL/I will be described later.

In the above, TOP is considered to be a simple variable whose value is a link to the first card. Given any non-nil link in TOP, node(TOP) refers to the complete node pointed to by TOP. Thus, node(TOP) is the node representing the ace of hearts. It consists of three fields, which can be referenced by SUIT(TOP) with value 2, RANK(TOP) with value 1 and LINK(TOP), which is a link to another node. Thus it makes sense to refer to node(LINK(TOP)), SUIT(LINK(TOP)) and so forth.

It is an error to make a reference like node(L) if link variable L contains the nil link 0.

1.1 Representing Nodes and Links Using Arrays

A maximum of 100 (say) nodes with three fields as depicted above can be implemented using three arrays:

```
DCL(SUIT(1:100),
    RANK(1:100),
    LINK(1:100)) FIXED;
```

A non-nil link value is then an integer between 1 and 100 (inclusive), and node(i) consists of the three array elements

SUIT(i), RANK(i), LINK(i)

The nil link can be represented by any value outside the subscript range of the arrays. However one often chooses the lower array bound 1 and uses 0 as the nil link. We adopt this convention throughout.

Note that value fields such as SUIT and RANK can be declared as arrays with any convenient type attribute, while link fields should be FIXED since they contain subscript values.

When using linked lists one must be extremely careful about using subscripts. In the example of a deck of cards, one cannot assume that if one card is in SUIT(I) and RANK(I), then its successor is in SUIT(I+1) and RANK(I+1); in fact its successor is SUIT(LINK(I)) and RANK(LINK(I)). One can only use the proximity of array elements with indices i and i+1 when such a use is explicitly allowed in the description of the data structure.

The three cards depicted on the previous page might appear in reverse order in the array:

TOP		SUIT	RANK	LINK
100	(98)	1	11	0
	(99)	3	2	98
	(100)	2	1	99

On the other hand, the cards might appear as follows:

TOP		SUIT	RANK	LINK
2	(1)	1	11	0
	(2)	2	1	3
	(3)	3	2	1

This will be discussed further in Section 2.3.

Section 1 Exercises

1. Consider the diagram above that represents the pile of three cards. What are the values of RANK(TOP), RANK(LINK(TOP)) and RANK(LINK(LINK(TOP)))? Is RANK(LINK(LINK(LINK(TOP)))) a valid reference (explain your answer)?

2. At the end of Section 1 three cards are represented in two different ways as linked lists using variable TOP and three arrays SUIT, RANK and LINK. Depict in the same manner three different ways that the same cards could be represented as linked lists using only the elements SUIT(1:3), RANK(1:3), and LINK(1:3).

Section 2 Stacks, Queues and Deques

2.1 Definition of Stack, Queue and Deque.

In Section 1 we introduced the idea of a sequence (X1,...,Xn) and described some possible operations on it. We now define three special kinds of sequences that differ in the operations we are able to perform on them. The differences are in where insertions and deletions can take place:

> A stack is a sequence for which elements may be inserted and deleted from one end only. We insert and delete from the front, or top, only.
>
> A queue is a sequence for which elements may be inserted only at the rear and deleted only from the front.
>
> A deque is a sequence for which insertions and deletions may only take place at the ends. (Deque stands for "double ended queue." It is pronounced as "deck".)

```
delete    ┌─────┐    ┌─────┐             ┌─────┐
   or-->| s1  +-->| s2  +--> ... -->| sn  |                stack s
insert    └─────┘    └─────┘             └─────┘
           top                           bottom


          ┌─────┐    ┌─────┐             ┌─────┐
delete-->| q1  +-->| q2  +--> ... -->| qn  |<--insert   queue q
          └─────┘    └─────┘             └─────┘
          front      second               rear


delete    ┌─────┐    ┌─────┐             ┌─────┐   delete
   or-->| d1  +-->| d2  +--> ... -->| dn  |<--or        deque d
insert    └─────┘    └─────┘             └─────┘   insert
         leftmost                        rightmost
```

Note that, with stacks, queues and deques, we are not allowed to insert and delete in the middle. For example, we are not allowed to change (x,y,z) into (x,z) in a single operation.

The stack is a common data structure in life. Consider for example a stack of cafeteria trays. The waiter puts clean trays on the top of the stack, and these top ones are the first to be taken off by customers. The bottom tray is used only if all others are already in use and there is only one in the stack. Another name for *stack* is *pushdown store*, because putting an element onto the stack "pushes" those on it down. One also hears the term *LIFO list*, meaning Last-In-First-Out list. Stacks play an important role in computing; for example they are used to implement recursive procedures (see Section IV.6).

While Americans stand in line, the British wait in a *queue*. The first person to buy tickets is at the front of the queue and latecomers must join at the rear. A queue is called a *FIFO list* (First-In-First-Out list). (The terms LIFO and FIFO are used by accountants to describe methods for pricing inventories.)

As can be seen from the above pictorial representation, we use different terminology for these structures. A stack s has a top and bottom, and elements are *pushed* onto the stack or *popped* from the stack. We will use the notation for stack operations

s <== A	push the value A onto stack s
A <== s	delete the top value of stack s and store it in variable A
s=();	set s to "empty", so that it contains no elements
empty(s)	a function that returns *true* ('1'B) if s is empty; *false* otherwise
top(s)	can be used to refer to or change top value on s

Thus if s contains (3,5,8) with 3 at the top, execution of s<==6 changes s to (6,3,5,8), while further execution of B<==s stores 6 in B and changes s back to (3,5,8). The operation A<==s cannot be performed if the stack is currently empty.

Top(s) can be used as follows. If s contains (3,5,8) with 3 at the top and 8 at the bottom, execution of

```
top(s)= top(s)+1;
```

would change s to (4,5,8).

These are, of course, *not* PL/I statements, and we will later have to show how to implement them for any given representation of stacks in PL/I.

A queue has a front and a rear. We use q<==A and A<==q to denote inserting the value of A into the rear of queue q, and deleting the front value of q and storing it in A, respectively. Similar to the above operations on stacks, we allow the operations q=();, empty(q), front(q) and rear(q).

2.2 Sequential Allocation of Stacks and Queues

We now show how to implement stacks and queues in a simple manner using PL/I arrays. In implementing a data structure such as a stack we must do two things: show how the various subparts (e.g. the stack elements) are represented in PL/I, and show how to implement the operations on the data structure (e.g. s<==A).

A stack s=(s1, s2, ..., sn) with n<100 (say), where the si are integers and s1 is at the top, can be implemented using variables as follows:

```
DCL TOP   FIXED INIT(0);   /*the no. of elements in stack.*/
DCL S(1:100)    FIXED;     /*s1 is in S(TOP), s2 in S(TOP-1),*/
                           /*..., sn in S(1).*/
```

Note that initially TOP=0, so that the stack is empty. Note also that since array S must have a lower and upper subscript bound (we have arbitrarily chosen 1 and 100), the size of the stack is limited.

We show below how to implement stack operations in PL/I. Note the explicit checks for overflow (too many elements) and underflow (attempting to pop an empty stack); when implementing a stack in a program, these should be replaced by statements that print error messages and stop. Underflow is usually a logical error while overflow can simply mean that not enough space was allocated for the stack. Executing the program again with a larger array might, in the latter case, result in correct execution. Finally, note the use of the HBOUND built-in function to refer to the upper bound of array S.

```
(2.2.1) Stack operation      PL/I implementation
        s <== A;             IF TOP=HBOUND(S,1)
                                 THEN overflow;
                             TOP=TOP+1;
                             S(TOP)=A;

        A <== s;             IF TOP=0
                                 THEN underflow;
                             A=S(TOP);
                             TOP=TOP-1;

        s=();                TOP= 0;
```

empty(s)	TOP=0	(a logical expression)
top(s)	S(TOP)	(S(TOP) refers to the top element, and S(TOP)=...; can be used to change top(s). It is an error to refer to S(TOP) if TOP=0.)

Implementing a queue q requires more ingenuity because we must keep track of both its front and rear. Furthermore, if we use an array Q(0:99) (say) and begin with q1, ..., qn in Q(0), ..., Q(n-1) (as in Fig. 1a) then a series of insertions and deletions will cause the queue values to migrate to the other end of Q. (See Fig. 1b, then 1c). Remember, deletions occur at the front and insertions at the rear.

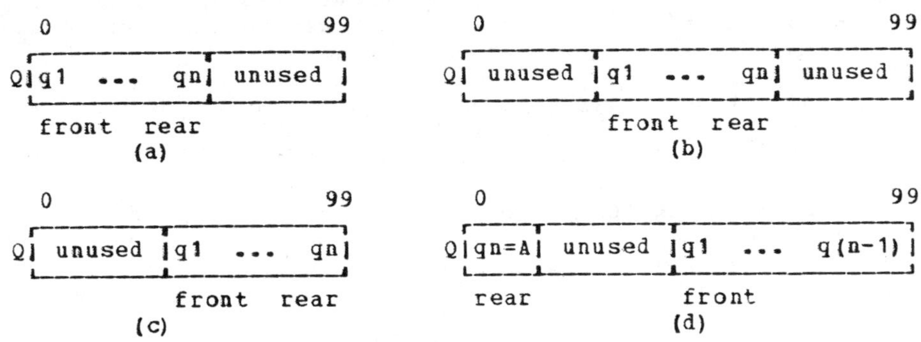

Figure 1. A queue q in an array Q

Suppose the state shown in Fig. 1c has been reached and suppose a new value A is to be inserted. We cannot put it after qn since Q(100) does not exist. We could move q1, ..., qn down one position in Q to make room for A, but this would be inefficient. A better solution is to put A in Q(0) -- in effect, we let the queue values "wrap around" and fill the front of the array, as shown in Fig. 1d. We give below the definition of the variables used in implementing q in this manner. The description uses the MOD function; for two positive integers i and j, MOD(i,j) is the remainder when i is divided by j. Thus, MOD(99,100)=99, MOD(100,100)=0 and MOD(101,100)=1. We can now see why the lower bound of Q is 0 rather than 1; it makes the use of Q to implement queue q easier to understand.

```
DCL (F,R) FIXED;          /*0≤F,R<100.  F=R means that q*/
DCL Q(0:99) FIXED;        /*is empty. If F≠R, q1 is in*/
                          /* Q(MOD(F+1,100)), q2 is in*/
                          /*Q(MOD(F+2,100)),...,qn in Q(R)*/
```

We now give operations on queues. The implementations are dependent on the size 100 of Q; we leave it to you to make it independent as was done for stack implementation.

```
Queue operation         PL/I implementation
q <== A;                R= MOD(R+1,100);
                        IF F=R
                            THEN overflow;
                        Q(R)= A;

A <== q;                IF F=R
                            THEN underflow;
                        F= MOD(F+1,100);
                        A= Q(F);

q=();                   F,R= 0;

empty(q)                F=R   (logical expression)

front(q)                Q(MOD(F+1,100))

rear(q)                 Q(R)
```

Suppose we want to implement two stacks sa and sb. We may do this with two arrays SA and SB, each of maximum size 100 (say). However, we may also do it with a single array S of size 200 and two simple variables SAN and SBN, as described by the following picture:

```
 S(1)    S(SAN)           S(SBN)   S(200)
┌───────────────┬──────────┬──────────────┐
│san  ...   sa1 │  unused  │sb1  ...   sbn│
└───────────────┴──────────┴──────────────┘
```

One stack grows up from S(1), while the other grows down from S(100). The advantage of this technique is that one stack may contain up to 200 elements as long as the other stack has correspondingly few elements. Thus overflow occurs not when one of the stacks reaches 100 elements, but only when the sum of the number of elements reaches 200.

2.3 Linked List Allocation of Stacks and Queues

In the sequential implementation of a stack described in Section 2.2 if a stack element was in array element S(i) then its successor, if any, was in S(i-1). We now discuss an implementation where this is not the case. Consider Fig. 2. Fig. 2a shows the stack s=(9,7,4) represented sequentially, while Fig. 2b shows a possible representation for s as a linked list.

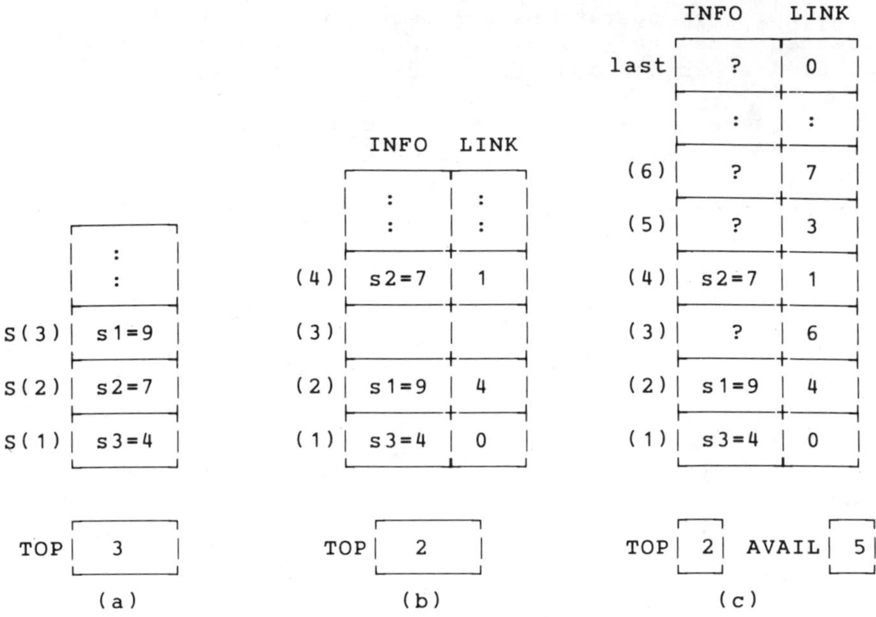

Figure 2. Sequential versus Linked Allocation

In the <u>linked list</u>, TOP=0 means the stack is empty; otherwise INFO(TOP) is the first element s1. Each element si of the stack is represented by a node j consisting of <u>two</u> values INFO(j) and LINK(j). INFO(j) is element si itself, while LINK(j) is the index of si's successor. The linked list of Fig. 2b could also be depicted as follows:

```
TOP     INFO(2) LINK(2)      INFO(4) LINK(4)       INFO(1) LINK(1)
┌─┐     ┌───────┬───────┐    ┌───────┬───────┐     ┌───────┬───────┐
│2┼--->│   9   │   4  -┼-->│   7   │   1  -┼--> │   4   │   0   │
└─┘     └───────┴───────┘    └───────┴───────┘     └───────┴───────┘
```

Thus the integers in TOP and the LINK fields act like arrows, directing one to the next node or "pointing at" the next node. Looking at Fig. 2b or the above, we deduce:

1. TOP=2. Therefore s1=INFO(TOP)=9. s1's successor is in node LINK(2)=4.

2. s2=INFO(4)=7. s2's successor is in node LINK(4), which is node 1.

3. s3=INFO(1)=4. LINK(1)=0, so s3 has no successor.

Using linked lists, the operation s<==A can be implemented as follows:

```
Find an unused node I (which is (INFO(I),LINK(I)));
INFO(I)= A;
LINK(I)= TOP;
TOP= I;
```

The problem is, of course, to find an unused node. Similarly, when executing A<==s; we must be able to indicate that the node being popped from s becomes unused. We solve these problems by keeping a second linked list or stack that contains all the unused or AVAILable nodes. Simple variable AVAIL will designate the top of this stack. This is shown in Fig. 2c, and we also show below the second way of picturing it:

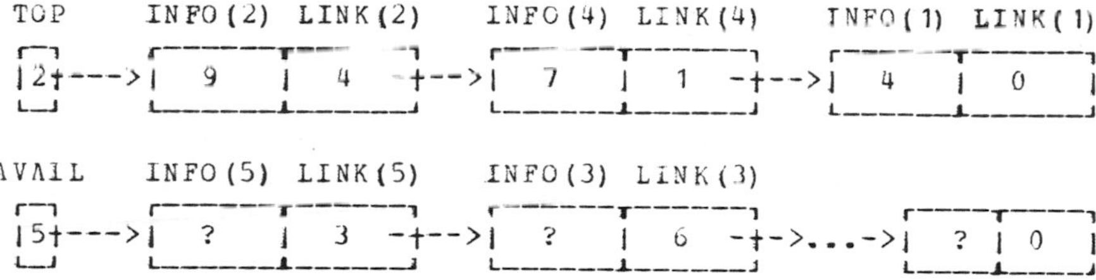

We designate by I<===AVAIL; the operation that takes an unused node from the AVAIL list, stores its index in variable I, and sets LINK(I) to 0. The corresponding operation AVAIL<===I puts a node I back onto the AVAIL list.

```
(2.3.1)  operation       PL/I
         I<===AVAIL      IF AVAIL=0
                            THEN overflow;
                         I= AVAIL;
                         AVAIL= LINK(AVAIL);
                         LINK(I)= 0;

         AVAIL<===I;     LINK(I)= AVAIL;
                         AVAIL= I;
                         I= 0;
```

The use of such an AVAIL list is important, and the operations of getting an "unused" node from it and putting a free node back on it are so frequent that we will always refer to them by their abbreviations I<===AVAIL; and AVAIL<===I;.

There are two points to consider about the implementation of I<===AVAIL. First, overflow means that there are no unused nodes, and if implemented in a program it should be replaced by statements that print an appropriate message and halt. Secondly, the statement LINK(I)=0; is not necessary, but it does protect against program errors. Suppose this statement is not present. Then after executing I<===AVAIL; node I is still linked, through LINK(I), to the AVAIL list; hence an error might cause the AVAIL list to be erroneously used. Setting LINK(I) to 0 localizes the effect of such errors. For the same reason, operation AVAIL<===I; includes setting I to 0.

We are now in a position to describe the variables used in implementing a single stack using linked lists:

```
DCL (AVAIL, TOP, I) FIXED;
DCL (INFO(100), LINK(100)) FIXED;
```

Variable I has been declared as part of the stack. This is to emphasize that it is a local variable used only in implementing the stack operations, and that it shouldn't be used elsewhere.

The following <u>must</u> be executed to initialize the stack to empty and to put all the nodes on list AVAIL.

```
TOP= 0;
AVAIL= HBOUND(LINK,1);
DO I= 1 TO HBOUND(LINK,1) BY 1;
    LINK(I)= I-1;
    END;
```

(2.3.2)

Stack operation	PL/I implementation

`s<==A;`	`I<===AVAIL;`
	`INFO(I)= A;`
	`LINK(I)= TOP;`
	`TOP= I;`

`A<==s;`	`IF TOP= 0`
	`    THEN underflow;`
	`I= TOP;`
	`A= INFO(TOP);`
	`TOP= LINK(TOP);`
	`AVAIL<===I;`

`s=();`	`DO WHILE(TOP¬=0);`
	`    I= TOP;`
	`    TOP= LINK(TOP);`
	`    AVAIL<===I;`
	`    END;`

`empty(s)`	`TOP=0` (a logical expression)
`top(s)`	`INFO(TOP)` (a variable)

The linked list scheme for a stack has at least two disadvantages compared to sequential allocation. It requires twice as much space because of the additional LINK field. (It may be less than twice the space if the INFO field consists of several values.) Secondly, only the successor operation is easy to implement (LINK(J) gives node J's successor), while in the sequential allocation scheme it was also easy to determine the predecessor. We shall see in Section 2.3 some advantages of the linked list scheme that in many contexts outweigh these disadvantages.

One advantage of the linked list scheme can be mentioned now: any number of stacks (or queues, or mixtures of both, for that matter) can be implemented in the same two arrays INFO and LINK. One just needs a different TOP variable for each one. This means that we need not give a maximum size for each stack; stacks can grow as large as they want as long as the pool of available nodes is not used up.

Let us see how to implement a queue using a linked list in the same arrays INFO and LINK. With a queue we must be able to refer to both ends, so that we need *two* simple link variables, say F and R for front and rear:

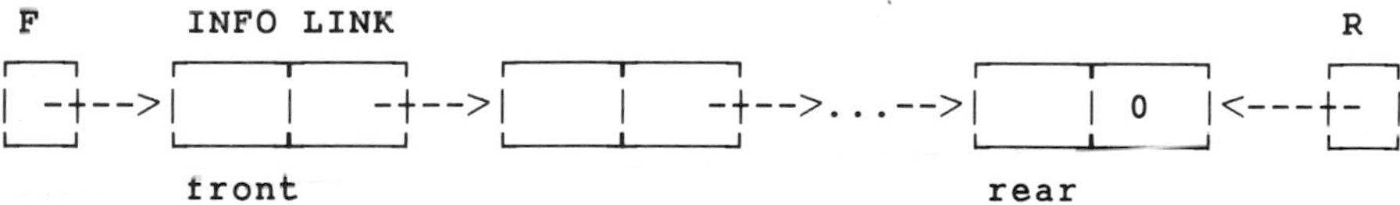

Remembering that nodes are inserted at the rear and deleted from the front, we give two of the operations on queues, of course making use of the AVAIL list.

```
(2.3.3)  Queue operation      PL/I implementation
         q<==A;               I<==AVAIL;
                              INFO(I)= A;
                              IF F=0
                                  THEN F=I;
                                  ELSE LINK(R)= I;
                              R=I;

         A<==q;               IF F=0
                                  THEN underflow;
                              I= F;
                              A= INFO(F);
                              F= LINK(F);
                              AVAIL<===I;
                              IF F=0
                                  THEN R= 0;
```

2.4 Examples of Implementations of Stacks

Writing algorithms with stacks and queues as values of variables (rather than simply in terms of PL/I numbers and strings) allows one to express ideas more clearly because many details can be suppressed. For example, consider a procedure to deal five playing cards to each of four players. Given is a variable DECK that contains a stack of cards -- how the cards are represented need not concern us -- and an array PLAYER(1:4), with each element containing the stack of cards that player holds. The purpose of the procedure is to deal five cards to each player, thus transferring cards from DECK to each of the elements PLAYER(I). In the procedure below upper case terms are PL/I, while lower case terms and non-PL/I operations refer to stacks; they must later be implemented in PL/I.

```
/*DEAL 5 CARDS FROM DECK TO EACH PLAYER IN PLAYER(1:4)*/
DEAL: PROC(DECK, PLAYER);
     DCL (DECK, PLAYER(*)) stack of card;
     DCL TEMP card;     /*HOLDS A CARD TEMPORARILY */
     DCL (I,J) FIXED;
     DO I= 1 TO 5 BY 1;
        DO J= 1 TO 4 BY 1;
           TEMP<==DECK;
           PLAYER(J)<==TEMP;
           END;
        END;
     END DEAL;
```

This procedure is written in terms of stacks because that is a simple, clear notation for the problem. We now show how to implement the procedure in PL/I using both sequential and linked allocation. Fortunately, procedure DEAL looks just as simple in PL/I; basically the operations TEMP<==DECK; and PLAYER(P)<==TEMP; are replaced by procedure calls and the declarations of stacks by suitable PL/I structures. Thus the main task is to design and implement the structures and procedures. Of course, this must be done only once; thereafter they may be used again wherever stacks of cards are needed.

Each card of a deck consists of a rank and a suit. It makes sense to combine them into a single unit of information using a PL/I structure:

```
DCL 1 CARD,
        2 (SUIT, RANK) FIXED;
```

Thus any part of the program dealing with cards as a whole need not mention the suit and rank directly; only those parts that must inspect the suit and rank need refer directly to them individually.

First consider <u>sequential allocation</u> of stacks. On the next pages we give an outline of the complete program, so that you can see how the various parts can be organized for understandability.

First is the declaration DECK of the deck of cards as a structure that includes both the array and the variable TOP that indicates the top of the stack. This has been done so that the entire deck of cards can be manipulated as a single unit, using the name DECK.

Second is the declaration of an array PLAYER(1:4), each element of which has exactly the same structure as DECK. Note, however, that the maximum size of each of these stacks is 5 since that is how many cards each player can have.

Next come the definitions of procedures that implement the stack operations. (We have written only two of them; the rest are left to you.) These can operate on any stack that has exactly the same structure as DECK.

Writing the declarations of parameters in such procedures can be a tedious job, for they are almost identical to those of earlier declared variables. PL/I has a facility to copy the form of a previous structure:

```
DCL 1 S LIKE DECK;
```

Unfortunately, LIKE has not been implemented in PL/C. (The PL/C macro facility can be used in its place.)

One consolation, and an important point, is that the procedures that implement the stack operations need only be written once. Thereafter, one can think of "stack of cards" as a new type, on the same level with FIXED and FLOAT and CHAR. In a sense, the language has been extended to include this type.

This point is illustrated in procedure DEAL, the PL/I implementation of the procedure given at the end of Section 2.1. Aside from the tedious declarations, the body of the procedure is simple and easy to understand.

```
/*ILLUSTRATION OF SEQUENTIAL ALLOCATION OF STACKS OF CARDS*/
X: PROC OPTIONS(MAIN);
   DCL 1 DECK                    /*STACK OF CARDS USING SEQUEN*/
         2 CARD(1:52),           /*TIAL ALLOCATION AS DESCRIBED*/
           3 (SUIT,RANK) FIXED,/*IN TEXT*/
         2 TOP FIXED INIT(0);

   DCL 1 PLAYER(1:4),            /*FOR 1<=I<=4, PLAYER(I) IS */
         2 CARD(1:5),            /*A STACK OF CARDS HELD BY */
           3 (SUIT,RANK) FIXED,/*PLAYER I.  SAME IMPLEMENTA*/
         2 TOP FIXED INIT(0);    /*TION AS FOR DECK */
```

```
/* S<==A;, FOR STACKS SEQUENTIALLY ALLOCATED(LIKE DECK) */
PUSH: PROC(S,A);
    DCL 1 A, 2 (SUIT,RANK) FIXED;
    DCL 1 S, 2 CARD(*),
                3 (SUIT,RANK) FIXED,
              2 TOP FIXED;
    IF S.TOP=HBOUND(S.CARD,1)
        THEN overflow;
    S.TOP= S.TOP + 1;
    S.CARD(S.TOP)= A;
    END PUSH;

/* A<==S;, FOR STACKS SEQUENTIALLY ALLOCATED(LIKE DECK) */
POP: PROC(A,S);
    [declaration of parameters as in PUSH]
    IF S.TOP=0
        THEN underflow;
    A= S.CARD(S.TOP);
    S.TOP= S.TOP-1;
    END POP;

...

[declaration of procedures for all other stack operations]
...

/*DEAL 5 CARDS FROM DECK D TO EACH PLAYER IN P(1:4).  */
DEAL: PROC(D,P);
    DCL 1 D,
             2 CARD(*),
                3 (SUIT,RANK) FIXED,
             2 TOP FIXED;
    DCL 1 P(*),
             2 CARD(*),
                3 (SUIT,RANK) FIXED,
             2 TOP FIXED;
    DCL 1 TEMP,
             2 (SUIT,RANK) FIXED;
    DCL (I,J) FIXED;

    DO I= 1 TO 5 BY 1;
        DO J= 1 TO 4 BY 1;
           CALL POP(TEMP,D);
           CALL PUSH(PLAYER(J),TEMP);
           END;
        END;
    END DEAL;

...
[main program, including initialization of DECK, PLAYER]
...

END X;
```

We consider an implementation of the same procedure using linked list allocation. The following program should be studied carefully, for it illustrates several points.

The implementation of the linked list allocation is the structure POOL, which includes the array of elements that represent cards. A deck of cards has a maximum of 52 cards and presumably this is all we need. We have included room for a few extra cards in case some procedure needs to hold cards temporarily.

POOL will be referenced globally by all procedures.

Directly after the declaration are initialization statements. We have previously required that all declarations precede all program statements; we now show one context where relaxation of this rule is reasonable. These initialization statements belong with the declaration of POOL and the linked list procedures OBTAIN and GIVEUP, for together they form a unit that can be placed in any program, as a whole, in order to extend the language of that program to include linked lists. Putting the initialization at the beginning of the main program would tend to destroy the desired unity.

Following the initialization are procedure definitions for the two linked list operations. The first procedure uses completely qualified names to reference parts of POOL, which reduces the chance of ambiguity but tends to make the program look cluttered and dense. The second procedure uses partly qualified names to illustrate the difference.

Following the linked list implementation we have the implementation of stacks using linked lists. This shows how one can easily build upon what has been done earlier. There are actually three levels of programming language here: PL/I itself, PL/I plus linked lists (implemented using arrays), and PL/I plus linked lists plus stacks (implemented using linked lists).

Finally we give procedure DEAL. Note that except for the declarations the procedure is exactly the same as in the sequential allocation case. This shows how programs can be written at a high level of notation to allow the possibility for trying out several different implementations of the high level concepts.

```
/*  ILLUSTRATION OF LINKED LIST ALLOCATION OF STACKS OF CARDS */
Y: PROC OPTIONS (MAIN);
   /** IMPLEMENTATION OF LINKED LISTS IN POOL*/
       DCL 1 POOL,
             2 CARD(1:60),
               3 (SUIT,RANK) FIXED,
             2 LINK(1:60) FIXED,
             2 AVAIL FIXED;

       /** INITIALIZATION OF POOL*/
           DO POOL.AVAIL= HBOUND(POOL.LINK,1) TO 1 BY -1;
              POOL.LINK(POOL.AVAIL)= POOL.AVAIL-1;
              END;
           POOL.AVAIL= HBOUND(POOL,LINK,1);

       /** J<===AVAIL, USING GLOBAL POOL OF CARDS*/
       OBTAIN: PROC(J);
           DCL J FIXED;
           IF POOL.AVAIL=0
               THEN overflow;
           J= POOL.AVAIL;
           POOL.AVAIL= POOL.LINK(POOL.AVAIL);
           POOL.LINK(J)= 0;
           END OBTAIN;

       /** AVAIL<===J, USING GLOBAL POOL OF CARDS*/
       GIVEUP: PROC(J);
           DCL J FIXED;
           LINK(J)= AVAIL;
           AVAIL= J;
           J= 0;
           END GIVEUP;

       /** END IMPLEMENTATION OF LINKED LISTS IN POOL*/
```

```
/* IMPLEMENTATION OF STACKS OF CARDS USING LINKED LISTS*/
/*FIXED VARIABLE S ALWAYS IS AN INTEGER GIVING THE HEAD*/
/*OF A LINKED LIST IMPLEMENTED IN GLOBAL STRUCTURE POOL*/
    /** S<==A*/
    PUSH: PROC(S,A);
        DCL S FIXED,
            1 A, 2 (SUIT,RANK) FIXED;
        DCL I FIXED;
        CALL OBTAIN(I);
        POOL.CARD(I)= A;
        POOL.LINK(I)= S;
        S= I;
        END PUSH;

    /** A<==S*/
    POP: PROC(A,S);
        DCL S FIXED,
            1 A, 2 (SUIT,RANK) FIXED;
        DCL I FIXED;
        IF S=0
            THEN underflow;
        I= S;
        A= POOL.CARD(S);
        S= POOL.LINK(S);
        CALL GIVEUP(I);
        END POP;

    [Procedures for other stack operations]

    /** END IMPL. OF STACKS OF CARDS USING LINKED LISTS*/

...

/** DEAL 5 CARDS FROM DECK D TO EACH PLAYER IN P(1:4)*/
DEAL: PROC(D,P);
    DCL (D, P(*)) FIXED;    /*TOPS OF STACKS IN POOL*/
    DCL 1 TEMP,
        2 (SUIT,RANK) FIXED;
    DCL (I, J) FIXED;
    DO I= 1 TO 5 BY 1;
        DO J= 1 TO 4 BY 1;
            CALL POP(TEMP,D);
            CALL PUSH(PLAYER(J),TEMP);
            END;
        END;
    END DEAL;

...

Main program

....

END Y;
```

Section 2 Exercises

1. Consider the stack s=(1,2). Execute the following sequence of operations on s: a<==s; b<==s; s<==5; s<==b; top(s)=top(s)+2; s<==a; s<==b; c<==s. After execution, what are the values of a, b, c, top(s) and empty(s)?

2. Do exercise 1 for s=(2,1) and the sequence a<==s; s<==a+5; s<==top(s)+2; top(s):=top(s)-1; c<==top(s); b<==s;.

3. Consider the queue q=(1,2). Execute the sequence of operations a<==q; b<==q; q<==5; q<==b; front(q)=front(q)+2; q<==a; q<==b; q<==a; c<==q;. What are the values of a, b, c, front(q), rear(q) and empty(q) before and after execution?

4. Do the same as exercise 3 for q=(2,1) and the sequence a<==q; q<==a+5; q<==front(q)+rear(q); rear(q)=rear(q)-1; b<==q;.

5. Do the same as exercise 3 for q=(2,1) and the sequence a<==q; b=front(q); c<==q;.

6. Section 2.1 defined *stack*, *queue* and *deque* but only gave notation for operations on stacks and queues. Develop a notation for manipulating deques in the spirit of Section 2.1.

7. Develop a sequential allocation implementation for deques based on your answer to exercise 6.

8. Section 2.2 showed how two stacks could be implemented sequentially using one array. Can two queues, or a stack and a queue, be similarly implemented? Explain your answer.

9. Let size(s) and size(q) be two new operations that denote the number of elements currently in a stack s and queue q. Augment the sequential allocation scheme for stacks and queues by showing how to implement the new operations. Do the same for the linked list allocation method.

10. In the sequential allocation method for a queue, F and R are initialized to 0. How else can they be initialized?

11. Consider a sequential allocation of a queue that uses, instead of variables F and R, two variables IN and OUT defined as follows: IN is the total number of elements inserted into the queue since the creation of the queue, while OUT is the total number taken out. Develop this sequential allocation method.

12. In the sequential allocation of a stack the implementation of s<==A includes an explicit check for overflow. Why is this explicit check not included in the linked list allocation of s<==A;?

13. In the sequential allocation of a queue how many elements can be in the queue without overflow occurring?

Section 3 Other Forms of Linked Lists

3.1 Inserting and Deleting Nodes in a Linked List

With stacks and queues, insertions and deletions are made only at the beginning and end. It should be clear, however, that in a linked list a node can be inserted after another node just as easily, as the following diagram shows.

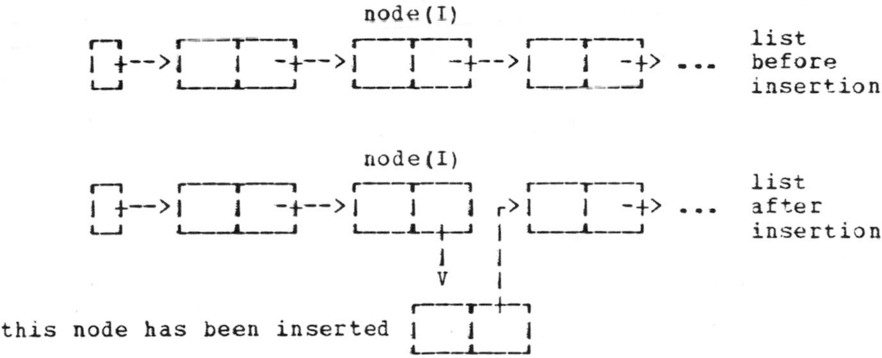

Similarly we can delete the node following a given node. The PL/I implementation of these operations, given below, uses a variable J that cannot be currently in use for some other purpose. Note that the delete operation makes sense only if there actually is a node following node(I).

Operation	PL/I implementation
Obtain and insert a node after node(I)	J<===AVAIL; LINK(J)= LINK(I); LINK(I)= J;
Delete and release the node following node(i)	J= LINK(I); LINK(I)= LINK(J); AVAIL<===J;

Note that inserting or deleting node(I) itself is more difficult and time consuming because it involves finding node(I)'s predecessor, and this can mean searching through the whole linked list.

The ease with which a node may be inserted into or deleted from a linked list makes the linked list much more attractive than sequential arrays for some applications. Inserting a value x after A(I) in an array A(1:N) typically requires moving the array segment A(I+1:N) into positions A(I+2:N+1). With linked lists no such time-consuming motion is required. In any program that requires ordered lists in which values will be continually inserted and deleted, linked lists should be considered.

3.2 Stacks and Queues with Headers

In the linked list allocation of stacks and queues an empty stack TOP (say) was represented by TOP=0. Particularly with queues, the PL/I implementation can be made simpler by always having at least one node at the beginning, called a header. Such a header is also useful whenever extra information about the linked list, such as its length, is needed. For example, a queue (q1,q2,q3) can be represented in this fashion as

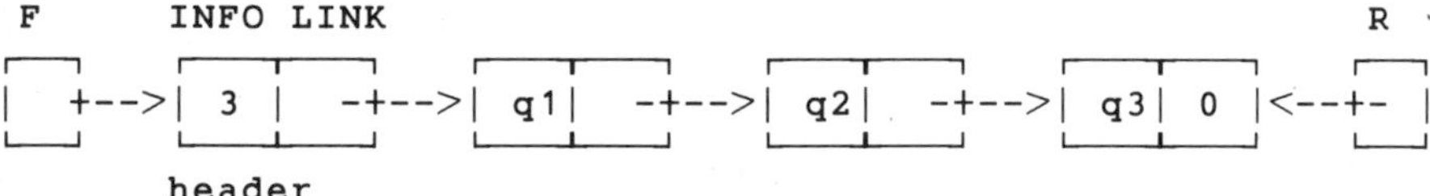

Let us introduce a second example of the use of a header, the implementation of variable precision integer arithmetic. In PL/C any fixed decimal number must lie in the range -99999 to +99999, and implementing variable precision arithmetic allows us to work with integers of almost any size.

A number like x = 543798 can be written as

$$x = 8 \cdot 10^0 + 9 \cdot 10^1 + 7 \cdot 10^2 + 3 \cdot 10^3 + 4 \cdot 10^4 + 5 \cdot 10^5,$$

that is, in the form

$$x = x0 \cdot 10^0 + x1 \cdot 10^1 + x2 \cdot 10^2 + x3 \cdot 10^3 + \ldots$$

where each xi satisfies $0 \leq xi < 10$. In this case 10 is called the base and x is being represented in the base 10, or decimal, system.

We can therefore represent any integer in a linked list with a header, where the header can be used to indicate the sign of the integer, as follows

1. The INFO field of the first node on the linked list contains +1 if the integer is positive, 0 if the integer is zero and -1 if the integer is negative.

2. The second, third, ... nodes contain the digits x0, x1, ... of the integer.

3. The last node must contain a nonzero digit xi.

We show below the internal representation of the integers x = 0, y = 582 and z = -32 using variables X, Y and Z to indicate the beginning of the linked lists.

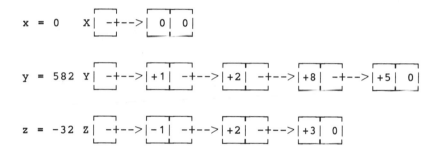

```
x = 0     X| -+-->| 0| 0|

y = 582   Y| -+-->|+1| -+-->|+2| -+-->|+8| -+-->|+5| 0|

z = -32   Z| -+-->|-1| -+-->|+2| -+-->|+3| 0|
```

To use integers effectively using this representation, it is necessary to write a set of procedures to (1) put a PL/I FIXED value into the linked list form, (2) print an integer that is in linked list form, (3) add, subtract, multiply and divide integers in linked list form, and (4) compare integers in linked list form.

Exercises 1 to 5 at the end of this section involve the implementation of variable precision arithmetic.

For ease of understanding we have represented integers in base 10 (decimal) notation. It should be clear to the reader already familiar with the idea of integers represented in different bases that using a larger base is much more efficient. For example, we show below the number x = 543798 in the base 100, 1000 and 10000 systems. In a PL/I implementation, the size of the base is limited by the size of the integer that can fit in the INFO field and perhaps by the size of the intermediate results produced by the multiply and divide operations.

```
X = 543798
in          X| -+-->| +1| -+-->| 98| -+-->| 37| -+-->| 54| 0|
base 100
```

```
X = 543798       ┌──┐    ┌─────┬──┐    ┌─────┬──┐    ┌─────┬──┐
in              X│ -+--->│  +1 │ -+--->│ 798 │ -+--->│ 543 │ 0│
base 1000        └──┘    └─────┴──┘    └─────┴──┘    └─────┴──┘

X = 543798       ┌──┐    ┌─────┬──┐    ┌─────┬──┐    ┌─────┬──┐
in              X│ -+--->│  +1 │ -+--->│3798 │ -+--->│  54 │ 0│
base 10000       └──┘    └─────┴──┘    └─────┴──┘    └─────┴──┘
```

3.3 Circular Lists

Consider a singly linked list as in the beginning of Section 3.1. If the last node of the list points back to the first we have what is called a circular list:

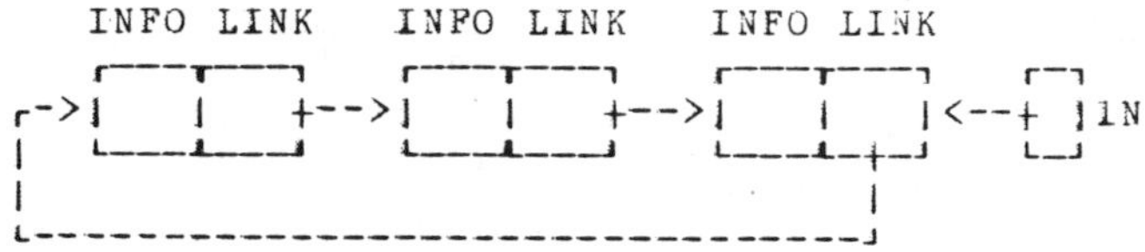

With a circular list it is possible to access all nodes starting at any point. Thus no importance need be placed on any particular node; there is no need to think of a "first" or "last" node. One simply needs a single variable IN (say) that contains a link to one of the nodes.

The diagram above has IN placed at the right instead of the left because this position allows us to think of inserting a new node at either the left or the right, as indicated in the following operations. The third operation below is used to delete an element from the linked list.

Operation	PL/I implementation
Insert a node with value Y at left	I<===AVAIL; INFO(I) = Y; LINK(I) = LINK(IN); LINK(IN) = I;
Insert a node with value Y at right	Insert node with value Y at left; IN = LINK(IN);
Delete the left node	I = LINK(IN); LINK(IN) = LINK(I); AVAIL<===I;

It should be noted that the two insert operations do not work if the list is initially empty, while the delete operation does not work if the list contains one or zero nodes. Exercise 6 is devoted to rectifying this problem.

Of course, another way to resolve the problem of empty lists is, again, to propose that every circular list always have at least one node called the list head as in Section 3.2. The list head would always be in a fixed place.

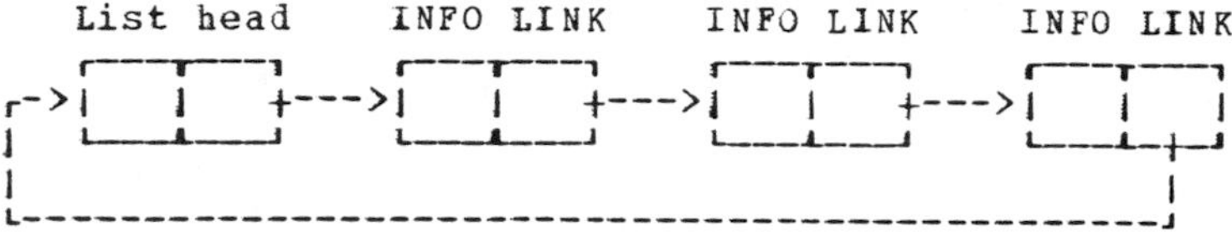

A study of the three operations described above reveals that a circular list can be used to implement a stack or a queue. Circular lists can also be used to efficiently implement other important operations on queues. As discussed in Exercise 7, it is easy to merge two disjoint circular lists into one. One can also put an entire nonempty circular list onto the list AVAIL with three simple assignment statements.

To end this section, let us outline a very simple application of circular lists. A common game is played as follows. A total of n players form a circle facing inwards, choose some positive integer m, and choose a starting player who is it. Players will now be deleted from the circle one at a time until one player is left, the winner. A player is deleted as follows. The player who is it counts around the circle beginning at his left and going counterclockwise until he reaches m. This mth player is deleted and his predecessor becomes it. The trick is, given n and m, to know how to choose the starting player to be it, relative to yourself, so that you will win.

While we will not give a solution to the problem, we can easily write a program that simulates the game. Using only arrays in the conventional fashion this might be difficult; using circular lists it is relatively simple. We first initialize a circular list to contain n nodes with INFO fields 1,2,...,n, and set IN to point to the node with value 1. The algorithm that simulates the game is then

```
DO WHILE (IN ¬= LINK(IN));  /* list has at least*/
                                  /* 2 nodes */
    /** SET IN TO PREDECESSOR OF PLAYER TO DELETE */
        DO I = 1 TO M-1;
            IN = LINK(IN);
            END;
    /** DELETE THE Mth PLAYER */
        I = LINK(IN);
        LINK(IN) = LINK(I);
        AVAIL <=== I;
    END;

[Player INFO(IN) is the winner]
```

3.4 Doubly Linked Lists

With a singly linked list one can easily delete the successor of a node I but not the node I itself. One also has difficulties determining the predecessor of node I. These problems dissappear if one uses a doubly linked list, in which each node has a link SUCC to its successor and a link PRED to its predessor:

```
         PRED    SUCC      PRED    SUCC      PRED    SUCC
┌─┐     ┌─────┬┬─────┐    ┌─────┬┬─────┐    ┌─────┬┬─────┐
│ +-->│  0  ││     +-->│     ││     +-->│     ││  0  │
│ │   │     ││     │<--+     ││     │<--+     ││     │
└─┘     └─────┴┴─────┘    └─────┴┴─────┘    └─────┴┴─────┘
```

When using a list header then, the successor of the last node is considered to be the header itself and the header's predecessor is considered to be the last node:

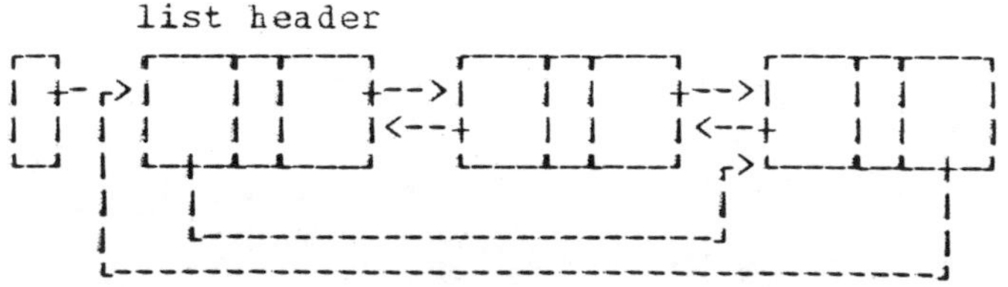

Deleting node I of a doubly linked list is now a simple process; only the predecessor's successor field and the successor's predecessor field need be changed, as the operation below shows. Similarly, inserting a node before node I becomes as easy as inserting one after node I. The operations below are designed to work on doubly linked lists with headers that always exist. Thus, in the delete operation the header itself may not be deleted.

Operation	PL/I implementation
Delete node I and return to AVAIL list	SUCC(PRED(I)) = SUCC(I); PRED(SUCC(I)) = PRED(I); AVAIL <=== I;
Insert a new node before node I	J <=== AVAIL; PRED(J) = PRED(I); SUCC(J) = I; SUCC(PRED(I)), PRED(I) = J;
Insert a new node after node I	K = SUCC(I); Insert a new node before node K

Many applications contain arbitrary insertion and deletion of elements in lists, as well as processing of lists elements in either direction (from front to rear and from rear to front). In such applications, the doubly linked list is a useful tool, and the extra flexibility and speed of basic operations more than make up for the extra space needed for the predecessor links.

Section 3 Exercises

Exercises 1-5 are projects that lead to an implementation of variable precision arithmetic as described in Section 3.2. They will increase your understanding of conventional arithmetic as well as of linked lists.

1. Implement a "package" of procedures to manipulate lists (with headers) of FIXED numbers. They will use a global structure.

```
DCL 1 LISTS,
      2 AVAIL FIXED,
      2 NODE(1:200),
         3 (INFO, LINK) FIXED;
```

The following five internal procedures will suffice; all parameters are FIXED:

1. INITSPACE: PROC; Initialize the list by putting all nodes on the AVAIL list.
2. STARTLIST: PROC(I); Set I to the index of a new list that consists solely of a header node.
3. INSERT: PROC(J); J is the LINK field of some node (i.e. the argument is LINK(K) for some K). Insert a new node (from the AVAIL list) after this node.
4. DELETE: PROC(J). J is the LINK field of some node. Delete the node following node J from the list and return it to AVAIL.
5. DELETELIST: PROC(J). Delete the entire list pointed to by J and return it to the AVAIL list. Set J to 0.

2. Using the list package of Exercise 1, write the following procedures to perform variable precision arithmetic. The procedures will all refer to a global variable B that will contain the <u>base</u> of the representation, as discussed in Section 3.2. Use B=10 initially, which yields the conventional decimal system. All parameters are FIXED.

1. CONVERT: PROC(X,I); Convert the ordinary FIXED value X into variable precision form and return the index of the header of the linked list result in I. The algorithm for converting is given in Exercise 1 of IX.1.
2. ADD: PROC(U,V,W); U and V are links to the headers of lists representing variable precision integers. Add the values together and return in W a link to the header of the list representing the result.
3. SUBTRACT:PROC(U,V,W); as in ADD, but perform W = U - V, instead of W = U + V.
4. PRINTB: PROC(U); U is as in the ADD procedure. Print out the variable precision value in radix B format.
5. PRINTDEC: PROC(U); U is as in the ADD procedure. Print out the variable precision value in conventional decimal notation. This routine is more difficult and may be given to you by your instructor.

3. Design and implement procedures MULTIPLY (U,V,W) and DIVIDE (U,V,W) to perform variable precision multiply and divide.

4. Use your results of Exercises 1-3 to print out N! = N·(N-1)·(N-2)·...·1 for as many values of N as you can. The following program segment to do this relies on the fact that N! = N·(N-1)!.

```
CALL CONVERT(1, OLDFACT);
DO I = 2 TO 1000 BY 1;
    CALL CONVERT(I, NEXTI);
    CALL MULTIPLY(OLDFACT, NEXTI, NEWFACT);
    CALL DELETELIST(OLDFACT);        /*WHY?*/
    CALL DELETELIST(NEXTI);          /*WHY?*/
    CALL PRINTDEC(NEWFACT);
    CALL PRINTB(NEWFACT);
    OLDFACT = NEWFACT;
    END;
```

Run the same program with different radixes: B=10, B=100, B=10,000, etc. and look for relationships between B, time and space.

5. Use the results of Exercises 1-3 to print out 2**N for N = 1,2,3,... (as many as you can in a reasonable amount of computing time).

6. Consider circular lists as described in Section 3.3. Let an empty circular list be represented by IN = 0. Change the operations "insert a node at left" and "insert a node at right" so that they would work correctly when the circular list is empty. Change operation "delete left node" so that it works properly if the list contains only one node.

7. Suppose IN1 and IN2 point to two disjoint circular lists. Write a program segment that merges the two into a single disjoint circular list that is pointed to by IN1. The nodes of IN1 should appear to the right of those of IN2 in the final list. Use only conditional and assignment statements (no loops). Be sure to take care of the cases IN1 = 0 and/or IN2 = 0.

8. Suppose IN points to a node in a nonempty circular list. Write a sequence of assignments that puts the entire circular list on the AVAIL stack.

9. The operation "Insert a new node after node I" on doubly linked lists, given in Section 3.4, is written in terms of the operation "Insert a new node before node K". Rewrite it as a sequence of assignments that do <u>not</u> need the local variable K.

10. The operations given in Section 3.4 for doubly linked lists work on lists with headers. Design similar operations for lists without headers and write their PL/I implementation. Be careful when dealing with an empty list.

Section 4 Trees

4.1 Binary Trees and Their Representation

In Section 3.4 we saw the use of two links in a node to form a doubly linked list. We now use this idea of having more than one link in a node in a different manner to represent so-called trees. For this introduction we restrict our attention to binary trees, which we define recursively as follows:

> A binary tree is a finite set of nodes that is either empty or consists of a root node and two disjoint binary trees, called the left and right subtrees, respectively.

Figure (4.1a) shows four trees. The first consists of a root node A and two empty binary trees. The second consists of a root node A, an empty left subtree and a right subtree; the right subtree consists of a root B and two empty subtrees. The third is different from the second because its right subtree, and not its left, is empty. The fourth tree consists of a root D, a left subtree containing the nodes B, A, C, and a right subtree containing the nodes F, G.

The idea of a tree in the sense given occurs often outside computer science, the main difference being that, for historical reasons, computer scientists tend to draw trees with the root at the top instead of the bottom. Computer scientists even call the nodes with empty left and right subtrees leaves. We use the term binary tree because each tree or subtree has at most two subtrees. One can of course use more general trees, but in an introduction the binary tree will suffice.

As an example of the use of "trees" in everyday life consider the "family tree", which shows the ancestors of a given individual. A root node denotes the individual, the left subtree the mother and her ancestors, and the right subtree the father and his ancestors, in a similar fashion.

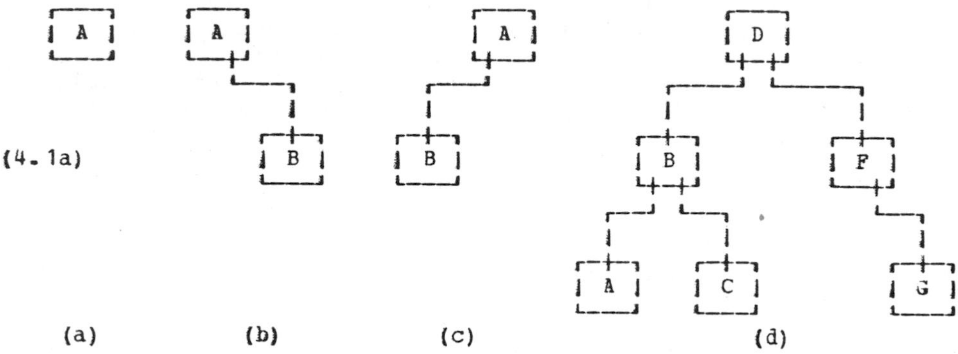

The table of contents of this book bears a strong resemblance to a tree -- it looks different simply because a different two-dimensional representation was used for it. The root node is the book itself; its subtrees are the Preface, Part I, Part II, etc. Part I contains the sections (subtrees) labeled I.1, ..., I.9, and each of these has its subtrees.

The following terminology is usually used in computer science. A root is called the *father* of the roots of its subtrees, the roots of its subtrees are *brothers* and are the *sons* of their father. In the same sense, all nodes in the subtree are called *descendents* of the root. Those nodes with no sons are called *terminal nodes* or *leaves*.

For example, in the tree d of Figure (4.1a), D has a left son B and a right son F. F has no left son and a right son G. A, C and G have no sons, and are leaves, or terminal nodes. The terminal nodes are A, C and G.

The root node is on *level 1*, its sons are on *level 2*, their sons are on *level 3*, and so on.

One can use a *linear representation* of a binary tree, which is also defined recursively. Let rep(T) denote the linear representation of T. If T is the empty tree then

rep(T) = ().

If T consists of a root node A, a left subtree T1 and a right subtree T2, then

rep(T) = (A rep(T1) rep(T2)).

For example, the trees of (4.1a) would be written as

```
(a) (A () ())
(b) (A () (B () ()))
(c) (A (B () ()) ())
(d) (D (B (A () ()) (C () ())) (F () (G () ())))
```

Obviously, the two-dimensional representation of Fig. (4.1a) is easier to understand than this linear representation, but where it is simple enough, we use the linear representation because it takes less space. One convention that helps is: if both subtrees of a tree with root A are empty, it is permissable to write (A) instead of (A () ()). The above examples would thus be written as

(a) (A)
(b) (A () (B))
(c) (A (B) ())
(d) (D (B (A) (C)) (F () (G)))

In this linear representation of trees, the <u>level</u> of a node is simply its level of nesting within parentheses.

We now look at how trees may be represented using linked list concepts. An empty tree can be represented by a <u>nil</u> (or 0, usually) link. A nonempty tree (A T1 T2) can be represented by a link to a node that contains three fields named INFO, LEFT and RIGHT:

(1) INFO contains the value A of the root node.
(2) LEFT contains the representation (a link value) of the left subtree T1.
(3) RIGHT contains the representation (a link value) of the right subtree T2.

Since we are using nodes and links essentially as discussed in Sections 3.2 and 3.3, nodes can be created, used and released using an AVAIL list. One must be careful about which of the two links is used to link nodes on the AVAIL list. To illustrate, we give below one possible representation of tree d of Fig. (4.1a), in which the LEFT link is used to link nodes on the AVAIL list. Simple variable TREE contains the link to the root node of the tree.

	INFO	LEFT	RIGHT
(1)	?	8	?
(2)	B	3	4
(3)	A	0	0
(4)	C	0	0
(5)	F	0	6
(6)	G	0	0
(7)	D	2	5
(8)	?	9	?
(9)	?	10	?
...	...	...	...

TREE	7
AVAIL	1

4.2 Traversing Binary Trees

Typical applications of binary trees (and we shall see one at the end of this section) often require that each node of a binary tree be "visited" in order to perform some operation on it. Thus, one traverses the tree, or walks through it. The order in which the nodes are visited may of course be important in an application. There are three main orders, which can be defined recursively as follows:

```
preorder traversal of tree (A T1 T2):
        visit the root A.
        visit the left subtree T1 in preorder.
        visit the right subtree T2 in preorder.

inorder traversal of tree (A T1 T2):
        visit the left subtree T1 in inorder.
        visit the root A.
        visit the right subtree T2 in inorder.

postorder traversal of tree (A T1 T2):
        visit the left subtree T1 in postorder.
        visit the right subtree T2 in postorder.
        visit the root A.
```

The names preorder, inorder and postorder are derived from when the root node A is visited: first, in the middle and last.

Consider the trees b, c and d of Fig. (4.1a). For each, we give its linear representation and the order in which the nodes would be visited in each of the traversal methods.

```
tree b:     (A () (B))
preorder:   A B
inorder:    A B
postorder:  B A

tree c:     (A (B) ())
preorder:   A B
inorder:    B A
postorder:  B A

tree d:     (D (B (A) (C)) (F () (G)))
preorder:   D B A C F G
inorder:    A B C D F G
postorder:  A C B G F D
```

Inspection of these examples discloses an interesting fact that applies to all binary trees: the preorder traversal visits the nodes exactly in the order they appear in the linear representation. The inorder traversal also has an interesting property, which we will discuss later, but first let us develop a PL/I implementation of a tree traversal.

We can make use of recursion in PL/I to implement preorder quite simply. Suppose we have a representation of a tree using a link variable TREE and three global arrays INFO, LEFT and RIGHT as described in Section 4.1. We would like a call

```
CALL PREORDER(TREE);
```

to perform an operation "Visit" on each node value INFO of tree TREE, in preorder. The PL/I procedure is simply the following:

```
/* PERFORM VISIT ON EACH NODE OF */
/* TREE IN PREORDER */
/* INFO, LEFT, AND RIGHT ARE GLOBAL ARRAYS */
PREORDER: PROC(TREE) RECURSIVE;
    DCL TREE FIXED;
    IF TREE = 0 THEN RETURN;
    Visit INFO(TREE);
    CALL PREORDER(LEFT(TREE));
    CALL PREORDER(RIGHT(TREE));
    END PREORDER;
```

This procedure requires a (recursive) call of PREORDER for each of the subtrees of TREE even when they are empty. With a slight change in the definition of the procedure, we can dispense with these useless calls:

```
/* TREE ¬= 0. PERFORM VISIT ON EACH NODE OF TREE, */
/* IN PREORDER.  INFO, LEFT AND RIGHT */
/* ARE GLOBAL ARRAYS */
PREORDER: PROC(TREE) RECURSIVE;
    DCL TREE FIXED;
    Visit INFO(TREE);
    IF LEFT(TREE) ¬= 0
        THEN CALL PREORDER(LEFT(TREE));
    IF RIGHT(TREE) ¬= 0
        THEN CALL PREORDER(RIGHT(TREE));
    END PREORDER;
```

How much time does it take to perform a preorder traversal of each node of a binary tree with n nodes? Note that the above procedure is called once for each node in the tree, and from this we see that execution takes time proportional to n.

Let us see how to write a procedure PREORDER without using recursion, assuming, as in the last procedure, that TREE $\neq$ 0. To do so we will write the body of the procedure as a loop. Each iteration of the loop will visit one node of the binary tree. We will use an array S(1:100) to keep track of which nodes are still to be visited; the procedure will only work if the number of levels of the tree is no greater than 100. The meaning of array S and simple variable N is as follows:

Consider the state of affairs just before each iteration of the loop. Some nodes of TREE have already been visited in preorder form. Each value S(i), $1 \le i \le N$, is nonzero and is the index of some node in TREE. S(1:N) describes the rest of the nodes to be visited, as follows:

> First visit the nodes in subtree S(N), in preorder,
> Next visit the nodes in subtree S(N-1), in preorder,
> ...
> Finally visit the nodes in subtree S(1), in preorder.

Using this as the definition of S and N, we write the procedure simply as follows:

```
/* TREE ¬= 0. VISIT THE NODES OF TREE */
/* IN PREORDER.  GLOBAL ARRAYS INFO, */
/* LEFT  AND RIGHT ARE USED TO REPRESENT THE TREE */
PREORDER: PROCEDURE (TREE);
    DCL TREE FIXED;

    DCL (N, S(1:100), NODE) FIXED;
    N = 1;
    S(1) = TREE;
    DO WHILE (N >= 1);
        NODE = S(N);
        N = N - 1;
        Visit INFO(NODE);
        IF RIGHT(NODE) ¬= 0
            THEN DO;
                N = N + 1;
                S(N) = RIGHT(NODE)
                END;
        IF LEFT(NODE) ¬= 0
            THEN DO;
                N = N + 1;
                S(N) = LEFT(NODE);
                END;
        END;
    END PREORDER;
```

4.3 Application of Trees

We now discuss a few applications of binary trees. One application has already been discussed elsewhere: in Section VI.2.7 binary trees, with a different representation, were used to develop the sorting algorithm known as heapsort.

4.3.1 Maintaining a List of Values

In some applications the program is to keep a list of values in such a way that finding and inserting elements is fairly efficient but so that at any time one can print the list of values in ascending order. No value occurs more than once in the list. A good example is a compiler for a language like PL/I. A list of identifiers in a program, together with their "meaning" -- whether they are labels, fixed variables, procedure parameters, etc., -- is searched once for each occurrence of an identifier in that program. And the list is printed out in alphabetical order in the "cross-reference" list.

A binary tree can be used to contain such a list of values, with one value in each node, if we put a simple restriction on it:

(4.3.1a) For any subtree (VALUE T1 T2) of the binary tree, including the tree itself, all values in T1 are < VALUE and all values in T2 are > VALUE.

Tree d of Fig. (4.1a), which is (D (B (A) (C)) (F () (G))), satisfies this restriction. T1 is (B (A) (C)) and all its values are alphabetically smaller than D; T2 is (F () (G)), and both F and G are larger than D. These two subtrees (B (A) (C)) and (F () (G)) also satisfy the restriction.

With this restriction, one sees that the values of a binary tree (VALUE T1 T2) can be printed in ascending order by:

```
Print the values in T1 in ascending order.
Print VALUE.
Print the values in T2 in ascending order.
```

The astute reader will notice that this corresponds to visiting the nodes in inorder and printing each when visited. Thus the values of a binary tree satisfying (4.3.1a) can be printed in ascending order in an inorder traversal, with "print value" corresponding to "Visit". Note that this takes time proportional to the number of nodes in the tree.

In order to complete the discussion we need to give PL/I procedures for finding and inserting values in the tree.

```
/* TREE = 0 OR IS THE INDEX OF THE ROOT IN GLOBAL */
/* ARRAYS INFO, LEFT AND RIGHT. TREE SATISFIES */
/* (4.3.1A).  RETURN IN NODE THE INDEX OF THE */
/* NODE IN THE TREE THAT CONTAINS THE VALUE; */
/* RETURN 0 IF VALUE IS NOT IN THE TREE */
FIND: PROCEDURE (TREE, VALUE, NODE);
    DCL (TREE, VALUE, NODE) FIXED;
    NODE = TREE;
               /* NOTE: AT EACH ITERATION */
               /* IF THE VALUE IS IN TREE */
               /* IT IS GUARANTEED TO BE */
               /* IN THE SUBTREE WITH ROOT NODE */
    DO WHILE (NODE ¬= 0);
        IF INFO(NODE) = VALUE
            THEN RETURN;
        IF INFO(NODE) > VALUE
            THEN NODE = LEFT(NODE);
            ELSE NODE = RIGHT(NODE);
        END;
    END FIND;
```

The insert procedure searches the tree in a similar fashion -- only the necessity to insert the value at the correct place causes a difference. The procedure could be lengthened a bit to cause an immediate return whenever the value has been inserted, but the difference in speed is not worth it. Note the use of procedure INS, which is called in three places.

```
/*  TREE = 0 OR IS THE INDEX OF THE ROOT OF A TREE IN */
/* GLOBAL ARRAYS INFO, LEFT, RIGHT THAT SATISFIES */
/* (4.3.1A).  RETURN IN NODE THE INDEX OF A SUBTREE */
/* WITH A ROOT VALUE, INSERTING IT IF NECESSARY.  */
/* SET INSERTED TO '1'B ('0'B) IF INSERTION */
/* WAS (NOT) NECESSARY */
INSERT: PROC(TREE, VALUE, NODE, INSERTED);
    DCL (TREE, VALUE, NODE) FIXED;
    DCL INSERTED BIT(*); /* ARGUMENT SHOULD BE BIT(1) */

    INSERTED = '0'B;
    IF TREE = 0
        THEN CALL INS(TREE, VALUE, INSERTED);
    NODE = TREE;
    DO WHILE (INFO(NODE) ¬= VALUE);
        IF INFO(NODE) > VALUE
            THEN DO;
               IF LEFT(NODE) = 0
                   THEN CALL INS(LEFT(NODE), VALUE,
                           INSERTED);
               NODE = LEFT(NODE);
               END;
            ELSE DO;
               IF RIGHT(NODE) = 0
                   THEN CALL INS(RIGHT(NODE), VALUE,
                           INSERTED);
               NODE = RIGHT(NODE);
               END;
        END;
    END INSERT;

/* GENERATE NODE WITH INFO=V, STORE ITS INDEX IN N, */
/* SET INSERTED = '1'B.  */
INS: PROC (N, V, INSERTED);
    DCL (N,V) FIXED;
    DCL INSERTED BIT(*);
    N <=== AVAIL;
    INFO(N) = V;
    LEFT(N),RIGHT(N) = 0;
    INSERTED = '1'B;
    END INS;
```

4.3.2 Representing and Evaluating Expressions

A binary tree can be used to represent arithmetic expressions consisting of unary and binary operations, as follows:

(1) A terminal node represents a simple operand -- an identifier or constant.
(2) A nonterminal node represents an operation. The value of the node is an operator; the left subtree represents the left operand of the operation (if any) and the right subtree the right operand (if any).

Examples are:

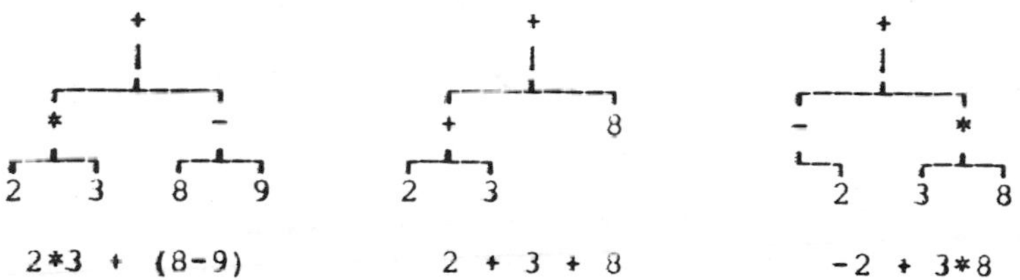

Hence, the binary tree is a natural way of representing the structure of an expression. Just as easily, we can write a recursive function EVAL that will evaluate an expression represented by a binary tree. To do this, let us look a bit closer at the PL/I binary tree representation of an expression. We will, as before, use arrays LEFT and RIGHT to designate left and right subtrees. The INFO array, however, will be a structure because we must be able to use integers as operands and characters as operators. Thus we have, for a maximum of 100 nodes,

```
DCL 1 INFO(1:100),
      2 OPERATOR CHAR(1) VARYING, /* '+', '-', *, '¬' */
                                  /* FOR UNARY MINUS, */
                                  /* OR 'I' FOR */
                                  /* INTEGER  OPERAND.  */
      2 VALUE FIXED;              /* VALUE OF OPERAND */
                                  /* IF OPERATOR='I' */
```

One assumption is that +, -, *, / all have two operands and ¬ only a right operand.

Following closely the definition of the representation of an expression as a binary tree, we write the following function EVAL.

```
/* TREE IS THE INDEX OF A BINARY TREE */
/* REPRESENTATION  OF AN EXPRESSION, USING GLOBAL */
/* ARRAYS LEFT, RIGHT, INFO.  */
/* RETURN THE VALUE OF THE EXPRESSION.  */
EVAL: PROC(TREE) RETURNS(FIXED) RECURSIVE;
    DCL TREE FIXED;

    DCL (L, R) FIXED; /* LEFT, RIGHT */
                      /* SUBTREE VALUES */
    IF LEFT(TREE) ¬= 0
       THEN L = EVAL(LEFT(TREE));
    IF RIGHT(TREE) ¬= 0
       THEN R = EVAL(RIGHT(TREE));
    SELECT;
        WHEN (INFO(TREE).OPERATOR = '+')
               RETURN (L + R);
        WHEN (INFO(TREE).OPERATOR = '-')
               RETURN (L - R);
        WHEN (INFO(TREE).OPERATOR = '*')
               RETURN (L * R);
        WHEN (INFO(TREE).OPERATOR = '¬')
               RETURN (-R);
        WHEN (INFO(TREE).OPERATOR = 'I')
               RETURN (INFO(TREE.VALUE));
        END;
    END EVAL;
```

This function performs a <u>postorder</u> traversal of the tree. First the left subtree is visited, then the right subtree is visited, and finally the root node is "visited" in order to determine which operations to perform.

This is no accident; there is a nice relationship between the various methods of traversal and the way people have viewed expressions. To see this, consider the nodes of the tree for 2 * 3 + (8 - 9) again,

```
in preorder:   + * 2 3 - 8 9
in inorder:    2 * 3 + 8 - 9
in postorder:  2 3 * 8 9 - +
```

The inorder list corresponds to our normal <u>infix</u> notation for expressions, except that parentheses have been removed. Exercise 18 asks you to rewrite the inorder traversal algorithm so that it prints out the expression fully parenthesized. Thus, the above expression would appear as ((2) * (3)) + ((8) - (9)).

The expressions printed in preorder and postorder are known as "Polish notation" because the notation first was introduced by the Polish logician Lukasiewicz (before the advent of computers). The expression in preorder is in <u>prefix notation</u>, because the operator precedes its operands, while the postorder expression is in <u>postfix</u> or <u>suffix notation</u>.

It is interesting to note that from the binary tree representation of an expression one can derive the prefix, infix and postfix notations with equal ease. Humans, of course, favor infix notation -- with use of parentheses to avoid ambiguity. The tree representation and prefix notation are used in compilers and assemblers as an "intermediate" form for expressions; they are easier to manipulate mechanically than infix notation.

Section 4 Exercises

1. Given the following linear representations of trees, draw them in two-dimensional form, as in Fig. (4.1a):

   (a) (A (B (C) (D)) (E (F) (G)))

   (b) (A (B (C (D) ()) ()) ())

   (c) (A () (B () (C () (D))))

2. In the linear representation of a binary tree, we can abbreviate (A () ()) as (A) -- if the two subtrees of a binary tree are empty, we write only the root. Why can't we simply leave out <u>all</u> occurrences of "()"? Hint: how many trees would (A (B)) represent?

3. How many different binary trees are there with three nodes, say A, B and C?

4. By inspection, we see that on level 1 of a binary tree there is a maximum of 1 node, on level 2 a maximum of 2 nodes, and on level 3 a maximum of 4 nodes. Prove (by induction on the level number) that on a level i there is a maximum of 2**(i-1) nodes, for $1 \le i$.

5. Prove that a binary tree with maximum level number i has a maximum of (2**i)-1 nodes. Hint: use the results of exercise 4 and prove it by induction on i.

6. Consider the three binary trees of exercise 1. Give a representation of each using the three arrays INFO, LEFT and RIGHT, as was done in Section 4.1 for the tree d of Fig. (4.1a).

7. List the nodes of the three trees of exercise 1 in the order they would be visited: (a) in a preorder traversal; (b) in an inorder traversal; (c) in a postorder traversal.

8. Consider the terminal nodes of a binary tree. Are they always in the same relative position in preorder, postorder, or inorder listings of all nodes? Explain your answer.

9. Write PL/I recursive procedures to visit the nodes of a binary tree in (a) inorder and (b) postorder, as was done in Section 4.2 for preorder.

10. Write PL/I procedures that are not recursive to visit the nodes of a binary tree in (a) inorder and (b) postorder, as was done in Section 4.2 for preorder.

11. Suppose you are given the nodes of a tree in both preorder and postorder. Prove that you can (or cannot) reconstruct the tree.

12. Suppose you are given the nodes of a tree in both preorder and inorder. Prove that you can (or cannot) reconstruct the tree.

13. A preorder traversal visits the nodes in the order they appear in the linear representation. Develop a new traversal method that visits the nodes in the reverse of this order -- last node first, next to last node second, etc.

14. What is the maximum depth of a tree with n nodes? Use this answer to determine how long it takes to find a value in a tree that satisfies (4.3.1a) with n nodes, in the worst case.

15. Suppose N is the index of a subtree of a binary tree that satisfies restriction (4.3.1a). It is known that N is not a terminal node (it has at least one nonempty subtree). It is desired to delete node N (but not its subtrees) from the tree, but the result should satisfy (4.3.1a). Write the algorithm to do this.

16. Write binary trees for the following arithmetic expressions:

(a) 1, 1 + 2, 2 * 1
(b) 1 * (2 + 3), 1 * 2 + 3
(c) 1 * (-2 + 3), 1 * (-2) + 3
(d) 1 + 2 + 3 + 4, 1 + (2 + (3 + 4))

17. In Section 4.3.2 appears a recursive function EVAL. Rewrite EVAL so that it uses no recursion. Hint: look at your answer to excercise 10.

18. Write a recursive procedure that, given a tree representing an expression as in Section 4.3.2, prints out the expression fully parenthesized. Hint: this is a version of an inorder traversal, with parentheses written out at the necessary places.

Part VIII
Database Systems

By any measure the most important computer application is the processing of business data. This involves:

1. maintaining the detailed operational and financial histories required by an organization;

2. processing the transactions that represent the activity of the organization;

3. making many of the low-level tactical decisions that guide and implement the routine activity of the organization;

4. producing the reports that relate the organization to others;

5. providing the information required to manage the organization.

The volume and complexity of these tasks is such that modern economic society has become completely dependent on its computers. It is hard to imagine how business, government, or even educational institutions could maintain their operations without computer systems.

In its early years -- the 50s and early 60s -- computer processing of business data could be regarded as the mechanization of recognizable tasks that had previously been performed by other means. But by now many organizations are in their second or third generation of computer-based processing and the tasks have evolved to take advantage of the new technology. Functions that were once relatively distinct, processing separate files, are being integrated into the processing of a common database. Increasingly, computer systems are involved in communication as well as the storage and processing of information.

In the past, business computing has been regarded by computer scientists with some condescension as technically uninteresting. But today there is probably more challenging developmental work in this field than in "scientific computing". There are formidable problems in achieving reliability and security in an integrated database system that is remotely and simultaneously accessed by many users.

Database systems are as varied as the organizations they serve, but there are some common distinguishing characteristics. One is the <u>longevity of the data</u>, relative to the programs. In our previous discussions we have concentrated on the program. There has been the implicit assumption that the program was relatively long-lived; that a good program would be repeatedly used for different sets of data. Now we consider systems where the database is long-lived and, in fact, is <u>permanently resident</u> in the auxiliary storage devices of the computer. Our previous programs have read their data from an external data list. Programs for database systems also read external data ("transactions") but the most important and voluminous part of their data is already present in the computer system when the program arrives.

Each individual program in a database system behaves much like the programs we have been discussing, with slightly different kinds of input and output statements, but the overall perspective of considering the <u>data to dominate</u> the system is significant and distinctive.

A second distinguishing characteristic is <u>volume</u>. Database systems consisting of 10^8 characters are commonplace, 10^{10} is not unusual, and 10^{12} is being contemplated. Transaction rates are comparably impressive. A system linked to a thousand terminals, all potentially active simultaneously, is not extraordinary today. As a direct consequence of these volumes, efficiency is critical. For example, in the terms of Section VI.2, an algorithm that runs in n^2 time is useless. It often turns out that tasks that would be conceptually simple for low volumes are very challenging for the dimensions characteristic of real systems.

A third distinguishing characteristic is the harshness of the environment in which a database system must survive. For example, you are used to an environment in which data is supplied by someone (yourself) who is familiar with the program's requirements and who has strong incentive to make the system operate successfully. Now imagine a situation in which the data is supplied by someone who is totally ignorant of programming, only vaguely aware of "user instructions" for the program, repeating the same task well past the point of boredom, and indifferent as to the success or failure of the process. Each program in a database system must contend with Murphy's Law -- that whatever can go wrong, will. Murphy, in this case, is aided by both time and volume. There is abundant opportunity for every conceivable disaster to occur, and many inconceivable disasters as well. Moreover, in addition to ignorance and clumsiness, the program must contend with deliberate subversion and maliciousness. These programs deal with objects of value, and many mistakes would reallocate certain objects to someone's advantage. Under such circumstances there is incentive to deliberately introduce such "mistakes" into the system.

Consequently, programs in a database system must include an order-of-magnitude more "checking", relative to actual "processing", than any of the sample programs we have exhibited. Yet this must still be done without making the program so inefficient that it cannot be used.

The following sections introduce a few of the basic ideas and problems of database systems. We recommend that you pursue the topic by reading Date or Kroenke (see References).

Section 1 Processing with Secondary Storage

Even a modest sized database system is too large to fit in main memory of a computer, so it is relegated to secondary storage, usually on magnetic disks or tapes. At least at present most computer systems do not regard such storage as a logical extension of main memory and it is managed in a completely different way from main memory. The programmer must be cognizant of this distinction and, in fact, it turns out to be a dominating characteristic of database programs.

A computer does not use secondary memory in the same manner as main memory. Main memory is said to be "randomly accessible" since arbitrary locations can be referenced. Secondary memory is only "block accessible" and, in the case of magnetic tapes, not every block is equally accessible. Consequently a computer does not really operate in secondary memory, it only transfers relatively large blocks of information from secondary to main memory, or vice-versa. The programming language must provide statements to perform these operations:

1. Copy a block of size k starting in main memory location m to secondary location memory location s.

2. Copy a block of size k from secondary memory location s to main memory starting in location m.

Once information is in main memory the computing process proceeds much as in our previous examples.

In other words, although the database is already in secondary memory the program regards the transfers as input and output, and regards the database as just an alternative source for input and destination for output.

In PL/I the GET and READ statements provide input, and the PUT and WRITE statements provide output, with various options to specify the source or destination. READ and WRITE are more efficient since they use what PL/I calls "record format" transfers, without editing or concern for format within the block.

While the idea is simple enough, the detail of these statements is formidable. We cannot justify space to describe them fully so you will have to resort to a PL/I reference manual.

● PL/CS: There is neither auxiliary storage capability, record format input/output, READ statement nor WRITE statement.

1.1 Record-at-a-Time Processing

The programmer considers a database to consist of a set of "logical records". This concept is discussed in Section 2, but at this point just think of a record as a convenient segment of information from the database. The basic strategy of most database processing is to process <u>one such record at a time</u>.

For example, to change information in one particular record the following algorithm would be used:

```
        Locate the appropriate record in the database.
        Copy the record from secondary storage into main memory.
        Modify the main memory version of the record.
        Copy the modified record back into secondary storage,
            replacing the earlier version.
```

As another example, to prepare a report with one line for each record that satisfies a certain criterion:

```
        For each record in the database:
            Copy the next record from database to main memory.
            If the record satisfies the criterion, copy
                information onto the output report.
```

Such processing is described in more detail in Section 3. Here you need only understand that there is a "buffer" area in main memory that holds one record at a time; that there are instructions that copy information between this buffer and the database; and that the program operates on the record in the buffer just as our previous programs have operated on variables, arrays or structures.

1.2 Timing Considerations

The devices used for secondary storage are electro-mechanical. They all involve some form for physical motion and, consequently, are relatively slow. The fastest current drums require a few milliseconds to find and transfer a block of information; the largest bulk storage devices require a few seconds for this task. On the other hand, main memories are solid-state devices that involve no physical motion and can be accessed in a fraction of a microsecond. Although both kinds of memory have gotten faster over the years, their relative speeds have not changed appreciably.

The consequence of these performance figures is that a GET, READ, PUT or WRITE statement takes something like 50,000 times as long to execute as an assignment statement that involves only main memory. Obviously, these instructions tend to dominate all others in the program and efficiency of a database program is judged largely in terms of the number of secondary storage transfer operations that are executed.

These numbers can lead to some surprising results. For example, suppose you have a student information system for a university with 15,000 students and there is one record in the database for each student. Now consider a course registration process with an average of, say, 5 courses per student.

Each course registration is to be recorded in the record for the appropriate student. Assuming that the registrations are in random order with respect to students this means that approximately 75,000 READs and 75,000 WRITEs must be executed. Say that this is going to be processed on an IBM 370/168, which is capable of executing several million arithmetic operations per second, and for your PL/C jobs has been executing several hundred thousand statements in a fraction of a second. 50 milliseconds is a reasonable estimate for a READ or WRITE statement and this job will take more than two hours. To be sure, the 168 will be doing many other jobs at the same time, but the elapsed time will still be surprisingly long.

1.3 Blocking and Buffering

An interesting and useful characteristic of block transfer operations is that the execution time does not vary appreciably with the amount of information transferred -- a large block is transferred almost as rapidly as a small one. In some cases this characteristic can be exploited to significantly speed up execution of a database program.

One way is to transfer several records at a time. Since a record is a logical unit of information from the programmer's point-of-view, and a block is the amount of information transferred by one operation, the trick is to place several records in each block. Then, at least for programs that must process all records, the number of operations is reduced by a factor equal to the number of records per block (called the "blocking factor").

Even when records are blocked in this way to gain efficiency the programmer still thinks of processing one record at a time. Ordinarily this blocking phenomenon is completely hidden from him by the operating system. A function of the operating system called an "access method" actually performs the physical transfer from secondary storage to a buffer area in main memory that is not part of the user's program. Then the GET or READ statements in the program are satisfied by transferring information from this buffer to the program area. This transfer is totally within main memory and takes place at memory speed. Whenever the buffer is depleted, another physical transfer from secondary storage is executed. An analogous buffering process in the other direction serves PUT or WRITE statements.

Note that while the mechanics of blocking and buffering are hidden from the programmer, the implications for the program strategy are not. Unless the program is designed so that the several records in a block can be processed consecutively, there is no benefit to be obtained. For example, in the student registration problem of Section 1.2 the assumption that registrations were processed in random order implied that each record access required a separate physical block transfer, regardless of whether or not the records were blocked.

Section 2 Logical Structure of a Database

The manner in which the information in a database is organized significantly affects the efficiency with which the database can be processed. Many different organizational strategies are available, and the proper choice is not easy.

For various reasons the programmer may be presented with a view of the organization that is quite different from its actual physical structure. In fact, different programmers may be provided with different views of the same database since not every programmer has the same requirements for information from the database.

A programmer's view is called the <u>logical</u> structure, in contrast to the actual <u>physical</u> structure. The central concept in this view is the logical record, discussed in the next section.

2.1 <u>Logical Records</u>

A database contains information about some set of <u>entities</u> in the real world. In general, it represents a number of entities of each of several differnt types. For example, a university database might contain information about one type of entity called students, another type called faculty members, another called courses, another called departments, etc.

A <u>logical record</u> consists of <u>all the information concerning one particular entity</u>. In the university database there would be a logical record type called "student" and one occurrence of this record type for each individual student. There would be a logical record type called "faculty" and one occurrence of this record type for each faculty member, etc.

Each entity possesses certain <u>attributes</u> (the same word, but with different meaning than the PL/I type attributes in a declaration). These attributes are reflected in the values of the individual <u>elements</u> or <u>fields</u> of the record. For example, the relevant attributes of a faculty member might be his/her name, social security number, age, rank, departmental affiliation, telephone number and salary. Each faculty record would then consist of seven fields. Usually a structure would be used to define the record type:

```
DECLARE 1 FACULTY,
            2 NAME CHAR(30) VAR,
            2 SSNBR CHAR(11) VAR,
            2 AGE FIXED,
            2 DEPT CHAR(3) VAR,
            2 TELNBR CHAR(8) VAR,
            2 SALARY FIXED;
```

This declaration in the program creates the working area in main memory into which faculty records can be copied from the database and from which they are copied into the database. It represents the programmer's logical model of a faculty record, which may or may not describe what such a record actually looks like in the database itself.

2.1.1 Repeating Groups

Often some attribute, or group of attributes, will be repeated some number of times. For example, a faculty member's publications might be relevant with each publication having attributes of title, journal and date. This could be reflected in the record structure by an array of minor structures:

```
DECLARE 1 FACULTY,
            ...
            2 PUBLICATION(n),
                3 TITLE CHAR(50) VAR,
                3 JOURNAL CHAR(40) VAR,
                3 DATE CHAR(12) VAR,
            ...
```

The number of publications will undoubtedly vary considerably from one faculty member to another so there is a question as to how large n should be in this declaration. The simplest solution is to pick some value that will accomodate most faculty members. This results in space being wasted in many records and requires either truncation or some means of handling overflow for individuals with very long publication lists. There are ways of allowing the size of a repeating group to vary dynamically, but they are beyond the scope of this brief introduction. (For example, see IBM's IMS database system, described in Date or Kroenke.)

2.2 Logical Files

The collection of all logical records of a certain type in a database represents a logical file. For example, our university database would contain a student file, a faculty file, etc. Many processing tasks are related to such a subset of a database. For example:

> For all student records:
> If the cumulative average is greater than 3.5,
> record the student name on the Dean's List.

The two types of file organization described in the next sections are dominatingly important.

2.2.1 Sequential Files

A field in a record may be designated as a "key" field. Candidates for this designation must have the property that the values of this field for all occurrences of this record type must be unique. That is, no two records can have the same key value. This uniqueness establishes a complete ordering of the records of a logical file. A logically sequential file is any file whose records have a key field, taking the records in order of increasing value of that key field. There is a first record (the one whose key value is a minimum), and for every record (except the last) there is a next record.

A file may be processed sequentially if it is logically sequential and if there is some reasonably efficient means of finding the next record. Examples are given in Section 3.

Many, but not all, logically sequential files are also physically sequential. That is, the records are actually arranged so that the key values form an increasing sequence. This is the most practical file organization for storage devices such as magnetic tapes that are inherently serial rather than randomly accessible. But this organization is also widely used with random-access devices since, by blocking the records, very efficient processing is possible.

In the early days of file processing by computer, all files were physically sequential since magnetic tapes were the only mass storage device available. Today other alternatives are available but a large fraction of all file processing applications still employ this strategy. It is simple, efficient and well-suited to the requirements of many of these tasks.

2.2.2 Indexed Files

The principal limitation of sequential files is the inability to access a particular record directly. The only access path is by exhaustive sequential examination, so this organization is not practical if direct record access is required.

An alternative access method, for a file that has a key, is to create an index, or directory, upon that key. This is simply a data structure that associates a physical location (a disk "address") with each key value. Given a particular key value, there is some routine that determines the corresponding record location and with that information the record can be accessed directly.

For example, the following function provides a simple indexing scheme:

```
/* RETURN LOCATION OF RECORD WITH KEY VALUE = VAL */
INDEX: PROCEDURE(VAL) RETURNS(FIXED);
    DCL VAL FIXED;           /* KEY VALUE TO BE INDEXED */
    DCL (KEY(N),             /* LOCN(I) IS ADDRESS OF RECORD */
        LOCN(N))             /* WITH VAL = KEY(I) */
          FIXED EXTERNAL; /* KEY(N) IS A SENTINEL, LOCN(N)=0 */
    DCL I FIXED;

    KEY(N) = VAL;
    DO I = 1 TO N BY 1;
        IF KEY(I) = VAL
            THEN RETURN(LOCN(I));
        END;
    END INDEX;
```

The linear search strategy shown here is just to give the idea of what indexing accomplishes and, in practice, a more efficient search strategy would be employed (for example, see Section VI.2.4).

Note that the concepts of sequential ordering and indexing are not mutually exclusive. For storage devices that permit direct record access (that is, everything except tape) a file can be both sequential and indexed. Such indexed sequential files are widely used.

An alternative way of determing the record location, given the key value, is to position each record so that its address is some computable function of its key value. The address can then be computed directly from the key, rather than obtained from the search of an index. (The simplest scheme is, of course, the identity function where the record address is taken to be the key value. This is not often practical and you usually have to work a little harder to obtain the transformation.) The transformation is called "hashing" and the overall process is called "direct address calculation". For our purposes it isn't important whether an address is obtained by calculation or search of an index, as long as a record can be located without exhaustive sequential search of the file itself.

2.3 Relationships Between Records

Some of the information in a database consists of relationships between records. For example, there might be an advisor-advisee relationship between a faculty member and a student. The question is how to represent this relationship in the database. The answer is more subtle and complex than you might guess.

The most obvious approach is to simply consider the adviser's name to be one of the attributes of a student, and hence provide a corresponding field in the student record:

```
DECLARE 1 STUDENT,
            ...
            2 ADVISER_NAME CHAR(30) VAR,
            ...
```

This provides convenient and efficient access to the adviser's name for a task such as the following:

> For all students:
> Print a list of student name, college, cumulative average, adviser name and campus telephone number.

But now suppose you wanted to add the adviser's telephone number to this list. That information is present in a field in the faculty record for each adviser, but it is not easily accessed by a program based primarily on student records.

Consider this task in more detail. Assume that the key to the faculty file is the social security number, since names are not generally used for keys. Then, since the name is the only information given in the student record, to find the adviser's faculty record in order to obtain the telephone number, we must <u>exhaustively search the faculty file</u> for a record with the proper name. If there are m faculty records this search will require m/2 record accesses, on the average. If there are n students this means a total of nm/2 accesses. This is effectively a quadratic process and is prohibitively expensive for the dimensions that are likely in this case.

Assuming the faculty file is indexed using social security number as the key, an alternative scheme would be to include the adviser's social security number rather than his name in the student record:

```
DECLARE 1 STUDENT,
          ...
          2 ADVISER_SSNBR CHAR(11) VAR,
          ...
```

Now we could directly access the faculty record using this key value, without having to search the faculty file. This would give us access to the faculty name, telephone number and anything else we might need to know about the adviser. The process would require only 2n accesses; that is, it is linear with respect to the number of students.

However, note that the previous task without the advisor telephone number now also requires 2n accesses, so it takes twice as long as before. What we have done is make the adviser's name relatively less accessible in order to make all other information about the adviser more accessible. If the name is frequently used and other information only rarely used this may not have been a wise decision.

You could, of course, include <u>both</u> the adviser name and the social security number (and any other frequently used information) in the student record. This would require a little more space, but space is cheap and worth using to reduce the number of accesses. However, it causes a more serious problem. The same piece of information -- the adviser name -- is now recorded in two places in the database, once in the faculty record and again in the student record. This is asking for trouble. When the necessity of changing such a field arises, what assurance have you that <u>all occurrences</u> have been changed?

Failure to change all instances means the database contains inconsistent information -- technically called "update anomalies". The difficulty tends to feed upon itself, and ultimately threatens the credibility of the whole system. Consequently, except for key values, a database should be designed so as to minimize the amount of multiple recording required.

We have been discussing a link from a student record to a faculty record. Links in the opposite directions would also be useful. The difference is that while a student presumably has one adviser, a faculty member has more than one advisee -- the number varying among different faculty members. We would still use a field in the faculty record containing the key value of a student, but now we require several such fields and, in effect, have a repeating group of fields that are pointers to other records.

The student -> faculty relationship is one-to-one; the faculty -> student relationship is one-to-many. The more general case of a many-to-many relationship is illustrated by students and courses. Each student takes several courses so the student record contains fields pointing to the course records for which the student is registered. Each course includes several students and the course record contains fields pointing to the records of students taking that course. The number of students taking a course can vary from a few to a few thousand, which might suggest the inherent difficulty of the repeating group problem.

Even from this brief introduction you might begin to see why design of an effective database is a non-trivial task. The designer must anticipate and analyze the different kinds of processing that the database must support. The relationships between records are a critical aspect of the design. Without effective links between records a database degenerates into a set of disjoint files. Moreover, the manner of implementing these relationships is significant in determining the ease with which processing tasks can be programmed and the efficiency with which they can be executed. This is currently a very active area of development and debate. There are two competing approaches called the "network model" and the "relational model" and one or the other might well dominate the design of database systems in the 1980s. The two models are well-described in either Date or Kroenke.

Section 3 Database Processing

Examples of typical database processing tasks have been given in the previous sections but there are still some general points to be made. Tasks can be classified by whether or not they alter the contents of the database, and by the pattern of record accesses they require.

3.1 Query Processing

Tasks called "queries" extract information from the database without changing its contents. They READ from, but never WRITE into, the database. Consider the following examples, all based on our previous example of a university database. Assume that each logical file in this database is indexed by some entity identification number, and that all interrelationships between records are given in terms of these indices.

(3.1a) Find the telephone number of a student whose identification number is 10694.

(3.1b) Find the telephone number of the student who lives in Room 104 of Boldt Hall.

(3.1c) Find the name and telephone number of student 10694's faculty adviser.

(3.1d) Find the age of the chairman of the department of which student 10694's adviser is a member.

(3.1e) Find the home address of student 10694's roommate.

(3.1f) Make a list of the names of all students whose cumulative average is greater than 3.5.

(3.1g) Make a list of the names of all students registered in the College of Engineering.

(3.1h) Make a list of the names of the students in the top half of the senior class in Engineering.

(3.1i) Make a list of the names of all students who are taking at least one course taught by their own advisor.

Now consider the record accesses required by each of these tasks. Assume there are a total of n student records in the database.

(3.1a) requires access to a single record for the particular student.

(3.1b) seeks a single record, but since the key value is not known an exhaustive search of the student file is required, testing each record for the value in a field representing residence. On the average, a search such as this will access n/2 records.

(3.1c) requires access to two records, the student record and a faculty record whose key value is given in the student record.

(3.1d) requires a path of four records: student -> faculty -> department -> faculty. It is like (3.1c) in concept but deeper in access. Note how difficult it is to precisely express a query of this complexity in English.

(3.1e) requires two records, both being student records. This differs from (3.1c) only in that the first student record contains a key value for another record of the same type.

(3.1f) requires access to all n student records. Unlike the search in (3.1b) this process must continue to the very last record, no matter how many qualifying records have been found.

(3.1g) is essentially like (3.1f), however the class of entity specified here has a relatively stable membership and is likely to be referenced fairly often. There are several ways that one could take advantage of this and structure the database so that it would only be necessary to examine records for Engineering students, without having to make an exhaustive search of the complete student file.

(3.1h) requires more than one pass over the student file, assuming that it is not known in advance exactly what cumulative average delimits the top half of the class. It is possible to determine the median student average in a single pass, and a second pass would be required to select those students whose average is greater than this value.

(3.1i) requires an exhaustive pass over the student file. For each student record, you must examine each element of a repeating group of key values for course records. Presumably the course record contains the key value of the faculty record for its instructor. This can be compared with the key value of the faculty record for the student's advisor. Note that the faculty record itself need not be accessed; comparison of the key values for faculty records is sufficient.

It should be evident in these examples how the cost of apparently similar queries can be vary different. A user who knows nothing of programming may not understand why it is significantly more difficult (and thus more costly) to list the students in the top ten percent of the class than those with average greater than 3.5. It is even harder to explain why sometimes information that is present in the database cannot be economically retrieved.

The information retrieved by these queries must be presented in a useful form. Sometimes the specification of the required output format is very precise and rigid -- for example, it may be necessary to position the output in the proper spaces of a preprinted form. The long sequences of PUT EDIT statements necessary to generate such output are tedious and uninteresting, but unfortunately are often required in database processing.

3.1.1 Information Retrieval Systems

Although the examples shown above clearly retrieve information, the area of computer science called "information retrieval" usually refers to a somewhat narrower subject. It is concerned with retrieval in a _library_ context, where the entities themselves are _documents_, and the records in the database contain descriptive information about the documents. The objective is to use the database to determine which documents are likely to be relevant for some purpose, or at least which are worth further examination.

The records in a typical system contain keywords that attempt to characterize the subject of the corresponding document. Queries specify which keywords or combinations of keywords suggest that a document would be relevant. These queries are characteristically quite different from those in a business database. For example, for a business query records are selected only if they _exactly_ meet the specified condition, where a library query would request the k records that _come closest_ to meeting the requirements.

A library system takes a probablistic view of its task and measures its success statistically. A query system is judged by its average "recall" -- the proportion of the relevant documents that are retrieved, and its average "precision" -- the proportion of the retrieved documents that are relevant.

Our purpose here is primarily to point out that Part VIII is _not_ concerned with information retrieval in the strict sense of the term. A good summary of that field is given by Salton (see References).

3.2 Update Processing

The other side of the processing task is the modification of the content of the database. The database must be "updated" to reflect changes in the attributes of the entities it represents. The messages that convey this information to the database are called "transactions".

A transaction can convey information that causes any of four types of change:

1. a change in the value of a field in an existing record,

2. a change in relationship between existing records,

3. the creation of a new record,

4. the deletion of an existing record.

Examples of events that produce such transactions are:

1. Student 10694 has paid $2000 toward his tuition bill.

2. Student 10694 has dropped out of course CS314.

3. The Computer Science Department has hired a new faculty member whose social security number is 298-28-6741.

4. Course CS711 has been discontinued.

Note that each transaction identifies a particular record by key value and then describes some change to be made in that record. If the record is not specified by key, then a search is required to identify the appropriate target record.

Note also that the second example is a <u>dual transaction</u>. It changes a relationship between two records and implies changes in both -- the deletion of a course record reference for the registration repeating group in the student record, and the deletion of a student record reference from the class list repeating group in the course record.

3.2.1 Update of a Sequential File

Suppose that a particular file in the database is sequential and there is a group of transactions to update this file. Even though each transaction specifies a particular record by key value, records cannot be located directly in this file; they can be found only by an exhaustive search. If a separate search had to be performed for each transaction the result would be prohibitively costly.

But suppose that the group of transaction was sorted so the record key values formed a non-decreasing sequence (non-decreasing rather than strictly increasing since several transactions can refer to the same record). Now begin a search for the record specified by the first transaction -- that is, the transaction with minimum key value. Whichever record this is, and whatever its relative position in the file, it provides the starting point for the search for the record for the second transaction, which provides the starting point for the search for the third, etc. Consequently, any number of transactions can be located and processed in a single pass through the file. This, coupled with the possibility of blocking the records, can provide very economical processing.

In effect, transaction processing for a sequential file is a merging process between a stream of transactions and a stream of records, both ordered by the same key values.

But note that this merging update process involves accumulating a batch of transactions to be sorted and then processed in a single run, and this accumulation implies some delay in processing. If you need to process transactions essentially as soon as they arrive, this strategy is not acceptable.

Type 3 transactions, requiring insertion of a new record, present a problem in a sequential file. If the file is logically but not physically sequential the record may be linked into place using the technique described in Section VII.3. But if the file is physically sequential how does one squeeze another record into the proper position between two others? The solution is simple and surprising. The update process simply produces a completely new version of the file. As the new "generation" is created the new records are inserted at the appropriate positions. Similarly, records are deleted just by failing to copy them from the old into the new generation. Even records that are entirely unaffected by the update -- those not referenced by any transaction -- are copied without change into the new generation. This sounds inefficient but in fact it tends to be just the opposite.

It is important to realize that the update of a sequential file does not actually change the file at all. The old generation is left entirely intact and a separate new generation reflects the new information. This has the considerable virtue of permitting simple recovery from disasters of all kinds. For example, suppose the update program is belatedly found to be faulty and to have produced numerous errors in the new file generation. Since the old file still exists unchanged, the update can simply be repeated whenever the program has been corrected.

3.2.2 Update of a Direct-Access File

When a file is indexed for direct access to individual records, transactions that identify the target record by key value can be processed without batching, sorting or delay. The usual strategy is to retrieve the specified record, modify it, and return the new version to overwrite the old version in the database. This "update-in-place" actually modifies the file, rather than produce an entirely separate new generation. This seems obvious and sensible, but it leads to some interesting problems.

For example, suppose the update program is found to be faulty. How do you recover the information lost when records were improperly overwritten? Or suppose the execution of an update program is aborted somewhere in the middle by a power failure, or some other computer "crash". How do you restart the program without having the initial transactions be processed twice? (For example, the first transaction may add 10 to field A in record B. It should not do so a second time in the restarted run.)

Then there is the question of "interference" between simultaneous users of the database. Suppose user C wants to add 10 to field A of record B, and user D wants to add 15 to the same field. Suppose they operate almost simultaneously. Each would copy the same old record, make his change, and then return the modified record to the database. Suppose C happens to get there first and his +10 version overwrites the old record. Then D arrives and his +15 version overwrites the +10 version. The consequence is that C's update has been nullified after he thought it had been successfully completed.

There are solutions to these problems, but some of them seem crude and inefficient and there is considerable room for improvement in these matters.

3.3 Programming Languages for Database Processing

The languages used for database processing today are obsolescent. They were designed for an earlier generation of file processing and lack well-developed facilities to support an integrated, shared, remote-access database system. The languages are supported by equally archaic operating systems, so the programmer is faced with an incredible patchwork of job control languages, operating system functions, data management services, access methods, database management systems, and programming languages. This makes a difficult task much harder. But the formidable problems of conversion and continuity makes progress in this area painfully slow.

For example, facilities that would make it convenient to prevent interference between two simultaneous users are rudimentary; facilities that would limit the privileges afforded different users are almost non-existent.

3.3.1 COBOL and PL/I

Without question the standard general-purpose language for file processing today is COBOL; it is much more widely used than PL/I. In the late 50's, envious of the success of FORTRAN, a group of computer users with file processing problems got together to define a language of comparable convenience and power. The result was COBOL. The United States Government was heavily represented in this effort, and computer manufacturers were encouraged to develop COBOL compilers by strong indications that sales to all government agencies would be contingent on having COBOL capability.

COBOL is comparable to PL/I, and you could read a COBOL program and have a general idea of what it accomplishes. The similarities between the two languages are more important than the differences (although one would not get this impression from listening to a militant advocate of either).

A COBOL program is divided into four "divisions". The first two, called "identification" and "environment", correspond to blocks of PL/I comments describing the purpose of the program and its operating requirements. Declarations are collected in the "data division", and the "procedure division" corresponds to the main procedure in PL/I.

Some COBOL statements are quite similar to their PL/I counterparts (IF and GOTO, for example); others look different but perform a familiar task:

```
PERFORM TAXLOOP VARYING I FROM 1 BY 1 UNTIL N
```

Comparable assignment statements in PL/I and COBOL are:

```
A = B + C;          ADD B AND C TO A

D = E * F;          MULTIPLY E AND F GIVING D

G = H * (U + V);    COMPUTE G FROM H * (U + V)

A = B;              MOVE B TO A
```

The most significant difference between the two languages (and the greatest weakness in COBOL) is the area of program structure. The procedure division can be subdivided into "sections" and "paragraphs" but the facilities provided to invoke paragraphs, pass arguments to them, and isolate them from other program actions, are very limited.

An example of a COBOL program paragraph is the following (from an IBM 360 COBOL manual -- C28-6516):

```
PROCESS-SORTED-RECORDS SECTION.
PARAGRAPH-3.  RETURN SORT-FILE-1 AT END GO TO PARAGRAPH-4.
IF FIELD-FF = FIELD-EE WRITE FILE-3-RECORD FROM
SORT-RECORD GO TO PARAGRAPH-3 ELSE
MOVE FIELD-EE TO FIELD-EEE MOVE FIELD-FF TO FIELD-FFF
MOVE FIELD-AA TO FIELD-AAA MOVE FIELD-BB TO FIELD-BBB
MOVE SPACES TO FILLER-A, FILLER-B WRITE FILE-2-RECORD.
GO TO PARAGRAPH-3.
PARAGRAPH-4.  EXIT.
```

The academic world tends to regard COBOL as verbose, clumsy and inelegant, and tries to ignore it, although there are more COBOL programs and programmers in the world than there are for FORTRAN, ALGOL and PL/I combined.

PL/I is the second most important general-purpose language for file processing. It was designed in the early sixties by a committee of IBM language specialists and users of IBM computers. Their objective was to provide a single language that would be useful for both mathematical computing and file processing, and would possess the structure and elegance that were present in ALGOL. Unfortunately, the design committee was under severe time constraints and the result was not as attractive as it might have been. Nevertheless, IBM embraced the new language and announced the demise of both FORTRAN and COBOL. That obituary turned out to be premature, to say the least. Even if PL/I is a better language than either FORTRAN or COBOL many users felt that it was not enough better to be worth the effort to retrain programmers and convert program libraries. This reluctance was encouraged by the fact that IBM neglected to provide an efficient translator for PL/I until 1971.

It now seems unlikely that PL/I will ever succeed in replacing either FORTRAN or COBOL. Instead of unifying a computing world that was divided in two by a language barrier, PL/I has created a three-language situation in the United States. (In the rest of the world ALGOL is also important.)

But it is equally unlikely that either FORTRAN or COBOL, at least in their present form, will continue in major use indefinitely. Both of these languages were pioneering efforts, and it would indeed be surprising if experience and research does not eventually lead to their retirement. Successor languages (whatever they may be called) are likely to offer many of the features now present in PL/I.

The CODASYL Committee that created COBOL is working to extend it to meet the demands of programming for modern databases. The Database Task Group of CODASYL is identified with the "network" database model and the COBOL community is clearly inclined in that direction.

3.3.2 Higher-Level Languages

Beginning in the late sixties various "database management systems" began to be offered, primarily by independent programming firms. Many of these systems included new programming languages, some of which provided interesting new features and approaches. Many of these languages are significantly "higher-level" than PL/I or COBOL. That is, for a given task their programs are shorter and more closely related to problem terms than machine operations. These languages lack the general capability of COBOL or PL/I, and are intended only for the more routine forms of query and transaction processing. But for these limited purposes these specialized languages are substantially easier to use than either COBOL or PL/I.

One of the least attractive is called RPG, but since it is distributed by IBM it is also the most widely used. An RPG programmer uses a variety of special forms, filling in designated spaces to specify the structure of the file, the format of transactions on punched cards, and the desired format of printed output. An experienced RPG programmer can write such "programs" in a fraction of the time required in PL/I. MARK IV is a language similarly dependant on special forms, but with much greater power and flexiblity.

Other languages do not use special forms, and some of these have a remarkably readable English-like syntax. For example, the following are programs in the ASAP language:

```
FOR ALL STUDENTS WITH COLLEGE = 'ENGINEERING' AND
        GRADE_AVG > 3.0,
    PRINT A LIST OF:
        NAME, ADDRESS, FACULTY_ADVISOR, GRADE_AVG,
    ORDERED BY GRADE_AVG.
```

```
FOR ALL STUDENTS SELECTED BY KEY IN FEBRUARY_DATA,
   FORMATTED BY BIOGRAPHICAL_CARD_FORMAT,
   UPDATE THE RECORD.
```

These ASAP programs are strikingly similar to the language we have been using for algorithms and statement-comments, suggesting some interesting possiblities for the future.

Part IX
Computer Solution of Mathematical Problems

by J. E. Dennis and Jorge J. Moré

Many people study computer programming because they are interested in implementing algorithms to extract quantitative information from mathematical models in engineering and the social or physical sciences. Our purpose in this part is to first discuss some of the difficulties that are encountered when implementing such algorithms, and then to study two representative mathematical problems in some detail.

We are faced with a problem in notation. The formulas in this part will generally be intended as mathematical rather than programming language statements. However, the computer text-editing system used to produce this book does not permit many of the usual mathematical notational conventions. In particular it does not permit subscripts, and permits only integer superscripts. Therefore, we have resorted to the usual programming convention for subscripts, and in order to increase the readability of our expressions, we restrict their generality, when possible, to use only integer superscripts. In all other cases we use mathematical symbols and conventions such as ≤ instead of <=. We indicate multiplication by proximity or · rather than *, and we use vertical lines | | to indicate absolute value (rather than concatenation or "or", as in PL/I.)

Section 1 Floating Point Numbers

Except for programming errors, the factors which usually account for unexpected results in numerical computations are as follows:

1. Most numbers cannot be represented exactly in the computer.

2. The results of the arithmetic operations performed by the computer are not, in general, exact.

3. Most mathematical problems require an infinite number of calculations.

In this section we will discuss how numbers are represented in the computer, and how this representation leads to a certain type of error called "roundoff error". We also discuss how roundoff error affects the different arithmetic operations.

1.1 Representation of Floating Point Numbers

We have already mentioned that some of the difficulties with executing numerical algorithms on the computer are due to the fact that most numbers cannot be represented exactly in the computer. Let us see what this means in terms of a specific example.

Consider a PL/I program which reads the number 69.4 from a data card, assigns the value to a variable which has been declared FLOAT DECIMAL and then prints the value of the variable. If you run the program you will find that the number printed out is 6.93999E+01, which is equivalent to 69.3999. On the other hand, if the number on the card is 69.5, then it is returned exactly, that is, as 6.95000E+01. The same results would have been obtained if the variable had been declared FLOAT BINARY.

To understand these results, we need to know how 69.4 and 69.5 are stored in the computer, that is, the internal representation of a floating point number. Since the situation is the same for FLOAT DECIMAL and FLOAT BINARY variables we will call their contents "floating point numbers". In this way the following discussion will apply to both cases.

A number can be written in terms of a base b, a fraction f, an exponent e, and a sign. If b=10 then this representation is just the number written as a decimal fraction times a power (the exponent) of 10. Most computers do not use base 10, but regardless of the base, any number can be written as a fraction f times a power of b. The fraction is also written in terms of powers of b, and this means that

$$f = d(1)\cdot b^{-1} + d(2)\cdot b^{-2} + \ldots, \text{ where } 0 \le d(i) \le b-1,$$

which in base b notation is abbreviated to

$$f = (0.d(1)d(2)\ldots)(\text{base } b).$$

The exercises at the end of this section will describe a method for finding the base b representation of a number.

A floating point number is also written in terms of a base and an exponent. In the IBM 360 and 370, b = 16. This means that 69.4 is (0.4566...)(base 16) because this number can be written as $f\cdot 16^2$ where

$$f = 4\cdot 16^{-1} + 5\cdot 16^{-2} + 6\cdot 16^{-3} + 6\cdot 16^{-4} + \ldots .$$

You can easily verify that 69.5 is just $(0.458)\cdot 16^2$ in base 16. By now you have probably guessed that 69.4 and 69.5 are treated differently by the computer because it can only hold finitely many digits of a fraction.

The representation of the fraction that the computer does save is called the mantissa and t, the number of digits in the mantissa, is the precision of the floating point number. Some computers, like the IBM 360 and 370, obtain the mantissa by truncating the fraction to t digits while for others the mantissa is obtained by rounding the fraction to the closest t digit number. For example, if b=16 and t=3 then the mantissa of 69.4 is 0.456 for truncation and 0.457 for rounding. In our discussion of floating point numbers we will assume that the mantissa is obtained by truncating the fraction to t digits, but regardless of the method used, the errors due to the finite precision of the computer are traditionally called roundoff errors. Since we are assuming that the mantissa is obtained by truncation, in our case a better name would have been "truncation errors", but this term is customarily used for another type of truncation error which is not associated with the finite precision of the machine.

PL/I on the IBM 370 allows t=6, called single precision, or t=14, called double precision. The default assumption is single precision, so in order to use double precision, it is necessary to declare attributes of DECIMAL FLOAT(16) or BINARY FLOAT(53). Since double precision was not specified in the previous example, 69.4 was represented internally in single precision as

$(0.456666)\cdot 16^{2}$(base 16)

and 69.5 was represented as

$(0.458000)\cdot 16^{2}$(base 16).

On output the computer prints the base 10 representation of these numbers.

Note that the internal representation of a floating point number has a mantissa with a non-zero first digit. This "normalized" form is always possible (unless the number is zero) and clearly leads to maximum accuracy.

The t-digit floating point numbers can be thought of as a finite subset of the real numbers. They are fairly densely packed about zero, but become more widely separated further from zero. The t-digit floating point representation T(x) of a real number x is the member of this subset which is nearest to x among all those members between x and 0. In particular, all real numbers between two adjacent floating point numbers will have the same floating point representation.

In the preceding paragraph we referred for the first time to there being finitely many t-digit floating point numbers. This is rather clear, for just as the computer must truncate the fractional part of the number, so it can't allow more than finitely many different exponents. The IBM 360 floating point numbers are approximately between

$5.4\cdot 10^{-79}$ and $7.2\cdot 10^{75}$

since the range of base 16 exponents is $-64\leq e\leq 63$. When the computer encounters a number not in this range it prints an UNDERFLOW or OVERFLOW message. OVERFLOW is a common problem in numerical computation, where it is often caused by dividing a large floating point number by a small one. UNDERFLOW signals a loss of accuracy since it warns that a number has been taken to be zero because in its normalized form the exponent required is too small. In general, when we see UNDERFLOW we <u>suspect</u> the results of the computation, and when we see OVERFLOW we <u>discard</u> them.

Unless the number of operations is rather large, the increased cost of double precision isn't noticeable, so double precision is generally advisable for small problems. In PL/C, you do not have this choice since all floating point variables are actually maintained in double precision form, and converted to the specified precision only on output. This is not true in PL/I.

You may wonder why we specify double precision variables as FLOAT DECIMAL(16) or FLOAT BINARY(53) when the computer represents them in either case with 14 base 16 digits. The answer is that 16 decimal digits, 53 binary digits, and 14 hexadecimal (base 16) digits all give essentially the same precision. We explain why in the next section.

1.2 Roundoff Errors and Significant Decimal Digits

In the previous section we showed how a computer represents any real number x in its floating point range by a floating point number T(x) obtained from the leading t terms of the number's expansion in powers of the base b. Clearly, this approximation of x by T(x) sets a limit on the accuracy of any subsequent calculations and we are thus led to ask what the maximum possible accuracy is when we approximate x by T(x). To answer this question we need a precise way to measure accuracy.

The generally accepted way to measure how accurately a number y approximates another number x is in terms of significant decimal digits. We would like to say that y has s significant decimal digits as an approximation to x if when x and y are represented as decimal numbers then the leading s digits agree and the (s+1)st digits do not differ by more than five. This definition suffices for x=10012, y=10034, or for x=10.012, y=10.034, since it gives the same reasonable answer of three significant decimal digits in either case. On the other hand, in the previous section we stated that if x=69.4 then on the IBM 360 the single precision T(x) is 69.3999. This is clearly a better approximation to x than 69.3 and yet in the above sense they both have two significant decimal digits. All this is meant to convince you that in order to give a precise and reasonable definition of significant decimal digits we will have to examine roundoff errors more carefully.

We begin by obtaining a bound on the magnitude of the error committed by replacing T(x) by x. The quantity |T(x)-x| is called the absolute error of T(x) as an approximation to x, while if x≠0 then |T(x)-x|/|x| is the relative error.

Theorem: If x≠0 lies in the range of the base b floating point numbers of precision t, then

(1.2a) |T(x)-x|/|x| < b**(1-t).

We will prove (1.2a) for the case when t=6. This will illustrate the general case, and you should prove (1.2a) in full generality as an exercise. It is only necessary to give a proof in the case that x>0 since the proof for a negative x differs only in sign.

Now take any x>0 and represent it as a normalized base b number. That is, set

$$x = (b**e)\cdot[d(1)\cdot b^{-1} + \ldots + d(6)\cdot b^{-6} + \ldots]$$

where $d(1)\neq 0$. Notice (since we will need it later) that $|x|>b**(e-1)$. Then since t=6,

$$T(x) = (b**e)\cdot[d(1)\cdot b^{-1} + \ldots + d(6)\cdot b^{-6}]$$

and thus,

$$T(x)-x = -(b**e)\cdot[d(7)\cdot b^{-7} + d(8)\cdot b^{-8} + \ldots].$$

Now make use of the fact that $0\leq d(i)\leq b-1$ to replace d(7), d(8), etc., by (b-1) and get

$$|T(x)-x| \leq (b**e)(b-1)[b^{-7} + b^{-8} + \ldots \quad].$$

However,

$$b^{-7} + b^{-8} + \ldots \quad = b^{-7}(1 + b^{-1} + b^{-2} + \ldots) = b^{-6}/(b-1)$$

since this is a geometric series. Therefore,

$$|T(x)-x| \leq (b**e)b^{-6} < b^{-5}|x|$$

where we have used the fact that $|x| > b**(e-1)$. Inequality (1.2a) now follows.

In general, if x and y are real numbers and y is an approximation to x, then $|y-x|$ is the <u>absolute error</u> of y as an approximation to x while $|y-x|/|x|$ is the <u>relative error</u> of y as an approximation to $x\neq 0$. Inequality (1.2a) indicates that if y=T(x) then the absolute error is not a very good measure of the agreement between y and x if the magnitude of x is very large or very small. This is also true if y is any approximation to x. For example, if $y=10^{-6}$ and $x=10^{-5}$ then $|y-x|<10^{-5}$ although y certainly isn't a good approximation to x. On the other hand, the relative error measures the number of fractional digits that x and y have in common. In fact, we will say that <u>the first s decimal digits of y are significant as an approximation to x</u>, if <u>$|y-x|/|x| \leq 5\cdot 10**(-s)$</u>. If you work out a few examples, you will see that this precise definition and the intuitive notion given at the beginning of this section essentially agree.

Now that we have these results we can determine the number of significant decimal digits in T(x) as an approximation to x. We will only consider double precision in the IBM 360 with b=16 and t=14 although essentially the same results hold if b=2 and t=53. For any real number x in the range of floating point numbers, (1.2a) implies that the relative error of T(x) as an approximation to x is bounded by 16^{-13} or about $2.2\cdot 10^{-16}$. Therefore, T(x) has 16 significant digits as an approximation to x so subsequent calculations which use T(x) in place of x can only be expected to have <u>at most</u> 16 significant decimal digits. This explains why only 16 digits are printed as output by the computer, and why FLOAT DECIMAL(16) and FLOAT BINARY(53) give the same precision.

1.3 Errors in Floating Point Arithmetic

We have already discussed how roundoff errors arise as the result of converting a number x into its floating point representation. Roundoff errors also arise because the results of arithmetic operations performed on the computer are, in general, not exact. In order to illustrate these errors we will assume that we are working on a computer with base b=10 and precision t=4. You can observe similar errors on any computer, but this simple scheme makes it easier to really see what is happening.

First consider addition and suppose we want to add 163.9 and 24.36. On our computer they would be represented in normalized form as $(0.1639)10^3$ and $(0.2436)10^2$. However, since the computer can only perform additions by adding the mantissas of numbers with equal exponents, these numbers will be added in the form $(0.1639)10^3$ and $(0.02436)10^3$. In other words, the exponent of the number with the smaller exponent will be increased, and its mantissa will be shifted right by the same number of places. You can see that the result is $(0.1882)10^3$ which is the correct answer truncated to our working precision, t=4.

Although the example shows that the addition of two numbers has a small relative error associated with it, this is not the case when several numbers are added. For example, consider adding 0.556, 3.294, 24.36 and 163.9. Adding in decreasing order of magnitude the sum is 191.9. But if we add in the opposite order the sum is 192.1. Since the true sum is 192.11, the relative error for the sum in decreasing order is 21 times larger than in the reverse order.

If you have to add many numbers and you want high precision then you should try to add them in <u>increasing order of magnitude</u>. For most mathematical problems this is not convenient, so instead the sums are usually <u>accumulated</u>. This means that each intermediate sum is stored in double precision and then added to the next summand in double precision. The final result is then truncated to the working precision. If the sum in the previous example had been accumulated, then the final sum would have been 192.1 regardless of the order in which the sum was carried out. PL/C's use of internal double precision, which we explained in Section 1.1, is more or less an extension of this idea.

Subtraction is similar to addition. However, note that if two almost equal numbers are being subtracted then there may be a loss of significance. For example, if x=136.5 and y=136.4 are approximations to 136.52 and 136.41, respectively, then both x and y have 4 significant digits. However, x-y=0.1 has <u>one</u> significant digit as an approximation to 0.11, the true difference.

It is not important to know precisely how the multiplication and division of two floating point numbers are carried out. It is important for you to know that these operations are carried out in such a way that the result equals the true answer truncated to the working precision. This means that the multiplication or division of two numbers gives rise to a small relative error. In fact, unlike addition and subtraction, it is even possible to prove that the relative error does not grow when several numbers are multiplied or divided. Unfortunately things aren't as good as they sound, since underflow and overflow occur much more frequently in this case and can be a source of error. For example, let x and y be floating point numbers and consider the calculation of $z = \text{sqrt}(x^2 + y^2)$. (Here and below, we intend "sqrt(arg)" to denote the nonnegative square root of arg.) If our machine with b=10 and t=4 restricts the exponent to $-9 \le e \le 9$, then you can verify that a straightforward calculation of z with $x = y = 10^{-6}$ gives $z = 0$ instead of $10^{-6} \cdot \text{sqrt}(2)$. This seems to be unavoidable in our computer, but in fact it isn't. We just have to be clever and see that the computation of z can also be carried out as follows:

Let $v = \max\{|x|, |y|\}$

and $w = \min\{|x|, |y|\}$.

Then, you can see that

$$z = v \cdot \text{sqrt}(1 + (w/v)^2),$$

and this time, for our example, we do obtain $z = 10^{-6} \cdot \text{sqrt}(2)$.

Now that we have talked about sums and products, we can discuss one of the most common numerical computations. From our discussion of the calculation of sums you can see that we should also be careful in the evaluation of inner products; that is, quantities of the form

$$(x(1) \cdot y(1)) + \ldots + (x(n) \cdot y(n)).$$

If high accuracy is desired, then inner products are usually accumulated. This means that each product $(x(i) \cdot y(i))$ is calculated in double precision and then this double precision number is added to the accumulated sum of the previous products. The final result is truncated to working precision. Again, this is more or less automatic in PL/C.

As a final word of warning we mention that the accumulation of sums and inner products is not guaranteed to result in small relative errors unless cancellation does not occur. For example, consider

$$1.002 \cdot (1.003) + 0.9999 \cdot (-.9995) + 0.02000 \cdot (-0.2803).$$

Forming the products in double precision, i.e. with t=8, gives

$$(0.10050060)10^{1} + (-0.9994005)10^{0} + (-0.56060000)10^{-2}$$

which is zero in floating point addition with t=8. The true sum is easily seen to be $-0.5\cdot 10^{-7}$.

Now that we have made you aware of roundoff errors, what can you do about them? Certainly it helps to work in extended precision, but still the best line of defense is to be aware of them so that you may be able to rearrange your calculations to lessen their effect.

Section 1 Exercises

1. Write a program that will perform the conversion between binary (base 2) and hexadecimal (base 16) numbers. An outline of the algorithm is as follows:

> To go from hexadecimal to binary, replace each hexadecimal digit by its binary representation and (since $16=2^4$) multiply the exponent by 4. For example,
>
> $$(.458)\cdot 16^2 \text{ (base 16)} = (.0100\ 0101\ 1000)\cdot 2^8 \text{ (base 2)}.$$
>
> To go from binary to hexadecimal, first increase the exponent and add leading zeroes to the fraction until the exponent is divisible by 4. Then replace each group of four binary digits by the corresponding hexadecimal digit and divide the exponent by 4. For example,
>
> $$(.10101)\cdot 2^{-6} \text{ (base 2)} = (.0010101)\cdot 2^{-4} \text{ (base 2)}$$
>
> $$= (.2A)\cdot 16^{-1} \text{ (base 16)}.$$
>
> We have used A (=10) for 1010, and similarly, B, C, D, E and F are used for the digits 11 through 15.

2. Let $x=1.0$ and $y=0.999$. Give the number of significant decimal digits, the absolute error and the relative error in y as an approximation to x. Repeat the exercise with the pairs $x\cdot 10^{-4}$, $y\cdot 10^{-4}$ and $x\cdot 10^4$, $y\cdot 10^4$.

3. a) Prove that $y=0$ never has any significant decimal digits as an approximation to any nonzero number x.

   b) Show that if $y\cdot x < 0$, then y has no significant decimal digits as an approximation to x.

4. Complete the proof of (1.2a) by showing that it holds for any precision t.

5. a) For an arbitrary x, what is the maximum number of significant decimal digits in its approximation by T(x) on a computer with $b=16$ and $t=6$?

   b) Since one hexadecimal digit can be represented by four binary digits it would seem that machines with $b=16$, $t=6$ and $b=2$, $t=24$ are equally accurate. Explain the fallacy in this argument.

6. a) Show that 0.2 has no significant decimal digits as an approximation to 0.1 but that 0.1 has one significant decimal digit as an approximation to 0.2.

b) Part a) shows that there is a lack of symmetry in the definition of significant decimal digits; prove that it can be removed by changing the definition to

$$|y-x| \le 5(10**-s)\cdot\min\{|x|, |y|\}.$$

7. Write a program segment to read a given value of x and compute the sum

$$1 + x/1! + x^2/2! + \ldots + x^{30}/30!$$

in ascending and descending orders. Compare the results for $x = \pm 10, \pm 5, \pm 0.1$. Explain any differences.

8. Consider the following segment of a PL/I program:

```
A = 20;
B = 0.1;
C = A * B;
DO I = 1 TO C BY 1;
     PUT SKIP LIST(I);
     END;
```

What values of I will be printed? Check your answer by running this program.

9. In real arithmetic (infinite precision), the two expressions

$$99-70\cdot\text{sqrt}(2) \quad \text{and} \quad 1/(99+70\cdot\text{sqrt}(2))$$

are equal in value. Which expression is more accurate in finite precision arithmetic? Why?

10. If x(1),...,x(n) are given numbers then m=(x(1)+...+x(n))/n is their mean or average and $v=((x(1)-m)^2+\ldots+(x(n)-m)^2)/n$ is their variance. Show that in real arithmetic $v=(x(1)^2+\ldots+x(n)^2)/n-m^2$. Which way of computing v is preferable in finite precision arithmetic? Hint: Consider b=10, t=3 and x(1)=...=x(n)=0.905. Now compute v both ways for n=1,2,..,5.

11. Write a program to convert a decimal integer x > 0 into base 2 notation. For example, since 69 = 1000101 (base 2), or

$$69 = 1\cdot 2^6 + 0\cdot 2^5 + 0\cdot 2^4 + 0\cdot 2^3 + 1\cdot 2^2 + 0\cdot 2^1 + 1\cdot 2^0,$$

execution of this program should deliver the sequence of bits

1 0 0 0 1 0 1

Let there be k + 1 significant bits in the answer. Then the result should be stored in an array A with A(0) being the least significant bit and A(k) being the most significant bit. With the case x = 69 the result should be

k = 6, A(6) = 1, A(5) = 0, A(4) = 0, A(3) = 0, A(2) = 1, A(1) = 0, A(0) = 1.

<u>Hints on writing the program</u>. With the notation given above, we can see that upon termination we should have

$$x = A(k) \cdot 2^{**}k + \ldots + A(1) \cdot 2^1 + A(0) \cdot 2^0$$

where A(k) = 1 and each other A(i) is either 1 or 0. Let us rewrite this equation using a new simple variable z, $z \geq 0$, as

$$x = z \cdot 2^{**}(k+1) + A(k) \cdot 2^{**}k + \ldots + A(1) \cdot 2^1 + A(0) \cdot 2^0$$

Now note that if we initialize k to -1 and z to x that this equation is true. Moreover, if z can be reduced to 0 while adjusting k and array A to keep this equation true, then the result has been achieved. Thus we use a loop

```
K = -1;
Z = X;
DO WHILE(Z > 0);
    Reduce z and adjust k and A to keep z ≥ 0
            and the equation true
    END;
```

In effect, each iteration of the loop will determine the next significant bit A(k+1) of the result, and thus causes an increase in k. To determine how to reduce z in the body of the loop one should use the fact that

$$z = \text{MOD}(z,2) + \text{FIXED}(z/2) \cdot 2$$

12. Write a program that will find the base 2 expansion of a decimal fraction. The algorithm for this program is very similar to the one described in Exercise 11, but now the number will be successively <u>multiplied</u> by 2.

Section 2 Library Functions (COS and SQRT)

Consider the statement Y = COS(X); where X is some floating point number, or the statement Y = SQRT(X); where X is now restricted to be nonnegative. When the computer executes these statements it will provide fast and accurate approximations to cos(x) and sqrt(x). How does it do this? Certainly, it does not have a table in which to look up the answer; this would require huge amounts of storage space and time. Instead for each value of x the computer generates an approximation to cos(x) or sqrt(x) by means of a few arithmetic operations.

2.1 Approximation by Polynomials

There are many methods for calculating a fast and accurate approximation to cos(x). Those readers with some knowledge of calculus are aware of a method based on Taylor's expansion of the cosine function. Since most people think that this is the way to calculate cos(x), we will first spend some time trying to convince you that this approach is not at all practical.

The approach that we have been referring to is based on the mathematical theorem that

(2.1a) $\cos(x) = 1 - x^2/2! + x^4/4! - x^6/6! + \ldots$

The right hand side of (2.1a) is called the "Taylor expansion" of the cosine function; the meaning of (2.1a) is that given any x and any accuracy factor ERROR, there is an integer n (which depends on x and ERROR) such that the sum of the first n terms on the right of (2.1a) is an approximation to cos(x) whose absolute error is less than ERROR. In other words, by adding enough terms we can get an approximation to cos(x) which is as accurate as desired.

There are many reasons why this approach is not reasonable. For one, how many terms do we need to take? In general, the larger $|x|$ is, the more terms you need to take and this will slow down the computation. Even if you are willing to spend the time to compute enough terms in the right hand side of (2.1a), there is no guarantee that we will obtain an accurate answer. Equality in (2.1a) is a mathematical fact which depends on infinite precision; in finite precision (2.1a) is not true. For example, if x=5.0 then with b=16 and t=6 the sum on the right of (2.1a) equals 0.283655 but cos(5.0) = 0.283662... in infinite precision.

It is fairly easy to see why we only obtain five significant decimal digits: All the terms in the sum are restricted to approximately seven decimal digits, but since the initial terms like $5^4/4! = 26.04...$ are large, their initial two digits will have to cancel in order to obtain an answer that is less than one, and therefore only five decimal digits really contribute to the accuracy of the sum. In addition, later terms will be small and only their initial digits will contribute to the sum; after the twelfth term they are negligible.

The cancellation that we have observed is due to the fact that |x| is large and it will get worse if |x| is increased. If |x| is small then (2.1a) is a reasonable way to compute cos(x). Therefore, it is reasonable that practical methods for evaluating cos(x) have an initial stage which allows you to avoid the direct computation of cos(x) for large values of |x|. The method that we will now describe shows that all the values of cos(x) can be obtained from those of cos(x) and sin(x) for x between 0 and (pi)/4 (where pi = 3.14159...).

First recall that the cosine is an even function, which means that cos(-x) = cos(x), so we only need to consider nonnegative x. Moreover, the cosine is a periodic function whose period is p = 2pi. This means that cos(x + p·k) = cos(x) for any integer k. To make use of this property first compute 4x/pi = q + f, where q is an integer and f is the fractional part of 4x/pi. Now express q as q = 8k + r where k and r are integers with 0≤r<8. Altogether, x = p·k + pi·(f+r)/4, so that periodicity implies that

$$\cos(x) = \cos(pi\cdot(f+r)/4).$$

Depending on the values of r we will have different results. For example, if r = 0 then

$$\cos(x) = \cos(pi\cdot f/4)$$

while if r = 1 then

$$\cos(x) = \cos(pi/2 - pi\cdot(1-f)/4) = \sin(pi\cdot(1-f)/4).$$

Similar relationships hold for any 0≤r<8, so that cos(pi·(f+r)/4) equals ±cos(pi·g/4) or ±sin(pi·g/4) where g = f or g = 1-f.

The process just described is known as "range reduction". Note that it consists of a clever use of the symmetries of the cosine function; for other functions range reduction would take a different form. If it is possible, range reduction is usually beneficial, but the operations involved have to be carried out with extreme care since they are very sensitive to errors.

Now that we have range reduction, the calculation of the cosine function will be complete if we can generate cos(x) and sin(x) for $0 \le x \le (pi)/4$. For simplicity we only discuss the cosine function. In this case (2.1a) is reasonable since cancellation will not occur. In fact, if

(2.1b) $$p(x) = 1 - x^2/2! + x^4/4! - x^6/6! + x^8/8!,$$

then some thought will show that (2.1a) implies that

$$|p(x) - \cos(x)| < (pi/4)^{10}/10! = (2.5)10^{-8}$$

for $0 \le x \le (pi)/4$. Moreover, since in this range $\cos(x) \ge 1/\mathrm{sqrt}(2)$, we also have

$$|(p(x) - \cos(x))/\cos(x)| < (3.5)10^{-8}.$$

This shows that p(x) always has eight significant decimal digits as an approximation to cos(x), so (2.1b) is adequate for single precision.

The function defined by (2.1b) is a polynomial of degree 8 in x, and degree 4 in x^2. Hence if we can find a polynomial of degree 3 in x^2 which approximates the cosine as well as (2.1b), then we should use this polynomial instead of (2.1b) since any work saving in a library function like the cosine is important because of the high frequency with which it will be used. It is indeed possible to find such a polynomial but the methods for doing this are beyond the scope of this book. The interested reader will find material on this topic in the references of Section 4.

2.1.1 Horner's Scheme

The point was made in Section 2.1 that any savings in the work required to execute a frequently performed task are generally worthwhile. Polynomial evaluation is certainly such a task if for no other reason than their frequent use in approximation.

Consider then the evaluation of a polynomial p of degree n

(2.1.1a) $$p(x) = a(0) + a(1)x + a(2)x^2 + \dots + a(n)(x^{**}n).$$

If we evaluate (2.1.1a) in what would seem to be the obvious way -- evaluate a(i)(x**i) for i=0,1,...,n and add these terms together -- then this would involve n(n+1)/2 multiplications and n additions. To see this, note that the evaluation of a(i)(x**i) involves i multiplications and therefore the number of multiplications is

$$1 + 2 + \ldots + n = n(n+1)/2.$$

In analogy with the terminology introduced in Part VII, we say that this is an n^2 algorithm. Note however, that if we evaluate (2.1.1a) from left to right, then each term needs only 2 multiplications and one addition. For example, if we have evaluated

$$a(0) + a(1)x + a(2)x^2,$$

then we only need one multiplication to compute x^3 from x^2, another multiplication for $a(3)x^3$, and an addition for

$$a(0) + a(1)x + a(2)x^2 + a(3)x^3.$$

In all, for (2.1.1a) we need 2n multiplications and n additions, so this is an order n algorithm.

However, there is a still faster algorithm, known as Horner's scheme. This method consists of a series of n nested multiplications such that at each stage only one multiplication and one addition occur. Thus Horner's scheme is also an order n algorithm but requires only half as many multiplications as the previous algorithm.

The idea of Horner's method is really simple. First note that a first degree polynomial can be evaluated in one multiplication and one addition. If we write a second degree polynomial in the form

$$a(0) + a(1)x + a(2)x^2 = a(0) + (a(1) + a(2)x)x,$$

then it can be evaluated in two multiplications and two additions. For a third degree polynomial, first write

$$a(0) + a(1)x + a(2)x^2 + a(3)x^3 = a(0) + (a(1) + a(2)x + a(3)x^2)x,$$

and then evaluate the polynomial in parentheses as above. The idea of the algorithm should now be clear; a version of it is as follows:

```
PX = A(N);
DO I = N-1 TO 0 BY -1;
   PX = X * PX + A(I);
   END;
```

Note that if the coefficients of the polynomials are decreasing in magnitude, as in (2.1b), then for $|x|\leq 1$, the sum in Horner's method will consist of an addition of terms of increasing magnitude. Therefore, in cases like this we expect an accurate evaluation of the polynomial.

2.2 Approximation by Iteration

The techniques discussed in Section 2.1 apply to the evaluation of most functions, and in particular, to the evaluation of sqrt(x). However, in this case we shall see that although range reduction is possible, the final approximation of sqrt(x) is not obtained from a polynomial, but by a technique called "iteration".

First let us consider the form taken by range reduction. If x is a floating point number in a base 16 computer then

x = m(16**e)

where $1/16 \leq m < 1$ is the mantissa and e is the exponent. If e is even, say e=2c, then

sqrt(x) = sqrt(m)·16**c,

while if e is odd, say e=2d-1, then

sqrt(x) = (1/4)sqrt(m)·16**d.

By combining both cases we see that it is only necessary to evaluate sqrt(x) for $1/16 \leq x < 1$.

At this stage, in analogy with the previous section, it would seem reasonable to try to approximate the square-root function on the reduced range by a polynomial. However, this turns out not to be practical.

The method used depends on the fact that the number we are after, sqrt(m), is the positive solution of the equation $-m+x^2 = 0$. Consider then the graph of the function defined by $f(x) = -m+x^2$. If we have an approximation x(0) to sqrt(m) with x(0) > sqrt(m), then it is easy to obtain a better approximation x(1) with x(1) > sqrt(m). Just draw the tangent line to f at x(0) and take x(1) to be the intersection of this line with the x-axis. Finding x(1) is not difficult. The slope of the tangent line to f at x(0) is just the derivative f'(x(0)) so that the y-intercept equation of the tangent line is

y = f'(x(0))(x-x(0)) + f(x(0)).

But f'(x(0)) = 2·x(0) and $f(x(0)) = -m + x(0)^2$ and thus

$$y = 2\cdot x\cdot x(0) - m - x(0)^2.$$

Finally, since x(1) is the x-intercept of this line,

$$0 = 2\cdot x(0)\cdot x(1) - m - x(0)^2$$

and rearranging terms,

x(1) = (x(0) + m/x(0))/2.

There is no reason why this process cannot be repeated to obtain a still better approximation x(2) where

$$x(2) = (x(1) + m/x(1))/2.$$

In general, if we have the kth approximation x(k), the (k+1)st approximation x(k+1) is given by

$$x(k+1) = (x(k) + m/x(k))/2. \tag{2.2a}$$

Geometrically, it is obvious that if $x(0) > \mathrm{sqrt}(m)$ then

$$\mathrm{sqrt}(m) < x(k+1) < x(k),$$

and that given any accuracy factor ERROR there will be an approximation x(k) such that

$$|x(k) - \mathrm{sqrt}(m)| < \mathrm{ERROR}.$$

Since $\mathrm{sqrt}(m) \geq 1/4$, we would also have

$$|(x(k) - \mathrm{sqrt}(m))/\mathrm{sqrt}(m)| < 4 \cdot \mathrm{ERROR}.$$

This would solve the problem of evaluating sqrt(m) if we could answer two questions: 1) How do you choose the initial approximation x(0)? 2) How do you decide which approximation to take as sqrt(m)?

These two questions are obviously related. We want an x(0) which is close to sqrt(m) because this may mean that our fourth approximation, say, will be the final one. On the other hand, we do not want to spend too many operations in trying to find an accurate x(0). In the following, these delicate matters will not be fully explored and we will limit ourselves to presenting reasonable solutions.

An acceptable x(0) can be found as follows: First find the straight line that best approximates (in the relative sense) the square root function for $1/16 \leq x \leq 1$; that is, determine constants a and b such that

$$\max\{\,|(\mathrm{sqrt}(x) - (a+bx))/\mathrm{sqrt}(x)| \;:\; 1/16 \leq x \leq 1\,\}$$

is minimal. Then set x(0) = a+bm. It turns out that a=2/9, b=8/9, and that the resulting x(0) always has one significant decimal digit as an approximation to sqrt(m).

Deciding which approximation to accept as the final one is a somewhat difficult question to answer theoretically. However, a little experimentation will convince you that the third and fourth approximations x(3) and x(4) will suffice for single and double precision, respectively. The rule of thumb is that each iteration roughly doubles the number of significant figures (and recall that x(0) has one significant figure).

To finish this section, we mention that the method used to find the zero of the function $f(x) = -m+x^2$ is known as "Newton's method". It can be used to find a zero of a general function f. In fact, the same argument in terms of tangent lines and x-intercepts yields that Newton's method is given by

$$x(k+1) = x(k) - f(x(k))/f'(x(k)).$$

If $f(x) = -m+x^2$ then it is easy to verify that Newton's method reduces to (2.2a).

Section 2 <u>Exercises</u>

1. Show that sqrt(2) does not have a finite or repeating decimal representation. Do the same for cos(1) by using (2.1a).

2. Write an algorithm which accepts a positive integer q and finds integers k and r with $0 \le r < 8$ and such that q = 8k + r.

3. Complete the discussion in the text by showing how cos(pi·(f+r)/4) can be expressed in terms of cos(pi·g/4) or sin(pi·g/4) where g=f or 1-f.

4. Verify the statements given in the text on the calculation of the right side of (2.1a). Evaluate it in three different ways: in ascending and descending order, and by Horner's method. In addition, evaluate the right side of (2.1a) for x=1.57 and explain why the result has a larger relative error than for x=5.0.

5. Let s(n,x) denote the sum of the first n terms on the right of (2.1a). Show that if $|x| \le 2n$ then

$$|\cos(x) - s(n,x)| \le (x**2n)/(2n)!$$

6. Write a procedure which, given an integer n and a float decimal x, will read in coefficients and evaluate the corresponding polynomial by Horner's method. Do not use any arrays.

7. a) Show that if x(0) = 2/9 + (8/9)m then x(1) > sqrt(m) for $1/16 \le m < 1$.

   b) Verify that $|(x(0) - \text{sqrt}(m))/\text{sqrt}(m)| \le 1/9$ for all $1/16 \le m \le 1$.

8. Verify, by experimentation, that the third iterate of (2.2a) suffices for single precision.

Section 3 Algorithms for Two Typical Problems

3.1 Simultaneous Linear Equations

The first of our typical problems is frequently encountered, not only for its own sake, but also as an intermediate step in the solution of other computational problems. It can be stated as follows: Given a vector (or one-dimensional array) b with n elements, and a matrix (or two-dimensional array) A with n rows and n columns, find a vector x of length n such that

$$
\begin{aligned}
&a(1,1)\cdot x(1) + \ldots + a(1,n)\cdot x(n) = b(1)\\
&\quad\ldots\\
&a(i,1)\cdot x(1) + \ldots + a(i,n)\cdot x(n) = b(i)\\
&\quad\ldots\\
&a(n,1)\cdot x(1) + \ldots + a(n,n)\cdot x(n) = b(n),
\end{aligned}
\tag{3.1a}
$$

or show that there is no solution to this problem.

If n=2 then (3.1a) represents two straight lines, and the problem reduces to finding whether two lines intersect and the point of intersection. Similarly, for n=3, we have three planes and the problem is to find a point (if any) shared by these planes. In general, given a vector b, the system of equations (3.1a) can either have no solution, a unique solution, or an infinite number of solutions. In this section we will assume that (3.1a) has a unique solution.

The problem may seem trivial, but this is not so. For example, (3.1a) might have a solution vector of real numbers, but not a solution in floating point arithmetic. Moreover, you should realize that roundoff errors will probably change the A and B arrays when they are read in, so that you will be solving a different system of linear equations. Clearly, all we can hope for is an approximate solution to (3.1a), but this problem is also not easy. For example, if

$$
\begin{aligned}
0.66666\cdot x(1) + 3.33334\cdot x(2) &= 4\\
1.99999\cdot x(1) + 10.00001\cdot x(2) &= 12,
\end{aligned}
\tag{3.1b}
$$

then you can verify that x = (1,1) solves this system exactly. Now consider the approximate solutions y=(1.1,0.9) and z=(6,0).

Although y appears to be the better solution since it is closer to x, substituting y for x in (3.1b) gives

(3.733332, 11.199998)

instead of (4, 12), while the substitution of z for x in (3.1b) gives

(3.99996, 11.99994).

Thus, from this point of view z seems to be the better solution.

Equations (3.1b) also illustrate another difficulty with linear systems. Suppose the right side of (3.1b) is changed to

(3.99996, 11.99994).

Then, as we have seen above, the exact solution is changed to (6,0). Thus, a small relative change in the equations leads to a large relative change in the answer. Clearly, such a system is "ill-conditioned" and will cause problems. We will have more to say about (3.1b) in Section 3.1.3.

3.1.1 Gaussian Elimination

Most of you have encountered linear systems before, and if so, you probably have solved them by Gaussian elimination. Rather than give a formal description we will discuss this algorithm in connection with a system (3.1a) with n=3, but in such a way that the general algorithm is clear.

Consider then

$$\begin{aligned} 5\cdot x(1) - 2\cdot x(2) + 3\cdot x(3) &= 10 \\ 10\cdot x(1) - 3\cdot x(2) + 4\cdot x(3) &= 16 \\ 15\cdot x(1) + 1\cdot x(2) - 3\cdot x(3) &= 8. \end{aligned} \tag{3.1.1a}$$

The first stage of Gaussian elimination consists of eliminating the unknown x(1) from the second and third equations. To do this, we multiply the first equation by 2, and subtract it from the second, then multiply by 3, and subtract it from the third to get

$$\begin{aligned} 5\cdot x(1) - 2\cdot x(2) + 3\cdot x(3) &= 10 \\ 1\cdot x(2) - 2\cdot x(3) &= -4 \\ 7\cdot x(2) - 12\cdot x(3) &= -22. \end{aligned} \tag{3.1.1b}$$

Thus, we have effectively reduced the problem to a smaller problem (in this case 2 by 2 but generally (n-1) by (n-1)) which doesn't involve x(1). If we can solve the smaller problem for x(2) and x(3) (generally x(2),...,x(n)) then x(1) could easily be determined by substituting these values back into the first equations.

At this point, we can apply the same elimination strategy to the smaller problem and eliminate x(2) from all except the first equation of the problem. In our example this results in

```
      5·x(1) - 2·x(2) + 3·x(3) = 10

(3.1.1c)       1·x(2) - 2·x(3) = -4

                        2·x(3) =  6.
```

In the general case we would now have n-2 equations in n-2 unknowns and we would continue. In our example, n=3 and so we have completed the forward elimination. From this you see that for the general system (3.1a), the ith stage of the forward elimination consists of eliminating x(i) from equations i+1 through n. This is done by forming the multipliers

m(i,j) = a(i,j)/a(i,i)

for j = i+1,...,n, then multiplying the ith equation by m(i,j) and subtracting it from the jth equation for j = i+1,...,n.

Now that we have reduced our original 3 by 3 system to the simple form of (3.1.1c) the solution can be obtained easily. The third equation yields x(3) = 3. Substituting x(3) back into the equation just above it yields x(2) = 2 and both of these values substituted back into the next equation above, in this case the first, results in x(1) = 1. This process is called back substitution; in the general case it would be carried out by the following program segment:

```
DO I = N TO 1 BY -1;
   SUM = 0;
   DO J = I+1 TO N BY 1;
       SUM = SUM + A(I,J) * X(J);
       END;
   X(I) = (B(I) - SUM)/A(I,I);
   END;
```

Things certainly don't always go so smoothly. If the coefficients of the second equation in (3.1.1a) had been 10, -4 and 6 then the second equation in (3.1.1c) would have been 0 = -4 and so no solution would exist. A good program would not merely terminate at this point but would return information to the user concerning the nature of the failure. Another hitch which could occur does not imply the nonexistence of a solution. Suppose A(2,2) had been -4 with all the other coefficients the same as in (3.1.1a). Then the second equation in (3.1.1b) would not involve x(2) and so it clearly couldn't be used to eliminate x(2) from subsequent equations. The remedy to this difficulty is simple; just interchange the second and third equations.

In general, this difficulty is caused by having a(i,i)=0 in the ith stage of the forward elimination, and thus, the multipliers can't be formed. The remedy is to interchange the ith row for any row j such that a(j,i)≠0, although in practice j is chosen so that

$$|a(j,i)| \geq |a(k,i)|$$

for k = i,...,n. This modification which is made even when a(i,i)≠0 is called Gaussian elimination with partial pivoting, and we will see in Section 3.1.3 that this is the method generally in use at present for solving (3.1a) except in those cases where A has some special property that makes special-purpose methods more suitable. Moreover, it can be shown that if (3.1a) has a unique solution then Gaussian elimination with partial pivoting will yield the answer provided all operations are performed in infinite precision arithmetic.

3.1.2 Efficiency -- Gaussian Elimination vs. Cramer's Rule

You have probably encountered Cramer's rule in your studies, and you may even have used it to solve systems of linear equations. If this is the case, you might want to know whether or not Gaussian elimination is more efficient than Cramer's rule in order to decide which algorithm to apply.

The standard way to measure efficiency in solving (3.1a) is in terms of the number of arithmetic operations necessary to obtain a solution. For linear equations, this is a reasonable measure since the only operations involved are arithmetic, but we shall see that the next problem we consider (in Section 3.2) requires a different criterion.

Cramer's rule depends on the calculation of the determinants of certain matrices. The determinant of a matrix A with n rows and n columns is given by

$$\text{(3.1.2a)} \quad \det A = a(1,1)\cdot\det M(1,1) - a(2,1)\cdot\det M(2,1) + a(3,1)\cdot\det M(3,1) \ldots \pm a(n,1)\cdot\det M(n,1)$$

where M(i,1) is the (n-1) by (n-1) matrix obtained by deleting the ith row and first column of A. To calculate det M(i,1) we can apply this definition again and express det M(i,1) in terms of determinants of (n-2) by (n-2) matrices. By repeating this process, we eventually obtain det A expressed in terms of the determinants of 2 by 2 matrices, and since

$$\det \begin{bmatrix} a & b \\ c & d \end{bmatrix} = ad - bc,$$

this completes the calculation of det A.

However, the efficiency of this method for evaluating determinants is very poor. To see this let m(n) be the number of multiplications necessary to evaluate the determinant of an n by n matrix. Then (3.1.2a) implies that

$$m(n) = n \cdot m(n-1) + n,$$

and in particular, $m(n) > n \cdot m(n-1)$. But by the same reasoning $m(k) > k \cdot m(k-1)$ for any $3 \le k \le n$, and therefore,

$$m(n) > n \cdot (n-1) \cdot \ \ldots \ \cdot (3) \cdot m(2).$$

Since m(2) = 2, we finally have m(n) > n!.

This is an impossibly-large problem (as described in Section VII.3), even for small values of n. For example, on an IBM 360/65 a single precision multiplication takes approximately four microseconds ($4 \cdot 10^{-6}$ seconds). Since $15! = (1.3) \cdot 10^{12}$ this means that the calculation of the determinant of a 15 by 15 matrix by (3.1.2a) would take at least 2.6 years of computing time.

Now Cramer's rule states that if det A ≠ 0, then the solution to (3.1a) is given by

$$x(j) = \det A(b|j)/\det A,$$

where A(b|j) is the n by n matrix obtained by replacing the jth column of A by b. Therefore, the above arguments would seem to imply that Cramer's rule is unreasonable. However, the correct conclusion is that if the <u>determinants</u> are calculated by (3.1.2a) then Cramer's rule is unreasonable. We shall later point out that it is possible to calculate determinants in about $n^3/3$ multiplications, but that even if the determinants are calculated in this manner Gaussian elimination with partial pivoting is more efficient.

To estimate the efficiency of Gaussian elimination, we will count the number of multiplications and divisions required by the forward elimination and the back substitution. It is important not to neglect the counting of additions and subtractions, since if this number is much larger, then it would determine the efficiency of the method. However, we shall let you verify that this is not the case in Gaussian elimination.

Since multiplications and divisions take almost the same amount of time to perform, we will count a division as a multiplication. Similarly, a subtraction is counted as an addition.

The ith stage of the forward elimination needs (n-i) divisions to form the multipliers. Moreover, to multiply the ith equation by m(i,j) for j = i+1,...,n requires (n-i)(n-i-1) multiplications. Altogether, the ith stage requires

$$(n-i) + (n-i)(n-i-1) = (n-i)^2$$

multiplications, and the complete forward elimination needs

$$(n-1)^2 + (n-2)^2 + \ldots + 1^2 = n(n-1)(2n-1)/6$$

multiplications.

From the program segment we gave for back substitution, it is easy to verify that this process uses

$$n + (n-1) + \ldots + 1 = n(n+1)/2$$

multiplications. So we see that the most expensive part of Gaussian elimination is the forward elimination, and this only involves approximately $n^3/3$ multiplications. Since this is also the most expensive in terms of additions, Gaussian elimination is an n^3 algorithm. Moreover, Gaussian elimination with partial pivoting is also an n^3 algorithm since there will be at most n(n-1)/2 comparisons.

It is interesting that Gaussian elimination with partial pivoting is used to find the determinant of an n by n matrix in approximately n^3 operations. In fact, the determinant of A is not changed during the forward elimination except when two rows are interchanged. However, even then only the sign is changed, and this happens only if the number of interchanges is odd. Since the forward elimination will reduce A to an upper triangular matrix -- a matrix such that a(i,j)=0 for i>j -- we only need to know how to calculate the determinant of an upper triangular matrix. But this is easy, since (3.1.2a) implies that the determinant of an upper triangular matrix is the product of the elements on the diagonal. In particular, the determinant of the matrix in (3.1.1c) is 10, and therefore the determinant of the matrix in (3.1.1a) is also 10. In summary, we have shown that the determinant of an n by n matrix is an immediate by-product of the forward elimination and therefore it can be calculated with an n^3 algorithm. Since Cramer's rule requires the calculation of n+1 distinct determinants, this makes Cramer's rule an n^4 algorithm.

3.1.3 Ill-Conditioned Problems and Stable Algorithms

You have already seen an ill-conditioned problem; in equations (3.1b) a small relative difference in the righthand side led to a large relative difference in the solution. Geometrically, it should be clear why this happens -- the lines represented by (3.1b) are essentially parallel. Computationally, there is not much that you can do with these problems except work in higher precision. However, if the problem is very ill-conditioned then even changing the data into the internal representation of the computer will drastically change the answer.

Let us now assume that our system of linear equations is not too ill-conditioned. Under this assumption, a method for solving (3.1a) is stable if it gives accurate results with respect to the working precision.

Without any pivoting, Gaussian elimination can't be considered stable since it can break down even in infinite precision arithmetic by having a(i,i)=0 at the ith stage of the forward elimination. Consider, for example, equations (3.1.1a) with a(2,2) replaced by -4. However, if a zero causes problems in infinite precision, then maybe a small number will do the same in finite precision. Here is an example that will show that this is the case:

$$\begin{aligned} 10^{-4}\cdot x(1) - x(2) &= -1 \\ x(1) + x(2) &= 2 \end{aligned} \qquad (3.1.3a)$$

We assume that we are working on a computer with base b=10 and precision t=4. The result of the forward elimination is

$$\begin{aligned} 10^{-4}\cdot x(1) - x(2) &= -1 \\ 10^{4}\cdot x(2) &= 10^{4} \end{aligned}$$

so that x(2) = 1 and x(1) = 0. However, to four decimal places the correct solution is x(1) = 0.9999 and x(2) = 1.0001.

Note that (3.1.3a) is well-conditioned since the corresponding straight lines are far from parallel. Therefore, the conclusion is that without pivoting Gaussian elimination is not stable even for well-conditioned systems.

It is pretty clear what happened in (3.1.3a). We found ourselves having to add numbers whose magnitudes were so different that excessive roundoff errors resulted. An indication of this can be found in the magnitude change from 1 to 10^4 in the coefficient of x(2) in the second equation. When Gaussian elimination is modified to be more stable, the changes are directed toward reducing the growth in the magnitude of the elements generated during the forward elimination. The partial pivoting strategy is one way to accomplish this. As mentioned in Section 3.1.1, this consists of interchanging rows at the ith stage of the forward elimination in such a way that

$$|a(i,i)| \geq |a(k,i)|$$

for k = i+1,...,n. It follows that the multipliers m(i,j) satisfy $|m(i,j)| \leq 1$, and therefore, at each stage of the forward elimination the elements can, at worst, double in size. In practice, however, this growth is usually not obtained, and Gaussian elimination with partial pivoting is a stable algorithm.

Let us consider one last example:

$$\begin{aligned} 10\cdot x(1) - 10^5\cdot x(2) &= -10^5 \\ x(1) + x(2) &= 2 \end{aligned} \qquad (3.1.3b)$$

Note that (3.1.3b) is well-conditioned, and that in fact, this example was obtained from (3.1.3a) by multiplying the first row by 10^5. Since in this case Gaussian elimination with partial pivoting does not interchange any rows, forward elimination gives

$$\begin{aligned} 10\cdot x(1) - 10^5\cdot x(2) &= -10^5 \\ 10^4\cdot x(2) &= 10^4 \end{aligned}$$

if the operations are carried out on a computer with b=10 and t=4. Therefore, x(2) = 1 and x(1) = 0 which is, of course, completely incorrect. What went wrong? The reason for the failure is that there is <u>already</u> a large difference in the magnitude of the elements of A. For this reason partial pivoting is usually implemented with a "scaling" or "equilibration" technique. Unfortunately this subject is not well understood, but at present scaling usually consists of dividing each row of (3.1a) by the absolute value of the element of maximum magnitude in that row. In (3.1.3b) this would amount to changing the system into (3.1.3a) which, as we have seen, can be adequately solved by Gaussian elimination with partial pivoting.

3.2 The Quadrature Problem

You are probably familiar with the problem of finding the area of a triangle or a circle. These are simple examples of the "quadrature problem", which is to find the area enclosed by a curve. This problem is not only geometrically interesting, but it is of great importance in science and engineering.

Instead of dealing with the completely general question, we will assume that we are given numbers $a < b$, and a procedure which accepts any x between a and b and returns a value f(x).

This is a very important special case and if we think of f(x) as the height of a curve, then we want the area enclosed between the curve and the x-axis from a to b. For example, if someone gives us a=0, b=1 and $f(x) = sqrt(1-x^2)$ then we are being asked to find the area of a quarter of a circle whose radius is one. Now, of course, you know the answer is pi/4 = 0.785398..., but suppose you had never seen the formula for a circle's area. How would you solve the problem then?

Those of you who have had calculus will probably recognize this problem as a special case of the more general problem of finding "the definite integral of a function". If this is the case, then you will realize, as you read this section, that the methods discussed here apply verbatim to this more general problem. Nevertheless, when the problem is treated from the point of view of finding an area, the methods for its solution become geometrically intuitive and therefore accessible to a wider audience.

Another remark is in order for the calculus student. A large percentage of the "indefinite integrals" which arise in practice can't be found in closed form. Furthermore, even when an antiderivative could be found it is often more accurate to ignore this and use a numerical quadrature method.

3.2.1 The Trapezoidal Rule

The simplest approach to solving our quadrature problem is to first subdivide the interval [a,b] into a series of smaller intervals in such a way that for each interval, say [c,d], the area of a trapezoid with a base of length d-c and sides of height f(c) and f(d), is a reasonable approximation to the area under the curve from c to d. Then the sum of the areas of these small trapezoids should be a good approximation to the area under the curve from a to b.

To illustrate this approach let us return to our example where a=0, b=1 and $f(x) = sqrt(1-x^2)$. As a first attempt we could divide [0,1] into two equal subintervals, calculate the areas of the corresponding trapezoids and take their sum as a tentative answer. Since the area of a trapezoid with base length of d-c and sides of height f(c) and f(d) is

```
T_AREA(c,d) = (d-c)(f(d)+f(c))/2
```

we would obtain 0.683 as our tentative answer. This is clearly not very good. To improve matters we could successively subdivide the interval into equal subintervals, calculate the corresponding area approximations and stop when two consecutive approximations agree to the desired accuracy. The result of this strategy is summarized in the table below:

Number of subintervals	Approximate areas
2	6.83012E-01
4	7.48927E-01
8	7.72454E-01
16	7.80813E-01
32	7.83775E-01
64	7.84824E-01
128	7.85195E-01
256	7.85326E-01
512	7.85372E-01
1024	7.85389E-01
2048	7.85394E-01
4096	7.85397E-01
8192	7.85397E-01

The results in this table were generated by the following method: The interval [a,b] was divided into n equal subintervals, each of length h = (b-a)/n. (In the above example n is a power of 2, but this is not important right now.) This introduces a set of partition points x(i), i=0,1,...,n where

(3.2.1a) $x(i) = a + h\cdot i.$

The area of the ith trapezoid is

$$(h/2)[f(x(i-1)) + f(x(i))],$$

and the sum of the areas of these trapezoids is

$$TR(n) = (h/2)\{[f(x(0)+f(x(1))] + [f(x(1))+f(x(2))] + \ldots + [f(x(n-1))+f(x(n))]\}.$$

This formula can also be written as

(3.2.1b) $$TR(n) = h[(1/2)f(a) + f(x(1)) + \ldots + f(x(n-1)) + (1/2)f(b)],$$

and in this form the formula is known as the <u>trapezoidal rule</u>. The results in the previous table were then obtained by using (3.2.1b) and double precision on an IBM 360. However, only single precision answers were printed out. Finally, the computation was terminated when

$$|TR(n) - TR(2n)| < 10^{-6}$$

for some integer n.

There is a good reason why n was always doubled from one calculation to the next. Consider, for example, TR(512). Equation (3.2.1b) shows that to calculate TR(512) we have to call the height procedure 513 times. However, if you think about it, 257 of these values were already used in TR(256) and so they will be repeat calls. Therefore you should be able to compute TR(512) from TR(256) with only 256 additional procedure calls. In fact, you should convince yourself that

(3.2.1c) TR(2n) = (1/2)TR(n) +
h[f(x(1)) + f(x(3)) + ... + f(x(2n-1))]

where h = (b-a)/2n and x(i) is defined by (3.2.1a).

Although in our example we first computed TR(2), and then used (3.2.1c) to compute the other values of TR(n), this is not necessary. Usually n is initially chosen so that h = (b-a)/n is relatively small; for example, choose n to be the smallest integer such that $n \geq 10(b-a)$. Then TR(n) is computed from (3.2.1b), and (3.2.1c) is used for the remaining values. Also note that the computation of TR(2n) by (3.2.1c) represents a real savings. Instead of 2n+1 procedure calls as (3.2.1b) requires, only n calls are required. There is also a corresponding decrease in the required number of arithmetic operations.

3.2.2 Efficiency - Fixed vs. Adaptive Quadrature

How should we measure the efficiency of an integration technique? Consider, for example, the following two methods for finding the area under a curve. The first method chooses n such that $n \geq 10(b-a)$ and then computes TR(n), TR(2n), TR(4n), ..., by (3.2.1b) until

$$|TR(m) - TR(2m)| < ERROR$$

for some integer $m \geq n$ where ERROR is a pre-specified accuracy. The second method only differs in the fact that TR(n), TR(2n),..., are computed by (3.2.1c).

In this case the second method is more efficient. The reason is that clearly the main cost of finding an accurate approximation to the desired area is measured by the number of calls to the height procedure. Since this is true in general, the efficiency measure for integration methods is usually taken to be the number of calls to the height procedure necessary to achieve some pre-specified accuracy.

We now would like to show that with this measure, the trapezoidal rule is not very efficient when used to find the area under certain curves. In fact, the example with a=0, b=1, and $f(x) = sqrt(1-x^2)$ shows that the trapezoidal rule can use up a tremendous number of procedure calls. To convince you that this behavior is not typical, consider the problem a=0, b=1, and f(x) = cos(x). In this case we have

n	TR(n)
20	8.41295E-01
40	8.41427E-01
80	8.41460E-01
160	8.41468E-01
320	8.41470E-01
640	8.41470E-01

The difference in behavior is due to the fact that for f(x) = sqrt($1-x^2$) the tangent line at x=1 is vertical. It is very difficult for a trapezoid to approximate the area of a curve near a point at which a vertical tangent line exists. In general, the trapezoidal rule is slow if the slope of the tangent line changes abruptly as the curve is traversed.

Another reason for the failure of the trapezoidal rule is that the points at which the height procedure is going to be evaluated are fixed in advance. These points are equally distributed throughout the interval [a,b] which means that the trapezoidal rule assumes that the curve behaves the same way throughout the interval, and this is not true for sqrt($1-x^2$).

Actually, it is not very difficult to modify the trapezoidal rule so that it adapts itself to the shape of the curve. The important modification that will be described below is called the <u>adaptive trapezoidal rule</u> while the trapezoidal rule as described in Section 3.2.1 is sometimes called the <u>fixed</u> trapezoidal rule.

The adaptive trapezoidal rule consists of a series of stages. In the first stage, subdivide the interval [a,b] into two equal subintervals by means of the midpoint m = (a+b)/2 and compare

```
T1 = T_AREA(a,b)
```

with

```
T2 = T_AREA(a,m) + T_AREA(m,b).
```

If T1 and T2 agree to the desired accuracy, then take T2 as the answer and stop. If they don't, then momentarily forget about the subinterval [m,b] and concentrate on [a,m]. The second stage is entirely analogous. The subinterval [a,m] is subdivided into two equal subintervals, and the corresponding T1 and T2 are computed. If T1 and T2 agree to the pre-specified accuracy then T2 is accepted as the area under the curve from a to m, and the above process is repeated on the interval [m,b]. If they don't agree, repeat the process on the left half of the interval [a,m].

Even from this vague description of the adaptive trapezoidal rule it should be clear that this scheme will concentrate the calls of the height procedure on the wiggly parts of the curve, and therefore the adaptive trapezoidal rule should be more efficient in the use of function values than its fixed counterpart. However, it should also be clear that we will have to keep track of the values produced by the calls to the height procedure in order to avoid repeat calls. Since it may not be clear how to save those values, we will now refine the description of the adaptive trapezoidal rule, and in doing so we will give a method for saving these values. You will probably not be surprised to learn that this method is sometimes implemented as a recursive procedure (see Section IV.6) although we will not take this approach.

To fix ideas suppose that a=0, b=1, and let us concentrate on the intervals being examined. For example, if T1 and T2 don't agree to the desired accuracy, then during the first three stages we successively generate

[0,1/2]   [1/2,1]

[0,1/4]   [1/4,1/2]   [1/2,1]

[0,1/8]   [1/8,1/4]   [1/4,1/2]   [1/2,1].

Note that the leftmost interval is the one that is currently being examined. At the fourth stage we would calculate

T1 = T_AREA(0,1/8),

and

T2 = T_AREA(0,1/16) + T_AREA(1/16,1/8).

If T1 and T2 agree to the desired accuracy, then T2 is accepted as the area under the curve between 0 and 1/8. The process would then start again, but now the list of intervals would be

[1/8,1/4]   [1/4,1/2]   [1/2,1],

while if T1 and T2 had not agreed, then we would have had

[0,1/16]   [1/16,1/8]   [1/8,1/4]   [1/4,1/2]   [1/2,1].

It is convenient to think of this list of intervals as being a last-in first-out stack, with the rightmost interval at the bottom, and the most recently generated intervals being inserted at the top. To represent these stacks on the computer let STK_A(J) be the left endpoint of the Jth interval on the stack, and let STK_B(J) contain the right endpoint. For instance, in our example, STK_A(1) = 1/2, STK_B(1) = 1, and at the end of the third stage STK_A(4) = 0, STK_B(4) = 1/8.

The height of the stack is related to the length of the smallest interval in the stack. In particular, if the length of the smallest interval is 1/(2**k), then the length of the stack does not exceed k+1. In the general case, the initial interval is [a,b] so the lengths of the subintervals are each of the form (b-a)/(2**k) for some integer k. Since this integer k indicates the size of the interval it is called the <u>level</u> of the interval. In our example, if on the fourth stage T1 and T2 do agree to the desired accuracy, then on the stack we have

level 1 intervals [1/2,1]

level 2 intervals [1/4,1/2]

level 3 intervals [1/8,1/4]

at the end of the fourth stage. If now, on the fifth stage, the interval [1/8,1/4] is divided into halves and the corresponding T1 and T2 don't agree then the level 3 interval [1/8,1/4] is replaced by the two level 4 intervals [1/8,3/16] and [3/16,1/4]. In particular, note that if a level k interval is subdivided then it is removed from the stack and replaced by two level k+1 intervals.

By now you should have a fair idea of how to implement the adaptive trapezoidal rule. In particular you may have realized that to keep track of the evaluations of the height procedure you will need two more stacks: STK_FA(J) and STK_FB(J) will contain, respectively, the height of the curve at the left and right endpoints of the Jth interval in the stack. Moreover, you will need another array to record the level of the jth interval on the stack.

There is, however, one last but very important point that must be made concerning the statement "T1 and T2 agree (or don't agree) to the desired accuracy". The whole idea of the adaptive trapezoidal rule is that, given a desired accuracy ERROR, the adaptive trapezoidal rule will <u>automatically</u> provide an estimate EST for AREA(a,b) -- the area under the curve from a to b -- such that

|EST - AREA(a,b)| < ERROR.

A technique for accomplishing this is based on the observation that if EST1 and EST2 are the corresponding estimates for AREA(a,m) and AREA(m,b) then we should require that

|EST1 - AREA(a,m)| < ERROR/2,

and

|EST2 - AREA(m,b)| < ERROR/2.

In general, the acceptable error for a level k+1 interval should be half of that acceptable for a level k interval. Thus, if we are examining a level k interval [c,d] we should accept T2 as an estimate for AREA(c,d) if

|T2 - AREA(c,d)| < ERROR/(2**k).

However, since we don't know AREA(c,d) we try to satisfy this requirement by asking that

(3.2.2a) |T2 - T1| < ERROR/(2**k).

Therefore, in our example, we should accept T2 as an approximation to AREA(0,1/8) if

|T2 - T1| < ERROR/2^3

since [0,1/8] is a level 3 interval.

Interestingly enough, in practice criterion (3.2.2a) is very stringent. In other words, the absolute error of your final estimate for AREA(a,b) will be much smaller than ERROR. Therefore, instead of (3.2.2a) you could use

|T2 - T1| < ERROR/(g**k)

where 1<g<2. Our limited experiments indicate that g=1.4 is a good value, but you should determine your own favorite choice of g. In some implementations, agreement is required between three, rather than two, successive levels.

Finally, as an example of the power of the adaptive trapezoidal rule, we mention that for a=0, b=1, and f(x) = sqrt(1-x^2) this algorithm (with g=1.4 and ERROR=10^{-6}) obtained a value of 7.85396E-01 in just 437 calls of the height procedure as opposed to 8192 calls for the fixed rule. For a=0, b=1, and f(x) = cos(x), it obtained 8.41469E-01 in 255 procedure calls versus 640 for the fixed rule.

3.2.3 Simpson's Rule

We have already noted that the trapezoidal rule is inefficient if at some point the area under the curve cannot be conveniently approximated by trapezoids. One way to deal with this defect is to localize the problem and concentrate the calls of the height procedure at points near the trouble spot; this philosophy leads to the adaptive trapezoidal rule. On the other hand, you may believe that the defect is due to the simplicity of the trapezoid, and that if the area under the curve were approximated by a more sophisticated shape, then the resulting rule would be more efficient. Let us consider this approach.

First note that an alternate way of looking at the trapezoidal rule on each subinterval is to say that we are approximating the curve by a straight line, and taking the area under this line as an approximation to the area under the curve. From this point of view it is easy to extend the trapezoidal rule by approximating the curve on each subinterval with a parabola instead of a line.

To apply this idea consider a curve f defined on an interval [a,b]. Now subdivide [a,b] into 2n equal subintervals by means of the partition points

$$x(i) = a + h\cdot i \qquad i=0,1,\ldots,2n$$

where h = (b-a)/(2n). The area under the parabola that goes through the points (x(j),f(x(j))) for j=2i-2,2i-1,2i is then

$$(h/3)[f(x(2i-2)) + 4f(x(2i-1)) + f(2i)],$$

and the sum of all these areas is

$$S(2n) = (h/3)[f(a) + 4f(x(1)) + 2f(x(2)) + 4f(x(3)) + \ldots + 2f(x(2n-2)) + 4f(x(2n-1)) + f(b)].$$

This last formula is known as Simpson's rule, and the geometrical arguments given above indicate that it will be more efficient than the trapezoidal rule. This often turns out to be the case. Also note that the two rules are closely related. In fact, given TR(2n) and TR(n) it is easy to calculate S(2n) by means of

$$\text{(3.2.3a)} \qquad S(2n) = (4TR(2n) - TR(n))/3.$$

Simpson's rule can also be used in the adaptive form. In this case we proceed as before subdividing intervals in halves, but now we make use of the formula

$$\text{(3.2.3b)} \qquad P\_AREA(a,m,b) = (b-a)[f(a)+4f(m)+f(b)]/6$$

where m is the midpoint of a and b. In fact, the first stage would consist of estimating the area under the curve from a to b by calculating

$$T1 = P\_AREA(a,m,b),$$

and

$$T2 = P\_AREA(a,p,m) + P\_AREA(m,q,b),$$

where p and q are the midpoints of the intervals [a,m] and [m,b], respectively. Of course, we can implement this adaptive Simpson's rule by using stacks as in the adaptive trapezoidal rule, but now we need another stack, say STK_FM. Then STK_FM(J) would contain f(m) where m is the midpoint of the Jth interval in the stack.

Section 3 Exercises

1. For Gaussian elimination:
   a) Find the number of additions and comparisons done during the forward elimination.

   b) Verify that the number of multiplications in the back substitution is n(n+1)/2.

   c) Find the number of additions in the back substitution.

2. Show that (3.1.2a) implies that the determinant of an upper triangular matrix is the product of the elements on the diagonal.

3. a) Find the solution to (3.1a) where

$$A = \begin{bmatrix} 1 & 2 & 2 \\ -1 & -3 & 2 \\ 2 & 0 & 6 \end{bmatrix}$$

   and b = (0, 4, 8) by Gaussian elimination with partial pivoting.

   b) What is the determinant of A?

4. Write and test a procedure that will solve (3.1a) by Gaussian elimination with partial pivoting. This procedure should have at least the following parameters:

   N, the order of the system
   A, the coefficient matrix
   B, the righthand side
   X, the solution vector.

There should be appropriate messages in case of failure.

5. Write and test a procedure that will execute the adaptive trapezoidal rule. This procedure should have at least the following parameters:

   A, the left endpoint of the interval
   B, the right endpoint of the interval
   EST, the final estimate for the area
   ERROR, the desired absolute error in EST
   MAX_LEVEL, the maximum number of levels allowed
   CALLS, the total number of calls of the height procedure
   MAX_CALLS, the maximum number of calls allowed.

The procedure should either run successfully, or terminate when

MAX_CALLS or MAX_LEVEL is exceeded. In either case appropriate messages should be printed. Note that A, B, ERROR, MAX_LEVEL, and MAX_CALLS have to be set by the user, but that the other parameters will be set by the procedure. You may also want to have other parameters; for example, the name of the height procedure, or MIN_LEVEL so that you will be assured that the height procedure will be called a sufficient number of times.

6. Write a procedure as in exercise 5 for the adaptive Simpson's rule and compare it with the adaptive trapezoidal rule.

7. The following applies to the procedures defined in exercises 5 and 6:

   a) Replace the use of STK_A and STK_B by the use of one stack for the length of the intervals and a variable which contains the left endpoint of the interval on top of the stack.

   b) Investigate the effect of calling these procedures with arguments A > B.

   c) Modify these procedures so that they will test for relative errors instead of absolute errors.

8. a) Verify equation (3.2.3a).

   b) Show that if f is a parabola then formula (3.2.3b) gives the area under this parabola from a to b.

Section 4 Suggestions for Further Reading

We hope to have whetted your appetite for numerical analysis and to this end we have compiled a very brief list of references in this section.

The books by Conte and de Boor, Shampine and Allen, and Forsythe, Malcolm, and Moler are excellent introductory books on numerical analysis; they should be intelligible to anyone who has had calculus. Moreover, they contain FORTRAN programs for most of the mathematical problems they discuss.

To find out more about the effects of finite precision arithmetic on mathematical computations read the standard reference book by Wilkinson. Fike's book is an excellent introduction to the topic of computer evaluation of mathematical functions. Linear equations are treated by Stewart in a very readable manner. Numerical integration, the more exact description of the topic of Section 3.2, is surveyed by Davis and Rabinowitz. Their last chapter is of special interest since it deals with automatic integration and contains several programs.

Finally, the book edited by Rice contains several good articles on the interaction between mathematics and computer programming.

Conte, S. and C. de Boor, Elementary Numerical Analysis, An Algorithmic Approach, 3rd edition, McGraw-Hill, 1978.

Davis, P. and P. Rabinowitz, Methods of Numerical Integration, Academic Press, 1975.

Fike, C., Computer Evaluation of Mathematical Functions, Prentice-Hall, 1968.

Forsythe, G., M. Malcolm, and C. Moler, Computer Methods for Mathematical Computations, Prentice-Hall, 1977.

Rice, J. (editor), Mathematical Software III, Academic Press, 1977.

Shampine, L. and R. Allen, Numerical Computing: An Introduction, W. B. Saunders, 1973.

Stewart, G., Introduction to Matrix Computation, Academic Press, 1973.

Wilkinson, J., Rounding Errors in Algebraic Processes, Prentice-Hall, 1963.

Appendix A Summary of PL/I

This Appendix describes much of the PL/I language. It includes all the features covered in the text, plus some others, but still not all of PL/I. This is presented as reference material, with limited examples and explanations.

The situation is complicated by the many dialects of PL/I. For example, there are:

1. The ANSI standard PL/I.
2. Release 3 of the PL/I Optimizer: the principal current IBM version.
3. PL/I-F: the original IBM version.
4. DOS-PL/I: a subset version for small IBM systems.
5. PL/C: the Cornell version, based on PL/I-F. The current version is Release 7.6.
6. PL/CT: the time-sharing version of PL/C.
7. PL/CS: a new (1978) Cornell version to support experimental test of new language features.
8. SP/K: University of Toronto's subset language for introductory instruction.
9. PLAGO: Brooklyn Polytechnic Institute's subset language for introductory instruction.
10. PLUM: University of Maryland's version for UNIVAC systems.

There are many others. A good comparison of the principal versions is given by Hughes (see References).

This Appendix is based on the old PL/I-F, with a few additions (such as SELECT, LEAVE, UNTIL) reflecting features of the current Optimizer. It also attempts to describe the differences between PL/C and these IBM versions. Not all PL/I constructs are shown in their full generality -- in some cases we opt for a simpler form in respect for simplicity and reliability of use. Appendix A.9 summarizes the differences between PL/I and PL/C-Release 7.6.

PL/CT and PL/CS are summarized separately in Appendicies A.11 and A.12.

Appendix A.1 Notation and Basic Definitions

A consistent "metalanguage" is used in the Appendices to concisely and precisely describe PL/I constructions. Points 1 - 3 describe the notation, while points 4 - 9 give basic PL/I definitions.

1. Square brackets [and] surround an option -- something that may be omitted if desired. For example

```
CHECK [(exp)];
```

means that either of the following is permitted:

```
CHECK;    or    CHECK(exp);
```

As another example

```
CHECK [ (exp [, exp ] ) ] ;
```

means that all of the following are valid:

```
CHECK;
CHECK(exp);
CHECK(exp, exp);
```

2. Braces ¦ and ¦ surround a construction that may occur 0, 1, 2, 3 or more times. For example

```
CALL entry-name [ (argument ¦ , argument ¦ ) ] ;
```

means that any of the following are valid:

```
CALL entry-name;
CALL entry-name(argument);
CALL entry-name(argument, argument);
CALL entry-name(argument, argument, argument);
```

3. Upper-case words are PL/I keywords and are used just as they appear in the model construction. Lower-case words denote general classes of elements, and are replaced by some specific member of the class. For example, if the model is

```
PUT [ SKIP [ (exp) ] ] LIST (exp ¦ , exp ¦ );
```

then an actual statement of this type might be:

```
PUT SKIP(2) LIST (VALUE, SUM/COUNT);
```

4. The principal classes of elements in PL/I are listed below, with references to the appendix sections where they are described:

<u>array-ref</u> A reference to an array or a cross section of an array (for example: C or C(*,2)).

<u>attribute</u> A property or characteristic of a name that helps determine how the name is to be used. Examples are FIXED, BINARY, and RECURSIVE. Appendix A.4.

<u>constant</u> Described later in this section.

<u>declaration</u> Appendix A.3.

<u>entry-name</u> An identifier used to define an entry point in a procedure. Appendix A.3.

<u>exp</u> Any expression.

<u>file-name</u> An identifier used to name an input-output file.

<u>label</u> An identifier used to label a statement.

<u>ON-unit</u> A substatement of an ON statement. Appendix A.2.

<u>procedure definition</u> A procedure; Appendix A.3.

<u>statement</u> Any <u>executable</u> statement; Appendix A.2. The BEGIN block, Compound statement, IF statement, Iterative statement (loop) and ON statement are "complex" statements, since they contain other statements as part of them. All others are called "simple" statements. Note that we do not consider such non-executable elements as END and BEGIN to be statements. This departure from normal PL/I practice makes the description clearer and shorter.

<u>structure-ref</u> A reference to a structure or part of a structure.

<u>variable-name</u> The name of a variable. For a simple variable this is just the identifier used to name it. For a subscripted variable this is the identifier followed by a (, followed by the constant subscripts separated by commas, followed by a). For example, A(1) and B(2,3), but <u>not</u> A(I) and B(2,K).

A variable name can also be a qualified name yielding part of a structure (e.g. X.Y.P).

variable-ref

1. A reference to a simple or subscripted variable.
2. A reference to an array.
3. A so-called "pseudo-variable", which is sometimes used to reference part of a value of a variable, or the whole value but in an unconventional way. These are: SUBSTR, COMPLEX, IMAG, REAL, and UNSPEC.
4. A cross section of an array (e.g. C(*,2)).
5. A qualified name, which refers to part of a structure (e.g. X.Y B(I).Z).

5. A program in PL/I has the following form:

```
entry-name : PROCEDURE OPTIONS(MAIN);
             |declaration|
             |statement|
             |procedure definition|
             END entry-name ;
```

The two entry-names must be the same. The declarations (see Appendix A.3) describe the variables used in the program. The statements are the algorithmic part of the program; they are executed, generally in the order they appear, to produce results. The procedure definitions define other subprograms that the statements can invoke to perform specific subtasks.

The statements of the program refer to and manipulate simple variables, arrays, labels of statements, and so forth. Statements are described in Appendix A.2.

6. A job submitted to the computer consists of a program, together with optional external procedures, as described in Appendix B.1.

7. Identifiers and Keywords of PL/I

An identifier is a single alphabetic character (A through Z, $, #, and @) possibly followed by 1 to 30 alphanumeric characters and/or break characters. The alphanumeric characters are the alphabetic characters and the digits 0 through 9. The break character is the underline character "_".

Examples: B FILE3 $21 @ PRICE_PER_DOZEN

A keyword is an identifier that, when used in the proper context, has a specific meaning. In PL/I keywords are not reserved and can be used as names of variables, etc. (although it is not wise to do so). In PL/C however, some of the keywords are reserved and may not be used as identifiers. We give a list of the reserved keywords below. A keyword in parentheses can be used as an abbreviation for the keyword preceding it.

ALLOCATE BEGIN BY CALL CHECK CLOSE DECLARE (DCL) DELETE DO ELSE END ENTRY EXIT FLOW FORMAT FREE GET GO GOTO IF NO NOCHECK NOFLOW ON OPEN PROCEDURE (PROC) PUT READ RETURN REVERT REWRITE SIGNAL STOP THEN TO WHILE WRITE

8. Use of Blanks in PL/I

Except for the following cases, blanks may appear anywhere and have no particular meaning.

1. They may not appear between adjacent characters of an identifier, keyword, constant, or composite symbol (one made up of two characters, like /* and **).

2. One or more blanks must separate adjacent identifiers, keywords, and/or constants.

3. Within a character string constant, a blank is treated as any other character. Thus 'A BC' is the string consisting of an A followed by a blank followed by a B followed by a C.

9. Comments in PL/I

A comment has the form

/* any sequence of characters */

where the sequence of characters may not include "*/". A comment has no effect on execution of the program, and is used only to make the program more understandable. A comment is permitted wherever a blank is permitted (except in a character string) and is logically equivalent to a blank.

In PL/C, a comment must fit on one card -- it may not extend to two or more cards. This restriction may be lifted by using an option on the *PL/C card; see Appendix B.2.

Because of PL/C's "pseudo-comment" facility (see Section V.5.4.1), it is wise to begin the text of normal comments with a blank.

10. Constants in PL/I

In PL/I the following kinds of constants can be used:

1. A decimal fixed point constant. Examples are: 831 003 .0016 391416

2. A decimal floating point constant. Examples are: 18E-2 4E+30 .001E6

3. An imaginary decimal number. This is a decimal fixed or floating point number followed directly by "I". Examples are: 18E-2I 003I

4. True, or false, which in PL/I must be written as '1'B and '0'B respectively. (They are bit strings.)

5. A literal, which is a quote ' followed by a sequence of characters, followed by a quote '. Examples are 'SIN TABLE' 'ABCD*$.' and '' (the null string). The characters within the quotes can be any punchable characters, including a blank. A quote to be placed in a string constant must be punched twice. Thus, 'A''B' is the string constant whose three characters are A, ', and B, in that order.

One can specify that a string is to be repeated several times. For example, (3)'AB' is shorthand for the string constant 'ABABAB'. (3) is called the "string repetition factor". String repetition factors cannot be used in PL/C.

6. A binary fixed point constant, which is like a decimal fixed point constant except that only the digits 0 and 1 may be used, and that the character B must directly follow the number. Examples are: 1011100B .0010B, and 1.10B, whose decimal values are 92, 0.125 and 1.5.

7. A binary floating point constant, which is a binary fixed point number, followed by E, followed by an optionally signed decimal integer exponent, followed by B. The exponent specifies a power of 2. Examples are: 1011E-31B 1.10E2B (which is equivalent to .110E3B)

8. An imaginary binary number. This is a binary fixed or floating point number followed directly by I. Examples are: 0.1BI 100001000E+200BI

9. A bit string constant. This is a sequence of 0's and 1's enclosed in quotes and followed by B. A repetition factor may be used as for character string constants, but not in PL/C. Examples are: '1'B '0'B '00000'B ''B

10. A label constant. Labels may be assigned to certain variables as values.

Appendix A.2 PL/I Executable Statements

This Appendix lists (in alphabetical order) all the statements included in either the IBM Optimizing Compiler or the Cornell compilers (PL/C, PL/CT or PL/CS). Some statements are not explained ("beyond the scope of this book"), and for many others not all the options are described.

Each statement described here can be optionally preceded by a series of labels, which serve to name that statement:

¦Label:¦ statement

ALLOCATE statement

Execution: Causes storage to be allocated for controlled or based data -- beyond the scope of this book.

ASSERT statement

(PL/CS only, see Appendix A.12)

Assignment statement

There are three forms of the assignment statement, discussed separately under "Assignment to scalars" (the conventional one), "Assignment to arrays", and "Assignment to structures".

Assignment to arrays

Form: array-ref ¦, array-ref¦ = exp [, BY NAME] ;

exp is a scalar expression or an array expression. The arrays referenced and array operands of the expression must have the same number of dimensions and identical bounds.

Execution: This is <u>not</u> executed as a conventional assignment statement. The expression is <u>not</u> first evaluated and then assigned to the arrays referenced. This statement is executed as if it were a number of nested loops (the number depending on the number of dimensions of the arrays) that evaluate an expression and assign to one array element at a time, in row-major order. For example, suppose A(1:20,1:40) is an array. The statement A = A / A(1,1); is executed as if it were

```
DO I = 1 TO 20 BY 1;
    DO J = 1 TO 40 BY 1;
        A(I, J) = A(I, J)/A(1, 1);
        END;
    END;
```

This execution first changes A(1,1) to 1, and then leaves the rest of the array elements unchanged since A(1,1)=1. As another example, A = 5*A(1,1); is executed as if it were

```
DO I = 1 TO 20 BY 1;
    DO J = 1 TO 40 BY 1;
        A(I, J) = 5*A(1, 1);
        END;
    END;
```

The statement inside the generated loops will be a scalar or structure assignment statement; in the latter case it will be further expanded as described under "Assignment to structures". If the original array assignment has BY NAME appended to it, then so will the generated statement inside the loops (this is used for assignment to structures).

Assignment to scalar variables

Form: variable-ref |, variable-ref| = exp ;

The variable-refs must reference scalar variables; evaluation of the expression must yield a scalar value.

Execution:

1. The variables referenced are determined in left to right order. This means evaluating subscripts, etc.
2. The expression is evaluated.
3. The value of the expression is assigned to the variables determined in step 1, in left to right order. The value is converted, if necessary, to the characteristics of each variable according to the rules given in Appendix A.5.

If the variable-ref is a fixed length string, the string exp is truncated on the right if too long or padded on the right (with blanks for character strings and zeros for bit strings) if too short. If the variable-ref is a VARYING string and the value of the expression is longer than the maximum length allowed, the value is truncated to this maximum length and assigned. Otherwise the length of the variable-ref is changed to the length of the value.

Assignment to structures

Form 1: structure-ref |, structure-ref| = exp ;

All structure-refs must have the same number k (say) of immediately contained items. The exp must yield a scalar or a structure value. All structure operands of the expression must have exactly k immediately contained items.

Execution: this is not a conventional assignment statement. The expression is <u>not</u> evaluated and then assigned. Instead, the statement is executed as if it were k simpler assignment statements. The ith one is derived from the original assignment statement by replacing each structure operand and reference by its ith contained item. For example, suppose we have

```
1 ONE                      1 TWO
  2 PART1                    2 PART3
    3 RED                      3 RED
    3 WHITE                    3 WHITE
  2 PART2                    2 PART4
```

The assignment statement ONE=TWO+2; is executed like the two assignments below. Note that the first is still a structure assignment statement, while the second is a scalar assignment.

```
ONE.PART1 = TWO.PART3 + 2;
ONE.PART2 = TWO.PART4 + 2;
```

Form 2: structure-ref |, structure-ref| = exp, BY NAME;

The exp must be a structure expression.

Execution: Execution is equivalent to execution of the assignment statements generated by the following rule: Each immediate item of the leftmost structure-ref is examined in turn, as follows:

If each structure-ref and each structure operand has an immediately contained item with the same identifier as the item being examined, an assignment statement is generated. It is derived by replacing each structure operand and reference with its immediately contained item that has that identifier. If the generated statement is a structure or array of structures, then BY NAME is appended.

For example suppose we have the structures

```
1 ONE                    1 TWO
  2 PART1                  2 PART1
    3 RED(30)                3 RED(30)
    3 BLUE                   3 WHITE
  2 PART2                    3 BLUE
```

The assignment statement ONE = TWO + 2 * ONE, BY NAME; is evaluated as if it were

```
ONE.PART1 = TWO.PART1 + 2 * ONE.PART1, BY NAME;
```

This in turn is evaluated as if it were the two statements below. Note that the first statement below is an array assignment statement.

```
ONE.PART1.RED = TWO.PART1.RED + 2 * ONE.PART1.RED;
ONE.PART1.BLUE= TWO.PART1.BLUE+ 2 * ONE.PART1.BLUE;
```

BEGIN block

```
Form: |label:| BEGIN; |declaration|
                      |statement|
                      |procedure definition|
                      END [label] ;
```

See Appendix A.2.1 concerning END.

PL/I allows the declarations, statements, and procedure definitions to be intermixed, but good practice is to order them as shown above.

Execution: The variables declared and the procedures defined may be referenced by their names only while executing the block. For more on scope rules, see Appendix A.5.1. The BEGIN block is executed as follows:

1. Variables are created and initialized according to the declarations.
2. The statements in the block are executed in order.
3. The variables in step 1 are destroyed.

See also the GOTO and RETURN statements.

CALL statement

```
Form: CALL entry-name [(argument |, argument| )] ;
```

Each argument can be a variable, constant, expression, file-name, label, label variable, entry-name or mathematical built-in function. The number of arguments must be the same as the number of parameters specified at the definition of the entry-name.

●PL/C: Scalars may not be used as arguments for array or structure parameters.

Execution:

1. A correspondence is set up between parameters and arguments, as described in Appendix A.5.5.
2. The variables of the called procedure are created.
3. The sequence of statements of the procedure, beginning at the entry point defined by entry-name, is executed, until the last one has been executed or until a RETURN is executed.
4. The variables created in step 2 are destroyed.

See also the GOTO statement.

CHECK statement

Form: CHECK [(exp1 [, exp2])] ;

The PL/I and PL/C versions of this statement are different. The following applies only to PL/C and PL/CT.

Execution: Execution causes resumption of printing that results from the raising of the CHECK condition. (The printing may have been suppressed by execution of NOCHECK.) Note that the normal action is to do the printing, so that the NOCHECK; statement is provided to override this normal action. (This is the opposite of the situation for the FLOW condition.)

With the form CHECK; there is no limit to the number of times printing will occur. When arguments are used the amount of output is limited as follows: exp1 specifies the maximum number of times that the printing resulting from raising of the CHECK condition in the current block will appear. After the specified number of instances, printing is suppressed.

Exp2 gives the maximum number of times the printing of the CHECK condition will be permitted in each block dynamically entered from the current block, provided NOCHECK; is not executed:

```
CHECK(N,M); is equivalent to
    CHECK(N); in the current block and
    CHECK(M,M); as the first statement in every block
        entered from the current block.

CHECK(N); is equivalent to
    CHECK(N); in the current block and
```

CHECK; as the first statement in every block entered from the current block.

Each time a CHECK; statement is executed the controlling counters are reset to the new limiting values.

<u>CLOSE statement</u>

Form: CLOSE FILE(file-name) ¦, FILE(file-name)¦ ;

Execution: Execution causes the files designated to be "closed" -- disassociated from the dataset with which it was associated upon opening. The file can be reopened. CLOSE need not be executed for each file, since all files are automatically closed upon termination of the program. Closing an unopened file has no effect.

<u>Compound statement</u>

Form: ¦label :¦ DO; ¦statement¦ END [label] ;

See A.2.1 concerning END.

Execution: The statements are executed, in order.

See also the GOTO and RETURN statements.

<u>Conditional statement</u> See "IF statement".

<u>DECLARE, DCL</u> This is not a statement. See Appendix A.3.

<u>DEFAULT statement</u>

Execution: Alters the default attributes in implicit declarations -- beyond the scope of this book.

<u>DELAY statement</u>

Execution: Suspends execution of a "task" -- beyond the scope of this book.

<u>DELETE statement</u>

Execution: Deletes a record from an UPDATE file -- beyond the scope of this book.

DISPLAY statement

Execution: Displays a message to the computer operator -- beyond the scope of this book.

DO See "Compound statement" and "Iterative statement".

END This is not an executable statement. See Appendix A.2.1.

ENTRY This is not an executable statement. See "Procedure definition" in Appendix A.3 and "ENTRY attribute" in Appendix A.4.

EXIT statement

Form: EXIT;

Execution: Causes immediate termination of a "task"; if it is a major task EXIT is equivalent to STOP.

●PL/C: Equivalent to STOP.

FETCH statement

Execution: Causes external procedures to be copied from secondary storage -- beyond the scope of this book.

FLOW statement

Form: FLOW [(exp1 [, exp2])] ;

The PL/I and PL/C versions of this statement are different. The following applies only to PL/C and PL/CT.

Execution: Execution causes resumption of printing that results from the raising of the FLOW condition. The normal action is not to do the printing that results from the raising of the FLOW condition, so that the FLOW statement is provided to override this normal action. This is the opposite of the situation for the CHECK condition.

Exp1 and exp2 have exactly the same interpretation as for CHECK as described above.

The FLOW condition is raised by any action that potentially alters the normal sequential flow-of-control -- that is, by the CALL, DO, GO TO, RETURN, and IF statements, by any exceptional condition (except FLOW) that would cause an ON-unit to be entered, and by in-line function references.

FORMAT declaration This is not an executable statement. See Appendix A.8.

FREE statement

Execution: Causes storage allocated for controlled or based data to be freed -- beyond the scope of this book.

GET statement

```
Form 1: GET LIST(variable-ref {, variable-ref} )
                    [input] [SKIP[(exp)]] [COPY] ;

Form 2: GET EDIT(variable-ref {, variable-ref} ) format
                    [input] [SKIP[(exp)]] [COPY] ;

Form 3: GET DATA   [input] [SKIP[(exp)]] [COPY] ;
```

Execution of all of these has to do with reading in or skipping data. "input" is usually left out, which means that the data are read from the standard input file SYSIN (that is, the data are taken from the cards following the *DATA card). If "input" has the form "FILE(file-name)" then the data are taken from that file. If "input" has the form "STRING(variable-ref)" then the variable-ref must be to a string variable. In this case, the data are taken from this string, beginning with the first character. This is useful in changing data previously read from character to arithmetic form.

The presence of COPY causes the data to be written onto the standard print file, as read. This is useful for debugging purposes. COPY may only be present if "input" is not STRING.

SKIP is equivalent to SKIP(1). SKIP may not be used when "input" is STRING.

The order of the options "input", SKIP and COPY is immaterial, and they may also be placed before LIST, EDIT, or DATA.

Execution:

1. If SKIP(exp) is present, the exp is evaluated and converted to yield an integer w. If w < 1, w is set to 1. w records (usually cards) are then skipped on the input file. (If in the middle of a record, the rest of the record is skipped; this counts as 1 skip).
2. The data are read into the variables specified, depending on the Form used, as described below. The difference lies in the format of the input data being read.

Form 1: GET LIST(variable-ref |, variable-ref|)

Constants are read and assigned to the variables in the list, in left to right order. Any necessary conversion occurs exactly as in an assignment statement.

The input must consist of constants separated by a comma and/or one or more blanks. Each constant is a signed or unsigned number (e.g. -32), a character string (e.g. 'AB C'), a bit string (e.g. '1'B), or a complex constant (e.g. 32-21I).

If the variable-ref is an array or structure, constants are read and assigned to each element of the array or structure, in order. For arrays, this is done in row-major order. For example, for an array A(1:2,1:2), the assignment proceeds in the order A(1,1), A(1,2), A(2,1), A(2,2).

Form 2: GET EDIT (variable-ref |, variable-ref|)
format

The data are read and stored into the variables using the format. See Appendix A.8 on formats. The variables are assigned in the same order described for GET LIST.

Form 3: GET DATA

The input must have the form

variable-name = constant |,variable-name =
constant|;

One or more blanks may be used in place of, or together with, the comma. In effect, the input looks like a sequence of assignment statements. The variable-names may be names of simple or subscripted variables. A qualified name must be <u>fully</u> qualified. The constants have the form described in GET LIST. The constants are assigned to the variables, which of course must be referenceable at the point where the GET DATA statement appears. For example, if the data contains

A(1)=3, B= 21 C(1,3)='AB' ;

then 3 is assigned to A(1), 21 to B and the string 'AB' to C(1,3).

GOTO statement

Form: GOTO label ; or GOTO variable-reference ;

"GO TO" may be used in place of "GOTO".

Execution: Statements are usually executed in the order in which they occur. This normal sequencing can be changed by executing a GOTO. Control is transferred to the statement labeled "label", or to the label that is the current value of the variable-reference. Execution cannot cause a transfer into an inactive block (one not currently being executed), or into a loop from outside the loop.

Execution causes the termination of any BEGIN block, procedure, IF statement, or compound statement whose scope does not include the target of the jump. This termination occurs just as if the block or procedure were exited normally, in the sense that all variables created at the beginning of the procedure or block are destroyed.

HALT statement

Form: HALT;

Execution: In interactive mode, causes execution to pause until resumed by user action; a null statement when not in interactive mode. Similar to PAUSE statement of PL/CT.

IF statement

Form: IF exp THEN statement1 [ELSE statement2]

The exp must yield a scalar value. IF statements can be nested. If so, an ELSE belongs with the closest possible preceding THEN. For example,

```
IF exp1
   THEN IF exp2 THEN s1
   ELSE s2
```

is equivalent to

```
IF exp1
   THEN IF exp2 THEN s1
                ELSE s2
   ELSE;
```

●PL/C: The exp must yield true or false (or any bit string value).

Execution:

1. The expression is evaluated to yield a value. This value is usually "true" ('1'B) or "false" ('0'B); if not, it is converted to a bit string (in PL/C it <u>must</u> be a bit string, no conversion is performed).
2. If the result of step 1 is true ('1'B or a bit string that contains at least one bit that is '1'B) then statement1 is executed; otherwise statement2 is executed if it is present.

<u>IGNORE command</u> A PL/CT debug command. See Appendix A.11.

<u>Iterative statement (loop)</u>

Form 1: ¦label:¦ DO WHILE (exp) ; ¦statement¦ END [label] ;

See Appendix A.2.1 concerning END.

Execution: This is exactly equivalent to execution of

```
L1: IF exp THEN
        DO; ¦statement¦ GOTO L1; END;
```

Form 2: ¦label:¦ DO UNTIL (exp); ¦statement¦ END [label];

See Appendix A.2.1 concerning END.

Execution: This is exactly equivalent to execution of

```
LI: ¦statement¦
    IF ¬ exp THEN GOTO LI;
```

```
Form 3: ¦label:¦ DO variable-ref = exp1 TO exp2 [BY exp3]
                          ¦statement¦
                 END [label] ;
```

If "BY exp3" is missing, "BY 1" is implied. "TO exp2 BY exp3" may also be written as "BY exp3 TO exp2".

Execution: Let V1, V2, and V3 be variables with the type attributes of exp1, exp2, and exp3 respectively, which are not used elsewhere in the program. Execution is exactly equivalent to executing the sequence:

```
Determine variable-ref -- say it is to variable VAR;
V1 = exp1;
V2 = exp2;
V3 = exp3;
VAR = V1;
LOOP:       IF (V3>=0) & (VAR>V2) THEN GOTO NEXT;
            IF (V3<0)  & (VAR<V2) THEN GOTO NEXT;
            ¦statement¦
            VAR = VAR + V3;
            GOTO LOOP;
NEXT:;
```

Form 4: ¦label :¦ DO variable-ref = spec ¦, spec¦ ;
¦statement¦ END [label] ;

Each spec (specification) has the following form (see Form 2):

```
exp1 TO exp2 [BY exp3] [WHILE exp4] [UNTIL exp5]
```

Execution: This is exactly equivalent to executing the following sequence of loops, where variable-ref and ¦statement¦ are as above, and the spec number denotes the order of the specifications above:

```
DO variable-ref = spec1 ¦statement¦ END;
DO variable-ref = spec2 ¦statement¦ END;
DO variable-ref = spec3 ¦statement¦ END;
                ...
```

LEAVE statement

Form: LEAVE [loop-label];

Execution: Causes exit from a loop. If loop-name is omitted, exit is from the innermost loop containing the LEAVE statement. LEAVE can only appear in a loop, and if loop-name is specified, only in the specified loop. Execution may cause BEGIN blocks and procedures to be terminated; see the GOTO statement for details.

LOCATE statement

Execution: Causes allocation of a based variable in an output buffer -- beyond the scope of this book.

NOCHECK statement

Form: NOCHECK;

The PL/I and PL/C versions of this statement are different. The following applies only to PL/C and

PL/CT.

Execution: Execution causes suppression of any printing that would occur from raising the CHECK condition. See the CHECK statement.

NOFLOW statement

Form: NOFLOW;

The PL/I and PL/C versions of this statement are different. The following applies only to PL/C and PL/CT.

Execution: Execution causes suppression of the printing that occurs from raising the FLOW condition. See the FLOW statement.

NOPAUSE command A PL/CT debug command. See Appendix A.11.

NOSTEP command A PL/CT debug command. See Appendix A.11.

Null statement

Form: ;

Execution: Execution of the null statement does nothing.

ON statement

Form 1: ON condition [SNAP] SYSTEM ;
Form 2: ON condition [SNAP] ON-unit

The possible conditions are given in Appendix A.6. The ON-unit may be any unlabeled statement except a compound, iterative, IF, RETURN, or another ON statement. It may be an unlabeled BEGIN block.

Execution: Execution of an ON statement indicates how an interrupt for the specified condition is to be handled. If Form 1 is used, or if no ON statement has been executed for a certain condition, the standard system action is taken. This is usually to print an error message and stop execution. In PL/C, the standard action is usually to print a message, to attempt a repair, and to continue execution.

If Form 2 is used, the condition's occurrence causes the ON-unit to be executed. After it has finished executing, control usually returns to the point where the interrupt occurred. (This varies according to the condition; see IBMFM for complete details.)

In effect, the ON-unit is a procedure, which is called into action not by an explicit call, but by the raising of some condition.

The presence of SNAP causes a list of all blocks and procedures active at the time the interrupt occurs to be printed, just before executing the ON-unit or the standard system action.

Note that execution of an ON statement does not cause the ON-unit to be executed; it causes the ON-unit to be associated with the condition. After execution of the ON-statement, the ON-unit is said to be "pending". That is, the ON-unit is awaiting the occurrence of the condition. If SYSTEM was specified, then the "standard system action" for that condition is pending. (When the program begins execution, the standard system action is pending for each condition.)

We use the term "ON-action" to mean either a programmer-defined ON-unit or the standard system action. Only one ON-action can be pending for any condition at one time. However, each active block or procedure in the program can have a different pending ON-action for each condition. When a block or procedure begins execution, the pending actions are what they were just before execution began. When that block or procedure is finished, the ON-actions revert to what they were before entry. If the exit is by way of a GOTO, the ON-actions are those of the block containing the statement jumped to.

Execution of an ON statement within a block or procedure changes the ON-action only for that block or procedure. Executing a second ON-statement within the block or procedure completely cancels the previously pending ON-action. It is possible to recover the ON-action of a surrounding or calling block using the REVERT statement.

See Appendix A.6 for more details on the ON-statement and conditions.

OPEN statement

```
Form: OPEN FILE(file-name) |options|
                           |, FILE(file-name) |options|| ;
```

In PL/C the possible options are: SEQUENTIAL STREAM RECORD INPUT OUTPUT TITLE(exp) PRINT LINESIZE(exp) and PAGESIZE(exp) . All exps must yield scalar values. These options need not be present; they augment the attributes specified in the file declaration.

Execution: Each file is opened by associating the file-name with the data set. The option INPUT or OUTPUT is used to indicate whether the file will be read or written.

Usually, the first eight characters of the file-name are used as the "ddname" of the dataset. If the file-name is a parameter, the identifier of the argument and not the parameter, is used. If the option TITLE(exp) is used, the ddname for the data set is assumed to be the first eight characters of the string expression.

The LINESIZE option can be used only with a STREAM OUTPUT file. The value of the expression is used as the length of each line of the file. If no LINESIZE is given for a PRINT file, 120 is used.

PAGESIZE(exp) is used to indicate the number of lines on one page. The default is 60. PAGESIZE can only be used for PRINT files.

●PL/C: The default attributes for all PL/C files are STREAM and EXTERNAL.

PAUSE command A PL/CT debug command. Appendix A.11.

PROCEDURE, PROC Not an executable statement. See "Procedure definition" in Appendix A.3.

PUT statement

```
Form 1: PUT                                [output] position   ;

Form 2: PUT LIST(exp |, exp| )             [output] [position] ;

Form 3: PUT EDIT(exp |, exp| ) format      [output] [position] ;

Form 4: PUT DATA (variable-ref |, variable-ref|)
                                           [output] [position] ;
```

The order of the options "output" and "position" is immaterial; they may also be placed directly after PUT.

Execution: Execution of all these have to do with writing data on an output file or into a variable. In the normal case, "output" is missing and the standard output file SYSPRINT is used. If "output" has the form "FILE(file-name)" the data are written out on that file. If "output" has the form "STRING(variable-ref)" then the data are not written out on a file, but are assigned to the string variable referenced, beginning with its first character. In the latter case the position option may not be present.

The forms for "position" are:

```
PAGE [LINE(exp)]        (only for PRINT files)
SKIP [(exp)]
LINE(exp)               (only for PRINT files)
```

The exps must yield integers. SKIP is equivalent to SKIP(1).

Execution:

1. If PAGE is present, the current output page is ended and a new one is begun.

2. If LINE(exp) is present, exp is evaluated and converted to an integer w. If w ≤ 0, it is changed to 1. Blank lines are written out so that line w of the current page is the <u>next</u> one to be formed and written out.

3. If SKIP(exp) is present exp is evaluated and converted to an integer w. w lines are then skipped. For non-PRINT files, w must be greater than 0. For PRINT files (like the standard output file SYSPRINT) w ≤ 0 has the effect of writing at the beginning of the current line again.

4. If Form 1 is used no transfer of data takes place.

5. The data are written out, depending on the form used. The form to use depends on the output format desired: as explained below:

Form 2: PUT LIST(exp {, exp})

For PRINT files (like the standard output file SYSPRINT) the values of the expressions are written out, 24 columns each, in a standard format. Each line has five fields and each field contains one value. If an exp is missing (but not the corresponding comma) a blank field is written. If a string value covers exactly 24 characters, the next field will be left blank. If a string value contains more than 24 characters, it uses as many fields as necessary.

Form 3: PUT EDIT(exp {, exp}) format

The values are written out according to the format. See Appendix A.8 for details.

Form 4: PUT DATA(variable-ref {, variable-ref})

Each reference may be to a scalar value, an array, or a structure variable. For PRINT files (like the standard output file SYSPRINT), the values are written out in the form

variable-name = constant

with a blank between each. The last one is followed by a semicolon. Arrays are written in row-major order.

● PL/C: There are additional forms of PUT statement:

PUT option |option| ;

Options are: ON OFF FLOW SNAP ALL ARRAY and DEPTH(exp) , and the PAGE SKIP and LINE options discussed above. If ON or OFF is used, it must be the only option.

FLOW, SNAP, ALL and ARRAY can appear in any combination with each other, and with the standard SKIP, PAGE or LINE options of PL/I. They are used as follows:

OFF -- suppresses printing of execution output on SYSPRINT.

ON -- resumes printing of execution output on SYSPRINT.

FLOW -- displays the recent FLOW history of the program.

SNAP -- displays the recent calling history of the program.

ALL -- displays the SNAP output as well as the current values of all automatic, scalar variables in the blocks active at the time of execution, and the current values of all static or external scalar variables.

ARRAY -- same as ALL but includes array as well as scalar variables.

DEPTH(exp) -- specifies the depth of block nesting for which the display is to be produced. It is used only with the SNAP, ALL and ARRAY options.

READ statement

Form: READ FILE (file-name) INTO (variable) KEY (exp) ;

Execution: Causes a record with key value "exp" to be transmitted from the RECORD INPUT or RECORD UPDATE flie named "file-name" to "variable" (usually a structure).

The full form is much more general than shown here.

RELEASE statement

Execution: Release memory occupied by specified procedures -- beyond the scope of this book.

RETURN statement

Form 1: RETURN ;

Form 2: RETURN [(exp)] ;

Execution: form 1 is used in a procedure invoked by CALL. Execution causes immediate termination of the procedure and the procedure call.

Form 2 is used in a procedure called as a function. Execution causes immediate termination of the function; the value of the expression is returned as the value of the function (converted to the attributes specified by the RETURNS option of the procedure definition). Execution may cause the termination of BEGIN blocks, etc.; see the GOTO statement for details.

REVERT statement

Form: REVERT condition;

Execution: Used in connection with the ON statement. Execution causes cancellation of the pending ON-action for the condition. The pending ON-action of the last block executed becomes pending again. See the ON statement.

REWRITE statement

Form: REWRITE FILE (file-name) FROM (variable) KEY (exp) ;

Execution: Overwrites an existing record with the key value "exp" in a RECORD UPDATE file named "file-name" with the value from "variable" (usually a structure).

SELECT statement

```
Form: |label:| SELECT [(exp1)] ;
              |WHEN (exp2 |, exp2| ) statement |
              [OTHERWISE statement]
              END [label] ;
```

See Appendix A.2.1 concerning END.

Execution:

Case 1: If exp1 is given it is evaluated and its value saved. Then the exp2's are evaluated in the order given. The <u>first</u> exp2 to be equal to exp1 causes the corresponding |statement| to be executed. If no exp2 is equal to exp1 then the OTHERWISE |statement| is executed (if present, otherwise the SELECT execution is null).

Case 2: If no exp1 is given the exp2's are evaluated in the order given. The <u>first</u> exp2 to evaluate to '1'B causes the corresponding |statement| to be executed. If no exp2 is '1'B then the OTHERWISE |statement| is executed (if present, otherwise the SELECT execution is null).

- PL/C: Not included in PL/C or PL/CT.

- PL/CS: Exp1 is not allowed, OTHERWISE is required, at least one WHEN is required, exactly one exp2 is required for each WHEN.

<u>SIGNAL statement</u>

Form: SIGNAL condition;

Execution: Simulates the interrupt specified by the condition. If the condition is enabled, the current ON-action for that condition is executed.

<u>STEP command</u> A PL/CT debug command. See Appendix A.11.

<u>STOP statement</u>

Form: STOP;

Execution: Causes execution of the program to be terminated.

<u>UNLOCK statement</u>

Execution: Makes a previously "locked" record accessible to other "tasks" -- beyond the scope of this book.

<u>WAIT statement</u>

Execution: Withholds execution of a block until a specified event occurs -- beyond the scope of this book.

WRITE statement

Form: WRITE FILE (file-name) FROM (variable) KEYFROM (exp) ;

Execution: Writes a record with key value "exp" in a RECORD OUTPUT or RECORD UPDATE file named "file-name" with value from "variable" (usually a structure).

A.2.1 The END delimiter

The BEGIN, compound, iterative, SELECT statements and the procedure definition all have the general form

```
|label:|    body END [label] ;
```

The label following the END (if it appears) must be the same as one of the labels proceding the statement or declaration. Be careful; the PL/I rules state that if a label follows the END, any ENDs missing within the body will be automatically inserted, without warning, just before the END following the body. Therefore, omit no ENDs.

- PL/C Restriction: if a label appears after the END, it must be the same as the first label preceding the body.

- PL/CS Restriction: a single label is required on iterative, SELECT and procedure definitions, and following the corresponding END. Labels are not allowed on compound statements.

Appendix A.3 Definitions and Declarations

Definitions and declarations are used to define attributes of

1) variables, arrays, structures, and files
2) procedures and entry points to procedures
3) parameters of procedures

Except for the entry point definition, declarations and definitions may be placed anywhere within a block or procedure; they are not executable statements but just descriptions of things. However, it is suggested that these definitions and declarations be placed as described under "BEGIN block" (Appendix A.2) and "Procedure definition" (Appendix A.3), so that they may be easily found by the reader.

Declaration (simple)

Form: DECLARE (name |, name|) |attribute| ;

1. If there is only one name, the parentheses are not needed. Thus the following two are equivalent:

```
DECLARE (A) FIXED;                  DECLARE A FIXED;
```

2. Each name has the form "identifier", in which case it is a simple variable name, a file-name, a label or an entry-name; or the form

```
identifier( exp1:exp2 | exp1:exp2| )
```

in which case it is an array named "identifier" of subscripted variables. It has as many dimensions as there are pairs "exp1:exp2". The exps are evaluated and converted to integers at the time the array is created. For each dimension, exp1 must not be greater than exp2. The subscript range is exp1, exp1+1, ..., exp2.

In a bound pair "exp1:exp2", "exp1" can be omitted if exp1 is the constant 1. Thus, A(50,20) is equivalent to A(1:50,1:20).

3. The typical attributes that will be used, together with their meanings in PL/C, are:

FIXED [DECIMAL]   The variable can contain integers

in decimal notation from -99999 to +99999.

FIXED BINARY The variable can contain integers in binary notation from (in decimal) -32767 to +32767.

FLOAT [DECIMAL] The variable can contain a floating point number of the form

±.ddddddE±dd

where the d's are digits 0-9. The exponent dd has the range -78 to +75 (approximately).

FLOAT BINARY The variable can contain a binary floating point number ±.bbbbbbbbbbbbbbbbbbbbbE±dd where each b is a bit 0 or 1, and the d's are digits. The exponent represents a power of 2. Binary floating point numbers range from 2^{-260} to 2^{252} (approximately).

CHAR(x) where x is an integer between 1 and 256. The variable can contain a string of x characters.

CHAR(x) VARYING where x is an integer between 1 and 256. The variable can contain a string of 0 to x characters. Upon creation of the variable, it is initialized to contain 0 characters (the null string). The number of characters in the variable at any point depends on the last assignment to it.

BIT(x) where x is an integer between 1 and 256. The value of the variable is a string of x bits.

BIT(x) VARYING As in CHAR(x) VARYING, except that the value is a string of bits instead of a string of characters.

4. Two (or more) declarations may be written as one by replacing the semicolon of the first and the DECLARE of the second by a single comma. For example,

```
DECLARE (A,B) CHAR(10), C FIXED BINARY;
```

is equivalent to

```
DECLARE (A,B) CHAR(10); DECLARE C FIXED BINARY;
```

5. PL/I allows implicit declaration of variables, but it is advisable to explicitly declare every name used in the program. It is also advisable to specify all the

data attributes for each variable; the defaults are too ad hoc to remember. See the beginning of Appendix A.4 for a list of default attributes.

6. See "Procedure definition" and "BEGIN block" for a discussion of where declarations go and what effect they have.

7. Possible attributes are listed in Appendix A.4.

Declaration (of structures)

A structure is a hierarchical collection of names. The names at the bottom of the hierarchy are names of simple variables or arrays. The name at the top is called the structure name. Space does not permit a full explanation of structures, and we restrict ourselves to discussing an example. Consider the declaration

```
DECLARE 1 STUDENT,
          2 NAME CHAR(20),
          2 ADDRESS,
              3 STREET CHAR(20),
              3 CITY CHAR(20),
              3 ZIP_CODE FIXED,
          2 TRANSCRIPT,
              3 NO_OF_COURSES FIXED,
              3 COURSE_NAME(50) CHAR(10),
              3 GRADE(50) CHAR(1);
```

The name of the structure is STUDENT. It can be used to refer to the whole structure. STUDENT.NAME refers to the part of the structure containing his name -- a CHAR(20) variable. STUDENT.NAME is called a qualified name -- it consists of the sequence of names in the hierarchy, beginning with the structure name, which ends up at that variable name. The qualified name STUDENT.ADDRESS refers to a minor structure of the whole structure. To reference the various parts of the address, use STUDENT.ADDRESS.STREET, STUDENT.ADDRESS.CITY, and STUDENT.ADDRESS.ZIP_CODE.

Note that two parts of the TRANSCRIPT structure are arrays of character variables. The (qualified) name of one of these arrays is STUDENT.TRANSCRIPT.COURSE_NAME. To refer, say, to the Ith element, use STUDENT.TRANSCRIPT.COURSE_NAME(I).

To declare an array of 100 structures, each capable of holding the record of one student, change the first line of the declaration to

```
DECLARE 1 STUDENT(1:100),
```

We could then refer, say, to the Ith grade of the Jth student using

STUDENT(J).TRANSCRIPT.GRADE(I).

Structures are useful in collecting several items of information together under one name. For example, to pass the student record to a procedure we need only give the argument STUDENT; it is not necessary to pass each of the individual parts as arguments.

It is not always necessary to use the complete qualified name to reference part of a structure. Only enough of it must be present to make the reference unambiquous. For example, if there is no identifier GRADE being used, except in this structure, then one can used the name GRADE instead of the qualified name STUDENT.TRANSCRIPT.GRADE. Generally, one should include the name of the structure; for example, write STUDENT.GRADE, OR STUDENT.CITY.

The only difference in structure declarations and normal declarations is in the use of _level numbers_ just preceding the name of a part of the structure. The structure name must have level 1; all its immediate subparts should have level 2, _their_ immediate subparts should have level 3, and so on. The immediate subparts are generally referred to as immediate _items_.

Entry definition

```
Form: entry-name : ¦entry-name :¦
               ENTRY [ (parameter ¦, parameter¦ )]
               [RETURNS( ¦attribute¦)] ;
               ¦parameter declaration¦
```

Use: This definition defines the entry-names to be "secondary entry points" of the procedure in which it appears. The procedure may be called using one of the entry-names, in which case execution begins at the statement following the entry definition. The placement of this definition is therefore important.

The parameters, RETURNS phrase and parameter declarations are as described under "Procedure definition".

Each parameter must be described in the parameter declarations, _unless_ it has the same name as a parameter of the procedure entry point or an earlier secondary entry point. In this case, the parameter has the attributes as specified in that earlier parameter declaration.

Care must be taken that execution of a procedure only references those parameters of the entry point for which it was called. Consider the procedure

```
A1: PROCEDURE (X, Y);
     DECLARE (X,Y) FIXED;
          ...
     A2: ENTRY (X,Z);
         DECLARE Z FIXED;
         IF Z = 0
             THEN X = X + 1;
             ELSE X = Y;
     END A1;
```

If the procedure is called with CALL A2(B,0); execution proceeds without an error and the value 1 is stored in B. If it is called with CALL A2(B,1); an error results during execution, because the statement X=Y cannot be executed since no argument exists for parameter Y.

Procedure definition (simple)

```
Form:  entry-name: PROCEDURE [ (parameter |, parameter| )] ;
           |parameter declaration|
           |declaration|
           |statement|
           END entry-name ;
```

1. The entry-name is used to call the procedure. See Appendix A.2.1 concerning END.

2. This simple form of the procedure definition does not apply to the main program definition. See Appendix A.1 or the general procedure definition which follows.

3. Each parameter is an identifier.

4. The parameter declarations describe the attributes of the arguments corresponding to the parameters when the procedure is called. All parameters should be specified here. The parameters are <u>not</u> variables and never receive a value of their own.

Parameter declarations look exactly like normal declarations, except that

a) The length of a string or bounds for an array may be specified by using *. Thus CHAR(*) would be the attribute used for a character string, while A(*,*) would describe a two-dimensional array. In PL/C one <u>must</u> use * in these positions for parameters.

b) Since a parameter is not a variable, it may not have storage attributes STATIC, AUTOMATIC, or BASED. PL/I allows a parameter to have the attribute CONTROLLED, but this attribute is not included in PL/C.

5. The declarations describe variables that are internal to this procedure, or EXTERNAL variables that the procedure may use. The non-STATIC variables (the usual ones) are created when the procedure is called, and are destroyed when its execution ends.

6. When the procedure is invoked, the statements are executed, in order, until either a RETURN; is executed or until the last statement has been executed. See also the GOTO statement. Upon termination, all variables created at the beginning of the procedure execution (see point 5 above) are destroyed.

Procedure definition (general)

```
Form: entry-name: ¦entry-name :¦
         PROCEDURE [ (parameter ¦, parameter¦ )]
         [OPTIONS(MAIN)]  [RECURSIVE]
         [RETURNS ( ¦attribute¦ )] ;
            ¦parameter declaration¦
            ¦declaration¦
            ¦statement, or entry point definition¦
            ¦procedure definition¦
            END [entry-name] ;
```

All the points discussed under "Procedure definition (simple)" apply here. In addition,

7. OPTIONS(MAIN) is used to designate the main procedure which the system should call to begin execution.

8. RECURSIVE must be specified if the procedure is to be invoked recursively -- if it may be called while it is still executing.

9. The RETURNS phrase is not used if the procedure is to be invoked using CALL. It is used only if the procedure is a function. The attributes in the RETURNS phrase specify the attributes of the value that will be returned as the value of the function. Only type attributes for arithmetic and string quantities are allowed; a function cannot return an array, structure, file-name, label or entry point.

10. The entry point definitions specify other points where execution of the procedure may begin. For example:

```
X1: PROCEDURE ...
        ...
    X2: ENTRY ...
          S1 S2 S3
    X3: ENTRY ...
          S4 S5 S6
    END X1;
```

If the procedure is called using the name X1, the whole procedure is executed. If it is called using the name X2, statements S1, S2, S3, S4, S5 and S6 will be executed. If X3 is used, only S4, S5, and S6 will be executed. (See also the GOTO statement.) See the CALL statement for a complete description of the procedure call.

11. The procedure definitions within this procedure define other procedures, which can only be called from within this procedure.

12. If the entry-name appears after the END, it must be the same as one of the entry-names preceding the PROCEDURE phrase. (In PL/C it must be the same as the first one preceding PROCEDURE.)

Appendix A.4 Attributes

This is a brief summary of the more important attributes of variables. Each scalar variable has _type_, _scope_ and _storage_ attributes and optionally, an _initial_ attribute. These classes of attributes are described below:

1. _Type attributes_. These indicate what kind of value the variable can contain.

   a) For arithmetic variables, these attributes fall into the following classes:

      1. A _base attribute_, DECIMAL or BINARY.

      2. A _scale attribute_, FIXED or FLOAT. One should always be given.

      3. A _mode attribute_, REAL or COMPLEX. The default is REAL. Almost all variables are REAL so there is no need to give this attribute explicitly.

      4. A _precision attiubute_. In general, this is not needed.

   b) For character variables, the attribute is CHARACTER, and perhaps VARYING.

   c) For bit strings, the attribute is BIT and perhaps VARYING.

   d) For labels, the attribute is LABEL.

2. _Scope attributes_. These are INTERNAL and EXTERNAL. They help indicate in what part of the program the variable can be referenced by its name.

3. _Storage class attributes_. These are AUTOMATIC and STATIC. They help indicate when and where the variable is to be created and destroyed.

4. _INITIAL attribute_. This specifies what the initial value of the variable is. This can be used only if the initial value is to be a constant.

PL/I provides _defaults_, in case a variable is not declared or only a partial list of attributes is given. For variables, the scope definition default is INTERNAL and the storage class default is AUTOMATIC.

The default for the other attributes defining a variable are rather ad hoc (they are historically grounded in FORTRAN). Default attributes for base, mode and type depend upon the identifier name. For identifiers beginning with any letter I through N, the default attributes are REAL FIXED BINARY (15,0). For identifiers beginning with any other character, the default attributes are REAL FLOAT DECIMAL (6). If BINARY or DECIMAL and/or REAL or COMPLEX are specified, FLOAT is assumed unless FIXED has been specified. If FIXED or FLOAT and/or REAL or COMPLEX are specified, DECIMAL is assumed unless BINARY has been specified. (Got it? Now forget it and give the attributes explicitly.)

Several attributes are not described here, either because they are not in PL/C, because they are beyond the scope of the book, or because they are not that useful for the space the explanation takes. They are:

1. "Parallel processing" or "multi-tasking" attributes. They are EVENT, EXCLUSIVE, and TASK.

2. File-name attributes. These are BACKWARDS, BUFFERED, DIRECT, KEYED, RECORD, SEQUENTIAL, STREAM, ENVIRONMENT and UNBUFFERED.

3. Attributes concerning programmer-control of storage and "pointer" variables. These are ALIGNED, BASED, CONTROLLED, DEFINED, OFFSET, PACKED, POINTER, POSITION, UNALIGNED, and UPDATE.

4. Attributes used to help the compiler "optimize" the program. These are IRREDUCIBLE and REDUCIBLE.

5. The LIKE attribute, which is used to help abbreviate structure definitions.

6. The PICTURE attribute, which is used to define special internal formats of data and to specify editing of data.

The following description of attributes is based on the version of PL/I defined by the IBM F-level compiler. If no form is given for an attribute, then the form is just the symbol itself. For example, the AUTOMATIC attribute is written "AUTOMATIC". Abbreviations for attributes are given in parentheses.

AUTOMATIC (AUTO) and STATIC attribute

Two other storage class attributes, CONTROLLED and BASED, are not included in PL/C.

1. AUTOMATIC means that the variable is created when the block in which it is declared is entered, and destroyed when

execution of the block is finished. This is the conventional default attribute, and it need not be given for any variable. An EXTERNAL variable may not be AUTOMATIC.

2. STATIC specifies that the variable is to be created when the program begins execution, and is to be destroyed only when the program terminates. The bounds of any STATIC array or string variable must be given as integer constants, since the variables are to be created before program execution begins. A STATIC variable can only be referenced within the block in which it is declared, but remains a variable and retains its value after the block execution is finished.

Note that STATIC affects only the storage class of the variable, and not the scope of its name (which is INTERNAL or EXTERNAL). For example, there can be several STATIC variables named X, each internal to a different block.

BINARY (BIN) and DECIMAL (DEC) attributes

Arithmetic values may be stored in the computer in decimal or binary representation. The number of bits (digits) of accuracy depends on the attributes of the variable as follows:

FIXED BINARY	15 bits plus sign. The range in decimal is -32767 to +32767.
FLOAT BINARY	21 bits plus sign for the mantissa. The range is approximately 2^{-260} to 2^{252}.
FIXED DECIMAL	5 digits plus sign (-99999 to +99999).
FLOAT DECIMAL	6 digits plus sign for the mantissa. The range is approximately 10^{-78} to 10^{75}.

See also the "Precision attribute".

BIT and CHARACTER (CHAR) attribute

Form 1: BIT(length) [VARYING]
Form 2: CHARACTER(length) [VARYING]

"length" must be an expression which when evaluated can be converted to an integer.

Use: The value of a variable with this attribute is a string of "length" bits for Form 1, or "length" characters for Form 2. In PL/C, "length" has a maximum of 256. If VARYING is present, the string consists of 0 to "length" characters, depending on the last assignment to it. Upon creation of the variable, its length is set to 0 -- the variable contains the null string.

For parameters, in PL/C use "*" instead of "length", since the length depends on the corresponding argument.

BUILTIN attribute

Any reference to a name with this attribute is a reference to the built-in function or pseudo-variable with the same name. The name can have no other attributes. A parameter may not have this attribute. This is used to reference a built-in function in a block contained in another block in which the name has a different meaning.

CHARACTER (CHAR) attribute See "BIT attribute".

COMPLEX (CPLX) attribute See "REAL attribute".

DECIMAL (DEC) attribute See "BINARY attribute".

Dimensioning of Arrays See "Declaration" in Appendix A.3.

ENTRY attribute

In PL/C, this attribute need be explicitly given only for a parameter which is to be a procedure or function. Otherwise, it is not needed.

Form: ENTRY [(|attribute| |, |attribute| |)] ;

A name associated with the ENTRY attribute is an entry point of a procedure. The first set of attributes describes the first parameter of the entry point, the second set of attributes the second parameter, and so on. If a parameter is an array a special attribute (*) for a one-dimensional array, (*,*) for a two-dimensional array, etc. must be used as the first attribute in the set.

Use: There are three reasons for using this attribute:

1. In PL/I an external procedure can be compiled separately. In this case, when a program contains a call on that procedure, it cannot know what its parameters are. The ENTRY attribute serves to indicate the attributes of the parameters. For example,

```
DECLARE P ENTRY(FIXED, (*,*) FLOAT) ;
```

indicates that procedure P has two parameters, a fixed decimal variable, and a float decimal two-dimensional array. The procedure P does not have to appear in this program, but may be compiled at a later time.

2. An argument may be the name of a procedure. In this case the declaration for the corresponding parameter must describe the procedure and its parameters using the ENTRY attribute.

3. In PL/I (but not in PL/C), argument attributes must match parameter attributes exactly unless an explicit ENTRY attribute is given for the entry point. If we want to call a procedure P(X) where the parameter X is fixed binary, with CALL P(2);, then we must write

```
PROGRAM: PROCEDURE OPTIONS(MAIN);
  DECLARE P ENTRY(FIXED BINARY);
        ...
          CALL(P2);
        ...
  P: PROCEDURE(X);
    DECLARE X FIXED BINARY;
        ...
    END P;
  END PROGRAM;
```

- PL/C: dimension and length attributes in the parameter list that follows ENTRY must be given as *.

EXTERNAL (EXT) and INTERNAL (INT) attributes

These are called scope attributes. They specify in which part of a program a name may be referred to. INTERNAL means that the name can only be referenced within the block in which it is declared (and of course within contained blocks). It is not necessary to give the INTERNAL attribute; it is the conventional, default scope attribute.

EXTERNAL specifies that the variable can be referred to within any block containing an external declaration for it. For example, if two external procedures and the main program all contain identical EXTERNAL declarations for the same variable I, then each can reference that same variable. There are not three variables I, but just one variable I which they can all reference. An EXTERNAL variable must be STATIC; its name can contain no more than seven characters.

FILE attribute

This indicates that the identifier is a file-name. The default attributes for all PL/C files are STREAM and EXTERNAL.

FIXED and FLOAT attributes

FIXED specifies that the value of the variable is to be kept in fixed point form. Typically, this means the value is an integer, but see the "Precision attribute" for more information. FIXED by itself is equivalent to FIXED DECIMAL.

FLOAT specifies that the value is to be kept in floating point. The number of digits (bits) of accuracy remains the same no matter what the value, but the value need not be in any certain range. See the "Precision attribute" and the "BINARY attribute". FLOAT by itself is equivalent to FLOAT DECIMAL.

<u>FLOAT attribute</u> See "FIXED attribute".

<u>GENERIC attribute</u>

This attribute allows different procedures to have the same name; which one is called will depend on the attributes of the arguments. It is not included in PL/C.

<u>INITIAL (INIT) attribute</u>

Form: INITIAL (item {, item})

Each item in the list can be a signed or unsigned constant (see Appendix A.1 for constants). The INITIAL attribute can be associated only with a variable or array. Only one constant can be specified for a simple variable; the multiple items are used for arrays.

Use: The constants are assigned as initial values to the corresponding variables at the time the variables are created. Thus, all three variables A, B and C in the following declaration are initialized to 3:

```
DECLARE (A,B,C) FIXED INITIAL(3);
```

For arrays, the constant values are assigned to the subscripted variables of the array in row-major order. Consider for example the declaration

```
DECLARE (A(1:2), D(1:2,1:2)) FIXED INIT(1,3,5,7);
```

Upon creation, the variables will be

A(1)	<u>1</u>	A(2)	<u>3</u>				
D(1,1)	<u>1</u>	D(1,2)	<u>3</u>	D(2,1)	<u>5</u>	D(2,2)	<u>7</u>

If not enough constants are supplied, the left-over array elements are not initialized. If there are too many constants, then the left-over constants are ignored.

One can supply an asterisk * instead of a constant for an item. This means that the corresponding array element will not be initialized. For example,

```
DECLARE E(1:3) FIXED INIT (3,*,2);
```

creates E(1) <u>3</u> E(2) <u>???</u> E(3) <u>2</u>

Iteration specification: To abbreviate a sequence of identical items an "iteration factor" may be used. For example, the item (4) 3 is equivalent to 3, 3, 3, 3.

The iteration factor is any expression that can be evaluated and converted to an integer. (For STATIC variables it must be an unsigned integer.) There are two forms for this:

1. (iteration-factor) item
   (this is equivalent to "iteration-factor" items.)

2. (iteration-factor) (item |, item|)
   (this is equivalent to the list of items repeated "iteration-factor" times.)

An iteration factor less than or equal to zero causes the item(s) to be skipped. For example, the following two are equivalent:

```
INIT( (2)*, (3)(*,3,6), 0(*), (3)8)
INIT(*,*, *,3,6,*,3,6,*,3,6, 8,8,8)
```

The item (2)'AB' is equivalent to 'ABAB', because (2) implies string repetition and is not an iteration-factor. With a string constant, to get an iteration-factor the string repetition must be there also. Thus (2)(1)'AB' specifies two elements and is equivalent to 'AB', 'AB'.

● PL/C Restriction: Iteration factors, but not string repetition factors are allowed in the INITIAL list. This means that the phrase (x) (1) '---' in PL/I-F would have to be given as (x) ('---') in PL/C. The phrase (x) '---' is not allowed.

LABEL constants: A label constant assigned an initial value must be known within the block where the declaration occurs.

INPUT and OUTPUT attributes

These are attributes of a file-name (see "FILE attribute"). INPUT specifies that the file is to be read; OUTPUT that it is to be written.

INTERNAL (INT) attribute

See "EXTERNAL attribute".

LABEL attribute

A variable or array with this attribute can contain only a label constant. It may not contain an entry-name of a procedure.

<u>Length of String Variables</u> See "BIT attribute".

<u>OUTPUT attribute</u> See "INPUT attribute".

<u>Precision attribute for arithmetic variables</u>

Form: (number-of-digits [, scale-factor])

1. The number-of-digits is an unsigned decimal integer; the scale-factor is an optionally-signed decimal integer.

2. The precision attribute must immediately follow a FIXED, FLOAT, DECIMAL, BINARY, REAL or COMPLEX attribute.

Meaning: The number-of-digits specifies the minimum number of decimal digits (or bits for binary) to be maintained for the value of the variable. The maximum allowable number is 15 for DECIMAL FIXED, 31 for BINARY FIXED, 16 for DECIMAL FLOAT, and 53 for BINARY FLOAT.

The scale factor may be specified only if the variable is FIXED; it must be in the range -128 to +127. It specifies the assumed position of the binary or decimal point -- that is, the number of fractional bits or digits. If omitted, 0 is assumed and the value is an integer.

The default precision attributes are:

(5,0)	for FIXED DECIMAL	(15,0)	for FIXED BINARY
(6)	for FLOAT DECIMAL	(21)	for FLOAT BINARY

Examples: some sample attributes and the corresponding format of a value. (d stands for a digit, and b for a bit.)

```
FIXED DECIMAL(5,0)     ddddd
FIXED DECIMAL(5,2)     ddd.dd
FIXED DECIMAL(5,7)     .00ddddd
FIXED DECIMAL(5,-2)    ddddd00.
FIXED BINARY(6,7)      .0bbbbbb
FLOAT DECIMAL(8)       .dddddddd*10**dd
FLOAT DECIMAL(6)       .dddddd*10**dd
FLOAT BINARY(10)       .bbbbbbbbbb*2**dd
```

<u>PRINT attribute</u>

The data file associated with a file-name with the attribute PRINT will eventually be printed. Each line (record) is written out with an extra character at its beginning, which is used by the printer to determine when to skip to a new page, to a new line, etc. See Appendix B.3 for the USASI codes and their meaning in the extra character.

REAL and COMPLEX (CPLX) attributes

REAL specifies that the value of the variable is a real number. REAL is the default attribute and need not be explicitly stated if FIXED, FLOAT, DECIMAL, or BINARY are used. COMPLEX specifies that the value is a complex number, consisting of real and imaginary parts.

RETURNS attribute

This is used in connection with the ENTRY attribute to help describe an entry-name. It indicates that the entry-name is called as a function, and describes the attributes of the value returned as the result of the function. The form of the RETURNS attribute is exactly the same as the form of the RETURNS phrase in a procedure definition (see Appendix A.3).

STATIC attribute See "AUTOMATIC attribute".

VARYING (VAR) attribute See "BIT attribute".

Appendix A.5 Variables, Values and Expressions

We consider how variables are referenced and changed. The kinds of values that can be assigned to variables have already been listed in Appendix A.3 under "Declaration (simple)", and in Appendix A.4 in the discussion of the Precision attribute. Constants for the different kinds of values have been described in Appendix A.1.

A.5.1 Scope and Recognition of Names

Assume for the moment that all identifiers are explicitly declared or defined. Note that the presence of a label preceding a statement, or an entry-name preceding PROCEDURE or ENTRY, constitutes its definition. "Block" means either a BEGIN block or a procedure definition.

The use of an identifier in a program always refers to a declared or defined identifier; it represents some entity -- a variable, array, entry point in a procedure, etc. That part of the program where an entity may be referred to by its identifier is called the scope of that entity. The scope has nothing to do with the question of when that entity is created or destroyed; it only indicates where it may be referred to by its name. The scope of an entity depends on where it is declared or defined relative to the blocks of the program.

The scope of an entity named with an identifier is the block in which its declaration or definition appears, including any contained blocks, except those blocks (and blocks contained in them) where another declaration or definition of that same identifier occurs.

For example, consider the program below, where the lines to the right show the scope of the corresponding identifiers. The identifiers X, W and B are each declared twice; we use superscripts to distinguish them.

PL/I allows the use of identifiers without having to declare them. For such undeclared identifiers, PL/I inserts a declaration with default attributes that are determined from the way in which the identifier is used. For an explanation of "contextual" and "implicit" declarations see an IBM PL/I manual.

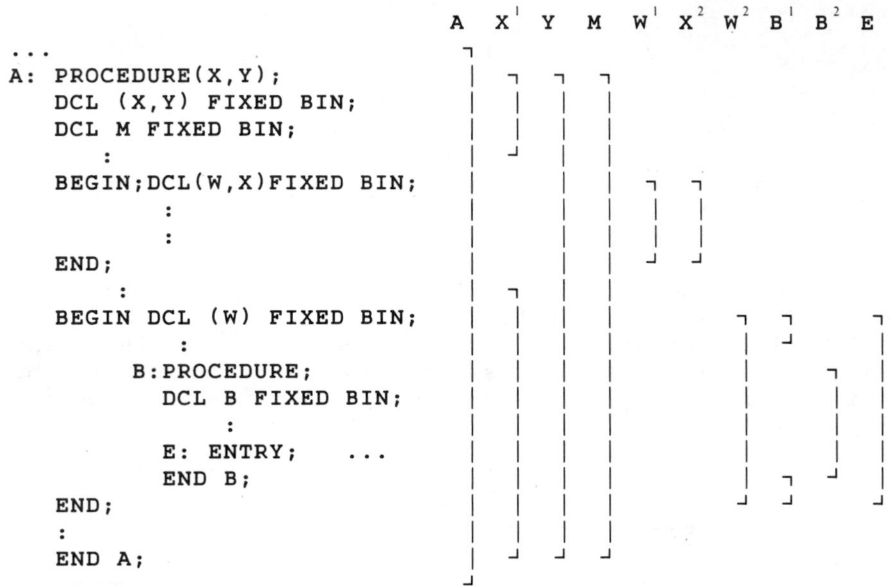

A X1 Y M W1 X2 W2 B1 B2 E
...
A: PROCEDURE(X,Y);
DCL (X,Y) FIXED BIN;
DCL M FIXED BIN;
:
BEGIN;DCL(W,X)FIXED BIN;
:
:
END;
:
BEGIN DCL (W) FIXED BIN;
:
B:PROCEDURE;
DCL B FIXED BIN;
:
E: ENTRY; ...
END B;
END;
:
END A;
...

A.5.2 Referencing Variables, Arrays and Structures

In Appendix A.1 we discussed variables, arrays and structure references briefly. We elaborate a bit more here. We illustrate assuming the declarations

```
DECLARE (A, B(1:20,1:20)) FIXED,
        C CHAR(20),
        D CHAR(20) VARYING;
DECLARE 1 PERSON,
        2 NAME CHAR(20),
        2 ADDRESS,
            3 STREET CHAR(20),
            3 CITY CHAR(20),
            3 ZIPCODE CHAR(5);
DECLARE 1 UNIVERSITY,
        2 NAME CHAR(20),
        2 ADDRESS(5),
            3 CITY CHAR(20),
            3 ZIPCODE CHAR(5);
```

Within the scope of a declaration, one references variables, arrays and structures declared in that declaration as follows:

1. To reference a simple variable use its name (e.g. A , C).

2. To reference an array, use its name (e.g. B).

3. To reference a subscripted variable, use the form

    array-name (exp ¦, exp¦)

The number of exps must equal the number of dimensions of the array. To find out which element of the array is referenced, evaluate the subscripts and convert to integers, from left to right. For example, if I has the value 1 and J the value 2, then A(I,J+1) refers to the subscripted variable A(1,3).

4. To reference a cross section of an array, use a form like that of a subscripted variable, but use an asterisk * for a subscript for which a whole "row" is wanted. For example, B(*,1) is the one-dimensional array consisting of B(1,1), B(2,1), ..., B(20,1). B(7,*) is the array consisting of B(7,1), B(7,2), ..., B(7,20). B(*,*) represents the whole array. A cross section is an array with as many dimensions as there are asterisks in the cross section reference.

The following program segment stores in array T(1:20,1:20) the transpose of the array B:

```
DO I = 1 TO 20;
    T(I,*) = B(*,I);
    END;
```

5. To reference a structure, use its name (e.g. PERSON).

6. To reference a part of a structure use a <u>qualified name</u>. This is the sequence of identifiers, starting from the name of the structure and leading down to the name of the structure part desired, separated by periods. For example, to refer to the value of STREET of the substructure ADDRESS of the structure PERSON, use

```
PERSON.ADDRESS.STREET
```

Note that the declaration for UNIVERSITY allows for 5 different addresses; UNIVERSITY.ADDRESS is a qualified name which refers to an array. UNIVERSITY.ADDRESS(1).CITY refers to the city for the first address.

It is not necessary to fully qualify such a reference; only enough names must be given to make the reference unambiquous. Thus STREET, PERSON.STREET, or ADDRESS.STREET would be equivalent to PERSON.ADDRESS.STREET. ADDRESS, however, is ambiquous since it could refer to either PERSON.ADDRESS OR UNIVERSITY.ADDRESS.

7. Pseudo-variables. A pseudo-variable is a phrase which allows one to reference a subpart of a variable, or two variables which are thought of as being one. For example, the SUBSTR pseudo-variable allows one to use part of a string as a variable, just as we use A(3) to reference part of an array.

Most of the pseudo-variables allow arrays as arguments, in which case the pseudo-variable refers to an array of values. Pseudo-variables may not be nested. Thus UNSPEC(REAL(A)) = '00'B is invalid.

The pseudo-variables COMPLETION, ONCHAR, ONSOURCE, PRIORITY, STATUS and STRING are beyond the scope of this book. The other pseudo-variables are:

1. COMPLEX(a,b) -- In an assignment statement like COMPLEX(A,B) = 1+2I; the real part "1" is assigned to variable A, while the imaginary part "2" is assigned to variable B. If either A or B is an array, they both must be arrays with identical bounds.

2. IMAG(c) -- This refers to the imaginary part of the complex variable c. If c is an array, IMAG(c) refers to the array of imaginary parts of c.

3. REAL(c) -- This refers to the real part of the complex variable c. If c is an array, REAL(c) refers to the array of real parts of c.

4. SUBSTR(string, i [, j]) -- This refers to the subpart of the character string or bit string "string", beginning with character (bit) i and ending with character (bit) i+j-1. No other characters (bits) of the string are changed by an assignment to SUBSTR. The pseudo-variable is always non-VARYING. Thus, execution of SUBSTR(C,1,1) = ''; does not delete the first character from C, but just sets it to a blank. If j is missing it is assumed to be i+LENGTH(string)-1.

   If one argument is an array, they all must be, with identical bounds.

5. UNSPEC(s) -- s can be a string or arithmetic variable or array. The value being assigned to it is evaluated, converted to a bit string (if possible), and assigned to s <u>without further conversion</u> to the attributes of s.

8. To reference a function, use the same format as the call of a procedure, except that the keyword CALL and the semicolon are omitted.

A.5.3 Expressions

An expression is something that, when evaluated, yields a value. The expression "2" yields the value 2; if A is a variable with current value 3, then the expression "A" yields the value 3 while the expression "A+2" yields the value 5.

An expression can be a single constant, a reference to a variable, or a combination of "operators" and "operands", with perhaps parentheses to indicate the order in which the operators should be evaluated.

Operands of Expressions

These may be

1. Constants.

2. References to variables, as described in Appendix A.5.2.

3. References to built-in functions, as described in Appendix A.7.

4. References to user-defined functions (procedures with RETURNS attributes).

Operators

PL/C allows the following operators:

```
+ - * / ** < ¬< <= =
> ¬> >= ¬= | & ||
```

Their descriptions appear below:

1. Arithmetic operators -- These operators have only arithmetic operands. Unless otherwise specified, if the operands of an operator have the same arithmetic attributes, so does the result. Thus addition of two fixed decimal numbers yields a fixed decimal number. The result of an operation in which the two operands do not have the same attributes is discussed in Appendix A.5.4. Remember that a constant like 3 or -2.45 is fixed decimal.

   a) + x -- The result is the value of x.

   b) - x -- The result is the negative of the value of x.

   c) x + y -- This is conventional addition: 1+5 is 6.

   d) x - y -- This is conventional subtraction: 2-5 is -3.

   e) x * y -- This is conventional multiplication: 2*5 is 10.

   f) x / y -- This is conventional division. Be very careful if both operands are fixed point. In this case the result is also fixed point but is not rounded to an integer. Because of the PL/I precision rules, 25+1/3 is 5.333333 and not 25.333333.

g) x ** y -- This is conventional exponentiation. That is, x is multiplied by itself y times. If y is not an unsigned integer constant, then x is converted to floating point and floating point exponentiation is performed. Some special cases are:

1. If $x=0$ and $y>0$ the result is 0.
2. If $x=0$ and $y \leq 0$ an error results.
3. If $x \neq 0$ and $y=0$ the result is 1.
4. If $x<0$ and y is not fixed (an integer) an error results.
5. If $x=0$ and y is complex with real part >0 and the imaginary part =0, the result is 0.
6. If $x=0$ and y is complex but does not fit (5), an error results.

h)
```
x < y,   x ¬< y,   x <= y,   x =  y
x > y,   x ¬> y,   x >= y,   x ¬= y
```

These are the arithmetic <u>comparison</u> operators. They yield the value "true" ('1'B) or "false" ('0'B), depending on whether the relation is true or not. "¬=" stands for not equal, "<=" for less than or equal, etc. For example,

```
1  < 2 yields true      1 ¬< 2 yields false
1 <= 2 yields true      1  = 2 yields false
1  > 2 yields false     1 ¬> 2 yields true
1 >= 2 yields false     1 ¬= 2 yields true
```

2. <u>Character string operators</u>

a) x || y -- The result of this concatenation is a character string consisting of the characters of x followed by those of y. For example,

```
'ABC' || 'DXY' yields 'ABCDXY'
'ABC' || ''    yields 'ABC'
'AB ' || 'DXY' yields 'AB DXY'
```

b)
```
x < y,   x ¬< y,   x <= y,   x =  y
x > y,   x ¬> y,   x >= y,   x ¬= y
```

These are the character string comparison operators. They have the same form as the arithmetic comparison operators. A comparison is evaluated as follows: first, the shorter of the two operands is extended with blanks until the two have the same length.

Then a left-to-right character by character comparison is performed until the result is determined. The result is '1'B if the relation is true; '0'B otherwise. The collating sequence given at the end of Section I.2.2.3 is used to make the comparison. Examples are:

```
'A' <= 'A'      yields true
'A' <= 'AB'     yields true
'AB'<= 'A'      yields false
'A'  = 'A '     yields true
```

3. <u>Bit string operators</u> -- These always take bit strings as operands, and always yield a bit string result.

   a) ¬ x -- The result is a bit string the same as x but with every bit reversed. ¬ '10011'B yields '01100'B.

   b) x | y -- If one operand is shorter than the other, the shorter is extended on the right with zeros until they are the same length. Then a bit-by-bit operation is performed to yield a bit-string with the same length. For each bit, the result is 1 if either operand has a 1 in that position, and is 0 otherwise. For example,

   ```
   '1010'B | '1100'B yields '1110'B
   '1'B    | '1101'B yields '1101'B
   ```

   c) x & y -- The shorter operand is extended with zeros until both operands have the same length. Then a bit-by-bit operation is performed to yield a value with that length. For each bit, the result is 1 only if both operands have a 1 in that position. For example,

   ```
   '1010'B & '1100'B yields '1000'B
   '1'B    & '1101'B yields '1000'B
   ```

   d) x || y -- The result is a string of bits consisting of those in x followed by those in y.

   e) x < y, x ¬< y, x <= y, x = y
   x > y, x ¬> y, x >= y, x ¬= y

   These bit comparison operators yield '1'B if the relation is true, and '0'B otherwise. The shorter operand is first extended with zeros until both operands have the same length. Then a left-to-right bit-by-bit comparison is made of the two operands until the result is determined. See also the arithmetic and character string comparison operators.

Expressions and the Priority of Operators

Expressions follow conventional mathematical notation, where parentheses may be used to indicate the order of evaluation of the operators. For example,

- A + B * C + D * (E + F)   is evaluated as follows:

1. Evaluate -A
2. Evaluate B*C
3. Evaluate -A + B*C (using the results of steps 1 and 2)
4. Evaluate E+F
5. Evaluate D*(E+F) (using the result of step 4)
6. Evaluate -A+B*C + D*(E+F) (using the results of steps 3 and 5)

Operations are performed using the following table of priorities of operators:

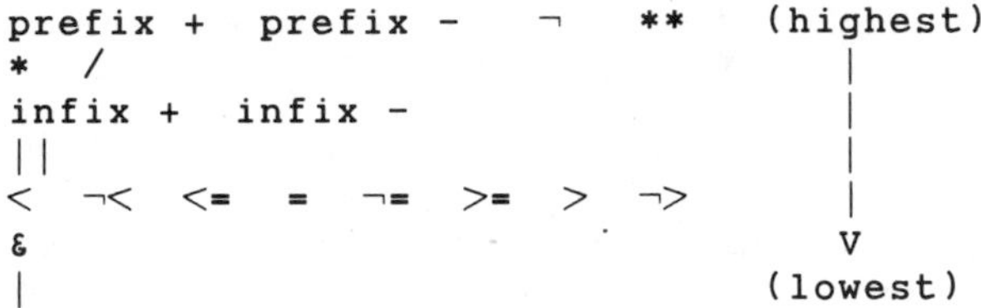

If two or more operators on the same level appear next to each other, the operations are performed in left-to-right order. The exception to this rule is the top line. If two or more operators from the top line of the table appear next to each other, the operations are performed in right-to-left order. For example:

```
A * -B is evaluated as A * (-B)
A + B + C is evaluated as (A + B) + C
A ** -B is evaluated as A ** (-B)
A ** B ** C is evaluated as A ** (B ** C)
```

Array and Structure Expressions

PL/I allows array expressions that yield arrays of values, and structure expressions that yield structures of values. An array expression is evaluated element by element. Thus if A(1:3) is (3 8 2) and B(1:3) is (2 1 2), then A*B is the array (6 8 4). This is <u>not</u> conventional array multiplication.

Any operator described for conventional expressions can also be used for arrays, but be careful. An array operation implies that same operation being applied to the individual elements of the array (or array operands), to yield an array of the same size. Read "Assignment to arrays" and "Assignment to structures" in Appendix A.2 before using array expressions.

In an array expression all array operands must have identical bounds. In a structure expression, each structure operand must have the same structure.

A.5.4 Data Conversion

Quite often, values have to be converted from one form to another -- FIXED DECIMAL to FLOAT DECIMAL, bit string to character string, etc. These conversions occur when evaluating an expression, when assigning a value to a variable, and in similar situations. In PL/I, evaluation of operations and conversion of values is a difficult problem, mainly because of the way precision attributes are defined and used. The typical programmer will not use these precision attributes; instead he will rely on the default attributes given by PL/I and PL/C. Fortunately, PL/C retains as many significant digits as possible, which greatly simplifies the explanation of conversion of values.

We describe only data conversion as it is done in PL/C, and assume that the precision attributes are not explicitly used. Those people who want to understand why 25+1/3 = 5.33333 are encouraged to read an IBM PL/I manual.

Remember that constants like 3.14 are actually fixed decimal values. To be sure of results, when using a constant as an operand of a division, write it with an exponent: 3.14E0.

Conversion During Arithmetic Operations

During evaluation of an operation like x*y, if the arithmetic attributes of the operands differ, some conversion must be performed before the operation can take place. The rules for the order of this conversion are:

1. If one operand is binary and the other decimal, the decimal operand is converted to binary.

2. If one operand is fixed and the other floating point, the fixed point operand is converted to floating point form. The one exception to this rule is with exponentiation. If in x**y, x is FLOAT and y FIXED, no conversion is necessary; the result is still FLOAT. If in x**y, both operands are FIXED, then x is converted to floating point form <u>unless</u> y is an unsigned integer constant.

3. If one operand is REAL and the other COMPLEX, the REAL operand is converted to COMPLEX. The one exception is exponentiation. If in x**y, y is a fixed point integer, no conversion is necessary.

Results of Conversion

Bit string to character string -- Each bit 1 becomes the character 1; each bit 0 becomes the character 0. The length of the result is the length of the original value.

Character string to bit string -- The character string should contain only the characters 1 and 0; any other causes an error message to be printed (the CONVERSION condition is raised). Each character 1 becomes the bit 1; each character 0 becomes the bit 0.

Mode conversion -- Conversion from complex to real is done by deleting the imaginary part of the complex number. When converting from real to complex, a zero imaginary part is added to the real value.

Base conversion -- Converting from DECIMAL FLOAT to BINARY FLOAT, or vice versa, causes no changes in the number, since both are internally stored in the same representation. Conversion from DECIMAL FIXED to BINARY FIXED can cause the number to be truncated, so significant digits may be lost. This is because DECIMAL FIXED has the range -99999 to +99999, while BINARY FIXED has the range -32767 to 32767. For example, the fixed decimal number 32769 will be converted to 1000000000000001B and then truncated to 1B. An error message will be printed if a significant digit is lost. (The SIZE condition will be raised.) Conversion from BINARY FIXED to DECIMAL FIXED causes no problems.

Scale conversion -- Conversion from FIXED to FLOAT causes no problem in PL/C, since the FLOAT representation allows more digits (or bits) than the FIXED representation. Conversion from FLOAT to FIXED may cause the least signicant digits (bits) to be discarded. Truncation, not rounding, is performed.

A.5.5 Parameter-Argument Correspondence

Suppose we have CALL P(A1); of a procedure defined as

```
P: PROCEDURE(P1);
     DECLARE P1 ...;
          :
     END P;
```

The parameter-argument correspondence is set up before the actual execution of the procedure statements. Once this link between parameter and argument is made, it is not changed for the duration of the procedure execution.

The way the correspondence between P1 and A1 is set up depends on the attributes of both P1 and A1. In general, P1 must be attached (by an arrow) to a line containing the value of the argument. The declaration of P1 does not indicate that P1 is a variable; it just indicates what the attributes of the corresponding argument must be. In the above example, an assignment to P1 changes A1 immediately.

We have generally indicated parameter-argument correspondence by an arrow from the parameter to the argument:

We now describe the way in which the parameter-argument linkage is done when a procedure is called, depending on the attributes of the parameter.

<u>Scalar parameter</u> The parameter represents a variable that is neither an array nor a structure. The argument must be an expression (a constant, scalar variable, or more general expression). The linkage is drawn as follows: if the argument is a simple or subscripted variable whose data attributes match those of the parameter <u>exactly</u>, then the arrow is drawn from the parameter to the argument:

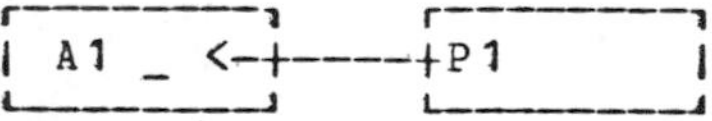

Note that the arrow is drawn before the procedure statements are executed. If the argument is a subscripted variable, the subscripts are evaluated just <u>once</u>, before execution of the procedure statements, in order to determine which variable is being passed to the procedure.

If the argument is <u>anything else</u> (a constant, an expression that is not a variable, a variable in parentheses, like (I), a variable with different attributes from the parameter), the following happens:

1. A new variable, say TEMP, is automatically created; its attributes are those of the parameter.

2. The argument is evaluated and assigned to TEMP. Normal conversion rules for an assignment statement apply.

3. An arrow is drawn from the parameter to TEMP:

```
┌─────────┐     ┌─────────┐
│ A1 _ ┌─┼─────┼P1       │
│TEMP_<┘ │     │         │
└─────────┘     └─────────┘
```

TEMP is called a "dummy argument".

If the parameter is a fixed length string and the argument a VARYING string, a dummy argument is created with a length equal to the <u>maximum</u> length of the argument.

If the parameter has the attribute LABEL, then the argument must be a label or a label variable.

<u>Array parameter</u> If the parameter is an array, the argument must be an array expression or a scalar expression. (Note: In PL/C the argument must be an array expression; we cover only this case here.) The array operands of the array expression must have the same number of dimensions as the parameter.

If the argument is an array or a cross section of an array with the same attributes as the parameter, then an arrow is drawn from the parameter to the argument:

```
┌────────────┐    ┌───┐
│ A(1)  _  <┐│    │   │
│ A(2)  _   ├┼────┼P1 │
│   :       ││    │   │
│ A(10)_  <┘│    │   │
└────────────┘    └───┘
```

In <u>any other case</u>, an array TEMP (say) with attributes of the parameter and dimension of the argument is created, the argument is assigned to the array TEMP and an arrow is drawn from the parameter to TEMP. Any conversion is performed as in an assignment statement. TEMP is called a "dummy array argument".

```
┌──────────────────────────┐    ┌───┐
│ A(1)  _   TEMP(1)  _<┐   │    │   │
│ A(2)  _   TEMP(2)  _ ├───┼────┼P1 │
│   :         :        │   │    │   │
│ A(10)_    TEMP(10)_<┘   │    │   │
└──────────────────────────┘    └───┘
```

<u>Structure parameter</u> If the parameter is a structure, then the argument must be a structure expression or a scalar expression. (In PL/C it may only be a structure expression.) The correspondence is similar to the correspondence for array parameters.

<u>Entry-name parameter</u> If the parameter is an entry-name, the argument must be the name of a procedure (or

function). It can be the name of a mathematical built-in function, like SIN. The number and attributes of parameters declared for the parameter and the argument must be the same.

File-name parameter The argument must also be a file-name. The attributes of the parameter are ignored.

Appendix A.6 Conditions and Prefixes

During execution of a program an exceptional condition such as OVERFLOW (a floating point number becoming too large) or ZERODIVIDE (division by zero) can cause an interrupt to occur. Execution of the program is temporarily halted, a certain statement is executed, and then the program terminates or execution resumes, depending on the condition and what the programmer wants. Generally, a standard system action is performed when the interrupt occurs. However, the programmer himself can indicate what should take place, using the ON statement. We will call the statement to be performed when the condition occurs the "ON-action" for that condition.

The typical programmer will usually use only the CHECK, FLOW, and ENDFILE conditions.

A.6.1 Prefixes and Their Use

For each possible condition that can occur, the programmer can indicate whether or not the ON-action should be executed if the condition occurs. The programmer does this by placing a "condition prefix" before the statement in which the condition may occur. If the ON-action should be executed, it is said to be "enabled"; of not, it is "disabled". For example, suppose we do not want an ON-action to execute if division by zero takes place in a statement A=B/C;. Then we should write

```
(NOZERODIVIDE) : A = B / C;
```

If division by zero does occur, the programmer won't know about it, and some undefined value will be stored in A.

The complete form of a statement is

```
|prefix :| |label :| statement
```

A prefix has the form

```
( cond |, cond| )
```

where each "cond" is a condition as specified in Appendix A.6.2. A "cond" may also be a condition with the letters NO immediately preceding it (no intervening blanks). A prefix attached to a statement signifies that each condition is to be enabled (if just the condition is used) or disabled (if NO precedes the condition). The statement can be any simple statement, BEGIN block, IF statement, or loop. A procedure definition may also be prefixed, which means the condition applies to the execution of the whole procedure. There are some restrictions on which conditions may be used as prefixes; these will be explained under the particular conditions.

One may of course enable a condition for a block, and disable it for part of that block. For example,

```
(ZERODIVIDE): BEGIN; ...
                 (NOZERODIVIDE): A=B/C;
                   ...
                 END;
```

A prefix applies to the statement to which it is attached, but <u>not</u> to any procedure called by that statement. The scope of a prefix is statically defined, like the scope of an identfier in a declaration. Prefixes attached to IF, ON, compound, and iterative statements are treated differently:

1. A prefix attached to an IF applies only to the evaluation of the expression following the IF, and not to the statements following THEN or ELSE.

2. A prefix attached to an ON statement does not apply to the ON-unit.

3. A prefix attached to a compound statement has no effect.

4. A prefix attached to an iterative statement does not apply to the substatements of the loop (except for FLOW).

A.6.2 Conditions

Unless otherwise noted, the following three points hold for an interrupt:

1. The standard system action when an interrupt occurs is to print a message and raise the ERROR condition. In PL/C, a message is printed, some sort of error recovery is performed, and execution continues. There is a limit to how many such errors can occur before execution terminates.

2. In PL/I, the result of the operation causing the interrupt is undefined. In PL/C, the result will be described in the error message.

3. Upon normal termination of a ON-unit, control returns to the point <u>following</u> the operation which caused the interupt.

The conditions are listed below. Permissible abbreviations are shown in parentheses. The PL/C default states are shown by underlining, and the differences in default between PL/C and PL/I are noted. Unless otherwise noted, the form of the condition used in a prefix or as a condition is the keyword itself. For example, the form of the FLOW condition is "FLOW".

The following conditions are not discussed here; see IBMFM for details: AREA, KEY, PENDING, RECORD and TRANSMIT.

CHECK Form: CHECK(name |, name|)

where each name is the name of a simple variable, array (but not a subscripted variable), a structure, an entry-name, or a label. A name cannot be a parameter in PL/I, but this is allowed in PL/C.

This particular prefix may only be attached to a BEGIN block or a procedure definition. The names appearing in the CHECK prefix refer to names known within that block or procedure.

The CHECK condition is raised in the following cases:

1. If a name is a variable, array or structure, the condition is raised whenever it is assigned a value, or whenever part of it is assigned a value, or after a return from a user-defined procedure which had that name as an argument which was not a dummy argument.

2. If a name is a label, the condition is raised just before execution of the statement with that label.

3. If a name is an entry-name, the condition is raised when the entry-name is invoked.

Raising CHECK has no effect on the statement being executed; it is used primarily to obtain output to help debug a program. The standard system action is to print out the name on SYSPRINT together with its value if it has one. If an ON-unit is given, upon its termination, execution continues at the point where the interrupt occurred.

CHECK is not raised if

1. An assignment occurs because of an INITIAL attribute.

2. An assignment is made through a parameter. (But CHECK will be raised upon return from the corresponding procedure if the argument is not a dummy argument.)

In PL/C the system action is different than in PL/I. When an element of a "checked" array is changed, only that particular element is displayed, and not the whole array. A similar action occurs when an element of a structure is changed. The timing of the PL/C display is also not exactly the same; PL/C displays the results immediately after the check condition is raised, and not after the whole statement has been executed. In addition, PL/C has additional CHECK and NOCHECK statements. See Appendix A.2.

CONDITION Form: CONDITION (identifier)

The identifier is given by the programmer. No declaration or definition can be given for it; its appearance with a CONDITION in an ON, SIGNAL, or REVERT statement constitutes its declaration. It is given the attribute EXTERNAL.

CONDITION is raised by execution of a SIGNAL statement that specifies the appropriate identifier. It cannot be disabled.

CONVERSION (CONV) NOCONVERSION (NOCONV)

This occurs whenever an illegal conversion is attempted on a character string value. (For example, when a character other than 0 or 1 occurs in a string being converted to a bit string.) Upon termination of an ON-unit, control returns to the beginning of the statement and the conversion is retried.

ENDFILE Form: ENDFILE(file-name)

This occurs when an attempt is made to read when no more data exists on the file. Another attempt to read from the same file will cause another interrupt. Upon normal termination of an ON-unit, the statement that caused the interrupt is immediately terminated. This condition cannot be disabled.

ENDPAGE Form: ENDPAGE(file-name)

where the file referred to is a PRINT file.

This occurs when an attempt is made to start a new line beyond the last line specified for the current page. The last line is the limit given when the file was opened, or the default of 60. When ENDPAGE is raised, the current line number is 1 greater than that specified. ENDPAGE is raised only once per page, and it is possible to continue writing on the same page by specifying a null ON-unit. An ON-unit can start a new page by executing PUT PAGE for that file.

The standard system action is to start a new page. Upon normal termination of the ON-unit, control returns to the point of the interrupt and the operation is performed again.

If it is raised while data is being written, the data is written on the current line after the ON-unit is executed. If ENDPAGE results from LINE or SKIP this action is ignored.

ENDPAGE may not be disabled.

ERROR

This is raised in the following cases:

1. As a result of the standard system action for an interrupt which is "print a message and raise the ERROR condition.

2. As a result of an error during execution for which there is no ON condition.

3. As a result of execution of SIGNAL ERROR;

The standard system action is to raise the FINISH condition. ERROR cannot be disabled. If there is an ON-unit associated with ERROR, upon its normal termination the standard system action is taken.

The PL/C ERROR condition is not entirely compatible with PL/I. In PL/C, the standard system action is to apply the automatic error correction and then continue execution.

FINISH

This is raised by execution of STOP and EXIT, and by execution of a RETURN in the main procedure. The standard system action is to do nothing. If an ON-unit is associated with FINISH, it is executed before program termination occurs. The ON-unit can avoid termination by jumping out of the ON-unit and continuing execution. FINISH cannot be disabled.

FIXEDOVERFLOW (FOFL) NOFIXEDOVERFLOW (NOFOFL)

This occurs when the length of a FIXED arithmetic operand exceeds 15 digits (or 31 bits).

FLOW NOFLOW

This is not a PL/I condition; it is included only in PL/C. See the FLOW statement in Appendix A.2.

NAME Form: NAME(file-name)

This is raised during execution of GET DATA when a name in the input cannot be referenced at the point GET DATA appears. The standard system action is to ignore the input item, print a message, and continue. Upon normal termination of an ON-unit, execution of GET DATA continues with the next item in the input. NAME cannot be disabled.

OVERFLOW (OFL) NOOVERFLOW (NOOFL)

This occurs when the magnitude of a floating point number exceeds approximately 10^{75} or 2^{252}.

SIZE NOSIZE

This occurs when the high-order (leftmost) significant bits or digits are lost in an assignment to a variable or temporary, or in an input-output operation. SIZE is raised when the size of the value exceeds the size declared for that variable, while FIXEDOVERFLOW is raised when the maximum allowed value for the computer is exceeded.

In PL/I the default is NOSIZE; in PL/C, SIZE.

When SIZE is raised the arithmetic results in PL/C will differ from those produced by PL/I. PL/I-F may truncate results to the user's specification, while PL/C always retains the implementation-defined maximum precision. That is, in PL/C there may be loss of precision due to OVERFLOW or FIXEDOVERFLOW, but not because of SIZE.

STRINGRANGE (STRG) NOSTRINGRANGE (NOSTRG)

This is raised whenever the lengths of the arguments of SUBSTR don't follow the rules. The standard system action is to change the SUBSTR reference to fit the rules, by increasing or reducing the position and length arguments in a fairly obvious manner. See an IBM PL/I manual. In PL/C the default is the opposite of PL/I's.

SUBSCRIPTRANGE (SUBRG) NOSUBSCRIPTRANGE (NOSUBRG)

This is raised when a subscript is evaluated and found to be outside its bounds. The PL/C default is the opposite of the PL/I default.

UNDEFINEDFILE (UNDF) Form: UNDEFINEDFILE(file-name)

This occurs if a file cannot be OPENed by execution of an OPEN statement. This may be caused by a conflict of attributes, no blocksize specified, no DD statement in the JCL for the file, and other similar reasons.

Upon normal termination of the ON-unit, control is given to the statement following the statement that caused the interrupt. UNDEFINEDFILE cannot be disabled.

UNDERFLOW (UFL) NOUNDERFLOW (NOUFL)

This occurs when the magnitude of a floating point number is smaller than the minimum allowed -- approximately 10^{-78} or 2^{-260}. A 0 is used instead.

ZERODIVIDE (ZDIV) NOZERODIVIDE (NOZDIV)

This occurs when a division by zero is attempted.

Appendix A.7 Built-in Functions

We describe briefly the PL/I built-in functions as they are evaluated in PL/C where the values are maintained in the largest precision possible. Unless otherwise specified, an argument may be an array as well as a scalar value. The result is then an array with the same bounds. The values in the array are the result of applying the function to each of the individual values of the original array. If two or more arguments are arrays, they must have identical bounds.

String handling built-in functions

BIT(exp, [size]) -- The exp is converted to a bit string of length "size". "size" must be a decimal integer constant. If "size" is missing, the length of the result depends on the attributes of the exp. As with the CHAR function, the argument cannot be arithmetic in PL/C.

BOOL(x, y, z) -- This is beyond the scope of this book.

CHAR(exp, [size]) -- The exp is converted to a character string representing the same value, of length "size". The same conventions apply for "size" as do with the function BIT. In PL/C, CHAR cannot be used to convert an arithmetic quantity to a string. Instead, use the PUT statement with the STRING option (see Appendix A.2).

HIGH(i) -- The result is a character string of length i, each character of which is the highest character in the collating sequence. i must be a decimal integer constant.

INDEX(string, config) -- string and config are bit or character strings. The result is a fixed binary integer which gives the leftmost position in string where the config begins. If config does not appear as a substring of string, the result is 0.

LENGTH(string) -- The result is a FIXED BINARY integer giving the length of the string.

LOW(i) -- The result is a character string of length i, each character of which is the lowest character in the collating sequence: hexadecimal 00. i must be an integer constant.

REPEAT(string, i) -- string is a character or bit string; i is a decimal constant. The result is "string" concatenated with itself i times. Thus REPEAT('ABC',2) is 'ABCABCABC'.

STRING(x) -- x is a variable, array name, or structure, composed entirely of character strings or entirely of bit strings. The result is the string resulting from concatenating all the elements of x together.

SUBSTR(string, i [, j]) -- The result is the substring of string beginning at character i and ending with character i+j-1. If j is missing, LENGTH(string)-i+1 is used.

TRANSLATE(s, r [, p]) -- All arguments are bit strings or character strings. If p is missing, the string consisting of all 256 possible EBCDIC characters in ascending order is used (from hexadecimal 00 to FF).

If r is shorter than p, r is extended with blanks (or zeros). The result is a string identical to s, except that any character of s which is also in p is replaced by the corresponding character in r. Thus if character i of s is the same as character j of p, then character i of s is replaced by character j of r. For example, the result of

```
TRANSLATE('XYZW', 'ABCD', 'VWXY')
```

is the string 'CDZB'.

UNSPEC(x) -- x is any expression. The result is a bit string containing the internal representation of x. The length depends on the attributes of x.

VERIFY(string, config) -- string and config are both character strings or both bit strings. The result is a FIXED BINARY integer which indicates the position of the first character in string which is <u>not</u> in config. If all characters are in config, the result is 0. For example,

```
VERIFY( 'b̸b̸b̸b̸BC', 'b̸')    yields 5, while
VERIFY( 'b̸b̸b̸b̸BC', 'ABCb̸') yields 0.
```

Arithmetic Built-in Functions

The result of an arithmetic built-in function is always an arithmetic value. Unless otherwise noted, the attributes of the result are the same as the attributes of the argument. If conversion is necessary because arguments differ, the conversions are performed as outlined for arithmetic operations in Appendix A.5.4. Unless otherwise noted, an argument may be an array as well as a scalar value, as explained in the introduction to Appendix A.7. The argument to the functions BINARY, DECIMAL, FIXED, and FLOAT may not be strings. Use the GET statement with the STRING option to convert strings to arithmetic quantities.

We omit descriptions of the functions ADD, DIVIDE, MULTIPLY and PRECISION.

ABS(x) -- The result is the absolute value of x.

BINARY(x) -- The value of x is converted to the binary base.

CEIL(x) -- x must not be complex. The result is the smallest integer that is greater than or equal to x. CEIL(3.5) is 4; CEIL(-3.5) is -3.

COMPLEX(x, y) -- The result is a complex number with real part x and imaginary part y. X and y must be real.

CONJG(x) -- The result is a complex number which is the conjugate of the complex number x.

DECIMAL(x) -- The argument is converted to base DECIMAL.

FIXED(x) -- The argument x is converted to fixed point.

FLOAT(x) -- The argument x is converted to floating point.

FLOOR(x) -- x must not be complex. The result is the largest integer not greater than x. FLOOR(3.5) is 3; FLOOR(-3.5) is -4.

IMAG(x) -- The result is the imaginary part of x.

MAX(x1, x2, ..., xn) -- The result is the maximum value of the arguments x1, x2, ..., xn, converted to conform to the highest characteristics of all the arguments. (FLOAT is higher than FIXED, BINARY is higher than DECIMAL.) No argument may be complex.

MIN(x1, x2, ..., xn) -- The result is the minimum value of the arguments, converted to the highest characteristics of all the arguments. (FLOAT is higher than FIXED, BINARY is higher than DECIMAL.) No argument may be complex.

MOD(x, y) -- x and y may not be complex. The result is the remainder when dividing x by y. If x and y have different signs, the operation is performed on their absolute values, and the result is then ABS(y)-remainder. For example, MOD(29,6) is 5, while MOD(-29,6) is 1.

REAL(x) -- the result is the real part of the complex value x.

ROUND(x, n) -- n is an optionally signed integer constant. If n is 0, x is rounded to the nearest integer. If n > 0, x is rounded at the nth digit to the right of the decimal (binary) point. If n < 0, x is rounded as the n+1th digit to the left of the decimal (binary) point.

If x is floating point, n is ignored and the rightmost bit of the internal representation of x is set to 1.

SIGN(x) -- x must not be complex. The result is a fixed binary value equal to 1 if x>0, 0 if x=0, and -1 if x<0.

TRUNC(x) -- x must not be complex. If x < 0 the result is CEIL(x); if x > 0 the result is FLOOR(x).

Mathematical Built-in Functions

All arguments to the mathematical built-in functions are floating point. If not, they will be converted to floating point. Unless specifically stated otherwise, an argument can be real or complex. The result is always a floating point value, with mode, base and precision attributes the same as those of the argument. An argument may be an array, as described in the introduction to Appendix A.7.

ATAN(x) -- The result is the arctangent of x. x must not be ±1I.

ATAN(x,y) -- Both x and y must be real; they must not both be 0. The result is the arctangent of x/y.

ATAND(x,y) -- x and y must be real, and not both be 0. The result is the arctangent of x/y, expressed in degrees.

ATANH(x) -- The result is the hyperbolic tangent of x. ABS(x) must be greater than or equal to 1.

COS(x) -- The result is the cosine of x, where x is expressed in radians.

COSD(x) -- The result is the cosine of x, where x is expressed in degrees.

COSH(x) -- The result is the hyperbolic cosine of x.

ERF(x) -- x must be real. The result is 2/SQRT(PI) multiplied by the definite integral from 0 to x of e**($-t^2$) dt.

ERFC(x) -- x must be real. The result is 1-ERF(x).

EXP(x) -- The result is e**x, where e is the base of the natural logarithm system.

LOG(x) -- If x is real, it must be greater than 0. If x is complex, it must not equal 0+0I. The result is the natural logarithm of x.

LOG10(x) -- x must be real and greater than 0. The result is the common logarithm of x (base 10).

LOG2(x) -- x must be real and greater than 0. The result is the logarithm to the base 2 of x.

RAND(x) -- RAND produces a sequence of pseudo-random numbers, one each time it is called, using the method of Coveyou and Macpherson in ACM Journal 14 (1967), 100-119. x should be FLOAT; if not it will be converted to FLOAT. It must be in the range $0 < x < 1$. The initial value of x should have nine significant digits, and be odd; this maximizes the period of the sequence. RAND is usually used in an assignment: X=RAND(X). RAND is not included in PL/I.

SIN(x) -- The result is the sine of x, where x is expressed in radians.

SIND(x) -- The result is the sine of x, where x is expressed in degrees.

SINH(x) -- The result is the hyperbolic sine of x.

SQRT(x) -- If x is real, it must be greater than or equal to 0. The result is the square root of x.

TAN(x) -- The result is the tangent of x, where x is expressed in radians.

TAND(x) -- The result is the tangent of x, where x is expressed in degrees.

TANH(x) -- The result is the hyperbolic tangent of x.

Array Generic Functions

All these functions require array arguments and return a single scalar value.

ALL(x) -- x must be an array of bit strings. The result is a bit string obtained by "and-ing" (as in the operator "&") all the bit strings of the array together.

ANY(x) -- x must be an array of bit strings. The result is the bit string obtained by "or-ing" (as in the operator "|") all the bit strings in the array together.

DIM(x,n) -- The result is a binary fixed integer giving the "extent" of the nth dimension of the array x. The extent is the upper bound minus the lower bound, plus 1.

HBOUND(x,n) -- The result is the upper bound of the nth dimension of array x.

LBOUND(x,n) -- The result is the lower bound of the nth dimension of array x.

POLY(a,x) -- This is not included in PL/C.

PROD(x) -- The result is the product of all the elements of array x.

SUM(x) -- The result is the sum of all the elements of array x.

Condition Built-in Functions

DATAFIELD, ONCHAR, ONCODE, ONCOUNT, ONFILE, ONKEY, ONLOC, and ONSOURCE are beyond the scope of this book. Three other functions, ONORIG, ONDEST, and STMTNO are included only in PL/C.

Based Storage Built-in Functions

ADDR, EMPTY, NULL, and NULLO are beyond the scope of this book.

Multitasking Built-in Functions

COMPLETION(event-name), PRIORITY(task-name), and STATUS(event-name) are beyond the scope of this book.

Miscellaneous Built-in Functions

ALLOCATION(x) -- This is beyond the scope of the book.

COUNT(file-name) -- This is beyond the scope of the book.

DATE -- The result is a character string of length 6, with the form yymmdd. yy is the current year, mm the current month, and dd the current day (e.g. 731225).

LINENO(file-name) -- The result is the number of the current line in the named file.

TIME -- The result is a character string of length 9 giving the current time of day. Its form is hhmmssttt, where hh is the current hour of the day, mm is the number of minutes, ss the number of seconds, and ttt the number of milliseconds in machine-dependent increments.

Appendix A.8 Formats

GET EDIT and PUT EDIT read and write values using a user-defined _format_ to control the editing and formatting of the values. The format is a list of "data items" which specify the format of each individual value in turn -- how many characters it uses, where the decimal point should go, and so on. Interspersed between the data items may be "control items", which specify things like skipping to the next line or page.

Input-output is done under the control of the list of variables or expressions being read into or printed, as follows. The format is searched for the first data item; any control items encountered are executed immediately. When the first data item in the list is found, the first value is read or written using that data item. Next, if there is a second value to read or print, the format is searched again, beginning at the item following the one just used. Any control items encountered are executed immediately. Upon finding a data item, the second value is read or printed. This process continues until the last value has been read or printed. Any excess data items or control items in the format are not used.

To make formats more flexible, one may specify "iteration factors". Thus "3 A(2)" is equivalent to a list of three items "A(2), A(2), A(2)", while "2 (A(2), X(1))" is equivalent to the four items "A(2), X(1), A(2), X(1)". Simple examples of formats and their use are given in Part I.4.

A format has the form

(specification |, specification|)

where each specification may be one of the following:

1. item -- Items are described below.

2. integer-constant item -- This is equivalent to "integer-constant" replications of the item. Thus "3 A(2)" is equivalent to "A(2), A(2), A(2)".

3. (exp) item -- At the point the specification is to be used, the exp is evaluated and converted to an integer. If 0 or negative, the item is skipped. If exp > 0, this is equivalent to "exp" replications of the item. Thus, if I has the value 4, "(I) A(3)" is equivalent to "A(3), A(3), A(3), A(3)". The expression is evaluated _each_ time the specification

is to be used to control editing.

4. integer-constant format -- This is equivalent to "integer-constant" replications of the format. Thus, "2 (A(2), X(1))" is equivalent to "A(2), X(1), A(2), X(1)". Note that this defines a format in terms of another format.

5. (exp) format -- The exp is evaluated as explained under specification 3 above. This is equivalent to "exp" replications of the format. If exp ≤ 0, the specification is skipped entirely.

The following items may be used. Any expressions in the item are evaluated each time the item is to be used. w, d, and s are used for expressions.

A -- Print a character string, in the next n columns. n is the current length of the string being written out.

A(w) -- Read or print a character string. For input, the next w columns of the input stream are assigned to the variable. If w ≤ 0, the null string is assigned and no columns are used in the input stream.

For output, the character string value is printed, left-adjusted, in the next w columns of the output stream. The string is truncated if too long. If w ≤ 0, no output results.

B -- Print a bit string in the next n columns of the output stream. n is the length of the value being printed.

B(w) -- Read or print a bit string. For input, the next w columns of the input stream are read in and assigned to the corresponding bit variable. Blanks may occur before or after the bit string value in the input, but they may not be imbedded within the value. Only 1's and 0's are allowed in the input value. If w ≤ 0, the null string is assigned and no columns are skipped.

For output, the corresponding bit string value is printed, left-adjusted, in the next w columns. If too long, the value is truncated on the right. If w ≤ 0, no output results.

C(real-format-item [, real-format-item]) -- Read or print a complex number. Each real-format-item is either F or E, as described below. If the second one is missing, it is assumed to be the same as the first.

For input, two numbers are read in and assigned to the real and imaginary part of the corresponding COMPLEX variable. No letter I may appear in the input. For output, the complex value is printed according to the format. No letter I is appended to it.

COLUMN(w) -- This control item causes columns to be skipped until column w of the current line is reached. On input, skipped columns are ignored; on output, they are filled with blanks. If the current line is already positioned <u>after</u> column w, the current line is completed and a new one started, in column w. If w ≤ 0, it is assumed to be 1. If w is greater than the size of a line, 1 is assumed.

E(w, d [, s]) -- Read or print a floating point number, in w columns. w must be large enough to include <u>all</u> parts of the number, including the preceding sign and the exponent. If the variable to be assigned or the value to be printed is not floating decimal, conversion will be performed on the number.

For input, the value on the line should have the form

[+ or -] mantissa [E [+ or -] yy]

where yy is any 1 or 2 digit number. The mantissa is a fixed point constant. If the mantissa has no decimal point, the decimal point is assumed to be just before the rightmost d digits of the mantissa. If the exponent is missing, a zero exponent is assumed. Blanks may precede or follow the number in the field of w columns, but may not appear within the number. "s" is not used for input.

For output, the number is printed in a field of w characters in the form

[-] <s-d digits> . <d digits> E <+ or -> exponent

s represents the number of significant digits and d the number of fractional digits. If s is missing, it is assumed to be d+1. Thus, one digit will be printed to the left of the decimal point. If d is 0 no decimal point is printed. s must be less than 17.

If necessary, the number is rounded to fit the format.

F(w, d [, s]) -- Read or print a fixed-point decimal number, in w columns. If the variable being assigned or the value being printed is not fixed decimal, suitable conversion will be performed.

For input, the number is an optionally-signed decimal fixed-point constant. It may be preceded or followed by blanks, but can contain no embedded blanks. If the entire field is blank, the number is 0.

If the number contains no decimal point, an implied decimal point is inserted d digits from the right of the number. If s appears, the number is multiplied by 10**s, <u>after</u> it is read in but before it is assigned to the variable.

For output, the value to be printed is first converted to fixed decimal form. It is then rounded to fit the format and printed out, right-adjusted, in a field of w columns. If d does not appear, the integer part of the number is written without a decimal point. If d appears, d digits will be printed to the right of the decimal point. If s appears, before writing out the value, it is multiplied by 10**s.

LINE(exp) -- This control item causes blank lines to be inserted so that the current line is the expth line on the page. If exp $\le$ 0, 1 is assumed. If the current line number $\ge$ exp, the ENDPAGE condition is raised (which usually causes a new page to be started).

PAGE -- This control item causes a new page to be started. It may be used for output only.

SKIP [(exp)] -- This control item causes exp lines (records) to be skipped (the current line counting as 1 skip). If exp is missing it is assumed to be 1. SKIP may cause the ENDPAGE condition to be raised (which usually causes a new page to be started on output).

On output, if exp $\le$ 0, SKIP causes the same current line to be used, starting at the beginning. This does <u>not</u> erase the previous contents of the current line, but can be used to cause overprinting of characters.

X(w) -- This control item causes w columns to be skipped (on input) or w blank characters to be printed (on output). If w $\le$ 0, it it is assumed to be 0.

Appendix A.9 Summary of Differences between PL/C and PL/I

PL/C is a product of a research project of the Department of Computer Science at Cornell University. This project has been concerned with high-performance compilers with special diagnostic facilities since 1961; PL/C development began in 1969.

PL/C is almost a subset of PL/I. It was designed to be "upward compatible" with PL/I in the sense that a program that runs without incurring error messages under the PL/C compiler should run under PL/I and produce the same results.

PL/C is not quite a proper subset of PL/I since some features have been added. However, since these are primarily diagnostic facilities they can presumably be removed after testing is completed in order to run the program under PL/I. Alternatively, incompatible features can be sheltered from PL/I in pseudo-comments. There is no effective way to shelter the PL/C macro facility from PL/I, so use of that feature usually precludes running the program under PL/I.

PL/C was designed to be compatible with the IBM PL/I(F) compiler. Although PL/I(F) is by now obsolescent, it is generally upward compatible with the PL/I Optimizing Compiler that has replaced it in IBM's library, so presumably PL/C is still more-or-less compatible with IBM's PL/I.

The current version of PL/C is designated "Release 7.6" and the characteristics of this version are reflected in this book. The following sections provide a brief summary of the omissions, restrictions and additions that distinguish PL/C-7.6 from PL/I(F).

A.9.1 PL/I(F) Features not Included in PL/C

1. REGIONAL auxiliary files.

2. Controlled and based storage, and list processing.

3. Multi-tasking.

4. Compile-time facilities.

5. 48 character set option.

6. Message DISPLAY to the operator.

7. DEFINED and LIKE attributes.

8. A few built-in functions and pseudo-variables.

A.9.2 Additional Restrictions Imposed by PL/C

1. 33 statement keywords and 6 auxiliary keywords are reserved and cannot be used as identifiers.

2. The names of built-in functions and pseudo-variables are not reserved and may be used as identifiers, but if they are to be used in this way they should be explicitly declared -- contextual declaration of these particular identifiers may succeed (depending upon context) but will produce a warning message.

3. Parameters cannot be passed to the MAIN PROCEDURE of a PL/C program from the OS EXEC card.

4. String constants and comments must be contained on a single source card unless the PL/C NOMONITOR=(BNDRY) option is specified.

5. String constants cannot have repetition factors.

6. There are restrictions on the END, ENTRY, FORMAT, PROCEDURE, READ and WRITE statements.

7. There are restrictions on dimension, ENTRY, ENVIRONMENT, INITIAL, LABEL and length attributes.

8. Not all PL/I(F) condition codes are used by PL/C and the default condition states under PL/C are not exactly the same as under PL/I(F).

A.9.3 Incompatible Features Added to PL/C

1. CHECK, NOCHECK, FLOW and NOFLOW statements; a FLOW condition; ONORIG, ONDEST, STMTNO built-in functions.

2. Diagnostic options on the PUT statement.

3. A built-in function to generate pseudo-random numbers.

4. Comments that are convertible to source text depending upon the first letter of their contents.

5. A text-replacement MACRO processor.

A.9.4 Differences in Internal Representation of Data

Internally PL/C carries out all floating point arithmetic operations in double-precision form, adopting user-specified precision only on output. This means that computation is often somewhat more precise than under PL/I(F). The result is usually a slight difference in the least significant figures of results, but of course it is possible for the differences to become highly significant.

PL/C assigns a full word of storage to each FIXED BINARY variable and a double word of storage to each FIXED DECIMAL variable, regardless of the declared precision. This means that PL/C variables may hold values larger than their PL/I(F) counterparts. However, the default state for the SIZE condition in PL/C is "enabled" so that the situations in which PL/C would give different results from PL/I(F) are detected.

Each bit in a PL/C bit-string is assigned an entire byte in storage. Each PL/C string variable also has an eight byte control block called a dope vector so that an array of short strings takes a surprising amount of core.

Decimal-base values in PL/C are maintained internally in floating binary form and are converted on output.

This internal representation does not apply to record files, which are written in standard PL/I(F) representation and assumed to be in that representation when read. This means that PL/C and PL/I(F) are compatible with respect to record files -- files written by either compiler can be read by either.

A.9.5 Order of Evaluation in Declarations

PL/I(F) will reorder the evaluation of bounds and lengths and the initialization of variables so that, in the absence of circular dependencies, variables will be allocated and initialized before they are used to allocate or initialize other variables. PL/C uses a simpler strategy, which depends upon the order in which the DECLARE statements appear in the block and the order in which variables are listed in a DECLARE statement:

1. First, all scalar arithmetic and label variables are given their initial value.

2. Then, proceeding in the order in which they are declared, strings, arrays and structures are allocated space and initialized. Any expressions in the bounds or length fields are evaluated before space is allocated. After space has been allocated, the variable is initialized before processing the next variable in the order of the declaration.

This strategy does not eliminate any allocation scheme available in PL/I(F) but does require the programmer to order his declaration of variables to avoid the use of unallocated or uninitialized variables declared in the same block.

A.9.6 Dimensional Limits in the PL/C Compiler

The internal structure of the PL/C compiler is very different from that of the PL/I-F compiler and it was not feasible to limit certain critical dimensions of the source program in exactly the same way. There are probably some unusually large and complex programs that would be accepted by PL/C but would exceed some dimensional limit in PL/I-F. The opposite is certainly true. The limits in PL/C are the following:

1. Maximum nesting of IF statements is 12.
2. Maximum static (syntactic) nesting of PROCEDURE, BEGIN and DO statements is 11.
3. Maximum nesting of factors in DECLARE is 6.
4. Maximum number of label prefixes on a statement is 87.
5. Maximum depth of parenthesis nesting in expressions is 14.
6. Maximum number of identifiers in a factor or structure in DECLARE is 88.
7. No single expression can contain more than 256 symbols.

These limits are fixed by the structure of the compiler and cannot be relieved by increasing the core made available to the compiler. In most other respects the compiler's limits are related to the amount of core available--for example, length of program and size of arrays. In these cases when the compiler indicates that a limit has been exceeded the user can resubmit the program with a larger core specification.

Appendix A.10 *PL/C Macros*

PL/C has a facility for automatically making *textual substitutions* in a program, just before the program is compiled and executed. This "macro" facility can aid the programmer in many ways. As a first example, suppose we have the following job to be run:

```
 1  *PL/C
 2  *MACRO
 3      FREE = LIBERATED %;
 4      PI = 3.14159 %;
 5  *MEND
 6      X: PROC OPTIONS(MAIN);
 7          DCL FREE FIXED;
 8          FREE = 1;
 9          PUT LIST( FREE, PI+1);
10          END X;
```

Cards 2-5 form a "macro packet", which describes two "macro-names" FREE and PI, and corresponding "macro-bodies" LIBERATED and 3.14159. Just before the program is compiled, each occurrence of a macro-name is replaced by the corresponding macro-body. Thus the above program is *exactly equivalent* to:

```
*PL/C
    X: PROC OPTIONS(MAIN);
        DCL LIBERATED FIXED;
        LIBERATED = 1;
        PUT LIST( LIBERATED, 3.14159+1);
        END X;
```

A.10.1 *Macro Definitions*

A macro packet has the form shown below. The control cards *MACRO and *MEND must begin in column 1; the other cards may *not* use column 1.

```
*MACRO
    macro-name = macro-body %;
    ...
    macro-name = macro-body %;
*MEND
```

Each *macro definition* defines a *macro-name* and corresponding *macro-body* that will replace it. The macro-name can be any PL/I identifier or reserved word; the macro-body is any sequence of characters not containing the sequence "%;". The macro-body may contain any number of characters; it may contain any number of cards.

A job usually has one macro packet, placed just before the program, but it can have any number of them and they may be placed anywhere. However, a macro with macro-name M (say) may *not* be defined if M has been used *previously* as an identifier in the program. The position of a macro-definition determines where it is effective, as explained under *macro-call*.

A.10.2 *Macro Calls*

The occurrence of a previously defined macro-name within a program constitutes a *macro call*; that macro-name is replaced by the corresponding macro-body. Macro-names used within comments or strings *are not replaced*. As an example, consider:

```
1   *PL/C
2   *MACRO
3       F =    G   %;
4   *MEND
5       X: PROC OPTIONS(MAIN);
6          DCL F FIXED INIT(1);
7          PUT SKIP LIST(F, 'F' /* F */);
8          END X;
```

This is executed as if it had been written as below. The first occurence of F on line 7 *has* been changed. The next two occurrences of F on line 7 have *not* been changed since they appear in a comment and string, respectively.

```
*PL/C
    X: PROC OPTIONS(MAIN);
      DCL G FIXED INIT(1);
      PUT SKIP LIST(G, 'F' /* F*/);
      END X;
```

The macro-name must of course appear as an identifier or PL/I reserved word in order to be replaced. Consider the program

```
1   *MACRO
2       E1 = XXX %;
3   *MEND
4       X: PROC OPTIONS(MAIN);
5         DCL E1 FLOAT;
6         E1 = 25E1;
7         END X;
```

The second occurrence of E1 on line 6 is not a macro call, since it is not recognizable as an identifier; it is part of the constant 25E1. This program is equivalent to, that is, is compiled as if it were:

```
1        X: PROC OPTIONS(MAIN);
2          DCL XXX FLOAT;
3          XXX = 25E1;
4          END X;
```

A.10.3 The Source Listing with Macros

Unless the NOSOURCE option is specified, macro definitions are always printed (with four asterisks in the lefthand columns to indicate they are macro definitions). These lines are not given STMT numbers, etc., because they are not really part of the program; they contain text to be inserted into the program at various places.

Two options are available to control printing of programs with macros: MCALL and MTEXT. Typically we want just the <u>calls</u> printed, in which case MCALL and NOMTEXT should be used. At times, however, we may also want to see the text that is substituted for a macro-name. In this case we specify MTEXT. When a macro body is printed within a program, it appears indented as in the macro definition itself. To illustrate, we show a section of the source listing for a small program with the three possible legal combinations of these options.

```
*PL/C MCALL,NOMTEXT
*MACRO
****        STRING =
****        'FFFFFF' ||
****          'GGGG' ||
****        'HHHHHH' %;
*MEND

        X: PROC OPTIONS(MAIN);
            PUT LIST(STRING);
            END X;
```

```
*PL/C NOMCALL,MTEXT
*MACRO
****        STRING =
****        'FFFFFF' ||
****          'GGGG' ||
****        'HHHHHH' %;
*MEND

        X: PROC OPTIONS(MAIN);
            PUT LIST(
                       'FFFFFF' ||
                         'GGGG' ||
                       'HHHHHH' );
            END X;
```

```
*PL/C MCALL,MTEXT
*MACRO
****        STRING =
****        'FFFFFF' ||
****          'GGGG' ||
****        'HHHHHH' %;
*MEND

        X: PROC OPTIONS(MAIN);
            PUT LIST(STRING
                        'FFFFFF' ||
                          'GGGG' ||
                        'HHHHHH' );
            END X;
```

PL/C also has a column to the left of the program in the listing, titled MLVL. This column indicates the "level of nesting" of statements on the line, within macro bodies. Usually, this column is left blank. But those statements that occur in a macro body being inserted in the program have MLVL=1. If a statement with MLVL=1 is a macro call, the statements in <u>its</u> corresponding body have MLVL=2, and so on.

A.10.4 Macros with Parameters

Macros, like procedures, become more flexible when arguments can be communicated to them. For example, a macro SWAP given as

```
*MACRO
    SWAP(X,Y,T) = /*SWAP VALUES X,Y USING GLOBAL T*/
        DO;
            T = X;
            X = Y;
            Y = T;
            END; %;
*MEND
```

can be used to interchange the values of any two variables.

The definition of a macro with parameters has the form

```
macro-name(par-1, par-2, ..., par-n) = macro-body %;
```

Each parameter par-i is a PL/I identifier (with 31 or fewer characters). The parameters are <u>local</u> to the macro-body; they follow scope rules exactly like parameters of a procedure. During the replacement of a macro call by a macro-body, each occurrence of a parameter (which can be recognized as such) is textually replaced by a corresponding argument. For example, in

```
*MACRO
    M(E) =   E = 12; /* SET E TO UPPER BOUND */ %;
*MEND
    ...
    M(V)
    ...
```

the macro call M(V) will be replaced by

```
V= 12; /* SET V TO UPPER BOUND */
```

Note that the two E's that can be recognized as identifiers have been replaced, while the two E's in the words SET and UPPER have not.

A macro call of a macro with n≥1 parameters has the form

```
macro-name( arg-1, arg-2, ..., arg-n)
```

Usually, each argument is a variable or expression, as is the argument of a procedure. But actually the argument can be practically any sequence of characters; remember, a <u>textual</u> substitution is made -- the sequence of characters making up the argument replace the parameter. Some conventions must be followed so that the commas separating adjacent arguments can be recognized. These conventions are:

1. Blanks surrounding an argument are ignored.
2. Any commas in the argument itself must come between matching left and right parentheses.
3. An argument may begin and end with a single quote "'". In this case, rule 2 need not be followed. Any quote within the argument must be represented by two consecutive quotes "''" (these are <u>not</u> compressed to one quote during replacement).
4. If an argument begins with a left parenthesis, all characters up to its matching right parenthesis are considered part of the argument. This pair of outer parentheses is <u>discarded</u> and not considered part of the argument.

Consider the macro packet

```
*MACRO
    ASGN(P,Q,R) = SUBSTR(P,Q) = R; %;
*MEND
```

Expansion of the macro call ASGN(X,(10,3), 'ABC''XYZ') yields

```
SUBSTR(X,10,3) = 'ABC''XYZ';
```

A.10.5 Uses of Macros

Macros can be used in many ways:

1. To change some name throughout a program to some other name.
2. To give mnemonic names to constants.
3. To aid in testing.
4. To extend PL/C in some fashion.
5. To aid in structuring a program in top-down fasion.

The first two uses were illustrated in the beginning of this Appendix. The reason for changing the name FREE in that example was because FREE is a reserved word in PL/C and cannot be used as an identifier. It is easier to change every occurrence of FREE with a macro than to repunch all cards containing that word. This effectively allows use of FREE as an identifier in the source listing; it is only behind the scenes that it has been changed.

The use of macros to aid in testing was discussed in Section V.5.4.2.

Macros can be used to overcome PL/I's lack of a facility for defining named constants. For example, given the packet:

```
*MACRO
    TRUE = '1'B %;
    FALSE = '0'B %;
*MEND
```

we can use statements such as A = TRUE; and DO WHILE(TRUE); ... END;.

Macros can be used to restrict or eliminate features as well as add them. For example, the following packet effectively eliminates the GOTO statement:

```
*MACRO
    GO = %;
    GOTO = %;
*MEND
```

We have seen earlier how procedures help "abstract the details away", and shorten the length of a program segment. Macros offer an alternative to procedures in this regard. For example, consider the following procedure (and macros) for sorting:

```
*MACRO
    SWAP_VARIABLES =
       BEGIN;
            DCL T FIXED;
            T = X;
            X = Y;
            Y = T;
            END; %;

    GET_LARGEST_OF_SEGMENT_1_THRU_I_IN_POSITION_I =
       BEGIN;
            DCL J FIXED;
            DO J = 1 TO I BY 1;
                 IF A(J) > A(J+1)
                      THEN SWAP_VARIABLES(A(J), A(J+1))
                 END;
            END; %;
*MEND

    SORT: PROCEDURE(A,N);
       /* SORT ARRAY SEGMENT A(1:N) */
            DCL (A(*), N) FIXED;
            DCL I FIXED;
            DO I = N TO 2 BY -1;
                 GET_LARGEST_OF_SEGMENT_1_THRU_I_IN_POSITION_I
                 END;
            END SORT;
```

Macros and procedures allow roughly the same power of abstraction. In fact, recall that procedures were first introduced using the idea of a textual substitution. Design your program without worrying whether procedures or macros will be used. Then, on the basis of the whole program, decide for each body whether it should be a macro or procedure, based on the number of calls upon it and the space and time requirements of your program.

A program with macro calls takes longer to "compile", since each call must be textually replaced. But execution is more efficient with macros than with procedures. A procedure call requires a jump to another set of instructions and processing for argument-parameter correspondence; there is a good deal of bookkeeping to be done. Macro argument-parameter correspondence, on the other hand, is done before the program is compiled, and the body of the macro appears "in-line", at the place of call. However, more space is used. If a macro is called from five different places, then a copy of that macro-body exists in five places.

With macros you must be more careful about the use of variables and identifiers. The macro feature is not built into PL/C, but should be thought of as a a "preprocessor" for it, something that transforms a program just before it is loaded and executed. Macros, therefore, do not follow the usual block structure and scope rules. A macro-name is global; once defined, it can be used only for a macro call.

Consider the sort procedure presented above. We have made variables J and T local to the statements in which they are used, which is as it should be. However, this procedure is compiled as if it were

```
SORT: PROCEDURE(A, N);
   DCL (A(*), N) FIXED;
   DCL I FIXED;
   DO I = N TO 2 BY -1;
       BEGIN;
           DO J = 1 TO I -1 BY 1;
               IF A(J) > A(J+1)
                   THEN BEGIN;
                       DCL T FIXED;
                       T = A(J);
                       A(J) = A(J+1);
                       A(J+1) = T;
                       END;
               END;
           END;
       END;
   END SORT;
```

This means that on the order of N^2 BEGIN blocks may be executed. In most PL/I implementations this can be quite costly, taking much more time than the rest of the program. Therefore, using macros in this fashion may be increasing the running time too much.

We can sacrifice a bit of clarity to gain efficiency by making these parameters global to the macros, as shown below. Now, no blocks are executed and the program is faster, but the macros are less usable since they refer to global variables. In effect, we have introduced more communication between the program segments, which should be explicitly described by comments.

```
*MACRO
   SWAP_VARIABLES(X, Y) = /* USES GLOBAL T TO SWAP */
       DO;
           T = X;
           X = Y;
           Y = T;
           END; %;

   GET_LARGEST_OF_SEGMENT_1_THRU_I_IN_POSITION_I =
       /* USES GLOBAL FIXED VARIABLE J */
           DO J = 1 TO I-1 BY 1;
               IF A(J) > A (J+1)
                   THEN SWAP_VARIABLES(A(J),
                                       A(J+1);
```

```
                    END; %;
*MEND


SORT: PROCEDURE(A, N);
       /* SORT ARRAY SEGMENT A(1:N) */
           DCL (A(*), N) FIXED;
           DCL (I, J, T) FIXED;
           DO I = N TO 2 BY -1;

GET_LARGEST_OF_SEGMENT_1_THRU_I_IN_POSITION_I
               END;
       END SORT;
```

Appendix A.11 The PL/CT Interactive System

This appendix is taken directly from the PL/CT User's Guide, distributed by the Department of Computer Science and the Office of Computer Services of Cornell University.

PL/CT - A Terminal Version of PL/C
Release 2

User's Guide to the Cornell-CMS Version

C. G. Moore III, S. L. Worona and R. W. Conway

PL/CT is a special version of PL/C designed to permit programs to be run interactively from a typewriter terminal. It is completely compatible with normal PL/C -- that is, the source languages accepted by PL/C and PL/CT are identical and the results of execution are exactly the same. Hence a program can be developed and tested under PL/CT and subsequently run under normal PL/C (or vice-versa).

PL/CT permits the user to interact with the program during its execution. Output will be printed on the terminal and input data may be requested from the terminal. The course and rate of execution can be controlled from the terminal. It is also possible to interrupt execution and display and alter the values of variables. However, the source program itself cannot be changed under PL/CT. PL/CT receives a complete program, compiles it, and then executes it in interactive mode. But to make any change in the program it is necessary to leave PL/CT, make the change under the CMS editor, and then present the modified program to PL/CT for complete recompilation.

This Guide provides only minimal information about CMS, perhaps sufficient for very straightforward programming tasks. For additional information see the following publications: IBM VM/370: Command Language Guide for General Users (GC20-1804); IBM VM/370: EDIT Guide (GC20-1805); IBM VM/370: Terminal User's Guide (GC20-1810).

Levels and Modes

The most complicated aspect of using CMS-PL/CT is understanding that you are communicating with the system at several different levels. Sometimes you are entering commands telling the command processor what to do, sometimes you are entering lines that are PL/I source statements, and sometimes you are entering data required for the execution of your PL/I program. It is essential that you understand the difference between these levels, and that you understand the means by which you indicate the proper level to the system.

CMS handles this problem of levels by establishing different "modes" of communication. The highest level is called command mode. When the system is in command mode it assumes that anything entered is a command (and not a program line or data). Two of these commands change the mode of the system: the EDIT command causes the system to enter EDIT mode; the PLC command causes it to enter PL/CT mode. When the system is in EDIT mode it assumes that anything entered is an EDIT sub-command. One of these sub-commands causes the system to shift to INPUT mode in which it assumes that everything entered is a line to be stored in a dataset. Similarly there are modes within PL/CT that determine whether input from the terminal is considered to be source program lines, execution data, or execution debugging sub-commands. It is difficult to describe, but it works fairly naturally in practice. The relationship between levels, modes, commands and sub-commands can be summarized in the following table:

```
CMS Command Mode
   Input:
       EDIT to enter EDIT mode
       ERASE to delete a dataset
       LISTFILE to list the names of datasets
       LOGOFF to end the terminal session
       PLC to enter PL/CT mode

   EDIT Mode
       Input: (sub-commands)
           INPUT to enter INPUT mode
           DELETE to delete 1 or more lines
           LOCATE to locate a certain line
           CHANGE to change part of a line
           TYPE to display 1 or more lines
           TOP, BOTTOM, UP, DOWN to move the line pointer
           SAVE to save a copy of a dataset
           QUIT to return to command mode

       INPUT Mode
           Input:
               Lines to be inserted in dataset
               Null line to return to EDIT mode
```

PL/CT Mode

Input:

Source program lines
Execution data
Debug commands

Returns to CMS command mode when program execution is completed, or STOPped, or two consecutive ATTNs occur.

Command Mode

The system indicates that it is in command mode with the prompting message 'R; T=runtime time-of-day'.

Commands (optional abbreviation below full form)

EDIT dataset-name PLC
E

"Dataset-name" is a string of not more than 8 characters, beginning with a letter.

If "dataset name" is the name of an existing dataset, then EDIT will retrieve that dataset and EDIT mode is entered to allow you to make modifications to that dataset. If "dataset-name" is not the name of any existing dataset, then EDIT will create a new dataset with that name. In this case, when you enter EDIT mode, EDIT will type "NEW FILE", to indicate it has created a new, empty dataset. You should then use the INPUT sub-command to enter lines into the new dataset.

ERASE dataset-name

Delete the indicated dataset.

LISTFILE * * A
L

List the contents of your dataset catalog -- the names of all your datasets. (The names will appear in "full" form, rather than the simple form that is sufficient for the purposes described here.)

LOGOFF

End the terminal session. The system will reply with a line giving the cost of the session. The system leaves command mode and will accept no further commands. Turn off the terminal and the coupler and replace the telephone handset.

PLC sp-list DATA(d-list) OPTIONS(op-list) PAUSE SAVE n

Cause the system to enter PL/CT mode to compile and execute a PL/C program. "Sp-list" specifies the source program; "d-list" specifies the input data for execution of the program; "op-list" specifies PL/C options; PAUSE causes a return to the terminal before beginning execution of the program;

"SAVE n" saves n lines of the source listing for display during execution. All of the phrases after PLC are optional; their order is immaterial except that sp-list (if given) must come first.

Because of CMS restrictions a PLC command must not contain a sequence of more than 8 characters without a blank character appearing. This will not be a problem if you use the following rules in typing a PLC command:

(1) always type a blank after a comma
(2) always type a blank before or after a parenthesis (left or right)
(3) use dataset-names of 6 characters or less

The source-program dataset (specified by sp-list) contains lines equivalent to the source program cards submitted to batch-PL/C -- including PL/C control cards (*PL/C, *PROCESS, etc.) Sp-list should be given in one of the following forms:

1. a dataset name
2. an asterisk, indicating program will be entered from the terminal. This is the default assumption if no source-program-list is given.
3. a list of dataset names, separated by commas and enclosed in parentheses. The datasets listed are "concatenated" -- the first line of one dataset follows the last line of the predecessor dataset on the list -- and presented as a single dataset to PL/CT.

Data for the execution of the program is obtained in one of the following ways:

1. If the concatenated source-program dataset contains a *DATA line, input data will be drawn from that dataset. The DATA option on the PLC command should be omitted.
2. If there is no *DATA line in the source-program dataset <u>and</u> the DATA option is omitted, then DATA(*) is assumed and PL/CT will return to the terminal for input data.
3. If there is no *DATA line in the source-program dataset and the DATA option is given on the PLC command then input data will be drawn from the dataset concatenated from the items given in d-list. Items may be datasets or asterisks, as in sp-list.

When a dataset is entered from the terminal, its end must be indicated by entering a null line consisting of simply a carriage return.

Op-list specifies PL/C options to be applied <u>after</u> any options that may be given on a *PL/C card in the source-program dataset. (This may be used to override the *PL/C options. A *PL/C card need not be present.) Remember when typing in this list that CMS will not accept more than 8 characters without a blank.

PAUSE is given if you want your program to enter debug mode just before program execution begins. It is equivalent to pressing "ATTN" just as program execution begins (which is hard to do). This will give you the opportunity to set PAUSEs in the program before it begins to execute.

PL/CT will save a copy of the source listing for display during execution unless the NOSAVE option is given. SAVE n saves the <u>first n lines</u> of the listing. The default is SAVE 200. This feature uses a lot of memory, so if you don't need it, specify NOSAVE; if you have a small program, specify an n < 200.

Examples:

PLC

Both source program and input data are to come from the terminal. The source program lines must conclude with a *DATA line to initiate execution, just as in batch-PL/C.

PLC PROB1

Source program is to come from dataset PROB1. If this includes a *DATA card it will also supply data, otherwise data will come from the terminal.

PLC * DATA (P1DATA) SAVE 50

Source program is to come from the terminal; input data from P1DATA. Save only 50 lines of the source listing.

PLC PROX4 DATA (XDATA) OPTIONS (ATR, XREF)

Source program is to come from PROX4, data from XDATA. The cross-reference and attribute listing is to be printed.

PLC (*, PRG1) PAUSE NOSAVE

Source program is to come first from the terminal (perhaps to supply a *PL/C card) and then from PRG1; input data is to come from the terminal (unless PRG1 includes a *DATA line). Return to the terminal before beginning execution. Do not save the source listing.

PLC (CS104, LIBR) DATA (INIT, *)

Source program is to come from CS104 followed by LIBR, data is initially to come from INIT and from the terminal when that is exhausted.

Special note: There is a difference between the two commands PLC * and PLC * DATA (*). The first command expects the input from the terminal to consist of the source program, followed by a *DATA card, followed by the program data. The second form expects the input to consist of the source program, followed by an end-of-file (carriage return), followed by the program data.

EDIT Mode

The EDIT facility permits the creation and modification of datasets. The following describes a portion of the full EDIT, assuming you are working with a relatively small dataset and that you have a listing of that dataset available. The full EDIT is much more powerful and flexible than what is described here -- see the IBM VM/370 EDIT Guide (GC20-1805).

The editor keeps track of a "current-line-pointer", which always points to the "current line" in your dataset. Most EDIT sub-commands use the current-line-pointer to determine where editing is to be done, and most alter the current-line-pointer as part of their action. For example, the DELETE command deletes lines beginning with the line pointed to by the current-line-pointer, and then sets the current-line-pointer to point to the next line after those deleted.

EDIT Sub-commands (optional abbreviation below full form)

INPUT
I

Enter the *input* sub-mode of EDIT. Subsequent lines are inserted into the dataset after the current line. To terminate this sub-mode enter a "null line" (carriage return only).

DELETE n
DEL

Delete n lines, beginning with the current line. If n is omitted, delete only the current line. The new current line is the first line *after* those deleted.

LOCATE /string/ or LOCATE 'string'
L

Beginning with the current line, search the dataset for the first line containing the sequence of characters given by "string", and make that line the new current line. Use the first form (delimited by slashes) if the string you are searching for contains no /; use the second form (delimited by quotes) if it contains a / but no quotes. If the search is unsuccessful (the string is not found in the portion of the dataset searched) the current-line-pointer is set to point to the last line of the dataset. For example: LOCATE /QQSV/ searches the dataset from the current line to the end of the dataset for the first occurrence of the string of characters "QQSV".

CHANGE /string1/string2/ or CHANGE 'string1'string2'
C

Replace the leftmost occurrence of "string1" in the current line with "string2". "String1" and "string2" do not need to be of the same length. For example, if the current line is: "THIS IS A LINE" the sub-command: CHANGE /IS/WAS/ would change the line to: "THWAS IS A LINE".

TYPE n
T

Print n lines of the dataset, beginning with the current line. The last line printed becomes the current line.

TOP

Set the current-line-pointer to an imaginary line before the first line of the dataset (so that INPUT can be used to insert lines at the beginning).

BOTTOM
B

Set the current-line-pointer to the last line of the dataset.

UP n
U

Move the current-line-pointer up n lines (1 line if n is omitted).

DOWN n
DO

Move the current-line-pointer down n lines (1 line if n is omitted).

SAVE or SAVE dataset-name PLC

First form: copy the current version of the dataset into the file whose name was given in the EDIT command, replacing the old version. Second form: copy the current version of the dataset into the file whose name is given in the SAVE sub-command. EDIT makes a <u>temporary copy</u> of the specified dataset when you give the EDIT command, and all <u>changes are performed on this copy</u>. Therefore, if you do not specify SAVE before QUITing, your changes will be lost.

QUIT

Terminates the EDIT command. Normally this will be given just after a SAVE sub-command.

PL/CT Mode

The PL/CT source language is identical to PL/C, but the following default options are different (to reduce the amount of printing):

CMPRS	NOHDRPG
NODUMP, NODUMPE, NODUMPT	NOOPLIST
FLAGE	NOSOURCE

PL/CT Source Program Entry

Programs can be entered in one of two ways:

1. directly to PL/CT from the terminal, or

2. by preparing a dataset which is then presented to PL/CT.

For all but trivial programs the second method should be used, since it provides a means of saving the source program for subsequent reuse and/or modification. If a program is presented directly to PL/CT it is not saved in the system and must be reentered to be re-run.

Note that once a source line has been presented to PL/CT (either from the terminal or from a dataset) there is no way within PL/CT to change that line. You must leave PL/CT, change the program, and then re-invoke PL/CT.

Terminal Use During Execution

During execution of a program the PL/CT terminal has two distinct roles:

1. It serves as the normal (that is, SYSIN/SYSPRINT) input/output device for the program. The printed output from PUT statements will appear on the terminal; GET statements will request input data from the terminal (assuming the d-list of the PLC command specifies the terminal). There is <u>no automatic prompt</u> when the program is requesting input data -- hence it is generally good programming practice to place a PUT statement with a prompting message <u>immediately before</u> each terminal GET.

2. In "debug mode" the terminal is used to enter PL/CT "debug commands" -- statements for immediate execution. Debug mode can be entered in the following ways:

   a. Give the <u>PAUSE option</u> on the PLC command that invokes PL/CT. This simulates an "attention interrupt" during the first statement of the program, and enters debug mode before the second statement. This gives you an opportunity to set PAUSEs in the program before its execution begins.

b. Strike the "attention" ("ATTN") key at any time during program execution. The program will complete execution of whatever statement is being executed and enter debug mode before beginning the next statement. If the statement being executed is a PUT causing printing on the terminal, the statement will be completed, but actual printing of the final lines will be suppressed. Moreover, because of the buffering of printed output both in PL/C and in the operating system, the handling of printed output on an attention interrupt is sometimes rather difficult to understand. Be careful that you hit attention only once, and then give the system a chance to respond. Hitting two consecutive attentions (without any intervening action) will cause the system to leave PL/CT and return to command mode, losing all trace of the program's execution.

c. After each non-fatal execution error, PL/CT will automatically enter debug mode. PL/CT prints the usual error message, makes the usual PL/C error repair, and then enters debug mode before beginning the next statement.

d. When a PAUSE, or "breakpoint" is encountered in the source program, PL/CT enters debug mode. PAUSEs may be set and removed by the debug commands, described below.

e. When a specified number of statements of the original program have been executed, PL/CT will enter debug mode. This "STEP interval" can be set by debug commands, described below.

In each case, PL/CT will print a message indicating the reason for entering debug mode, and the statement number of the next statement to be executed. This message will end with the prompting symbol "DBC:", indicating that PL/CT is in debug mode, waiting for a debug command to be entered on the terminal. After each debug command line the prompt "DBC:" will be repeated to indicate that the system is still in debug mode and is ready to receive another debug command.

The "debug mode" and the "input data mode" are completely distinct -- you cannot enter data when PL/CT expects a debug command, and you cannot enter a debug command when it expects data.

PL/CT Debug Commands

When the system is in debug mode any of the following commands may be given. Each command is executed immediately; it is not saved, and does not become part of the source program. The format for commands is free-field -- essentially the same as for statements in PL/C, except:

1. Comments are not allowed.
2. Commands may begin in position 1 of the line.
3. Commands cannot be continued onto a second line.

PUT SKIP LIST(variable, ...);
PUT SKIP DATA(variable, ...);

A restricted form of the PL/C PUT statement. The variable specified can be a scalar, an array, a structure or a subscripted variable with a constant subscript. Variables must be accessible at the point of interrupt under normal PL/C scope rules. Neither expressions nor literals can be given.

SKIP is assumed and need not be given.

If neither LIST nor DATA is specified the default output format will be used. If either LIST or DATA is specified, either in a PUT or as a separate command (see below), this sets the default output format. Initially the default is LIST.

This command may be abbreviated as just "PUT variable;" or just as the variable name alone. That is, assuming that LIST is the default output format, "X;" and "PUT X;" are equivalent to PUT SKIP LIST(X);".

LIST;

Set the default output format (for debug commands only) to be LIST.

DATA;

Set the default output format (for debug commands only) to be DATA.

PUT m, n;

m is a statement number from the source listing, and n is an integer. Display n source lines beginning with the line on which statement m started. If n is omitted from the command, 1 is assumed.

m can also be given as a label or entry-name, accessible from the point of interrupt under the normal PL/C scope rules.

Variable = constant;

A restricted form of the PL/C assignment statement. The target variable must be a scalar or a subscripted variable with constant subscript(s). It cannot be a label variable, an array or a structure. Structure elements must be fully-qualified. Multiple left sides and BY NAME assignment are not allowed. The right side can only be an arithmetic or string constant -- neither a variable nor an expression is allowed.

STEP n;

n is an integer. Reset the STEP interval to n, so that PL/CT will re-enter debug mode after execution of n statements of the source program. If n is omitted, 1 is assumed. This STEP interval remains in effect until changed -- it does not just apply to the first RETURN. Note that statements are counted in a manner comparable to PL/C numbering -- that is, END, PROCEDURE, DO are also counted as statements.

NOSTEP;

Reset the STEP interval to the default value: STEP 2^{16}.

PAUSE AT s;

Establish a PAUSE before statement(s) s. s can be given in several forms:

-a statement number, as given on the PL/C source listing

-a label or entry-name, which is accessible at the point of interrupt under normal PL/C scope rules

-an accessible label or entry-name modified by an integer. For example:

```
PAUSE AT ERRORPROC+6;
PAUSE AT TERMLOOP-3;
```

-an inclusive range of statements: "s^1 TO s^2" where s^1 and s^2 are any of the forms listed above. s^2 can also be the word END, implying the last statement of the program. For example:

```
PAUSE AT 14 TO TERM_LOOP;
PAUSE AT EVALPROC+3 TO EVALPROC+14;
PAUSE AT PRINT+6 TO END;
```

-ALL, which means "1 TO END".

The PAUSE command may be abbreviated by giving s (or s^1 TO s^2) alone. That is, if a command consists of any of the valid forms for s, "PAUSE AT s;" is assumed. For example, "36;" is equivalent to "PAUSE AT 36;".

PAUSEs are maintained in a list of fixed length within PL/CT. When this list is full, further PAUSE commands will be rejected. You will have to remove some PAUSEs before new ones can be added.

NOPAUSE AT s;

Remove the PAUSE (if any) before statement(s) s. s is given in the same forms as for the PAUSE command. Note that NOPAUSE can have a range but not a list of arguments. That is, "NOPAUSE AT s^1, s^2;" is not valid. (s2 will be considered a separate command -- an abbreviation of "PAUSE AT s^2;".) Also note that since removing the middle of a PAUSE range actually creates two ranges, it is possible for NOPAUSE to cause overflow of the PAUSE list.

IGNORE n;

n is an integer. During program execution ignore the first n PAUSEs encountered; re-enter debug mode on the n+1st PAUSE. If n is omitted, 2^{16} is assumed. This IGNORE count remains in effect until changed -- it does not just apply to the first RETURN. Initially, the IGNORE count is 0 -- that is, PL/CT will stop on every PAUSE unless you set the PAUSE count to some non-zero value.

NOCHECK;

Suppress the printing of CHECK output, exactly as in PL/C.

CHECK;

Resume the printing of CHECK output, as in PL/C except that no parameters are allowed on the command.

NOFLOW;

Suppress the printing of FLOW output, exactly as in PL/C.

FLOW;

Resume the printing of FLOW output, as in PL/C except that no parameters are allowed on the command.

PUT OFF;

Suppress printing of SYSPRINT output, exactly as in PL/C.

PUT ON;

Resume printing of SYSPRINT output, exactly as in PL/C.

PUT ALL;

Display the current values of all automatic, scalar variables in the blocks active at the point of interrupt, as well as the current values of all static and external scalar variables, exactly as in PL/C.

PUT ARRAY;

Same as PUT ALL but also includes arrays, exactly as in PL/C.

PUT FLOW;

Display recent FLOW history, exactly as in PL/C.

PUT SNAP;

Display recent calling history, exactly as in PL/C.

RETURN;
Leave debug mode and resume execution of the source program. RETURN can be indicated by a null line. That is, after the "DBC:" prompt a carriage return with an empty line is equivalent to a RETURN command.

GOTO label;
Leave debug mode and resume execution of the source program starting with the statement whose label is given. This label must be accessible from the point of interrupt under the normal PL/C scope rules.

STOP;
Terminate execution of the PL/CT program, exactly as in PL/C.

PL/CT Errors

When errors are detected during compilation of a program the usual PL/C action is taken. That is, a message is printed, some repair is automatically effected, compilation continues and execution will be attempted. (There are a few cases in which these errors are "fatal" and execution is suppressed.) If the repair is not satisfactory you must leave PL/CT mode, alter the source program, and then re-submit it to PL/CT.

Similarly, during execution of the program PL/CT gives the standard PL/C response -- message and repair -- but then returns control to the terminal (before executing the next statement of the program) and requests a debug sub-command.

An error in a debug command will cause a message to be printed, followed by a prompt "DBC:" for re-entry of the command. The complete command must be re-entered -- not just from the point of error. However, if several debug commands were given on the line containing the error, commands to the left of the erroneous command will have already been executed and should not be re-entered.

Appendix A.12 The PL/CS Language

The following is a summary of PL/CS. Except as noted below, PL/CS syntax and semantics are identical to the corresponding PL/C statement.

Statements

ASSERT

1. Form is: ASSERT (condition) [quantifier]:
2. Quantifier is either:
   FOR ALL index-var = exp1 TO exp2 BY exp3;
   FOR SOME index-var = exp1 TO exp2 BY exp3;
3. If satisfied, ASSERT has no side-effects; if not satisfied, ASSERT prints a message.
4. The ASSERT sub-option of MONITOR determines whether or not ASSERTs are executed.

Assignment

1. No multiple left-hand-sides.
2. In array assignment, the right-hand-side must be an array or a constant.
3. In assignment to a bit variable, the right-hand-side must be enclosed in parentheses.
4. Assignment to READONLY variables or parameters is not allowed.

CALL

1. Neither labels nor entry-names are allowed as arguments.
2. Types of arguments and parameters must match exactly.
3. Arguments cannot be READONLY parameters or variables.
4. Arguments cannot be control variables of a loop.

DATAEND

1. Form is DATAEND:;
2. Can appear at most once per procedure.
3. Must be positioned after the last GET statement in procedure.
4. Must be at "top-level" -- cannot be in compound statement or loop, or in IF or SELECT unit.

DECLARE

1. Explicit declaration of variables and parameters is required, and must be positioned at the beginning of the procedure.
2. Variables and parameters must be given in separate declarations.
3. Form is: DECLARE (identifier-list) attributes;
4. Array dimensions are as in PL/C.

5. Attributes for variables:
   a. Exactly one of the following is required: FLOAT, FIXED, CHARACTER (length) VARYING, BIT (1)
   b. The following are optional: INITIAL (list), STATIC, EXTERNAL, READONLY
   c. Required order: type INITIAL STATIC READONLY EXTERNAL
   d. Combinations: READONLY requires EXTERNAL or INITIAL
   e. Only one level of repetition is allowed in the INITIAL list.
6. Attributes for parameters:
   a. One of the following is required: FLOAT, FIXED, CHARACTER (*) VARYING, BIT (*)
   b. Optional: READONLY
   c. Required order: type READONLY
7. FLOAT implies FLOAT DECIMAL(16), FIXED implies FIXED DECIMAL(15,0)

DO

1. Compound statement as in PL/C, but no label.
2. DO WHILE as in PL/C, with single label required.
3. DO UNTIL (condition); with single label required.
4. DO index-var = exp1 TO exp2 BY exp3;
   a. Single label required.
   b. Form shown above is required; TO-BY phrases must be in the order shown.
   c. Index-var must be numeric.
   d. Index-var cannot be a READONLY variable or parameter.
   e. Index-var cannot be EXTERNAL.
   f. Index-var and all variables in exp1, exp2, and exp3 (that is, the control variables) are READONLY in the body of the loop. They cannot be the target of an assignment, cannot appear in the variable list of a GET statement or CALL statement, and cannot be the index-var of another (nested) loop.
   g. The value of the index-var after normal termination of the loop is uninitialized.
   h. Exp3 must have a non-zero value.

END

1. ALL ENDs are explicit.
2. ALL ENDs except for compound statements must be named.

GET

1. Only the LIST, DATA and EDIT options are allowed. Only single level repetition is allowed in format lists.
2. No DO iteration is allowed in the variable list.
3. GET cannot appear after DATAEND.
4. READONLY variables and parameters cannot appear in the variable list.

GOTO	1. Only forward references are allowed. 2. Target must be a labeled null statement. 3. Target can be in loop or compound statement only if all references are also in that loop or compound statement.
IF	1. Form is: IF (condition) THEN s1 [ELSE s2] 2. Neither s1 nor s2 can be null.
LEAVE	1. Form is: LEAVE loop-name; 2. Can only appear in the body of the named loop.
Null	1. Form is: label:; 2. Used only as a target for a GOTO statement.
ON	1. Form is: ON ENDFILE GOTO DATAEND; 2. Can appear at most once per procedure. 3. Must be positioned immediately after declarations.
PROCEDURE	1. MAIN procedure must be the first procedure. 2. All procedures are external. 3. All parameters and variables must be explicitly declared at the beginning of the procedure. 4. Types of arguments and parameters must match exactly. 5. Lengths and dimensions are dynamic as in PL/C. 6. Function procedures have no side effects: a. All parameters are READONLY. b. STATIC and EXTERNAL variables are READONLY. c. Body cannot contain CALL, GET or PUT. 7. Function procedures must have at least one parameter. 8. Character-string function must have: RETURNS(CHARACTER(256)VARYING) 9. Bit-string function must have: RETURNS(BIT(1)) 10. Single entry-name is required. 11. Explicit RETURN before the END is required.
PUT	1. Only the SKIP, LIST, DATA, and EDIT options are allowed. Only single level repetition is allowed in format lists. 2. No DO iteration in the variable list.
RETURN	1. Explicit RETURN is required before the END of a procedure.
SELECT	1. Form is: select-name: SELECT; WHEN (condition1) s1; WHEN (condition2) s2; ... OTHERWISE sn; END select-name; 2. At least one WHEN must be given.

3. OTHERWISE is required.

Comments

1. Procedure comments (/*) print at left.
2. Ordinary comments (/*) print in MSGCOL; They can only follow statements.
3. Declaration comments (/*) print in MSGCOL; Can follow identifiers.
4. Pseudo-comments (/*: or /*i i=1-7) are included; Depending on CMNTS options, they are converted to ordinary comments or normal source text (Without comment delimiters).
5. Statement comments (/** or /*+); Printed in source text as a DO statement would be. /*+ implies (but does not generate) a closure of the last /**.

Miscellaneous

1. *OPTIONS card is not included.
2. Macro facility is not included.
3. *INCLUDE facility is included.
4. Trace is deferred.

Abbreviations

CHAR	CHARACTER
DCL	DECLARE
EXT	EXTERNAL
GO	GOTO
INIT	INITIAL
OTHER	OTHERWISE
PROC	PROCEDURE
READ	READONLY
VAR	VARYING

Reserved Words

ALL	DCL	FIXED	LEAVE	PUT	THEN
ASSERT	DECLARE	FLOAT	LIST	READ	TO
BIT	DO	FOR	MAIN	READONLY	UNTIL
BY	EDIT	GET	ON	RETURN	VAR
CALL	ELSE	GO	OPTIONS	RETURNS	VARYING
CHAR	END	GOTO	OTHER	SELECT	WHEN
CHARACTER	ENDFILE	IF	OTHERWISE	SKIP	WHILE
DATA	EXT	INIT	PROC	SOME	
DATAEND	EXTERNAL	INITIAL	PROCEDURE	STATIC	

Built-in Functions

ABS	COSH	FLOOR	LOG2	ROUND	SUM
ALL	DATE	HBOUND	LOW	SIGN	TAN
ANY	DIM	HIGH	MAX	SIN	TAND
ATAN	ERF	INDEX	MIN	SIND	TANH
ATAND	ERFC	LBOUND	MOD	SINH	TIME
ATANH	EXP	LENGTH	PROD	SQRT	TRANSLATE
CEIL	FIXED	LOG	RAND	STRING	TRUNC
COS	FLOAT	LOG10	REPEAT	SUBSTR	VERIFY
COSD					

Options

CMNTS	DUMPT	HDRPG	MONITOR	MSGCOL	TIME
CMPRS	DUMPS	ID	ASSRT	OPLIST	
CTIME	ETIME	IDENT	BNDRY	PAGES	
DUMP	ERRORS	LINES	CONV	SORMGIN	
DUMPE	ERRLV	LINECT	DFLTS	SOURCE	
		LIST	UDEF	TABSIZE	

Format Items

A	COL	E	LINE	PAGE	X
B	COLUMN	F			

Appendix B Operating Procedures for PL/C

B.1 Program Deck Structure

1. The control cards described below are only those for PL/C. Other cards may be required in front of these to invoke PL/C, or after the program to end the "job". Control cards have * in column 1 and a keyword starting in column 2 (see B.3.1):

```
*PL/C or *PLC       *MACRO      *INCLUDE
*PROCESS            *MEND
*OPTIONS            *DATA
```

2. *PL/C precedes each separate program (several programs may be run together as a single job). If a program has more than one external procedure the procedures are separated by *PROCESS.

3. If data cards are needed, a *DATA card follows the program and the data follows *DATA (but not on the same card as *DATA). If no data is present, *DATA is optional.

4. *MACRO and *MEND enclose macro definitions. See Appendix A.10.

5. *INCLUDE permits source card images to be inserted. See the <u>PL/C User's Guide</u>.

6. PL/C uses whatever space or "region" is assigned to it by the operating system. A minimum of about 100K is required. Methods of specifying region size vary; get local instructions.

B.1.1 Examples of PL/C Card Decks

1. Single program without data:

```
*PL/C options
    source program cards
```

2. Single program with data:

```
*PL/C options
    source program cards
*DATA
    data cards
```

3. Program with 2 external procedures and data:
```
*PL/C options
    source program cards for 1st external proc
*PROCESS options
    source program cards for 2nd external proc
*DATA
    data cards
```

4. Three independent programs run as one job:
```
*PL/C options
    source program cards for program 1
*DATA
    data cards for program 1
*PL/C options
    source program cards for program 2 (main proc)
*PROCESS options
    source program cards for program 2 (ext. proc)
*DATA
    data cards for program 2
*PL/C options
    source program cards for program 3
```

B.2 Program Options

Options may be specified on *PL/C, *PROCESS or *OPTIONS cards. Options may be given in any combination, in any order, separated by blanks and/or commas. They may be continued onto a card with * in column 1 and columns 2-3 blank. But an individual option may not be split over a card boundary. Options may be abbreviated or misspelled; only a few key letters are significant, as indicated in the listing of options below. The prefix letters N or NO designate negated options. Certain options can only be given on the *PL/C card, as noted.

Options on the *PL/C card, and the default values for options not specified, are in effect throughout the program, except as temporarily overridden on *PROCESS and *OPTIONS cards. *PROCESS options apply only to the one external procedure following that card. *OPTIONS options apply only to the remainder of the external procedure in which the card appears. After each external procedure, options are reset to the "global" *PL/C and default values.

In the listing below the normal default value of each option is underlined, but these choices are easily changed by each installation, and yours may be different from what is shown here. In addition, each installation can override options so that user specification of such options is ineffective.

ATR, NOATR, A
Produce attribute listing.

ALIST, NOALIST, AL
Produce assembler listing of generated object code.

AUXIO=n, AU (on *PL/C only)
Limit on number of auxiliary input/output operations. Supplied default n=10000.

CMNTS, CMNTS=(n1,n2,...), NOCMNTS, C
Contents of comments beginning with : considered source text. If parameter(s) are given (1<=ni<=7) comments beginning with ni are also considered source text.

CMPRS, NOCMPRS, CP
Source listing to be given in compressed form (certain page ejects replaced by 3 line skips).

CTIME=(m,s,h), CT (on *PL/C only)
Time limit for compilation.
- m is minutes; assumed zero if omitted.
- s is seconds; assumed zero if omitted.
- h is hundredths of seconds; assumed zero if omitted.

DUMP, DUMP=(d1,d2,...), NODUMP, D (on *PL/C only)
Produce post-mortem dump.
Dump options d1, d2, ... are:
- BLOCKS, B
  Traceback of blocks active at termination.
- SCALARS, S
  Final values of scalar variables in active blocks. (Implies B.)
- ARRAYS, A
  Final values of arrays in active blocks. (Implies S and B.)
- FLOW, F
  History of last 18 transfers of control.
- LABELS, L
  List of labels with frequency of encounter.
- ENTRIES, E
  List of entry-names with frequency of call.
- REPORT, R
  Statistics on run (time, core usage, auxiliary I/O operations, etc.)
- UNREAD, U
  List of first 5 or fewer unread data cards.
- Depth
  An integer giving limit on number of active blocks for B, S and A dump options. If 0 is given, depth is unlimited.

Supplied default DUMP options are (B,S,F,L,E,R,U,0).

DUMPE, DUMPE=(d1,d2,...), NODUMPE, DE (on *PL/C only)
Produce post-mortem dump only if error was encountered

during execution.
Supplied default DUMPE options are (B,S,F,L,E,R,U,O).

DUMPS, NODUMPS, DS, |NO|DUMPS=(d1,d2,...), |NO|DUMPS=1112...
(on *PL/C only) Specifies all three of DUMP, DUMPE, and DUMPT.

DUMPT, DUMPT=(d1,d2,...), NODUMPT, DT (on *PL/C only)
Produce post-mortem dump only if execution was terminated by an error.
Supplied default DUMPT options are (B,S,F,L,E,R,U,O).

ERRORS=(c,r), E (on *PL/C only)
Suppress execution if c or more compile errors.
If c=0 suppress execution unconditionally.
Terminate execution after r runtime errors.
If r=0 there is no limit on runtime errors.
Supplied default c=50, r=50.

ETIME=(m,s.h), ET (on *PL/C only)
Time limit for execution.
m is for minutes; assumed zero if omitted.
s is seconds; assumed zero if omitted.
h is hundredths of seconds; assumed zero if omitted.

FLAGE, FLAGW, FE, FW
FLAGW prints both warnings and error messages.
FLAGE suppresses warnings.

HDRPG, NOHDRPG, H (on *PL/C only)
Print header/ separator page before program.

ID='name', I (on *PL/C only)
Program identification name (20 characters maximum).
Supplied default name = '*** NO ID ***'

LINES=n, L (on *PL/C only)
Maximum number of lines to be printed.
Supplied default n=2000.

LINECT=n, LC
Lines to be printed per page during compilation. Supplied default n=60. (Use PAGESIZE option of OPEN statement to control runtime page size.)

MCALL, NOMCALL, MC
Print macro calls.

MONITOR, NOMONITOR, M, |NO|MONITOR=(d1,d2,..), |NO|MONITOR=1112..
The MONITOR option specifies that an error message is to be given whenever a program uses a MONITORed feature. The error will count toward the compile or run-time error limit, and the standard PL/C correction will be applied.
MONITOR options are given below. For d1,d2,... use the single-letter or full-name form. For 1112... only the

single-letter form may be used.

BNDRY, B

Monitor strings and comments extending over card boundaries.

UDEF, U (on *PL/C only)

Monitor use of uninitialized variables.

SUBRG, S (on *PL/C only)

Monitor subscripts (i.e. disallow the NOSUBRG condition prefix).

AUTO, A (on *PL/C only)

Monitor implied arithmetic/string conversion.

DFLTS, D (on *PL/C only)

Equivalent to specifing the installation defaults.

Only the listed options are altered (i.e. turned on or off) <u>except</u> when MONITOR is used on the *PL/C card. In this case, the designated options are turned on, and all others are turned off.

For compatibility with previous releases of PL/C, the BNDRY, UDEF, and FREE options will be accepted outside of a MONITOR specification.

MTEXT, <u>NOMTEXT</u>, MT

Print macro text expansion.

M91, <u>NOM91</u>, M9 (on *PL/C only)

Generate code to run on 360 Model 91.

<u>OPLIST</u>, NOOPLIST, O

Print list of options in effect.

PAGES=n, P (on *PL/C only)

Maximum number of pages to be printed.
Supplied default n=30.

SORMGIN=(s,e), SORMGIN=(s,e,c), SM

Establish source card margins:

s is first column scanned; supplied default s=2.
e is last column scanned; supplied default e=72.
c is carriage control column; supplied default c=1.

<u>SOURCE</u>, NOSOURCE, S

Print source program listing.

TIME=(m,s.h), T (on *PL/C only)

Time limit (compilation + execution).

m is minutes; assumed 0 if omitted.
s is seconds; assumed 0 if omitted.
h is hundredths of seconds; assumed zero if omitted.

Supplied default is TIME=(0,15.00)

The CTIME, ETIME, and TIME options serve to limit the compilation, execution, and job times, respectively. The order in which the options are specified is irrelevant. The time limit for the compilation phase is equal to the CTIME limit if it is specified, or to the TIME limit if it is not. The CTIME limit must not be greater than the TIME limit. If ETIME is specified, the time limit for the execution phase is the smaller of the ETIME limit and the TIME limit less the actual compilation time. The ETIME limit may not be greater than the TIME limit. If both CTIME and ETIME limits are specified, but TIME isn't, then CTIME is simply the compilation limit, and ETIME is the execution limit.

TABSIZE=n, TS (on *PL/C only)
Determines the amount of PL/C region allocated to symbol table. N given in fullwords.
Supplied default is 1/2 of usable area, up to 32768 fullwords.

XREF, NOXREF, X
Produce cross-reference listing.

B.3 Card Formats

For all types of cards the contents of columns 1 and 2 may be significant to the "operating system" and cause a card to be intercepted and never reach PL/C. The characters // in columns 1 and 2 are significant to most IBM systems and the characters /* are significant to some. Both combinations should be avoided in columns 1-2 of all cards (data cards as well as program). A common error is to begin a comment in column 1. If a card with // in 1-2 reaches PL/C the following happens:

1. If 3-80 are blank it is treated as an end-of-file and it terminates the program. PL/C expects either a *PL/C card to begin a new program or to have the job ended by the operating system. Any number of consecutive // cards with 3-80 blank are equivalent to one.
2. If 3-80 are not blank the entire card is ignored.

B.3.1 Control Cards

Control cards have * in column 1. (Some installations may use another character instead of *.) The control keyword -- PL/C, PROCESS, OPTIONS, DATA, MACRO, MEND or INCLUDE -- begins in 2. The continuation of a control card has * in 1 and blanks in 2-3. Control cards are not affected by SORMGIN. Options on control cards can be in any order, separated by blanks and/or commas, but not split over a card boundary.

B.3.2 Program Cards

1. The default card field for source statements is 2-72. The contents of 73-80 are ignored, but appear on the source listing.

1a. Columns to the right of the right margin (default 73-80) can be used for identification and numbering. A four-character abbreviation of the program name can be punched in 73-76 and automatically duplicated from one card to the next (see Appendix B.3.4). Cards should be serially numbered in 77-80 with initial numbers in intervals of ten or more to leave room for later insertions. For example, a sorting program might be identified and initially numbered:

```
SORT0010
SORT0020
SORT0030
...
```

Card numbering seems unnecessary until you or the computer operator drops one of your decks.

2. The default position for the specification of carriage control for the listing of the source program is column 1. Carriage control characters do not appear on the source listing. Only 5 of the USASI codes are recognized for this purpose:

blank	space 1 line before printing (normal mode)
0	space 2 lines before printing
-	space 3 lines before printing
+	do not space before printing (overprint)
1	skip to channel 1 (page eject)

2a. If any character other than these five appears in column 1 PL/C assumes that text accidentally began in 1 instead of 2.

3. The default source card format can be altered by specifying SORMGIN on the *PL/C, *PROCESS or *OPTIONS card. The form is:

```
SORMGIN = (s,e,c)
    where: s is the leftmost column to be included
           e  is the rightmost column to be included
           c  is the column for carriage control
```

The maximum column specification is 100, and the carriage control column must be outside of the s,e field. If SORMGIN is used paragraphs 1 and 2 above must be altered accordingly. The correction in 2a only applies when s=2 and c=1.

4. When the default MONITOR=(BNDRY) is in effect PL/C does not permit any element to be split over a card boundary. That is, keywords, identifiers, constants and <u>comments</u> cannot start on one card and continue on the next. This limits the length of literals, and means that for long comments each card must be a separate comment.

When NOMONITOR=(BNDRY) is specified, literals and comments may be continued over a card boundary (as in PL/I). The maximum length of a literal is then 256 characters. There is no limit on the length of a comment. Note that the card boundary is as defined by the SORMGIN option and not the physical card boundary. For example, with the default SORMGIN of (2,72,1) column 2 directly follows 72 of the previous card -- no blank is supplied. Note also that NOMONITOR=(BNDRY) applies only to literals and comments. In PL/C one still cannot continue a keyword, an identifier or an arithmetic constant over a card boundary.

B.3.3 Data Cards

The card field for data cards is always 1 to 80. Data cards are not affected by the SORMGIN or BNDRY options. Data cards are considered to be a continuous stream of characters and the card boundary is of no significance. That is, column 1 of a card directly follows 80 of the previous card, and any element may be continued over a card boundary.

B.3.4 Format Control on the Keypunch

The use of program format to emphasize the structure of a program requires a convenient means of indenting. The keypunch offers a facility comparable to the "tab stops" on a typewriter for this purpose. The "stops" are set by a control card that is placed around a drum in the upper center of the IBM 029 keypunch. When the "star wheels" are lowered onto the face of this drum (by depressing the left side of the toggle switch just below the drum), pushing the SKIP key on the keyboard will cause the card to advance to the next "stop" position, specified by a field-starting punch as shown below.

The drum control card also controls automatic skipping, automatic duplication (copying from one card to the next), and the alpha/numeric shift of the keyboard. Consider the control card to be divided into sets of adjacent columns called "fields". One character is used to start a field (in the left-most column), and another to continue the field:

Type of field:	To start:	To continue:
alpha shift	1	A
numeric shift	blank	&
automatic skip	-	&
automatic duplicate	/	A

The alpha/numeric shift in the control card can be overridden by the ALPHA and NUMERIC keys on the keyboard. For the automatic skip and automatic duplicate to be effective the AUTO SKIP DUP switch at the left top of the keyboard must be ON (in the up position).

The following is a generally useful drum control card:

1; automatic skip
2-5, 6-9, 10-13, 14-17, ...; alpha fields with stops every four columns
73-76; automatic duplicate (for program identification)
77-80; numeric (for card serial number)

The control card would be punched as follows:

```
                   1         2         3         4
columns   1234567890123456789012345678901234567890
cont.char -1AAA1AAA1AAA1AAA1AAA1AAA1AAA1AAA1AAA1AA

          4         5         6         7         8
columns   1234567890123456789012345678901234567890
cont.char AAAAAAAAAAAAAAAAAAAAAAAAAAAAAAAA/AA &&&&
```

With this drum card, to punch a PL/C control card with a * in column 1 you have to momentarily turn off the AUTO SKIP DUP switch to suppress the skip over column 1.

If you do not want to use columns 73-80 for card identification, columns 73-80 of the control card would be punched as follows, to automatically release the card as soon as column 72 is punched, and feed a new card:

```
                                            7      8
columns                                     34567890
cont.character                              -&&&&&&&
```

Without an automatic skip or duplicate in column 73 it is easy to accidentally continue punching program text beyond column 72 and the result can be mystifying. Characters in 73-80 are not scanned by PL/C (unless directed to by the SORMGIN option), but since they are printed it is not obvious that they have been ignored. This often produces errors for a statement that looks correct on the listing.

B.4 Efficient Programming in PL/C

PL/C was designed to emphasize speed of compilation rather than execution. If execution is substantial it may be worthwhile running under the IBM Optimizing Compiler once the program has been thoroughly tested. However, if a program is to be run under PL/C and the execution time is significant, a number of options and devices can be employed to improve execution speed. These all have the effect of suppressing or disabling diagnostic provisions that are normally compiled into PL/C programs. While this will improve execution speed it obviously reduces the degree of protection and the amount of information provided. Execution speed will be increased by each of the following (if these are not already the defaults at your installation):

1. Disable the FLOW condition. This is done by giving a (NOFLOW): prefix for each external procedure. Even if the FLOW events are not being printed (as a result of execution of a FLOW statement) the tracing code is present and active if the FLOW condition is enabled. (Similarly the CHECK condition must be disabled -- by removing CHECK prefixes. Suppressing printing with the NOCHECK statement does not eliminate the checking code.)

2. Disable the SUBSCRIPTRANGE condition. This is done by giving a (NOSUBSCRIPTRANGE): prefix on each external procedure. This is only possible if the NOMONITOR=(SUBRG) sub-option is specified. Note that some installations inhibit (overide) this sub-option since subscript testing is vital to ensure the integrity of the compiler. If you can run in NOMONITOR=(SUBRG) mode, the elimination of subscript testing will make a substantial improvement in the execution speed of a program with frequent references to subscripted variables.

3. Disable the SIZE condition. This is done by giving a (NOSIZE): prefix on each external procedure.

4. Specify the MONITOR=(UDEF) sub-option. This will eliminate the code required to test for the use of uninitialized variables. All variables (including strings) will be initialized to (hex) zero.

In order to limit the amount of printing from a PL/C program, consider the use of the CMPRS, NODUMP, FLAGE, NOHDRPG, NOOPLIST and NOSOURCE options. To reduce the amount of printing during execution of the program, consider using the PUT OFF and PUT ON statements in the sections that are not of current interest.

Because of the differences in internal representation in PL/C, certain operations are relatively inefficient (in comparison to PL/I). These are <u>RECORD I/O, bit-string operations</u>, and the <u>UNSPEC and TRANSLATE built-in functions</u>. To the extent that a program can avoid use of these features, its execution speed relative to PL/I will be improved.

References

References on PL/I, PL/C, PL/CT and PL/CS

IBM: OS PL/I Optimizing Compiler: Language Reference Manual, Form GC33-0009

IBM System 360 PL/I Reference Manual, Form C28-8201

IBM System 360 OS PL/I-F Programmer's Guide, Form C28-6594

IBM System 360 DOS/TOS PL/I Programmer's Guide, Form GC24-9005

IBM PL/I Language Specifications, Form C28-6571

PL/C User's Guide, Release 7.6, Department of Computer Science, Cornell University, 1977

PL/CT User's Guide, Release 2/7.5, Department of Computer Science, Cornell University, 1975

PL/C and PL/CT Installation Instructions, Release 7.6, Department of Computer Science, Cornell University, 1977

Constable, R. and J. Donahue, "An Elementary Formal Semantics of the Programming Language PL/CS", Technical Report 76-271, Department of Computer Science, Cornell University, 1976

Constable, R. L. and M. J. O'Donnell, A Programming Logic - with an Introduction to the PL/CV Verifier, Winthrop, 1978

Conway, R., and D. Gries, Primer on Structured Programming, Winthrop, 1976

Conway, R., Programming for Poets: A Gentle Introduction Using PL/I, Winthrop, 1978

Conway, R., A Primer on Disciplined Programming, Winthrop, 1978

Conway, R. and R. Constable, "PL/CS -- A Disciplined Subset of PL/I", Technical Report TR 76-293, Department of Computer Science, Cornell University, 1976

Conway, R. W. and T. R. Wilcox, "Design and Implementation of a Diagnostic Compiler for PL/I", Communications of the ACM, March 1973

Germain, Clarence B., PL/I for the IBM 360, Prentice-Hall, 1972

Hughes, Joan K., PL/I Programming, Wiley, 1973

Pollack, S. V. and T. D. Sterling, A Guide to PL/I, Holt Rinehart Winston, 1969

References on Programming

Aho, A. V., J. E. Hopcroft and J. D. Ullman, The Design and Analysis of Computer Algorithms, Addison-Wesley, 1974

Alagic, S. and M. A. Arbib, The Design of Well-Structured and Correct Programs, Springer-Verlag, 1978

Dahl, O. J., E. W. Dijkstra and C. A. R. Hoare, Structured Programming, Academic Press, 1972

Dijkstra, E. W., A Discipline of Programming, Prentice-Hall, 1976

Dijkstra, E. W., "GO TO Statement Considered Harmful", Communications of the ACM, March 1968

Dijkstra, E. W., Notes on Structured Programming, Eindhoven University, 1970 (also in Dahl, Dijkstra and Hoare)

Dijkstra, E. W., A Short Introduction to the Art of Programming, Eindhoven University, 1971

Gries, D. (editor), Programming Methodology: a collection of articles by members of IFIP WG2.3. Springer Verlag, 1978.

Kernighan, B. W. and P. J. Plauger, Elements of Programming Style, McGraw-Hill, 1974

Kernighan, B. W. and P. J. Plauger, "Programming Style: Examples and Counterexamples", ACM Computing Surveys, December 1974

Knuth, D. E., "Structured Programming with GO TO Statement", ACM Computing Surveys, December 1974

McGowan, C. L. and J. R. Kelly, Top-Down Structured Programming Techniques, Petrocelli/Charter 1975

Mills, H., "Top Down Programming in Large Systems", in Rustin (ed.), Debugging Techniques in Large Systems, Prentice-Hall, 1971

Minsky, M., Computation: Finite and Infinite Machines, Prentice-Hall, 1967

Polya, G., How to Solve It, Princeton, 1945.
(Also excerpted in Newman, The World of Mathematics, Vol. 3, Simon & Schuster, 1956)

Van Tassel, D., Program Style, Design, Efficiency, Debugging and Testing, Prentice-Hall, 1974

Weinberg, G. M., The Psychology of Computer Programming, Van Nostrand, 1971

Wirth, N., Algorithms + Data Structures = Programs, Prentice-Hall, 1976

Wirth, N., "On the Composition of Well-Structured Programs", ACM Computing Surveys, December 1974

Wirth, N., "Program Development by Stepwise Refinement", Communications of the ACM, April 1971

Wirth, N., Systematic Programming: An Introduction, Prentice-Hall, 1973

Yeh, R. (editor), Current Trends in Programming Methodology, Prentice-Hall, 1977

Yohe, J. M., "An Overview of Programming Practices", ACM Computing Surveys, December 1974

References on Database Systems

ASAP System Reference Manual, Compuvisor Inc., Ithaca N. Y.

Brightman, R. W., and J. R. Clark, RPG Programming, MacMillan, 1970

Date, C. J., An Introduction to Database Systems (2nd Edition), Addison-Wesley, 1977

Kroenke, D., Database Processing, SRA, 1977

MARK IV Reference Manual, Informatics Inc., Sherman Oaks, CA.

Martin, J., Computer Data-base Organization, Prentice-Hall, 1975

Martin, J., Principles of Data-base Management, Prentice-Hall, 1976

Maurer, W. D., and T. G. Lewis, "Hash Table Methods", Computing Surveys, March 1975

Salton, G., Dynamic Information and Library Processing, Prentice-Hall, 1975

Severance, D. G., "Identifier Search Mechanisms: A Survey and Generalized "model", Computing Surveys, September 1974

Wiederhold, G., Database Design, McGraw-Hill, 1977

References on Mathematical Problems

See Section IX.4.

References on Statistical Systems

Barr, A. J, J. H. Goodnight, J. P. Sall, J. T. Helwig, A User's Guide to SAS 76, SAS Institute, Inc., Raleigh, N. C., 1976.

Nie, N. H., C. H. Hull, J. G. Jenkins, K. Steinbrenner, D. H. Bent, SPSS - Statistical Package for the Social Sciences, 2nd Edition, McGraw-Hill, 1975

Index

A format item, 68, 663
A option, see ATR, ARRAYS, AUTO, and ASSERT options
Abbreviations, 695
ABS function, 44, 57, 657
Absolute error, 557
Abstraction, 152
Access method, 535
Accounting problem, 226
Accumulated sums, 559
Ackermann's function, 362
Active block, 323
Active procedure, 290
Adaptive trapezoidal rule, 584
Adaptive quadrature, 583
ADD function, 657
Addition, 40, 639
Address, 12
AL option, 699
ALGOL, 6
Algorithm, 199
  exponential, 460
  linear, 460
  logarithmic, 460
  quadratic, 460
    source of ideas for, 262-270
  stable, 579
ALIST option, 699
ALL function, 58, 660
ALL option, see PUT ALL
ALLOCATE, 598
Allocation,
  sequential, 493
  linked list, 495
ALLOCATION function, 661
Analysis of a problem, 4-6, 196
Ancestor, of a node, 474
And, 53
ANY function, 58, 660
Approximation, 565-571
  by iteration, 569
  by polynomial, 565
AREA condition, 650
Argument, 43, 287
  array, 295
  constant, 294
  dummy, 293, 645
  expression, 294
  matching, 287, 291, 644
  with different type, 293
Arithmetic expressions, 39-45
Arithmetic operators, 40, 639
Array-ref, 595
Array expressions, 56-58, 642
ARRAY option, see PUT ARRAY
Arrays, 23
  as arguments, 295
  as parameters, 295
  assignment to, 56-58, 598
  built-in functions for, 660
  cross section of, 637
  declaration of, 23, 25
  dynamic, 335
  expressions, 56-58, 642
  extent of, see DIM function
  external assignment to, 77
  input-output, 77
  mode of, 480
  of labels, 99
  of structures, 30-31
  referring to, 24, 636
  space for, 455
ARRAYS dump option, 699
ASAP, 551
Arrows, parameter, 288-293, 645
ASSERT statement, 414, 598, 692
Assertions, 414
Assignment, 34-39, 599, 692
  BY NAME, 59
  from external data, see GET
  logical, 50
  multiple, 36
  swimming, 354
  to arrays, 56, 599
  to scalar variables, 34-39,

600
to strings, 45
to subscripted variables, 37-39
to structures, 58, 601
ATAN function, 44, 658
ATAND function, 658
ATANH function, 658
ATR option, 82, 387, 699
Attention, 424, 686
ATTN_FLAG, 424
ATTN key, 687
Attribute listing, 82, 374
Attributes, 595
AUTOMATIC, 302, 628
base, 626
BINARY, 620, 628
BIT, 620, 628
BUILTIN attribute, 629
CHAR, 20, 620, 628
CHAR VARYING, 20, 620, 628
COMPLEX, 634
DECIMAL, 620, 628
default, 21, 627
ENTRY, 629
EXTERNAL, 303, 630
FILE, 630
FIXED, 20, 620, 628, 630
FIXED BINARY, 620, 628
FIXED DECIMAL, 620, 628
FLOAT, 20, 620, 628, 631
FLOAT BINARY, 620, 628
FLOAT DECIMAL, 620, 628
GENERIC, 631
INITIAL, 26, 302, 626, 631
INPUT, 632
INTERNAL, 630
LABEL, 99, 632
length, 20, 628, 633
mode, 626
OUTPUT, 632
precision, 626, 633
PRINT, 633
READ, see READONLY
READONLY, 29
REAL, 634
RECURSIVE, 346
RETURNS, 316, 634
scale, 626
scope, 626, 630
STATIC, 302, 628
storage class, 626
type, 13-19, 626
VAR, see VARYING
VARYING, 20, 620
AUTOMATIC attribute, 628
Automatic diagnostic services, 370
Automatic indentation, 138-139
Automatic repair of errors, 373
Automatic storage, 302, 456
Automatic variable, 302
Automatic verification, 447
AUTO option, 701
AUXIO option, 699
AVAIL list, 497
Average case analysis, 461
Averaging program, 165-169

b̸, 16
B format item, 663
B option, 699, 701
Back substitution, 575
Backing up, 259-262
Base, 508, 555
conversion, 562, 644
Base attributes, 626
BASIC, 6
Basic step, 457
BEGIN block, 602
BINARY attribute, 628
BINARY function, 657
Binary search, 263, 440, 462
Binary tree, 516, 473
Bit, 19, 454
BIT attribute, 20, 620, 628
BIT function, 655
Bit string, 13, 19
Bit string operators, 641
Bit-string variables, see Variables, bit
Bit values, 19
BIT VARYING attribute, 620, 628
Blank character, 16, 597
extension on right with, 52
use of, 597
Block,
active, 322
nested, 323
external, 323
internal, 322
BEGIN, 330, 602
physical, 534
tracing execution of, 327
use of, 337
Blocking, 534
BLOCKS dump option, 699

Block structure, 330
BNDRY options, 701
Body,
  of a loop, 103-108
  of a compound statement, 94
  of a procedure, 285
BOOL function, 655
Boolean operations, 53, 641
Boolean values, 19
BOTTOM sub-command, 685
Bottom-up testing, 380
Boundaries, see SORMGIN option
Bounds, see Declarations, arrays
Branch, of a tree, 473
Branching, see GOTO
Breakpoint, 424, 687
Brother, 517
Bubble sort, 261
Buffering, 534
Built-in functions, 43, 655, 696
BUILTIN attribute, 629
Business data processing, 529
BY NAME, 59, 601
Byte, 454

C format item, 663
C option, 699
Call, of a macro, 413, 671
CALL statement, 287, 603, 692
  argument of, see Argument
  execution of, 289
  nesting of, 299
Card boundaries, see SORMGIN option
Card deck, 8
Card formats, 702
  control cards, 702
  data cards, 703
  drum card, see Drum card
  program cards, 703
Card reader, 71
Carriage control characters, 703
CEIL function, 55, 57, 657
CHANGE sub-command, 685
CHAR attribute, 20, 620, 628
CHAR function, 655
CHAR VARYING attribute, 20, 620, 628
CHARACTER attribute, see CHAR
Character, 16-18
  blank, 16
  collating sequence of, 52
  constant, see Literal
  legal, 52
  ordering of, 52
  string, 16
Character-valued variables, see string variables
CHECK command, 690
CHECK condition, 650
CHECK prefix, 403, 406
CHECK statement, 406, 603, 690
Chess-playing program, 356
Circular list, 510
CLOSE statement, 603
CMNTS option, 410, 699
CMPRS option, 699
CMS commands, 680
COBOL, 6, 44, 549
Coercion of values, 42, 55, 643
COL format item, 75, 664
Collating sequence, 52
COLUMN format item, 75, 664
Command mode, 680
Commands,
  PL/CT debug, 688
  CMS, 680
Comments, 3, 134, 597, 695
  in declarations, 137, 143-146
  pseudo-comments, 410
  statement-comments, 135, 151-155
  in PL/C, PL/CS, 138
  useless, 138, 145-146
  user instructions, 137, 143-146
COMMENTS option, 699
Comparison, 640
  of characters, 52, 640
  of values, 51-53
Comparison of PL/I and PL/C, 666
Compiler, 8
  for PL/C, 669
Compiling, 8,81
COMPLEX attribute, 634
COMPLEX function, 657
COMPLEX pseudo-variable, 638
Component, of a structure, 29
Compound condition, 54
Compound statement, 94, 604, 693
  indentation conventions

for, 94
termination of,
Concatenation, 47, 640
Condition, 50, 54
CONDITION condition, 651
Conditional execution, 88-98
Conditional statement, see IF, SELECT
nesting of, 95-97
Conditions, 649-653
AREA, 650
CHECK, 650
CONDITION, 651
CONV, 651
CONVERSION, 651
ENDFILE, 120, 158, 651
ENDPAGE, 651
ERROR, 652
FINISH, 652
FIXEDOVERFLOW, 652
FLOW, 652
FOFL, 652
KEY, 650
NAME, 652
OFL, 653
OVERFLOW, 653
PENDING, 650
RECORD, 650
SIZE, 653
STRG, 653
STRINGRANGE, 653
SUBRG, 653
SUBSCRIPTRANGE, 653
TRANSMIT, 650
UFL, 654
UNDEFINEDFILE, 653
UNDERFLOW, 654
UNDF, 653
ZDIV, 654
ZERODIVIDE, 654
CONJG function, 657
Constant, 13, 597
algorithm, 460
as an argument, 294
decimal, 13-15
integer, see Integer
named, 28
string, see Literal
Consultants, 383
Control cards, 81, 702
*DATA, 81, 697
*INCLUDE, 697
*MACRO, 697
*MEND, 697
*PLC, 81, 697
*PL/C, 81
*PLCS, 697
*PROCESS, 697
*OPTIONS, 697
Control-item, 68
Control section, 339
CONV condition, 651
Conversion, between bases, 563
CONVERSION condition, 651
Conversion of values, 42, 55, 643
Conway, J., 386
COPY option, 606
Correctness, 9, 432
confirmation of, 9, 369
meaning of, 366
proof of, 432
functional, 366
syntactic, 366
testing for, 9
verification of, 447
COS function, 44, 565, 658
COSD function, 658
COSH function, 658
Cosine function, see COS
COUNT function, 661
CP option, see CMPRS option
Cramer's rule, 576
Creation of a variable, 19-31
Cross reference listing, 82, 374
Cross section of array, 637
CT option, see CTIME option
CTIME option, 699
Current value, 13

D option, 699, 701
Data base, 529
network model, 542
relational model, 542
programming language for, 549
*DATA card, 81, 697
Data cards, format of, 73, 703
DATA command, 688
Data conversion, 643
DATAEND, see ENDFILE
Data format, 73
Data item, 68
Data list, 80
Data refinement, 257
DATA statement, see GET, PUT
Data structure, 487

choice of, 200
DATE function, 661
DBC prompt, 426
DCL, see DECLARE
Debug commands, 426, 428, 688
DEC, see DECIMAL
DECIMAL attribute, 628
Decimal base, 508
Decimal numbers, 13, 597
DECIMAL function, 657
DE option, 699
Declaration, 619-621, 692
ENTRY, 317
form, 19
comments for, 137, 146
grouping of, 143-146
implicit, 21
integers, 19
numbers, 19
of character variables, 20
of a function, 316
of a parameter, 281-283
of arrays, 23-25, 619
of string variables, 20
of structures, 29, 621
organization of, 143
position of, 280
DECLARE, see Declaration
Default attributes, 19-21
Default on-unit, 120-123
Default options,
Default precision, 14
DEFAULT statement, 605
Definition, recursive, 346
of a function, 316
of a macro, 670
of a procedure, 280, 316, 346, 623
of an entry-name, 622
DELAY, 605
DELETE command, 684
DELETE, 605
DEPTH dump option, 699
Deque, 491
Direct access file, 548
Descendant, of a node, 474
Design considerations, 4-6, 252-272
Design of a program, 4, 252-272
Design of test cases, 376
Detection of errors, 370
Determinant, 576
Development, of a program, 4-6
examples of, see Examples of Development
ideas for, 262-271
phases of, 4, 195, 202-207
top-down, 5, 203, 252-256
Devices, storage, 62, 75, 533
DFLTS option, 701
Diagnostic services, 403, 410-412, 370
Dijkstra, E. W., 445
DIM function, 660
Dimension, 25
Dimensional limits in PL/C, 669
Display, see PUT
DISPLAY, 605
DIVIDE function, 657
Division, 40, 639
DO, see compound statement
indexed, 108, 150, 609
DO group, see Iterative statement
DOS-PL/I, 593
DO UNTIL, 106, 150, 609
DO WHILE, 104, 150, 609
DOWN sub-command, 685
Double precision, 555
Doubly linked list, 512
Driving routine, 380-381
Drum card, 704
DS option, see DUMPS option
DT option, see DUMPT option
Dummy argument, 293, 645
Dummy procedures, 382
Dump, 83, 374, 409, 699
DUMP option, 83, 374, 699
DUMPE option, 374
DUMPS option, 700
DUMPT option, 700
Dynamic arrays, 335
Dynamic version of a program, 147, 432

E format item, 69, 664
E option, 699, 700
EDIT, see GET, PUT
command, 681
mode, 680, 684
sub-commands, 680
Editor, CMS, 680
Elimination,
forward, 575
Gaussian, 574
ELSE, see IF
Empty string, 18, 47

Empty tree, 516
END, see block, compound statement, iterative statement, loop, procedure definition, SELECT
END delimiter, 618
ENDFILE condition, 120, 158, 651
End node, 473
ENDPAGE condition, 651
ENTRIES dump option, 699
Entry-name, 595, 622
  as a parameter, 646
ENTRY attribute, 629
ENTRY declaration, 317
Entry definition, 622
Entry-point, 622
ERASE command, 681
ERF function, 659
ERFC function, 659
ERROR condition, 652
ERROR_FLAG, 424
Errors, 365
  absolute, 557
  automatic repair of, 373
  detection of, 370
  during execution, 372
  handling input errors, 271
  in floating point, 14
  invalid operations, 372
  levels, 366
  locating, 378
  messages, 82
  relative, 557
  roundoff, 555, 557
  truncation, 555
  syntax, 371
  types of, 368
ERRORS option, 700
ETIME option, 700
ET option, see ETIME option
Evaluating programs, 453
Evaluating expressions, 358, 525
Examples of program development,
  Accounting problem, 226
  Binary search, 263
  Bubble sort, 261
  KWIC index, 468
  Listing program, 208
  List search, 214
  Sorting, 222
  Successive maxima, 265
  Symbol scanning, 237-245
  Text editing, 266
Examples of programs, see also Examples of program development
  Binary search, 440, 462
  Exponentiation, 441
  Expression evaluation, 358
  Factorial, 346
  Game of Life, 386
  Heap sort, 473-478
  Insertion sort, 440
  Linear search, 297
  Merge sort, 363
  Mode calculation, 480-481
  Partition, 443
  Primeness test, 464
  Quicksort, 353, 442
  Successive minima, 434
  Swapping values, 37, 276
  Swimming assignment, 354
  Towers of Hanoi, 351, 363
Execution, 80-87
  conditional, 88-93
  of a program, 8, 80-87
  order of, 459
  output from, 82, 85, 87
  repetitive, 103-125
  recursive, 350
  sequential, 86, 147-158
  tracing, 86, 123, 327, 350
Execution speed, 457
Exit from terminal, see LOGOFF, QUIT, STOP
  from loop, 114, 118-123
EXIT statement, 605
EXP function, 44, 659
Exponent, 13, 555
Exponential algorithm, 460
Exponential notation, 13
Exponentiation, 40, 440, 640
Expressions, 39-57, 639
  arithmetic, 39, 639
  array, 642
  as arguments, 294
  as subscripts, 24
  evaluation of, 31, 358, 525
  functions in, 43
  in output, 67
  logical, 50
  operators for, 40, 47
  mixed type, 41
  string, 45-53
  structure, 642
Extending with blanks, 48, 52

Extent, see DIM function
EXTERNAL attribute, 303, 630
External block, 323
External procedure, 273-282
  placement of, 280

F format item, 69, 664
F option, see FLOW option
Factorial function, 346
  algorithm, 460
False, see Values
Family tree, 516
Father, of a node, 517, 474
FE option, 700
FETCH, 605
Fibonacci numbers, 362
Field, of a node, 489
FIFO, 492
File, 529-552
  direct access, 548
  indexed, 539
  logical, 538
  sequential, 538, 547
  update to, 546
  structure of, 538
File-name, 613, 645
FILE attribute, 630
FILE option, 75
File processing,
  characteristics of, 529-552
FINISH condition, 652
Finite sequence, 488
FIXED attribute, 20, 619, 630
FIXED BINARY attribute, 620
FIXED DECIMAL attribute, 619, 630
FIXED division, 41
FIXED function, 44, 55, 657
FIXEDOVERFLOW condition, 652
FLAGE option, 700
FLAGW option, 700
FLOAT attribute, 20, 620, 630
FLOAT BINARY attribute, 620
FLOAT DECIMAL attribute, 620, 630
FLOAT function, 44, 55, 657
Floating point error, 14
Floating point format, 14
Floating point notation, 14
Floating point number, 13, 554
FLOOR function, 44, 55, 57, 657
FLOW condition, 652
FLOW option, see PUT FLOW, 699
FLOW prefix, 407
FLOW statement, 407, 605, 689
Flow trace, 403
FOFL condition, 652
Ford, 483
FOR ALL, see ASSERT
Format, 662
  of a job, 596
  of a program, 80, 596
  of cards, 702
  of input data, 607
Format control on the keypunch, 704
Format list, see Items, format
FOR SOME, see ASSERT
FORTRAN, 6, 22, 44
Fraction, 555
FREE, 606
Forward elimination, 575
Fulkerson, 483
Function, 314-320, 624
  argument of, 43
  built-in, 43, 696
  conditions, 660
  definition of, 316
  logical, 343
  ENTRY declaration for, 317
  reference to, 317
  side effects, 318
  user-defined, 316
Functional notation, 43
Functions,
  ABS, 44, 57, 657
  ADD, 657
  ALL, 58, 660
  ALLOCATION, 661
  ANY, 58, 660
  array, 660
  ATAN, 44, 658
  ATAND, 658
  ATANH, 658
  BINARY, 657
  BIT, 655
  BOOL, 655
  CEIL, 55, 57, 657
  CHAR, 655
  COMPLEX, 657
  CONJG, 657
  COS, 44, 565, 658
  COSD, 658
  COSH, 658
  cosine, see COS
  COUNT, 661

DATE, 661
DECIMAL, 657
DIM, 660
DIVIDE, 657
ERF, 659
ERFC, 659
EXP, 44, 659
factorial, 346
FIXED, 44, 55, 657
FLOAT, 44, 55, 657
FLOOR, 44, 55, 657
HBOUND, 660
HIGH, 655
IMAG, 657
INDEX, 49, 655
LBOUND, 660
LENGTH, 49, 655
LINENO, 661
LOG, 44, 659
LOG10, 659
LOG2, 463, 659
LOW, 655
MAX, 43, 58, 657
MIN, 44, 657
MOD, 44, 658
MULTIPLY, 657
POLY, 660
PRECISION, 657
PROD, 58, 660
RAND, 659
REAL, 658
REPEAT, 656
ROUND, 658
SIGN, 658
SIN, 44, 57, 659
SIND, 659
SINH, 659
SQRT, 43, 569, 659
STRING, 656
SUBSTR, 47, 656
SUM, 57, 660
TAN, 44, 659
TAND, 44, 659
TANH, 659
TIME, 661
TRANSLATE, 656
TRUNC, 658
UNSPEC, 656
VERIFY, 49, 656
FW option, 700

Game of Life, 386
Gaussian elimination, 574
with partial pivoting, 576
GCD, 362, 451
GENERIC attribute, 631
GET statement, 71, 606, 693
GET DATA, 73, 607
GET EDIT, 74, 607
GET LIST, 71, 607
with STRING option, 76, 606
Global variables, 324
GO, see GOTO
GOTO command, 691
GO TO, 116, 157, 608, 694
GOTO statement, see GOTO
Greatest Common Divisor, see GCD
Grouping declarations, 143-146

H option, see HDRPG option
Habits, testing, 385
HALT, 608
Handling input errors, 271
Hanoi, towers of, 351, 363
Hashing, 539
HBOUND function, 660
HDRPG option, 700
Header, 508, 512
Heap, 474
Heap sort, 473
Hexadecimal, 562
HIGH function, 655
Hierarchical structure, 151-155
Horner's scheme, 568

I option, 700
ID option, 700
Identifier, 11, 596
reserved, 12
scope of, 324, 635
IF, 88, 95, 608, 694
indentation for, 89, 99, 150
IGNORE command, 429, 609, 690
IGNORE, 426
IGNORE_RESET, 426
Ill-conditioned problem, 579
Ill-defined problem, 482
IMAG function, 657
IMAG pseudo-variable, 638
Imaginary number, 598
Implicit declaration, 19-21
Impossibly large problem, 483
Improper subscripts, 38
*INCLUDE card, 697
Increment of a loop, see Loop
Indentation conventions, 150-

153
automatic, 138
for BEGIN blocks, 330
for compound statements, 94, 150
for IF, 88, 95, 150
for loops, 105, 108, 150
for repetition unit, 105-108, 150
for conditional statement, 88, 150
for SELECT, 91, 150
Indexed file, 539
Indexed loop, see Loop
Indexed sequential file, 539
INDEX function, 49, 655
Index variable, 108
Infix notation, 526
Information retrieval, 545
INIT, see INITIAL
INITIAL attribute, 26, 302, 631
Initial value, see Initial attributes
Initialization,
of variables, 26-28
Inorder traversal, 519
Input, see GET
Input data format, 607
Input device, 71, 75
Input errors, handling of, 271
INPUT attribute, 632
INPUT option, 613
INPUT sub-command 684
Insertion sort, 440
Integer, 13,15
value as a subscript, 23-25
variables, see Variable
Interactive systems, 179-186
Interactive testing, 423, 430
Interchange of values, see Swapping values
INTERNAL attribute, 630
Internal block, 323
Internal procedure, 322, 328
Internal string variable, 76
Interrupt, 120, 648
Invalid operations, 372
Invariant relation, 434-446
of a loop, 434
simple examples of, 439
theorem of, 436
use in programming, 444
Item, format, 68, 662, 696
A, 68, 663
B, 663
E, 69, 664
F, 69, 664
C, 663
COL, 75, 664
COLUMN, 664
LINE, 665
PAGE, 665
SKIP, 665
X, 68, 665
Iteration factor, 632
Iterative statement, 103-125, 609
DO WHILE, see DO WHILE
DO UNTIL, see DO UNTIL
exit problems with, 114
indentation conventions for, 118
indexed loop, 108-112
nesting of, 113
invariant relation of, 434
proof of correctness, 434
termination of, 114
Iteration, approximation by, 569

JCL, 75
Job, 596
Job Control Language, 75
Job format, 81

K, 454
KEY condition, 650
Keypunch, format control on, 704
Keypunching, 704
Keypunch, efficient use of, 704
Keyword, reserved, 12, 596
Kilobyte, 454
KWIC index, 468

L option, 699, 700
Label, 116-118, 598
counts, 83,
local, 284
scope of, 325
Label arrays, 99
LABEL attribute, 99, 632
LABELS dump option, 699
Labeling results, 65-67
Languages for file processing, 549
LBOUND function, 660

LC option, see LINECT option
Leaf, of a tree, 516, 473
LEAVE statement, 114, 156, 609, 694
  simulation of, 116
Left son, of a node, 517, 474
Left subtree, 516
Length attribute, 16, 20, 628
Length, of a string, 16, 45
LENGTH function, 49, 655
Level, of a node, 517, 474
LEVEL number, 621
Library system, 545
Life, game of, 386
LIFO, 492
Limitation of output, 409
Line control, see SKIP LINECT option
LINECT option, 700
LINE format item, 665
LINE option, 614
Linear algorithm, 297, 460-461
Linear equations, 573
Linear list, 488
Linear search, 219, 461
Linear tree representation, 517
LINENO function, 661
LINES option, 700
LINESIZE option, 613
Link, 489
Linked list, 495
  allocation, 495, 508
  circular, 510
  doubly linked, 512
LISP, 6
LIST, see GET, see PUT
LIST command, 681, 688
LISTFILE command, 681
List, linear, 488
  LIFO, 492
  FIFO, 492
  circular, 510
  doubly linked, 512
Literal, 17, 66, 598
Loading, of a program, 8
Local variable, 283, 290, 302, 333
Local label, 284
LOCATE, 609, 684
LOG function, 44, 659
Logarithm, 463
Logarithmic algorithm, 460
LOG10 function, 659
LOG2 function, 463, 659
Logical file, 538
Logical function, 343
Logical operators, 53, 641
Logical record, 536
Logical values, 19
LOGOFF command, 681
Loops,
  Body, see Body, loop
  exit from, 114, 118
  increment, 108
  indexed, 108, 609
  nesting of, 113
  termination of, 118
  tracing, 123
  UNTIL, see DO UNTIL
  WHILE, see DO WHILE
LOW function, 655
Lukasiewicz, 526

M9 option, 701
M91 option, 701
M option, see MONITOR option
*MACRO card, 412, 670, 697
Macros, 412, 670
  call of, 671
  definition of, 412, 670
  packet, 670
  source listing for, 672
  uses of, 675
  with parameters, 413, 673
Macro level, 673
MAIN in OPTIONS(MAIN), see Procedure
Main memory, 454
Main procedure, 274
Major structure, 30
Mantissa, 555
Margins, see Card formats
Match-snatch program, 182, 356
Matrix, 25
MAX function, 44, 58, 657
MC option, 700
MCALL option, 672, 700
Meaning of correctness 366
Meaning of variables, 143-146, 257-258
Measuring execution speed,
Measuring space, 454
Median, 309
Megabyte, 454
Memory, 2, 11, 454, 532
  address, 11
  two-level,

secondary, 454
Memory dump, 409
*MEND card, 412, 670, 697
Merge sort, 363
MIN function, 44, 657
Minor structure, 30
Minus, 40, 639
Minsky, M., 486
Mixed type expression, 41
MLVL numbers, 673
MOD function, 44
Mode, of an array, 480
Mode attributes, 626
Mode conversion, 644
Modes, system, 680
Modular testing, 379
MONITOR option, 700
MT option, 701
MTEXT option, 672, 701
Multiple assignment, 36
Multiple subscripts, 25
Multiple test cases,
Multiplication, 40, 639
of arrays, 57
MULTIPLY function, 657
Murphy's law, 530

NAME condition, 652
Named constants, 28
Names,
qualified, 31, 637
scope of, 635
variable, 11
Negation, 40
Nesting,
conditional, 95-99
of blocks, 323
of iterative loops, 113
of procedure calls, 299
Network model, 542
Newton's method, 572
Nil link, 489
NIM-playing program, 356
NO-prefixes, see Conditions
NOALIST option, 699
NOATR option, 699
NOCHECK statement, 406, 609, 690
NOCMNTS option, 699
Nodes, 516, 473, 489
NODUMP option, 699
NODUMPE option, 700
NODUMPT option, 700
NOFLOW command, 689
NOFLOW prefix, 407
NOFLOW statement, 407, 609
NOMCALL option, 672
NOMTEXT option, 672
NO-- options, 648
NOPAUSE command, 429, 690
Normalized, 14
NOSOURCE option, 701
NOSTEP command, 689
Not, 53
Notation,
floating-point, see Floating-point
for data, 257
for statements, 255
scientific, see Scientific
NOUDEF option, 701
NOXREF option, 702
Null statement, 93, 116, 611, 694
Null string, see Empty string
Numbers, 13, 597
floating point, 554

O option, see OPLIST option
OFF option, see PUT OFF
ON, see ENDFILE
ON-action, 612
ON-condition, 612
ON option, see PUT ON
ON-unit, 120, 611, 694
default, 120-123
pending,
ON statement, 120, 611, 694
OPEN statement, 613
Operand, 639
Operating procedures for PL/C, 697
Operations, invalid, 372
Operators, 639
arithmetic, 40, 639
bit string, 53, 641
Boolean, 53, 641
logical, 53, 641
precedence of, 40, 47, 642
relational, 51, 640
string, 47, 640
OPLIST option, 701
*OPTIONS card, 697
Options, in a job, See Program options
OPTIONS(MAIN), 80, 274, 624
Or, 53
Ordering a list, see Sorting
Ordering of characters, 52
Order of execution time, 459

Organization,
  of declarations, 143
  of statements, 147
OTHERWISE, see SELECT
Output, see PUT
  attribute listing, 82, 374
  cross-reference listing, 82, 374
  device, 62, 64, 75
  from PL/CS, 85
  post-mortem dump,
  execution, 82, 374
  limiting, 409
  source listing, 82, 672
  temporary, 377
OUTPUT attribute, 632
OUTPUT option, 613
OVERFLOW, 556,653

P option, 701
PAGE format item, 665
PAGE option, 613 701
PAGES option, 701
PAGESIZE option, 613
Parameter, 280
  -argument correspondence, 287, 293, 644
  array, 295, 646
  arrows, 288-293, 645
  attribute matching, 287, 293
  character-string, 281, 646
  declaration of, 281
  entry-name, 646
  of a macro, 413, 673
  read-only, 283
  scalar, 645
  structure, 646
Partial pivoting, 576
Partition algorithm, 443
PASCAL, 6, 28, 120
PAUSE command, 428, 689
PAUSE, 426
PAUSE option, 686
PENDING, 650
Performance evaluation, 453-484
Placement of procedures, 274, 280
PLAGO, 593
PL/C, 7, 593
  additions to PL/I, 667
  automatic repair in, 373
  compiler for, 669
  dimensional limits, 669
  dump, 409
  examples of card decks for, 697
  flow facilities, 407
  operating procedures for, 697
  postmortem dump, 374
  pseudo-comments, 411
  restrictions, 667
*PL/C card, 697
  options on,
PLC comment, 681
PL/CS, 7, 692-696
  assertions, 414
  automatic repair in, 373
  comparison to PL/I, see PL/I
  indentation for, 138-139
  output from, 85
  postmortem dump, 374
  pseudo-comments, 411
*PLCS card, see Control card
PL/CT, 7, 679-691
  Debug commands, 688
  Terminal procedure, 424
PL/I, 6-7
  dialects of, 593
  comparison to PL/CS,
  for data base processing, 549
PL/I-7, 593
PLUM, 593
Pointer, 489
POLY function, 657
Polish notation, 526
Polya, G., 199
Polynomial approximation, 565
Post-assertion, 414
Postfix notation, 526
Post-mortem dump, 83, 374
Postorder traversal, 519
Pre-assertion, 414
Precedence, 40, 47, 642
Precision, 14, 555
  default, 14
  double, 555
  single, 555
  variable, 508
Precision attributes, 626, 633
PRECISION function, 657
Prefix, 648
  scope of, 648
Prefix notation, 526
Prefixes, see Conditions

Preorder traversal, 519
Prime number, 464
Print, see PUT
PRINT attribute, 633
Priority of operators, see Precedence
Problem,
  ill-defined, 482
  ill conditioned, 579
  impossibly large, 483
  undecideable, 484
Problem analysis, 4, 196
Problem clarification, 4, 196-198
PROC see PROCEDURE
PROCEDURE, 80, 273-363, 694
  active, 290
  body, 285
  call of, 287
  control section, 339
  definition, 280, 314, 623
  dummy, 382
  entry-name, see Procedure name
  external, 273, 331
  form of, 280
  function, 314-320, 343
  independence of, 342
  internal, 322, 328, 330
  labels in, 284
  local variables in, 283
  main, 274
  name, 281, 595, 622
  nested calls of, 299
  OPTIONS(MAIN), 80
  parameter of, see Parameter
  placement of, 274, 280, 328
  procedure-name, 281
  recursive, 346
  stub, 382
  terminal, 424
  testing of, 380-383
  use of, 330, 337
*PROCESS card, 274
PROD function, 58, 660, 697
Program, 1, 199, 595
  as a dynamic object, 147
  as a static object, 147
  as data, 485-486
  bottom-up testing,
  compiling, 8
  confirming correctness of, 9
  design, 4-6
  development, 4-6, 195, 202
  dynamic version of, 147, 432
  examples of, see Examples of programs
  execution, 8, 86
  evaluation of, 453
  format, 80
  loading, 8
  schema, 188-193
  similarities between, 208
  static version of, 147, 432
  structure, 141, 158, 697
  testing, 369, 375, 386
  translation of, 8
  units, 204
  well-structured, 185
Program card, see Drum card
Program options, 698
Programming by test cases, 445
Programming language, 6-7
  ALGOL, 6
  ASAP, 551
  BASIC, 6
  COBOL, 6, 44, 549
  for data base processing, 549
  FORTRAN, 6, 22, 44
  LISP, 6
  PASCAL, 6, 28, 120
  PL/C, 7
  PL/CS, see PL/CS
  PL/CT, see PL/CT
  PL/CV, see Verifier
  PL/I, 6-7, 549
  PL/I-F, 593
  PLAGO, 593
  PLUM, 593
  RPG, 551
  SNOBOL, 6
  SP/k, 593
Prompting, 181, 686
Proof of correctness, 432
Proportional to, 460
Pseudo-comments, 410
Pseudo-variable, 48, 637
  COMPLEX, 638
  IMAG, 638
  REAL, 638
  SUBSTR, 48, 638
  UNSPEC, 638
Pushdown store, 492
PUT ALL, 409, 615, 690
PUT ARRAY, 409, 615, 690
PUT commands, 429, 688, 690

PUT DEPTH, 615
PUT FLOW, 615, 690
PUT OFF, 615, 690
PUT ON, 615, 690
PUT SNAP, 690
PUT statement, 62-70, 613, 694
  PUT DATA, 67, 615, 688
  PUT EDIT, 68, 614
  PUT LIST, 64, 614, 688
  PUT SKIP, 72
  with STRING option, 76-77

Quadratic algorithm, 460
Quadrature, 580
  adaptive, 583
  fixed, 583
Qualified name, 31, 621, 637
Query, 543
Question marks, as value, see Undefined value
Queue, 491
Quicksort, 353, 442
QUIT sub-command, 685
Quotes, around literals, 17
Quotes, in literals, 18

R option, see REPORT option
RAND function, 659
Random access, 532
Read, see GET
READ, 616
READONLY attribute, 28, 283
REAL attribute, 634
REAL function, 658
REAL pseudo-variable, 638
Real variable, see Variable
Record, 489
  logical, 536
  relations between, 540
RECORD, 650
Record input/output, 62
Record processing, 533
Recursion, 346-361
RECURSIVE attribute, 346, 624
Recursive definition, 346
Recursive procedure, 346, 624
Referring to functions, 317, 638
Referring to variables, 636
Refinement,
  ideas for, 262-271
  limitations for, 254
  of data, 257-258
  of statement-comments, 152, 253
  of statements, 253-256
  stepwise, 203
Relational model, 542
Relational operators, 51, 640
Relations, 50-53, 640
Relative error, 557
RELEASE, 616
Repair of errors, 373
REPEAT function, 656
Repetition factor, 28, 598
Repetition of statements, 103-125
Repetitive statement, see Iterative statement
REPORT dump option, 699
Reserved keywords, 12
Results, labeling of, 65-67
RETURN command, 691
RETURN statement, 285, 316, 616, 694
RETURNS attribute, 316, 624, 634
Reversing a string, 362
REVERT statement, 616
REWRITE, 616
Right son, of a node, 517, 474
Right subtree, 516
Root node, 516, 473
ROUND function, 658
Roundoff error, 555
Row-major order, 27
Running time, 460
RPG, 551

S option, 699, 701
SAVE sub-command, 685
Scalar variable, 23
Scalar parameter, 645
Scalar variable assignment, 34-36, 600
SCALARS dump option, 699
Scale attributes, 626
Scale conversion, 644
Scale factor, 633
Scanning symbols, 236, 242-243
Schemata, 188-193
Scientific notation, see Exponential notation
Scope,
  of a block-name, 325
  of a label, 325
  of a prefix, 648-649

of a variable, 324
of an entry-name,
of identifiers, 324, 635
Scope attributes, 630
Searching a list, see Linear Search, Binary Search
Secondary storage, 454, 532
SELECT statement, 91-93, 98-100, 617, 694
indentation for, 91, 150
simulation of, 98
Sentinel, 179, 220
Sequence, 488
Sequential execution, 86-87, 147-158
Sequential allocation, 493
Sequential file, 538, 547
Severity level of errors, see Error levels
Side effects, 318
SIGN function, 658
SIGNAL statement, 617
Significant digits, 557
Similarities between programs, 206
Simple-variable, see Variable
Simpson's rule, 588
Simultaneous linear equations, 573
Simulation, of SELECT, 98
of LEAVE, 116
SIN function, 44, 57, 659
SIND function, 659
SINH function, 659
Sine function, see SIN
Single precision, 555
SIZE condition, 653
SKIP option, see PUT SKIP
SKIP format item, 665
SM option, 701
SNAP, 611
SNOBOL, 6
SNAP option, see PUT SNAP
Solving related problems, 270
Solving simpler problems, 265-269
SOME, see ASSERT
Son, of a node, 517, 474
SORMGIN option, 701
Sorting, 222
bubble sort, 261-262
heap sort, 473
insertion sort, 440
merge sort, 363
quicksort, 353
successive maxima, 223-224, 265
successive minima, 434
Source listing, 82, 672
SOURCE option, 701
Space efficiency, 454
Space, measuring, 454
Speed of execution, 457
SQRT function, 44, 57, 659
approximation to, 569
Square root, see SQRT
Stable, 579
Stack, 491
with header, 508
Standard deviation, 170
Standard input device, 71, 75
Standard output device, 62, 75-76
Statement, 595
ALLOCATE, 599
ASSERT, 414, 599
assignment, see assignment statement
block, 330, 602
CALL, see CALL
CHECK, see CHECK
CLOSE, 604
comments, 135-136, 151-155
compound, 94-95, 604
conditional, see IF, SELECT
DEFAULT, 604
DELAY, 604
DELETE, 604
developing notation for,
DISPLAY, 605
DO UNTIL, see DO UNTIL
DO WHILE, see DO WHILE
EXIT, 605
FETCH, 605
FLOW, 605
FREE, 606
GET, see GET
GOTO, see GOTO
HALT, 608
IF, see IF
IGNORE, 609
input, see GET
iterative, see Iterative statement
LEAVE, see LEAVE
LOCATE, 610
NOCHECK, 406, 611
NOFLOW, 611
NOPAUSE, 611
NOSTEP, 611

null, 93, 116, 611
numbers, see STMT
ON statement, 120-123, 611
OPEN, 613
organization of, 147
output, see PUT
PAUSE, 613
PUT, see PUT
READ, 616
refinement of, 253-256
RELEASE, 616
repetitive, see iterative statement
RETURN, 285, 316, 616
REVERT, 616
REWRITE, 616
SELECT, see SELECT
SIGNAL, 617
STEP, 617
STOP, 617
UNLOCK, 618
WAIT, 618
WRITE, 618
Statement keywords, 12
STATIC attribute, 302-304, 628
STATIC variables, 302-304
Static version of a program, 147, 432
Statistical system, 170-175
STEP, 426
STEP command, 428, 689
STEP interval, 426-427
STEP_RESET, 426
Step-wise refinement, 203
STMT numbers, 82, 424
STOP command, 691
STOP statement, 617
Storage, see Memory
automatic, 302, 506
of arrays, 455
secondary, 532-535
static, 454
Storage class attributes, 626
Storage devices, 62, 75, 533
Storage space, measuring, 454
STRG condition, 653
Stream input/output, 62
String, 13
as argument, 281-282
assignment, 45-46
character, 13, 16-18
bit, 13, 598
comparison, 52, 640
constants, see Literal
empty, 18, 47
expression, 45-53, 640
function, 49
length, 16, 45-47
null, 18, 47
repetition factor for, 598
variable, internal, 76
STRING function, 656
String operators, 47, 52
STRING option, 55, 76-77, 606, 613
STRINGRANGE condition, 653
Structure, 29-31, 621
array of, 30-31
as a parameter, 646
assignment to, 58-59, 601
component of, 29-30
declaration of, 29-31, 621
expressions, 642
hierarchial, 151-155
input of, 78
level number, 621
major, 30, 621
minor, 30, 621
name, 621
of arrays, 30
output of, 78
referring to, 637
Structure, of a program, 141-142, 158
Structure-ref, 595
Stubs, 382
SUBRG condition, 653
SUBRG option, 701
Subroutine, 337
Subscript, 24-25
Subscripted variables, 23-25, 636
assignment to, 37-39
improper, 38-39
SUBSCRIPTRANGE condition, 653
SUBSTR function, 47, 656
SUBSTR pseudo-variable, 48, 638
Subtraction, 40, 639
Subtree, 516
Successive maxima, 223-224, 265
Successive minima, 434
Suffix notation, 526
SUM function, 57, 660
Swapping values, 37, 276
Swimming assignment, 354
Symbol, in PL/C,
Symbol Scanning, see Scanning

Symbol
Syntax errors, 82, 371
SYSIN, 75
SYSPRINT, 75-76
SYSTEM, 122, 611

T option, 701
TABSIZE option, 702
TAB stops, 64
TAN function, 44, 659
TAND function, 659
TANH function, 659
Target label, see Label
Taylor expansion, 565-567
Terminal, 8
Terminal procedure, 424
  statements in, 428
Test cases, design of, 376
  programming by, 445
Testing, 369, 375, 386
  bottom-up testing, 380
  independent, 380
  interactive, 423, 430
  modular, 379
  top-down, 382
Testing habits, 385
Text-editor problem, 266-269
THEN, see IF
TIME function, 661
TIME option, 701
Timing considerations, 533
TITLE option,
Titling, 65-67
Top-down programming, 203, 252-256
Top-down testing, 382
TOP sub-command, 685
Towers of Hanoi, 351, 353, 363
Tracing execution, 86-87, 327
  of a block, 327
  of a loop, 123-125
  of recursion, 350
Transaction, 226, 546 226
TRANSLATE function, 656
Translation, of a program, 8
Translation program, 175-179
Translator, 8
TRANSMIT, 650
Trapezoidal rule, 581
  adaptive, 584
Traversal,
  of a tree, 519
Tree, binary, 516, 473
Tree Traversal, 519
True, see Values
TRUNC function, 658
Truncation, 43, 46
Truncation error, 555
TS option, see TABSIZE option
Turing, A., 486
TYPE command, 685
Type attributes, 13-21
Types of errors, 368
Types of values, 13-21

U option, see UDEF and UNREAD options
UDEF option, 701
UFL condition, 654
Undecidability, 486
Undecideable problem, 484
Undefined value ???, 20
UNDEFINEDFILE condition, 654
UNDERFLOW, 556
UNDF condition, 654
Units,
  of a program, 204
UNLOCK, 618
Update, of file, 546
UP sub-command, 685
UNREAD dump option, 699
UNSPEC function, 656
UNSPEC pseudo-variable, 638
UNTIL loop, see DO UNTIL
Useless comments, 138, 145-146
Use of blanks, 597
Use of procedures, 330, 337
User defined values, 19
User instructions, 136

Values, 13-20
  ???, 20
  assignment of, 34-39
  bit, 19
  Boolean, see Values, true-false
  character, 16-18
  coercion of, 42
  constant, 28
  conversion of, 55
  current, 13
  empty string, 18, 47
  initial, 26-28
  literal, 17-18
  logical, 19
  numeric, 13-15
  structured, 29-31

  true-false, 19, 50
  undefined, 20
  user defined, 19
Variable, 11
  assignment of value, 34-39, 600
  ATTN_FLAG, 424
  attributes, 13-20
  automatic, 302
  bit, 19
  creation of, 19-31
  current value of, 13, 34
  decimal, 13-14
  declaration of, 19-31
  description of, 143-146
  ERROR_FLAG, 424
  EXTERNAL, 303
  floating point, 13-14
  global, 324
  identifier, 11-12
  initialization of, 26-28, 302
  integer, 15
  internal, 76
  LABEL, 99
  local, 283, 290, 302, 333
  meaning of, 143-147
  multiply-subscripted, 25
  names, see Identifier
  pseudo-variables, see Pseudo-variable,
  READONLY, see READONLY
  referring to, 636
  reserved keywords, 12
  scalar, 23
  scope of, 324
  simple, 23
  space for, 455
  STATIC, 302-304
  structured, 29-31
  subscripted, 23, 636
VAR, see VARYING
Variable-name, 595
Variable precision, 508
Variable-ref, 595
VARYING attribute, 20
Verification, 447
Verifier, 447
VERIFY function, 49, 656
Vertical bar, 47

WAIT, 618
Well structured program, 158
WHEN, see SELECT
WHILE loop, see DO WHILE
Worst case analysis, 461
WRITE, 618
Write, see PUT

X option, 702
X format item, 68, 664
XREF option, 82, 387, 702

ZDIV condition, 654
ZERODIVIDE condition, 654